New Perspectives on Philosophy and Education

Gerald L. Gutek

Loyola University Chicago

Columbus, Ohio
Upper Saddle River, New Jersey

This book is dedicated to the memory of my uncle,
Ralph Joseph Novotney, a man who was excellent in all things.

Library of Congress Cataloging-in-Publication Data

Gutek, Gerald Lee.
  New perspectives on philosophy and education / Gerald L. Gutek.
     p.   cm.
  Includes bibliographical references and index.
  ISBN-13: 978-0-205-59433-7
  ISBN-10:   0-205-59433-6
  1. Philosophy.   2. Education.   I. Title.
  B72.G88 2009
  107.1—dc22   2008018826

Publisher: *Kevin M. Davis*
Acquisitions Editor: *Meredith D. Fossel*
Series Editorial Assistant: *Maren Vigilante*
Marketing Manager: *Erica DeLuca*
Production Editor: *Mary Beth Finch*

Editorial Production Service: *TexTech International*
Composition Buyer: *Linda Cox*
Manufacturing Buyer: *Megan Cochran*
Electronic Composition: *TexTech International*
Cover Administrator: *Elena Sidorova*

This book was set in Times by TexTech International. It was printed and bound by R. R. Donnelley, Harrisonburg. The cover was printed by Phoenix Color Corporation, Hagerstown.

Pearson® is a registered trademark of Pearson plc.
Merrill® is a registered trademark of Pearson Education, Inc.

Pearson Education Ltd.
Pearson Education Singapore Pte. Ltd.
Pearson Education Canada, Ltd.
Pearson Education—Japan

Pearson Education Australia Pty. Limited
Pearson Education North Asia Ltd.
Pearson Educación de Mexico, S.A. de C.V.
Pearson Education Malaysia Pte. Ltd.

Photo Credits: p. 1, Michael Pole/Corbis; p. 18, Courtesy of the Library of Congress; p. 40, Getty Images; p. 73, Courtesy of the Library of Congress; p. 99, National Historical Museum, Frederiksborg/Danish Embassy; p. 132, Stanford University Library; p. 161, Courtesy of the National Archives and Records Administration; p. 192, AP Images; p. 214, Courtesy of the Library of Congress; p. 249, Michael Evans/The White House Photo Office; p. 271, Courtesy of the Library of Congress; p. 296, LILO/SIPA Press; p. 308, Courtesy of the Teachers College, Columbia University; p. 336, Courtesy of the author; p. 360, Courtesy of the Teachers College, Columbia University; p. 393, Jaimie Trueblood/Paramount/Picture Desk, Inc./Kobal Collection; p. 420, Kamenko Pajic/AP Images.

Printed in the United States of America

Merrill
is an imprint of

10 9 8 7 6 5 4 3 2 1
ISBN-13: 978-0-205-59433-7
ISBN-10:   0-205-59433-6

www.pearsonhighered.com

Contents

4 *Pragmatism and Education*   **73**

5 *Existentialism and Education*   **99**

14   *Progressivism and Education*   336

15   *Social Reconstructionism and Education*   360

16   *Critical Theory and Education*   393

17   *Globalization and Education*   420

Preface

In writing a textbook, there is always the overriding issue that all authors face—what should be included and what should be excluded? In response to this question, I relied on reading about trends in philosophy of education, on the advice of reviewers, and what I think is important for teachers to know to reflectively construct their own philosophy of education. However, I took the author's prerogative to include topics of my own special research and interest. Throughout the book, I encourage teachers to reflect on their experiences and to use their reflections in constructing their own philosophy of education. I took my own advice and am occasionally autobiographical in the book.

New Perspectives on Philosophy and Education is based on my continuing interest in the cultural foundations of education, especially the interrelationships between philosophies, ideologies, and theories of education. The book is divided into three parts: Part I—Philosophies of Education, Part II—Ideologies of Education, and Part III—Theories of Education.

Part I introduces philosophy of education. It describes and analyzes Idealism, Realism, Pragmatism, Existentialism, and Postmodernism. It distinguishes the philosophies that are based on metaphysics from those that are not. Each chapter identifies founders of the philosophy, its major principles, and its relationships to education and schooling, especially to curriculum and instruction. As a teacher who began his career as an instructor in Western Civilization, I think we cannot begin to understand philosophy without returning to its origins with Plato and Aristotle. Therefore, I include Idealism and Realism. Pragmatism, especially Dewey's Experimentalism, has had such a pervasive influence on American education that it has to be included in any book on the subject. As I reread books on Existentialism, I felt once again its dramatic appeal and believe that it will touch a responsive chord with today's readers. Because we live in what is called the postmodern era, Postmodernism, because of its pervasive influence on contemporary humanities and social science, needed to be included.

Part II examines the relationships between ideology and education. It begins by defining ideology and comparing and contrasting it to philosophy. It discusses and comments on Nationalism, Liberalism, Conservatism, and Marxism and draws out their educational implications. Because of my work in history of education and comparative-international education, I consider ideology to be one of the important influences in shaping educational policies and practices. The debates between American Conservatives and Liberals over policy, both at home and abroad, cannot be understood without an examination of their ideological origins and development. I include Marxism because it is an important tool of analysis for many professors teaching the foundations of education. While I note how

Marxism became Marxist-Leninism, the official ideology in the now-defunct Soviet system, I also examine Marxism, especially Neo-Marxism, as an important analytical tool.

Part III examines theory and discusses Essentialism, Progressivism, Social Reconstructionism, Critical Theory, and Globalization. After some internal debate with myself, I followed the advice of the manuscript's reviewers that Perennialism should be included in the chapter on Realism rather than presented as a separate chapter. I have noted a revival of interest in and research on Essentialism, especially in the books by Diane Ravitch and J. Wesley Null. My own doctoral dissertation at the University of Illinois examined the educational ideas of George S. Counts, who originated Social Reconstructionism when he asked, "Dare the school build a new social order?" The research and writing of Karen Riley and her colleagues convinced me that Social Reconstructionism is still highly relevant for teachers and educational policymakers. As I attend conferences and sample the recent books in the field, I note pervasive interest in Critical Theory, and so a chapter on it is indispensable. Globalization is also a frequent topic in foundations of education. I debated with myself—is it a philosophical topic or not? Taking a broad view of philosophy of education, I decided that a chapter on globalization should be included in the book.

I understand that there are many ways to organize and to teach courses in the Foundations of Education, especially Philosophy of Education. During my career, I experimented with teaching one particular philosophy, such as Realism or Experimentalism, in depth. I also used several selected books, advocating a particular philosophy, as primary source readings. Over time, I became convinced that teachers need what I call a cognitive map, a guide to the field, that is useful in placing educational ideas, innovations, and trends in perspective and in relating them to the broader philosophical and ideological contexts from which they come and of which they are a part. I have used this approach in this book and also in my earlier ones. What makes this book somewhat unique is the relationship that I make between philosophies, ideologies, and theories of education.

The organization of the chapters in this book is based on how I taught the philosophy of education course at Loyola University Chicago and at other institutions. Each chapter moves from a general overview of the philosophy, ideology, or theory; a discussion of its leading founders or proponents; identification and discussion of its major principles about truth, knowing, and values; and its implications for education, schooling, curriculum, and instruction. I have included some figures or charts that I used when I diagrammed or identified key points on the chalkboard.

Professors who use the book, of course, have their own designs and approaches to instruction. They might want to use the book as a structural framework that relates philosophies, ideologies, and theories of education. Because each chapter can be used as a free-standing text, professors might wish to use them selectively and develop their own sequence of presentation.

As I wrote the book, I had some autobiographical moments and some recollections from my past rose to the surface of my consciousness. I had particularly strong remembrances of my high school teachers. I learned much about writing from some talented teachers of English—Gwendolyn Harris, Faye Homrighous, and Grace Magierski—at Streator High School back in the early 1950s. These teachers worked persistently at getting us to express ourselves as clearly and directly as possible in our writing. We had numerous exercises in précis writing—taking large and often ambiguous statements and rewriting them so that they were succinct and clear. I later found out that Thomas Jefferson used the same method in his writing. These teachers were all proponents of gathering evidence and interpreting it in required term papers. So for me, writing a book is an extension of research and writing those required term papers.

When I was working on my master's degree in American history at the University of Illinois, my thesis director was J. Leonard Bates, a distinguished historian of the Progressive period. I wrote a thesis on the Illinois delegation at the Democratic National Convention in 1924—it was the longest convention in American political history. Professor Bates was a busy scholar but a patient one. He read several drafts of my thesis, carefully editing and correcting it with his red or blue pencil. Like my high school teachers, he wanted the narrative to be clear, succinct, and direct.

I am very grateful to the Foundations of Education professors in the School of Education at the University of Illinois who introduced me to the history and philosophy of education: Harry S. Broudy, William O. Stanley, Joe R. Burnett, and Archibald Anderson. My book, in many ways, draws on and continues what they taught me and my colleagues. I especially remember how Professor Anderson encouraged me to write my doctoral dissertation on George S. Counts.

I also want to thank Steven I. Miller, my colleague at Loyola University, who always replied to my e-mails and calls about questions I had such as: What is a good source for Scientific Realism? Why are so many professors in the field attracted to Neo-Marxism? What is the continuing relevance of the Essentialists?

I would also like to thank the reviewers of the manuscript: Jerry Bowling, Harding University; Erskine S. Dottin, Florida International University; Vincent R. McGrath, Mississippi State University; and Joseph R. Nichols, Arkansas State University.

Writing this book took me some time. I missed due dates and deadlines as I put it aside for other projects. However, Steve Dragin, my editor at Allyn and Bacon, made sure that I stayed with the project. His timely calls would get me back on track. Steve's persistence overcame my procrastination. For his efforts, I thank him.

Finally, I come to my family, especially my wife, Patricia, who is always steadying and encouraging of my work. My grandchildren—Claire, Abigail, Luke, Drew, Mills, and Anna Hope—keep giving me new insights into the mysteries of childhood and learning. I am especially awed by my four-year-old grandson Luke's question about dinosaurs. He asked, "What happened to the dinosaurs?" His mother told him that they were gone—they were extinct. He, of course, then had another question, "What comes after people?" I end with this child's question—hoping that as a people we will find a way to sustain our lives and pass on a green and peaceful planet to future generations.

Gerald Gutek

1

Philosophy and Education

Students and professor in a college course engaged in a discussion on education.

Chapter Preview

In this chapter, philosophy of education is introduced in terms of its relationships to its components—philosophy and education. We can begin our discussion with a preliminary and tentative definition of philosophy as the most general way of reflecting on the meaning of our lives in the world and reflecting deeply on what is true or false, good or evil, right or wrong, and beautiful or ugly.[1]

As we move through the book, we will return to our initial definition, restating, expanding, and revising it. You will notice that in the first paragraph we invite the reader to reflect on the meaning of life, education, and schooling. Philosophical reflection causes us to think deeply and profoundly about meaning in the world, in our country, and in our schools. Another way of reflecting is to ask yourself, "What difference does it make that I am here and am a teacher? What difference does it make to my students and to me?"

Although reflection begins with us as persons, it also has professional implications for us as teachers. Professional teacher organizations such as the National Council on the Accreditation of Teacher Education (NCATE) encourages teachers to reflect on their work. When we begin to put into practice the various ideas that we have formed during reflection, we arrive at what the NCATE standards call a "conceptual framework," a philosophy of education that gives meaning to teaching by integrating its daily demands with long-term professional commitment and direction.[2]

A conceptual framework, essentially a philosophy of education, can provide teachers with a sense of coherence in which various elements and episodes in teaching and learning are placed in relationship and perspective to each other. It is a strategy for fitting short-term objectives into long-term goals. To become reflective educators, teachers need to think philosophically about the broad cultural and ethical implications of education.

The chapters in this book that examine philosophies, ideologies, and theories of education are designed to provide a conceptual map to help you focus your reflections on education. You can move from the conceptual framework to constructing your own philosophy of education. There are many ways to develop your philosophy of education. You can keep a log of classroom events and relate them to the philosophies examined in this book. Or you can begin by writing an essay to yourself about what you believe is true and valuable and how your educational experiences up to this time have shaped these beliefs. As you then proceed through the book, you can add to, delete from, reaffirm, or revise your beginning ideas about philosophy of education. To begin reflecting on your own philosophy of education, you might ask yourself the following questions: What do I believe is real and why do I believe this? What do I believe is true and why do I believe this? What do I value and why do I value it? Is there some system of logic that guides me? How does my conception of reality, truth, knowledge, values, and logic affect my ideas about education and my teaching?

You can determine whether the philosophies, ideologies, and theories discussed here are reflected in your own experience. You can see whether your encounters with them cause you to revise or rethink your beliefs about what is true, good, and valuable. When you have finished, you should have a statement of your own philosophy of education, a conceptual framework for your teaching.

To begin the process of constructing a personal philosophy of education, we need to expand our initial definition and discussion of philosophy. To do this, we examine philosophy's major subdivisions: metaphysics, epistemology, axiology (ethics and aesthetics), and logic. We then relate these philosophical areas to education. The chapter next considers education as both a formal process in the school and as an informal process that takes place through agencies in society such as the home, church, and media. Schooling is discussed in terms of curriculum, methods of instruction, and teacher–student relationships. These areas of formal education are then related to the subdivisions of philosophy. The chapter examines the following major topics:

- Areas of philosophy
- Education in terms of curriculum, methodology of instruction, and teachers and learners
- Philosophies of education

Areas of Philosophy

During a person's early teaching experience, there is little time to examine the deeper philosophical meaning that results from being a teacher. Often, teaching is a hurried series of episodes in which the teacher reacts to the immediate demands of students, parents, administrators, colleagues, and community and school organizations. In the first years of a teaching career, the teacher must meet the day-to-day demands of lesson planning, conducting classes, and attending conferences both in and out of school. Little time is free to reflect on education. For the teacher to become a genuine professional, however, exclusive attention to daily routine and detail is insufficient. Every teacher knows that education is a powerful instrument for the shaping of individual lives and society. When the teacher begins to reflect on his or her role, that person is moving from preoccupation with the immediately practical to an examination of the theory that underlies and sustains practice. Teaching requires the careful blending of theory and practice. Theory without practice is insufficient; practice unguided by theory is aimless.

Blending theory and practice, teaching has both a reflective and an active dimension. It has effects that transcend the immediate instructional episodes of the classroom. The way in which teachers relate to their students depends on their conception of human nature. Instruction is about something; it is about a skill or about knowledge. One's view of reality shapes one's beliefs about knowledge. When the teacher begins to reflect on the conception of reality, of human nature, and of society, he or she is philosophizing about education. In its most general terms, philosophy is the human being's attempt to think speculatively, reflectively, and systematically about the universe and the human relationship to that universe.

Metaphysics

Metaphysics, the study of the nature of ultimate reality, involves speculation about the nature of existence. It asks the question, After all the nonessentials of life have been stripped away, what is genuinely real? Our beliefs about the nature of reality determine how we perceive our relationships to the universe and to society. These beliefs raise our most important questions—what is and what is not real—and also begin to provide the answers to these questions. Is there a spiritual realm of existence or is reality material? What is the origin of the universe? Is it inherently purposeful by its own design or do we create our own purposes?

In their speculations into the nature of reality, metaphysicians have drawn varying conclusions. Whereas an Idealist defines reality in spiritual or nonmaterial terms, a Realist sees reality as an order of objects that exist independently of human beings. Conversely, a Pragmatist rejecting metaphysics, holds that the human conception of reality is based on experience.

Metaphysics relates to educational theory and practice in many ways. The subjects, experiences, and skills in the curriculum reflect the conception of reality held by the society that supports the school. Much formal schooling represents the attempt of curriculum-makers, teachers, and textbook authors to describe certain aspects of reality to students. For example, subjects such as history, geography, chemistry, and so on, describe certain dimensions of reality to students.

Epistemology

Epistemology, the theory of knowing and knowledge, is of crucial importance to educators. Defining the foundations of knowledge, epistemology considers such important questions as: (1) How do we know what we know? (2) On what process of knowing do we base our knowledge of the world and society? (3) What is the authority on which we base our claims to truth? (4) Do our knowledge claims derive from divine revelation, empirical evidence, or personal and subjective experience?

Historically, much authority has rested on a belief in God or the supernatural and revelations of divine truths to inspired men and women. Civilization's great religions—Judaism, Christianity, Islam, Hinduism, and Buddhism, for example—rest on knowledge claims arising from a holy book or scriptures, such as the Bible or the Koran. Implied is the believer's faith in a transcendent, universal, spiritual authority, which, while prior to and independent of human experience, is life's true guide. These divinely revealed truths are universally valid in every time and place. While not necessarily religious, philosophies such as Idealism and Realism also claim to represent universal knowledge. Other philosophies, such as Pragmatism, base knowledge claims on human experience, especially publicly verifiable empirical evidence. Highly subjective, Existentialism roots knowledge in a person's intuitive perception of one's own needs and psychological disposition.

Dealing with the most general and basic conceptions of knowing, epistemology is closely related to methods of teaching and of learning. For example, an Idealist may hold that knowing, or the cognitive process, is really the recall of ideas that are present latently in the mind. The appropriate educational method for Idealists would be the Socratic dialogue in which the teacher attempts to bring latent ideas to the student's consciousness by asking leading questions. Realists hold that knowledge originates in the sensations we have of objects in our environment. We arrive at concepts from these sensations. Through the abstraction of sensory data, we build concepts that correspond to these objects in reality. A teacher who wishes to structure instruction based on the Realist sensation–abstraction formula might use classroom demonstrations to explain natural phenomena to students. A Pragmatist, in contrast, holds that we create knowledge by interacting with our environment in problem-solving episodes. Thus, problem solving is the appropriate method of instruction for those who accept the Pragmatist's view of knowledge. Existentialists contend that we create our own knowledge by choosing what we wish to believe and appropriating it as our own. Postmodernists challenge universal claims to knowledge as the historical constructions of powerful groups at particular times in history.

Axiology

Axiology is concerned with value theory and attempts to prescribe what is good and right conduct. The subdivisions of axiology are **ethics** and **aesthetics**. Ethics refers to the philosophical study of moral values and conduct. Aesthetics is concerned with the study of values in the realm of beauty and art. Whereas metaphysics attempts to describe the nature of ultimate reality, axiology refers to prescriptions of moral behavior and beauty. Educators have always been concerned with the formation of values in the young and with the encouragement of certain kinds of preferred behavior.

In a general way, each person is influenced by those who seek to shape his or her behavior along certain lines. Children are continually told that they should or should not do certain things. Statements such as "you should wash your hands before eating," "you should not break the school's windows," or "you should love your country" are all obvious value statements. In the process of growing to maturity, an individual encounters countless attempts to mold behavior along preferred modes of action. In a very direct way, parents, teachers, and society reward or punish behavior as it conforms to or deviates from their conceptions of correctness, goodness, or beauty.

Cultural ethos refers to the value core that provides a sense of identity, purpose, and community to a society. In the contemporary United States, strong cultural divisions exist in defining the nation's ethos and character. James Hunter, a noted author on American values, has found these divisions to be so deep that they constitute a veritable "culture war."[3] Among the divisive value issues that impact contemporary U.S. society are the following: Is the national character religious or secular? Should there be prayer in the schools? What is the role of women in U.S. society? What is the nature of the family? These fundamental issues are intertwined with issues of national identity. Is there and should there be a national character? Or, should the United States be a place of many diverse identities, cultures, and lifestyles? Further, how does this clash of values impact schooling? What is the role of schools in transmitting and cultivating values?

The classical conflict in values is that of objective versus subjective value theory. Advocates of objective value theory assert that what is good is rooted in the universe itself and is applicable everywhere for all time. In contrast, subjectivists assert that values are group or personal preferences—likes or dislikes—that depend on particular circumstances, times, and places. For them, values are not universally valid but are relative to particular situations.

The aesthetic dimension of life frequently has been neglected in U.S. education. In its broadest sense, aesthetic theory refers to the cultivation of taste and appreciation for what is beautiful. Although aesthetic theory is concerned with the human attempt to objectify insights and feelings in various art forms, it is equally concerned with the cultivation of persons whose lives are harmonious, balanced, and beautiful. Aesthetic values have an obvious place in art, drama, music, and dancing classes; they are also relevant to the cultivation of the public taste and style of life.

Logic

Logic is the subdivision of philosophy that deals with correct thinking. It is concerned with how we organize and sequence our thinking and frame our arguments according to a coherent pattern, that is, how we organize our supporting evidence to make a case for or to explain something. The two major patterns of logic are deduction and induction. In **deductive logic**, or deduction, reasoning moves from general statements or principles to specific cases or examples. We are all familiar with the classic statement of deduction: (1) All men are mortal; (2) Socrates is a mortal; (3) therefore, Socrates is a man. We can also think of how Thomas Jefferson framed his arguments in the Declaration of Independence: (1) All men are endowed with inalienable rights of life, liberty, and happiness; (2) the American colonists had these inalienable rights; (3) because George III was violating these rights, the colonists had the right to rebel against British rule. In the above examples of deductive logic, if the premises are true, then, if we reason correctly, the conclusions will also be true.

Inductive logic, or induction, moves from specific instances, cases, or situations to a larger generalization that includes and encompasses them. For example, a particular suburban high school spends more funds on each student than a particular urban high school in a particular county in a state. Further research shows that same expenditure pattern is found at other suburban and urban high schools throughout that state. The general conclusion is that this trend occurs in high schools throughout the state.

Instructional materials—manuals, books, handouts, videos, computer programs—are organized according to some kind of logic. Some state general principles and then illustrate these principles with specific examples. Others introduce a number of specific examples and then lead the student to make a generalization.

The traditional curriculum, in its general organization, follows a pattern of logic that tends to be deductive in that it is sequential and cumulative. Experiences and courses are organized so that they follow each other in a sequence—often moving from the simple and easy to the more complicated and difficult. They are cumulative in that each skill or subject learned is a foundation for the next higher order skill or subject. Progressive or constructivist curricular strategies, in contrast, are inductive. By examining objects or issues in their environment, the students are expected to generalize from their experience.

Subdivisions of Philosophies of Education and Questions They Raise

Metaphysics	*Epistemology*	*Axiology (Ethical Values)*	*Axiology (Aesthetic Values)*	*Logic*
Examines what ultimately is real.	Examines what is knowledge and how do we know.	Examines what is right and wrong; good and evil.	Examines what is beautiful or ugly.	Examines rules of correct thinking.
Is reality mental or spiritual?	Is truth intuitive, subjective, and personal?	Are ethics, the standards of behavior, objective and universal, reflecting the nature of the universe?	Is beauty a reflection of the universal, absolute, and unchanging?	Is logic deductive, from the general principle to the specific example?
Is reality objective, existing outside of our minds?	Is truth revealed from God in a sacred or holy book?	Are ethics subjective, personal likes and dislikes?	Is beauty subjective, in the eye of the beholder?	Is logic inductive, from the specific example to the general principle or finding?

Metaphysics	*Epistemology*	*Axiology (Ethical Values)*	*Axiology (Aesthetic Values)*	*Logic*
Is reality based on our experiences?	Is truth revealed from reasoning?	Are ethics culturally relative, depending on cultural norms at given time?	Is beauty determined by cultural preferences?	
Do we construct or make our own reality?	Is truth empirical, constructed by using our senses and the scientific method?			

Education

The word **education** refers very broadly to the total social processes that bring a person into cultural life. The human species reproduces biologically as do all other living organisms. Biological reproduction, however, is not cultural reproduction. By living and participating in a culture, the immature human being gradually becomes a recipient of and a participant in a culture. Many persons and social agencies are involved in the process of enculturation of the young. The family, the peer group, the community, the media, the church, and the state all have formative effects on the individual. By living with other people, the immature child learns how to deal with them. He or she takes on their language, their manners, and their behavior. Educational theorists and philosophers have long recognized the educative role of interactions of human beings and society, and they have tried to indicate the kind of social order that is based on and fulfills human potentiality.

Education, in a more formal and deliberate sense, takes place in the **school**, a specialized social agency established to cultivate preferred skills, knowledge, and values in the learner. The school is staffed by teachers who are regarded as experts in the learning processes. Informal education, or milieu, is related to formal education, or schooling. If the school is to succeed in its program of instruction, its curriculum and methods must be viable in relation to society.

Curriculum

As the vital center of the school's educational efforts, the **curriculum** is the locus of the sharpest controversies. Decision making in curricular matters involves considering, examining, and formulating the goals of education. Those concerned with curriculum planning and organization ask such questions as: What knowledge is of most worth? What knowledge should be introduced to the learner? What are the criteria for selecting knowledge? What is valuable for the learner as a person and as a member of society? The answers to these questions not only determine what is included and what is excluded from the school's curriculum, but also rest on assumptions about the nature of the universe, of human beings, of society, and of the good life. In the philosophies examined in this book, we will find a variety of basic and general assumptions that provide alternatives to making the curriculum.

Curriculum has been defined in various ways. Throughout most of the history of education, the curriculum consisted of the basic skills of reading, writing, and mathematical computation at the primary or elementary level, and the arts and sciences at the secondary and higher levels. For many educators, the curriculum remains essentially a program of studies, skills, and subjects offered to a learner in a formal sequence. Since the appearance of the activity, experience, process, or constructivist approach, many educators have moved to a more generalized conception of curriculum. For them, the curriculum includes all of the learner's experiences for which the school assumes responsibility.

In the broadest sense, the curriculum can be defined as the organized experiences that a student has under the guidance and control of the school. In a more precise but restricted sense, the curriculum is the systematic sequence of courses or subjects that forms the school's formal instructional program. These two major definitions of curriculum, as well as the variations that lie between them, are based on particular conceptions of knowledge and value. The philosophies of education examined in this book hold conceptions of the curriculum that range from the broad view that includes all of the learner's experiences, to the more specific view that sees it as academic subject matter.

There can be no question that curriculum designers, regardless of their philosophical convictions, attempt to seek that which is of the greatest worth to the learner. The problem lies in identifying and agreeing on what is of the greatest truth, beauty, and goodness. This question has metaphysical, epistemological, axiological, and logical dimensions. Philosophers and educational theorists, however, have responded to this question with different answers, and their disagreements have resulted in a variety of curricula.

For the Idealist, Realist, and Thomist philosophers, as well as for the Essentialist and Perennialist theorists, the curriculum consists of skills and subjects organized in a systematic and sequential fashion. They regard learning basic skills as necessary tools that have generative power for the later study of the more sophisticated subjects based on such learned disciplines as mathematics, science, and history. For these more traditional philosophies, the preferred curricular design focuses on subject matter. Their major goal is the transmission and preservation of the cultural heritage. Scientists and scholars, through their research, have developed the learned disciplines that explain the various dimensions of reality. The curriculum, then, is the means of transmitting this heritage, in learnable units, to the immature so that they can participate in the culture. The survival of civilization is believed to hinge on the ability to transmit tested truth and values to the young. The subject-matter curriculum is a form of the conscious and deliberate transmission of the adult view of reality to children. Although children may be initially imposed on, the acquisition of knowledge will lead to their eventual freedom by multiplying their alternatives of action. The subject-matter curriculum is arranged in a hierarchy with priority given to subjects regarded as more general, and hence more significant, than other subjects. This arrangement of the subject-matter hierarchy depends on the particular conception of reality and values that is the background for constructing the curriculum.

In contrast to the subject-matter design, various other curricula have been proposed as desirable ways of organizing the school's instructional program. Experimentalists, Progressives, and Reconstructionists are more concerned with the process of learning than the acquisition of subject matter. This process-oriented curricular design is often called the activity, the experience, or the problem-solving curriculum. In contrast to the differentiated knowledge in the subject-matter curriculum, the process approach concentrates on developing methodological skills to work through and organize undifferentiated human experience.

According to John Dewey's experimental mode of learning, the method of scientific inquiry can be applied to all human problems. The curriculum that evolved from Dewey's methodological premise is a series of problem-solving episodes based on the learner's needs and interests as well as on social situations and issues.

Methodology of Instruction

The **method of instruction** is closely related to the goals or ends specified in the curriculum. *Methodology* refers to the processes of teaching and learning by which the learner is brought into relationship with the skills and knowledge specified and contained in the curriculum. In the school, methods are the procedures a teacher uses to aid students in having an experience, mastering a skill or process, or acquiring an area of knowledge. If efficient and effective, the methods of instruction will achieve the desired end.

John Colman has defined *method* as, "An ordered system by which a teacher puts educative agents to work on humans to produce certain changes or results." He has identified five necessary elements in instructional methodology: (1) an aim, or the specific objective or purpose of instruction; (2) an introduction that relates the particular lesson to previous learning or experiences; (3) content, or the substance or subject of a lesson; (4) a summary to reinforce the particular learning; and (5) an evaluation that determines whether the particular aim has been achieved by the learner.[4]

Because teaching implies the use of a technique to achieve a desired objective, educators are involved in methodological questions. In programs of teacher education, attention is given to courses in techniques and methods of teaching. For example, courses exist in teaching reading, language arts, science, social studies, mathematics, music, and art. Supervised student or practice teaching is designed to provide the prospective teacher with experience in integrating content and methodology in a classroom situation. Experienced teachers are involved in programs of in-service training designed to familiarize them with new methods. School administrators devote much of their time and resources to introducing and experimenting with methodological innovations. Even a cursory examination of the literature of professional education gives evidence of a keen interest in methodology. One will find articles on the Socratic method, the project method, the discovery method, the inquiry method, collaborative learning, constructivism, and other approaches to instruction.

The methods of teaching and of learning are most closely related to epistemology, or knowing, and to logic, the correct patterns of thinking. Once again, the study of educational philosophy provides clues to learning strategies that relate to the conception of knowing embodied in the philosophical system. If knowledge, or ideas, are innately present in the mind, then the most effective instructional strategy is one that brings them to consciousness, such as the Socratic method. If, however, learning is transactional between the person and the environment, as Dewey asserts, then the most effective method is problem-solving.

Teachers and Learners

Formal education involves a teacher and a learner. The conception of the roles and functions of the teacher and the learner depends on one's view of human nature. The Thomists' view of a human being as an "incarnate spirit-in-the-world" is very different from the Pragmatist

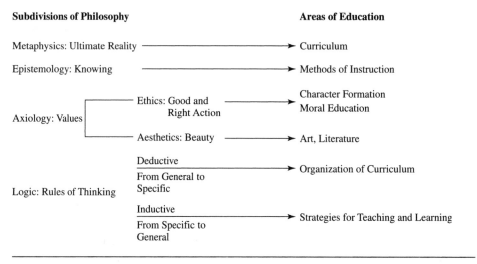

Relationships of Philosophy and Education

conception of the human being as a biological-sociological-vocal phenomenon. The Existentialist view that the person creates his or her own essence differs from the philosophies that see the human being as a category in a metaphysical system. From each of these perspectives, the roles of the teacher and the learner would be seen quite differently.

In the subject-matter curriculum, the teacher is an authority figure who is expert in the content and teaching of a body of organized knowledge. In regard to that knowledge, the learner is an immature person who is in the school to acquire and to master that knowledge. In such a curricular framework, the teacher–learner relationship depends substantially on the logic of the subject matter.

In contrast to the subject-matter approach, the process-oriented educator looks to the child's interests to provide the basis of the teacher–learner relationship. The child, not the subject matter, is the center of the relationship. The teacher is a guide to the learning process but does not dominate it.

The teacher's assumptions about learners influence his or her behavior toward learners and determine the curriculum he or she will plan for them. Assumptions about human nature influence the type of curriculum, the particular method of instruction, and the school's climate.

Philosophies of Education

Over time, a number of systematic philosophies have been developed. Idealism and Realism represent major philosophies that have had a long history in Western civilization. They remain vital philosophies that guide educational processes and give substance to various curricular designs. Closely related to these more traditional philosophies are the educational theories of Perennialism, which emphasizes the human being's rationality, and Essentialism, which stresses basic skills and subjects.

In contrast to the more traditional philosophies, John Dewey's Pragmatism emphasizes the educational process as a transaction between the person and the environment. Among the educational theories that are related to Pragmatism are Progressivism and Reconstructionism. Progressivism, a reaction against traditionalism in schooling, stresses the liberation of the child's needs and interests. Reconstructionism urges that schools play a significant role in cultural criticism and change.

Two contemporary approaches to educational philosophy are Existentialism and Postmodernism. The Existentialist is concerned about the rise of a mass society and bureaucratic schools that dehumanize students by reducing them to objects or functions. The Postmodernist is most concerned with a critique of existing rationales of knowledge and values. Postmodernism challenges universalizing views by deconstructing the rationales that support them.

In addition to examining significant philosophies of education, in later chapters we will also examine several ideologies that have shaped the Western political, social, and educational perspective. Based on political and social contexts, ideologies such as Nationalism, Liberalism, Conservatism, and Marxism have shaped schools, curricula, and styles of teaching and learning. At times, elements of philosophical systems have been fused with particular ideologies. The text concludes with a discussion of theories of education and then examines Essentialism, Progressivism, Social Reconstructionism, and Critical Theory.

Reflecting on Autobiographical Exercises

Several years ago, I was a visiting summer professor at the University of Northern Michigan in Marquette, in the Upper Peninsula. It was a change from my home university, Loyola in Chicago. Loyola is an independent, Jesuit, Catholic institution whereas Northern Michigan is a state-supported public institution. Loyola is an urban university located in a major metropolitan area; Northern Michigan is located in a very natural area with abundant forests and wildlife, and a small population.

I was teaching a course in philosophy of education and as a beginning exercise asked my students to write short educational autobiographies. As a starting point to examine their philosophies of education, the exercise was designed to stimulate them to think about how they had constructed their ideas about education in general, the purposes of schools, and why they were

teachers. After I had read their autobiographies, I planned to return them to the students, who were then to revise them in terms of their reactions to lectures, readings, and discussions in the course. In reading the initial autobiographies, I discovered some things about my students and had new insights into their thinking about education. Although there were variations in the autobiographies, some general common themes emerged.

My students saw their lives and interpreted their education in terms of their place—the Upper Peninsula. They were shaped by growing up in an environment where the winters were long and snowy. They delighted in the recreational activities of the region—hiking, fishing, hunting, snowmobiling. They were educated in the Upper Peninsula and wanted to spend the rest of their lives there. I was amazed by the importance of place in their lives. I appreciated the genuineness of their commitment

(Continued)

Reflecting on Autobiographical Exercises   *(Continued)*

to their home area. I thought that in reflecting on philosophy of education I would need to draw insights on the importance of a place in a person's life. The desire to be rooted in a place was very different from the urban mobility that I found in many of my students at Loyola. I also thought about how place, while creating identity, also can be a cause of looking inward rather than outward. Perhaps, there was a need to extend horizons.

My students saw education largely in terms of processes—how to teach in ways that they found engaging. Many essays contained the term *process-based education.* They were highly interested in methods of teaching. This gave me a problem to work on in my own teaching. I felt that I had to make a definite connection between my course, which was basically content-oriented to philosophy of education, and the aspects of teaching and learning that most concerned my students. I used discussions in which I linked students' comments about process to my course. For some of the philosophies (e.g., Pragmatism) and theories (e.g.,

Progressivism), there was a natural relationship. It took more work on my part to make the linkage to the more traditional philosophies.

Another thing I learned was that the students felt that they were in a situation that was changing economically. Many of their grandparents and parents had worked in the fishing or lumber industries, or in the copper and iron mines. However, these industries had seriously declined. There was significant unemployment and the students knew that earning a living would be a challenge. As I now reflect on their reactions, I am struck by how economic change, such as globalization, affects personal lives.

There were many more things that I learned from my students that summer. I recently saw the motion picture *Freedom Writers,* in which a teacher used autobiographical writing with her students in a depressed Los Angeles high school. Maybe, I thought, my idea about autobiography as an entry into constructing a philosophy of education had merit.[5]

Conclusion

It is valuable for teachers to recognize various philosophies of education and to identify curricula and methods in their relationship to particular philosophical positions. This competency helps educators to examine and to criticize educational policies and programs. For example, many of the proposals made in educational reports such as *A Nation at Risk* and in the No Child Left Behind Act rest on philosophical and ideological assumptions. In many respects, these proposals represent a revival of Neo-Conservatism and Essentialism.

Philosophical inquiry can aid the educator in examining decisions and problems. In turn, philosophy of education may draw heavily from the experiences, practices, and observations of the educator. For example, as we shall see in later chapters, educational goals, practices, methods, and ends can be extrapolated from such systems of philosophy as Idealism, Realism, and Thomism. The converse is also true, however. It is possible to create educational theories by examining educational practices and generalizing about their most general consequences for personal and social growth as the Essentialists, Progressives, Perennialists, and Critical Theorists have done.

Throughout history, and particularly in recent years, education has been the subject of much debate and conflict. In many ways, the presence of divergent views is a sign of vitality. As a social institution, the school is the focal point of conflicts. Numerous recommendations have been made for school reform. Some have even suggested that the school be abandoned as society's primary educational institution. Others argue that schools should deliberately instill religious and spiritual values in the young; still others plead for an emphasis on law and order. Some voices proclaim that schools must return to the intellectual virtues, to the liberal arts and sciences, or to basic education. Others see schools as agencies of social criticism or vehicles for initiating social and political reform. Behind these proposals lie assumptions about the nature of the universe, human life, and society. By examining these assumptions in their philosophical matrix, these various alternatives in education may be explored and illuminated.

Using this discussion of definitions of philosophy and education and their relationships, you can proceed to your project of constructing your own philosophy of education. First, reflect on and record your beliefs about reality, knowledge and knowing, and values and how your own education helped to form these beliefs. This initial statement is a "formative" expression of philosophy of education, that is, a starting point that can be re-formed, reshaped, and revised until it becomes more complete. Expressing your beginning thoughts about philosophy of education, your statement is likely to be based on your experiences with education up to this point. You may wish to reflect on your own formal education, your schooling, and how it contributed to shaping your ideas. You may wish also to reflect on how informal agents shaped your ideas about education. Consider how parents, family members, friends, teachers, and classmates shaped your ideas about education—its purposes, processes, and outcomes. You may also wish to consider how books, movies, television, and the Internet influenced your view of education.

Then, as you read the book, analyze each philosophy, ideology, and theory that is presented and discuss it in class. Reflect on how the ideas and themes developed in each chapter relate to your initial expression of your philosophy of education. They may either reinforce or challenge your initial ideas and first reflections about philosophy of education. They may confirm them or possibly cause you to change your mind.

You can begin to construct your own philosophy of education by reflecting on and answering such questions as:

1. Do you believe that knowledge is based on universal and eternal truths or do you think that it is relative to different times and places?
2. What is the purpose of education? Is it to transmit the cultural heritage; to provide economic and social skills; to develop critical thinking; or to criticize and reform society?
3. What are schools for? Why does society support schools as institutions? Are they to teach skills and subjects, encourage personal self-definition, develop human intelligence, or create patriotic and economically productive citizens?
4. What should be contained in the curriculum: basic skills and subjects, experiences and projects, the great books and classics, inquiry processes or critical thinking?
5. What should be the relationship between teachers and students? Transmitting the heritage, teaching and learning skills and subjects, examining great ideas, encouraging self-expression and self-definition, constructing knowledge, or solving problems?

As you think about and answer these questions you will be constructing your own philosophy of education. After you read each of the following chapters, you can revisit your philosophy and revise or enlarge it.

Questions for Reflection and Discussion

1. Reflect on your ideas about knowledge, education and schooling, and teaching and learning. What would you say is your philosophy of education? If you have the opportunity, share your thoughts with your classmates and listen to their philosophies. Discuss the agreements and disagreements that emerge.

2. Reflect on how your philosophy of education has been influenced by significant teachers in your life or by books, motion pictures, or television programs about teachers and teaching. Share and discuss such influences with your classmates.

3. What underlying philosophical orientations can you identify in your teacher-education program as a whole?

4. Reflect on your educational experience. What value conflicts have you observed in schools, between teachers and teachers, between teachers and students, and between students and students?

5. How is teaching both reflective and active?

6. Reflect on values in contemporary American society and culture. Do you find evidence of conflict between those who subscribe to universal and objective values and those who take a relativistic or subjective view?

Inquiry and Research Projects

1. Maintain a journal that identifies the philosophy or theory underlying the school, curriculum, and teaching–learning methods you are experiencing.

2. Create and maintain a clippings file of articles about education that appear in the popular press—newspapers and magazines—either critiquing schools or proposing educational reforms. Analyze the philosophical and theoretical positions underlying these critiques and proposed reforms.

3. Analyze the district philosophy of education approved by the board of education in your school. What does it say about knowledge and values?

4. Visit several elementary and secondary school classes. Direct special attention to the curricular and instructional strategies being used. In a report to the class, reflect on your observations in terms of underlying philosophical assumptions.

5. Read and review a book that is used in teacher education in terms of the author's view of reality and human nature.

6. Read a novel about teaching and analyze the author's perception of the teacher–learner relationship.

7. Analyze several academic majors described in the catalogue of your college or university. What conceptions of knowledge are implied in the course requirements for these majors?

As you begin to read the next chapters on Idealism, Realism, Pragmatism, Existentialism, and Postmodernism, you might wish to refer back to the Overview table on the following page.

Overview of Philosophies of Education

Philosophy	Metaphysics	Epistemology	Axiology	Educational Implications	Proponents
Idealism	Reality is spiritual or mental and unchanging, eternal and universal.	Knowing is reminiscence, the recollection of latent ideas through introspection and intuition.	Values are universal, absolute, and eternal and are based on the goodness of the World Mind.	A subject-matter curriculum that includes the culture's most noble and enduring ideas. Socratic method. Teachers as exemplars.	Plato Hegel Emerson
Realism	Reality is objective and is composed of matter and form; it is fixed, based on natural law.	Knowing consists of conceptualization based on sensation and abstraction.	Values are absolute and eternal, based on universal laws.	A subject-matter curriculum emphasizes humanistic and scientific disciplines. The great books of Western civilization. Methods that demonstrate reality.	Aquinas Aristotle Hutchins Adler Maritain
Pragmatism (experimentalism)	Concepts of reality are based on experience, the interaction with environment; it is always changing.	Knowing results from experiencing, use of scientific method.	Values are situational or relative.	Instruction is organized around problem solving according to the scientific method.	Dewey James Peirce
Existentialism	Reality is subjective, with existence preceding essence. Existence creates essence.	Knowing is to make personal choices. To choose or appropriate what I want to know.	Values should be freely chosen.	Classroom dialogues stimulate awareness that each person creates a self-concept through significant choices.	Sartre Marcel Morris Kierkegaard
Postmodernism	Rejects metaphysics as historical constructions used for socio-economic domination.	Deconstructs texts (canons) to find their origin and use by dominant groups and classes.	Emphasizes the values of marginalized persons and groups.	Schools are sites of democratic criticism and social change to empower dominated groups.	Derrida Foucault

Building a Philosophical Vocabulary

Aesthetics: the subdivision of axiology that examines questions of beauty.

Axiology: the subdivision of philosophy that examines ethical and aesthetic values.

Curriculum: the deliberately organized experiences presented to learners in a school; or, a program of skills and subjects.

Deductive Logic: reasoning that proceeds from the general principle to the specific case, example, or illustration.

Education: the learned social processes that contribute to participation in a society and a culture.

Epistemology: the subdivision of philosophy that examines knowledge and knowing.

Ethics: the subdivision of axiology that examines right conduct.

Inductive Logic: reasoning that proceeds from the particular instance, case, or example to a generalization.

Metaphysics: the subdivision of philosophy that examines the nature of ultimate reality.

Method of Instruction: the process that teachers use to bring about learning in students.

School: a formal educational agency, established and supported by a society, to educate children; it is staffed by teachers, experts in curriculum and instruction, who deliberately instruct students.

Internet Resources

For commentaries on philosophers and philosophies, consult the Internet Encyclopedia of Philosophy at www.utm.edu/research/iep.

For commentaries and analysis of the educational philosophies and theories of selected educators, consult the Gallery of Educational Theorists organized and maintained by Edward G. Rozycki at www.newfoundations.com/GALLERY/Gallery.html.

For discussions of informal education in the philosophies and theories of selected educators, consult www.infed.org/thinkers.

For an extensive repository of materials on philosophy of education, access "Materials on the Philosophy of Education, Metropolitan Community College, Omaha, Nebraska, at http://commhum.mccneb.edu/PHILOS/phileduc.htm.

The home page of the Philosophy of Education Society is http://philosophyofeducation.org.

Further Readings

Achterhuis, Hans, ed. *American Philosophy of Technology: The Empirical Turn.* Bloomington: Indiana University Press, 2001.

Apple, Michael W. *Democratic Education in a Conservative Age.* New York and London: Routledge, 2000.

Barrow, Robin, and Ronald G. Woods. *An Introduction to Philosophy of Education.* New York: Routledge, 2006.

Carr, David. *Making Sense of Education: An Introduction to the Philosophy and Theory of Education and Teaching.* New York: Routledge Falmer, 2003.

Curren, Randall. *ed. A Companion to the Philosophy of Education.* Malden, MA: Blackwell, 2006.

The Freedom Writers, with Erin Gruwell. *The Freedom Writers Diary: How a Teacher and 150 Teens Used Writing to Change Themselves and the World Around Them.* New York: Doubleday/Random House, 1999.

Gutek, Gerald L. *Philosophical and Ideological Voices in Education.* Boston: Allyn and Bacon, 2004.

Kaminsky, James S. *A New History of Educational Philosophy.* Westport, CT: Greenwood Press, 1993.

Kammen, Michael. *Contested Values: Democracy and Diversity in American Culture.* New York: St. Martin's Press, 1995.

Kelly, Elizabeth A. *Education, Democracy & Public Knowledge.* Boulder, CO: Westview Press, 1995.

Noddings, Nel. *Educating Moral People: A Caring Alternative to Character Education.* New York: Teachers College Press, 2002.

Noddings, Nel. *Philosophy of Education.* Boulder, CO: Westview Press, 2006.

Titone, Connie, and Karen Maloney. *Women's Philosophies of Education: Thinking Through Our Mothers.* Columbus, OH: Merrill/Prentice-Hall, 1999.

Watras, Joseph. *Philosophical Conflicts in American Education, 1893–2000.* Boston: Allyn and Bacon, 2004.

Endnotes

1. For further reading on philosophy of education, see Robin Barrow and Ronald Woods, *An Introduction to the Philosophy of Education* (New York: Routledge, 2006); Sheila G. Dunn, *Philosophical Foundations of Education: Connecting Philosophy to Theory and Practice* (Upper Saddle River, NJ: Pearson, Merrill, Prentice Hall, 2005); and David Carr, *Making Sense of Education: An Introduction to the Philosophy and Theory of Education and Teaching* (New York: Routledge Falmer, 2003).

2. Available at www.ncate.org/public/standards.asp (2006).

3. James D. Hunter, *Culture Wars: The Struggle to Define America* (New York: Basic Books, 1991), pp. 3–29, 44.

4. John E. Colman, *The Master Teachers and the Art of Teaching* (New York: Pitman, 1967), pp. 5–11.

5. The Freedom Writers, with Erin Gruwell, *The Freedom Writers Diary: How a Teacher and 150 Teens Used Writing to Change Themselves and the World Around Them* (New York: Doubleday/Random House, 1999).

2

Idealism and Education

Ralph Waldo Emerson (1803–1882), an American philosopher, who developed Transcendentalism, a version of Idealism.

Chapter Preview

Idealism, which asserts that reality is essentially spiritual or ideational, is one of humankind's oldest and most enduring philosophies. The belief that the world and human beings within it are part of an unfolding universal spirit has long been a cosmic principle in Asian religions such as Hinduism and Buddhism. It was probably through cultural interactions between East and West that Idealist concepts entered Western thought. Buddhism often is found in the contemporary movement in which individuals seek a spiritual basis for their lives. Spiritualism, highly compatible with Idealism, offers an alternative to the materialism and consumerism of contemporary globalization.

In Western philosophy, Idealism's origins are usually traced to the ancient Greek philosopher Plato. Idealism has often dominated philosophical discourse in the past. In eighteenth- and nineteenth-century Germany, Idealists such as Johann Gottlieb Fichte (1762–1814), Friedrich Schelling (1775–1854), and Georg Wilhelm Friedrich Hegel (1770–1831) dominated philosophy. Hegel's monumental work, *The Philosophy of History,* influenced philosophical thought both in Germany and abroad. Both Karl Marx (1818–1883) and John Dewey (1859–1952) studied Idealism in their education as philosophers. Friedrich Froebel (1782–1852), the founder of the kindergarten, created a method of early childhood education based on Idealist philosophy.

In the United States, the New England Transcendentalists Ralph Waldo Emerson (1803–1882) and Henry David Thoreau (1817–1862) used Idealism as the basis of their concepts of the Oversoul, or Macrocosm, and of Nature. William Torrey Harris (1835–1909) used Hegelian Idealism as a philosophical rationale for school organization and curriculum.

While Idealism is historically significant, certain current educational practices have their origin and rationale in the Idealist perspective. The notion that education is a process of unfolding that which is present but latent in the child is grounded in Idealist epistemology. The concept of the teacher as a moral and cultural model, or exemplar, also originated in Idealism, as did the **Socratic method**, which includes the skillful asking of probing questions to stimulate the student's recollection.

Idealism is a historically significant philosophy that continues to hold implications for education. This chapter examines the following topics:

- Plato, Hegel, and Emerson as founders of Idealism
- Idealism as a systematic philosophy and its view of metaphysics, epistemology, axiology, and logic
- Idealism's educational implications for education, schooling, curriculum and instruction, character formation, and teacher–student relationships

As you read the chapter, think about Idealism and how it relates to the construction of your own philosophy of education. In your reflection on philosophy of education, determine whether Idealism, or some of its parts, is meaningful to you.

Plato: Founder of Western Idealism

The origins of Idealism in Western thought are generally traced to Plato, the famous student of Socrates. Whereas Socrates raised fundamental questions about reality, knowledge, and human nature, Plato went beyond his teacher to construct fundamental answers. Plato sought to answer the metaphysical question, What is the nature of reality? and the epistemological question, What is the nature of knowledge and how do we come to know? From these fundamental questions, Plato moved into values, asking, What is the relationship between knowledge and ethical, moral, and aesthetic behavior?

In this section, we examine how Plato established the basic philosophical foundation for Idealism that remains with us today. In Idealist education, the notion that the teacher is a learned master and that the student is a disciple in learning the master's wisdom is a powerful concept that was true in the case of Socrates, the master, and Plato, the disciple.

In ancient Athens, the intellectual gadfly and social critic Socrates (469–399 B.C.) had attracted a circle of students, one of whom was Plato. Rejecting the Sophists' materialistic opportunism and moral relativism, Socrates sought to discover the universal principles of truth, justice, and beauty that govern all humankind. The basic conflict between Socrates and the Sophists points to a recurrent issue in education. The Sophists claimed that ethical principles are relative to a given time and place, and given circumstances; in other words, moral behavior is a response to changing circumstances. Socrates disputed this situational ethics, claiming that what is true, good, and beautiful is the same throughout the world.

Socrates asserted that human beings should seek to live morally excellent lives. Rather than training people in a particular vocational or professional skill like the Sophists, Socrates argued that a genuine education cultivates the knowledge every person needs as a human being. It is the kind of education that cultivates morally excellent persons who act according to reason. Once again, Socrates' assertion that there is a general education for every free human being provides a strong argument for liberal education and against vocational training.

Unlike the Sophists, Socrates denied that true wisdom would result from merely telling a student about some body of information or training him or her in a particular technique. He asserted that concepts, the basis of true knowledge, exist within the mind and can be brought to consciousness. Probing questions stimulate the learner to discover the truth in his or her mind by bringing latent concepts to consciousness.

Socrates' basic epistemological goal was that human beings define themselves in terms of the criteria of universal truth. Through rigorous self-analysis, each person should seek the truth that is universally present in all members of the human race. As a teacher, Socrates asked probing questions that stimulated his students to investigate the perennial human concerns about the meaning of life, truth, and justice.[1] Through dialogue, Socrates and his students dealt with basic questions by defining them, criticizing them, and developing more adequate and comprehensive definitions.

Socratic education involved mentoring, a close personal relationship between teacher and student to create within the student's character an ethical predisposition to discover and use truth to order and govern his or her life. In the past, this kind of ethical formation was called character building. Contemporary educators refer to it as modeling. That is, the teacher personifies desirable character traits and dispositions that are worthy of the learner's imitation.

Our knowledge about Socrates comes from Plato (427–347 B.C.), who was Socrates' student and a speculative philosopher in his own right. Plato, who founded the Academy in Athens in 387 B.C., wrote a number of philosophical works that established the foundations of Western philosophy. Among them were *Protagoras,* which examined the issue of virtue; *Phaedo,* which examined the soul's immortality; and ***The Republic*** and the *Laws,* which considered political and educational issues.

Like his mentor Socrates, Plato rejected the Sophists' claims that ethical behavior is situationally determined and that education could be reduced to specialized vocational or professional training. Plato based his metaphysical beliefs on the existence of an ideal, hence unchanging, world of perfect ideas, such as universal and timeless concepts of truth, goodness, justice, and beauty.[2] The individual examples or cases of these general concepts are imperfect reflections or representations of the perfect forms upon which they are based. All of the perfect forms are contained in a great all-inclusive and highly general form which Plato called the **Form of the Good**. The Form of the Good is a metaphysical and universal form that contains all truth, goodness, and beauty. In structuring a philosophy based on such an unchanging order or reality, Plato was attacking the Sophists' relativism and reliance on sensory perception. In contrast, he asserted that human beings are good and honorable when their conduct conforms to the ideal and universal concepts of truth, goodness, and beauty.

Plato's epistemology, or theory of knowledge, is based on the concept of **reminiscence** or recollection by which human beings recall the truths that are latently but unconsciously present in their minds. Reminiscence implies that every human being possesses a soul, which prior to birth lived in a spiritual world of perfect forms or ideas. With the shock of birth—actually, an imprisoning of the psyche in a material flesh-and-blood body—this knowledge of the perfect ideas is repressed within the unconscious part of the mind. However, the ideas of the perfect forms are still there and can be brought to consciousness. Knowing requires effort, however. The learner has to be ready and willing to learn, to discard false opinion, and needs to seek truth in a conscious fashion.

Genuine knowledge, according to Plato, is immaterial, intellectual, and eternal as are the perfect forms on which it is based. There is but one idea of perfection common to all human beings regardless of where and when they live or the circumstances under which they live. Like truth itself, a genuine education is also universal and timeless. Because reality can only be discovered intellectually, the best kind of education is also intellectual. Although Plato developed his educational philosophy in ancient Greece, his ideas have been reiterated many times since then. Defenders of liberal education often rely on Plato's ideas, which are also the basis for the contemporary educational theory of Perennialism. For example, Allan Bloom, in his noted attack on relativism in *The Closing of the American Mind,* calls Plato's *Republic* "the book on education" that really explains genuine teaching and learning.[3]

In his famous allegory of the cave, Plato depicted humans as prisoners, who, chained in a dark cave, can only glimpse shadows reflected against a wall, rather than the objects of which they are reflections. Like these shadows, the perceptions of our senses are not reality but distorted images of it. True knowledge comes as we escape the cave of sensation and opinion and go into the light where the sun, the light of reason, shows things as they truly are.

While his allegory of the cave encouraged human beings to liberate themselves by finding universal truth, Plato's Idealism also stressed the importance of the political state. Plato compared the well-ordered political state with the well-functioning human organism. The perfectly functioning political state and the perfectly functioning person both conformed to the form of justice. In *The Republic,* Plato wrote about a perfect society ruled by an intellectual elite of philosopher-kings.

Plato's ideal state existed to cultivate truth and virtue in its citizens. His political and educational theory rested on the assumptions that only knowledgeable persons should govern society and that all the republic's residents should contribute, according to their aptitude, to the general welfare. Education and educational agencies would have a key role in determining the role and functions that the individual exercised in the community.

An examination of the class composition of Plato's republic provides an idea of the functioning of the organic state and education's role in ensuring that the state functioned properly. Plato divided the inhabitants of his republic into three basic classes: the philosopher-kings, the intellectual rulers of the state; the auxiliaries, the state's military defenders; and the workers, who performed the services and produced the economic goods that the state needed. By way of analogy, the philosopher-kings could be compared to the state's mind, the auxiliaries to its limbs, and workers to its stomach. Assignment to one of these three basic classes depended on one's intellectual ability.

In Plato's republic, the educational system exercised a selecting role as it assessed the person's intellectual potentiality. Once the individual's intellectual potentiality had been determined, he or she received the education appropriate to this ability and ultimately to the function to be exercised in the political state.

The philosopher-kings, the supreme rulers of the political state, were highly educated intellectuals who, after a long period of training in philosophy and dialectic, had attained a vision of the truth. In Plato's political design, the philosopher-kings were virtuous, intelligent, and talented persons who had the capacity for leadership. They had the important assignment of determining the kind of education a person needed for his or her future role in the state.

The auxiliaries, or warriors, who comprised the second class were subordinate to the state's intellectual rulers. More willful than intellectual, the auxiliaries—because of their courage—were to defend the republic. Based on their capacities, the education of the auxiliaries was primarily military. The third class of people, the workers, who produced the state's goods and services, had a limited capacity for intellectual abstraction. Their education consisted of vocational training.

Plato's Idealist philosophy originated in ancient Greece's classical period; centuries later, Idealism had a strong resurgence in the nineteenth century in the works of Hegel, a German philosopher, and Emerson, an American philosopher.

Hegel's Idealist Philosophy of History

Georg Wilhelm Friedrich Hegel (1770–1831) developed an Idealist philosophy of history that influenced Western thought throughout the nineteenth and early twentieth centuries. A professor of philosophy at the University of Heidelberg and then at the prestigious University of Berlin, Hegel attracted numerous students to his lectures on Idealism.[4] Among his works were *The Science of Logic, The Encyclopedia of Philosophical Sciences,* and *The Philosophy of History.*[5] In this section, we examine how Hegel, as an important Idealist, views history and change.

Hegel believed that as individuals our minds are attuned to and related to the Divine Mind, which he called the **Absolute Mind**, the Mind of the Creator. The Absolute Mind, with its perfect intelligence and rationality, gives order to a purposeful world. Not aimless, nor a series of random happenings, history, governed by the Absolute Mind, is purposeful and is moving forward to the goal that is established in the Absolute Mind. People, living through the stages of history (prehistory, ancient, medieval, and modern), march forward along the historical paths that lead to one harmonious destination, which Hegel saw as the modern, rationally organized state. For him, the epitome of a rationally organized state, analogous to Plato's Republic, was Prussia, then a constitutional monarchy.[6]

For Hegel, it is the idea of freedom, in the Absolute Mind and in the minds of human beings, that drives history's forward movement. The idea of perfect freedom is in the Absolute Mind and the minds of human beings striving to achieve it in their lives. The history of humankind is the story of how that idea unfolds from the Absolute Mind and continuously develops, over time, in human cultures.[7]

The movement from one historical period to another, for Hegel, is caused by the dialectical process, in which a regnant idea (a thesis) is challenged by its opposite (an antithesis). The clash of these two ideas results in a higher level and more complex idea, a synthesis, which combines elements of both ideas. The synthesis is then a thesis that contains its antithesis, and the dialectical process continues in increasing comprehensiveness and complexity. This process resembles the way in which the Absolute Mind works in history, moving it forward, until it reaches its conclusion.[8]

With Hegel's dialectical process comes the concept of change as gradual development, an unfolding of what is contained in the Absolute Mind through history. The concept of development as unfolding is significant in education. It means that human growth and development is the unfolding of what is already present in the child, who possesses a spirit that is manifesting itself outward. The stages of human development, when seen as a spiritual progression, give a dignity to children's play and activities. The development is from within outward. For example, in Friedrich Froebel's kindergarten, the teacher is to facilitate development. Froebel designed a series of kindergarten materials, which he called the "gifts." The gifts included balls, blocks, rods, and other items that children were to use in their play and constructive activities. As an Idealist, Froebel believed that the child's activity with a gift would stimulate bringing the underlying concept to consciousness. For example, the ball would lead to the recall of the idea of a sphere or circle. The child's use of

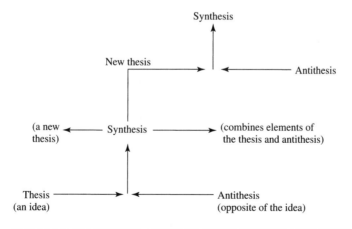

Idealism: Hegel's Dialectic

the gifts was serial and cumulative. In constructing a tower, it was important that the child learn to build on what existed rather than knock the tower of blocks down.

Further, in a broader political and sociological sense, Hegelian development emphasized gradual, slow, steady unfolding as change. It absolutely rejected human social engineering through revolutionary action such as the French Revolution. Such attempts to interfere with the dialectical process of unfolding resulted in discord, disorder, and a tyranny that interfered with human freedom. Hegelian Idealism would reject the Marxist use of dialectic as class conflict, as it would Social Reconstructionist attempts to rapidly build a new social order.

On history's forward march, the emergence of Christianity was a profound development as human beings came to understand that they are spiritual and have an infinite value and an eternal destiny. A crucial historical development was the Protestant Reformation, inaugurated by Martin Luther, which ushered in the modern period.[9] Now, the human being realizes more fully that he or she has a direct spiritual relationship with God. With each person as a free spiritual agent, history has developed to the point that human beings can enjoy their true freedom by giving their rational assent to a culture and society that conforms to rational standards. Notice that the person reaches true freedom not by rejecting culture and society but by conforming to it. In the modern state, exemplified by Prussia, all social institutions now conform to the general principles of reason. Plato's Republic is now realized on earth. In this rationally organized state, individuals, following their inner consciences, will freely choose to act in accord with law and morality of the objective state order and perfect harmony will be achieved between the freedom and society.

The perfect state for Hegel, as for Plato, is an organic community that integrates individuals with the society, the state. In the organic community, discord ends and there is harmony between private interests and community welfare. Personal identity comes from membership in the community.[10]

Before leaving Hegel, we need to consider how his philosophy has shaped the ideas of later philosophers. Most philosophers of the nineteenth and early twentieth centuries studied Hegelian Idealism, which was dominant in the universities of the period. Karl Marx studied Hegel as a student in Germany and incorporated the dialectic into his philosophy of dialectical materialism. He transferred the concept of the dialectic from the realm of ideas into the material world. He retained the idea that history was preordained and would reach a perfect state, which for him was not the Platonic or Hegelian organic society but the classless society in which the state would wither away.

John Dewey, too, studied Hegelian Idealism as a doctoral student at Johns Hopkins University. Like Marx, he would abandon Idealism to create his own Experimentalist version of Pragmatism. However, his great society, much like Hegel's rational state, was one in which private interests would be absorbed in the good of the community based on mutual and reciprocal shared interests.

American Transcendentalism

In the nineteenth century, Idealism was the dominant philosophy in the United States. American Idealism marked a movement away from John Locke's empiricism, especially its emphasis on sensation as the origin of ideas. A revival of Plato's Idealism in England entered the thinking of American philosophers, especially Ralph Waldo Emerson and the Transcendentalists in New England.

Transcendentalism was named after the philosophy of Emmanuel Kant, a German philosopher, who argued in the *Critique of Pure Reason* (1781) that ideas, or transcendent imperative forms, exist in the mind prior to experience. These preexisting transcendental intellectual structures, similar to Plato's forms or latent ideas, are the mental structures by which people locate their experience and construct concepts. Knowledge is possible because our minds organize and systematize what we experience within a framework of space, time, and substances. Space, time, and substance are not outside of us but are creations of our intuition that make it possible to comprehend the world.[11]

Ralph Waldo Emerson

Foremost among the Transcendentalists, Ralph Waldo Emerson (1803–1882) was the nineteenth century's most prominent American intellectual. He was an unusual blending of essayist, poet, mystic, orator, and philosopher. His ideas about individualism and self-reliance were so influential in shaping American character that Emerson's essays were required reading in high school courses in American literature throughout the nineteenth and twentieth centuries. Indeed, Emerson is more often discussed in English rather than in philosophy courses. Emerson's Idealist individualism appealed to Americans who wanted to freely shape their own lives and not be forced to conform to external pressures and authorities. There was no place for external doctrines or dogmas in Emerson's philosophy. The truth came from within the person.

Emerson's Harvard Divinity School Address.   Though once a Unitarian minister, Emerson abandoned denominational Christianity, which he believed had become mired in theology and ritual. Rejecting denominational creeds, he believed that all religions originated in Nature, the one universal world religion. In his 1838 address at the Harvard University Divinity School, his alma mater, Emerson argued that philosophy's overriding challenge was to extricate the great doctrines of the higher law, individual freedom, and human progress from traditional religion's dogmas.[12] True religion, he said, is based on personal intuition and comes from a person's heart and mind and not from revelation. Through the soul, every person can reach the great Mind and Heart of the universe.

Emerson's Divinity School address gives us a clear idea of his views on values and ethics. For him, moral laws are above and beyond the contingencies of time and the relativism of place and culture. Universal moral laws are found in the nature of reality. People intuitively know these laws in their conscience and personal virtue comes from the reverence and awe of being in the presence of these divine laws. The operations of the interior principle of justice are instant and entire. The person who performs a good action is instantly ennobled whereas the one who does a mean deed is instantly contracted.

With philosophy as his primary undertaking, Emerson developed the following overriding Transcendentalist principles: (1) Reality originates in, emanates from, and is unified in the **Oversoul**, the Macrocosm, similar to Plato's Form of the Good; (2) each individual possesses a microcosm, an individual spiritual essence, that is vitalized by the spiritual energy that flows into them from the Universal Spirit, the Oversoul; (3) Nature, a universal reality, is the way by which the Oversoul is manifested to human beings and through Nature we discover the truth that is in us; and (4) we find our truth by our own introspection, contemplation, and intuition of the ideas within our minds.[13]

In searching for the truth, Emerson advises us to go beyond, indeed to see through, the everyday world of sensation and consumerism and to look to Nature to find the truth present in our minds.[14] The world of Nature corresponds to the world mind and to our individual minds. It connects us to the world mind. If we work at it, we can discover the truth through contemplation and meditation but we need to overcome the external pressures of materialism and consumerism that distract our quest for the truth.

Education and "The American Scholar."   Although educational themes abound in Emerson's essays, his treatise "The American Scholar" directly addressed education. His "scholar" is the educated person, who enjoys literature and philosophy, but also leaves the library to learn from Nature.[15] An Emersonian teacher would use books as intellectual sources and Nature, the natural environment, to stimulate students' search for the truth. Through intuition, the person can grasp the truth, as it is: a unified and integrated whole. As a universalist, Emerson, discounting relativism, saw the truth as one in all places and at all times. When we empirically dissect or deconstruct the truth, its unity, too, is ripped apart. Science can give us a partial view of the truth, but only parts and not the whole. Science misses the beauty of truth. When we transcend the immediate and the partial, we are able to unite our cognitive knowing and our aesthetic feeling into a unified experience of reality.

Though much of the teacher's language is descriptive and narrative, Emerson advises teachers to also use metaphors, allegories, and poetry to inspire and provoke students to look into their own minds. Emerson wrote, "Life is good only when it is magical and musical, a perfect timing and consent, and when we do not anatomize it. . . . You must hear the bird's song without attempting to render it into nouns and verbs."[16]

Transcendentalism as a Green Philosophy.   In many respects, the Transcendentalists, especially Henry David Thoreau, were naturalists and environmentalists who anticipated the contemporary "green" movement. The Transcendentalist idea of Nature seeks to correct the view that Nature is something to be exploited by those who seek profits from tapping and selling its resources. In many ways, the Transcendentalists were among the country's early environmentalists and conservationists. They regarded the American's natural landscape—plains, mountains, forests, rivers, deserts—not only as a rich source of natural resources but also as the means by which people could transcend their own experiences and feel, or intuit, something greater than themselves but of which they were an intricate and unique part. Nature was much more than trees to be cut into lumber or oil to be drawn to the earth's surface for fuel; it was an intricate totality that touched the human spirit.[17]

For them, education needs to impress on people that they and the animals and plants, the air and water, are related and connected to each other. Nature needs to be seen in terms that transcend the material and enter into the poetical—seeing the reflection of trees on the surface of a quiet and glassy lake, for example.

Extrapolating Emerson's concept of transcendent knowing to teaching and learning requires us to step back from current educational trends such as the use of technology and process learning. It requires us to think about education as providing the quiet times, the uncluttered spaces, that allow students to contemplate, meditate, and reflect on their ideas and when these ideas originate. Though not in tune with today's instantaneous information, and scattered bits of information called factoids, Emersonian teaching involves leading students, through probing questions, to examine themselves and the world in which they live.

Idealism as a Systematic Philosophy

In this section, we address the following components of Idealism: (1) metaphysics, (2) epistemology, and (3) axiology.

Idealist Metaphysics

Idealism asserts the primacy of the mental, the spiritual, and the ideal as the basis of reality. It affirms that reality is essentially spiritual or mental and denies the possibility of knowing anything except ideas. In explaining the universe, Idealism posits ultimate reality solely in the mind and argues that the universe is an expression of a highly generalized intelligence and will.[18]

In explaining human nature, the Idealist holds that the human being's spiritual essence is its essential and permanent characteristic. The mind provides the elemental life force that gives the person vitality and dynamism. Mind is evidenced by doubting; doubting is thinking; thinking gives evidence of the presence of intellect or of mind.

The person's real self is nonmaterial, spiritual, or mental. Selfhood, an integrating core of personal values, provides identity for the person because it separates that which *is* from that which *is not* the self.

Reality is spiritual in substance rather than material. Although it may exhibit nonmental entities, the universe definitely contains spiritual or mental realities that are irreducible and hence really existent. Spirit is more inclusive than matter and encompasses it. Matter is dependent on spirit for spirit both energizes and vitalizes matter.

Although the spiritual is ultimately real, it is possible to speak of the "real" world and the world of "appearance" in the Idealist's perspective. The real world of mind and ideas is eternal, permanent, regular, and orderly. Representing a perfect order of reality, the eternal ideas are unalterable because change is inconsistent and unnecessary in a perfect world. It is possible, then, to assert the existence of absolute, universal, and eternal truth and value in contrast to changing sensations or opinion.

In contrast to eternal truth, the "world of appearance" or of opinion is characterized by change, imperfection, irregularity, and disorder. In terms of the real and the apparent, the educational task is to redirect students from sensation and opinion to the reality of ideas. Just as Socrates and Plato argued against the relativism of the Sophists, today's educators need to create in their students a readiness to undertake the continuous and arduous search for the truth. Today's students need to free themselves from the relativism and shoddiness of opinion that says anything goes. They need to embark on a Socratic-like journey to find the universal truths that are present but latent in their minds.

Idealist metaphysics involves a transition from the notion of an individual mind to the assumption that the entire universe is itself also a larger and more comprehensive spiritual mind. Through the principle of relationship, the individual mind is related to other minds and to the Universal Mind. In other words, the individual comes to realize that what is occurring in the universe is also occurring within the self. The subjective individual mind can know other minds and can understand them. To know and interpret other minds implies that an order of intelligibility exists that can be comprehended. This leads to the assumption that there is a Universal Self, an all-encompassing entity from which all reality comes. Thus, the individual human mind is related to and is of the same spiritual substance as the Universal Mind.

The principle of intelligibility or the relationships of mind to mind can be explained by the concepts of the Macrocosm and the Microcosm. Idealists have given various names to the concept of the World or Macrocosmic Mind such as the ground-of-being, the Absolute Self, the World Mind, the First Cause, or the Universal. Regardless of the name, the Macrocosmic or Absolute Mind transcends all limiting qualifications. Because the Absolute Mind is underived, complete, perfect, and unconditioned, it cannot be changed in any way. The universe is one all-inclusive and complete mind of which the lesser minds are limited parts. The Universal, or Macrocosmic, Mind is an absolute person, which is continually thinking, valuing, perceiving, and willing. The Macrocosmic Mind or Self is both a substance and a process. Although the language may seem vague or poetical, the Macrocosm can be said to be thought thinking, contemplation contemplating, and will willing.

Although composed of the same substance as the whole, the Microcosm is a limited part of the whole, an individual, lesser self. A qualitative relationship exists between the Absolute Mind and the individual Microcosmic Self. The individual self, or mind, is a complete entity insofar as it is a self. However, in relationship to the universe, it is part of the whole. In the sense that the part is less than the whole, the individual self is qualitatively less than the whole.

Although subtle metaphysical distinctions run through Idealism, the following constitute the underlying basis of Idealist philosophy: (1) the universe is spiritual and contains distinctively mental, or nonmaterial, realities; (2) these mental realities are personal; and (3) the universe is one all-inclusive and complete part in which the lesser selves are genuine and identical parts or constituent members.

Idealist Epistemology

In order to explain Idealist epistemology, it should be remembered that the Absolute Mind is eternally thinking. The Finite Mind, or the Microcosmic human mind, though of the same spiritual substance as the Absolute Mind, is limited. Nevertheless, the individual mind can communicate with and share the ideas of the Absolute Self or the Macrocosmic Mind, whose knowledge is complete. The human mind is emergent but limited. As an emerging personality, the individual human mind is on a quest to be united in the Absolute.

In Idealism, knowing is recognition or reminiscence of latent ideas that are preformed in the mind. By reminiscence, the human mind may discover the ideas of the Macrocosmic Mind in its own thoughts. Through intuition, introspection, and insight, the individual looks within his or her own mind and therein finds a copy of the Absolute. What is to be known is already present in the mind. The challenge of teaching and learning is to bring this latent knowledge to consciousness.

Idealist Logic

For the Idealist, the basic logic underlying the metaphysical and epistemological processes is that of relating the whole and the part. Mind is essentially a process by which relationships are ordered on the basis of whole–part logic. Truth exists within the Macrocosm, or the Absolute, in an order or pattern that is logical, systematic, and related. Each proposition is related to a larger and more comprehensive higher proposition. While the whole includes the parts, the parts must be consistent with the whole.

According to the Idealists, truth is a set of closely related, orderly, and systematic relationships. To be, or to exist, means to be involved systematically in the whole–part, or Macrocosmic–Microcosmic, relationship. As an assimilator and arranger, mind locates consistency and exposes inconsistency. The properly functioning intellect seeks to establish a perspective based on relating the parts to the whole. The Whole Mind, or the Macrocosmic Mind, is contemplating the universe according to a total perspective that orders time and space. The properly functioning individual mind, striving to imitate the Universal Mind, seeks to fashion a coherent perspective into the universe. The consistent mind, because of its intellectual structures, is able to relate the parts—time, space, circumstance, event—into a coherent pattern or whole. Inconsistency occurs when time, place, circumstance, and condition are unrelated and cannot be put into perspective.

Idealist Axiology

In the preceding sections, it was emphasized that Idealists see the person as essentially spiritual and intellectual. Because the origin of this spirituality and intellectuality is found in a Supreme Supernatural Being or an Absolute Principle, values, like truth, are universal, eternal, and unchanging. They are rooted in the nature of the universe's underlying spirituality and intellectuality. They definitely are not culturally relative as Pragmatists and many Progressives and Liberals claim. Neither are they based on materialism as Marxists assert. In Idealist axiology, values are more than mere human preferences; they really exist and are inherent intrinsically in the universe. Value experience is essentially an imitation of the Good, which is present in the Absolute. As such, values are absolute, eternal, unchanging, and universal. It is lack of perspective produced by sensation, opinion, or confusion that causes people to err in their ethical and moral behavior.

Because they reject cultural relativism, Idealists see values as general ethical standards. Further, some values, those that possess greater generality and uniformity, rank highest in the hierarchy of values. Values that relate most directly to our defining spiritual and intellectual nature rank highest and are most important. Our higher order intellectual and spiritual values should regulate our lower order and more material needs.

In our search for values, Idealists tell us to look to the ethical core found in the wisdom of the human race that has persisted over time. Ethical conduct grows out of the permanent aspects of a social and cultural tradition that in reality is the wisdom of the past functioning in the present. Rich sources of value education can be found in history, literature, religion, and philosophy.

For the Idealist, our aesthetic experience comes from the idealization of the world around us. Art portrays our ideas about reality. Art succeeds when it portrays the idealized representations of that which appears commonplace in our life. Good art—literature, drama, painting, sculpture—succeeds when it creates perspective and harmony. Like a work of art, an aesthetic personality is one of harmony and balance. In aesthetic education, the student should be exposed to the great works of art and literature and should try to find the essence that makes them timeless.

The Educational Implications of Idealism

In the following section, we examine (1) the educational goals of Idealism, (2) the school, (3) the Idealist curriculum, (4) the attitudinal dimension, (5) Idealist methodology, and (6) the teacher–learner relationship.

Idealism's Educational Goals

The goal of an Idealist educator is to seek and to find the truth. All other goals are subordinate to that overarching goal. At the outset, notice that the truth is singular and not plural. There is one truth, not many claims to truth. Truth is universal and not dependent on different cultures in different places. Truth is absolute and not contingent on a claim that needs to be constantly tested and revised. Neither do we make the truth, as Constructivism asserts. Education is to lead us on our journey to the truth. Idealism's absolute, eternal, and universal truth runs against the trends of many approaches to education in the twenty-first century.

To seek the truth and to live according to it means that people must first want to find the truth and then be willing to work to attain it through profound thought and rigorous study. Idealist education aims at a personal conversion to the good, true, and beautiful. Idealist education has the following objectives to help students find truth:

1. The teaching–learning process should assist students to realize fully the potentialities inherent in their human nature.
2. The school, as a social institution, should expose students to the wisdom contained in the cultural heritage so that they can know, share in, and extend it through their own personal contributions.

The goal of an Idealist education may seem too abstract and altruistic for today's society. Just as Socrates and Plato combated the relativism of the Sophists in ancient Greece, so too do contemporary Idealists battle against materialism, acquisitiveness, and vocationalism.

The Idealists see a genuine education as being general rather than training for a specific occupation or profession. The goal of vocationalism is expertise in job performance rather than wholeness and excellence as a human being. While Idealists want people prepared to earn their livelihood and contribute to the economic well-being of society, they oppose—as a matter of educational policy—giving vocational training priority over general education.

Acquisitiveness and a crude vocationalism stem from what Idealists would diagnose as a major ill of modern times—namely, a lack of wholeness caused by a myopic vision and a limited perspective. From the time of Plato, Idealists have condemned materialism as an obstacle to a true vision of reality. Such a true vision comes from establishing a proper distance from the sensory world of things so that one can see objects, causes, motives, and ambition in a broad and long-range vista and with a sense of relationship. Whether or not we agree with the metaphysical and epistemological underpinnings of Idealism, the sense of perspective and relationship that Idealism cultivates is a worthy educational goal.

The Role of the School

What can be seen in Idealism is a universal **principle of generality** according to which more specific, immediate, and particular goals are derived from those that are higher, more abstract, general, and inclusive. If the primary goal of education is the student's spiritual or intellectual development, then the school's primary function also becomes quite clear. Schools are institutions, established by society, for the primary purpose of developing a student's spirituality or intellectuality. Just as God or the Absolute is eternal and universal, the purpose of education, too, is universal and unchanging. It remains the same from generation to generation. According to the principle of generality in which specific goals are to agree with more general goals, all other goals and aims are subordinate to the general goal of spiritual and intellectual development. Nothing should be permitted to interfere with or obscure that primary goal.

Idealists see development as the historical evolution of human culture from its primitive origins to successive and cumulative stages of higher and more advanced levels of civilization. Throughout the centuries of human history, the corpus of knowledge has grown as each generation transmits and adds to it. The words *successive* and *cumulative* have a special meaning for the school. Its administrators and teachers are to arrange knowledge as a structured curriculum in which subjects, that is, organized bodies of knowledge, succeed each other in increasingly complex and sophisticated content. As students progress through schooling, their learning is cumulative in that the knowledge attained at one level or grade is added to in the next higher level.

Civilization preserves truth and knowledge by institutionalizing them. In this way, the achievements of each generation are transmitted to the succeeding generation. In particular, it is the task of the school to preserve knowledge by transmitting the cultural heritage in a deliberate fashion by way of systematically ordered, sequential, and cumulative curricula.

Curriculum

Because metaphysics deals with questions of what is ultimately real, it has a strong influence on curriculum, or the "whatness" of education. What do we hold to be most real and important? How does our belief about reality determine what skills and subjects are taught in the school curriculum? In considering these questions from an Idealist perspective, be guided by the major principles already discussed: (1) that which is ultimately real is spiritual or ideational; (2) that which is immediate and particular agrees with that which is more abstract and general; and (3) schools are to cultivate spirituality or intellectuality.

To these three principles, we now add another working assumption about human history and culture. For Idealists, human history represents the unfolding or revealing of the ideas that are present in the mind of God or the sum of concepts that exist in the great unifying idea of the Absolute. These ideas, like their source, are eternal, universal, and unchanging and not dependent on or relative to changing times, situations, or circumstances. What is good, true, and beautiful now has always been good, true, and beautiful. These enduring truths and values have been encased in great works of literature, art, and music, for example, that have existed and been enjoyed and used by people across the generations. These **classics** are permanent sources of God's or the Absolute's unfolding or revelation to human beings over time. These constitute the knowledge that is of most worth and should form the core of the curriculum. A book's current popularity is not a criterion for including it in the curriculum. The real test is that of time—has it captured something that touches people across the ages.

Conceptual systems derived from the Universal Absolute constitute the cultural inheritance, a legacy that should be added to by each generation. The Idealist curriculum can be viewed as a hierarchy in which the summit is occupied by the most general disciplines, namely philosophy and theology, which explain humankind's most essential relationships to God and to the Cosmos. According to this hierarchical principle, the more particular subjects are justified by their relationship to the more general subjects. The more general subject matters are abstract and transcend the limitations of a particular time, place, and circumstance. Because they are general and abstract, they can transfer to a wide variety of situations. Mathematics, in its pure form, is a very useful discipline that provides the opportunities for dealing with abstractions. History and literature are also ranked high in the curriculum hierarchy. In addition to being cognitive stimuli, the historical and literary disciplines are value laden. History, biography, and autobiography can be examined as sources of moral and cultural models, exemplars, and heroines and heroes. History can be viewed as the record of the Absolute unfolding over time and in the lives of persons, especially those men and women of heroic dimension.

Throughout history, humankind has developed bodies of related concepts, or conceptual systems, such as the clusters of linguistic, mathematical, and aesthetic systems. Many conceptual systems and their corresponding learned disciplines exist; these various subject matters form a larger synthesis. The various subject matters represent the varying dimensions of the Absolute that have unfolded and been discovered over time by human beings. However, their cause, origin, and culmination are in the underlying unity. For example, the liberal arts are arranged into many conceptual systems, or learned disciplines, such as history, language, philosophy, mathematics, chemistry, and so forth. However, the highest degree of knowledge is that which sees the relationships of these various subject matters as an integrated unity.

Idealists subscribe to the doctrine of preparation. The school curriculum is designed to prepare students for adult life. It helps students to develop the skills and knowledge to recognize and, indeed, to want to learn that which it is important to learn. Preparation supposes that the adults—the administrators and teachers—who organize the curriculum are knowledgeable. Students are immature but eager to learn. The doctrine of preparation implies that teachers, as knowledgeable adults, know what is in the interests of students to learn, whether or not they are interested in learning at that time.

For Idealists, the elementary school curriculum cultivates the basic skills of literacy, numeracy, and civility that prepare a person for more advanced learning, especially the study of the classics. In this respect, the Idealists can be considered supporters of basic education (i.e., learning to read, write, and calculate) as these are tool skills that enable one to study the important philosophical, historical, and literary works of the cultural heritage. The Idealists would also accept the use of computer skills as another tool in acquiring knowledge. In art, they would encourage the study of the great paintings and musical compositions for both appreciation and creative inspiration. Civility, defined as a respect for spirituality, learning, and art, also is an important behavior.

The principle of a hierarchy of generality operates most evidently when organizing the curriculum—the most general and abstract subjects are higher in the curriculum, deserving of the most time and effort. The tool skills learned in elementary school prepare the student to read, study, and discuss the great works of literature, philosophy, politics, and history at the secondary and higher levels. Mathematics, especially algebra, geometry, and calculus, with their high abstract power, also would rank high in the curriculum. Idealists would also include the sciences but with an emphasis on theory. If the Idealist operates from a religious orientation, then the holy and sacred books of the particular religion (e.g., the Hebrew scriptures, the Christian Bible, the Hindu Gita, and the Islamic Koran) would be placed at the summit of the curricular hierarchy.

Idealists can be identified with those who see the curriculum as a body of subjects organized around basic principles. Although subjects are taught as separate disciplines, students are encouraged to develop integrative and interdisciplinary insights into the unity of knowledge. It is thorough knowledge of individual disciplines, however, that makes true interdisciplinary knowledge a possibility.

Idealist Methodology

Idealist instructional method is derived from its epistemology. The thought process is essentially that of recognition, an introspective self-examination in which learners examine their ideas and therein find the truth shared by all others because it reflects the universal truth present in the World Mind. Idealist educators such as Friedrich Froebel, the founder of the kindergarten, have emphasized the principle of the learner's own self-activity. The learning process is made more efficient by the stimulation offered by a teacher and school environment committed to intellectual activity. Immersion in the cultural heritage, via the curriculum, is part of formal schooling, according to Idealists.

The learner's own self-activity is related to his or her interests and willingness to expend effort. Students have their own intuitive self-interests, which attract them to certain acts, events, and objects. With such intrinsic interests, no external prodding is needed. When interest is intrinsic, or internal to the learner, the positive attraction of the task is such that no conscious exertion is needed.

Although learners have their own interests, not all learning is easy. Students may be distracted by the world of appearance and may seek ends not genuinely related to their own self-development. At these times, effort is required when the task does not elicit sufficient interest on students' parts. At such a time, the teacher, a mature model of cultural values, should encourage every student's redirection to truth. After an expenditure of interest and the application of self-discipline, the student may become interested in the learning task. Again, the cultural heritage comes into play to generate the student's interests. The broader the exposure to the cultural heritage, the more likely it is that the student will have many interests. The more interests that are present, the greater are the possibilities for further self-development.

Although no one particular method can be specified, the Socratic dialogue is certainly appropriate to the Idealist classroom. The Socratic dialogue is a process in which the mature person, the teacher, acts to stimulate the learner's awareness of ideas. The teacher must be prepared to ask leading questions about crucial human concerns. When using the Socratic dialogue in a classroom situation, the teacher must be able to use the group process so that a community of interest develops in which all students want to participate. The Socratic method requires skillful questioning on the part of the teacher and thus is not a simple recall of facts that have been memorized in advance. However, this may be a necessary first step so that the dialogue does not degenerate into a pooling of ignorant and uninformed opinion.

Idealist Value Education

Because the ethical core is contained within and is transmitted by the cultural heritage, subjects such as philosophy, theology, history, literature, and artistic criticism are also rich sources of value. These subjects, which fuse the cognitive and the axiological, are the bearers of the human moral tradition and represent the generalized ethical and cultural conscience of civilization. The humanities can be closely studied and used as sources of cognitive stimulation. At the same time, these historical and literary sources can be absorbed emotionally and used as the basis for the construction of models of value. Value education, according to the Idealist conception, requires that the student be exposed to worthy models and exemplars so that their styles might be imitated and extended. Therefore, the student should be exposed to and should examine critically the great works of art and literature that have endured through time.

Idealist character education accentuates the importance of having a sense of **perspective** that comes from studying the great works of civilization. The Idealist sense of perspective can be compared to perspective in art. In a painting, for example, the artist portrays the subject on a flat surface but is able to use her or his brush and oils to convey a sense relationship not only of color and stroke but also of depth, dimension, and distance. In viewing the painting, it is necessary that we stand back a bit so that we can capture the artist's perspective and see the painting as a whole and unified work of art. In addition and more important, the artist needs to capture something in the painting that conveys her or his aesthetic insights in a way that is meaningful to the viewer and elicits a response in people across time and place (e.g., the timelessness of the Mona Lisa).

In education, perspective means that the student has learned how to take a long-range view of ethical and aesthetic values rather than acting on fleeting short-term popular images. The sense of perspective is not developed quickly but instead comes from gradual and steady exposure to enduring works of literature, music, and art. It means that the person has developed a sufficient psychic distance to appreciate the wholeness and relationships of ethical and aesthetic choices. By studying the great works of art, literature, and history, students can acquire a sense of perspective that unites them and places them within the cultural heritage.

Developing the Idealist sense of perspective is obviously difficult in the contemporary world of rapid and vivid images and loud sounds that bombard us constantly. Think about how a commercial on television is often more vividly conveyed at higher sound decibels that the rest of the program. The sensual bombardment is instantaneous and works in a way that is contrary to building perspective. It shortens our attention span and get us to act impulsively rather than taking our time and creating a distance that places things in a relationship of perspective—from the most general and important to the most immediate and least important. Although the contemporary situation is very challenging to the building of perspective through education, the Idealist would seek to inspire us to accept the challenge and run against the tide, as Emerson urged. The more the external society works against building perspective, the more important it is that schools and teachers be agents of helping students to gain it.

Imitation of the model or exemplar is also a part of the Idealist axiology. Students are exposed to valuable lessons based on worthy models or exemplars from history, literature, religion, biography, and philosophy. They are encouraged to study and to analyze the model so that the particular person being studied serves as a source of value. The teacher is also a constant model in that he or she is a mature embodiment of the culture's highest values. Although the teacher should be selected for competency in both subject matter and pedagogy, he or she should be an aesthetic person who is worthy of imitation by students. Students imitate the model by incorporating the exemplar's value schema into their own lives. Emulation is not mimicry; rather, it is an extension of the good into one's own life.

The Teacher–Learner Relationship

J. Donald Butler, in *Idealism in Education,* has identified some of the desired qualities of the good teacher. According to Butler, the teacher should (1) personify culture and reality for the student; (2) be a specialist in human personality; (3) as an expert in the learning process, be capable of uniting expertise with enthusiasm; (4) merit students' friendship; (5) awaken students' desire to learn; (6) realize that teaching's moral significance lies in its goal of perfecting human beings; and (7) aid in the cultural rebirth of each generation.[19]

In the teacher–learner relationship, emphasis is placed on the teacher's central and crucial role. As a mature person, the Idealist teacher should be one who has established a cultural perspective and has integrated various roles into an harmonious value orchestration. Although the learner is immature and seeks the perspective that the culture can provide, this does not mean that the student's personality should be manipulated by the teacher. The student is striving to gain a mature perspective into his or her own personality. As in the case of all people, the learner's spiritual nature and personality are of great worth. Thus, the teacher should respect the learner and help him or her to realize the fullness of his or her own personality. Because the teacher is a model and mature representative of the culture, selection of the teacher is of great importance. The teacher should embody values, love students, and be an exciting and enthusiastic person.

When schooling's primary goal is students' spiritual and intellectual development, the teacher's role becomes very clear. Teachers are to help students unfold their potentiality and thereby achieve their fullest spiritual and intellectual development. To perform their role, teachers need to realize that they are more than classroom managers. They are spiritual and intellectual agents who are engaged in the great moral calling of assisting students in their spiritual and intellectual self-development.

Students, too, are spiritual and intellectual persons who, though they may be immature physically and socially, have the innate power within them to externalize and fulfill their potentiality. All education is a kind of self-education that is stimulated by skilled teachers, much in the way that Socrates provoked his students to search within themselves to find the truth that is latently present in all persons. The true student, aided by the teacher, then is on a spiritual and intellectual journey to discover what is true, and good, and beautiful—first by looking inward and then moving with all the inner resources possible to achieve the fullness of her or his human nature.

Contemporary education emphasizes the concept of mentoring in which the more experienced, often older, teacher acts as a guide for the inexperienced younger teacher. Some universities have mentoring programs for their faculty in which established senior scholars guide beginning instructors in teaching, research, and publication. The concept of mentoring is not new and can be traced to the Idealist educators. In the history of philosophy, one of the great mentoring situations occurred in ancient Athens when Plato became Socrates' student. Plato learned his basic strategy of probing for truth through dialogues—a conversation in which the participants ask and answer each other's leading questions—from Socrates. Plato, in turn, was a mentor for Aristotle. The American Transcendentalist Emerson was a mentor for the young Thoreau. All positive teacher–student relationships have an element of mentoring in them. As mentors, Idealists teachers are to be models of the culture, persons who inspire students and are worthy of their emulation.

An Idealist Scenario

To illustrate an Idealist classroom situation, I have constructed this scenario about a high school English teacher who is discussing Mark Twain's *Huckleberry Finn* in a course in American literature. The class is examining the moral dilemma that Huck encounters when he must either follow the law of the state or the higher law of his conscience. Specifically, Huck must decide whether he should surrender the escaped slave Jim to the authorities for return to his slave master, or help Jim escape to a free state. Huck's dilemma reveals the apparent conflict between the more general and abstract values and those that are more immediate and particular.

The teacher uses *Huckleberry Finn,* a classic work of the American experience, to represent perennial values. It is important that the teacher place the story in its historical and literary context so that the students are aware of its relationship to the American experience. The relationships of the book to the history of the Dred Scott decision and the fugitive slave law should also be made clear.

It is important that students have read the book before discussing it. While welcoming a free-flowing discussion, the Idealist teacher does not encourage misinformation or permit unfounded opinion to obscure the real meaning of the learning episode. Once the students are aware of Mark Twain's own life, the context of the novel, the characters, and the plot, then the serious exploratory learning can take place through the asking of stimulating questions. Avoiding those questions that can be answered with a simple yes or no, the teacher's questions should lead to still other questions.

The conflict between civil law and higher law is a crucial issue that has persisted throughout human history. What should a person do when the law of the state and the dictates of his or her conscience conflict? Is there a distinction between the good person and the good citizen? Should the person follow his or her conscience and take the risks attendant to such a decision? Should he or she seek to change the law? Is the inner law of conscience part of a universal and higher law that binds all human beings?

Once the students have explored the theme of the human conflict presented by Huck's dilemma, other instances of the same conflict can be illustrated by pointing to examples of civil disobedience as practiced by Henry David Thoreau, Mohandas Gandhi, and Martin Luther King, Jr. The moral questions raised by the Holocaust during World War II and the Nuremberg trials of the Nazi leaders can be examined to illustrate the persistence of these broad moral issues.

Conclusion

Idealism, a philosophy proclaiming the spiritual nature of the human being and the universe, asserts that the good, true, and beautiful are permanently part of the structure of a related, coherent, orderly, and unchanging universe. Idealist educators prefer a subject-matter curriculum that emphasizes truths gained from enduring theological, philosophical, historical, literary, and artistic works. The following concepts, rooted in Idealist philosophy, have a special relevance for educational practice:

1. Education is a process of unfolding and developing that which is a potential in the human person.
2. Learning is a discovery process in which the learner is stimulated to recall the truths present within the mind.
3. The teacher should be a moral and cultural exemplar or model of values that represent the highest and best expression of personal and humane development.

Constructing Your Own Philosophy of Education. As a result of reading about Idealism, you may wish to relate Idealism to constructing your own philosophy of education. Are there aspects of Idealism that you might wish to include or exclude from your personal philosophy of education? For example, do you believe, like Plato, that universal truth and values really exist and good people incorporate these universal standards in their lives?

Questions for Reflection and Discussion

1. Do you believe Idealism as a philosophy of education is too abstract and removed from the real problems of education to be relevant to today's teachers and students?

2. Why do Idealists reject the assumption that values depend on situations and circumstances? Do you agree or disagree with them?

3. Have you encountered teachers who used the Socratic method? If so, how did they use the method and what were the consequences of its use?

4. Have you had teachers who were exemplary models of the educated person? Why do you think they are models? What was their influence on you?

5. Do you think contemporary culture makes it difficult to see things in perspective and to separate what is important from what is trivial? What do you think teachers should do about this issue?

6. Have you ever had a mentor? What made this person a mentor?

7. In Plato's *Republic,* education was used to sort people by their intellectual ability. Have you seen this kind of selection function in contemporary education? What is your opinion of the selective function of education?

Inquiry and Research Projects

1. Develop an outline for a secondary school curriculum that is organized according to the Idealist principle of a hierarchy of generality.

2. Read Henry David Thoreau's *Walden.* What method and processes did he use to develop his insights about Nature?

3. Devise a lesson plan for a unit on the environment that is based on the Transcendentalist idea of Nature.

4. Develop a bibliography of ten books in American literature that you consider to be classics. Annotate each book with a short statement indicating why it is a classic.

5. In a short description, list the qualities that you would expect in a teacher-mentor.

6. Read an autobiography written by a teacher about teaching or see a movie about a teacher in a school situation. Do you find any evidence that the author acted as a model or a mentor to her or his students?

Building an Idealist Vocabulary

Absolute Mind: Hegel's concept of the most general, most abstract, complete, and perfect idea in the universe from which all other ideas are derived.

Classics: great and enduring works of art, literature, and philosophy that are permanent sources of God's or the Absolute's unfolding or revelation to human beings over time; should form the core of the curriculum.

Form of the Good: Plato's metaphysical and universal form or all-embracing construct that contains all truth, goodness, and value.

Hegelian History: human history is the development of cultural and institutions as the ideas in the mind of the Absolute are unfolded and revealed over time.

Idealism: a philosophy that asserts that reality is essentially spiritual, ideational, and nonmaterial.

Oversoul: Emerson's name for the great idea of the universe, the Macrocosm.

Perspective: the process of studying the classics of art, literature, and history to gain a long-range view and understanding of the cultural heritage.

Principle of Generality: An Idealist principle that more specific, immediate, and particular subjects are derived from those that are higher, more abstract, general, and inclusive.

The Republic: Plato's book that argues that the perfect society is an organic one in which each class performs the functions for which it is suited by its nature.

Reminiscence: Plato's epistemology that we know by remembering or recalling ideas already present but unconscious in our minds.

Socratic Method: Socrates' method of asking probing questions about truth, beauty, and justice.

Transcendentalism: a very influential American variety of Idealism developed by Ralph Waldo Emerson in the nineteenth century.

Universalism: the assertion that truth and values are unchanging in every place and at every time, in contrast to cultural relativism, which claims that they depend on particular times and places and their cultures.

Internet Resources

For Idealism in America, access www.Radicalacademy.com/amphilosophy6.htm.

For Philosophy as Idealism, access www.stanford.edu/group/dualist/vol9/pdfs/irani.pdf.

For Idealist philosophy, access www.divinity.library.vanderbilt.edu/rosenzw/idealist.html.

For Plato, access www.plato.stanford.edu/entries/plato.

For Emerson, access www.transcendentalists.com/emerson.html.

For Hegel, access www.philosophypages.com/ph/hege.htm.

Suggestions for Further Readings

Ahrensdorf, Peter J. *The Death of Socrates and the Life of Philosophy: An Interpretation of Plato's* Phaedo. Albany: State University of New York Press, 1995.

Annas, Julia. *An Introduction to Plato's* Republic. Oxford, UK: Clarendon Press, 1991.

Bloom, Allan. The Republic *of Plato*. New York: Basic Books, 1968.

Blondel, Maurice. *The Idealist Illusion and Other Essays.* Translated by Fiachra Long. Dordrecht, Netherlands: Kulwer Academic, 1997.

Budner, Rudiger, ed. *German Idealist Philosophy*. New York: Penguin Books, 1997.

Butler, J. Donald. *Idealism in Education*. New York: Harper and Row, 1966.

Graham, William. *Idealism: An Essay, Metaphysical and Critical*. Bristol, UK: Thoemmes, 1991.

Henrich, Dieter. *Between Kant and Hegel: Lectures on German Idealism*. Edited by David S. Pacini. Cambridge, MA: Harvard University Press, 2003.

Irwin, Terence. *Plato's* Ethics. New York: Oxford University Press, 1995.

Myerson, Joel. *Transcendentalism: A Reader*. New York: Oxford University Press, 2000.

Plato. *Symposium of Plato*. Translated by Tom Griffith. Berkeley: University of California Press, 1989.

Pinkard, Terry B. *Hegel: A Biography*. Cambridge, UK: Cambridge University Press, 2000.

Richardson, Robert D. *Emerson: The Mind on Fire*. Berkeley and Los Angeles: University of California Press, 1995.

Schott, Gary A. *Plato's Socrates as Educator*. Albany: State University of New York Press, 2000.

Singer, Peter. *Hegel: A Very Short Introduction*. Oxford, UK: Oxford University Press, 2001.

Stauffer, Deven. *Plato's Introduction to the Question of Justice*. Albany: State University of New York Press, 2001.

Endnotes

1. John E. Colman, *The Master Teachers and the Art of Teaching* (New York: Pitman, 1967), pp. 28–34.
2. Robert S. Brumbaugh and Nathaniel M. Lawrence, *Philosophers on Education: Six Essays on the Foundations of Western Thought* (Boston: Houghton Mifflin, 1963), pp. 10–48.
3. Allan Bloom, *The Closing of the American Mind* (New York: Simon and Schuster, 1987), p. 381.
4. For Hegel's biography, see Terry P. Pinkard, *Hegel: A Biography* (Cambridge, UK: Cambridge University Press, 2000).
5. For Hegel's works, see Stephen Houlgate, ed., *The Hegel Reader* (Oxford, UK, and New York: Blackwell, 1998).
6. Peter Singer, *Hegel: A Very Short Introduction* (Oxford, UK: Oxford University Press, 2001), p. 15.
7. Singer, *Hegel: A Very Short Introduction*, p. 21.
8. Singer, *Hegel: A Very Short Introduction*, p. 104.
9. Singer, *Hegel: A Very Short Introduction*, p. 24.
10. Singer, *Hegel: A Very Short Introduction*, pp. 45–46.
11. Singer, *Hegel: A Very Short Introduction*, p. 4.
12. Ralph H. Gabriel, *The Course of American Democratic Thought* (New York: Ronald Press, 1956), p. 41.
13. Ralph Waldo Emerson, *Emerson on Transcendentalism* (New York: Continuum, 1994).
14. Gabriel, *The Course of American Democratic Thought*, p. 45.
15. For an analysis of Emerson's "American Scholar," see Kenneth Seeks, *Understanding Emerson: "The American Scholar" and His Struggle for Self-Reliance* (Princeton, NJ: Princeton University Press, 2003).
16. Frederick Mayer, *American Ideas and Education* (Columbus, OH: Charles E. Merrill, 1964), pp. 165–189.
17. For an analysis of Transcendentalism's relationships to environmentalism, see Andrew McMurry, *Environmental Renaissance: Emerson, Thoreau & the System of Nature* (Athens: University of Georgia Press, 2003).
18. For an analysis of Idealism, see "Idealism: A Clarification of an Educational Philosophy," *Educational Theory*, 25 (Summer 1975), pp. 263–271.
19. J. Donald Butler, *Idealism in Education* (New York: Harper and Row, 1966), p. 120.

3

Realism and Education

Aristotle (384–321 B.C.), Greek philosopher-teacher who founded Realism.

Chapter Preview

Realism as a philosophy of education argues that we inhabit a world, an objective order of reality, that we can come to know. We can discover the truth about this reality and organize it as knowledge. This knowledge is our best guide to action. We begin our discussion by returning to Realism's origins in ancient Greece with Aristotle and then move historically to the Middle Ages to examine Thomas Aquinas's Theistic Realism as a synthesis of

Aristotle's philosophy with Christian doctrines. We then explore Realism as a philosophy and consider its implications for education. The chapter is organized into the following major components:

- Aristotle as a founder of Realism
- Theistic Realism or Thomism
- Maritain's Integral Humanism
- Realism's philosophical and educational relationships
- Realism's educational implications
- Perennialism as an educational theory derived from Aristotelian Realism

As you begin to read the chapter, you might recall the suggestion to construct your own philosophy of education. Reflect on Realism as you read and ask yourself whether it appeals to you as a philosophy of education. Are there elements in Realism that you might wish to incorporate into your own philosophy of education?

Aristotle: Founder of Realism

Aristotle (384–321 B.C.), a student of Plato, like his teacher was a leading founder of Western philosophy and education. Plato established Idealism's foundations; Aristotle developed Realism. Aristotle was born in the northern Greek kingdom of Macedonia, where his father, Nichomachus, was court physician to King Amyntas II. Encouraged by his father, a collector of scientific and medical materials, young Aristotle developed his lifelong fascination with scientific research.[1] At age seventeen, Aristotle journeyed to Athens, where he studied for twenty years with Plato. As many students do with their mentor's teaching, Aristotle revised Plato's philosophy. Aristotle, theory builder and philosophical synthesizer, combined his scientific curiosity about nature with Plato's more speculative Idealism in which truth resided in a perfect metaphysical realm beyond and superior to the natural world. Whereas Plato's worldview rested on a perfect and unchanging view of reality that could be glimpsed by those expert in philosophical speculation, Aristotle began his inquiries with his senses. The young philosopher-scientist was driven by a desire to know how things developed and changed. Aristotle set out to reconcile Plato's theory of perfect forms or ideas with his own findings about natural development.[2]

Aristotle replaced Plato's belief that reality consists of pure ideas, derived from the Form of the Good, with a metaphysical dualism in which reality consists of matter and form. Plato believed that knowing means using intuition to recall innate ideas; Aristotle's epistemology begins with sensation of objects in the environment and is completed by forming, or abstracting, concepts from that experience. In 343 B.C., Aristotle went to Macedonia as tutor to King Philip's son, who as Alexander the Great would conquer the then known world. Aristotle returned to Athens and established a school, the Lyceum, where he taught from 336 B.C. to 323 B.C.

Aristotle, like Plato, was a philosopher-teacher, whose search for truth led him to research many areas—metaphysics, ethics, rhetoric, logic, natural science, psychology, and language. An early prototype of the traditional university professor, Aristotle closely connected research and teaching. He would do his research, reflect and digest his findings, and then transmit his discoveries to his students in his lectures. Aristotle's teaching, however, differed from Plato's. Whereas Plato, following his own mentor, Socrates, used the dialectical process to probe large questions about reality with his students, Aristotle, who believed that there was much to know, turned to lecturing as an efficient process of transmitting knowledge to students. All his treatises, generally based on his lectures, held important ideas for education; his most significant writings about educational themes are *Metaphysics, Nichomachaean Ethics, On Justice, On the Sciences, Political Theory* and *Art of Rhetoric*. Aristotle died in 321 B.C. in retirement on the island of Chalcis.

Aristotle and Scientific Realism

Aristotle was an early research scientist as well as a philosopher. He investigated a range of natural areas—astronomy, meteorology, zoology, botany, and biology—and collected data in all these areas. Although his method was crude in comparison to modern science's controlled experimentation in a laboratory setting, Aristotle made the whole natural world his laboratory. His method involved reviewing what was known about an area, identifying questions to be probed, careful observation and collecting of specimens, recording his findings, and then reaching some generalizations or conclusions—all of which remain germane to modern science.[3]

Aristotle's review of earlier Greek scientists' work gave him his point of entry into scientific exploration. He studied the work of his famous predecessors before beginning his own investigations of natural phenomenon. From Thales of Miletus, Aristotle adopted the idea that the universe operates according to a rational plan that humans can discover. From Anaximander, Aristotle took the view that nature is a balance of forces. Aristotle was aware of Parmenides' atomic theory and of Heraclitus' theory of a constantly changing reality. Building on the work of these earlier Greek scientists, Aristotle developed his own scientific theory.[4]

Aristotle developed his own theory of progression in which natural phenomenon is organized in a hierarchy. At the lowest level in the order are lifeless things, inanimate objects such as rocks and minerals. Upward, in the next higher order, came plants, which, although alive in comparison to inanimate objects, lack many of the powers of the animals. In the animal kingdom, there was a continuous scale of ascent upward to human beings, who were the highest in the hierarchy because of their rationality.

Based on his hierarchy of natural progression, Aristotle devised a system to classify and categorize natural phenomena. Using the crude but important large categories of mineral, plant, and animal, he moved to develop a more specialized schema of classification that could be finely tuned and divided into an immense array of subcategories. The information derived from the study of these subcategories could be classified into biology, zoology, anthropology, anatomy, physiology, and so on. In the Aristotelian system, everything that exists can be categorized and classified.

Running through Aristotle's science is the belief that we can understand the world objectively. Using our intelligence, guided by rationality, and with sufficient patience, we can discover considerable verifiable information about the world. We can formulate theories about what the world contains and how it works. Our theories can be revised to become more accurate; this does not change the object but enables us to refine our understanding of it. Further, although there are various social uses, and often technological changes in how we use objects, these utilitarian factors do not change the nature and structure of objects. In fact, how we use objects depends on their composition.

Contemporary Scientific Realists are concerned with investigating and researching the objects in the world to discover their constituent makeup, how they function, and how they may or may not relate to us. They discount the metaphysical aspects of Aristotle's philosophy and instead focus on the observable aspects of reality—that which can be seen, examined, and tested. For them, the aim of science is to provide the most accurate description possible at a given time. As the scientific instruments of observation are further improved, the findings about reality will become more detailed and give a more complete picture of reality. This means that our scientific knowledge will be revised, made more comprehensive and more accurate, if we continue to pursue objective scientific research. Scientific experimentation is to keep filling in the details through improved observation. The more details we have, the more we know and the more accurately our concepts will conform to what is really out there. In genetics, for example, scientists have made significant discoveries about DNA in which we have acquired increasingly detailed information about human genes. Certain combinations of genes result in differences in the physical appearance and health of individuals. Genetic scientists can study these genes and make generalizations and principles from which we can make deductions about specific instances. For example, certain genes in certain combinations may cause specific kinds of inherited disease. By identifying these combinations in individuals, physicians can make accurate diagnoses and prescribe appropriate treatment plans.

Aristotle's Ethics

Aristotle was also an early ethicist. We are all familiar with his ethical principle to act in moderation and to take the middle course and avoid extremes. In *Nichomachean Ethics,* Aristotle sets forth his ethical theory in which he examines the relationship between knowledge and virtue: We live in a purposeful and orderly universe and so our actions, too, should be purposeful. In human character formation, ethical behavior originates in predispositions, early habits, learned from parents and teachers, that incline us, as children, who have not yet developed our rational potentiality, to virtue. An important predisposition to virtue is coming to understand that what we do will have a consequence.

In *De Anima* and *Nichomachean Ethics,* Aristotle asserted that certain general principles of human nature and behavior were discernible. Along with other animals, humans share the functions of nutrition, locomotion, reproduction, and respiration. But as a more complex and sophisticated being, humans also have functions of sense, imagination, habit, pain, and pleasure. Following his dualistic worldview, Aristotle described the two planes of human existence. As a rational being, human beings are abstractive, symbolic, and choice-making creatures. However, a nonrational component also exists in human nature in that the same person who is rational is also emotional and volitional. The human being's reason for being is to recognize, cultivate, develop, and use his or her rationality. The greatest source of human happiness lies in the active cultivation of rationality, which contributes to self-actualization or self-cultivation and self-perfection. The person who truly acts as a human being is governed by his or her highest and defining power—reason. Although emotions are the means to experience pleasure, and will is the instrument of obtaining ends, both the emotions and the will are governed properly by reason. When governed by appetites, emotions, and will, the human being acts unintelligently, is unreasoning, and debases his or her own essential humanity. When governed by reason, human beings can develop the excellence of moral character that is a mean between the extreme of repression and the uninhibited expression or indulgence of passions and appetites.

For Aristotle, the individual's ultimate goal is happiness, which he defined as the cultivation of rationality, the power that both defines and contains the purpose of human existence. The virtuous life is governed by reason. The exercise of virtue is the means of attaining happiness. Aristotle divided values into moral and intellectual virtues. Moral virtue is a habit by which the individual exercises a prudent choice, that which a rational person would make. Moral virtues favor moderation, lying between extreme excess and extreme inhibition. For example, the prudent person would develop a balanced diet based upon the consumption of foods that promote physical health and well-being. Gorging oneself leads to obesity, which has deleterious consequences for health such as impaired circulation, diabetes, and other illnesses. At the other extreme, starving oneself into a state of anorexia impairs health by depriving the body of proper nutrition.

Aristotle, like his mentor Plato, was motivated by an intense desire to know, to acquire knowledge and to know the truth. He believed that his desire for the truth was not his alone but was shared by all other human beings who by their rational nature wanted to know. As reasoning beings, humans essentially were led to philosophy, the love of wisdom. Indeed, he saw the greatest human activity and the source of human happiness to be the intellectual engagement with reality.[5] The intellectual virtues contribute to the perfection of the human intellect or power of reason through which the person seeks to discover the truth that is genuine knowledge. Aristotle, a consistent categorizer and classifier, subdivided knowledge into three categories: theoretical, practical, and productive. Theoretical knowledge is the highest form of knowledge in that its end is the truth. Practical knowledge guides us in our political and social affairs, advising us about moral and ethical action. Aristotle was the least concerned with productive knowledge about how to make things.[6] Realist educators, like the founder of their philosophy, give the highest priority to theory that, for them, is the surest guide to rational choice and ethical behavior.

For Aristotle, cultivation of both intellectual and ethical virtues takes place in human community. In the *polis,* the Greek locus of the human community, shared perceptions of human life arose. The city-state, Aristotle argued, existed so that its inhabitants would have a place to experience happiness, or to live well. The constitution and laws of the city-state should be designed to foster virtue. It is education that creates a commonality among a city's citizens.[7]

Knowing the World

Unlike his mentor Plato, who searched for a perfect world beyond the senses, Aristotle began with the natural and social environments in which he lived but continued his search upward to discover the underlying structure of this world in the higher realm of metaphysics. His search led him to formulate the classical supposition of Realism—we live in an objective order of reality, a world of objects that exists outside of our mind but that we can come to know. Using their senses and their power to reason, human beings can acquire knowledge about objects and develop generalizations about their structure (what they are) and their function (what they do).

Matter and Form

In explaining the meaning of an objective order of reality, Aristotle developed his **matter–form hypothesis**. All the objects that we perceive through our senses are composed of matter. Matter, the stuff of every object, however, is organized into different objects—rocks, plants, trees, animals—that have different structures, which Aristotle called *forms*. Everything that exists has matter but matter needs to take a form. At this point, Aristotle began to create the dualism—the division of everything into two elements—that is basic to Realism. Recall that for the Idealists, reality possesses a unity—a singularity—a oneness with the Absolute. Now, Aristotle has departed again from his mentor, Plato, in seeing the universe as two elements. Later philosophers such as the Pragmatists would wage a continual battle against Aristotelian dualism. Aristotle also devised two explanatory principles: potentiality, which means that matter has the possibility, the potentiality of becoming something; and actuality, when matter takes a form its potential to become an object is actualized.

So far, Aristotle has given us two essential and necessary components of the objects that comprise the objective reality—their matter, their material component, and their form, their structural component or design. He also has given us two principles—matter can become an object by being actualized. How actualization occurs led Aristotle to consider the process of change—what caused matter to move from the potential of being something to actually being it. He explained change through his theory of the four causes: material, formal, efficient, and final. Every object has a **material cause**—the matter from which it is made. For example, the chair on which you are sitting may be made of wood—the chair's material cause. (We are simply calling the material cause in this instance wood. If we wish we can call it the hard fibrous material from the trunk of a tree made into lumber; we can push this back further into an analysis of its chemistry, if we wish.) The **formal cause** gives the object its structure. In our example, the wood has been structured into a chair, which gives it its definition. We now have a definition, which means we have conceptualized the structural component of the object. In this case, it belongs to the concept of chair—a seat for a person, supported by four legs, and a rest for the person's back. It is in the class of the same objects that have "chairness" about them. The formal cause, or form, constitutes the essence of an object, what it needs to be in a particular class of objects. Although chairs may be made of wood, metal, or plastic and come in different colors, these are accidental or incidental in that they do not constitute the essence of what is always needed to be a chair. It is the essence that is the object of our intellectual knowledge. The **efficient cause** refers to the agent who actualized the matter's potentiality. In the case of the chair, it is the woodworker who made the wood into the chair. The **final cause** is that purpose for which the action is done. For the woodworker, the final cause is making the chair.

Aristotle's belief that we live in a purposeful universe rested on his conception of causation, the movement from potentiality to actuality. What occurs in Nature—the seasons of the year, the sprouting and growing of plants from seeds, and human conception, birth, and growth—are all meaningful, not accidental or random, processes that are purposeful. They are moving toward an end during which potentiality is actualized. Aristotle's affirmation of a purposeful universe supposes that there is a First Cause, a principle of rationality, that operates in a purposeful way in the universe. The reality of an orderly and purposeful universe has immense implications for education. It means that human life has a purpose and is meaningful rather than meaningless. It means that human beings, inherently defined as rational beings, can realize their potential. The meaning of human life in Aristotelian terms is the pursuit of happiness, defined as the fulfillment of all human potentiality, especially the power and quality of reason. In Aristotelian terms, the purpose of education is to cultivate, to develop, and to exercise each child's potentiality to be a fully rational human being.

Epistemology as Sensation and Abstraction.   Just as he had divided reality into two parts, form and matter, Aristotle's epistemology is also dualistic and divided into two sequential phases: sensation and abstraction. **Sensation** is the process human beings use to acquire sensory information and data about the material, the matter, of an object. **Abstraction** is the process that we use to sort out sensory information and extract the necessary qualities, the essence, of an object that makes it what it is. When we have discovered these necessary qualities we have formed a concept about an object.[8]

We first begin our process of knowing through our senses, our bodies' physical organs that bring us into contact with objects. Our eyes give us sight of an object, our nose its smell, our ears its sound, our tongue its taste, and our fingers its tactile qualities. Our senses, perceiving the matter of the object, carry information about the object's size, color, hardness or softness, sound, and other data to our minds. Somewhat like a computer, the mind sorts out information into those qualities or conditions that are always present, or necessary to the object, as distinct from those that are sometimes or occasionally found in the object. The necessary conditions that give us the idea of an object's form are the basis of a concept. For Aristotle, a concept is based on the formal or essential qualities abstracted from an object. These are the qualities that it shares with other members or individuals of its class but with no other objects.

To illustrate Aristotle's process of **conceptualization**, we can return to our example of a chair. Chairs come in a variety of sizes—children's chairs and adult chairs—colors, and materials. Their styles are variations on a theme—straight back, Windsor, Hitchcock, folding, Shaker, and so on. Underlying these differences that appear to the senses, the mind is able to abstract a common set of conditions that are necessary for an object to be a chair—a seat for a person, supported by four legs, and a rest for the person's back.

Aristotle's epistemology carries educational implications for instruction. Because we know through our senses and abstraction, we should use this pattern as the basis of our teaching. Instruction—teaching and learning—should provide occasions for students to examine, observe, and deal with objects. It should provide situations in which students create categories of objects that share certain essential characteristics and also recognize those objects that are similar and different.

Dualism

Dualism, seeing reality as composed of two constituent elements, is a very important concept in Aristotle's metaphysical system. **Dualism** means that two related entities exist, neither of which can be reduced to the other. For example, mind and body are two separate entities. Metaphysical dualism asserts that the two essential components of reality, while related, remain distinct. Thus, Aristotle viewed existence as the uniting of the two elements of actuality and potentiality, of form and matter. This dualistic conception of reality profoundly affected Western thought. Human beings are viewed as composite creatures composed of spirit and matter, or mind and matter. Such a dichotomous view of human nature leads to distinctions that have significant educational consequences. Knowledge can be separated into the theoretical and the practical arts; aesthetic experience can be viewed as dealing with either the fine or applied arts; education can be categorized as either liberal or vocational. In the context of these Aristotelian dualisms, that which was abstract, theoretical, fine, and liberal was given priority over that which was practical, applied, and vocational. In the chapter on Pragmatism, we will examine John Dewey's attack on dualism.

The Aristotelian conception of a dualistic universe can also be seen in the categories of substance and accident. *Substance* is the ultimate "element," that which exists of and by itself, of which any object is made; it is the underlying reality to which the primary qualities of an object adhere. Substance is the continuing essence of an object that remains constant through all the alterations in the object's accidental characteristics.

In contrast, *accident* refers to the variable changes that do not alter the essence of a being but individuate it. In various treatments of Pragmatism, one often encounters the statement that reality is constantly changing. The Realist would observe that to measure change, there must be some stable object that is changing. For the Realist, that which undergoes change is substantial, whereas the changes themselves are accidental. For example, all human beings share a common rational human nature, which is their essence. Particular persons, however, are of different races, ethnic groups, weights, and heights. These individualistic characteristics are accidents.

When Aristotelians refer to the essence of a human being, they mean those substantial elements that are unchanging, regardless of time, place, and circumstances. It is from these universals that educators should establish the curriculum. For example, Aristotelians define humans as rational beings who possess an intellect that enables them to abstract from experience and to frame and act on various choices. Regardless of their race, nationality, occupation, or sex, all human beings have the power to reason. Nevertheless, particular persons live at various times and in different places. Varying environmental and social conditions contribute to cultural variations within the common human experience. Although a particular person may be American, Chinese, Russian, or Nigerian because of the accident of being born in a particular place, all people share a common human nature. As a result of being born in a certain location, some people will speak a particular language, such as English, Russian, Swahili, or French. But regardless of their particular languages, all people use language as a means of communication.

Aristotle and the Liberal Arts and Sciences

One of ancient Greece's most significant legacies to Western education, to which Aristotle contributed, is the liberal arts and science tradition. Aristotle was familiar with the Greek curriculum of higher education, which included grammar, rhetoric, literature, poetry, mathematics, and philosophy. Intrigued by science, his curiosity led him to the natural sciences—biology, botany, physiology, and zoology—areas that he developed in his own teaching and writing. Aristotle's system of classification of objects and of creating bodies of information about them helped organize the liberal arts and sciences. It is these bodies of knowledge that make a person liberally educated or free to make rational choices. Over time, people could construct vast arrays of related concepts that could be built into a storehouse of knowledge and provide a cognitive map of reality. The liberal arts and science tradition of education profoundly shaped Realist education and Thomism and Perennialism, which are discussed later in the chapter.

Theistic Realism or Thomism

We now turn to **Theistic Realism**, a synthesis of Aristotle's natural Realism and Christian doctrine developed during the Middle Ages. Realism's belief in an objective order of reality and the capability of human beings to acquire knowledge of it applies equally to Theistic Realism. In addition, we add the term **Theism**, the belief in the existence of an omnipotent, omniscient, and personal God who created the world and all its creatures, including human beings, and keeps them in existence.

Theistic Realism represents the fusion of the ideas of Greek rationality, represented by Aristotle, and Christian theology. Although Christianity had earlier entered the Western world in the Roman period, Christian intellectuals, or scholastics, such as Thomas Aquinas, worked to formulate a rational organization of religious doctrines to render them logically coherent and philosophically meaningful.

It should be pointed out at the onset of our discussion of Theistic Realism that Thomism, its dominant form, has been associated historically with Roman Catholicism; however, not all Theistic Realists or Thomists are Roman Catholics. Also, not all Christians are Theistic Realists. Saint Augustine and other fathers of the Christian Church subscribed to Idealism. In addition, some philosophers associated with Christianity have been Existentialists.

Thomas Aquinas: Founder of Theistic Realism

The development of Theistic Realism by Thomas Aquinas (1225–1274) can best be understood in the context of the scholastic movement that began in A.D. 1100 and reached its zenith in the thirteenth century. Scholasticism, the doctrines articulated by religious scholars, developed when some of the ancient Greek classics, including the philosophical works of Aristotle, were rediscovered and studied in Western European schools and universities, especially the University of Paris. Scholastic philosophers such as Anselm of Canterbury (1033–1109), Bernard of Clairvaux (1091–1153), Peter Abelard (1079–1142), Albertus Magnus (1200–1280), and Thomas Aquinas sought to create a synthesis of Greek rationalism, especially Aristotle's philosophy, and Christian doctrines.

The philosophy developed by the scholastics should be viewed in terms of the hierarchical system of governing the Christian church and its doctrines. The Bible, the writings of the church fathers, the councils of the church, and the body of tradition were authoritative sources for Western Christianity. From these sources, doctrines were articulated, interpreted, and enforced by church councils. As the primary medieval educational agency, the church, through its teachers and schools, transmitted the corpus of Christian doctrine to Western men and women. According to the medieval scholars, the church's divinely sanctioned teaching authority rested on sacred scripture and inspired doctrine.

From this body of theological doctrines, certain basic beliefs that characterized the Christian life can be identified. God is an omnipotent, perfect, and personal being who created all existence; human beings, possessing a spiritual soul and a corporeal body, were created to share in divine happiness. Endowed with an intellect and will, the human being has freedom of choice. Because of Adam's sin, his descendants who inherited the legacy of original sin were spiritually deprived. God sent his son, Jesus Christ, to redeem humankind through his death and resurrection. To aid human beings in achieving salvation, Christ instituted the church and charged it with administering the grace-giving sacraments. These core Christian beliefs held great importance for medieval education and continue to influence contemporary Roman Catholic education.

Scholastic philosophy and education reached its high point in the writings of Saint Thomas Aquinas, a Dominican theologian. Born into an Italian noble family, Aquinas was enrolled at the age of five in the Benedictine abbey of Monte Cassino, where he received his education. Between the ages of fourteen and eighteen, he attended the University of Naples, where he studied Aristotelian philosophy. Aquinas entered the Dominican order, studied at the monastery of the Holy Cross at Cologne from 1246 to 1252, and was ordained as a priest. In 1252, he entered the University of Paris, Western Europe's major theological center, where he taught and earned his master's degree in theology. In 1256, he became a professor of theology. From 1269 until 1272, he wrote *Summa Theologiae,* his most important philosophical work, which sought to create a synthesis of Aristotelian philosophy and Christian doctrine.

In the tradition of medieval scholasticism, Aquinas was both a theologian and a philosopher. Using both faith and reason, he sought to answer questions dealing with the Christian conception of God, the nature of the universe, and the relationship between God and humans. A philosopher-theologian, Aquinas devoted his life to reconciling the claims of faith and reason.

Following Christian doctrine, Aquinas asserted that the universe and life within it had been created by God, a supreme being who, in creating human life, had endowed it with an immaterial and deathless spiritual soul, which is the basis of human self-awareness and freedom. God had also given human beings a physical body, which on earth was temporal, that is, existing at a particular time, and spatial, existing in a particular place. Although the human being lives for a time on earth, the purpose of life was that the soul should live eternally with God in heaven.

Like Aristotle, Aquinas construed human beings to be rational creatures distinguished by their intellectual powers. Again, like Aristotle, Aquinas asserted that human knowledge begins with sensation and is completed through conceptualization or abstraction. However, the natural process of knowing is enhanced by the human being's cooperation with supernatural grace and acceptance of the truth of Christian doctrine.

Again, like Aristotle, Aquinas held a teleological conception of the universe, agreeing that the universe functioned in a purposeful way rather than by mere chance or accident. Human history—indeed, every person's life—expresses purposeful movement to a goal.

Aristotle saw the "good life of happiness" as the human being's reason for being. While accepting the good life as the human being's purpose on earth, Aquinas believed in an even higher purpose—the beatific vision, or the experience of being in the presence of God.

Thomism's Theological and Philosophical Bases

In contrast with Natural Realism, Thomists embrace supernaturalism and find revelation, recorded in the Bible, to be an authoritative source of divinely inspired truth. Thomists assert that human beings have as their ultimate goal the beatific vision of God, which is the final, highest, and most complete happiness. However, through their own actions, human beings sinned and were alienated from God, their creator. This "estrangement" or "alien-ation" was overcome through the redemptive act of Jesus Christ, the son of God, who insti-tuted grace and founded a new "people of God." As a free agent, the individual can choose either to cooperate with or to oppose the work of his or her own salvation.

Because it draws from both Aristotelian Natural Realism and from Catholic Christian theology, Thomism represents the interpenetration of the two. Thomism asserts a dualistic view of reality, which has both a spiritual and a material dimension. Possessing both a body and a soul, human beings exist on both a supernatural and a natural plane. God, the first cause and creator, the source of all existence, is a personal and caring creator, not an imper-sonal "ground of being."

William Cunningham, in *Pivotal Problems of Education,* has referred to this synthe-sis of Realism and Theism as "Supernaturalism." He asserts that human beings, possessing a soul and body, are properly guided by faith and reason. For him, education has a perennial and unchanging character. For Cunningham, an educational philosophy founded on Super-naturalism can specify educational aims in terms of human origin, nature, and destiny. Humankind originated from God through the act of creation; human nature was created in God's image and likeness; the human destiny is to return to God.[9]

Thomism and Knowledge

Like Aristotle, Aquinas asserted that the highest human activity is rationality, the exercising of intellectual and speculative powers. Through conceptualization, we can overcome the restrictions of a primitive and natural determinism and transform our environment. To trans-form the environment, we can formulate plans and structure ends. Through art, science, and technology, we can use our intelligence to humanize the material environment.

Aquinas agreed with Aristotle that humans act most humanely when reasoning. How-ever, Aquinas qualified his agreement; while reason is the human being's highest and most satisfying earthly power, it is nevertheless an incomplete and imperfect happiness. Perfect happiness comes after the death of the body when, through the gift of divine elevation, the human being experiences an immediate cognitive and affective union with God.

Thomist educators, like most Realists, emphasize the intellectual function of the school as an agency designed to cultivate and exercise human reason. Formal schooling's greatest goal is to transmit subject-matter disciplines. For Thomists, a subject-matter discipline is called **scientia,** which means that it is a body of accumulated, demonstrated, and organized knowledge. For Thomists, such subject matters are organized on the basis of major premises that are either self-evident, derived from experimentation, or derived from a higher science. These bodies of knowledge are transmitted by teachers, who expert in the disciplines they teach to students, are expected to use their intellectual powers in understanding, mastering, and applying the principles contained in the subject matter.

The interpenetration of Realism and Theism in Thomistic philosophy has pronounced educational implications. Following dualistic principles, education has two complementary aims based on the human being's nature: to provide the knowledge, exercises, and activities that cultivate both human spirituality and human reason.

Moral Education

Thomist education is deliberately committed to cultivating supernatural values. In its goal of forming Christlike individuals, it encompasses religious and theological studies. Value formation that takes place in religious studies is also reinforced by the school milieu and activities that involve an exposure to religious practices, habits, and rituals.

Aquinas was careful to point out, however, that knowledge does not necessarily lead to morality. Although a person may know the principles of religion and may know about religious observance, knowledge cannot be equated with goodness. However, intelligent men and women can distinguish between moral right and wrong in making choices. The exercise of freedom means that every person possesses the ability to frame, recognize, and evaluate alternative courses of action.

In the Thomist context, moral education is a process of habituating the learner to a climate of virtue. Such an environment should contain models of value worthy of imitation. The Christian school milieu should provide the exercises and conditions that help to form dispositions inclined to virtue.

Curricular Implications of the Thomist Conception of Human Nature

Aquinas defined the human being as a "spirit-in-the-world," an incarnate spirit who also possesses an animated body. Unique among creatures, women and men are composed of both a corporeal and spiritual substance and live between two worlds, with their souls situated on the boundary between heaven and earth. Possessing an immortal, deathless, and immaterial soul that vitalizes each person's self-awareness and freedom, the soul's embodiment affords each person a historical time and social place, or temporal and spatial contexts, in which to know, love, and choose.

In continuity with nature, all people create their own personal biographies over the course of their lives. The human being is a social creature who is born, grows, matures, and dies within families and communities. As social beings, humans have developed communication systems, such as speaking, writing, and reading. These communication systems, needed in community life, are acquired and must be learned. As social agencies, schools contribute to human development as they encourage reasoning, communicating, and participating in community life.

Thomists recognize that people live in a particular place at a particular time. Because of historical variations and social adaptations to changing conditions, various cultures, societies, and polities exist. While recognizing these variations, the Thomist, rejecting culturally relative truth and values, asserts that the commonality of human nature and culture is more important than these variations. All people possess a common human nature, as a result of the underlying spiritual and material realities in which they participate. This assertion makes it possible to speak of universal human rights and responsibilities. Thomists contend that culturally or situationally relative theories of ethics evade the claims that universal moral and ethical standards should have on us.

The Thomist conception of human nature, or "spirit-in-the-world," provides a curriculum rationale in which the principle of the hierarchy of generality operates. Those aspects of existence that are most general, abstract, and durable are located at the summit of the hierarchy. Those aspects of life that are particular, specific, and transitory are located in a lower position. Because the person's soul is immortal and destined for the perfect happiness of the beatific vision of God, subjects leading to spiritual growth and formation such as theology and scriptural and religious studies receive curricular emphasis. Because the person as a rational being is a free agent, knowledge and exercises that cultivate reason, such as philosophy and logic, are emphasized so that each person will be prepared to exercise freedom of choice. And because humans live in a natural and a social environment, knowledge and skills that sustain economic well-being should be included in the curriculum.

Living in society, people need knowledge of legal, political, and economic systems that contribute to personal and social well-being. Because we are social and communal beings, the language and literary skills that contribute to communication and community are also a major foundation of formal education. The skills of reading, speaking, and writing are an important part of every person's basic education.

The Thomist Teacher–Learner Relationship

Thomist educational philosophy provides useful definitions of and distinctions between education and schooling and thinking and learning even for those who do not share its theological premises. Although recognizing that education and schooling are related concepts and processes, Thomists carefully distinguish between education, the broader and more inclusive concept, and schooling, its more limited form. These distinctions help to define areas of competence and responsibility for teachers.

For Thomists, education—the complete formation of a person—is a lifelong process that involves many persons and agencies, such as the family, the church, and the community. Schooling, or formal education, is the responsibility of teachers who are deliberately responsible for instructing children and youth in the school, a specialized institution.

Although the Thomist distinction between education and schooling may seem obvious, it has often been ignored or neglected by educators. When it is ignored, areas of responsibility are blurred and confused. By recognizing that other agencies, such as the family, perform educational functions, Thomists argue that these agencies have responsibilities for educating children. In fact, Thomists strongly assert that parents should exercise the primary role in their children's education. This parental role is primarily informal, involving the cultivation of values that support morality, religion, and education. These values are supportive and conducive to the school's and the teacher's more specific and formal educational role. The Thomist distinctions between education and schooling also make clear that the school is not an all-powerful educational institution. Its effectiveness as an instructional agency depends on other agencies, such as the family, performing their educational responsibilities well.

For the Thomists, **educatio**, or education, is defined as a person's general formation in the broadest possible sense—spiritually, intellectually, socially, morally, politically, economically, and so forth. In the case of children, education refers to the child's total upbringing. Education, as a total process of human development, encompasses more than the formal instruction that takes place in the school's more limited environment. Because a person's total formation rests on both informal and formal educational agencies, the school's role must be considered in relationship to total human development.[10] In the school, a student is exposed to **disciplina**, or a deliberate instruction such as when a teacher teaches some knowledge or imparts some skill to the learner. The success or failure of such deliberate instruction depends at least in part on its relationship to the general formation taking place outside of the school.

In the Thomist school, the teacher, a mature person, possesses a disciplined body of knowledge or skill and through deliberate instruction seeks to impart this to a learner. Instruction is a verbal process by which the teacher carefully selects the appropriate words and phrases to illustrate the principles or demonstrate the skill that the learner is to acquire. The teacher's language is a stimulus that serves to motivate and to explain so that the student can exercise his or her intellect. The student must be an active participant in the teacher–learner relationship, for he or she possesses the potentiality for intellectually grasping and appropriating knowledge.

The Thomist teacher should be a skilled communicator. To communicate effectively, the teacher has to select the correct words, use the proper speaking style, and cite appropriate examples, illustrations, and analogies. The teacher should be careful that instruction does not degenerate into mere verbalism or preachment in which the words used are remote from the learner's experience. Instruction should always begin with what the student already possesses and should lead to an outcome which is new. As such, teaching involves a careful structuring and organizing of lessons.

Thomas Aquinas saw teaching as a vocation, a calling to serve humanity. Because of a desire to serve others, the good teacher should be motivated by a love of truth, a love of persons, and a love of God. Unlike the emotionalism of such romantic naturalist educators as Rousseau, who also preached a doctrine of love, the Thomist teacher prizes the cultivation of rationality. As true Aristotelians, Thomists emphasize that genuine love comes from knowing and is based on reason. Therefore, teaching is not allowed to degenerate into a merely emotional relationship. It is always about some knowledge, some truth, that is worthy of being known by a learner.

In the Thomist conception of the teacher, the art of teaching integrates the contemplative and the active life. As a contemplative, the teacher must spend time researching and planning instruction. Much of this research takes place in the serenity of a library. The teacher is to know the subject matter thoroughly, be it theology, mathematics, or science. The teacher is also an active person who is involved with students and who communicates knowledge to them.

Maritain's Integral Humanism

In this section, we consider the educational ideas of Jacques Maritain (1882–1973) a leading twentieth-century interpreter of Thomist philosophy. Maritain developed **Integral Humanism**, a philosophy derived from the Theistic Realism of Thomas Aquinas that emphasizes the spirituality and personalism of the human being.[11] Maritain's Integral Humanism is also a variety of **Perennialism**, a theory of education that asserts that truth is universal and that human nature, in terms of its defining rationality, is the same regardless of time and place. Maritain's educational ideas are closely affiliated with Thomism, so we discuss them here. Later in the chapter, we shall examine other varieties of Perennialism, especially the ideas of Robert Hutchins and Mortimer Adler.[12]

Maritain, born in France in 1882, was educated at the University of Paris. He was born into a Protestant family but became a convert to Roman Catholicism in 1906. Dissatisfied with the skepticism among academic philosophers, Maritain was attracted to Thomism. He urged a reconciliation of faith and reason in philosophy, as exemplified in the works of Thomas Aquinas. Maritain wrote *Education at the Crossroads* (1943), *Man and the State* (1951), *On the Use of Philosophy* (1961), and *Integral Humanism* (1968).

In *Education at the Crossroads,* Maritain argued that the purposes of education are twofold: to educate persons to cultivate their humanity and to introduce them to their cultural heritage. He emphasizes cultivation of rationality and spirituality, which define human character. Vocational and professional training are subordinate to the cultivation of the intellect.

Maritain condemned certain misconceptions that distort education's true purposes. Pragmatism, by overemphasizing means, failed to distinguish between means and ends. The obsession with means produced an aimless education without guiding principles. Maritain asserted that the proper end of education is to educate people to realize their human potentialities. Genuine education rests on a conception of human nature based on the Judeo-Christian heritage. According to Maritain, education should guide individuals to shape themselves as human persons "armed with knowledge, strength of judgment, and moral virtues" while transmitting the "spiritual heritage" of their "nation and the civilization." Thus, it preserves "the century-old achievements of generations." While the vocational aspect of education is not disregarded, it "must never imperil the essential aim of education"[13]

Maritain attacked Rousseau and the Progressives who exaggerate instincts and emotions in education. In seeking to educate the good-hearted person, Rousseau neglected intelligent judgment. In contrast, Maritain argued that the properly functioning person is governed by intellect rather than emotionalism. Even more dangerous than Rousseauean voluntarism, according to Maritain, was the modern emphasis on the complete liberation of the emotions and that makes education a matter of feeling rather than thinking.

Maritain viewed the teacher as an educated, cultivated, and mature person who possesses knowledge that the students do not have but wish to acquire. Good teaching should begin with what students already know and lead them to what they do not know. Maritain saw the teacher as a dynamic agent in the learning process.

The student, a rational and free being possessing a spiritual soul and a corporeal body, is endowed with an intellect that seeks to know. The good teacher should establish an orderly but open climate of learning that avoids the excesses of both anarchy and despotism, for the anarchical classroom rejects any kind of discipline and, with a misguided permissiveness, caters to childish whims. The despotic classroom, through fear of corporal or psychological punishment, reduces students' individuality to a standardized conformity in which spontaneity and creativity are punished as undesirable deviations.

The teacher's task is to foster those fundamental dispositions that enable students to realize their human potentialities, which according to Maritain are (1) love of truth, goodness, and justice, (2) simplicity and openness to existence, (3) a sense of a job well done, and (4) a sense of cooperation.

Maritain's Curriculum

Maritain recommended a subject-matter curriculum based on the systematic learned disciplines, the arts and sciences. Primary education is to cultivate the basic skills needed for the successful study of the more systematic disciplines. Maritain argues against the view that the child is a miniature adult. The child's world, instead, is one of imagination. Primary teachers should begin their instruction within the child's own world of imagination and, through the use of stories and storylike narrations, lead the child to explore the objects and values of the rational world. Although the child's initial stimulus is through imagination, he or she gradually comes to exercise intellect in grasping the realities of the external world.

Maritain believed that both secondary education and higher education should cultivate judgment and intellectuality through the study of the humanities. Secondary education, in particular, is to introduce the adolescent to the world of thought and to the great achievements of human civilization. Among the subjects that Maritain recommends for study in the secondary schools are grammar, foreign languages, history, geography, and the natural sciences.

Maritain divides the college curriculum into four years of study: (1) a year of mathematics and poetry, when students study both these subjects as well as literature, logic, foreign languages, and the history of civilization; (2) a year of natural science and fine arts, which is devoted to physics, natural sciences, fine arts, mathematics, literature, poetry, and the history of science; (3) a year of philosophy, which includes the study of metaphysics, philosophy of nature, epistemology, psychology, physics and natural science, mathematics, literature, poetry, and fine arts; and (4) the last year—the year of ethical and political philosophy, which examines ethics, political and social philosophy, physics, natural science, mathematics, literature, poetry, fine arts, the history of civilization, and the history of science.

Realism's Philosophical and Educational Relationships

We have discussed the origins of Realism in Aristotle's Natural Realism and examined how Thomas Aquinas developed a synthesis of Aristotle's principles and Christian doctrines called Theistic Realism in the medieval period. As we discussed its origin and development, we also commented on Aristotle's and Aquinas's ideas about education. With this more historical introduction in place, we now turn to a general discussion of Realism's philosophical and educational relationships. In the following sections, we consider Realism

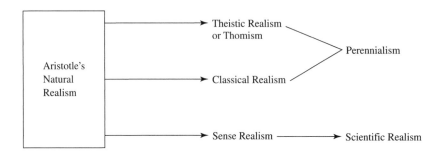

Development of Realism

as a philosophy, especially in terms of metaphysics, epistemology, axiology, and logic and relate these subdivisions of the philosophy to education. We then consider Realism's more direct educational implications for education, the school, curriculum, and teaching and learning.

Realist Metaphysics

Realism's essential metaphysical proposition is that we live in an objective order of reality that exists independent of and external to our minds. Objects, that is, material things, exist in time and in space, and we can come to know something about them. An object, then, is outside of us, and consists of two dimensions—matter and form. Matter, the material substratum of an object, has the potential of becoming something. To become an object, matter has to be organized according to some design or structure.

Realist Epistemology

For the Realist, knowing is a twofold process involving sensation and abstraction. This process corresponds to the Realist conception of a dualistic universe composed of a material and a structural, or formal, component. Whereas sensation has to do with matter, abstraction relates to form or structure. Cognition, or knowing, involves an interaction between the human mind and the world outside of the mind.

Sensation concerns the material component of an object, or matter. Because the material is changing, sensation varies from time to time and from place to place. It is contingent and circumstantial. Sensation is the beginning of knowing, but it is not the end of knowledge. Our knowledge about an object originates with sensations such as light, sound, pressure, heat, cold, vapor, or taste that come from the object. Each of our senses has a proper object of sensation. Touch apprehends pressure or physical resistance; temperature reveals whether the object is hot or cold; taste, localized in the tongue, detects flavors; smell, localized in the nasal passages, informs us of odors; the object of hearing is sound; sight, the highest and most objective sense, has color as its proper object. Sensation, then, first involves the physical action of something impinging on our sensory organs.

We first experience the immediate qualities of the object such as color, odor, taste, hardness, softness, and pitch. Needing no other senses to mediate for them, these immediate qualities are conveyed to us from the outside by the different energy patterns that activate the sensory organs. The mediate sensory qualities of size, distance, position, shape, motion, and weight are conveyed to us by the immediate sensory qualities.

As a result of sensation, we acquire sensory data, which our mind sorts out and arranges in computerlike fashion. Our common sense, the intellectual power of abstraction, sorts out our sense perceptions into the necessary conditions, those qualities that are always present in an object, and the contingent conditions, those sometimes found in the object. The necessary qualities, which are always present in the object, are its essential constituents and form the basis of our concept of the object. A concept, a meaning that applies to all things of the same class, has qualities that it shares with other objects in the same class but with no other objects.

Conceptualization, or concept formation, takes place when our mind has extracted and abstracted the form of an object and recognized it as belonging to a class. Objects are classified, or put in a category, when we recognize them as possessing qualities that they share with other members of the class but not with objects belonging to different classes.

For example, in our experiences, we encounter other human beings. Some of these people are of different heights and weights, speak different languages, and are of different ethnic origins. They may be Chinese, Russian, English, Nigerian, or Mexican, to name only a few of the many nationalities of people. However, underlying the variations of size, weight, height, ethnic origin, and nationality, there is something, some "whatness" or "quidity," that is common to all human beings. A common human nature identifies them as members of the class *Homo sapiens* and not of other classes of objects. A human being is different from a horse, a tree, a house, or a rock. The varieties of human beings share something that is common to them all. This commonness is what differentiates them from other objects; it is their defining quality or characteristic.

Realist epistemology has been called a "spectator theory," which means that we are observers of reality. While we all commonly share the same cognitive process, our "spectating" can range from the crudely unsophisticated to highly precise data gathering. As childlike watchers of reality, we begin early to sort out objects into mineral, vegetable, and animal. Through the course of time, humankind has developed a range of sophisticated instruments—telescopes, microscopes, X-ray machines, spaceprobes, and so on—that have enhanced our knowledge and rendered it more accurate. For example, the moon, as a

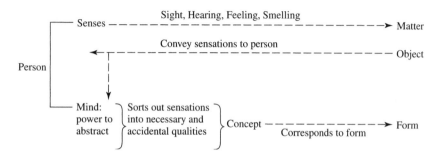

Realist Epistemology

physical entity, exists independently of us and prior to our knowing about it. The moon has figured in many religious rituals and festivals; it has been the object of poetry and song. With the coming of the space age and interplanetary exploration, astronauts have journeyed to the moon and, with sophisticated instruments, have made our knowledge of this heavenly body more accurate. Although the process of knowing remains the same, the instruments that we develop are dynamic. Our knowledge about the moon becomes accurate when it corresponds correctly to the moon in reality.

The "spectator theory of knowing" may appear to be passive, but it has many dynamic educational implications. Education should provide the experience, training, and practice that will cultivate our potentiality to be accurate observers, discoverers of reality. It should assist us in using the instruments and technology that contribute to the accuracy of our knowledge of the universe and the world. While Realists would still agree with Aristotle that human beings intrinsically seek to know, they would also recognize the instrumental, or use, value of knowledge. For scientific Realists, accurate knowledge about the world helps us to structure choices—to make decisions—that contribute to our continuing liberation from ignorance, superstition, disease, famine, and other human impediments.

As a systematic spectator, the Realist is concerned with discovering the essential plan or design of the universe. The philosophical and educational problem is that of extracting or abstracting the structures that explain the workings of the universe, of human beings, and of society. The discovery of structure involves extracting it from the matter that conveys it. Such organized spectating, involving the scientific method, deals with the discovery of principles and laws.

In humankind's long and continuing quest to discover the structures of reality, bodies of knowledge—learned and scientific disciplines—have evolved and been added to by researchers over time. For example, linguists have worked to extract the structure of speech by analyzing various languages; the natural and physical sciences—zoology, botany, chemistry, physics, astronomy—have sought to identify the structure and patterns of natural and physical phenomena; the social sciences—sociology, economics, political science, anthropology, and psychology—have as their object of inquiry the structure of human interaction. Bodies of knowledge that are the products of this quest for structure—the liberal arts and sciences—constitute the Realist curriculum.

As a spectator searching to discover structure in reality, the Realist is a discoverer of reality that is preexistent, independent, and antecedent to his or her experience of it. Through careful observation, we can discover the structures of objects and determine how they interact with each other. We can frame generalizations based on the patterns and regularities that occur in these interactions between objects. For instance, meteorologists have observed and recorded daily temperatures. As a result of this careful observation, variations in temperature can be detected over time, and thus it is possible to generalize about temperature variations and speak about seasons. Such generalizations form basic meteorological theory that can guide such practical activities as planting crops, wearing clothes, and constructing dwellings.

The Realist theory of knowledge is also referred to as a "correspondence theory." Our ideas are true when our concepts conform to or correspond with the object in reality. Because knowledge is to conform to reality, what is taught should also conform to reality. For example, Newton's law of universal gravitation corresponds to the way the universe actually works. It is true and should be both transmitted to the young and perpetuated.

Realist Axiology

Realist value theory is an objective one that asserts that we can estimate the value nature of objects through knowledge. The value of an act lies in the object or in the relationships among objects in such a way that it can be known, judged, or estimated. Realists contend that our actions and appreciations can be estimated and judged by criteria external to us.

Prizing rationality as the human being's distinguishing characteristic and defining power, Realists encourage us to shape our values in terms of the structures of reality. By knowing the structures of physical, natural, social, and human reality, we can frame realistic and viable alternatives. Through knowledge, we can rationally frame choices about life. The ability to develop such choices is at the core of a liberal, or liberating, education.

Harry S. Broudy, a Classical Realist, illuminated the value dimension of education, especially ethical and aesthetic concerns. For Broudy, the ultimate aim of education is "living the good life," which consists of cultivating human potentialities to their highest levels through processes of self-determination, self-realization, and self-integration.[14] The role of education and of schooling is to transform life through knowledge. The source of values lies in the relationship between the structure of objects and the structure of human nature. An object's structure makes it intrinsically as well as instrumentally valuable. Like Aristotle, Broudy asserted that our ethical decisions should be made on rational grounds. To be self-determined means that we have framed or defined our potentialities so that we can achieve worthy goals; to be self-integrated means that we have organized our values hierarchically and have resolved conflicts and inconsistencies.

Aesthetic judgment involves an interaction between a person, the perceiver, and an art object—a painting, drama, musical piece, dance, or sculpture, for example. Education enhances our aesthetic experience by cultivating our readiness to appreciate art, by providing a range of previous experience, and by providing us with some expertise in enjoying art forms.[15] Although art forms may exhibit cultural variations, Realists hold that the human desire for artistic expression and aesthetic enjoyment is universal.

Logic

For the Realist, logic is both inductive and deductive. We use induction as part of our cognitive process as we acquire sensory information about objects in the environment. From these sensations, our minds inductively create concepts as we abstract the various data into classes and categories. Teachers can use the inductive processes by which learners study the objects they encounter in the environment and arrive at concepts and generalization about them. Sense Realists, such as Johann Heinrich Pestalozzi, devised object lessons designed to facilitate concept formation based on sensation. In the process of moving from sensation to abstraction, there is a logic of going from the specific to the general and from the concrete to the abstract that is used in teaching and learning strategies. Through induction, they are discovering knowledge about reality but not constructing it as Constructivists assert. This kind of knowing and the logic based on it is inductive in that it moves from specific elements of sensory information to general concepts.

We also noted that, over time, scholars and scientists have arranged these concepts into conceptual systems: the theoretical framework of disciplined knowledge, or subject matters, as in the arts and sciences. Deductive logic is used in Realist instruction when the teacher designs lessons that begin with generalizations and principles already established in prior research. Using deduction, the teacher can begin with these authoritative generalizations, provide examples that illustrate them, and then conclude with their current application.

The Educational Implications of Realism

In the following section, we will examine the educational implications of Realism in terms of educational goals, the role of the school, the nature of the curriculum, instructional methodology, and the teacher–learner relationship.

Realism's Educational Goals

The ultimate educational goal of Realism remains that articulated by Aristotle—namely, to aid human beings to attain happiness by cultivating their potentiality for excellence to its fullest. As such, education is to

1. Cultivate human rationality, the human's highest power, through the study of organized bodies of knowledge; and
2. Encourage human beings to define themselves by framing their choices rationally, to realize themselves by exercising their potentiality for excellence to the fullest, and to integrate themselves by ordering the various roles and claims of life according to a rational and hierarchical order.

The Realist Conception of the School

Realists generally believe that each institution has a primary role and function in society. The government, the church, and the family perform definite roles. As such, the school has the primary mission of advancing human rationality. As a formal institution, it should be staffed by competent teachers who possess knowledge of a subject or skill and who know how to teach it to students who are immature in terms of that knowledge and are seeking to acquire it. The school has the well-defined and specific intellectual function of transmitting bodies of knowledge and inquiry skills to students. Although the school may perform recreational, community, and social functions, these are secondary and should not interfere with the efficient performance of its primary intellectual function. In such a setting, the educational administrator's role is to ensure that teachers in a school are not distracted from their primary task or unnecessarily burdened with noneducational duties that detract from it. The administrator is especially charged with maintaining the academic freedom of the faculty to teach and of students to learn.

The Realist conception of the school clearly prescribes policies designed to protect the school from interference that detracts from its central mission. Realists reject the residual theory of schooling that asserts that schools are responsible for providing services neglected or no longer performed by other institutions. They argue that the more schools act as medical, recreational, or employment agencies, the less time, money, and energy will be available for their primary function. To use schools as social service agencies not only confuses their purpose, but is also inefficient and costly.

The Realist Curriculum

As indicated earlier, the Realist conceives of an objective order of reality. The objects that comprise reality can be classified into categories on the basis of their structural similarities. The various learned disciplines, or subjects, of history, geography, language, mathematics, biology, botany, and chemistry, for example, consist of clusters of related concepts and of generalizations that interpret and explain interactions among the objects that these concepts represent. Each discipline as a conceptual system has a structure. **Structure** refers to a framework of related conceptual meanings and their generalizations that explain physical, natural, social, and human realities. For instance, biology consists of a number of necessary concepts appropriate to the study of plants and animals.

The role of the expert scientist and scholar is crucial in defining curricular areas. The scholar or the scientist is an expert who studies and carefully observes certain well-defined sections of reality. For example, the historian studies the past and analyzes documents explaining past events. By using the historical method, he or she re-creates events and develops generalizations or interpretations that explain and give them meaning. The historian as an expert in explaining the past has mastered a particular area of reality. He or she knows the limits of his or her expertise and is aware of what is appropriate to history and what lies in another learned discipline. The scholar or scientist is also skilled in the inquiry method, which is an efficient mode of discovery in the particular research area. Through monographs, lectures, and books, scholars make their findings available to the public and to other experts in their fields. Although scholars and scientists may disagree on interpretations, they are expected to follow the appropriate methods of investigation and conceptual framework of their disciplines.

Scientists and scholars are often, but not always, found in universities or research centers. Institutions of higher learning are expected to encourage, support, and reward research and teaching. Scholars and scientists are expected to make their findings known by publishing their research. Underlying scholarship in the Realist mode is the assumption that generalizations about reality are most accurately made by experts who have carefully investigated certain selected aspects of reality. In universities, these experts are usually organized into academic departments of history, language, chemistry, physics, English, political science, and so on. Students attend colleges and universities to study with and to obtain knowledge from these academic experts. Prospective teachers, especially secondary teachers, study academic subject matters, usually referred to as majors. They, in turn, use the descriptions, concepts, and generalizations provided by the expert to organize subject matter into instructional units for their students.

Basic to the Realist curriculum is the rationale that the most efficient and effective way to find out about reality is to study it through systematically organized subject-matter disciplines. The liberal arts and science curriculum of the undergraduate college and the departmentalized secondary school curriculum represent the subject-matter mode of curricular organization. The subject-matter curriculum consists of two basic components: (1) the body of knowledge that is the structure of a learned discipline—an organized way of viewing a certain aspect of reality, that is, historically, sociologically, biologically, chemi-cally, psychologically, geographically, and so on; and (2) the appropriate pedagogical ordering of the subject matter according to the readiness, maturation, and previous learning of the student. In such a curricular design, teachers are expected to be knowledgeable about their subject matters and well prepared in the methods of teaching them to students.

The Realist curriculum at the primary level involves instruction in the tools of read-ing, writing, and computation needed for subsequent successful study and inquiry into the systematic subject-matter disciplines. It is equally important that early childhood and pri-mary schooling foster predispositions and attitudes that value learning as a positive goal. Children should also gain experience with research methods, such as using the library and the computer, which aid in later learning.

Realist Instructional Methods

Instruction in the Realist school involves a teacher teaching some skill or subject to a stu-dent. While this may appear to be a simple statement, it carefully defines and prescribes the instructional act. Notice that there are three elements in the act of instruction: the teacher, the skill or subject, and the student. Because each of these components is essential to the teaching or instructional act, we will comment on all three.

The teacher is knowledgeable in the content of the subject; he or she is a generally educated person who knows how the subject relates to other areas of knowledge. The teacher also knows the limits of his or her competence. Thus, the goal of instruction is to provide the student with the body of knowledge possessed by the teacher.

The second element in instruction is some body of knowledge, such as history, or some skill, such as reading, that is to be taught to the student. In some situations, this sec-ond element is missing in schools, for example, in therapy or sensitivity sessions, or during entertainment or unfocused talking. Situations such as these, which lack the knowledge or skill element, diminish and often distort teaching. Realist teachers, like any teacher, need to know their students' backgrounds and how to motivate them. They can be entertaining as well as informative. However, they also need to be knowledge givers.

The third element in instruction is the student, the person who is present to learn the skill or knowledge. Students are expected to be ready to learn and willing to expend the effort required. While students may have many interests, they are expected to focus their attention on what is being taught.

The Realist teacher should command a variety of methods that may include lecture, discussion, or experiment. The teacher should use the method appropriate to the learner's background and situation. An ideal method, which needs to be used with great skill, would structure a learning situation that replicates the research activity of the scholar or scientist. For example, students in a history course would use the historical method to analyze and interpret primary sources.

The Realist Teacher–Learner Relationship

In our discussion of Realist philosophy, curriculum, and methodology, we have already sug-gested the basis of the teacher–learner relationship. The teacher, possessing subject-matter knowledge and instructional skill, is a professional educator. Teachers should be generally educated in both the liberal arts and sciences; this general knowledge is designed to assist them in being educated persons who appreciate the relationships of bodies of knowledge to each other and to the cultivation of human rationality. In addition to being generalists, teachers should be specialists in educating students.

The learner is regarded as an individual who has the essential human right to self-determination, self-realization, and self-integration. Seeking to grow in maturity in the areas of human knowledge, students have the right to have educated and professionally prepared experts as teachers. Learning, however, which requires commitment and application, is the student's primary responsibility.

Perennialism: An Educational Theory Derived from Aristotelian Realism

In this section, we continue our discussion of Perennialism, a theory of education derived from Realism, especially its Aristotelian version. Perennialism, based on its root, *perennial,* means perpetual, everlasting, continuing, or recurrent. In education, it is based on the Aristotelian premise that human beings are endowed with the power of rationality, which is the defining aspect of their human nature. The power of human rationality recurs with each new generation. It also is based on Aristotle's belief that truth is the same throughout the universe and is not determined by culture, place, or time. For the Perennialist, education should be based on the following universal characteristics of human nature:

- Our rationality defines us human beings.
- People everywhere frame their thoughts in symbolic patterns and express them in language.
- People everywhere have developed ethical, aesthetic, religious, social, and political principles that give direction to their private and public lives.
- Our human intellect enables us to frame alternative propositions and to choose between them; our choice is informed when it conforms to knowledge.

Because human nature is universal, so is education. Foremost, education's aim is to cultivate our rational powers and transmit truth. And because that which is true is universal and unchanging, a genuine education should also be universal and constant. The school's curriculum should emphasize the universal and recurrent themes of human life. It should contain cognitive materials designed to cultivate rationality; it should be highly logical and enable students to use the symbolic patterns of thought and communication. It should cultivate ethical principles and encourage moral, aesthetic, and religious criticism and appreciation. The Perennialist educational theory seeks to develop the intellectual and spiritual potentialities of the child to their fullest extent through a subject-matter curriculum based on such disciplines as history, language, mathematics, logic, literature, the humanities, and science. These subjects, regarded as bearing the knowledge of the human race, are the tools of civilized people and have a disciplinary effect on the human mind.

Perennialist educational theory emphasizes the humanities as providing insights into the good, true, and beautiful. In these works, humankind has captured a glimpse of the eternal truths and values. Such insights, found in science, philosophy, literature, history, and art, persist as they are transmitted from generation to generation. Works such as those of Plato, Aristotle, and Aquinas, for example, possess a quality that makes them perennially appealing to people living at different times and in different places. Other ideas, which may be popular to a particular time but fail to meet the test of time, fade quickly.

Our earlier discussion of Theistic Realism examined the ideas of Jacques Maritain, a religious Perennialist. Now, we turn to the more secular Perennialist theories of Robert Hutchins and Mortimer Adler.

Robert M. Hutchins

Robert Maynard Hutchins (1899–1977) argued forcefully that education is properly devoted to the cultivation of the human intellect. Hutchins received his higher education at Yale University. From 1927 to 1929 he was a professor of law at Yale. At age thirty, he became president of the University of Chicago and served until he became chancellor of that university in 1945. In 1954, Hutchins was named head of the Fund for the Republic. He was associated with the Center for the Study of Democratic Institutions, a nonprofit educational enterprise established by the Fund for the Republic to promote the principles of individual liberty in a democratic society. Hutchins's major educational works include *The Higher Learning in America* (1936), *Education for Freedom* (1943), *Conflict in Education in a Democratic Society* (1953), *University of Utopia* (1953), and *The Learning Society* (1968).[16]

As an Aristotelian, Hutchins described the purpose of education as drawing out

the elements of our common human nature. These elements are the same in any time or place. The notion of educating a man to live in any particular time or place, to adjust him to any particular environment, is therefore foreign to a true conception of education.

Education implies teaching. Teaching implies knowledge. Knowledge is truth. The truth is everywhere the same. Hence education should be everywhere the same. . . . I suggest that the heart of any course of study designed for the whole people will be, if education is rightly understood, the same at any time, in any place, under any political, social, or economic conditions.[17]

When asked his opinion as to the ideal education, Hutchins replied:

Ideal education is the one that develops intellectual power. I arrive at this conclusion by a process of elimination. Educational institutions are the only institutions that can develop intellectual power. The ideal education is not an *ad hoc* education, not an education directed to immediate needs; it is not a specialized education, or a pre-professional education; it is not a utilitarian education. It is an education calculated to develop the mind.

There may be many ways, all equally good, of developing the mind. I have old-fashioned prejudices in favor of the three R's and the liberal arts, in favor of trying to understand the greatest works that the human race has produced. I believe that these are the permanent necessities, the intellectual tools that are needed to understand the ideas and

ideals of our world. This does not exclude later specialization or later professional education; but I insist that without the intellectual techniques needed to understand ideas, and
without at least an acquaintance with the major ideas that have animated mankind since the
dawn of history, no man may call himself educated.[18]

Hutchins believed that American education, especially higher education, was not fulfilling its primary intellectual purpose. Immersed in materialism and catering to the shifting
whims of students, donors, business interests, alumni, and politicians, Hutchins claimed that
the university had lost its integrity in the frantic search for funds. In contrast, Hutchins
argued for a university whose sole purpose is to pursue, discover, and teach the truth.

Hutchins believed that a confused conception of democracy had resulted in the commonly held belief that everyone should receive the same amount and degree of education. He
would reserve higher education for students who have the interest and ability for independent
intellectual activity. A false notion of progress had led to the rejection of the wisdom of the
past, which had been replaced by a belief that progress comes only from empiricism and
materialism. A superficial empiricism had confused knowledge with the mere collection of
information and data. This confusion had produced an anti-intellectualism that regarded the
most worthwhile education as that bringing the greatest financial return.

Overspecialization has isolated specialist from specialist, Hutchins said. Without the
integrating core of a common education, specialists lack the ideas and language that came
from shared and communicable experience. Anti-intellectualism stems from an emphasis on
the purely utilitarian at the cost of sacrificing theory and speculation.

Hutchins claimed that vocationalism and specialized education had entered the curriculum prematurely and had distorted the purposes of general education. An overemphasis
on specialization had pushed the liberal arts out of the general curriculum. Some educators
had tied education to specific political and social programs that led to either superficiality
or indoctrination rather than to critical intelligence.

The Curriculum: The Permanent Studies

Hutchins argued that the curriculum should be composed of permanent studies that reflect
the common elements of human nature and connect each generation to the best thoughts of
humankind. He particularly recommended the study of the "great books"—classics contemporary in any age that embraced all areas of knowledge. He believed that four years
spent reading and discussing the great books would cultivate standards of judgment and
criticism and prepare students to think carefully and act intelligently.

In addition to the great books of Western civilization, Hutchins recommended the
study of grammar, rhetoric, logic, and mathematics. Grammar, the analysis of language,
contributed to the understanding and comprehension of the written word. Rhetoric provided the student with the rules of writing and speaking needed for intelligent expression;
logic, the critical study of reasoning, enabled a person to think and express him- or herself
in an orderly and systematic fashion. Mathematics was of general value as it represented
reasoning in its clearest and most precise form.

In order to restore rationality in higher education, Hutchins advocated revitalizing of
metaphysics. As the study of first principles, he believed metaphysics pervaded the entire

range of intellectual pursuits. Proceeding from the study of first principles to the most current concerns, higher education should examine fundamental human problems. Whereas the social sciences embrace the practical sciences of ethics, politics, and economics, the natural sciences deal with the study of natural and physical phenomena.

Hutchins, who was critical of the specialization that had occurred in teacher education, believed that prospective teachers should have a good general education in the liberal arts and sciences. Such an education contained the basic rules of pedagogy. The liberal arts—grammar, rhetoric, logic, and mathematics—were potent instruments in preparing the prospective teacher to organize, express, and communicate knowledge.

Mortimer Adler

Mortimer J. Adler (1902–2001) was an American Aristotelian philosopher and author. Closely associated with Hutchins, he supported the idea of curriculum based on reading and discussing the so-called great books of Western civilization. Adler founded and served as director of the Institute for Philosophical Research in 1952. He also served on the board of editors of *Encyclopædia Britannica* since its inception in 1949, and succeeded Robert Hutchins as its chairperson in 1974. He developed the Paideia Proposal and Program.

The Paideia Proposal: A Revival of Perennialism

Derived from the Greek, *paideia* refers to the "upbringing of children" and signifies the general learning that all human beings should have. True to Perennialist principles, the Paideia proposal argues that a genuinely equal educational opportunity should be the same for all children; it should provide the "same quantity," "the same number of years" of schooling, and the "same quality of education."[19] Paideia proponents argue that to divide students into tracks or to create special programs for some students but not for others denies the same quality of education for all.

Stressing the commonality of human nature, Paideia advocates do not propose that schooling be a leveling process that reduces the differences in human capacities to a common denominator. Education's ultimate goal, they assert, is to see that "human beings become educated persons."[20] Construed in Aristotelian terms, schooling not only provides skill and knowledge but also cultivates the habits or dispositions for lifelong education.

Schooling in the Paideia Proposal

For the Paideia proponents, the school, as an institution, provides a one-track rather than a multitrack system of education for all. The issue of a multitrack versus a single-track system raises complicated social, political, economic, and educational dimensions. Advocates of a multitrack system have varying motivations. Some believe that because of students' different intellectual capacities, socioeconomic backgrounds, and physiological–emotional needs, schools need to provide educational options to educate a widely differing student population. Still other advocates of multitrack education believe that schools should sort students according to their academic abilities and provide the intellectually gifted with a special kind of education that prepares them as a leadership elite, especially a technological and scientific one. In contrast, Paideia proponents, like Perennialists in general, concentrate on the universality of human nature.

Schooling, according to Paideia proponents, has three major objectives common for all students: (1) it should provide the means of mental, moral, and spiritual growth; (2) it should cultivate the civic knowledge and virtues for responsible citizenship; and (3) it should provide the basic skills needed for work rather than particular job training for a single occupation.[21]

Paideia proponents warn against premature vocational training, which weakens or diminishes general education. Based on the liberal arts and sciences, all people should have a general education to cultivate their human nature and its undergirding rationality. Specialized vocational training, at the expense of general education, limits a person to one economic undertaking that can quickly become obsolete.

The Paideia Curriculum

Paideia advocates argue that all students should follow the same common curriculum for the twelve years of basic schooling. Students, however, would have a choice regarding their second language. The curriculum consists of three related learning modes, which have as their goals: (1) developing learning and intellectual skills, (2) enlarging the understanding of ideas and values, and (3) acquiring organized knowledge.[22]

To develop learning and intellectual skills, Paideia proponents emphasize basic skills such as "reading, writing, speaking, listening, observing, measuring, estimating, and calculating."[23] Not taught in isolation, these skills are integral to the entire curriculum.

In enlarging the understanding, the Paideia proponents return to a basic Perennialist theme—one long associated with Robert Hutchins and continued by Mortimer Adler—that the reading and discussion of the great books or classics are vital to the development of a truly educated person. In Adler's *The Paideia Proposal,* the scope of the great literature encompasses not only the enduring "historical, scientific, and philosophical" works but also the great works in film, drama, dance, and music.[24]

Teaching and Learning in the Paideia School

Teachers in schools following the Paideia theory of education are expected to be liberally educated persons. In teaching the organized subjects that lead to the acquisition of knowledge, the method used is essentially didactic, or instructional, using well-organized narratives. To instruct students to master the essential foundational skills, the teacher uses coaching, which refers to organizing and correcting students to perform skills such as reading or listening correctly. In studying the great works of art and literature that enlarge human understanding, teachers and students enter into the Socratic mode, which uses probing questions and directed discussions.

Contemporary Neo-Perennialism

Perennialism's contemporary popularity rests with its emphasis on universal truth and values and its rejection of relativism. Perennialists contend that general intellectual and ethical standards have eroded because of relativism. For example, Allan Bloom's *The Closing of the American Mind* argued forcefully that relativism in higher education had seriously weakened Americans' sense of intellectual and moral judgment.[25]

Lynne Cheney has argued against relativism in education by asserting that models of excellence in history and literature rest on truths that transcend time and circumstance. These objective truths, which transcend class, race, and gender, are appropriate to all human beings.[26] It is necessary to protect these models of objective truth and value against those who would subvert and use them as ideological tools.

Perennialists claim that their educational theory is rooted in universal concepts of truth and justice and is not subservient to any particular ideology. They reject an ideological foundation for education because ideology is tied to particular social, political, and economic contexts, to the contingencies of human culture, rather than its universal character. Claiming that education is designed to cultivate the essential character of a universal human nature, they argue that they can speak about human rights and freedom in universal terms that are transcultural and transnational.

Remembering Professor Harry S. Broudy

Throughout this book, I encourage readers to construct their own philosophy of education. To help in this process, I have recommended reflecting on your own educational experiences to recall persons who influenced your thinking about education. As I was writing this chapter on Realism, I thought back and reflected on a person who shaped my ideas about education, especially philosophy of education.

When working on my doctorate at the University of Illinois, I was enrolled in several seminars on philosophy of education with Professor Harry S. Broudy (1905–1998), who had a formative influence on my thinking about education. My recollection of these seminars also provides an example of a Realist mode of teaching and learning. The seminars were focused on a topic in philosophy of education, such as value theory, with assigned primary sources readings. Professor Broudy would introduce the topic, give some explanation, relate it to the field historically and to contemporary issues, and then ask questions to stimulate discussion. We were to write short papers on a particular aspect of the topic and a longer one based on our research. True to Realist teaching principles, we stayed with the subject. Professor Broudy did not let the seminar degenerate into

a sharing of uninformed opinions. Although he led us to relate the topic to contemporary issues, Dr. Broudy always structured the discussion in a larger philosophical perspective. In fact, the perspective was a very large in-depth one that began with the ancient Greek philosophers Plato and, especially, Aristotle.

As a teacher, I recall Professor Broudy maintaining what I would call a "professorial distance" from the students. The subject matter was always there between us. I don't recall the entry of personal matters into the class. However, I found out that he did know his students. His knowledge was based on how we related to the subject, how we expressed ourselves, and the kinds of questions we raised.

Professor Broudy introduced me and other doctoral students to the field of philosophy of education. He encouraged us to attend meetings of the Midwest Philosophy of Education Society and the Philosophy of Education Society. When I went to these meetings, I discovered that Professor Broudy was not just an ordinary professor of philosophy of education but was a prominent and respected leader in the field who was widely recognized for his work on general, teacher, and aesthetic education. I came to realize that taking his courses was a rare experience that not many graduate students had. I found out that he had earned his doctorate at Harvard University and that his own professors had been famous scholars such as William E. Hocking, C. I. Lewis, Alfred North Whitehead, and John Wild.

Although I did not realize that Professor Broudy had noticed much about me, I was very wrong. As I was finishing my doctoral dissertation and searching for my first job, Professor Broudy did take a definite interest. He wrote letters of support and recommended me for a position at Loyola University in Chicago. I got the job and began teaching philosophy of education. In looking for a textbook, I came across Professor Broudy's book *Building a Philosophy of Education,* which I adopted as my text.[27] I now learned more about my distinguished teacher. Professor Broudy called himself a Classical Realist who was a modern Aristotelian. Now I understood why he kept on a steady course and did not latch on the many current fads that often inflict themselves on education. Now I understood his responses to some of the clichés in education. When people said everything is constantly changing and education, too, is constantly changing, Broudy would counter with—if everything is changing, then there has to be something that is changing. A true Aristotelian, he looked beyond the cliché to ask what it is that is changing. When people said education is life, Broudy would ask—if the school is life, why do we need it? Why not just live? As a Realist, he saw the school as having a primary academic function—the cultivation of our intellect through an encounter with knowledge.

Broudy was committed to the proposition that all students had the right to a general academic education. Our civic democracy, like the Athenian *polis* of antiquity, required the shared and common understandings based on knowing what is real.

Conclusion

Our discussion introduced Realism as a philosophy of education, beginning with Aristotle's Natural Realism, which argues that we live in an objective order of reality that we can know. Knowledge of this reality is our best guide to action. We then examined Theistic Realism, or Thomism, a synthesis of Aristotle's philosophy and Christian doctrines by Thomas Aquinas in the Middle Ages, and proceeded to examine Realism's philosophical principles and their implications for education. Among the most important educational implications are: (1) a belief in universal truth and values; (2) knowing as a twofold process of sensation and abstraction; (3) the constructing of conceptual systems that are organized into subject-matter disciplines; and (4) the proposition that genuine teaching involves teaching a skill or subject to a learner. These led to a discussion of Perennialism, a theory of education derived from Aristotle's Realism that asserts the universality of truth and education. Perennialism argues that education is everywhere the same and the Great Books are important in conveying the meaning of truth to each new generation.

Constructing Your Own Philosophy of Education. After reading this chapter, you may wish to relate Realism to constructing your own philosophy of education. Are there aspects of Realism that you might wish to include or exclude from your personal philosophy of education? For example, do you believe, like Aristotle, that reality is objective to us and is knowable and that knowledge about it is our best guide to action? Do you endorse a subject-matter curriculum and see the teacher's primary role as teaching these subjects?

Questions for Reflection and Discussion

1. Do you believe that Realism as a philosophy of education is too abstract and removed from the real problems of education to be relevant to today's teachers and students?

2. Why do Realists reject the assumption that values depend on situations and circumstances? Do you agree or disagree with them?

3. Have you encountered Realist teachers? Describe their teaching methods.

4. Do you agree or disagree with Realism that the act of teaching involves a knowledgeable teacher instructing students in a skill or subject?

5. Do you find religiously based philosophies, such as Thomism and Maritain's Integral Humanism, relevant to public education or should these faith-based theories of education be reserved for private education?

6. What are the strengths and weaknesses of the Realist view of a subject-matter curriculum? Do you endorse, modify, or reject the Realist subject-discipline curriculum?

7. Do you believe that educational experiences are equal or are some more important than others? Defend your answer.

8. Aristotle believes that we live in a purposeful and meaningful world. What do you think?

9. Do you agree or disagree with Aristotle that desired ethical behavior follows a mean of moderation between excess and repression? Consider your answer in terms of the standards of behavior found in contemporary American society and education.

Inquiry and Research Projects

1. Review the catalogue of your college or university. How is it organized? Would Realists agree with its organization?

2. Access Web sites dealing with the Paideia Project such as www.paideia.org/content.php/system/index.htm. Determine the aims of this approach to education. What is its underlying philosophy? Do you agree or disagree with it?

3. Access Web sites dealing with Realism. You might begin with the Stanford Encyclopedia of Philosophy at http://plato.stanford.edu/entries/realism. Identify the philosophers identified with Realism and their major philosophical ideas.

4. In outline form, construct a plan for a secondary school curriculum based on the Realist principles of subject-matter disciplines and a hierarchy of generality.

5. Examine a textbook used in a course you are taking. Determine whether the book is organized according to Realist principles.

6. Examine the liberal and science requirements in your degree program. In a position paper, indicate how you think a Realist would react.

Building a Realist Vocabulary

Abstraction: In Aristotelian cognition, the process by which the mind forms concepts by extracting what is necessary for them to be what they are from sensory information.

Concept: a general idea that represents a class of objects that possess the same necessary or essential qualities.

Conceptualization: for Realists, a twofold process of sensation and abstraction by which the human mind arrives at concepts.

Contingent Conditions: also called *accidental conditions* that are sometimes found in an object but that do not define them as to class.

Disciplina: According to Aquinas, formal education or schooling in which a teacher deliberately teaches a skill or a subject to a learner.

Dualism: a conception of reality that sees it in two parts.

Educatio: Aquinas's Latin term that refers to a person's general education and formation both in and out of school.

Efficient Cause: According to Aristotle, the agent who actualizes matter's potential to become an object.

Final Cause: For Aristotle, the purpose for which an action is done or an object is made.

Formal Cause: According to Aristotle, the form that gives an object its structure or design and puts it in a class with similar objects.

Integral Humanism: Maritain's neo-Thomist philosophy.

Material Cause: According to Aristotle, the matter that is at the base of an object.

Matter–Form Hypothesis: Aristotle's concept that objects consist of matter, a material cause, and form, the formal cause.

Necessary Conditions: characteristics that are always present in a particular class of objects, hence necessary for them.

Perennialism: an educational theory derived from Aristotle's Realism that asserts that education is universal and is based on a recurrent rational human nature.

Realism: a philosophy that asserts the reality of an objective order of reality that exists independently of the knower but that can be known.

Scientia: According to Aquinas, an organized body of knowledge in which first principles were logically developed and illustrated by analogies, cases, and examples.

Scientific Realism: emphasizes the use of the scientific method in acquiring knowledge and sees the physical and natural sciences as the most accurate sources of truth.

Sensation: the process by which the senses convey information about the external world to the mind.

Structure of a Subject: a subject-matter discipline's framework of related concepts, their definitions and meanings, and generalization about them that explain an aspect of reality.

Theism: the belief in the existence of a supernatural and omnipotent God; Aquinas combined theism and realism in Theistic Realism.

Theistic Realism: also known as Thomism; developed by Thomas Aquinas, a medieval Christian scholastic in the thirteenth century in Western Europe, as a synthesis of Aristotle's natural realism and Christian (Roman Catholic) doctrine.

Internet Sources

For a discussion of Realism, access the Stanford Encyclopedia of Philosophy at http://plato.stanford.edu/entries/realism.

For Realism and education, access www.pdst.purdue.edu/georgeoff/phil_am_ed/Realism.html.

For a general overview of Aristotle, access www.iep.utm.edu/a/aristotl.htm.

For the Jacques Maritain Center, access http://maritain.nd.edu.

For the Paideia Project, access www.paideia.org/content.php/system/index.htm.

Suggestions for Further Reading

Adler, Mortimer J. *Aristotle for Everybody.* New York: Touchstone, 1997.

Adler, Mortimer J. *How to Think about the Great Ideas: From the Great Books of Western Civilization.* Peru, IL: Open Court, 2000.

Anagnostopoulos, Georgios. *Aristotle on the Goals and Exactness of Ethics.* Berkeley: University of California Press, 1994.

Barnes, Jonathan. *Aristotle: A Very Short Introduction.* Oxford, UK: Oxford University Press, 2000.

Blanchette, Olivia. *The Perfection of the Universe According to Aquinas: Teleological Cosmology.* University Park: Pennsylvania State University Press, 1992.

Broadie, Sarah. *Ethics with Aristotle.* New York: Oxford University Press, 1991.

Davies, Brian. *The Thought of Thomas Aquinas.* New York: Oxford University Press, 1991.

Fatula, Mary Ann. *Thomas Aquinas: Preacher and Friend.* Collegeville, MN: Liturgical Press, 1993.

Gilson, Etienne. *The Christian Philosophy of St. Thomas Aquinas.* Notre Dame, IN: University of Notre Dame Press, 1994.

Hall, Pamela M. *Narrative and the Natural Law: An Interpretation of Thomistic Ethics.* Notre Dame, IN: University of Notre Dame Press, 1994.

Kenny, Anthony J. *Aquinas on Mind.* New York: Routledge, 1992.

Maritain, Jacques. *An Introduction to Philosophy.* New York: Sheed and Ward, 2005.

McInerny, Ralph M. *Aquinas on Human Action: A Theory of Practice.* Washington, DC: Catholic University of America Press, 1992.

McInerny, Ralph M. *A First Glance at St. Thomas Aquinas: A Handbook for Peeping Thomists.* Notre Dame, IN: University of Notre Dame Press, 1990.

Rankin, Kenneth. *The Recovery of the Soul: An Aristotelian Essay on Self-Fulfillment.* Montreal: McGill-Queen's University Press, 1991.

Reeve, C. D. C. *Practices of Reason: Aristotle's Nicomachean Ethics.* New York: Oxford University Press, 1992.

Selman, Francis J. *Saint Thomas Aquinas: Teacher of Truth.* Edinburgh: T&T Clark, 1994.

Spangler, Mary Michael. *Aristotle on Teaching.* Lanham, MD: University Press of America, 1998.

Swanson, Judith A. *The Public and the Private in Aristotle's Political Philosophy.* Ithaca, NY: Cornell University Press, 1992.

Verbeke, Gerard. *Moral Education in Aristotle.* Washington, DC: Catholic University of America Press, 1990.

White, Stephen A. *Sovereign Virtue: Aristotle on the Relation Between Happiness and Prosperity.* Stanford, CA: Stanford University Press, 1992.

Endnotes

1. G. E. R. Lloyd, *Aristotle: The Growth and Structure of His Thought* (Cambridge, UK: Cambridge University Press, 1968), p. 3.
2. E. W. Tomlin, *The Western Philosophers* (New York: Harper and Row, 1967), p. 62.
3. Jonathan Barnes, *Aristotle: A Very Short Introduction* (Oxford, UK: Oxford University Press, 2000), p. 30.
4. H. D. F. Kitto, *The Greeks* (Baltimore: Penguin Books, 1962), pp. 169–194.
5. Barnes, *Aristotle: A Very Short Introduction,* p. 3.
6. Barnes, *Aristotle: A Very Short Introduction,* p. 30.
7. Tomlin, *The Western Philosophers,* p. 62.
8. John Wild, *Introduction to Realistic Philosophy* (New York: Harper and Brothers, 1948), pp. 441–468.
9. William Cunningham, *Pivotal Problems in Education* (New York: Macmillan, 1940).
10. John W. Donohue, *St. Thomas Aquinas and Education* (New York: Random House, 1968), pp. 58–64, 82–89.
11. For commentaries on Maritain and education, see the articles by Wade A. Carpenter, Gerald L. Gutek, Peter A. Lawler, Alice Ramos, and Madonna Murphy in Wade A. Carpenter, guest editor, *Educational Horizons,* 83, No. 4 (Summer 2005).
12. In response to reviewers' recommendations, I am discussing Perennialism, a theory of education, in this chapter on Realism and education rather than later in the book when other theories of education, such as Essentialism and Critical Theory, are examined. Reviewers believed that because it is so closely related to Aristotle and to Realism that Perennialism should be discussed at this point in the book.
13. Jacques Maritain, *Education at the Crossroads* (New Haven, CT: Yale University Press, 1960), p. 10.
14. Harry S. Broudy, *Building a Philosophy of Education* (Englewood Cliffs, NJ: Prentice Hall, 1961), pp. 3–20.
15. Broudy, *Building a Philosophy of Education,* pp. 202–231.
16. Biographies of Hutchins are Harry S. Ashmore, *Unseasonable Truths: The Life of Robert Maynard Hutchins* (Boston: Littlefield, Brown, 1991); and Mary Ann Dzuback, *Robert M. Hutchins: Portrait of an Educator* (Chicago: University of Chicago Press, 1991).
17. Robert M. Hutchins, *The Higher Learning in America* (New Haven, CT: Yale University Press, 1962), pp. 66–67.
18. Robert M. Hutchins, *A Conversation on Education* (Santa Barbara, CA: Center for the Study of Democratic Institutions, 1963), pp. 1–2.
19. Mortimer J. Adler, *The Paideia Proposal: An Educational Manifesto* (New York: Macmillan Co., 1982), p. 4.
20. Adler, *Paideia Proposal,* p. 10.
21. Adler, *Paideia Proposal,* pp. 10–17.
22. Adler, *Paideia Proposal,* pp. 22–23.
23. Adler, *Paideia Proposal,* p. 26.
24. Adler, *Paideia Proposal,* pp. 28–29.
25. Allan Bloom, *The Closing of the American Mind* (New York: Simon and Schuster, 1987).
26. For Lynne Cheney's ideas on education, see Lynne V. Cheney, *Humanities in America: A Report to the President, the Congress, and the American People* (Washington, DC: National Endowment for the Humanities, 1988) and Cheney, *Telling the Truth* (New York: Simon & Schuster, 1995).
27. Harry S. Broudy, *Building a Philosophy of Education* (Englewood Cliffs, NJ: Prentice-Hall, 1961).

4

Pragmatism and Education

John Dewey (1859–1952), a leading American Pragmatist philosopher who developed Experimentalism.

Chapter Preview

Our discussion of **Pragmatism** focuses on John Dewey's Experimentalist or Instrumentalist version and examines Pragmatism's major concepts and their implications for society, education, schooling, curriculum, and teaching and learning. Dewey's philosophy of education is called **Experimentalism** because it sees human beings, who exercise their **social intelligence**, engaged in problem-solving according to the scientific experimental method.

Instrumentalism means that people can use their ideas as instruments, or tools, to solve problems. Dewey rejected the **dualism** that presented human beings as divided into antecedent categories such as mind and body and bifurcated education into theory and practice. He worked to remove the barriers that separated school from society, curriculum from community, and content from method. He discarded the doctrine of preparation that defines education as preparing for something in the future—the next stage in schooling, a job, or even a specific definition of nationality or citizenship. Integrating social life and education in the unifying concept of experience, Dewey redefined the school as a setting in which students, actively engaged in solving problems, added to their ongoing experience. Dewey reformulated the concept of the school from a strictly academic institution into a socially charged miniature community. Dewey's Pragmatism continues to be one of the world's leading educational philosophies. The following major topics are examined in the chapter:

- Pragmatism in the American experience
- John Dewey as a Pragmatist educator
- Experimentalism's philosophical bases
- Experimentalism's educational implications
- Pragmatism's philosophical opponents

As you read the chapter and think about constructing your own philosophy of education, consider whether Pragmatism, especially Dewey's Experimentalism, in its entirety or in its parts, appeals to you as a teacher. Do you plan to use it in constructing your own philosophy of education?

Pragmatism in the American Experience

Whereas Idealism and Realism date back to ancient Greece, Pragmatism developed in twentieth-century America. Whereas the older traditional philosophies rested on an antecedent conception of reality in which truth is *a priori,* or prior to and independent of human experience, the Pragmatists contended that a "truth" is a tentative assertion based on human experience. Pragmatism's originators were Charles S. Peirce (1839–1914), William James (1841–1910), and John Dewey (1859–1952).

Peirce, a mathematician, calling his philosophy *pragmaticism,* argued that our actions are really based on our estimates. When we act, we are basing our action on an estimate of the best hypothesis about something, namely, that our action will produce the results that we want. However, as estimates, we know these hypotheses will need to be revised to make them into more accurate tools or instruments that will improve our chances of getting the desired results. Instead of a certain and unchanging world in which truth is universal and eternal, as Plato claimed, Peirce's world is changing and in flux, and is indeterminate, not determined in advance. Because our world is indeterminate, our lives and our actions in it are also changing, relative, and indeterminate. To make sense of this kind of world, Peirce argued that we need to do the best job with it that is possible. Possibility, however, is not certainty. We need to estimate what we can do by using the theory of probability—what is likely to happen if we act in a certain way. Because certain actions bring about reactions in a way that can be quantified, we can estimate them. It is probable that such reactions will occur in the future. It is necessary to understand, however, that actions and reactions, themselves, never occur in exactly the same way. Our knowledge about something is probable rather than certain. However, probability provides us with a sense of intelligent direction and possible action.[1] With enough work, investigation, and thought, it is possible that we can formulate tentative generalizations—never ironclad laws—about how the world works.

James, a psychologist turned philosopher, regarded ideas as stimulated by the human need to choose between possible ways of acting in a situation. When we choose and think, James reasoned, our conclusions can guide our actions but they are also provisional and subject to further revision. Our beliefs give us rules that we can call good and true, right and wrong, while realizing that we may and likely will keep revising the guidelines as we encounter different situations in the course of life.[2] (Dewey's Experimentalism will be discussed in detail later in the chapter.)

The Pragmatists challenged traditional philosophical assumptions that a completed and perfect universe could be approached, only distantly and abstractly, through metaphysical speculation into the nature of ultimate reality. Rejecting the philosophical security provided by absolute and unchanging truth and values, the Pragmatists saw the world, much as Darwin did, as evolving and changing. People lived by successfully interacting with their environment and with each other in flexible relationships that could be examined, reappraised, and, when necessary, reconstructed. For the Pragmatists, ideas were not fixed in time and space as the universal and eternal reflections of an ultimate intelligence, as the Platonic and Hegelian Idealists believed. As human-made instruments, ideas were mental tools that could be used to solve the problems of real life. Ideas are to be judged by their consequences when acted on; truth is a **warranted assertion**, a tentative statement based on the application of hypotheses to solving problems; logic, following the scientific method, is experimental; values are experienced within the context of ethical and aesthetic problems and issues charged by the unique features of particular situations.

Pragmatism was a philosophical expression of America's frontier experience in which westward-moving pioneers migrated through varying natural environments that they transformed, but that also changed them and their society. The frontier experience caused Americans to judge success in terms of the consequences that came from transforming the environment for human purposes. Over time, the openness of an expansive frontier was translated into a wider vision of an open universe, charged by the dynamics of constant flux, change, and movement. Pragmatism appeared at a time when science and industry were creating a new technological society, the outlines of which were still emergent and flexible. As the nineteenth century yielded to the twentieth, the scientific temperament was exalted as a positive force for making a better life on earth. The legacy of the old frontier of open land in the West and the new frontier of a scientifically functioning technology made the time ripe for the new, hardheaded philosophy of Pragmatism. Pragmatism proclaimed the American propensity to discard purely speculative philosophy as an empty metaphysical meandering.

The formulation of Pragmatism coincided with that period of energetic social, political, and educational reform known as the Progressive movement, from the late 1890s to the United States' entry into World War I in 1917. The pragmatic outlook, which argued that problems, if capable of definition, were also capable of solution, fitted the social reformist attitude of Progressive Americans.[3]

Our examination of Pragmatism focuses on John Dewey's Experimentalism, or Instrumentalism. For Dewey, philosophy, like science, is experimental. Dewey was a philosopher who concentrated much of his effort on educational problems.

John Dewey: Pragmatist Educator

John Dewey was born in Burlington, Vermont, in 1859, the year when Charles Darwin's *Origin of Species* appeared. Dewey's father was a local businessman, and his family was active in the social and political life of the late nineteenth-century Vermont community, which was characterized by a spirit of democratic neighborliness.[4] Dewey's social philosophy would stress the significance of the face-to-face community in which people shared common concerns and problems. His democratic vision was shaped by the New England town meeting, where people met to solve their mutual problems through a peaceful and shared process of discussion, debate, and decision making. When he developed his social and educational philosophy, Dewey's theory of social intelligence embraced the concepts of the participatory community and the application of the scientific method.

Dewey's religious upbringing as a Congregationalist shaped his social and ethical outlook. Evangelical Protestantism was being infused with the "social gospel," which emphasized a person's ethical responsibility of working for the social and economic betterment of society. Although he would later end his formal adherence to organized religion, Dewey, like many Progressives, was a social reformer who believed that people had a mission to make the earth a better place to live, by reform and education.[5]

Dewey attended the University of Vermont, where he received his bachelor's degree. He then taught school in Oil City, Pennsylvania, and later in rural Vermont. Dewey pursued doctoral studies at Johns Hopkins University, a graduate institution founded on the German research model. Also attending Johns Hopkins was the future political scientist, academic and political reformer, and U.S. president, Woodrow Wilson.

As a graduate student at Johns Hopkins, Dewey studied the Hegelian Idealism of his mentor, George Sylvester Morris, which he would later abandon for Pragmatism. Although he abandoned Idealist metaphysics. Dewey's attraction to the Hegelian theme of a unifying "great community" continued. For him, the Idealist ethic that accentuated human self-realization remained a guiding possibility but he no longer believed that it was to be achieved in a spiritual realm.[6] Rather, Dewey believed that it would be achieved in human experiences transformed by larger transactions that embraced human relationships and democratic participation in the community.[7] After receiving his doctorate, Dewey joined the philosophy department of the University of Michigan, where he taught from 1889 to 1894.

In 1894, Dewey joined the faculty of the University of Chicago, which, under the leadership of William Rainey Harper, its president, was emerging as an internationally recognized institution for graduate research and study. At Chicago, Dewey served as head of the Department of Philosophy, Psychology, and Education. These three disciplines, then jointly organized in a single academic unit, held a special interest for Dewey, who studied and wrote on each of them.

Dewey's Chicago years, from 1894 to 1904, were especially significant for his philosophical development and for his educational experiment at the University Laboratory School. Dewey's association with George Herbert Mead, a colleague in his department, and his involvement in Jane Addams's Hull House helped to shape his emerging Pragmatism. Mead, sometimes called the most original of the Progressive philosophers, argued that ideas and actions ought to be fused and directed toward social reform. Among Mead's ideas shared by Dewey were that (1) democracy, as an ideal, required a public educated to understand the social duties and responsibilities of political life; and (2) morality should be applied to the problems of daily life—to personal, political, social, and educational behavior.[8]

Like Dewey, Mead was interested in child development, particularly in early childhood education. Mead developed a theory of play as an activity whose purposes create connections to later activities, including work. Mead, who saw play as a natural way to learn argued that the child's environment provided myriad opportunities for play.[9] Teachers should arrange children's learning environment so that it stimulated interest and elicited activity. Mead also advocated experimental learning in which students engaged in field studies and laboratory work. His ideas were congenial to Dewey's thought and stimulated Dewey's philosophical and educational work at the University of Chicago.

University of Chicago Laboratory School

The University of Chicago Laboratory School, an experimental school Dewey established, had a profound influence on his evolving philosophy of education, especially its relationship to teaching and learning.[10]

The school enrolled children ages four through fourteen and sought to provide experiences in cooperative and mutually useful living through the "activity method," which involved play, construction, nature study, and self-expression. These activities were designed to stimulate and exercise learners' active reconstruction of their own experiences. Through such activities, the school would function as a miniature community and an embryonic society. The children's individual tendencies were directed toward cooperative living in the school community.

True to his Experimentalist philosophy, Dewey's Laboratory School was an experimental school in which theories about education were tested. Educational hypotheses that were effective in aiding the students to reconstruct their experiences in terms of larger social outcomes could then be disseminated to a larger professional and public audience. In describing the Laboratory School at the University of Chicago, Dewey wrote:

> The conception underlying the school is that of a laboratory. It bears the same relation to the work in pedagogy that a laboratory bears to biology, physics, or chemistry. Like any such laboratory it has two main purposes: (1) to exhibit, test, verify, and criticize theoretical statements and principles; and (2) to add to the sum of facts and principles in its special line.[11]

Dewey's experiment emphasized the social function of the school. As a "special social community," the complexity of the "social environment" was "reduced and simplified." According to Dewey:

> The simplified social life should reproduce, in miniature, the activities fundamental to life as a whole, and thus enable the child, on one side, to become gradually acquainted with the

structure, materials, and modes of operation of the larger community; while upon the other, it enables him individually to express himself through these lines of conduct, and thus attain control of his own powers.[12]

The Laboratory School's curriculum integrated three of Dewey's concepts: critical reflective thinking, the scientific method, and the educative role of the group in constructing children's social intelligence. Unlike the conventional school curriculum organized around skills such as reading, writing, and arithmetic and academic subjects such as history, mathematics, and chemistry, the Laboratory curriculum focused on three broad sets of activities: making and doing, history and geography, and science. **Making and doing** referred to children's activities in their early years of schooling, the primary grades. To maintain continuity in their experience between home and school, children engaged in activities that grew out of their familiar experiences and interests and led them to the larger society's relationships and occupations. Making and doing was followed by **history and geography**, taught not as conventional school subjects, but designed to expand children's perspectives into time and space. The curriculum's third stage, **science**, broadly meant investigating various subject-matter disciplines, not in isolation from each other, but for their instrumental use in solving problems.

After testing his early ideas about education at the Laboratory School, Dewey proceeded to construct the philosophical scaffolding of Instrumentalism, or Experimentalism, his version of Pragmatism. Dewey's Laboratory School, which commanded national and international attention during its years of operation, still fascinates historians and philosophers of education. Despite the school's acclaim and perhaps because of it, Dewey ran into administrative conflicts, especially over his employment of his wife, Alice Chipman Dewey, as the school's principal. The University of Chicago's president, William Rainey Harper, began to challenge Dewey's administrative decisions.

Dewey's Chicago period, especially his Laboratory School, identified him with Progressivism as a social, political, and educational movement. He collaborated with Jane Addams, the founder of Hull House, a social settlement house, where Dewey was a consultant and lecturer. Dewey's conversations with Addams helped him to refine his philosophy. When he came to Chicago, Dewey still retained some ideas about the inevitability of social conflict. Addams convinced him that conflict was unnecessary and often interfered with the socially intelligent solving of problems. Conflicts generally arose when individuals interjected their personal biases into a controversial issue. The genuine resolution of conflict, Addams advised Dewey, came when people acted in a unified way to resolve a problem or issue.

While in Chicago, Dewey broadened his insights into the relationships between schools and children's learning. He collaborated with Colonel Francis Parker, a leading progressive educator, who was principal of the Cook County Normal School and the Chicago Institute of Education. He worked closely with Ella Flagg Young, the first woman to be a superintendent of a major urban school district. It was Young who encouraged him to put his ideas into practice at the Laboratory School.

Dewey left the University of Chicago to become a professor of philosophy at Columbia University in New York City in 1905, where he taught until he retired in 1930. At Columbia, Dewey was closely associated with such prominent Progressive professors of education as William Heard Kilpatrick, the founder of the project method, George S. Counts, the originator of social reconstructionism, and Harold Rugg, a pioneer in issue-based social studies.

Dewey's Major Philosophical and Educational Works

Because Dewey was such a prolific author, we comment only on a selected number of his books that are most relevant for Pragmatism as an educational philosophy.[13] Drawing on his experiences at the Laboratory School, Dewey, in *The School and Society* (1899), commented on the need for schools to assume a larger social function.[14] Dewey's *The Child and the Curriculum* (1902) examined the teacher's role in relating the curriculum to the child's interest, readiness, and stage of development.[15] Emphasizing experience as the basis for learning, Dewey recommended instruction that facilitated the child's immediate and personal use of knowledge.

In 1910, Dewey's *How We Think* argued that thinking is experimental in that it involves a series of problem-solving episodes that occur as we attempt to survive and grow in an environmental context.[16] Employing the scientific method, thinking occurs when we conjecture hypotheses designed to make an indeterminate situation into a determinate one. Thinking, as defined by Dewey, had implications for a method of educational inquiry based on problem solving. (Later in the chapter, we shall comment more extensively on *How We Think* in relationship to Dewey's epistemology.)

Democracy and Education (1916), Dewey's most complete rendition of educational philosophy, identified the foundational ideas of a democratic society and applied them to education.[17] Essentially, Dewey, who consistently rejected dualism, argued that genuine education proceeded more effectively in an open or **democratic environment** that is free of absolutes that blocked freedom of inquiry. In *Individualism, Old and New* (1920) he rejected the inherited notion of "rugged individualism" as an archaic historic residue.[18] In place of a competitive economy and society, Dewey urged social planning and action that would make the emergent corporate social order congenial to human growth and purposes. In *Art as Experience* (1934), Dewey elaborated an aesthetic theory that asserted that art was properly a public means of shared expression and communication between the artist and the perceiver of the art object.[19]

Among Dewey's other major books were *Interest and Effort in Education* (1913), *Human Nature and Conduct* (1922), and *Freedom and Culture* (1939).[20] Through his writings, lectures, and presence on the U.S. and world scene, Dewey contributed to political and social liberalism that urged social reform based on pragmatic planning. His work stimulated the rise of an Experimentalist educational philosophy that profoundly influenced U.S. educational theory and practice.

Dewey and Progressive Education

Although often called the father of progressive education, Dewey's identification with progressive education must be carefully considered. Dewey's influence on Progressivism came as he contributed to the general emphasis on social and educational reform. He agreed with many elements in progressive education and rejected others—especially the naive romanticism of the neo-Rousseaueans.

Although many Progressives were influenced by Dewey's Experimentalism, others were not. The Progressive Education Association, an umbrella organization, encompassed a variety of individuals and groups ranging from neo-Rousseauean child-centered educators to neo-Freudians. The publication of many of Dewey's educational writings coincided with the Progressive education movement, and similarities existed between Dewey and the Progressive reformers who opposed a static conception of learning and schooling. Although Dewey and many Progressive educators agreed on the importance of experience, continuity, and the cultivation of the child's interests and needs, Dewey challenged the sentimental, romantic neo-Rousseauean Progressives who dogmatically asserted child-centered doctrines. Dewey's *Experience and Education* (1938) criticized Progressive educators for failing to elaborate a positive educational philosophy based on experience.[21] He cautioned educators against a simplistic categorization of educational theories and practices into "either-or" polar opposites. He also challenged Progressives to move beyond merely opposing traditional school practices and urged them to develop a positive and affirmative educational posture.

Experimentalism's Philosophical Bases

Dewey's Experimentalism held a special relevance for education. Among its philosophical bases are (1) Dewey's rejection of metaphysical absolutes; (2) the organism and the environment; (3) Dewey's Experimentalist epistemology; (4) the complete act of thought; and (5) axiology as experimental valuation.

Dewey's Rejection of Metaphysical Absolutes

In earlier chapters on Idealism and Realism, we examined metaphysics as speculation about the nature of ultimate reality. Pragmatists, such as Dewey, rejected such speculation as being unverifiable in terms of human experience. In this section, we examine Dewey's attack on philosophical systems based on absolute metaphysical positions, dualism, and a quest for certitude.

Although *Democracy and Education* most completely stated Dewey's educational philosophy, the key to Dewey's system of thought is found in *The Quest for Certainty*.[22] Dewey argued against a dualistic conception of the universe, which he claimed was merely a human contrivance designed to postulate a theoretically unchanging realm of complete and perfect certitude. The more traditional Idealist, Realist, and Thomist philosophies, based on metaphysical propositions, grounded reality in a world of unchanging ideas for the Idealist or structures for the Realist. Based on these conceptions, Western thinkers had devised a bipolar, dualistic view of reality that divided it into ideational, or conceptual, and material dimensions. While ideas and spirit are higher in the chain of being, work and action are lower in the hierarchy. Priority is given to the immaterial and unchanging order. Thus, such classical dualisms as spirit–matter, mind–body, and soul–body came to permeate Western thought. These metaphysical dualisms had an impact on life and education in that they created distinctions between theory and practice, between liberal and vocational education, between fine and applied arts, and between thought and action.

The bifurcation between theory and practice, or thought and action, was not only a matter for speculation by philosophers, but it also had an impact on educational practice. Philosophical dualism contributed to patterns of hierarchical curricular organization in which the most theoretical subjects were given priority over practical ones. Distinguishing between theory and practice, the traditional curriculum required learners to first master symbolic and literary skills such as reading, writing, and arithmetic. Learning these tool skills prepared children to study systematically such subjects as history, geography, mathematics, and science at the secondary and higher levels. In the traditional subject-matter curriculum, disciplines were organized deductively as bodies of principles, theories, factual content, and examples. Formal education became excessively abstract and bore little relationship to the learner's own personal and social experience. Furthermore, the subject-matter curriculum aimed to prepare students for future situations after the completion of formal schooling. According to Dewey's critique, the traditional subject-matter curriculum, based on the dualism between theory and practice, created additional bifurcations that separated the child from the curriculum and the school from the society.

Dewey's social conception of education was basic to his Experimentalism, which saw thinking and doing as a unified flow of ongoing experience. Thinking and acting were not separable; thinking was incomplete until tested in experience. To understand Dewey's pragmatic philosophy, it is necessary to examine his antagonism toward the dualism that supported traditional philosophical beliefs in a higher, transcendent, and unchanging reality.

According to Dewey, human beings inhabit an uncertain world that contains threats to survival. In their minds, human beings sought to create a concept of certainty to give them a sense of permanence and security. Because actual living contains risk, traditional theorists differentiated between the uncertainty of everyday life and the security that came from an unchanging and perfect reality. Early religio-philosophical systems, such as Idealism and Thomism, created a worldview that posited reality in a perfect, unchanging, and eternal universal being. In this *Weltanschauung,* the inferior level of existence was mundane, changing, and uncertain, and the superior order was that which was beyond the scope of the empirical, experiential, and everyday existence, or, in other words, beyond the physical.

Traditional philosophies, derived from Platonism, or Aristotelianism, were occupied with speculation about permanent, eternal, and self-sufficient being. According to the doctrines of an immutable good and fixed order of being, speculative philosophers were concerned with describing metaphysical systems of immutable and necessary truths and principles that lay beyond human experience. According to philosophical dualism, a higher realm of fixed and permanent reality existed in which truth was absolute; there was also an inferior world of changing objects and persons that was the realm of experience and practice.

Dewey emphasized a changing and evolutionary universe where the human situation was not to transcend experience but rather to use it to solve human problems. Rejecting dualistic epistemologies, Dewey emphasized a continuum of human experience that related rather than separated thinking and acting, fact and value, and intellect and emotion.[23] He argued that philosophy should recognize, reconstruct, and use experience to improve the human condition. In such a reconstruction of experience, theory and practice were fused and used in ongoing human activity. Derived from experience, theory was tested in action. Instead of a dualism between the immutable and the changing, experience was a continuum in which individuals and groups dealt with a successive sequence of problematic situations.

In such a sequence, theory was derived from and was tested in practice; mind was a social process of intelligently solving problems rather than an antecedent and transcendent category; education was liberal, or liberating, as it freed human beings by giving them a methodology for dealing with all kinds of problems, including the social and vocational; and the distinction between the fine and useful arts was dissolved by integrating beauty and function. Dewey's thesis was that existence was uncertain. To exist meant to be involved in a changing world. The human quest was not for certainty but rather for a means, or a method, of controlling and directing the process of change insofar as this could be done in an imperfect world.

The Organism and the Environment

As indicated earlier, Dewey's birth in 1859 coincided with the publication of Charles Darwin's *Origin of Species*. The revolutionary implications of Darwin's biological theory reverberated throughout the late nineteenth and early twentieth centuries. Initially, Darwin's theory of evolution appeared to challenge the traditional Judeo-Christian version of creation, based on the book of Genesis, that God had created species in a fixed form. Those who accepted Genesis in a literal way found themselves in conflict with Darwinian science. For some fundamentalist Protestant Americans, the impact of Darwin's theory was a shattering experience.

According to Darwin's thesis that species evolved slowly and gradually, members of the species, or organisms, lived, adjusted, and adapted to their environments to survive. Those species that succeeded in surviving did so because they possessed favorable characteristics that enabled them to adjust satisfactorily to environmental changes. The transmission of these favorable characteristics to their offspring guaranteed the particular species' continuation. Darwin's theory emphasized the competition of individuals for survival in a frequently challenging environment.

To appreciate Darwin's impact on Dewey, it is necessary to examine briefly the initial adaptation of evolutionary theory into a sociology of knowledge by Herbert Spencer (1820–1903), who applied Darwinian principles to socioeconomic and political life. Spencer viewed the human being as an individual social atom who was locked in a fiercely competitive struggle against other individuals. Through individual competition and initiative, some individuals adapted to the environment more efficiently than others. These intelligent and strong competitors climbed upward in society to positions of social, economic, and political leadership. Those who were unintelligent in their behavior, who could not compete effectively or efficiently, descended on the rungs of the social ladder to become the dregs of society. For Spencer, competition was the natural order of life with the prize going to the fittest individuals.

Spencer and his many followers in business and in academia regarded the laissez-faire economic and social order as the natural state of affairs and argued against tampering with nature's laws of competition. Society was composed of independent, autonomous, and competitive individuals, who at the most direct level struggled for economic survival. In the Social Darwinist view, schools best performed their social role by preparing individuals for a competitive society. Progress occurred as individuals invented and perfected new ways of competing against each other in exploiting the natural and social environments.

Both biological and Social Darwinism influenced Dewey's developing Experimentalist philosophy. Although he accepted some of Darwin's basic biological conceptions, Dewey rejected Spencer's application of competitive ethics to society. Darwin's notion of an evolutionary process was accepted by Dewey, who had rejected fixed, final, and transcendent Hegelian metaphysics. Dewey's educational philosophy, drawing on an organismic psychology, applied the terms of organism and environment to life and to education. For Dewey, the human organism was a living and natural creature, physiologically composed of living tissue and possessing life-sustaining impulses and drives. Every organism lives within an environment, or habitat, which has elements that both enhance and threaten its life.

For Dewey, the sustaining of human life required interactions with the natural environment. Rather than becoming one with nature, as Rousseau suggested, or being locked in struggle with nature, as Spencer argued, Dewey recommended that human beings instrumentally use nature to transform parts of the environment to increase life-sustaining possibilities. Through the application of scientific intelligence and through cooperative social activity, humans can use certain elements in nature to solve problems with other aspects of the natural environment.[24]

As the individual human being, or human organism, lives, he or she encounters problematic situations of an indeterminate character that interfere with the ongoing march of experience. Upon encountering such an indeterminate situation, the organism's activity is blocked or impeded until it can render the novel situation determinate and resume activity. The successful person is able to solve problems and add the elements of his or her solution to the reserves of experience. As a result of this network of interaction between the organism and its environment, the human organism acquires experience. In Dewey's Experimentalism, the key concept of **experience** is best thought of as the interaction of or the transaction between an organism and its environment. We know through our experiences, or environmental interactions; each experiential episode adds to our experience. When confronted by problematic situations, we examine our experience for clues, which suggest the means for resolving the present difficulty.

At this point, several basic components of Dewey's educational philosophy can be identified: (1) the learner is a living organism, a biological and sociological phenomenon, who possesses drives or impulses designed to sustain life; (2) the learner lives in an environment, or habitat, which is both natural and social; (3) the learner, moved by personal drives, is an active person engaged in constant interaction with the environment; (4) environmental interaction produces problems that occur as the individual seeks to satisfy his or her needs; and (5) learning is the process of solving problems in the environment.

From his days at the University of Chicago Laboratory School onward, Dewey emphasized the school's social function as a miniature community or embryonic society. Although holding that society was composed of separate and discrete individual human beings, he rejected Social Darwinism's competitive ethic of social atomism. For Dewey, human beings lived in both a social and a natural environment. In striving to live, human beings found that group life, or human association, most effectively contributed to their welfare and survival. **Associative** living, or community, enriched human experience and added to it as the group mutually engaged in problem-solving activities. Collective human experience provided the individual with a more complex set of experiences, or interactive

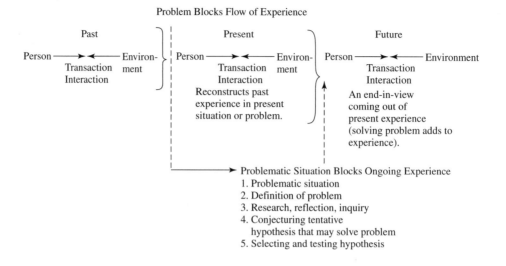

Pragmatic Continuum of Experience

___

episodes. Barriers to full human association blocked free interaction. They impeded the ability of individuals and groups to contribute to cultural growth by mutual sharing experiences.[25]

Although Dewey's model of experience arising from the interaction of the organism with the environment has often been interpreted in socio-educational terms, some scholars broaden the interpretation to include an ecological-educational dimension as well. According to this view, which emphasizes Dewey's humanist Naturalism, the human organism is interacting then with "an integrated social and biophysical environment."[26]

This naturalistic element in Dewey's thought, while not romantic in the Rousseauean sense, argued against a dualism that saw human beings occupying two separate spheres of existence—one social and the other natural. It also rejects a crude Darwinism that sees human beings as combatants locked in struggle against nature. Such a broadened conception of environmental interaction encourages an ecological sensitivity to the earth as a biosphere, which opens the educational process to a wide range of world problems such as pollution, conservation of natural resources, preservation of endangered species, and ultimately arms control.

Dewey's Experimentalist Epistemology

Rather than dealing with metaphysical issues, Dewey was concerned with epistemology. For him, as well as other Pragmatists, knowing as an experimental and commonsense way followed the method of scientific inquiry. In the next section, we will examine Dewey's concepts of intelligence and experimental inquiry and his rendering of the scientific method into the "complete act of thought."

In breaking with the more traditional Idealism and Realism, which rested on a metaphysical conception of antecedent reality, Dewey believed that these speculative philosophies had constructed a static theory of mind that was isolated from life's personal and social realities. Dewey proposed an active social conception of human intelligence, which, while conditioned by societal institutions, could dynamically affect social change.

For Dewey, intelligence is socially built as people share their experiences in dealing with common concerns. Intelligence, the ability to define and solve problems, is acquired through the experience of persisting and working through problem-solving situations. Within the problem-solving context, intelligence results from shared activity in making and using instruments, in fashioning plans of action, and in acting on hypotheses. Human beings use their intelligence to invent and fabricate instruments or tools. The more complex and sophisticated the society, the more instruments are available to use in solving problems. Unlike Rousseau's glorification of the primitive state of nature, Dewey found the savage or primitive human being to be limited by a paucity of instruments that could be used in solving problems. In contrast, civilized society possessed the instruments that enhanced group problem-solving efforts and cultivated and enriched social intelligence.

Dewey's view of the human being as a fabricator of tools, as an instrument maker, had implications for education. Children in a civilized society needed to develop familiarity with the use of instruments. Through schooling, they could experience in a relatively short time much of the human experience that involved making and using instruments.

Dewey's insightful *How We Think* (1910) develops his Experimentalist epistemology, psychology, and logic. He argues that (1) philosophy's true purpose is to help people solve their real problems that arise in experience; (2) "truth" is not the result of metaphysical speculation but is constructed from our tentative "warranted assertions" that guide us in a constantly changing environment; and (3) we verify our ideas when we test them to see whether their consequences resolve our problems. Relating epistemology to teaching and learning, Dewey argues that we use our ideas as instruments to solve our personal, social, and political problems.

Dewey, in *How We Think,* introduces the concept of "reflective thinking," which approximates the scientific method. He defined reflective thinking as the "active, persistent, and careful" examination of our beliefs in terms of the evidence that supports them and to the conclusions to which they lead. Reflection, for Dewey, is not daydreaming, listening to a teacher or professor lecture, or passive contemplation. Thinking is based on reflection during which the person, like a scientist, actively engages in experimentation about what ideas do when acted on. When we think reflectively, our thoughts are "persistent," which means that each element in them grows out of, relates to, and is connected in a chain, or continuum, to the proceeding one. The term *careful* means the willingness not to jump to a conclusion but to gather the evidence needed to support it and to defer a judgment, or a conclusion, by conjecturing about its consequences and testing it. Reflective thinking, like the scientific method, does not take beliefs for granted because of custom, tradition, or opinion, but puts them to the test of critical inquiry and action. For Dewey, generating a complete reflective thought replicates the scientific method.[27]

How We Think was written to guide teachers in developing students' reflective or scientific thinking habits and skills. Dewey believed that children's intrinsic curiosity, imagination, and activities are how they begin to use experimentation. Curious about their environment, children are eager to explore it; their explorations provide occasions for thinking about what they are experiencing. Children's natural curiosity has a social and educational connection. Children learn to ask others—parents, friends, and teachers—to add to their experience. When they see something new, they ask, "What is that?" When they don't understand what something does, they ask, often repeatedly, "How does it work?" or "What does it do?" These important leading questions verbalize their thinking process and seek to engage others in moving it from an internal process to a social one with many educational possibilities. "What," "why," and "how" are the questions children use to begin what, if encouraged and properly guided, leads to complete, reflective, and scientific thinking. In this process of moving from curiosity to critical thinking, Dewey observed that the "teacher has usually more to learn than to teach."[28] Dewey encouraged teachers to use children's open and flexible interests as the avenue to reflective thought. Too often, he warned, dogma and routine blight the learning process.

Complete Act of Thought

According to Dewey, genuine thought occurred as the individual encountered and solved problems according to the scientific method. Although informed by the bodies of scientific knowledge accumulated by experts, Dewey's concept of the scientific method was a broadly conceived procedure of scientific intelligence that was applicable to human affairs.[29] Dewey's problem-solving method, or **complete act of thought**—the scientific method broadly conceived—consisted of five steps:

1. The **problematic situation**, in which the person is confused because he or she is involved in an incomplete situation of indeterminate character. In the problematic situation, the individual's ongoing activity is blocked by some unique situational element that deviates from past experience.

2. In *defining the problem,* the individual examines the problematic situation and identifies that aspect of the situation, the deviant particular, that blocks continuing activity.

3. *Clarification of the problem* involves a careful survey, examination, inspection, exploration, and analysis of the elements involved in the problematic situation. At this stage of inquiry, the individual systematically and reflectively researches the problem to locate the ideas, materials, and instruments that could resolve the difficulty.

4. By *constructing tentative hypotheses,* the individual establishes a number of generalizations, if-then statements, that are possible means of solving the problem. This process involves mentally projecting oneself into the future and seeing the possible consequences of action. As a result of hypothesizing and conjecturing, the individual frames tentative solutions that could resolve the difficulty and have the greatest possibilities for securing the desired consequences.

5. This crucial step involves *testing the preferred hypothesis by acting on it.* If the hypothesis resolves the problem and brings the desired consequences, then the individual resumes activity until encountering another problem. If the problem remains, then another hypothesis is needed.[30]

In considering Dewey's five steps, it is important to realize, as Dewey states, that reflective thought is an ongoing and cumulative process and not just a sequence of mechanical steps. Each phase in thinking through a problem grows out of the preceding phase and the following phase to which it is connected and related. Amassing, reciting, and recalling facts as information is not reflective thought. The facts, or evidence, need to be organized, referenced, and used. The process needs to point to an end: solving the problem that was identified and defined at the beginning of the process. Having a direction means that the problem-solver is flexible and alert to new leads in how to use the materials to solve the problem. It also means that the learner needs the perseverance to stay with the project and not jump from one phase to another or to abandon it when it becomes difficult.

Reflective thinking might begin with children's instincts and impulses; it did not mean, however, that teachers should stay with them. Rather, they were to guide the thinking process from impulsivity to reflection. Reflective thinking did not mean that children should jump to conclusions; rather, it meant staying with the process, researching the problem, and conjecturing about ways to solve it. Children became reflective thinkers when they learned to take their time, pause, step back, and reflect on the consequences of their actions. Encouraging reflective thinking also meant that adults, particularly teachers, anxious that children get the right answer, were not to become impatient with the process and pressure children to get it done quickly. Education was truly progressive when children learned to think reflectively by formulating plans, gathering evidence pertinent to the problem, and avoiding being diverted into incidental and irrelevant matters.

Dewey's experimental epistemology is the format for the method of problem solving in which the learner, as an individual or in association with others, uses the scientific method to solve both personal and social problems. Each problem-solving episode becomes an experimental situation in which the learner applies the method of intelligence to real problems arising in his or her own experience. For Dewey and his followers, the problem-solving method is transferable to a variety of problematic situations.

Dewey's fifth step, the testing of the hypothesis, represents the greatest departure from the learning pattern of the traditional subject-oriented school. Teachers and students in the more conventional schools might explore problems and frame tentative solutions, but rarely do they attempt to solve these problems by acting on them directly. Although they might act on problems encountered in their chemistry and mathematics lessons, the solutions to these problems are already determined. It is most unlikely that students would be encouraged to act on the pressing social, economic, and political problems of the day. Although such problems as war, poverty, and pollution might be discussed in the conventional classroom, the students' active attempt to resolve these problems is deferred to times and situations outside the school. It might, in fact, be deferred until the student reached adulthood and became a voter. In contrast, Dewey held that the validation of an idea occurred only as it was tested in experience. Thought is incomplete until acted on and the consequences of action are assessed.

Axiology as Experimental Valuation

Dewey's Experimentalism applies as well to value issues as to inquiry. When Dewey abandoned Idealism for Pragmatism, he began to develop a non-metaphysical value theory. He saw ethical and aesthetic sensibilities and actions as coming from human experience rather than a vision of ultimate reality.[31] Unlike the more traditional Idealist and Realist philosophers who found a hierarchy of values inherent in the universe, Dewey was a moral relativist who believed that values arose as outcomes of human responses to varying environmental situations. For Dewey, a major defect of hierarchical value systems was that humans are confronted by wide varieties of conflicting hierarchies. Each hierarchy rests on a basic assumption that is supposed to be self-evident according to some principle of "right reason."

In addition to rejecting hierarchical values, Dewey also turned away from theories that relied on tradition and custom as value determinants. The major weakness in the customary validation of values is that, by justifying whatever exists at a particular time and place, it becomes a rationale for preserving the status quo. In an interdependent modern world, a methodology of valuation is needed to adjudicate cross-cultural conflicts. In a technological society characterized by rapid social changes, customs and traditions are inadequate determinants of values.

In contrast to value systems founded on universal hierarchies of tradition and custom, Dewey argued that the method of shared scientific intelligence should be applied to axiological questions of morality, ethics, and aesthetics. He postulated a criterion of valuation based on the relationships of aims, means, and ends. Experimentalist valuation begins in human preferences, wants, wishes, desires, and needs. Evaluation arises when a conflict occurs in these raw materials of value. If a person had only a single desire, then he or she would act to satisfy that desire. In the case of value conflict, it was necessary to unify the apparently conflicting desires. If the desires could not be unified, then one had to choose between conflicting alternatives. Choice is made by evaluating the possible consequences of acting on the chosen preference.

Dewey's method of valuation was designed to unify aims, means, and ends. When an end was attained, it became a means for the satisfaction of still another end. If a person desired a given end, it was necessary to ask questions about the appropriate and efficient means of attaining that end.

Although Dewey's theory of valuation followed an experimental design, it also embraced a conception of democracy that held broad implications for society and education. Democracy meant more than the particular political arrangements associated with representative, popular governments. It was both an ethical and a methodological necessity in Dewey's thought. A democratic society embraces the widest possible human sharing, participation, and involvement in institutional life and processes. Dewey's opposition to dualism in philosophy extended to dualisms in society in which individuals or groups were segregated and marginalized. Societies that practiced segregation on the basis of class, race, sex, or ethnicity lost the opportunity for the growth of social intelligence and enrichment that came from a sense of community life in which all people participated.

Just as he opposed metaphysically based value criteria, Dewey challenged the strong classical liberal orientation in U.S. society that argued for values being based on individual self-interest. He opposed the trend toward a fractured polity of special interest groups. For him, human beings were communal participants who defined and tested collective goals.[32]

Democratic social arrangements are also a methodological necessity for experimental inquiry. Such arrangements are free of philosophical absolutes that blocked inquiry into what were regarded as immutable first principles. They also were free of the restrictions to inquiry imposed by regimes that closed off public discussion and debate.

In educational situations, Dewey's value theory encourages inquiring minds in an open classroom. Such openness carries with it the risk that long-standing ideas and values may be discarded or reconstructed. Openness, however, does not mean educational anarchy or naive romanticism. Rather, openness requires social arrangements conducive to using the method of intelligence, the experimental method, to deal with human issues.

Experimentalism's Educational Implications

In the following section, we will examine certain aspects of Dewey's educational philosophy. These include: (1) education as conservation and reconstruction, (2) schooling and society, (3) the democratic society and education, (4) Experimentalist teaching and learning, (5) growth as the end of education, and (6) the experiential curriculum.

Education as Conservation and Reconstruction

In *Democracy and Education,* Dewey's primary concern is the relationship between society and education. Education occurs informally as the person matures within the cultural milieu and acquires the language, skills, and knowledge common to group life. In the more formal sense of schooling, education is a deliberate process of bringing the immature person into cultural participation by providing the necessary symbolic and linguistic tools needed for group interaction and communication.

Dewey conceived of education as having both a conservative and a reconstructive, or renewing, dimension. Education is conservative because it provides cultural continuity by transmitting the heritage from adults to children, the immature members of the group. In both its formal and informal aspects, education is always a value-laden process that involves cultural imposition because it takes place within the context of a particular culture with its unique customs, mores, folkways, and language. Although cultural imposition is always contextual to a given time and place, it provides the communicative and expressive means by which individuals liberate themselves through group participation.

As a transmitter of the cultural heritage, education is the means by which the group reproduces the cultural type and thus perpetuates itself. In the Deweyan context, the child is socialized by acquiring and using the cultural instruments and values through association with the members of the group. Thus, education becomes the process whereby the group transmits its cultural skills, knowledge, and values and reproduces the desired cultural type of person, who will perpetuate the heritage.

Although clearly recognizing that the conservative aspects of education provided cultural continuity, Dewey saw education as broader and more dynamic than preserving the status quo. Cultural conservation, for Dewey, did not mean that adults in a society used the school to reproduce currently held beliefs and values. Rather, it meant that the young were provided the cultural skills and tools by which they could improve social conditions.[33] The very cultural instrumentalities such as the language and technology that were imposed on the young carried the possibilities for altering or changing the inherited culture. Just as he conceived of the universe as undergoing constant change, Dewey believed that human culture was also changing. By using the scientific method, human beings possessed the ability to direct the course of change.

Dewey took an instrumental view of the past. Precedents were instruments in analyzing present situations rather than prescriptions to be followed implicitly in dealing with the present.[34] When reconstructed they were useful in framing new hypotheses for solving human problems.

Schooling and Society

The cultural heritage, a vast complex that includes the accumulated experience of the human race and the particular experience of the group, has elements that are both worthy and unworthy of perpetuation. Formal education is one of society's means of selecting those aspects of the cultural heritage that are worthy of perpetuation.

For Dewey, the school is a specialized environment established to enculturate the young by deliberately bringing them into cultural participation. As a social institution, the school is a selective agency that, while transmitting the culture, also seeks to reconstruct it to meet contemporary needs. For Dewey, the school's threefold functions are to simplify, purify, and balance the cultural heritage.[35] Simplification means that the school, really curriculum makers and teachers as social agents, select elements of the heritage and reduce their complexity by designing units appropriate to the learner's maturity and readiness. As a purifying agent, the school selects and transmits those elements of the cultural heritage that enhance human growth and eliminate unworthy aspects that limit it. Balancing the cultural heritage refers to integrating the selected experiences into a harmonious core. Because society is composed of many diverse groups, children need assistance in understanding individuals from other groups. The genuinely democratic society as an integrated and balanced community rests on mutually shared understanding.

Although problem solving is individualized and personalized, it is also a social process. Group experience is a cooperative enterprise in which all the participants share their experiences. The more sharing occurs, the greater are the possibilities for growth. Dewey recognized that the rise of an industrial, urban, and technological society had created a number of socioeducational problems that schools needed to address. The more complex the society becomes, the greater is the gap between the child's activities and the requirements of responsible adult life. Dewey's school society, based on mutually shared activities, was designed to be the embryo of an associative democracy. He anticipated that the school's problem-solving techniques would transfer to the larger society.

Democratic Society and Education

Dewey rejected the Perennialist assumptions, such as those of Robert Hutchins, that education is everywhere the same or is intrinsically good. Rather, he reasoned that the quality of education varies as does the quality of life experienced by the group that establishes and supports the school. Dewey's conceptions of democratic social arrangements and democratic education were related to an experimenting society that used a process-oriented philosophy. Not particular to the U.S. form of government or to particular political institutions, Dewey's conception of democratic education was rather an epistemological and sociological one characterized by the presence of an experimental temperament. In the experimenting society, citizens are free from the impediments erected by absolutist governments or a priori philosophies. Because educational institutions socialize the young in group values, genuinely democratic education occurs within the milieu of the experimental or inquiry-oriented school.

Dewey emphasized the cooperative nature of shared human experience. The more sharing that occurs among individuals, the greater are the possibilities for human interaction and growth. Dewey's emphasis on human association embraced three key elements: the common, communication, and community. The **common**, representing shared objects, instruments, values, and ideas, arises in the context of group experience. Communication occurs when people frame and express their shared experiences in symbolic patterns, in a common language. When individuals communicate, they take the perspective of the other person in developing their own understanding and behavior. Communication thus develops a commonly shared context; this context, in turn, frames the basis of community.[36] Community is the human association that results as individuals come together to discuss their common experiences and problems through shared communication. Dewey preferred the free, open, and humane arrangements of the democratic community in which the experimental processes operated without the interference of absolutist or authoritarian structures.

Although Dewey emphasized the importance of the like-minded community characterized by shared experience, such a community did not rest on conformity. A genuinely democratic community honored cultural pluralism and diversity within a shared context. For Dewey, education helped to create the sense of community.

In the current debates over multiculturalism, it is possible to extrapolate a Deweyan position. Dewey would see U.S. society and culture as being composed of smaller communities within a larger encompassing community. Each of the smaller communities—racial, ethnic, gender—has its own common communication and sense of membership. Each has a potentially enriching contribution to make to the greater community. Viewing the genuine American as an international composite, he stated that the American

> is not American plus Pole or German. But the American is . . . Pole-German-English-French-Spanish-Italian-Greek-Irish-Scandinavian-Bohemian, Jew—and so on. . . . the hyphen connects instead of separates. And this means . . . that our public schools shall teach each factor to respect every other, and shall . . . enlighten us all as to the great past contributions of every strain in our composite make-up.[37]

For Dewey, the smaller cultural communities could be expected to differ with each other as their interests clashed. It was crucial to the larger community, the great society, and especially to its democratic sensibilities and arrangements, that this conflict be contained within a communal framework and not become noncommunal. Communal conflicts should be resolved in a procedural, nonviolent, nondestructive way. The larger community, the greater society, is governed by commonly shared processes of conflict resolution. For Dewey, there is a communal, or communitarian, American core of beliefs and values. This core, however, rests on commonly agreed-on and shared democratic procedures.

Experimentalist Teaching and Learning

Although his critics have often accused him of encouraging disorderly permissiveness in schools, Dewey's views of the learner, like his relationships to Progressive education, must be considered carefully. The learner's freedom was not anarchy or doing as one pleased without regard to consequences. Freedom, rather, required an open classroom environment that facilitates using experimental inquiry to examine and test beliefs and values.

Dewey's group problem-solving method differs from traditional classroom management in which instruction is based on the teacher's authority. Questioning externally imposed discipline, Dewey preferred an internal discipline designed to cultivate self-directing and self-disciplining persons. This kind of task, or problem-centered discipline, originates within the activity needed to solve the problem. Control comes from the cooperative context of shared activity, which involves working with instruments and people. Rather than *controlling* the learning situation, the teacher, as a resource person, *guides* the situation.

In Dewey's learning situation, the starting point of any activity is the learner's felt needs. Such intrinsic interest, related to a real concern, is effective in eliciting the effort needed to satisfy the need and to solve the problem.

Based on Dewey's conception of learning, educational aims are of two kinds: intrinsic and extrinsic. Internal to the learner's experience and interests, intrinsic aims arise from the problem or the task. In contrast, extrinsic aims are extraneous to the person's problem, task, or interest. For example, externally administered rewards or punishments, often used to motivate learning in traditional school situations, are extrinsic and often distort genuine learning. For Dewey, intrinsic aims are always superior to extrinsic ones because they are personal, problematic, and relate to the individual learner's own self-direction, self-control, and self-discipline. Intrinsic educational aims, arising within the context of the learner's own experience, are flexible, capable of alteration, and lead to activity. Such an experimental aim is a tentative sketch, or plan of action, capable of being reconstructed and redirected.

In Dewey's problem-centered school, the teacher, as a resource person, guides rather than directs learning. The teacher's role is primarily that of guiding learners who need advice or assistance. Direction comes from the requirements of solving the particular problem. Educational aims belong to the learner rather than the teacher.

Teachers using the problem-solving method need to be patient with their students. Although coercion might force students to arrive at immediate results, it is likely to limit the flexibility needed for future problem solving. The teacher's control of the learning situation is ideally indirect rather than direct. Direct control, coercion, or external discipline fails to enlarge the learner's internal dispositions and does not contribute to the learner becoming a self-directed person. Teachers, motivated by a false sense of instructional efficiency, often err when their anxiety to have students arrive at the "correct answers" in the shortest possible time causes them to bypass the procedural requirements of experimental inquiry.

As resource persons, teachers need to allow students to make errors and to experience the consequences of their actions. In this way, students are more likely to become self-correcting. Dewey did not mean that childish whims should dictate the curriculum, however. The teacher, as a mature person, should exercise professional judgment and expertise so that the consequences of action do not become dangerous to the student or to his or her classmates.

Growth as the End of Education

For Dewey, the sole end of education is **growth**, or that reconstruction of experience that leads to the direction and control of subsequent experience. Education as a process has no end beyond growth. Particular experiences should be assessed according to the degree to which they contribute to growth, or to having more experience. Desirable experiences lead to further experience, whereas undesirable ones inhibit and reduce the possibilities for subsequent experiences. It might be recalled that intelligence involves the ability to solve problems, which, in turn, involves recognizing the connections and interrelationships among various experiences. Growth, in Dewey's context, means that the individual is gaining the ability to understand the relationships and interconnections among various experiences, between one learning episode and another. Learning by experience, through problem solving, means that education, like life, is a process of continuously reconstructing experience.

Dewey's educational goal of growth for the purpose of directing subsequent experiences rejects the traditional school's emphasis on the doctrine of preparation. According to the doctrine of preparation, students learn their lessons and master subject matter to prepare for events or situations that are to occur after the completion of school. In contrast, Dewey, who conceived of life as taking place in a changing universe and society, argued that deferring action until schooling had been completed would prepare students for a world that would be far different from the one for which they had been prepared. Instead of waiting for some remote future date, students are to act on their interests and needs to resolve present problems. By using day-to-day experiences, students would internalize a method of intelligence that is situationally applicable to the present and future.

The Experiential Curriculum

Dewey challenged the traditional subject-matter curriculum associated with formal schooling. Critics of the subject-matter curriculum charge that the teaching of such separate bodies of information as history, geography, mathematics, science, and language often degenerates into past-centered, highly verbal bookishness and pedantry. Formal schooling then becomes abstract in that it is separated from the child's own interests, needs, and experiences.

Dewey emphasized that methodology is intimately related to the curriculum when, in *Democracy and Education,* he recommended three levels of curricular organization: (1) making and doing; (2) history and geography; and (3) organized sciences.[38] Making and doing, the first curricular level, engages students in activities or projects based on their direct experience and requires using and manipulating raw materials. While the students are actively engaged in manipulating raw materials, these activities contain intellectual possibilities that expose children to experience's functional aspects.

Dewey regarded history and geography, the second curricular level, as two great educational resources for enlarging the scope and significance of the child's temporal and spatial experience, from the immediate home and school environments, to the larger community and the world. For Dewey, history and geography should not be taught as discretely organized bodies of information but rather should begin with the child's immediate environment and then be extended so that the learner gains perspective into time and place.

Dewey recognized that all learning is particular and contextual to a given time, place, and circumstance. Although cultural particularities imposed themselves onto learning, he recognized a distinction between imposition and indoctrination. Imposition reflected the concrete contingencies of living in a particular culture and environment with its unique heritage and values, whereas indoctrination closed the mind to divergent thinking and to alternative ways of acting.

Dewey's third stage of curriculum is organized subjects, the various sciences, consisting of bodies of warranted assertions. Students gain exposure to the various bodies of scientific information as they use them in researching their problems. Knowledge from the various sciences is a necessary component in identifying problematic elements and in formulating hypotheses of action. This view of curriculum construes knowledge to be interdisciplinary and instrumental.

Dewey challenged the traditional view of curriculum, embraced by Idealists and Realists, that knowledge should be organized into academic subjects and that teaching transmits this knowledge. He rejected the traditional curriculum that divided knowledge into separate subjects. He rejected the Idealist and Realist conception that certain bodies of knowledge, or subjects, are intellectual and that others are not. According to the Idealist-Realist view, also found in Essentialists and Perennialists, some subjects, such as the great books, are academic in that they have the power to make us think. In contrast, Dewey argued that all experience, whether labeled or catalogued as intellectual or academic, can generate thinking, not by its internal structure as a great book, but by its power to stimulate inquiry and reflection.

Dewey opposed the traditional view of teaching, prized by Perennialists, that it is the transmission of knowledge. Transmission is a method that tells students what they are to think about by having them memorize books, recite what has been memorized, and then regurgitate that information on a test.

Pragmatism's Philosophical Opponents

Although Dewey inspired Liberal and Progressive educators, his experimentalism also generated strong opposition. Philosophical opponents such as the Idealists and Realists, who remained committed to metaphysics, dispute Dewey's contention that we live in an open-ended universe where everything is changing and relative to particular situations. They see Dewey and the other Pragmatists as undermining the true role of philosophy as a search for universal truth. For them, Dewey's dismissal of the a priori principles found in the metaphysics of Idealism, Realism, and Thomism was an attack on the concept that human beings are the rational inhabitants of a purposeful universe. Dewey challenged the older philosophies in his relativist argument that truth, goodness, and beauty are not absolutes, inherent in the nature of the universe, but are projects to be worked out in human experience. Human experience arises in concrete and particular events and situations; therefore, the values that arise in these experiences are also relative to particular situations, to people living and acting at a particular time, at a given historical moment, in a particular place. The ethical and moral relativism associated with Pragmatism provokes criticism from those who believe that action should be guided on universal ethical and moral standards. Instead of prescribing and proscribing behavior on universal standards as do Idealists, Realists, and Thomists, the Pragmatists argue that our values arise as we find satisfactory and satisfying ways to live that enrich our experience.

Dewey's Experimentalism encountered opposition from some Realists, especially Perennialists, who see it as negating the essential cultural heritage of Western civilization. Educational philosophers, especially the Perennialists—Jacques Maritain, Robert Hutchins,

Mortimer Adler, and Allan Bloom—see Western civilization as carrying with it the importance of reason as a human universal. They see Dewey's blurring of the distinction between the theoretical and the practical as a dangerous anti-intellectualism. Regardless of changing times and circumstances, they believed that certain truths would be forever valid and certain values would be universally applicable. For them, good and bad and right and wrong do not depend on changing circumstances but are the moral standards that schools should perennially convey to each new generation.

Conclusion

Pragmatism represented a dramatic change in philosophy in that it focused on a changing universe rather an unchanging one as the Idealists, Realists, and Thomists had claimed. The Pragmatists, especially Dewey, waged a relentless struggle against the traditional philosophical dualisms that presented human beings as divided into antecedent categories such as mind and body and bifurcated education into theory and practice. Rejecting metaphysics, the Pragmatists' emphasize what we know, how we think, and how we use our hypotheses as tentative plans to control and direct change. In particular, Dewey's Experimentalism suggested significant changes in American education such as using the scientific method as the basis of problem solving and using experience as the basis of activity. Dewey's Experimentalism is a broad-based philosophy of education that argues that education is directly related to democracy—an environment free of absolutes and dogmas that block inquiry. In a democratic society, individuals are free to use their social intelligence to devise strategies to solve their problems and improve their lives and society. Dewey worked to remove the barriers that separated school from society, curriculum from community, and content from method. Dewey's pragmatism continues to be one of the world's leading educational philosophies.

Constructing Your Own Philosophy of Education. Now that you have read about Pragmatism and Dewey's Experimentalism, think about how Pragmatism relates to constructing your own philosophy of education. Consider whether Pragmatism, especially Dewey's Experimentalism, in its entirety or in its parts, appeals to you as a teacher. Do you plan to use it in constructing your own philosophy of education?

Questions for Reflection and Discussion

1. Do you agree with the Realists that we live in a purposeful universe or do you agree with Dewey that we construct our own purposes?

2. Consider Dewey's rejection of dualism. How does dualism operate in education? Why was Dewey so opposed to dualism in education?

3. Do you agree with Dewey that values are relative to time, place, and culture? Or, do you agree with the Idealists and the Realists that values are universal and unchanging?

4. Do you prefer Dewey's experience-based curriculum or do you favor the subject-matter curriculum of the Idealists and Realists?

5. Some of Dewey's critics contend that he emphasized anti-intellectualism in education. Do you agree or disagree with these critics? Defend your answer.

6. Do you agree with Dewey that to have a complete thought we must act on it to test it? Explain your answer.

7. Apply Dewey's concepts of the common, communication, and community to the current debates over multiculturalism and bilingualism in education.

8. Do you think that most Americans are pragmatic and experimental?

Inquiry and Research Topics

1. In an opinion paper, present your views on the question, Is the American character still pragmatic and experimental?

2. Develop a character analysis of John Dewey.

3. In a paper, write a character sketch of a typical Progressive reformer.

4. In an essay, comment on the evidences of dualism in contemporary education.

5. Prepare an extended review of Dewey's *Democracy and Education.*

6. Design a lesson plan that follows Dewey's complete act of thought method of problem solving.

7. In an essay, analyze the contemporary conditions of the American community.

Building an Experimentalist Vocabulary

Associative Activities: collaborative group activities such as problem solving, planning, and implementation that enhance social intelligence.

Common: group identification that is generated by the sharing of objects and engagement in shared activities that, in turn, leads to communication and community.

Complete Act of Thought: Dewey's concept of thinking completely according to the use of the scientific method in which we are in a problematic situation, define it, research it, develop hypotheses to solve it, and choose and act on a particular hypothesis.

Democratic Environment: an environment free of dogma and absolutes that block truly experimental inquiry.

Dualism: Dewey opposed dualism, or seeing the world in two dimensions—a superior one that was perfect, timeless, and unchanging and an inferior one that was temporary, finite, and changing.

Experience: the interaction of the person with his or her environment.

Experimentalism: Dewey's version of Pragmatism that asserts that human intelligence and education should use the scientific method of experiment and experimentation.

Growth: Dewey's sole end of education, which means to have more experience, more problems, more resolutions to problems, and a greater network of social relationships that makes life more effective, meaningful, and satisfying.

History and Geography: Dewey's second level of curriculum designed to expand children's perspective into time and space.

Instrumentalism: another name for Dewey's Pragmatism, which holds that ideas are instruments that can solve human problems.

Making and Doing: Dewey's first level of curriculum, consisting of learning activities that lead children from their immediate families and homes into the larger society.

Pragmatism: The philosophy developed by Charles S. Peirce, William James, and John Dewey that emphasizes the practical application of ideas by acting on them to actually test them in human experience.

Problematic Situation: a person's encounter with something that is different from previous experience and blocks ongoing activity.

Science: Dewey's third level of curriculum; refers to the interdisciplinary nature of various subjects in problem solving.

Social Intelligence: the process by which individuals create meaning through their association and participation in a community based on sharing experiences.

Warranted Assertion: a generalization based on existing evidence that could direct action for a time but is subject to further testing and revision.

Internet Sources

John Dewey Project on Progressive Education at the University of Vermont available at www.uvm.edu/dewey.

The Pragmatism Archive, Oklahoma State University, John R. Shook, Director; available at www.pragmatism.org/archive.

Suggestions for Further Reading

Dewey, John. *A Common Faith.* New Haven, CT: Yale University Press, l934.

Dewey, John. *Art as Experience.* New York: Minton, Balch, and Co., 1934.

Dewey, John. *Democracy and Education: An Introduction to the Philosophy of Education.* New York: Macmillan, 1916.

Dewey, John. *Experience and Education.* New York: Collier Books, l963.

Dewey, John. *Experience and Nature.* New York: Dover, 1958.

Dewey, John. *Freedom and Culture.* New York: Capricorn Books, 1963.

Dewey, John. *How We Think.* Mineola, NY: Dover, 1997.

Dewey, John. *Individualism: Old and New.* New York: Capricorn Books, l962.

Dewey, John. *The Early Works: 1882–1898.* Edited by Jo Ann Boydston, 5 vols. Carbondale and Edwardsville: Southern Illinois University Press, 1969–1972.

Dewey, John. *The Later Works: 1925–1953.* Edited by Jo Ann Boydston, 17 vols. Carbondale and Edwardsville: Southern Illinois University Press, 1981–1990.

Dewey, John. *Lectures on Ethics, 1900–1901.* Carbondale: Southern Illinois University Press, 1991.

Dewey, John. *Liberalism and Social Action.* New York: G.P. Putnam's Sons, 1935.

Dewey, John. *Logic: The Theory of Inquiry.* New York: Henry Holt, 1938.

Dewey, John. *The Middle Works: 1899–1924.* Edited by Jo Ann Boydston, 15 vols. Carbondale and Edwardsville: Southern Illinois University Press, 1976–1983.

Dewey, John. *The Public and Its Problems.* Athens: Ohio University Press, 1994.

Dewey, John. *The Quest for Certainty: A Study of the Relation of Knowledge and Action.* New York: Minton, Balch, 1929.

Dewey, John, and James H. Tufts. *Ethics.* New York: Henry Holt and Co., 1932.

Dewey, John. *Reconstruction in Philosophy.* Boston: Beacon Press, 1957.

Dewey, John, and Evelyn Dewey. *Schools of Tomorrow.* New York: E. P. Dutton and Co., 1915.

Diggins, John P. *The Promise of Pragmatism: Modernism and the Crisis of Knowledge and Authority.* Chicago: University of Chicago Press, 1994.

Feffer, Andrew. *The Chicago Pragmatists and American Progressivism.* Ithaca, NY: Cornell University Press, 1993.

Haskins, Casey, and David I. Seiple. *Dewey Reconfigured.* Albany: State University of New York Press, 1999.

Hickman, Larry A. *John Dewey's Pragmatic Technology.* Bloomington: Indiana University Press, 1990.

Hoy, Terry. *The Political Philosophy of John Dewey: Towards a Constructive Renewal.* Westport, CT: Praeger, 1998.

Kadlec, Alison. *Dewey's Critical Pragmatism.* New York: Lexington Books, 2007.

Martin, Jay. *The Education of John Dewey: A Biography.* New York: Columbia University Press, 2002.

Menand, Louis. *The Metaphysical Club.* New York: Farrar, Straus and Giroux, 2001.

Paringer, William A. *John Dewey and the Paradox of Liberal Reform.* Albany: State University of New York Press, 1990.

Putnam, Hilary. *Pragmatism: An Open Question.* Cambridge, MA: Blackwell, 1995.

Ryan, Alan. *John Dewey and the High Tide of American Liberalism.* New York: W. W. Norton, 1995.

Tanner, Laurel N. *Dewey's Laboratory School, Lessons for Today.* New York: Teachers College Press, 1997.

Welchman, Jennifer. *Dewey's Ethical Thought.* Ithaca, NY: Cornell University Press, 1995.

West, Cornel. *The American Evasion of Philosophy: A Genealogy of Pragmatism.* Madison: University of Wisconsin Press, 1989.

Westbrook, Robert B. *John Dewey and American Democracy.* Ithaca, NY: Cornell University Press, 1991.

Endnotes

1. Louis Menand, *The Metaphysical Club* (New York: Farrar, Straus and Giroux, 2001), pp. 188–189, 222–223.
2. Menand, *The Metaphysical Club,* pp. 141–143.
3. Lawrence A. Cremin, *The Transformation of the School: Progressivism in American Education, 1876–1957* (New York: Alfred A. Knopf, 1962), pp. 105–126.
4. Jay Martin, *The Education of John Dewey: A Biography* (New York: Columbia University Press, 2002).
5. Robert M. Crunden, *Ministers of Reform: The Progressives' Achievement in American Civilization, 1889–1920* (Urbana: University of Illinois Press, 1984), pp. 56–57.
6. Robert B. Westbrook, *John Dewey and American Democracy* (Ithaca, NY: Cornell University Press, 1991) pp. 42–43.
7. Walter Feinberg, "Dewey and Democracy at the Dawn of the Twenty-First Century," *Educational Theory,* 43, no. 2 (spring 1993): 199.
8. Crunden, *Ministers of Reform,* pp. 34–38. Also see John D. Baldwin, *George Herbert Mead: A Unifying Theory for Sociology* (Newbury Park, CA: Sage, 1986).
9. Lawrence J. Dennis and George W. Stickel, "Mead and Dewey: Thematic Connections on Educational Topics," *Educational Theory,* 31 (summer/fall 1981): 320–321.
10. Dewey's Laboratory School is discussed in the following sources: John Dewey, *The School and Society* (Chicago: University of Chicago Press, 1923); John Dewey and Evelyn Dewey, *Schools of Tomorrow* (New York: E. P. Dutton, 1915); Katherine C. Mayhew and Anna C. Edwards, *The Dewey School* (New York: Appleton-Century-Crofts, 1936); Arthur G. Wirth, *John Dewey as Educator: His Design for Work in Education (1894–1904)* (New York: John Wiley & Sons, 1966); and Herbert M. Kliebard, *The Struggle for the American Curriculum, 1893–1958* (Boston and London: Routledge & Kegan Paul, 1986).
11. John Dewey, "The Laboratory School," *University Record,* 1, 32 (November 6, 1896): 417–422.
12. Dewey, "The Laboratory School."
13. A useful guide to Dewey's publications is Jo Ann Boydston, ed., *Guide to the Works of John Dewey* (Carbondale: Southern Illinois University Press, 1970).
14. John Dewey, *The School and Society* (Chicago: University of Chicago Press, 1899).
15. John Dewey, *The Child and the Curriculum* (Chicago: University of Chicago Press, 1902).
16. John Dewey, *How We Think* (Boston: D. C. Heath, 1910); also see John Dewey, *Logic: The Theory of Inquiry* (New York: Henry Holt, 1938).

17. John Dewey, *Democracy and Education* (New York: Macmillan, 1916).
18. John Dewey, *Individualism: Old and New* (New York: Minton, Balch, 1930).
19. John Dewey, *Art as Experience* (New York: Minton, Balch, 1934).
20. John Dewey, *Interest and Effort in Education* (Boston: Houghton Mifflin, 1913); *Human Nature and Conduct* (New York: Holt, Rinehart & Winston, 1922); and *Freedom and Culture* (New York: G. P. Putnam's Sons, 1939).
21. John Dewey, *Experience and Education* (New York: Macmillan, 1938), pp. 25–31.
22. John Dewey, *The Quest for Certainty: A Study of the Relation of Knowledge and Action* (New York: Minton, Balch, 1929).
23. Hilary Putnam and Ruth Anna Putnam, "Education for Democracy," *Educational Theory,* 43, no. 4 (fall 1993): 364.
24. Feinberg, "Dewey and Democracy," pp. 204–205.
25. Putnam and Putnam, "Education for Democracy," p. 364.
26. Tom Colwell, "The Ecological Perspective in John Dewey's Philosophy of Education," *Educational Theory,* 35, no. 3 (summer 1985): 257.
27. John Dewey, *How We Think,* introduction by Gerald Gutek (New York: Barnes and Noble, 2005), p. 6.
28. John Dewey, *How We Think,* introduction by Gerald Gutek pp. 31–33.
29. Westbrook, *John Dewey and American Democracy,* p. 141.
30. Dewey, *Democracy and Education,* pp. 163–178.
31. Feinberg, "Dewey and Democracy," pp. 203–204. Also see Jennifer Welchman, *Dewey's Ethical Thought* (Ithaca, NY: Cornell University Press, 1995).
32. Putnam and Putnam, "Education for Democracy," p. 367.
33. Putnam and Putnam, "Education for Democracy" p. 365.
34. Gail P. Sorenson, "John Dewey's Philosophy of Law: A Democratic Vision," *Educational Theory,* 30, no. 1 (winter 1980): 57.
35. Dewey, *Democracy and Education,* pp. 22–26.
36. Sandra Rosenthal, "Democracy and Education: A Deweyan Approach," *Educational Theory,* 43, no. 4 (fall 1993): 377.
37. The quote is abridged from John Dewey, "Nationalizing Education," in *The Middle Works,* vol. 10, ed. Jo Ann Boydston (Carbondale: Southern Illinois University Press, 1985), p. 205, as quoted in Putnam and Putnam, "Education for Democracy," p. 362.
38. Dewey, *Democracy and Education,* pp. 228–270.

5

Existentialism and Education

Søren Kierkegaard (1813–1855), the Danish philosopher whose ideas contributed to Existentialism.

Chapter Preview

Existentialism, a philosophy that challenges the traditional philosophies of Idealism, Realism, and Thomism, also raises objections for Pragmatism. It questions the Pragmatist reliance on the scientific method as an exclusive way of empirically validating our ideas. It also challenges Dewey's emphasis on the group. The Existentialists offer a different approach to education, schooling, curriculum, and teaching and learning. The following major topics are examined in the chapter:

- How Existentialism's rejection of systems differs from other philosophies
- Identification of the major Existentialist philosophers
- The human situation in the twenty-first century, especially the context of the global mass society
- The major Existentialist themes
- Existentialism's educational implications for curriculum and teaching and learning

As you read the chapter and think about constructing your own philosophy of education, consider whether Existentialism, in its entirety or in its parts, appeals to you as a teacher. Or, do you reject it or parts of it as possibilities in constructing your own philosophy of education?

Not Like Other Philosophies

Existentialism differs from Idealism and Realism and other more traditional philosophies. Its proponents chose not to construct a philosophical system and did not concern themselves with the traditional questions of metaphysics, in particular, questions about the nature of ultimate reality or the structure of the universe. Existentialists oppose using philosophy to speculate about the structure and secrets of the universe; for them, this speculation is a strategy to avoid grappling with the real issues of how people deal with the concrete, everyday situations of their lives. For them, the speculative philosophers, retreating into a metaphysical world, produced numerous abstract and highly theoretical books about what, in the end, really doesn't matter to individuals living in the real world. The genuine pursuit of philosophers, as well as ordinary persons, is philosophizing about what it means to exist, to be alive, in a concrete situation at a particular time in history. Philosophizing is a matter of raising axiological questions about values, about ethics, morality, and aesthetics. The real question is not the ultimate structure of the universe but what is it that makes one's life valuable to the person who lives it? How does a person's life become true, good, and beautiful? Although they asked the same question, Existentialists, who in their response deliberately refrained from systemizing their thought, chose not to come up with a unified answer.

Because of the refusal to systematize their philosophy, it is very difficult to provide a succinct and ironclad definition of Existentialism. The dictionary provides some help as we begin to explore Existentialism, which it defines as a modern philosophical movement that encompasses a variety of themes. Among these themes are the belief that individuals exist and determine their essences; that the human being has absolute freedom of choice but no rational criteria serves as a basis for choice; that individuals live with **angst**, anxiety and alienation in an absurd universe. When we go to the root of the word *exist,* the dictionary tells us that it means to have actual being, to have life, and to have being in the conditions of a specified place at a particular time in history.[1] Aided by the dictionary's definitions, we can stipulate some starting points for our discussion about Existentialism:

1. Existentialism is a movement, albeit a sometimes disconnected one, about philosophizing.
2. Human beings first exist—come on the scene—living in a concrete place, a context, at a given time, and through freedom of choice they construct their own essence, their own meaning of life.
3. Human choices, especially significant life-determining ones, are made freely without a guide that is outside of the person.
4. Individuals know that their existence is temporary and that they will disappear; living with this knowledge is a source of anxiety.

Rejection of Systems

Existentialism, embracing a variety of philosophical perspectives, is not a traditional systematic philosophy. It rejects both the desirability and possibility of constructing an all-explaining architectonic or systematic philosophy. Existentialists distrust philosophical systems that seek to construct an all-encompassing worldview that categorizes human experience according to conceptions of antecedent reality that exists prior to the person's entry on the world scene. According to traditional views, the human being enters the world, and is defined, catalogued, and assigned a role or place in it. For example, Aristotelian natural Realists assert the existence of an objective order of reality independent of human plans and purposes. The human being, a part of this reality, has an assigned place in it as a rational creature who possesses an intellect and naturally seeks to know. The descriptive assertion of human rationality also prescribes—asserts the value—that human beings ought to act or behave rationally. In countering Aristotle's premise, Existentialists contend that if reason is asserted as the primary element in defining the human being, then there is no genuine freedom in the human condition. If reason is an antecedent constituent and determinant of human nature, then humans cannot really choose reason as a value. In contrast, Existentialists contend that humans are choosing and valuing beings who can reason if they so choose. The Existentialist sees life as too varied, complex, confused, and unpredictable to be arranged in neatly structured philosophical categories.

In abandoning the metaphysical system building of Idealists, Realists, and Thomists, the Existentialist examines the most significant and persistent doubts from the perspective of the individual human person. Existentialist involvement calls for individual philosophizing about the persistent human concerns of life, love, death, and meaning. Accepting the fact that we live in a physical environment as an evident fact of life, Existentialists view this world as an indifferent phenomenon, which, while it may not be antagonistic to human purposes, is nonetheless devoid of personal meaning. In this world, each person is born, lives, chooses his or her course, and creates the meaning of his or her own existence.

Existentialism not only questions the architectonic traditional philosophies, but it also questions Pragmatism's reliance on the scientific method. Dewey's Experimentalism stresses the efficacy both of the scientific method and of social intelligence arising from shared human association. It stresses the individual's ability to use the empirical procedures of science as the exclusive means of establishing tentative truths. For Existentialists, the scientific method, so prized by Pragmatists, is only one of many ways in which individuals construct their own truth. Indeed, the scientific method can inform us only about the brute facts of the world, the "givens" that describe natural and physical reality. The most important way to make the truth is not through the scientific method but through personal, subjective choice. The person can choose to be scientific or not.

Experimentalism also asserts the individual's ability to participate in meaningful group interaction. Although Dewey believed that the individual gains freedom through group association, some Existentialists find the "like-minded" group to be a coercive agency in which the individual is subordinated to the group will. The group can overwhelm the individual who is forced to yield to its decisions and dictates.

Postmodernism and Critical Theory, discussed in later chapters, are related contemporary movements in educational thought that, like Existentialism, reject philosophical systems. Indeed, one of Postmodernism's major pursuits is their deconstruction. Paulo Freire and some Critical Theorists have incorporated the claim that human beings are unfinished projects, not categories in a predefined system, who are free to choose who they will be and to write their own autobiographies. Existentialists and Critical Theorists would endorse the contemporary educational pursuit of encouraging students to write their own life stories as a means of developing their self-understanding. However, an important difference is how the Critical Theorist and the Existentialist see the individual. Critical Theorists view individuals as members of socioeconomic classes and racial, ethnic, gender, and religious groups that largely define them. For them, education is a process that develops a person's consciousness about her or his group membership and how being a member of a dominated group marginalizes them. (For more discussion of marginalization, see the chapters on Postmodernism and Critical Theory.) Existentialists take a different view of group membership. Certainly, they say, the groups of which we are members are "givens" of our social, political, and economic lives that shape us but that do not define us. Regardless of class, gender, race, or ethnicity, the person is free to define him- or herself by making significant life choices.

Although early Existentialism appeared in such nineteenth-century writers as Søren Kierkegaard (1813–1855), Friedrich Nietzsche (1844–1900), and Fyodor Dostoyevsky (1821–1881), its greatest philosophical popularity was in the twentieth century, especially during and after World War II. Among the leading Existentialists of the twentieth century were the German philosophers Karl Jaspers (1883–1969) and Martin Heidegger (1889–1976), the Israeli philosopher Martin Buber (1878–1965), and the French philosophers Gabriel Marcel (1889–1973), who took a Christian perspective, and Jean-Paul Sartre (1905–1980), an atheist.[2] In addition, the eminent Protestant theologian Paul Tillich (1886–1965) examined the relationship between Christian theology and Existentialist philosophy. Like Kierkegaard, Tillich saw the human being facing the free but awesome choice of whether or not to enter into a personal relationship with God.

Many Existentialists found the **phenomenological method** developed by Edmund Husserl (1859–1938) philosophically congenial to their work. According to Husserl, every conscious act is directed toward or intended for another person or object already existing in the world.[3] Our way of intending these objects will vary according to our individual perceptions, images, and memories of them. Thus, our concepts are not mirror images of reality as Idealists assert, nor do they correspond with the structure of objects in reality as Realists claim. They are the results of our subjective ways of experiencing them. According to Husserl, philosophy should be a method of analyzing phenomena, our conscious awareness in experience of how objects and events appear to us. This careful analysis of our awareness is to occur without limiting conditions imposed by metaphysical assumptions. Human consciousness, our awareness of phenomena, is the basis for our understanding and interpretation of our situation.

From this diverse and often conflicting array of writers of literature and philosophy, it is evident that Existentialism was and is a philosophical perspective or inclination rather than a complete system of thought.

In discussing the Existentialists, we concentrate on two of the most significant philosophers, Søren Kierkegaard, a nineteenth-century Dane, and Jean-Paul Sartre, a twentieth-century French writer. These preeminent philosophers illustrate two varieties of Existentialism: Kierkegaard, Theistic, or Christian Existentialism; and Sartre, Atheistic Existentialism. In addition, we include several other philosophers such as Gabriel Marcel and Simone de Beauvoir who exemplify certain aspects of these varieties of Existentialism.

Søren Kierkegaard

Søren Kierkegaard (1813–1855), regarded as the leading founder of religious Existentialism, was born, educated, and lived in Copenhagen, Denmark. He recalled his childhood home as one of gloom and guilt, presided over by his father, Michael Pedersen Kierkegaard, who demanded unquestioned obedience. His mother and five of his siblings died before Søren was twenty-one and he grew up with the feeling that death was constantly present in the household. Initially aiming for a career as a Lutheran minister, Søren studied theology and philosophy at the University of Copenhagen. He moved slowly through his studies, taking ten years to complete his courses and his dissertation, *On the Concept of Irony with Constant Reference to Socrates* (1841).[4] He was awarded his degree in theology in 1840. Kierkegaard appeared to be moving toward a conventional upper-middle-class Danish lifestyle when he announced his engagement to Regine Olsen, the daughter of a well-connected government official.[5]

Dissatisfied with what he saw as the emptiness of his life, Kierkegaard made a dramatic change in course as he determined to take a new and self-affirming path. Not wanting to be pushed into a marriage, he ended his engagement to Miss Olsen. Instead of joining the dominant power structure as a minister, he challenged both the official Lutheran state church and the reigning philosophy, Hegelian Idealism.[6] Although critical of the institutionalized church-based Christianity of his day, Kierkegaard, remained intensely religious. For him, belief came not from conforming to the officially sanctioned doctrines of the state church, but from a "leap of faith," a personal conversion experience, to embrace the truth and live by it, regardless of the consequences. For the converted person, faith, the experience of recognizing the awesome majesty of God, was a total experience that united thinking, feeling, and imagining.[7] Kierkegaard, an iconoclast, who some regarded as an eccentric, challenged the religious and educational establishment. He became a prolific author of philosophical and theological books and articles that featured Existentialist themes. Among his most important books were *Either/Or* (1843), *Repetition* (1843), *Fear and Trembling* (1843), *Philosophical Fragments* (1844), *The Concept of Anxiety* (1844), *Stages on Life's Way* (1845), *Unscientific Postscript* (1846), *Sickness Unto Death* (1849), and *Training in Christianity* (1850).

A personal risk-taker, Kierkegaard confronted what he saw as the major sources of conformity that were stifling individual choice in nineteenth-century Denmark: the media of the time—the press; the officially established Lutheran state church; and Hegelianism, the philosophy that dominated intellectual life and education.[8] He believed that the press—the popular journals and newspapers—had created a pervasive climate of opinion in which individual thinking was twisted into a conformist mass mind. In response to his criticism, *The Corsair,* a popular weekly magazine, launched a series of scurrilous attacks on Kierkegaard, criticizing his ideas as ludicrous ravings of a madman and running cartoons that caricatured his appearance.[9] Officially established state churches, such as the Lutheran Church in Denmark, enjoying their government support and subsidies, Kierkegaard argued, had substituted rote dogmas and empty ceremonies for what should be a vital personal faith in God. The ministers, paid members of the state bureaucracy, like all bureaucrats were most occupied with maintaining their privileged status rather than living according to Christ's Gospel. The reigning philosophy, Hegelianism, based on the work of the German philosopher G. W. F. Hegel (1770–1831) had confined higher education in an intellectual conformist straitjacket. (For Hegel, see the chapter on Idealism.) Professors and students were constrained by the leading holders of intellectual power to frame their thinking, teaching, articles, and books to meet the guidelines of the Hegelian dialectic—the correct way of thinking. Kierkegaard argued that the Hegelian notion that history was the unfolding of the Absolute through a dialectical process had removed the personal—the autobiographical and biographical—from the past. It had replaced personal responsibility with abstract collective concepts that generated a pervasive philosophical fatalism of being part of the human group that was merely following the spirit of a particular age.[10]

Kierkegaard's critique of Hegelianism can be broadened to include a more general commentary on contemporary education. Although himself an intellectual, he was critical of the professional intellectuals, especially university professors, who were preoccupied with abstraction, theory, and claims of scientific objectivity. The academic tendency to interpret and fit human life into abstract theories, he felt, ignored what was most important about being alive—living, choosing, and acting in a concrete situation. Dominated by Hegelian philosophy that interpreted the human past as highly abstract layers of history, Kierkegaard felt Hegel's academic disciples had replaced the dynamism of personal auto-biographies with a lifeless dialectic of countervailing intellectual forces. Rather than being paramount, individuality was squeezed out of the historical narrative by the impersonal clash of ideas—the thesis and antithesis. Academics sought credibility by claiming their accounts to be true because they were scientifically objective and not personally subjective. These academic trends—abstraction, the theoretical layering of history, and claims of scientific objectivity—had devitalized education by neglecting or misinterpreting the person as the center of life.[11] The occupation of professors as constructing and deconstructing theories turns education into learning information and digested concepts of others, often those of the professor who is making a case for her or his pet theory rather than making genuine decisions that matter in students' concrete lived experiences.

Kierkegaard's critique of his own society in nineteenth-century Copenhagen bears many parallels to twenty-first-century America. The contemporary mass media—television, motion pictures, radio, newspapers, and magazines—usually tell us the same story with the same sensational interpretation of events. This media-shaped message is repeated incessantly until the mantralike refrain is echoed by members of the mass audience. The result is that what should be many voices, speaking independently of each other, becomes one mass voice that speaks slogans and clichés. Though no secularist, Kierkegaard had no sympathy for state-sponsored churches. He believed in the free exercise of religion, which for him was a private, not a public matter. Today, he would be likely to warn Americans against connecting churches to government. Institutionalized religion, today, often is geared to generate social conformism, especially when churches seek to influence politics and encourage their members to vote in a block on a single issue. Kierkegaard's admonition about the domination of intellectual life by a particular philosophy or ideology is an especially telling comment that applies to theory and methods of education, particularly when it becomes doctrinaire and dogmatic. In the foundations of education, a particular philosophy such as Pragmatism, Language Analysis, and now Critical Theory dominates teaching and writing to the extent that it smothers alternative perspectives. In methods, a particular style of instruction such as the project method, constructivism, or portfolio usage becomes so dominant that it too limits the use of alternative approaches.

Stages of Becoming

In his *Either/Or* and *Stages on Life's Way,* Kierkegaard identified three spheres or stages in the process of becoming an authentic person: the aesthetic, the ethical, and the religious.[12] Although every individual who is becoming an authentic person moves through these stages, this movement to moral development does not take place for all individuals. Some people stay locked by their own inclination in a particular stage and do not grow to moral fulfillment. Neither are the stages cumulative in that one variety of experience is subsumed into the next stage as the Pragmatists would assert. Neither are the stages a dialectical synthesis of the thesis of one stage and the antithesis of the next stage into a still higher and more comprehensive synthesis as Idealists, especially Hegelians, would argue. Rather, for Kierkegaard, the movement from one stage to another is not made by transitions; it is made only by a deliberate personal choice between incompatible alternatives.[13] Kierkegaard personifies each stage by using a model who exemplifies it: the pleasure-seeking, adventurous lover Don Juan, who seeks immediate sensual pleasure and instant gratification, for the aesthetic stage; the inquiring and provocative Socrates for the intellectual stage; and the Biblical Abraham for the religious stage, that of complete fulfillment.[14]

Don Juan lives in the sphere of the immediate, for the present and its pleasures, with little concern for past and future and with no sense of responsibility. Living for the moment, Don Juan is involved in momentary interests and excitements. His life is without continuity or direction. When it comes to enhancing his pleasures, however, Don Juan the seducer can be cunning and manipulative. Using persons, especially unsuspecting young women, as objects for his pleasure, he has no concern for them as individuals. With no interest in the higher modes of experience, Don Juan rejects anything that may free him from his insatiable quest for pleasure.[15]

Socrates is the model for the ethical stage in which an individual growing toward authenticity has gained a perspective on time that Don Juan lacks. The ethical person looks backward on the past and reflects on misdeeds with a sense of sorrow and repentance for having committed them. Ethical persons are willing to project themselves into the future with a sense of personal commitment and obligation to do the right thing as they conceive of it. For example, Socrates is willing to risk searching for truth regardless of where the search will take him. His search put him up against the Athenian authorities, who punished his intellectual pursuit of truth by sentencing him to death. Although an admirable stage, the ethical is still not the highest sphere for Kierkegaard.

For Kierkegaard, the "leap of faith" into the religious sphere is the highest stage of personal authenticity. Intensely and intimately personal, faith is beyond ethical or rational explanations. To personify the religious sphere, Kierkegaard chooses the Biblical character Abraham, whom God, in a test of his faith, calls on to sacrifice his son, Isaac. Abraham could find no justification for this act in philosophical or theological principles. Despite this, he stands alone before God and prepares to make the sacrifice. Seeing Abraham's "leap of faith" to unconditionally obey his Divine command, God no longer requires the sacrifice; He stays Abraham's hand and spares Isaac.[16] Abraham's act of faith ran against his love of his son and against all ethical proscriptions against taking an innocent life.[17] Abraham stood alone, before God, without the possibility of trying to justify his action on moral or ethical grounds. God's command to sacrifice Isaac was a duty that Abraham accepted but because of his acceptance—his faith—God released him from his dreadful task. Kierkegaard's "leap of faith" provided a point of origin for other theistic varieties of Existentialism.

Theistic Existentialism

Theistic Existentialists, arguing that human beings are more than accidents of nature, see the person as being of God-created intrinsic hope and value. Kierkegaard's leap of faith provides a means by which the person can choose openness to and a willingness to commit to a caring God. The leap of faith is not explainable through dogma, doctrine, or ritual but comes from the person's conversion of heart to seek God.

Gabriel Marcel

A leading voice for Theistic Existentialism was Gabriel Marcel (1889–1973), a French philosopher and writer, who was a contemporary of Sartre. Whereas Sartre argued that a human being is born into a world without meaning, Marcel contends that human existence is a gift from God. A Roman Catholic, Marcel integrated his religious faith into his philosophy of Existentialism. Like Sartre, Marcel was a poet and playwright as well as a philosopher. His major works, *The Mystery of Being* (1950) and *The Philosophy of Existentialism* (1961), express his Theistic Existentialism.[18] Unlike the pessimism and angst of other Existentialists, Marcel emphasizes faith and hope in God's promises. Urging an abiding charity for human beings, Marcel warns against falling into the process that turns one's human companions into objects or functions. In educational terms, Marcel's admonition against turning people into others is similar to arguments against "othering," labeling and classifying children into categories in schools rather than holding them present as persons.

Marcel in *Man Against Mass Society* (1951) made a strong argument against mass society, directing his pen against totalitarianism and materialism.[19] As a Theist, Marcel distinguished his Existentialism from Sartre's atheistic and semi-Marxist perspectives. Marcel shared his abhorrence of totalitarianism, however, especially that of Nazism and Fascism, which Europe had just experienced in World War II. His book, written six years after the end of World War II, struck out against how the Nazi regime mobilized Germans into a collective mass mind controlled by one man, Adolph Hitler. Writing in the midst of the cold war, Marcel saw Soviet totalitarianism as an equally pernicious force in the modern world. Totalitarian regimes sought total mind control as they whipped up hysteria against enemies relegated to the caste of the threatening outsider. For Hitler, the outsiders who threatened the Aryan race were the Jews. For the Soviet regime, the outsiders were the capitalists who surrounded the Soviet state and were determined to destroy it. Censoring what came in and controlling the internal mechanisms of the police, military, and schools, the totalitarian state operated and sustained itself by denying freedom. Indeed, it proclaimed the value that worthy members of the state were to surrender their freedom to the leader of the Nazi or Communist Parties. The totalitarian state promotes a mass fanaticism that is exalted as faithful and good citizenship. Fanaticism is substituted for a consciousness about the reality of a situation.

Marcel's warning against fanaticism is especially relevant given the contemporary anxiety generated by the rise of religious fundamentalists and ethnic and racial purists worldwide. Fanatical Islamic fundamentalists resort to terror, bombing, maiming, and killing innocent people, whom they condemn as "others" who need to be subdued in the name of religion. The recent history of ethnic cleansing in Bosnia, in the former Yugoslavia, and in Rwanda and Burundi in Africa is an example of the extremism that turns people into others, potential victims who are selected for killing or expulsion because they are members of a different ethnic or tribal group. As the United States fights its "War on Terrorism," there needs to be a warning that, in the name of self-defense, people who are different from us are not categorized as suspect others.

Materialism in its various forms—the denial of the spiritual or the lust for consumer products—though less overt than the totalitarian state, is an equally pernicious and perhaps more pervasive threat to individual freedom of choice. Materialism (denying the spiritual), and consumerism (exalting possession of things as the highest value) is dangerous in that it appears to offer choices in an array of consumer goods. However, the choices are merely slightly altered duplicates of each other that deflect the person from recognizing the real and most important choices about how to live life. The mass condition of humanity, constructed by a pervasive media and advertising, generates and sustains itself in a circular fashion. The media, paid for by advertisers, creates a blitz of commercials telling people what they need and should have. The individual, being submerged in a mass society and conditioned by the media, reacts by wanting what is advertised and creating a greater demand for it. Consumer demands, actually created by the forces who control the manufacturing and marketing system, stimulates still another round of advertising, buying, and charging purchases on credit.

While warning of the dangers of the mass society, be it totalitarian or materialist, Marcel is still hopeful and expresses an optimism that it is possible for human beings to choose to be free and overturn the conditions that jeopardize true personal authenticity. There is a need to be conscious of the dangers posed by the mass society. Rather than a mass society, it is possible to create a society which is a community of free people. The word *communion,* on which such a community is based, has both a religious and a social meaning. For Marcel, it means to be in communion with God and the faith community. It also means being in a society in which individuals have an abiding and nonexclusive mutual respect for each other so that no one is "demonized" as a dangerous other because of class, race, religion, ethnicity, or gender.[20] There is also a highly spiritual sense of communion in Marcel's Existentialism in which human beings, in communion with each other, are also in communion with God.

Marcel's theistic Existentialism has important implications for education. Education can bring about consciousness of the human condition in the mass society. This consciousness-raising is difficult, however, because schools and curriculum in a mass society reflect and mimic the conditions of the larger society. Schools are large and impersonal with students categorized by ability or disability. Older schools resemble industrial factories; newer schools, in affluent neighborhoods, may appear to be modern media centers, mimicking the information diffusion centers of the mass advertising. Neither of these types of school, however, is designed to facilitate an education that recognizes the conditions of the mass society and provide ways to escape and overcome them. Educational outcomes in a mass society are described as products—units or credit hours to be accumulated—rather than a conscious state of mind. Regardless of the conditions that pervade the educational setting, Marcel argues that there is still the hope of overcoming them. Teachers and students can work their way through them and come to recognize them for what they are—ways of shaping behavior that are not freely chosen.

Marcel's analysis of mass society that is applicable here is the creation of educational settings, or spaces, in which teachers and students are willing to empower themselves to transcend the limitations of mass educational institutions and processes by creating a community in which persons, respecting one another, are in communion. Public institutions can become centers of this kind of self-empowerment, but it is the faith-based private and parochial schools that have a unique opportunity to move beyond instilling doctrine to become places where students have hope to make the leap into true faith in God and in which they are in communion with their teachers and peers.

Jean-Paul Sartre

Jean-Paul Sartre (1905–1980), regarded as the leading Existentialist of the twentieth century, was a prolific author of plays, novels, and political and philosophical works. He was a graduate of the prestigious École Normale in Paris. He taught philosophy for a time but preferred the life of a writer. His novel *Nausea* was published in 1938, followed by *L'Imaginaire,* his first book on philosophy, in 1940. Sartre related his philosophy to the human imagination and sense of aesthetics. For him, exercising the imagination is the way to human freedom and choice. When France declared war on Germany in 1939 as a consequence of Hitler's invasion of Poland, Sartre was mobilized into the French army. He was captured and held as a prisoner of war. After his release, Sartre returned to Paris, then under German occupation, and joined the resistance movement.[21]

World War II, especially the Nazi conquest of much of Europe, vividly portrayed, not in fictional terms but in reality, the existential situation of modern humanity. Western Europe, especially France, was regarded as the citadel of culture, civilization, and rationality. Then, the rise to power of Hitler and the Nazis brought on the world scene a fanatical and ruthless totalitarianism that, boasting of its barbaric irrationality, demanded the total subjugation of the individual to the state. With the inherited traditions of Western culture and civility rendered meaningless by the irrationality of Hitler's new barbarianism, the Europe of the 1940s became a place of human repression and of the extermination of millions of people in technologically efficient death camps. It was in the chaos of the world turned upside down that individuals faced the choice of collaborating with Nazi totalitarianism, shutting their minds to it, or actively resisting it. Even in Nazi-occupied Europe of the time, human beings still had a choice—often the ultimate choice between life and death.

Sartre's famous work *Being and Nothingness* (1943) made him a paramount figure in the Existentialist movement that flowered in France after its liberation in 1945. Sartre's 1945 lecture, "Is Existentialism Humanism?" became a manifesto of the Existentialist movement. In it he proclaimed what became the leading principle of Sartrean Existentialism, "existence precedes essence." These three words signaled that individuals create their own essence, their own meaning and values, through their choices. Further, there was no authority to which to appeal other than the person who is making the choice.[22] Sartre answered his question affirmatively. Existentialism is humanistic because it focuses directly on the freedom of the individual human person to create his or her own values.

Although sharing many attributes with Kierkegaard's and Marcel's Theistic Existentialism, Sartre constructed a version of the philosophy that was essentially atheistic. To give Sartre's Existentialism some perspective, we need to consider the ideas of Friedrich Nietzsche (1844–1900), a German philosopher who is regarded as a founder of atheistic Existentialism. Nietzsche proclaimed that "God is dead" to signify that modern science had made belief in the supernatural irrelevant. In his *Zarathustra,* Nietzsche argued that some exceptional individuals could, in the name of their own absolute freedom, create their own higher ethics.[23] He replaced Aristotle's dictum that "man is a rational animal" with the claims that "man is an evaluating animal." The human project, especially for the extraordinary person, is to create by free choice a life that is a noble and beautiful self-construction.[24]

Against this background, Sartre examined the predicament of the human being in an absurd world devoid of meaning, except what people create for themselves. In coining the phrase "existence precedes essence," Sartre challenged the dictum of traditional philosophies that preached that human behavior is based on an antecedent definition of human nature. Unlike Aristotle's assertion that the human being is antecedently a rational creature who inhabits a purposeful, hence meaningful, universe, Sartre countered that each person exists—comes uninvited on the world scene—and creates his or her own meaning or essence. Because no universal truths, no absolute rules, no ultimate destiny exist to guide us, each person is totally free to choose. With this total freedom comes total responsibility for our actions or choices.

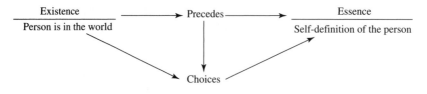

Existentialist Creation of Essence

Simone de Beauvoir

Simone de Beauvoir (1908–1986), the lifelong companion of Jean-Paul Sartre, had an illustrious career as a writer, playwright, novelist, and philosopher.[25] A graduate of the prestigious French educational institution, the École Normale Supérieure, she also taught in a *lycée*, a French academic secondary school. Her important book, *The Second Sex,* provides a feminist perspective on Existentialism.

Like other Existentialists, Beauvoir argues that human experience takes place in concrete contexts, lived in unstable and ambiguous situations. These contextual situations are the sites in which gender is constructed. She makes a distinction between a person's sex and gender. Sex is a biological given: A person is born as either a female or male. However, the lived-in situation, the context, constructs the meaning of being a woman or a man. For the female, becoming a woman is traditionally defined by men who are masters in patriarchal societies.[26]

Beauvoir attacks the mytho-history that portrays women as possessing a defining female essence that makes them what they are. Because of the female essence, women are traditionally portrayed as passive personalities who find fulfillment by being a dutiful daughter, a loving wife, and a caring and nurturing mother. The traditional concept of the patriarchal defined woman is a clear example of essence preceding existence—creating an a priori definition of what it means to be a woman. Historically, this definition has been constructed by men and imposed on women. Beauvoir argues to accept this definition is to impose a prior definition on women that severely limits their freedom to choose who they will be; in other words, it seeks to deny them the freedom to construct their own choices through the choices that they make. Beauvoir argues further that the historical construction of the feminine can be examined and deconstructed and be socially, politically, and economically dismantled.[27]

There are many examples of women who, in their lives, challenged the concept of a male-defined feminism. Two stand out in particular—Jane Addams and Maria Montessori. In her autobiography, Addams tells of being the dutiful daughter of her respected father and of being encased in the strictures of a Victorian-era family and upbringing. Coming of age during a time when a young woman's expectations were made by others—usually males—Addams eventually made the choices that led to her found Hull House, a pioneering social settlement. Montessori, too, had to run against the tide of the late nineteenth century in an Italian middle-class family structure and to challenge the conventional educational strictures. A single parent, she chose to define herself as one of Italy's first women physicians and to create the worldwide renowned method of early childhood education that bears her name.

The Human Situation in the Twenty-first Century

Existentialists argue that we need to philosophize in the concrete situations in which we live rather than speculate about metaphysical systems. We now examine the human context in the twenty-first century, especially identifying the trends and forces that deter us from philosophizing about the importance of our free choice. These self-limiting trends can be examined historically in terms of the modern mass society created during the modern industrial period from the 1830s to the 1980s and the postmodern period from the 1980s to the present. This examination emphasizes that the trends of modernity and postmodernity represent a continuum rather than a sharp break in history from one period to another.

The Modern Industrial Mass Society

Existentialism's philosophical origins coincided with disaffection against the nineteenth-century's optimistic view of science, technology, and progress after World War I. The rise of a mass society and technological culture, causing the depersonalization of the individual, aggravated the feeling of alienation. The industrial revolution introduced innovative mechanisms that facilitated both efficient production and massive consumption. The logic of the machine age and the efficiency of the assembly line required that machine parts be both standardized and interchangeable. When a machine part wears out, it is replaced by an identical part that fits the machine and allows it to function effectively. The logic of interchangeable machine parts was gradually extended to individuals who are designated by their functions in the system. When such functioning individuals wear out or become obsolete, they are discarded and replaced by other standardized individuals who have been trained to perform the same functions. The logic of interchangeable parts and interchangeable people has profound implications for education, especially for schooling. The school, as a system, becomes an assembly line that turns out products—namely, graduates trained to perform specific functions for the larger corporate system.

The rise of mass production–consumption systems, technological society, and scientific engineering attitudes produced an urban, corporate, and mass society. At the root of the mass society is mass production, which creates mass housing, communications, media, and entertainment. The thrust of the global corporate structure and its subsidiaries is to ascertain the material needs of the average person and persuade him or her to prefer certain goods. In gearing its energies to satisfying the needs of people, the corporate structure both creates and caters to the needs of a standardized human being, a composite of statistical and sampling techniques. As a consumer and as a citizen, the private person is reduced to a standardized unit whose needs, desires, and wishes can be measured and quantified.

Modern technological society, created by applying science to industrial processes, is characterized by an emphasis on science as the means of verifying truth and of solving problems. The scientific method deliberately minimizes the subjective and the value-laden aspects of life. Personal wishes and preferences are not allowed to interfere with scientific objectivity. The demand for scientific objectivity has led to the quantification of human experience. While quantities are measurable, qualities are not. Following the physical sciences, social science, sociology, social psychology, and behaviorism also attempt to examine individuals in objective terms. The consequences of emphasizing science and de-emphasizing the humanities have been the objectification and reduction of the human being to an entity or unit that can be weighed, measured, and quantitatively analyzed. In its behavioral aspects, the use of the scientific method has contributed to a reductionism that analyzes people by breaking down the quality of human experience into measurable and quantified responses.

The public life of mass society has been extended into what had once been the private preserve of human life, a person's unique lifestyle. The impersonal forces of industrialization, standardization, and globalization isolate the unique elements of human life, detaching them from the realm of meaningful activity, and eventually eroding them. Uniqueness is labeled as eccentricity rather than as the means of achieving self-definition. Success is measured quantitatively in terms of power, possessions, or control. Standardization objectifies, quantifies, and reduces human beings to objects or functional adjuncts of the corporate mechanism.

The corporate and standardized features of a mass global society are not restricted to economic, political, and social life; they also extend into education. The technology of corporate industry and advertising has encouraged an educational technology and technocracy that seeks to emulate the efficiency of the corporate sector. Assembly-line logic has extended into the educational complex serving the mass society as schools attempt to apply the logic and techniques of mass production to learning. Although the urban and corporate society educates larger numbers of students than ever before in human history, it does so in large buildings that resemble educational factories producing a standardized product.

Maintaining a massive corporate structure requires trained managerial and engineering elites who can apply their planning and administrative expertise to stimulating increased production and consumption. The managerial administrators in corporate industry have their counterparts in the educational administrators who staff the bureaucracies of school systems. In seeking to educate or train large numbers of students in massive educational complexes, educational administrators and curricular specialists have devised methods designed to make the learning process more efficient. Educational technology, or innovative media, has entered the school. Teaching machines, televised instruction, multimedia instructional packages, computer-assisted learning, and standardized tests are some of the tools of educational technology introduced to make instruction efficient in the vast educational complexes of the mass society. Large class sizes, impersonal bureaucracies, and little student–teacher contact have resulted from the extension of impersonality into education.

In education, Existentialists seek to reduce the impersonalization that has affected schooling and to assert an "I–Thou" relationship between the teacher and the learner. Although disagreeing on particulars, Existentialists share a common commitment to reshaping the human situation to encourage the freest and most genuine assertion of human personality.

The emphasis on science, objectivity, and standardization has had pervasive and profound consequences for American education that begin in the elementary schools, run through the high schools, and continue on through colleges and universities. In order for school districts to be eligible for federal funds, the No Child Left Behind Act requires that students be examined annually using standardized tests in mathematics and reading. Test data are used to determine whether teachers and schools are performing competently in achieving the standards in these skill areas. Schools that score below the norms set by the federal standard may be remediated. One consequence of this requirement is that teachers spend more instructional time preparing students to pass the standardized tests and less exploring other subjects such as social studies and the arts. The kind of standardization required by the act also penetrates into the methods used in classrooms. Standardized tests leads to standardized teaching; methods that vary from the requirements set by the standards are discouraged and may, indeed, be penalized. The primary and intermediate grades generally have been the years when teachers have had the greatest freedom to recognize students' individual needs and to experiment with creative teaching methods. Existentialists warn that the teachers' emphasis on students' subjectivity and individual needs and the freedom to experiment with creative and innovative methods decreases as the extent of standardization increases.

When education is institutionalized and structured in a system in which students move from lower to higher levels, the entry requirements for the higher level determine what is taught and how it is taught at the lower level. For example, the entry requirements for law, medical, and other professional schools shape the curriculum of the college and university; college and university entry requirements shape the curriculum and teaching method at the high school. In turn, the requirements of the high school to a large extent shape the curriculum of the middle schools, and so on.

Existentialist Themes

In this section, we examine the philosophical themes that run through Existentialism.

Existentialism's Relevance

Some readers might argue that the high tide of Existentialism is over and that the philosophy has become irrelevant to people in the early twenty-first century, when philosophy is largely dominated by Postmodernism and Critical Theory. On the contrary, Existentialism is especially relevant in the age of globalization with its mass marketing and mass information and with the increasing standardization of education. Focusing on the living person who is engaged in coping with a concrete situational reality, it is relevant because it still asks the questions about how we can choose to live self-examined and self-defined lives in whatever situation or context in which we find ourselves. It is especially relevant to philosophy of education because it raises the possibility of creating or constructing authentic learning experiences that can lead to personal authenticity for students and teachers. It offers a different kind of philosophical experience as it engages individuals to examine and address what matters most—their personal lives—and to take responsibility for either acting or failing to act.

An Epistemology of Appropriation

Asking the question, "What does it mean to me?" Existentialists want the truth to be a personal **appropriation** that is chosen, lived, and acted on rather than a speculative abstraction in the Platonic sense.

Knowing and learning, for Existentialists, means to appropriate, to choose, and to take what is known or learned and to make it one's own by giving it a personal meaning. This is very different from the Realist view that one's knowledge, to be valid and valuable, needs to correspond to the object that is external but knowable to the learner. It is also different from the Pragmatist concept that we can have tentative "truths" based on their probability of occurring in experience and that acting on them scientifically or empirically is likely to bring about predictable consequences. For Existentialists, knowing as appropriation is subjective, personal, and individualized, not objective, probable, predictable, or standardized.

Existentialists accept the validity or usefulness of objective or scientific information about the concrete world; it is up to the person to choose it, appropriate it, and determine how to use it. In other words, it can be chosen as something to use in our personal construction of reality. For example, one can think of the road map with its major expressways and highways, its smaller and slower two-lane roads, or its meandering scenic back roads, the "blue roads," as providing objective information. If scientifically plotted, the road map provides accurate information that may guide our choice of how to reach a destination, but the choice of what road to take constitutes the meaning of a journey and of what we might encounter on our way. Our choice of which road to take reveals how we have defined space, time, and direction. However, in making the journey, there is also the possibility of encountering the unexpected, the surprise, which can be exciting, engaging, or dangerous. For the Existentialist, the traveler who determines the way chosen is more important than the logistical specificity of the map.[28]

Space and Time

The analogy of the map engages us in the issues of space and time. The map is a graphic representation of the places within a given space (e.g., a state, a country, or the world). Distances on the map require so much time to reach depending on our mode of transportation (e.g., walking, driving, or flying). We can think of the questions—Where am I? Where am I going? How long will it take to get there?—as matters of practical logistics or in the broader sense of life determinations.

It is interesting to note that two primary goals of early childhood learning—to understand the meanings of space and time—are also important philosophical issues. It is a striking coincidence that how children learn to construct the meanings of space and time bear strong relationships to how Existentialists look at space and time. For children, the construct of space comes from where I am and where I live; for Existentialists, space is a concrete personal lived-in place. My personally meaningful construction of space is largely determined by how I choose to arrange my life. Note how the persistent issue between parents (usually mothers) and children (especially teenagers) is about how they keep their rooms. Notice, too, how your friends furnish and decorate their rooms and homes. In a school, observe how teachers have arranged and decorated their classrooms. These different patterns of arranging space mean more that moving chairs and desks around. They reveal how a person has decided to make a space a personally lived-in place.

Similar to space, Existentialists define time as lived time rather than as the ticking of an impersonal mechanical clock or the inexorable passage of the months on a calendar.

The value and meaning of the minutes, hours, days, months, and years of our lives is a consequence of how we choose to live and use our time. Although we have no power over how much time we will have in our lives (i.e., we don't know the time of our death), we are free to choose to do what we wish with the time that we have. Our decisions to put off, procrastinate about, and flee action or to seize the day as our own determines much of who we are. It is a matter of how we establish our temporal priorities.[29]

Becoming an Authentic Person

Sartre's short sentence, "existence precedes essence," clearly states the basic Existentialist premise. It means that who you are (your meaning or essence) is the result of your choices in a concrete situation, in a time and space. Your essence is self-constructed, self-made; it does not come from being defined as an a priori category as Idealists and Realists claim. Neither are you determined by and predestined to an inevitable future by some psychological, sociological, or political ideology. You are who you choose to be.

Existentialists hope that, as individuals construct their own essence, they will make choices that lead to **authenticity**. The dictionary defines *authentic* as not false or copied, as being genuine or real; *to authenticate* means to establish something as genuine, valid, or authoritative. As well as being a writer, the word *author* also means being the maker or creator of something.[30] Using these definitions, the quest to be authentic means that the person needs to recognize and understand the human situation as one being lived in a concrete context, but to resist being defined by the historical, psychological, social, political, and economic aspects of that context. As we live in the context of a global mass society and attend schools that reflect it, we face pervasive and rampant standardization, conformity, and consumerism that makes the challenge of becoming an authentic person perilous. The contemporary drives for instant notoriety on television that result in a parade of short-lived celebrities; bumper sticker slogans of religiosity and patriotism that claim to be moral dicta; and the belief that the big questions of life can be framed in a box on the computer screen, a PowerPoint program, or a textbook reduce life's mysteries to simplistic formulas.

Authenticity in Situational Contexts

Existentialists recognize that human beings live in **situations**, in contexts. These contexts set up the facts of our existences—who we are in terms of gender, race, socioeconomic class, ethnicity, and religious groupings. These bodies of facts, organized as the subjects of science, social sciences, history, and so forth, are important constituents of the formal school curriculum. Teacher education programs, too, are based on the historical, sociological, and psychological foundations of education that purport to describe, analyze, and predict students' development, behavior, and learning. Further, dominant philosophies such as Postmodernism and Critical Theory emphasize gender, race, class, and ethnicity as key factors in which schools are used as agencies of social control by dominant groups to establish conditions that marginalize members of oppressed and repressed groups and classes. For the Existentialists, these factors cannot be ignored by persons striving for authenticity. However, they cannot be used as excuses to avoid making critical choices, or to abandon these choices to others. While these contextual facts set the stage, they are not the determinants of our authenticity—they do not create us as persons. As authors of our own autobiographies, our evaluations, our choices, make us who we are.

Along with the formal curriculum, the hidden curriculum or the school milieu also contains pressures that work against authenticity. The individual in the global mass society and economy, and in the schools that reflect it, is constantly buffeted by pressures to conform, think, dress, speak, and behave the same as everyone else. In junior and senior high school, the pressures to conform are intense because subgroups identify themselves by how they dress, how they talk, what clubs they join, the type of music they listen to, the movies they see, and with whom they sit in the cafeteria. The fear is that one will be recognized as unique. It is all right to be different if that difference has the security of belonging to a group comprised of other people who share that differentiating feature.

Existentialism runs against the strong currents of group-identification found in educational institutions. Rather than accepting group designation as our primary identification, Existentialists urge us to recognize the facts in a context but to move beyond them. An Existentialist education involves examining and becoming conscious of how the forces in the context in which we live often impose their own definitions on us rather than being our genuine choices. It seeks to enliven our consciousness that we are our own authors, our own creators, and that we write our own story by facing and not avoiding the choices, though often difficult ones, that we find in our situations. This kind of education leads us to face our excuses for not acting and our rationalizations for acting in other-defined ways that often disguise our fear of being responsible for our choices. It alerts us to the true meaning of the clichés of "following the crowd," "going with the flow," "not making waves," and "that's just the way things are." Acceptance of the clichés means that I have resigned myself to something, to some situation, that I don't want to think about or face. In this challenge of creating one's self-definition and meaning by making significant choices, the goal cannot be found in ends that are stipulated or proposed by others; it needs to be self-framed and self-defined. Becoming an authentic person is a challenge to be accepted, undertaken, and sustained, but most likely, never really permanently achieved. Creating one's own agenda and purpose in life is dynamic and often filled with risks.[31] Existentialism challenges us to recognize and act on our self-defining, essence-creating choices. This requires us to be conscious of our situation, to know where we are and what we are, and to move forward in making us into what we want to be. Being the author of our own story means that we need to recognize that while we are the principal character who makes the plot, the story is a continuous work in progress, an unfinished symphony, that we write and rewrite as we face the choices that define us. Despite whatever context we find ourselves in, being alive also means that we have the possibility of moving through and beyond it.[32] An example of moving through and beyond the facts can be found in the life and choices of Helen Keller, who, though left blind and deaf by a childhood illness, moved beyond these facts to make herself into what she wanted to be—an independent person and a contributor to society. One also can think of Jane Addams, who recognized the facts of her Victorian era that limited women's choice but who went through and beyond them to define herself as the creator, or author, of Hull House in Chicago and to become a voice for women's rights and world peace.

The Axiology of Making Meaning in Ambiguous Situations

Existentialism shows a definite preference for ambiguity—the cognitive and evaluative awareness that individuals understand that they are free and not already defined, or determined. Ambiguity means that we do not have the security of a context in which everything is defined and prescribed: We have to work our way through a situation by defining it for ourselves. No matter who or what you are, you still have the power to redefine yourself and to create your essence. The Existentialist preference for the ambiguous strikes against determinism of all kinds. It argues against the metaphysical systems that define the person as a being within a preordained, a priori system of reality. Unlike Aristotle, who defines the human being as rational, the Existentialist argues that rationality is a state of mind that the individual must define and freely choose. Arguing against Marxist economic determinism, which defines people as members of a class, Existentialists say that individuals are free to define themselves regardless of their economic status. An individual may be a citizen of a nation-state, yet he or she still may choose to remain a citizen or to redefine citizenship in personal terms. A classic example of redefining citizenship occurred when Henry David Thoreau acted on his belief in civil disobedience when he was jailed for not paying taxes to support what he regarded as an unjust war, the war against Mexico. Although Existentialists recognize the importance of gender, race, ethnicity, and class to human beings, unlike the Critical Theorists, these are not the ultimate factors that define persons. The human being, an individual person, may be predisposed but is not predetermined. Predetermined social, economic, or philosophical theories fall before the ambiguity of life, which has many roads leading to many destinations. Indeed, ambiguity is not something to be feared and reduced by accepting a clear but confining a priori definition of the human being; it is a situation that holds the promise of opening the way for the free choice that only the individual has the power to make.

In educational terms, the recognition that the human being is continuously defining her- or himself in an undetermined life project means that the person is more than a composite of physical, social, economic, historical, and social forces. These forces are important conditioning factors in human choice but they are not fated nor ultimate ones. We can study and be informed by the physical, natural, and social sciences for the information and insights that they provide as background for assessing our choices but these fields, or subjects, cannot make the decisions for us.

Aesthetic Choice.   Existentialists, such as Sartre and Marcel, employed Existentialist themes in developing their novels, plays, and short stories. The Existentialist emphasis on the dramatic element in human experience resonates well in the fine arts. Our process of choice-making is aided by the fine and dramatic arts, which make it possible to express our feelings and our creation of value. Existentialism and Postmodernism both are closely related to the fine arts—literature, drama, art, music, dance, poetry, and architecture. Both philosophies are closely interwoven with literature, especially its style, meaning, and interpretation. However, the Existentialist emphasis on subjectivity is different from the Postmodernist tendency to determine what a literary work means by deconstructing it in terms of its origins, supporters, and opponents.

Many Roles But Only One Self

As Rousseau distinguished between the natural and the artificial in education in *Émile,* formal, institutionalized education—elementary, secondary, and higher education—often consists of learning about the different roles one plays in society, especially those that contribute to how society defines success, especially social and economic success. Those who master this role playing can enter the right college or university, prepare for the right profession, marry the right partner, live in the right neighborhood, and enjoy the good things of life, especially consumer goods—a "McMansion," a second home on the beach, several large cars, and so on. Playing roles means doing what is needed to satisfy the requirements to join a prestigious corporation and to become a member of a high-status country club. For the Existentialist, these roles, though chosen by the role player, are not defined by him or her. They are imposed by others. Unlike the Critical Theorist, the Existentialist does not see this multiplicity of roles as a capitalist conspiracy to ensnare the unsuspecting into the dominant economic web. Rather, the Existentialist wants to bring to the individual's consciousness the dramatic realization that the human condition involves the need to navigate between the many social and economic roles, taught so well in schools, and to choose personal authenticity over role determination.

For Existentialists, the tyranny of role playing may lead to unauthentic stage acting in which the person wears the mask, speaks the words, and exhibits the behavior required by the role rather than being true to him- or herself. The danger is an unintegrated personality, who is constantly shifting roles and adrift—carried along by eddies and currents rather than by self-direction. Without freely determined authentic choice, there is the danger that the roles will conflict and the individual will become an unhinged, disintegrated personality. The Existentialists constantly remind us we need to take off the mask of the role that hides our true identity. We make our true identity, not by retreating into a socially or economically determined success role, but by facing the reality that we are what we choose to be. Taking off the mask can be risky—it may mean losing the job, the fancy car, and the mansion.

Ethics and Social Justice

Social justice issues are an important ethical concern in contemporary education. Commitments to social justice are found in the mission statements of educational institutions and professional societies. Existentialism has often been accused of being a selfish, hedonistic, self-centered philosophy that ignores social justice needs and ideas. It is true that Existentialists place primary responsibility on the individual person and warn that persons must look to their own choices to create their own essences. Indeed, Sartre warned that the "other person is hell." And yet despite the charges made against it, Existentialism is concerned with human rights and social justice issues.

Often accused of putting individual preferences before social needs, Existentialists respond that personal ethical conduct—not making speeches or writing articles—reveals a person's true commitment to social justice. Sartre, for example, a determined anticolonialist, staunchly opposed European imperialism, especially French repression of the Algerian independence movement.[33] Acts of social injustice are perpetrated by oppressive regimes, but repression is not solely the consequence of an institutionalized political or economic system. It also needs to be seen in the subjective sense of the officials, who administer the instruments of repression, and the larger body of people who ignore it or condone it. This means that repression, marginalization, and other forms of oppression need to seen as acts committed by individuals, who are agents of such regimes, and as the responsibility of the larger public who support it through taxes. In other words, oppression has a human face no matter how well it is hidden within a system.

Existentialists such as Sartre see the control and marginalization of one group by another as a serious cause of personal alienation in society. Those social, economic, and political factors that repress human freedom cause both the suppressed and suppressor to be alienated from social justice. Alienation asserts that conditions of repression are necessary and that those who are repressed deserve this treatment because they are inferior or not like us. As part of the raising of consciousness needed for authentic choices, Existentialist educators encourage students to examine their social contexts—both the school community and the larger society—to identify conditions of repression and to expose the ideological factors that justify this repression.

Existentialists would make human rights and freedom a personal issue in that I as a person can be free only when you are free. This kind of freedom between persons means that the other persons are not objectified or turned into the functions that they perform. In other words, a teacher, physician, truck driver, and grocery check-out clerk are more than how they function in society or the economy. They, too, are persons who have the right to self-identification and self-determination.

Finally, Existentialists would resist the move to standardize social justice issues in much the same way that the curriculum has been standardized. It is insufficient to merely list social justice themes in the standards of professional societies and the mission statements of educational organizations and institutions. Justice between individuals at base is always personal and must resist being encased in standards or slogans that make one feel good but take away the responsibility of doing what is right.

Existentialism's Implications for Education

In this section, we examine Existentialism's implications for education. In particular, we consider its critique of educational trends and its suggestions for an Existentialist pedagogy, curriculum and teaching and learning.

An Existentialist Critique of Educational Trends

Philosophizing in the Existentialist style provokes a critique of certain social and educational trends that have influenced contemporary society and schools. Among the trends that reduce personal choice and self-definition are standardization, categorization, the inculcation of socioeconomic roles, and the tyranny of the average. Each of these trends works against creating opportunities for authenticity.

As educational institutions in a mass society emulate the larger corporate system, they depersonalize the teaching–learning relationship. There is also another sense in which formal education systems impede personal authenticity. Various subdivisions of professional education, such as educational psychology, instructional methodology, measurement, and evaluation, borrow heavily from the social sciences of psychology, sociology, and political science. Emulating the physical sciences, these various social sciences and their educational derivatives seek to predict and control behavior. Instruction is structured according to behavioral objectives so that outcomes can be measured to the degree that behavior has changed. Such a conception of learning views the learner as a social object or phenomenon and elicits responses that are quantified and rendered into measurable statistical and otherwise standardized responses.

Contemporary U.S. education has become highly group-centered as a result of the progressive educator's stress on shared activity in learning situations and because of the dominance of educational psychologies that emphasize social acceptance and adjustment. The aims of socialized education are such objectives as learning to cooperate with others, functioning successfully in group situations, and working as an effective collaborative team member. According to group-centered educational theories, the individual becomes more effective and efficient by identifying with and participating in group activities.

Existentialist educators are cautious about the glorification of the group. In the midst of crowds, human beings are still lonely and anxiety-ridden. Some group-centered learning situations may become so coercive of the individual that personal authenticity may be sacrificed to the pressure to achieve like-minded consensus. When a person freely chooses to join and to participate in a group, opportunities still exist for authentic choice. However, many group-centered situations in schools are not freely chosen. Learning situations organized around groups should be such that they permit and encourage opportunities for individuals to assert the unique aspects of their personalities.

In their desire to be scientific and efficient, modern educators have demonstrated a decided proclivity for standardization. Standardized tests, designed to measure student aptitude and achievement, are used to assign students to educational categories from which there is often little movement or mobility. School records and reporting systems deal in categories that encourage little or no recognition of students' uniqueness and creativity. Mass-produced instructional materials, ranging from basal readers and textbooks to videos, are geared to categories of students in clearly defined groups. For their organization, schools rely on routinized and standardized schedules. While contributing to efficiency, the standardization of educational institutions has fostered social control that is suspicious of individual uniqueness or creativity. Whereas some teachers willingly become agents of institutional standardization, other search for opportunities to encourage their students' self-expression and self-definition.

The tendency to standardization that comes from within educational institutions threatens individuality; the movement for standards and standardization that comes from outside of the school and is imposed on teachers and students is a significant contemporary threat to what Existentialists would consider to be an authentic education. The contemporary standards movement is largely a political phenomenon that seeks to identify certain specific skills (reading) and subjects (mathematics and science) as the essential curriculum components that every person should study and master. State legislatures and the U.S. Congress have enacted legislation that mandates standardized testing of students to determine whether they have achieved a basic and minimal competency in the specified skills and subjects.

The test results of mass student cohorts at specified grade levels are used as evidence that schools and their teachers are performing adequately. When students perform below the benchmark prescribed in the standard, this is taken as evidence of schools' and teachers' incompetence as instructors of academic skills and subjects.

Devoted to preserving and enhancing students' personal individuality and uniqueness, Existentialists are suspicious of, and indeed apprehensive about, state and national governments' drive to endorse and impose standardized tests to determine teachers' and students' academic competency. The standards give priority to specific skills and subjects that external authorities have determined are necessary in a person's education. The standards carry with them an expected desirable outcome, a benchmark that is determined to verify competence; however, the outcome that is expected also sets what is to be done, the lessons needed to meet the benchmark. The internal choice of teachers and students, which the Existentialists prize, is reduced to other-directed prescriptions that come to signify competency in academic instruction and learning. Because so much is riding on meeting the external standards, more time, effort, and resources are expended on the tested skills and subjects and less on other subjects and skills. The curriculum area that is likely to suffer de-emphasis is the fine arts, exactly the area that the Existentialists see as vital to providing opportunities for student self-expression and creation.

In addition, the movement to externally imposed standards also encourages teachers to teach for the test. That is, they concentrate their efforts on the skills and subjects featured on the various standardized tests. Their choices in designing and choosing different points of emphasis and different teaching strategies are limited to teaching specifically what is needed for their students to score well on standardized tests.

The general effect of externally imposed standards is to standardize what takes place in classrooms. Because a standard is generalized and uniform, classrooms, too, will become uniform. Uniformity means that uniqueness and difference has been eliminated for a new kind of lockstep approach in schools. Whereas Existentialists see ambiguity, openness, and indeterminacy as positive aspects of education, advocates of standards and standardization view them negatively. Standards emphasize specific academic expectations and outcomes that reduce ambiguity and hypothesizing, and reduce the possibilities of seeing education as an open-ended personal project: the more standardized, the less ambiguous; the more specific, the less open-ended.

It is not only the school's impetus toward standardized efficiency that threatens students' self-definition. Students themselves, seeking the security that comes from group identification, often become conformists who eagerly consign their peers to categories. In the typical high school, students often identify as "brains" or "grinds," students who are studious academic achievers; "jocks," those who are athletes and cheerleaders; "freaks" or "druggies," those who are on drugs; and then there are the "nobodies" who are without group identification. Once assigned to a school caste, the adolescent is identified as a member of a group, stays within that group, and often abandons the opportunities to cultivate his or her own uniqueness or to appreciate others for their own worth.

Still another tendency of contemporary society and education that limits self-definition comes from socioeconomic pressures that have shaped schooling into role playing. Schools define the role for economic success—getting a good-paying job and moving up the economic ladder; they define what it means to be a good citizen; they define what it means to be socially successful; and so on. Students are expected to study these roles and to play them well. In so doing, the opportunities for genuine self-determined choice are fewer. Authenticity becomes too risky because it may not lead to success as others have defined it.

Among the most pervasive but most subtle of the contemporary trends that erode the possibilities of human authenticity comes from the "tyranny of the average." The tyranny of dictatorial and authoritarian rulers, regimes, and institutions is a patently obvious kind of oppression. Less obvious, the tyranny of the average appears initially to be democratic but in actuality is a symptom of mass thought and preferences. In a consumer-oriented society, products are made and marketed for the largest possible group of consumers. Mass media, art, and entertainment—television, radio, movies, newspapers, magazines, popular books— are also designed to attract the largest possible audience. Again, marketability dictates that the widest appeal will come from catering to the average. These agencies of informal education both reflect and create popular tastes. In a mass society, deviations from the average do not sell well; uniqueness either becomes so expensive that it can be enjoyed only by a privileged elite or so unpopular that it is pushed to the margins of society.

It may be argued that standardization, categorization, role playing, and the tyranny of the average are the inevitable by-products of a mass society and that contemporary schooling only mirrors these irresistible trends. An Existentialist educator would argue, however, that as society becomes more conformist, standardized, and categorized, it is the responsibility of teachers to expose these trends by having students examine and analyze them. This exposé is not merely for sociological interest; it is to raise students' consciousness so that they at least are aware of the dangers that modern technological society poses to authentic freedom.

Toward an Existentialist Education

Van Cleve Morris argues that education should cultivate an "intensity of awareness" in the learner. Such an awareness means that students should recognize that as individuals they are constantly, freely, baselessly, and creatively choosing. Such an awareness carries with it the responsibility for determining how one wants to live and for creating one's own self-definition.[34]

In developing an Existentialist educational psychology, Morris identified a "pre-Existential" period of human development and the "Existential Moment."[35] During the **pre-Existential period** prior to puberty, the child, not really aware of his or her human condition, is not yet conscious of a personal identity and destiny. The pre-Existentialist years coincide with elementary education when children learn to read, write, do arithmetic, and acquire physical, recreational, communicative, and social skills. Children also learn some subject-matter and problem-solving skills.

For Morris, the **Existential Moment** arises when people become conscious of their presence as a self in the world. Although the experience of the Existential Moment varies with individuals, it generally occurs around the time of puberty and is characterized by an awareness of one's presence in the world, and an insight into one's own consciousness and the responsibility for conduct. At times, the Existential Moment is a period of great power and thrust; at other times, the adolescent seeks to escape adult responsibilities and to return to childhood's innocence.

Existentialist education would begin in the years of the junior high school and continue onward through the senior high school and the undergraduate college. Concerned with those elements of experience that are subjective, personal, and affective, an Existentialist education encourages involvement in situations conducive to the knowledge that human choices involve personal questions of good or bad and right or wrong.

An Existentialist Curriculum

Attempting to describe an Existentialist curriculum is an interesting and difficult challenge. Determining what students study and teachers teach prior to their engagement in the classroom jeopardizes the Existentialist of personal freedom of choice. However, given the legal reality of compulsory school attendance, it is still possible to consider how an Existentialist curriculum might be constructed. In making the curriculum, it is important to recall some key Existentialists themes:

- the need to arouse consciousness about the human situation;
- the need to maximize individual freedom and choice;
- the need to recognize the desirability of ambiguity; and
- the need to refrain from turning persons into objects or functions.

In exploring the Existentialist possibilities for curriculum construction, we might divide the curriculum into two broad areas: the "given" and the "open."

The Givens

The Existentialists emphasize that it is a given fact of existence that we live in specific, concrete contexts—spaces—at a particular time. Though not a technical term, **givens** refer to the skills and subjects that describe and explain the social and physical reality of our local, national, and global contexts. The givens as subjects such as the natural and physical sciences (e.g., biology, botany, chemistry, physics), mathematics, and the various social sciences (e.g., political sciences, sociology, and psychology) provide knowledge about our contexts. The skills—reading, writing, languages, arithmetic, research competencies, and computer literacy—provide the means to access the information contained in the subjects. The givens as skills and subject help explain our contexts. We need to know them as bodies of existing knowledge, but givens are one part only of our education and not the most important piece in constructing our self-definition as persons. Even though they are existents in the curriculum and the Existentialists still advise us that we need to know them, givens do not determine who or what we can make of ourselves. From an Existentialist educational perspective, they can inform us but do not determine us. Even though they are there, the Existentialists apply the strategy of appropriation to how they are taught and learned. We can choose to give them the relevance that we wish.

The Open Areas

For Existentialists, the key areas of the curriculum for raising consciousness about the human condition, freedom and choice, are the **open areas**, which include the humanities and the fine and expressive arts. The open areas include literature, music, dance, filmmaking and film studies, creative writing, autobiography, biography, art, drawing, painting, poetry, history, philosophy, and religion. This large array of open areas, dealing with values, is often neglected, given low priority, or squeezed out in schools and colleges by the more job-oriented saleable skills or the mandated required subjects, especially those related to standards. For the Existentialists, the humanities and the arts are of crucial importance in raising consciousness and encouraging self-definition because they are the most axiological, ethical, and aesthetic areas of the curriculum. As indicated, the Existentialists see a self-affirming education as leading to personal evaluation and valuation.

The arts, designed to cultivate and express aesthetic experience, include music, drama, dance, creative writing, painting, and film. The aim of aesthetic education, according to Existentialists, is not to imitate the styles of selected classical artists, although these might be studied, but rather to evoke creative expression. In aesthetic education, the teacher is to evoke the learner's sense and desire for aesthetic expression. Although not knowing what the learner will create, the teacher provides a variety of creative media so that the learner will have the raw materials from which to create his or her own art object. The learner uses the various media to portray the world as experienced in one's own consciousness and to produce the art that comes from the center of one's private existence.

Literature and the humanities also receive emphasis in an Existentialist curriculum. Relevant for awakening the learner to the significance of choice making, literature portrays persons facing basic human issues. Through literature, drama, and film, the learner places his or her capacities for feeling at the disposal of the author or artist. The vicarious involvement of the learner in the profound human questions of love, death, suffering, guilt, and freedom are excellent means for portraying the human condition and for constructing personal meaning in an apparently indifferent world.

Existentialism and History

History as a subject presents an interesting issue for Existentialists because it is not really a science, yet not quite an art. The sources—the documents and artifacts—historians use to construct their version of the past need to meet the requirements of validity that is somewhat empirical. Written history is also literature, somewhat akin to the novel; the historical narrative, though purporting to be based on a recital of the facts of an actual event, tells a story of individuals, their conflicts, choices, successes, and failures. As with other subjects, teaching and learning history involves the appropriation of the narrative in which the student can make it her or his own and either accept or reject the historian's interpretation of the meaning of the past.

In considering history as a subject in their curriculum, Existentialists would use the strategy of **emplotment**, in which the student is encouraged to appropriate, internalize, and interpret the narrative's plot—as the unfolding story of individuals who face the facts of their context and strive for meaningful action.[36] Through emplotment—the acts of appropriating and internalizing—individuals can acquire beliefs, attitudes, or behaviors from external sources and make them their own by transforming them into personal attributes, values, or styles.[37]

For example, students might engage with the months immediate to the onset of the American Civil War, and consider the hesitation and inaction of President James Buchanan, Abraham Lincoln's predecessor, and the action taken by Lincoln when he became president. The process of emplotment involves the student's participation in reflecting on the choices made by the two men. The educational philosopher George Kneller wrote:

> The student should therefore learn to handle his history with passion, personal thrust, and in the manner of a stage director, talently manipulating the human scene, with all its heroes, villains, and plots.[38]

Existentialism, Philosophy, and Education

Philosophy	Reality	Epistemology	Axiology	Educational Implications	Leading Philosophers
Existentialism	Existence precedes essence; we live in concrete situations and define ourselves through our choices.	Choosing what we want to know by appropriating it; making it our own.	Living is a process of open-ended evaluation and the construction of values through our choices.	Curriculum and activities, especially in humanities and arts, to stimulate an awareness that each person creates a self-concept through significant choices	Kierkegaard Sartre Marcel Morris

Existentialist Epistemology, Humanist Psychology, and Teaching and Learning

In describing the Existentialist classroom, we need to consider the relationship of epistemology and psychology to teaching and learning.

Existentialist Epistemology

Traditional philosophies such as Idealism, Realism, and Thomism emphasize the human being as a thinking and reasoning being. For example, Plato's philosopher-kings were an intellectual elite who possessed the keenest powers of speculative abstraction; Aristotle, identifying the power to reason as unique to the human being, called the human being a rational animal. Traditional educational philosophies and school practices based on the philosophies of Plato and Aristotle have stressed cognitive development as an overriding educational outcome. Unlike these philosophies, Existentialism sees the human being in more ambiguous but more varied terms. The human person is rational but also irrational, thinking but also feeling, cognitive but also affective.

Existentialist epistemology assumes that the individual is responsible for constructing his or her own knowledge.[39] Knowledge originates in and is composed of what exists in the individual's consciousness and feelings as a result of one's experiences. Human situations have both rational and irrational components. The validity of knowledge is determined by its value and meaning to the individual. An Existentialist epistemology emerges from the recognition that human experience and knowledge are subjective, personal, rational, and irrational. Whereas Pragmatists emphasize using the scientific method of problem solving, Existentialists prefer to probe human aesthetic, moral, and emotional concerns as well as cognitive ones.

Humanist Psychology

Existentialism has been influential in shaping humanist psychology, which has implications for educational psychology and counseling. Existentialists such as Sartre have criticized mechanistic and deterministic psychologies that reduce the human being to sets of instincts and impulses and neglect human freedom and choice. Arguing that human purpose is not determined, Sartre contended that it comes from personal choice arising in situations unique to each person.

Abraham Maslow, Gordon Allport, Carl Rogers, and Rollo May have been the leaders of the humanist psychology movement in the United States. Rogers, who developed the concept of client-centered counseling, emphasizes that the individual should create his or her own self-concept. This process of creating self-identity means that the person exists in, or is at the center of, a changing world of experience, which, while including social interaction, is ultimately private. As a result of environmental and social interaction, the structure of the self, that is, personhood, emerges but is self-formed or self-defined rather than other-directed.[40]

According to humanist psychology, Existentialist teaching seeks to stimulate and to facilitate learning, or self-examination and definition, in the broadest sense. Maintaining the Existentialist classroom requires a delicate balance in which both teacher and students maintain their identities as persons. This means that the teacher must constantly struggle against falling into a situation in which students are defined simply by their age, academic ranking, status, or group membership. It also means that students need to be conscious that they, too, can define a teacher, not as a person, but as one who performs custodial, instructional, and supervisory functions. In other words, the delicate Existential balance breaks down when teachers reduce students to objects and students reduce teachers to functions.

Existentialist Teaching and Learning

Although the Existentialist teacher may choose to use a variety of educational methods, none of these methods should obscure the personal I–Thou relationship between teacher and learner. The Socratic dialogue is an appropriate method for Existentialist teachers. The dialogue can bring questions to the learners so that they become conscious of the condition of their lives. Unlike the Idealist's use of the Socratic dialogue, the Existentialist teacher does not know the answers to the questions posed. Indeed, the best kind of question is answerable only in the student's own construction of meaning.

In an Existentialist methodology, the teacher seeks to stimulate an "intensity of awareness" in the learner, encouraging the quest for a personal truth by asking questions that concern life's meaning. It is the teacher's task to create the learning situation in which students can express their subjectivity. It is only the learner who can come face to face with his or her responsibility for self-definition. The creation of the intensity of awareness is as much the learner's own responsibility as it is the teacher's. Such an awareness involves the sense of being personally involved in the ethical and aesthetic dimensions of existence.

Students should be free to create their own modes of self-expression. They should be free to experiment with artistic media and to dramatize their emotions, feelings, and insights in short stories, poems, plays, drawings, and paintings. Educational technology that enhances personal choice and freedom can also be useful in existentialist education. For example, students might benefit from expressing themselves by creating multimedia productions, videos, and movies. Prepackaged programs that create conformity in thinking and in accessing information, on the other hand, would be viewed with suspicion.

An Existentialist Lesson

Literature, history, drama, and film are especially powerful subjects in existentialist teaching. One example might be a junior high school class reading *The Diary of Anne Frank*, the story of a young Jewish girl, her family, and others who hide in an attic in Amsterdam, which was under Nazi occupation, during World War II. Anne and her family live in an absurd and dangerous world. They must hide to avoid being rounded up and sent to a German concentration camp. They are aided by several Dutch friends who are loyal to Anne's father, their former employer. Anne and her family find themselves in a situation, a context, that is fraught with the everyday danger of their arrest simply because they are Jewish. If sent to a concentration camp, they face extermination. The danger represents the Existentialist theme of the dread of eventual disappearance. Anne makes a choice to turn her cramped refuge into lived space and to use her time, in which night and day have no meaning, to write her diary, which records growing up as a teenaged girl in a world that makes no sense. In the end, the family is betrayed by a collaborator. The Gestapo find the hiding place and

Anne and her family are seized and transported to the concentration camp in which Anne will die.

Students can consider the ethical meaning of Anne's situation. There are those righteous gentiles who, at the risk of their own lives, provided the Frank family and the others hidden in the attic with the food they needed to survive. Then, there is the choice made by the Nazi collaborator who revealed their hiding place. Students can ask themselves what they would have done under the circumstances. What choices would they make?

The lesson deals with an Existential situation being lived out in a concrete situation—the reality of surviving in a cramped attic. It crosses back and forth from history, biography, literature, and ethics. It uses the strategy of emplotment, by which students appropriate, internalize, and interpret the plot as the unfolding story of individuals facing the facts of their context and striving for meaningful action. Through emplotment, individuals can acquire beliefs, attitudes, or behaviors from external sources and make them their own by transforming them into personal attributes, values, or styles.

Conclusion

Although the high tide of Existentialism was in the decades following World War II, especially the late 1940s, 1950s, and early 1960s, Existentialist philosophy has made its mark on how we think today. The Existentialist themes of mutual respect, the freedom to define oneself by making significant choices, and the idea that life and education are open-ended and indeterminate resonate throughout thinking on education. Contemporary efforts to resist conformity and standardization echo the arguments of Sartre, Marcel, and de Beauvoir. The contemporary search for a spirituality that is free from dogma also reminds one of Kierkegaard's "leap of faith." Aspects of Postmodernism and Critical Theory reveal selected Existentialist origins. The terms *choice, commitment, authenticity,* and *freedom* resonate throughout political, social, and educational discourse that runs counter to establishment thinking. Arguments that an authentic education means that students have the right to construct their own identities, write their own stories, and bring their lived-in situations into the classroom reflect the Existentialism argument that persons come before definitions and actions before theories.

Most likely where the Existentialists part company with contemporary education is in their belief that persons are more than the sum of their social, political, economic, religious, class, race, ethnic, and gender parts. Although these aspects of living may illuminate who we are, we are not defined by them. In its abhorrence of determinism, its assertion that we are a self-constructed human project flies in the face of the many determinist theories that are taught and preached in academic lecture halls and classrooms. A major difference that the Existentialists offer to us is facing up to and accepting our own responsibility for who we are and what we do.

Constructing Your Own Philosophy of Education.   As you reflect on constructing your own philosophy of education, what themes or elements of Existentialism appeal to you as a teacher? Which appeal least? Why? Are there elements of Existentialism that you would like to incorporate into your philosophy?

Questions for Reflection and Discussion

1. Assume you are an Existentialist teacher. How would you respond to a student who asks, "What difference does it make to you that I am here in your classroom?"

2. A student says, "I want to make a difference." What would this statement mean to an Existentialist?

3. What does it mean to create your own self-definition without defining others?

4. Give some examples of antecedent definitions that define persons prior to their own individual existence. Do you find these examples present in contemporary schools?

5. Have you been involved with groups that limited your freedom to define yourself? Identity these groups and analyze how they operate in society and schools.

6. Have you known an authentic person, one who is completely self-directed? Describe this person.

7. Reflect on current trends in education such as the standards movement, multiculturalism, women's studies programs, authentic assessment, and constructionism. Do these trends encourage or discourage Existentialist themes such as authenticity, cultivating an intensity of awareness, and self-definition?

Inquiry and Research Projects

1. Review a book by one of the following in which you identify the work's Existentialist themes: Søren Kierkegaard, Friedrich Nietzsche, Fyodor Dostoyevsky, Martin Buber, Jean-Paul Sartre, Gabriel Marcel, or Simone de Beauvoir.

2. Identify and review movies, television programs, and novels that portray Existentialist themes or situations.

3. Write a script for a short play that exemplifies an Existentialist teaching situation; invite your colleagues to portray the various characters in the play. If possible, videotape the play and then analyze it as a classroom activity.

4. Arrange a group discussion on the topic, "Is Existentialism a relevant educational philosophy?" After the discussion, have the participants reflect on pressures that they experienced from being involved in the discussion.

5. Identify and describe in a journal entry how specific situations in your school either encourage or discourage freedom of choice and expression.

6. Select a current trend in education such as the standards movement, multiculturalism, women's studies programs, authentic assessment, or constructionism. Review the literature about this trend and determine how an Existentialist would relate to it.

Building an Existentialist Vocabulary

Angst: the German word for a deep and Existential anguish that arises when a person becomes conscious of freedom of choice in a world in which he or she is temporary.

Appropriation: an Existentialist epistemology that means to personally choose what is learned and to give it a personal meaning.

Authenticity: the state of being original or genuine and not a copy.

Emplotment: studying history by appropriating, internalizing, and interpreting the narrative's plot.

Existence: simply being present, or being there; as being present in the world.

Existential Moment: occurs sometime during puberty when we become aware of our personal responsibility for defining who we are.

Givens: skills and subjects that describe and explain the biological, social, and economic context. Scientific subjects that describe the world of physical realities.

Open Areas of Curriculum: the humanities, fine arts, and expressive arts, which hold great potential for raising consciousness about the human condition and freedom and choice.

Phenomenological Method: a philosophical method founded by Edmund Husserl that seeks to describe the objects of consciousness.

Pre-Existential Period: when children really do not know who or what they are and decisions are made for them by adults.

Situations: being in contexts of givens of birth, nationality, class, and gender but also having the power to transcend these facts of existence through self-defining choice.

Internet Resources

For a useful discussion of Existentialism, access www.plato.stanford.edu/entries/existentialism.

For an introduction to Existentialism, access www.allaboutphilosophy.org/existentialism.htm.

For Existentialism as a recent philosophy, access www.radicalacademy.com/adiphiexistentialism.htm.

Suggestions for Further Reading

Barrett, William. *Irrational Man: A Study in Existentialist Philosophy.* New York: Anchor Books, 1990.

Billington, Ray. *East of Existentialism: The Tao of the West.* London and Boston: Unwin Hyman, 1990.

Catalano, Joseph S. *Good Faith and Other Essays: Perspectives on Sartre's Ethics.* Lanham, MD: Rowman and Littlefield, 1996.

De Beauvoir, Simone. *The Ethics of Ambiguity.* New York: Citadel, 2000.

De Beauvoir, Simone. *The Second Sex.* New York: Knopf, 1989.

Dobson, Andrew. *Jean-Paul Sartre and the Politics of Reason: A Theory of History.* New York: Cambridge University Press, 1993.

Dreyfus, Hubert L., and Mark A. Wrathall, eds. *A Companion to Existentialism and Phenomenology.* Oxford, UK: Blackwell, 2006.

Flynn, Thomas. *Existentialism: A Very Short Introduction.* Oxford, UK: Oxford University Press, 2006.

Garff, Joakim. *Søren Kierkegaard: A Biography.* Princeton, NJ: Princeton University Press, 2005.

Golomb, Jacob. *In Search of Authenticity: From Kierkegaard to Camus.* London: Routledge, 1995.

Guignon, Charles, and Derk Pereboom, eds. *Existentialism: Basic Writings.* Indianapolis, IN: Hackett, 1995.

Kierkegaard, Søren. *Either/Or.* Translated by Alastair Hannay. London: Penguin Books, 1992.

Kierkegaard, Søren. *Papers and Journals: A Selection.* London: Penguin Books, 1996.

MacDonald, Paul S., ed. *The Existentialist Reader: An Anthology of Key Texts.* New York: Routledge, 2001.

Marcel, Gabriel. *The Philosophy of Existentialism.* New York: Citadel, 1961.

Marcel, Gabriel. *Man Against Mass Society.* Chicago: Gateway, 1970.

Sartre, Jean-Paul. *Being and Nothingness.* New York: Citadel, 1984.

Santoni, Ronald E. *Bad Faith, Good Faith, and Authenticity in Sartre's Early Philosophy.* Philadelphia: Temple University Press, 1995.

Westphal, Merold. *Becoming a Self: A Reading of Kierkegaard's Concluding Unscientific Postscript.* West Lafayette, IN: Purdue University Press, 1996.

Endnotes

1. *The Random House Dictionary of the English Language* (New York: Random House, 1968), p. 464.
2. Thomas Flynn, *Existentialism: A Very Short Introduction* (Oxford, UK: Oxford University Press, 2006), pp. 17–20.
3. Alastair Hanny, "Søren Aabye Kierkegaard" in Ted Honderich, ed., *The Philosophers: Introducing Great Western Thinkers* (Oxford and New York: Oxford University Press, 2001), p. 149.
4. Patrick Gardiner, *Kierkegaard: A Very Short Introduction* (Oxford and New York: Oxford University Press, 2002), pp. 8–9.
5. For a biography of Kierkegaard, see Joakim Garff, *Søren Kierkegaard: A Biography* (Princeton, NJ: Princeton University Press, 2005).
6. Flynn, *Existentialism: A Very Short Introduction,* pp. 3, 10.
7. Flynn, *Existentialism: A Very Short Introduction,* p. 25.
8. Gardiner, *Kierkegaard: A Very Short Introduction,* p. 13.
9. Gardiner, *Kierkegaard: A Very Short Introduction,* pp. 90–91.
10. Gardiner, *Kierkegaard: A Very Short Introduction,* p. 2.
11. Søren Kierkegaard, *Either/Or,* trans. Alastair Hannay (London: Penguin, 1992) and Kierkegaard, *Stages on Life's Way,* trans. Howard V. Hong and Edna H. Hong (Princeton, NJ: Princeton University Press, 1988).
12. Gardiner, *Kierkegaard: A Very Short Introduction,* pp. 52–53.
13. Flynn, *Existentialism: A Very Short Introduction,* pp. 26–27.
14. Gardiner, *Kierkegaard: A Very Short Introduction,* pp. 48–49.
15. Flynn, *Existentialism: A Very Short Introduction,* pp. 34–36.
16. Gardiner, *Kierkegaard: A Very Short Introduction,* p. 60.
17. Gabriel Marcel, *The Philosophy of Existentialism* (New York: Citadel Press, 1961).
18. Gabriel Marcel, *Man Against Mass Society* (Chicago: Gateway, 1970).
19. Flynn, *Existentialism: A Very Short Introduction,* pp. 90–91.
20. Thomas Baldwin, "Jean-Paul Sartre" in Ted Honderich, ed., *The Philosophers: Introducing Great Western Thinkers* (Oxord and New York: Oxford University Press, 2001), p. 245.
21. Jean-Paul Sartre, "Is Existentialism a Humanism?," in Walter Kaufmann, ed., *Existentialism: From Dostoevsky to Sartre* (New York: Penguin Books, 1988).
22. For Nietzsche, see Friedrich Nietzsche, *The Anti-Christ, Ecce Homo, Twilight of the Idols: and Other Writings* (Cambridge, UK: Cambridge University

Press, 2005) and Nietzsche, *Beyond Good and Evil* (Cambridge, UK: Cambridge University Press, 2001).

23. Flynn, *Existentialism: A Very Short Introduction,* p. 40.
24. For de Beauvoir's impressions of the French Existentialist movement, see Simone de Beauvoir, *The Force of Circumstances* (New York: Putnam, 1965) and Beauvoir, *All Said and Done* (New York: Putnam, 1974).
25. Flynn, *Existentialism: A Very Short Introduction,* pp. 98–99.
26. Flynn, *Existentialism: A Very Short Introduction,* pp. 101–102.
27. My analogy of the map is derived from Flynn's discussion of Kierkegaard's "fork in the road" commentary on truth in Flynn, *Existentialism: A Very Short Introduction,* pp. 9–10.
28. Flynn, *Existentialism: A Very Short Introduction,* pp. 5–7.
29. *The Random House Dictionary of the English Language* (New York: Random House, 1968), p. 91.
30. Flynn, *Existentialism: A Very Short Introduction,* pp. 24–25.
31. Flynn, *Existentialism: A Very Short Introduction,* pp. 65–67.
32. Flynn, *Existentialism: A Very Short Introduction,* p. 92.
33. Van Cleve Morris, *Existentialism in Education* (New York: Harper and Row, 1966), p. 110.
34. Morris, *Existentialism in Education,* pp. 116–117.
35. For discussions of history, meaning, and memory, see Peter N. Stearns, Peter Seixas, and Sam Weinburg, eds., *Knowing, Teaching and Learning History: National and International Perspectives* (New York: New York University Press, 2000).
36. James Wertsch, "Is It Possible to Teach Beliefs, As Well As Knowledge about History?" in Peter N. Stearns, Peter Seixas, and Sam Weinburg, eds., *Knowing, Teaching and Learning History,* pp. 38–50.
37. George F. Kneller, *Existentialism and Education* (New York: John Wiley and Sons, 1966), pp. 129–130.
38. Morris, *Existentialism in Education,* pp. 120–122.
39. Frank Milhollan and Bill E. Forisha, *From Skinner to Rogers: Contrasting Approaches to Education* (Lincoln, NE: Professional Educators, 1972), pp. 98–113.

6

Postmodernism and Education

Michel Foucault (1926–1984), a French philosopher whose ideas were highly significant in the development of Postmodernism.

Chapter Preview

Postmodernism is an important contemporary philosophy in both general conversation and in academic discussion. We often hear that we live in the postmodern, postindustrial, and poststructural era that followed the modern period of history. The term **postmodern condition** is used to describe the cultural changes caused by the contemporary information society. Among academics, postmodernism exerts a strong contemporary influence in literature, architecture, education, humanities, and the arts as well in multicultural, feminist, and gender studies. We now take a closer look at this important philosophy. We begin with two terms, *post* and *modern*. The prefix *post* means coming after some event, such as being a postgraduate, meaning after one graduates, or postsurgical, the recovery period needed to recuperate after surgery. *Modern* as an adjective has been applied to Western history from the Renaissance through the end of the Cold War, roughly from the fifteenth through the twentieth century. Postmodernists, in their critique of modernism, focus on the period from the eighteenth-century Enlightenment to the end of the twentieth century. Postmodernists are especially critical of the emphasis in Western history and culture that is given to the Enlightenment as the "age of reason" and its consequences for scientific discovery, European exploration and imperialism and industrialism, the two World Wars, the nuclear era, the cold war, and the current trend to globalization. The chapter examines the following aspects of Postmodernism:

- Postmodernist Philosophers
- Postmodernist Themes
- Postmodernist Education

As you read about Postmodernism, use it to critique your ideas about education, schooling, curriculum, and teaching and learning. Determine whether there are elements of Postmodernism that you would like to incorporate into your philosophy of education.

Postmodernist Philosophers

Rather than pointing to a particular founder of Postmodernism as we did with Plato for Idealism, Aristotle for Realism, and Dewey for Pragmatism, we examine the work of several philosophers. Postmodernism's early expressions are identified with the philosophers Nietzsche and Heidegger; contemporary Postmodernism is associated with such theorists as Jacques Derrida and Michel Foucault.

Antecedents of Postmodernism

Friedrich Nietzsche (1844–1900), an iconoclastic German philosopher, expressed ideas that anticipated Postmodernism. Nietzsche attacked traditional philosophical assumptions that metaphysical speculation could discover the universal truths of ultimate reality.[1] For Nietzsche, metaphysics was merely a human construction designed to fill the void when ancient myths and supernaturalism imploded because of modern science. Metaphysicians—Idealists, Realists, and Thomists—had constructed an unchanging otherworld of certitude that is always good, true, and beautiful. Their cosmic invention provided a philosophical tranquilizer for anxious people who could not accept the reality of a world that was incomplete, changing, and always in the ferment of becoming. Metaphysical statements were human-made rationales constructed at a given time in history that should be analyzed for their genealogy—for the historical, psychological, economic, sociological, and educational situations in which they occur.[2] Certain heroic individuals, "the supermen," Nietzsche claimed, accept the incompleteness of life and make their own rules.

Martin Heidegger (1899–1976), another German philosopher, constructed a philosophy called Existentialist Phenomenology. Heidegger developed an Existentialist theory of the self-defined authentic person, who lived with ever present feelings of dread, disappearance, and the awareness of death as a consciously known inevitability. Truth is not found in some universal category such as Plato's "Form of the Good." Rather, we construct our own "truths" from the intuitions, perceptions, and reflections that arise in our experience. Free from metaphysical antecedents, we are not born into an existing reality but construct it from our intuitions and experiences. There remains an Existentialist tendency in Postmodernism that emphasizes a personalism that is highly suspicious of the claims of objective rationality.

Karl Marx

Though Postmodernists would question and likely reject Karl Marx's universalizing dialectical materialism and his claims about the inevitability of class war, revolution, and the eventual construction of a classless society, much in his ideology informs their thinking. (Marx is more thoroughly discussed in a later chapter.) French Postmodernists sought to construct a version of Marxism that was free of the earlier connections between Marx and Soviet Communism. One important theme that entered Postmodernism from Marxism is the concept of **false consciousness**, an ideological smoke screen constructed by dominant classes and conveyed by their media and educational agencies to confuse and mislead oppressed people from recognizing who and what is exploiting them. False consciousness, for example, is the workers' false belief that they are free economic agents who are freely contracting to sell their labor on an open market. In reality, workers are imprisoned by the economic structures controlled by the upper economic classes.[3] False consciousness can be instilled, according to Marx, by the capitalist-controlled information systems—the media, entertainment, religious, and educational institutions and processes. Peter Sloterdijk identifies "enlightened false consciousness" as a pervasive symptom in postmodern society's ways of thinking.[4] In education, those holding political and economic power construct a curriculum of "official knowledge," the approved subject matter that is transmitted to the young to indoctrinate them in this false consciousness. Unless they are conscious that they are being indoctrinated, subordinate groups may mistake this imposition as a valid rendition of their situation.

Contemporary Postmodernists

In this section, we discuss the ideas of two leading contemporary philosophers, Jacques Derrida and Michel Foucault, who have shaped Postmodernism.

Jacques Derrida.   Jacques Derrida (1930–2004), an Algerian-born French philosopher, is often identified as a major contributor to Postmodernism, especially to poststructuralism, because of his development of **deconstruction** as a method of analyzing texts. To understand Derrida's deconstruction, we first need to understand how he views the construction of philosophical or texts in Western civilization. Examining Western philosophy's origins in ancient Greece, Derrida found that philosophers such as Plato and Aristotle, and their later disciples, sought to discover the general rational purposes, or **logos**, they believed were inherent in and that ordered and governed the universe. From its classical Greek origins, later philosophers continued to search for universal principles of rationality, inherent in the universe itself. They believed that the human being, as defined by Aristotle, possessed a reasoning mind that made it possible to discover the logi, the universe's rational principles, and act according to them. To deconstruct logos, it is necessary to analyze its origins in the ancient Greek philosophical tradition and its continual replay in Western philosophy. What is assumed to be the principle of rationality in the universe, according to Derrida, is not found in an objective reality but is rather how philosophers represented it in their writings, their texts. A text, as used by Derrida and the Postmodernists, may be, but is not necessarily, a work in print. Many philosophical works are unscripted, or recorded; other texts may be oral dialogues, or movies, videos, plays, or some form of cultural representation. In direct educational terms, a text can be a curriculum guide, a syllabus, a video, or a book, including a textbook.

Despite continued attacks on metaphysics by the Pragmatists and now by the Postmodernists, Derrida finds that metaphysical assumptions about rational principles, the logi, remain deeply embedded in Western culture. Indeed, meaning in Western cultures is logocentric, centered in and often controlled by these inherited metaphysical principles. Deconstruction is a method of getting inside and penetrating the texts to explore different shades of meaning in addition to those designated as an officially sanctioned canon. Getting inside the text is to: (1) identify its logocentric principles; (2) trace the origin and development of meanings conveyed, with special sensitivity to justification by appealing to the logi; and (3) determine how the knowledge claims, meanings, and interpretation in the text affect our ideas, beliefs, interpretations, and meanings. The aim of deconstruction is not simply to engage in language analysis but to understand how texts, rather than reflecting metaphysical principles, are historically and culturally specific constructions that involve political power relationships. The idea of power as an instrument of control is a persistent theme in Postmodernist philosophy.

For Derrida, philosophers need to liberate themselves from metaphysics and its remnants and stop their futile efforts to construct colossal worldviews, new world orders, and the like that claim to be based on some kind of universal principles. What they can do is to conduct a rigorous analysis, a deconstruction, of the language used to provide the theoretical foundations for social, cultural, political, economic, and educational institutions. These supposed foundations are conveyed in discourses—oral and written narratives—that promise to explain reality and are used to justify allegiance to existing institutions and situations. What we must deal with is not reality, but rather how the authors, the originators and users of the discourses, have interpreted reality. Because interpretation comes from a person's experience, we need to examine how individuals and groups have used language to construct meaning, to interpret, and to justify their position in society.

The philosopher's task is to deconstruct ideas about institutions and culture in order to uncover the rationale builder's underlying assumptions, presuppositions, and meanings. These rationales, often referred to as the foundations of culture, are expressed in the language of a text and assume the authority or special status of a canon. All discourse, including philosophical, historical, and scientific ones, is presented in texts. A text, itself, is not reality but what an author may think is true and valuable. Deconstruction involves identifying and explaining the author's meaning, her or his version of reality, as well as what the reader brings to the text in terms of experience. To deconstruct a text means to identify and analyze, "unpack" the author's assumptions and meanings as they are expressed by word choices, examples, metaphors, and puns.[5] In other words, deconstruction involves analyzing language as it is used in social relationships; it is a socially charged study in grammar.[6]

Derrida coined the term *differance,* to combine the words *difference* and *defer.* The efforts to deconstruct language involve identifying and analyzing the differences in how people understand and use language. To deconstruct requires us to find the differences in meanings and relationships in the various voices engaged in discourse. Language is a complex body of differences and nuances in which the meaning of a word can be determined only by comparing it and contrasting it with other words. Establishing meaning requires the act of interpreting—using other words to tell us what it is not.[7] At the same time that the search for meaning takes places in its various shades and nuances, there is a need to defer final results in establishing a central meaning because of the complexity, fluidity, and drift of language—how it is used at different times in different places.[8]

Michel Foucault. Michel Foucault (1926–1984), a French social philosopher and historian, shaped Postmodernism through his analyses of history, society, culture, politics, economics, and education. Foucault argues that notions of "truth" are not universal but arise in historical contexts and express power relationships in society, politics, economics, and education. To understand Foucault's complex philosophy, we begin with three of his major working premises: (1) the relationship of "truth" and power; (2) **"regimes of truth"**; and (3) the use of discourse.

Foucault, like Derrida, dismisses the possibilities of universal truth, based on traditional metaphysical speculation, but also the claims of the eighteenth-century Enlightenment that science and social science can provide objective and unbiased truths. Foucault rejects the Enlightenment assumption that rational individuals, using the scientific method, can discover the truth as an objective body of knowledge. He also discounts the Enlightenment premise that this kind of objective knowledge is open to all and that it can fairly and equally benefit all people.[9] The various social and behavioral sciences that originated in the Enlightenment and were developed in the modern period—sociology, economics, political science, anthropology, psychology—professed to be objective, empirical, and scientific ways of describing and examining human behavior. Note how much of modern educational theory and practice rests on these social sciences. From this allegedly objective research, social scientists developed prescriptions, guidelines that told how "normal," socially sound, good citizens—men, women, and children—should behave. Modern social sciences rest on probability and predictability—which in turn rest on the human being as a complex of observable, predictable, and measurable behaviors. As such, behavior can be controlled and manipulated, rewarded and punished.

The social sciences categorized people into roles and functions based on a standard of the normal, which led to norms or rules of behavior. Just as there are approved norms there are also disapproved forms of deviant behavior. Foucault examined how institutions such as law courts, hospitals, prisons, and asylums are controlled by the officially sanctioned norms established by experts.[10] Legal norms determine who is innocent or guilty of crimes (indeed what constitutes a crime); medical norms determine who is healthy or sick and how patients should be treated; psychiatric norms determine who is sane or insane, and so on. Depending on the degree of deviancy from the norm, individuals in these categories could be remediated or reeducated and, if need be, institutionalized in hospitals, asylums, and prisons. In setting norms, people can be classified into those who meet the norm and act appropriately and those who do not and behave inappropriately. The categories of "the others" are those who need to be confined, helped, corrected, or remediated. Note that schools, too, are institutionalized settings, designed to "educate" an age-specific group of children and adolescents. For example, historically defined concepts of childhood and adolescence were used in defining an appropriate education for these stages of life and then creating the appropriate institutions—schools in which to perform this education. Rather than analyzing institutions from the perspectives of the experts who control them, Foucault analyzes them from the viewpoint of those subject to the experts' norms—prisoners, patients, and plaintiffs. Schools should be analyzed from the perspectives of students—children and adolescents. The kind of analysis Foucault recommends offers an alternative to what is proclaimed as officially appropriate. The process of empirically based standard setting, characteristic of the modern era, became a way in which one group categorized, manipulated, and exercised power over others. The Enlightenment orientation, especially its claims to scientific objectivity, merely represents the discourse used by a regime of truth, by those who hold power.

Foucault examines how claims to possess "truth" are used to legitimate power relationships. To know, or to possess, the truth asserts a claim to knowledge that others do not have. At certain historic periods and in certain places, however, the truth–power formula favors, or empowers, some groups over others.

In his historical analysis, Foucault looks for what he calls the **episteme**, the assumptions that govern the intellectual outlook of a society at a particular time in history. These assumptions condition how people view their society, its social and economic conditions, and its institutions. They set the parameters for how discussion is to take place. For example, in the medieval period, church-approved doctrines set the framework for discourse. In the Soviet Union, under Communism, Marxist-Leninism set parameters for discussion. To be discussed, a topic had to fit the parameters set by the episteme. These truth–power relationships produce "regimes of truth," the ideologies, institutions, and practices by which people control, regulate, govern, and even define, each other. The truth–power regime implies that those who hold and use power have a right to do so because they know or possess some truth, unknown to others. Texts that contain the claims of one group over another are used to justify the power relationships.[11] By analyzing the texts, the power relationships can be stripped to their essentials—of who is exerting power and why they are doing so.

In understanding the truth–power relationship, Foucault is not arguing that relationships should be free of power. Nor is he arguing that it is always good to overthrow the power relationship. Rather, he is advising us that such a relationship is always present in social discourse, institutions, and relationships, no matter how often power holders claim that they are fair, objective, or disinterested. He advises us to recognize the existence of power in the relationship. He wants to challenge those who claim to know universal truth, to be altruistic in its application, and to justify their actions on universal principles. Instead of one truth that is universally manifested, he argues that there are many claims to truth, found in all societies, in all situations. There are multiple discourses, representing multiple regimes of truth. Discourses can justify one group's claim to truth but also can be used by another group to resist it.[12] Relationships of truth to power are slippery and shifting, with one group's claim ascendant and the other's suppressed or inarticulate. The interplay of discourses, each representing a truth claim by some groups, can be examined. A consequence of applying analysis to discourse is to locate the relationships of knowledge and power in a given society at a given time. Perhaps, those who are currently marginalized can use their insights to resist the imposition of dominant groups and liberate themselves. Analysis of truth–power relationships might be used to identify those that are negative and pernicious and those that have possibilities of liberation and to avoid the rule of dogmatism by those who claim to know it all.

Postmodernist Themes

Deconstructing Metaphysics and Universal Principles

Postmodernists are most concerned with deconstructing, actually deflating, the claims of scientific objectivity that stem from the Enlightenment, but they also attack the belief that there are universal metaphysical principles that transcend particular cultures and times. Postmodernists are particularly interested in deflating the claims of education that are based on eternal truths that are neither limited by, nor dependent on time, and universal, not bound by place or culture. They contend that claims to be universal and eternal statements of truth and value actually construct philosophical fogs, "cover-ups" of social conflict, that justify the power of one group or class over another subordinated group at a particular time in history.

For Postmodernists, many philosophical works of the past, such as Plato's *Republic,* Aristotle's *Nichomaechean Ethics,* and Aquinas's *Summa Theologiae,* are metanarratives constructed by a ruling group at a particular time in history rather than universal, totalizing, metaphysical explanations of reality, truth, and values. Plato's Idealism, for example, provided a conservative rationale against the rival sophists who represented a more democratic, but materialist, culturally relative orientation in Athens. They argue against those, including Hutchins and Adler, who argued that the great books of Western civilization should frame the culture core in education.

Postmodernists challenge the grand philosophical systems purported to explain reality as an architecture of the universe and the metaphysical assumption that an ultimate ground of being, a transcendent cosmic reality, exists beyond and above the physical world. The most concerted attack on philosophical systems is directed against Realism, especially its assertion that there is an objective reality that is knowable and this knowledge is the best guide to human conduct. For Postmodernists, traditional philosophical systems, resting on metaphysical foundations, are not explanations of ultimate reality. They are rather the discourses—the written texts—produced by the intellectuals of a given period of history that rationalized and explained the knowledge that gave power to some but denied it to others. Metaphysics has helped to impose constraints from which, with its demise, we are well liberated.[13]

Postmodernism reacts against the traditional philosophers' call for us to think deeply, to search for, to speculate, and to penetrate the surface of culture to find the ultimate, metaphysical nature of reality. For them, there is no ultimate nature of reality to find. Their reaction discounts those (e.g., Plato, Aristotle, Aquinas, and Emerson) who looked for a deeper metaphysical understanding that penetrates the surface to reach the true nature and meaning of underlying reality. These traditional philosophers misled people by proclaiming grand universal metaphysical designs, which the Postmodernists call **metanarratives**, which argue that there are universal and timeless principles that are superior to personal, group, and cultural norms.[14] We do not need to try to find some deeper hidden reality that lies beneath the surface of our experiences, such as Plato's "Form of the Good" or Emerson's Oversoul, because we can trust ourselves in our personal and communal relationships.

Postmodernism is not the first philosophy to reject metaphysics. Earlier in the twentieth century, the Pragmatists—William James, Charles Peirce, George H. Mead, and John Dewey—had abandoned metaphysics as empirically unverifiable "non-sense." Dethroning metaphysics, the Pragmatists put their trust in scientific method, to either verify or disprove the claims to "truth," now reduced to a probability or a warranted assumption rather than a universal. The scientific method, derived from Enlightenment thinking, was proclaimed to be a public, dispassionate, and objective process of solving problems. Postmodernists, unlike the Pragmatists, reject the claims that the scientific method is really objective. It is "scientific" and "objective" only for those who share the commitment to use its terminology. Scientific knowledge is merely what is acceptable to a particular group, the circle that shares a commitment.[15]

Postmodernists look with disdain at philosophers who try to seek the universalizing authority of grand metaphysical narratives, single processes of empirical verification, or the development of an all-embracing social consensus. They are highly skeptical of metanarratives, the universalizing and legitimizing bodies of theology, philosophy, and scientific theory. You may ask why the issue of metanarratives concerns us as teachers. The concern is that you or members of a group do not fit in or have a place in the metanarrative and are marginalized by it. Also, think about the power of those who proclaim a metanarrative as official, legitimate knowledge and have the means to disseminate it.

Instead of grand, universalizing metanarratives, Postmodernists look to the specific discourses or local narratives constructed by individuals in their immediate relationships in their groups and communities—the different expressions found in the varieties of human experiences. Each of these different expressions exists freely without a need to constrain experience by conformity to some contrived universal principles.

The Postmodernist call to celebrate the different expressions of human experiences in ourselves and local communities (racial, ethnic, and gender groups) has important implications for education. It relies on an Existentialist orientation to live and let live and not to fear those who are different from us as threats but to learn about and respect them. The Postmodernist antagonism to universalize—be it in the guise of metaphysics, empiricism, or consensus—contributes to multicultural education that celebrates and respects the differences between ethnic, racial, and gender experiences. Rather than being deduced from some grand metaphysical system or exclusive reliance on a single method of inquiry, such as the scientific method, the curriculum should be constructed from the "lived experiences," the autobiographies of persons and groups. The school, in the Postmodernist scenario, is the gathering site for members of the local community to voice their experiences and share their life stories. The school should be locally managed by its teachers, adminis-trators, students, and community members.

Critique of the Enlightenment

You may well ask—why give such attention to critiquing a long gone historical period such as the Enlightenment? In education, especially in the ideology of American public school-ing, the Enlightenment has had a pervasive impact. The Enlightenment philosophers believed that it was possible for the human race to improve their life—their society, politics, and economy—if they applied the scientific method to solve problems. It was possible for human society to be progressive and look to a better future. Education needed to be scientif-ically based, forward-looking, and progressive and not tied down to the obsolete classical and religious dogmas of the past. Pragmatism, the philosophy, and Progressivism, the ideol-ogy, which were so important in shaping modern American education, were permeated by the belief in progress and the scientific method. (See the chapters on Pragmatism and Pro-gressivism for the emphasis on the scientific method.)

Although the liberal Enlightenment ideology proclaimed "liberty, equality, and frater-nity," Postmodernists allege that it was subverted to become the political and economic justi-fication for a new capitalist ruling class, the bourgeoisie or middle class that overturned the privileged political position and ascribed social status of landed aristocrats. Science com-bined with technology generated the nineteenth-century industrial revolution, which contin-ued through the twentieth century and now drives globalization. Science, touted as an objective mode of inquiry, was applied to technology, which generated a spiraling cycle of new techniques to exploit natural resources and produce goods for a mass market of consumers. Linked together, the Enlightenment ideology, scientific rationales, and technolog-ical discoveries gave the capitalist class the economic power to control society and politics and to dominate other classes and groups either through the domestic structures in their home countries or through imperialism and colonialism in other countries, especially those in Latin America, Africa, and Asia. The capitalists, now the ruling class, constructed canons, the vari-ous texts, that through philosophy, ideology, politics, literature, and education served as ratio-nales for their taking of power and subordinating other groups such as the working class in their own countries or indigenous people, usually of color, in their colonies overseas. Post-modernists argue that we have moved into the postindustrial era in which industrial produc-tion has been replaced by a service and information age of rapid communication, especially by electronic means. Postmodernists are especially interested in critically examining, or in deconstructing, the canons, which pass for philosophical or ideological rationales, that justify, often in universal terms, the control of one class over another. Now that we are in the infor-mation age, they are concerned with who controls a text—how information is selected and transmitted by the media and by the school in a curriculum.

De-Enlightening the Enlightenment

In the Postmodernist critique, the Enlightenment theorists wrote the texts that repre-sented modern philosophy and ideology. (A text is the format such as a document that represents a group's rationale.) Enlightenment philosophers argued that humans using reason, enlightened by science, can discover the natural laws on which the universe, the world, and society operates. Enlightenment philosophers claimed that the scientific method, relying on empirical discovery and verification, is the most accurate instrument to discover the laws, the principles, that govern humankind's physical and social worlds. The application of these principles to society, politics, economics, and education will bring about continuing progress.

Although many Enlightenment theorists rejected traditional philosophical metaphysics, they constructed a new metanarrative that proclaimed that reasonable people, by using science, can discover the principles that govern the universe and by doing so can bring about progress. Postmodernists see the Enlightenment philosophers' turn to reason as a mechanism of social and political control. By asserting that certain knowledge claims are reasonable, the Enlightenment theorists also ruled that other claims are unreasonable. Those who do not follow the rules of reason are irrational and can be either ignored, purged, or marginalized. Postmodernists assert that what is claimed to be universal natural law is really a construction made by certain people (in the case of the Enlightenment, the scientific and political elites) at a given time in history. Postmodernists assert that the scientific method is but one of many methods of constructing one of many "truths." Postmodernists assert that the prescriptions for human behavior are established by groups, not nature, and are contested between dominant and subordinate groups. The groups or classes in control of society at a given time try to set standards and values that they claim are universal but, in reality, are a specific means of social, political, and educational control.

Postmodernism, like Pragmatism, is a relativistic philosophy, with an epistemology that rejects universal, absolute, and eternal truths and values. For Postmodernists, the claim of any statement to be true or valuable depends on the culture, time, situations, and conditions in which it is made. The claim to be representing what is true or valuable must be communicated by language—words presented in speech or in writing—in the form of a text. The language that conveys the claim can be deconstructed or "unpacked" to reveal the time and setting in which it was stated and its author's socioeconomic and political status and motivations. Thus, much Postmodernist deconstruction looks for clues that explain motivation such as the author's sex, race, class, or ethnicity. For example, is the statement being made by a male or female, a person of color or a white, a member of the upper or lower socioeconomic class? Whereas a universalist such as an Idealist, Realist, or Thomist says that the truth is what it is regardless of who states it, the Postmodernist argues that what is claimed to be the truth depends on who is making the statement. In education, the "official knowledge" conveyed through the school's mandated and approved curriculum represents the opinion of those in charge of the school system rather than those outside of the corridors of power.

The Postmodernist holds that no universal knowledge exists but rather that there is a variety of claims to knowledge, which arise in different cultural and social contexts. Although certain cultures may claim to be superior to others, the argument for preferential treatment is a fiction. In the variety of cultures, no one is better or preferred. Even within a particular society, or country such as the United States, various groups are contesting for control of the social, political, and educational systems. Those who base the curriculum on one culture (e.g., Western culture for the Perennialists) in reality are using schools to dominate other cultures. Postmodernists argue that the variety of different cultures in American society should be recognized in a celebration of multicultural differences, with respect for local and long-suppressed views and voices.[16]

Canons and the Canonical

In situating Postmodernism, we have emphasized its attack on the power that the Enlightenment has had in Western thought, especially on philosophy, ideology, and education. Postmodernists see the Enlightenment's endorsement of reason and science as a method to discover objective truth as a rationale contrived by a dominant class to justify their power and control. Postmodernists call these rationales, as represented in Enlightenment texts, **canons**.

A discussion of the genealogy of a canon's meaning illustrates its power in establishing meaning as a rationale for authority and power. The claims to authority, expressed in a canon, have an interesting origin and development that helps one to understand how canons are used to rationalize why power is held by some and not by others. In ancient Greece, a canon (*kanon*) was a rod used to measure something, especially property. Measurements based on the *kanon* were regarded as legally accurate in establishing the dimensions of something, especially property boundaries and limits. By the fourth century, canon had taken on a broader meaning as an authoritative rule or a law that was to guide and govern correct interpretations and practices. During the Middle Ages, the term *canonical* was used to designate an authentic religious text, officially sanctioned by the church. For example, the governing legal code of the Roman Catholic Church is referred to as canon law. Over time, a more general use of *canon* developed to refer to the great texts that have official acceptance and carry authority in a culture, political order, or in a learned discipline. For example, the "great books" curriculum, espoused by the Perennialists, is given an authority as "classics" that other lesser books, especially "popular" ones, do not have.

Although the discussion of canons may seem to be overly theoretical, it is important in establishing policy and practices in society, politics, and education. A canon gives something authority; in education it claims that an established interpretation of a discipline or subject matter is correct; if that interpretation is correct, then alternative versions are likely to be incorrect. Note that a great deal of teaching in traditional schools is devoted to correcting what is incorrect in students' work. This correcting is done so that students' work corresponds to the canon—to the correct interpretation. In other words, a canon sets a standard.

Going back to the word's origins, a canon marked something off; it established a parameter or a boundary. It indicated what belonged within a boundary. First used to mark property boundaries, the concept of a canon was extended to set the definitions and boundaries of bodies of knowledge. In the traditional curriculum, these boundaries set off one subject from another and identify who is an expert in that subject and what texts are canons, the bases of official knowledge. Postmodernists attack the concept that disciplines and subjects are demarcated by boundaries and that teachers and students to do their work properly have to stay within boundaries. In contrast, Postmodernists urge teachers and students to freely cross these arbitrary boundaries erected by educational elites.

If we think of the curriculum as a contested area as the Postmodernists do, we can see how the construction and deconstruction of canons operates. There have been many arguments about the need for a cultural core in education. Some advocates of a core curriculum refer to the core as containing those ideas or subjects that are indispensable to an educated person. Some, like the Perennialists, base the core on what they identify as the major ideas that have shaped Western civilization. Still others call for a core that represents what they call "traditional American values"—family, home, and country. Postmodernists challenge these canons that stand for a cultural core as setting boundaries not only between subjects but also between people. They see them as representing male-dominated, **Eurocentric**, Western culture, which takes on an added capitalist dimension in the United States. They contend that these canons have no intrinsic authority or value over alternatives. It is time, they argue, that the works of underrepresented groups—African, Asian, Hispanic, and Native Americans; feminists; those in the so-called third world; and gays and lesbians—be included in the curriculum, even at the core, if there is still to be a core.

Postmodernists regard canons as being constructions by a given group or class at a particular time in history and not being endowed with an enduring, universal authority. As mere historical pieces, they can be analyzed, or deconstructed. In deconstructing a canon, or text, Postmodernists ask: What events and situations gave rise to the canon? Who gives a canon a privileged status in a culture or society? Who benefits from the existence and acceptance of a canon? Why do lists of canons in a particular culture exclude those who are underrepresented and marginalized in a given society? Postmodernists want to know the criteria being used to establish some but not other works as canons. They argue that the criteria for analyzing and appraising a canon are internal to the work. There is no legitimate external—spiritual, natural, or universal—criteria for giving a canon a privileged authoritative status in a culture and society. Postmodernists conclude that canons are established—raised to authority—by those who hold social, economic, political, and educational power.

Discovering or Constructing Knowledge— Epistemological Questions

Important for epistemology and methods of teaching and learning is the question: Do we discover or do we construct our knowledge? For example, Realism, especially Scientific Realism, asserts that what we know is objective, or outside of us. Our knowledge, Realists say, is based on what we discover through our observations and that, by using science, as the Enlightenment philosophers claimed, we can discover the structures, functions, and patterns of how nature works. For example, we can discover how the blood circulates through the body and the patterns of bird migration during the year. The popular film *March of the Penguins,* for example, which documents the nesting, birth, and nurture of generations of emperor penguins, was a way to discover this bird's patterns of behavior. In teaching and learning, the "discovery method" is based on the assumption that there is something outside of us, outside of our minds that we can know if we use the correct methods.

Postmodernism argues against traditional philosophies' metaphysical claims that we can know objects as they correspond to reality. Rather than looking outside of human experience and history for truth, we need to look within the human past and present to see how claims to truth have been constructed and expressed. What people claim to be true is meaningful only when it is expressed in conceptual and symbolic form through language. Concepts do not correspond to objects existing in some supernatural or metaphysical realm, as the Realists claim, but are human constructions based on experience. Knowledge claims are constructions used to explain and control human life and institutions. Claims to knowledge, the constructions that explain and control, are expressed symbolically using sounds, signs, gestures, words, and language.[17] These language-expressed and language-bound claims of truth can be approached, dissected, decoded, or deconstructed by "unpacking" what is asserted to be true. Working through language reveals that what purports to be knowledge is a human-made construction. The language that a group uses to express its knowledge beliefs is a construction, a text that involves how the language is to be expressed and used. Language expression and use is a means of controlling knowledge and of giving control to those who purport to understand and interpret it. Historically, certain texts or metanarratives—religious and philosophical works, great books, the classics—have been given a prominence and status as speaking of universal truths to a universal audience that is transgenerational. Challenging the universal claims of these metanarratives, Postmodernists contend that they, too, are the constructions of once-powerful historical elites that are now used to empower new elites by investing them with the signs and symbols of the old order. Further, there are many ways to describe human experience, each of which has its own validity, rather than those that claim to speak in universal terms.

Closely related to the attack on metanarratives is how the Postmodernists conceive of language. The metanarratives in the Western cultural tradition, especially in philosophy, history, and literature, assert that the relationship between the great texts and the world reflects the structure of reality, civilization, and art. Postmodernists reject the assumption that words that describe this reality are valid definitions that mirror and accurately explain an objective reality. Instead, Postmodernists argue that the traditional language used to express beliefs about the universe, the world, society, politics, economics, and education are not accurate statements that correspond to reality but are social constructions arising from how a group decides to use them. Words are meaningful only in terms of the cultural systems of which they are a part.[18]

Deconstructing or decoding the text is a relentless effort to discern meaning and relationships. Deconstruction rests on the assumption that all claims to truth are relative and dependent on the intellectual and cultural outlook of the groups or individuals making the claim. Because claims to be stating something that is true are conveyed by language, Postmodernists are highly concerned with analysis of language. As they analyze language, they reject the assumption that the meaning of our words (their definitions), are fixed, final, and definitive. All statements require further statements and definitions. Language is variable, contextual, and shaped by its users. Indeed, every knowledge claim or statement can be deconstructed by looking at the various contexts in which it is used and how it is used. What did the text mean at the time of its origination or construction? What groups established and used the meaning of the text at its origination? What has the text come to mean over the course of history? What does the text mean at the present time for different groups? Turning to formal education, these questions focus on how curriculum is constructed. What texts represent official knowledge in the curriculum? How are these texts interpreted to establish and maintain the power relationships between different groups? What texts, meaning what experiences, are excluded? Postmodernists see the curriculum as a locus of struggle, a cultural war, between contending groups to establish knowledge claims and to assert power.

In contrast, "to discover," "to construct," as in constructionist psychology and instructional methods, means that we construct, make, or build what we know through our own explorations of our environment. As a construction, our knowledge is personal, subjective, and temporary, in that we keep revising it as we have more experiences. Unlike the discovery of knowledge, the construction of "knowledges" (note the plural use of the term) means that there is no one true knowledge but rather a variety of knowledges, each of which is meaningful to the person or group that constructs them. Again, it is important to note that these knowledge claims are all conveyed or represented by our use of language.

Philosophy of History

For Postmodernists, history is constructed by individuals and groups who write it in terms of their experience. For them, history is not the unfolding of the Absolute over time as Idealists contend; nor can it ever be an objective account of what has happened. Although revisionist histories may detect and attempt to revise earlier historical accounts, they, too, are subject to the same errors that plague all efforts to construct a "truthful" and "more accurate" account. This occurs because history is a set of competing stories, laden with myths and metaphors, that are more like literature, especially novels with fictional plots created by historians, than empirically grounded or documented accounts of the past. The sources on which history is based, primary sources and documents, are texts that can be deconstructed and have multiple meanings and interpretations. The past is simply what historians say it is and what they say can be disputed, reinterpreted, accepted, or rejected. It is story.

Dominant groups use history to validate their past actions and to use that interpretation of the past to legitimate their present practices and future projects. Dominant groups tend to impose their view of the past on others, especially marginalized groups. History, written by historians of the dominant group and made part of "official knowledge," can be used to maintain and extend the privileged position to exert control over marginalized people who are put in the historical situation of being a member of the "other" group. Historical accounts can set up a dichotomy between us and them—between members of lesser, more primitive, less developed (i.e., "less civilized") peoples and people in technologically-developed societies. Concepts such as the "other," the "primitive," the "less technologically developed," and the "non-Western," often found in the literatures of economics, political science, and education, on analysis reveal a stereotypic view of society in which the alternatives to these terms are regarded as higher and better and those included in these categories as subordinate and placed at the margins of institutions and society.[19] Still another example of the use of history to construct a false consciousness comes from the "official" history of American public education. For example, the educational establishment in writing the history of public education in the United States celebrates it as creating socioeconomic mobility and opportunity for all groups. In reality, Postmodernists would contend that the hidden history of public education is as much or even more about maintaining the socioeconomic status quo and of upper- and middle-class domination of lower socioeconomic classes. As Foucault argued, history examines the use of power in specific contexts. We study history by constructing a "genealogy" of the use of power and control. A genealogy provides historical understandings from within specific historical events, from the perspective of **eventualization**. Eventualization discounts the principle of uniformity of events and looks at breaks in the historical flow—those distinct and separate occurrences that are significant in how we define ourselves and organize our relationships. Events have multiple causation. Rather than looking for universal causal factors or forces to explain history, the challenge is to look for multiple influences within historical events or periods. Power is found in the manner in which people conduct and govern themselves and how they perceive and define themselves and the society in which they live. Situations such as power regimes that pass themselves off as necessary and historically determined are not the result of inevitable destiny but of human invention within specific historical contexts.

Postmodernists see a relationship between historical knowledge and power—who controls the interpretation of the past sets the standard for the present. They see traditional historical narratives—with a beginning, middle, and end—as constructions expressed by language that conforms to its own rules. For Postmodernists, the past has no beginning, middle, or end; it has no meaning except that imposed by historians. Historiography is an attempt to impose meaning on a meaningless past. Postmodernism questions historians' claims to be able to stand as unbiased observers outside of the flow of history. All historical accounts and interpretations are positioned and politicized. With its method of deconstruction, Postmodernism calls attention to sources, particularly to the questions of the conditions of their production and how they are used. Historians construct interpretations but never the past.[20]

For Postmodernists, genuine history, especially historical narratives or stories, are personal, local, and group accounts of past lived experience. There is no standard that exists "out there" such as reliance on historical method. The most genuine judgment that can be made is the meaning that the local story has for those who tell it. This assertion presents a different way of reading, writing, teaching, and learning history than has been done traditionally. As a local story, history begins at the grassroots, in the lives of students, in their families, and in their racial, ethnic, and language groups. What purports to be a national history, such as the history of the United States or France, is often a glossed-over presentation of selected events, designed to create an "official" and "privileged" account of the past that either ignores or marginalizes local stories.

Philosophy of Science

Postmodernists are more concerned with culture, literature, philosophy, and history than with science. Unlike the Pragmatists who share their relativism, Postmodernists are suspicious of the motives of those who emphasize the scientific method and empirical verification as objective and unbiased ways to construct warranted claims to truth. Dewey's insistence that the scientific method is the most reliable test of "truths" (i.e., warranted assumptions) for them is another effort to create a methodological metanarrative. Given their opposition to claims that truth is objective and "out there," Postmodernists are skeptical of scientists (e.g., Scientific Realists) who claim to construct theories describing reality. In particular, they attack the claims of Scientific Realists that (1) they can objectively describe the physical phenomenon that surrounds us and (2) scientific investigation is unbiased, objective, and a universal explanation of reality.[21] Postmodernists see scientific inquiry not as completely objective but rooted in the cultural and ideological locations and orientations of the scientist. For them, there are as many candidates for truth as there are individuals and groups who make truth claims. They are alert to how scientists are funded by powerful corporate elites who use the findings of science and technology to advance agendas of economic profit and international globalism. Scientists, especially those committed to empirical experimentation and public verification, contend that the validity of scientific claims needs to be free of politics and ideology. The question of what is science has important implications for science education. Should science be taught as a quest for empirically verified and testable assertions about reality, or should it be seen as highly influenced by politics, ideology, and economics?

Philosophy of Technology

The Postmodern era is called the time of the information society and of the technological revolution. Throughout society, politics, and education, technology has brought about a revolution in how information is defined, accessed, stored, retrieved, and disseminated. State and professional education mandates require that teachers and students be computer literate and that schools be linked electronically to the Internet and the World Wide Web. Postmodernists do not distrust technology and electronic information retrieval as a process, but they are suspicious of those who simplistically regard technology to be an instrument of liberated communications. While it provides a means for like-minded people to share information about oppressive conditions and to organize to liberate exploited people, technology, as a instrument, can be used to either empower or dominate. What is important to understand is that what is conveyed electronically is a text that needs to be deconstructed. Much of what purports to be information in reality is a formula for manipulative image-making by those in power to create a mass consumer-oriented society.[22]

Information conveyed by the media in terms of the "news," "factoids," interviews, and "infomercials," including visual images, either on the television or computer screen, is typically screened, selected, interpreted, and manipulated. Key questions are who decides that something is newsworthy, how much time should be allotted for its presentation, and when should it be transmitted? The events that we see on our television or computer screens or read about in print, though presented as unfolding on the scene as actual events, are often semifictionalized narratives, selected and edited for political or commercial purposes.[23] They are distorted by corporate business sponsors. Further, in the capitalist system, media control is concentrated in a few wealthy and powerful persons. The result is manipulated news, based on selected visual images, reaching a manipulated audience of consumers steeped in false consciousness. The mass audience, so conditioned by the mass media, seeks not to work at a more accurate portrayal of information but rather to buy television sets with larger screens or software that makes it possible to download programs more rapidly.

Postmodernists are alert to dangers that a mass technology presents when it is controlled by dominant groups; they also see that this technology, if critically used, can be an instrument of liberation. The World Wide Web and the Internet provide a means for persons to join in critical dialogues about their own uncensored analysis of issues and conditions in their communities. The "blogosphere," if used critically, can express a wide variety of opinions and transmit these opinions to other bloggers in almost any part of the world. The Internet, at this time, is an open forum for the free expression of ideas about any subject.

The educational issues created by a technologically manipulated mass society are myriad. How difficult it is for teachers to resist being caught up in the manipulative web of a managed technology. The same issues that relate to the impact of technology in the larger society also affect its entry and use in schools. Further, students, often spending as much time watching television or viewing computer programs, are all contaminated by the pervasive false consciousness that has been vividly and dramatically presented to them. Critical examinations of issues in schools pale in comparison!

Postmodernism and Education

False Consciousness Versus Lived or Authentic Consciousness

As indicated, Postmodernism emphasizes education as a critique of existing social institutions and conditions so that people can free themselves from domination. An important part of the Postmodernist critique is to deconstruct the texts—the official knowledge or approved subjects—that are used to rationalize the status quo. The official knowledge is approved by educational authorities, which for public elementary and secondary schools are boards of education, school administrators such as superintendents and principals, and curriculum committees. For higher education, the authorities are boards of trustees, university president, vice presidents, deans, and often committees of tenured faculty. The texts, conveying official knowledge, find their way into schools and colleges via national testing and state mandates, and through textbook publishers. Within this system, teachers are to transmit the official knowledge to students through lectures, discussions, and workbooks. In the system, teachers are held accountable for successfully transmitting the official knowledge to students. Successful transmission is registered on standardized achievement tests. When teachers succeed in transmitting the official knowledge, they are designated as competent by their supervisors in the educational bureaucracy; when they fail, they are judged incompetent and require remediation to improve their performance. Educational technology, such as computerized instruction, represents a way of making the transmission of official knowledge to students more current, rapid, dynamic, and colorful. Regardless of the method used, the aim is the same—to transmit official knowledge.

Official Knowledge as False Consciousness

The transmission of official knowledge in schools has two major effects. First, it provides the rationale that justifies the position of the dominant class or group; it states the reasons why this class's position is historically, economically, socially, politically, and often religiously, valid and justified. Official knowledge in the curriculum often is "privileged" and given hierarchical priority status. *Privileged* means that it is accorded a high status in the curriculum as better—more accurate, more scientific, more objective—than other academic subjects or educational experiences. Further, privileged knowledge is hierarchically ranked in priority—given more funding, more instructional time, and greater value than other subjects or experiences. Recall that Idealists and Realists argue that the subjects in the curriculum should be arranged hierarchically in terms of their generality, their abstract nature. In other words, regardless of students' interests or a group's needs, privileged knowledge has official preference and sanction.

The subjects that convey the official knowledge are typically history, literature, political science, economics, sociology, and psychology. From these subjects, elementary and secondary curriculum areas such as language arts, social studies, consumer education, and history are derived. Although they are part of the official curriculum, mathematics and the natural and physical sciences are less likely to carry the official ideology. However, the illustrations, cases, and examples used in mathematics and the sciences may convey the official ideology. Second, and very important, the transmission of official knowledge has the effect of creating a sense of false consciousness in the minds of dominated groups. All countries and societies have dominant and dominated groups: those dominated in American schools tend to be women; African, Asian, and Hispanic Americans; and the poor. Using the Postmodernist critique, we can identify four ways in which the transmission of official knowledge creates false consciousness: (1) reiterating universals and absolutes; (2) maintaining and transmitting social and cultural consensus; (3) transmitting the traditional curriculum; and (4) relying on "scientific" testing and standards to reinforce academic achievement that requires mastering the preceding items.

Reiterating Universals and Absolutes

For Postmodernists, the curriculum is a contested area that various groups seek to control. However, the dominant groups—typically white male, Euro-American, and upper and upper middle classes—have controlled it historically. The contemporary arena of curriculum-making has seen a struggle, a "cultural war" over what constitutes its required official core. The battle lines have been between those who want to perpetuate a Western cultural tradition and those who want a variety of multicultural experiences represented. Postmodernists take issue with the Western civilization canon that argues that education's major objective is to transmit the cultural heritage of great ideas, derived from the cultures of ancient Greece and Rome and Western Europe, to the young. Schools and colleges that mandate, or privilege, a curricular core derived from the canons of traditional Western philosophy, theology, literature, and history that claims their universal validity and applicability are engrafting "false consciousness" on the minds of their students.

The aim in asserting the supremacy of Western civilization is to form the intellectual matrix of the young and to root it in what are claimed to be universal truths and values. Some educators who argue for these universal canons are sincerely committed to them; they, nonetheless, are fostering a false consciousness on the young. Others, realizing these universal canons are obsolete and archaic, continue to indoctrinate the young in them to maintain their institutional positions of power and control.

Postmodernists argue for a multicultural perspective that cuts across, broadens, and integrates the humanities and social sciences to focus on what they call hitherto dominated peoples and voices and that gives a fuller account of women, working people, ethnic and racial groups, and includes other regions of the world along with the West. Rather than portraying a false universalism, the curriculum is particularized to reflect a variety of human experiences. Each culture has its own coherence, integrity, and logic and no particular culture or civilization is superior to another. In other words, there is an equality of experience rather than the hierarchically designed stratification of experience that locates Western above African or Asian, or male above female.

Maintaining and Transmitting Social and Cultural Consensus

A pervasive element in American public education, especially in public schools, is that it is based on a national consensus and, in turn, promotes, or builds, a general social consensus. Common-school leaders in the nineteenth century such as Horace Mann, Catharine Beecher, and Henry Barnard argued that public schools would be the welders of a great American feeling of national identity and the shapers of an all-embracing social consensus—an overarching agreement on the role of government, society, and the economy and on what constitutes appropriate behavior. The theory of consensus operates in two ways and is a key element in the public school philosophy/ideology. First, the presence of a consensus is regarded as necessary for the establishment, continuance, and support of public schools as well as other institutions of government, industry, and society. People need to agree that public schools are necessary for the common good, especially to educate people who are committed to the political and economic institutions and processes of American society. Second, public schools, once established, act as agencies that contribute to maintaining a national consensus—a shared agreement—on what to believe and how to act as Americans. The Postmodernist critique of the role and function of consensus in public education is that this broad agreement masks serious contradictions and conflicts in American society between dominant and subordinate classes and groups. Although many people in public education—administrators and teachers—know that the boasted consensus is false, they continue to give public allegiance, or lip service, to it, while harboring private doubts. The idea of a national consensus patches over and suppresses differences of class, gender, race, and ethnicity.

Maintaining the Traditional Curriculum

Still another instance of transmitting an "enlightened false consciousness" comes from those—often politicians, parents, organizations, and teachers—who seek to keep, maintain, and transmit the traditional curriculum. Those who fight curriculum change may point to education in the "good old days" when parents knew what the schools were teaching, when teachers controlled their classrooms, and when students obeyed, studied, and learned. Some define the traditional curriculum as the basics—reading, writing, arithmetic, history, geography, language (especially and often exclusively English), wholesome and uplifting literature, and science. The school milieu is charged with traditional values that reflect the family, patriotism, and the free enterprise economy.

In addition to the "good old days" approach, there is also another way of maintaining the traditional curriculum that is vested in the educational establishment—especially administrators and many teachers. The traditional curriculum is built around reiterating consensus values about American history and society throughout the system. The traditional curriculum presents "official knowledge" according to the school's curriculum guide, state mandates, or standards. The transmission of the official curriculum constitutes passing on and engulfing students in a false consciousness that minimizes their lived experiences or the experiences of their group. It becomes an "enlightened false consciousness" when teachers who understand that the old curriculum represents official knowledge that is often irrelevant for students continue to require it as rite of passage through the school system. They do so for a variety of reasons: to protect their positions and fields, because they are uncomfortable about change, or because they no longer care.

Relying on Standardized Tests

Still another instance of creating false consciousness comes from transmitting and requiring students to learn the "information," "subjects," or "knowledge" that purports to be the truth and then testing them to determine whether they have "mastered" the officially approved doctrines. With the standards movement and "no child left behind," standardized tests touted to be "fair," "objective," and "scientific" are administered to students. The test results are then used to indicate the degree of students' academic achievement and their teachers' competency in effectively transmitting official knowledge. The result is that false consciousness is legitimized as scientifically validated knowledge. Those who support standardized testing, including educators, do so because they may be carrying on an embedded false consciousness that, once learned, is difficult to unlearn. Although some educators may realize that the "official knowledge" is false, archaic, or inauthentic, they, nonetheless, publicly endorse and teach it as a comfortable way to maintain the status quo that ensures their position and authority.

The use of standards and standardized testing as a mandate illustrates the impact of a politically generated false consciousness on educational practice. It also illustrates how a canon is used to validate the mandate. The discourse used to validate the standards movement, especially No Child Left Behind, states as truth that: (1) all children, in a democratic society such as the United States, have a right to an education that is excellent and no child should be left behind; (2) an excellent education, a qualitative concept, is one in which students achieve academically; (3) academic achievement can be measured fairly and objectively, using the principles of science, by standardized tests; (4) these tests will identify those students who are achieving a quality education and those who are being left behind; (5) the tests will identify the schools that have a high record of academic success as well as those whose students fail to score well on the tests; (5) schools with high failure rates can be remediated; (6) if the remediation is unsuccessful, students in these schools can transfer to schools with higher test results with the assumption that this transfer will enable them to have an excellent education.

Using Postmodernist deconstruction, we can analyze the canon and the false consciousness that is operating in using standardized tests as measures of academic achievement to point to receiving an excellent education. It begins with political claims, based on a democratic ideology, that children have a right to an excellent education. An excellent education is a universalizing qualitative statement. Specifically, who defines an excellent education and is it excellent for all students? The general claim quickly shifts, however, to an assertion that standardized tests provide objective, scientifically unbiased findings, presented in impersonal statistics, about who is meeting and who is failing to meet academic standards. Now, the knowledge claim begins to relate to power relationships such as: Who is setting the standard? Who is mandating the testing? Who is making up the test? Who is interpreting the test results? How will the results be used? What roles do politicians, parents, teachers, and students play in setting standards and using tests to verify whether they have been met?

Based on the canon of scientific objectivity, the statistics about meeting or failing to meet the empirically measurable and verified standard discount the importance of individual specificity about the students taking the test. It discounts the importance of race, ethnicity, gender, and socioeconomic class.

Curriculum

Postmodernists critique the ways in which the curriculum has been organized in Western (including American) schools, according to which knowledge has been separated into either Aristotelian categories or on demarcations derived from Enlightenment science and social science. According to the Aristotelian categorization of knowledge, subject matters, reflecting metaphysical reality, correspond to the objects as they exist in nature. That is, an area of knowledge discloses something that exists in nature. Further, those subjects that are more theoretical and more abstract are more important, located higher in the curriculum hierarchy, and given greater priority in instruction than those that are more direct and immediate. (See the chapter on Realism for the hierarchical concept of curriculum.) For Postmodernists, Aristotelian categorization, though premodern, has had a lingering historical power in Western thought. Subjects are not an accurate representation of nature but rather represent how classical and scholastic elites constructed knowledge. For several thousand years, this Aristotelian categorization contributed to the control of formal education by dominant political aristocracies and religious elites. Domination, based on Aristotelian metaphysics, is still found in Realism, Thomism, and Perennialism.

In addition to rejecting the universals derived from premodern metaphysics, Postmodernists also reject the scientific construction of knowledge that began in the modern age with the Enlightenment. Growing out of their search to discover the natural laws that governed the universe and society, eighteenth-century theorists turned to empiricism, as in the case of John Locke, rather than to metaphysics as did the earlier Aristotelian Realists and Thomists. However, modern science and social science, too, represented a construction of knowledge by new elites—scientists, economists, and political scientists. The scientists of the Enlightenment and post-Enlightenment periods claimed that the scientific method, to be used correctly, had to be used in a neutral, uncommitted, and objective manner. Modern versions of science in the social studies, psychology, and education also claim to be scientific and objective. Postmodernists argue that scientific claims to objectivity are either a delusion or are contrived. Claims to knowledge, they allege, are never neutral but represent the establishment of a relationship of power between those who claim to know the truth and those on whom they impose their version of the truth. For Postmodernists, the modernist construction of knowledge, along with the language used to convey it, represented the strategy of modernist elites to take and keep power.

Both the premodern Aristotelian metaphysical categories and modern sciences and social sciences remain encased and encoded in subject-matter disciplines. The controlling elites have constructed "canons," texts that contain definitions, cases, and illustrations that demarcate subjects, boundaries, or borders, where a subject begins and ends. Like any boundary, these canons give a sense of ownership to the experts who control them and to the interests they serve. In academic institutions, the experts in each subject matter have constructed theoretical moats that act as impenetrable boundaries that protect their power and their "turf."[24] Often, educational reforms and efforts at change are weakened by academics who fight boundary wars to protect their subject matters and prevent curriculum reconstruction.

Based on an ideology stemming from the Enlightenment, the controlling elites, once colonialist, have fashioned a neocolonialist curriculum that is **Eurocentric**, patriarchal, and class-based. By subjecting the canons of the vested subjects to rigorous critical analysis, they can be seen as historically constructed rationales that justify dominant groups' racial, gender, and class biases. Once they are seen as rationales rather than as descriptions of universal truths, these canons can be deconstructed so that the purposes of those who originated them and use them can be examined. Further, the canons and the texts that convey them can be unmasked as the representation of a dominant class or group rather than having a larger, broader, universal legitimacy. With such official knowledge dethroned, it becomes possible to replace it with the representations of those groups, the marginalized, whose voices have been excluded by those who constructed what was passed off as official knowledge.

For Postmodernists, an important curriculum issue is the relationship between a discourse and the exercise of power. A discourse is a set of related, interlocking, and mutually supporting statements, which define and describe a particular subject. In curriculum, a discourse describes a subject matter. It is based on the belief that some authorities possess expert knowledge to set boundaries between subjects, to describe their structures, define their terms, construct appropriate interpretations and explanations, and select appropriate examples and illustrations. Such expertise gives the authority the power to define what belongs and what does not belong. More important, the authority has the power to determine what is an appropriate and inappropriate question in a subject. The power to set the range of questions determines the answers. For example, historians have the expertise to tell us what history is and political scientists to tell us what politics is. Literary critics tell us what literature is, and so forth. What is implied is that for each subject, there is a cadre of experts. These experts have the authority to set standards for a field. The relationships between discourse, experts, and power lead to demarcations in the curriculum.

To construct an authentic education, it is necessary to deconstruct and to restructure the curriculum. The Postmodernist educator is suspicious of certain catchwords or phrases such as *objective, unbiased, scientific,* or *neutral* that are used to justify the existing curriculum. Postmodernists attack the idea that the curriculum subjects are a means of introducing students to the bodies of knowledge that represent humankind's funded or refined experiences. Rather than inducting young people into the officially approved culture, the curriculum should feature experiences in which teachers and students unpack, deconstruct, and resist the transmission of approved information and knowledge. The teacher of history, for example, does not see history as a chronology with approved meanings. History is a "constructed" rather than an unbiased narrative about the past. It is important to ask whose past and whose interpretation is being conveyed in the history text; or whose story is being told in the literature course. The goal of Postmodernist teaching is to engage students in constructing their own history or writing their own literature. The science teacher will represent science not as a body of objective propositions about physical and natural reality but rather as a set of constructed propositions about the world that we are part of rather than one that exists apart from us. Scientific theories, like all theories, are human constructions.[25]

Instruction involves representation, a Postmodernist term that has a larger meaning for any kind of cultural expression or discussion. **Representation** refers to the "processes" that individuals and groups "use to interpret and give meaning" to their experience; this meaning is conveyed by "language, stories, images, music, and other cultural constructions."[26] Much teaching, especially the transmission of the official curriculum, involves making representations to students through language as teachers purport to provide students with descriptions of reality. However, the official curriculum—the approved representation—is only one version of reality, usually that of the dominant group in society. Teachers need to become conscious of the powerful role that they exercise and critical about the representations that they make. The official curriculum neglects the experience of marginalized groups, especially African, Hispanic, and Native Americans; women; and gays and lesbians. Rather than the transmission of officially approved knowledge, the process of representation needs to be used critically and reflectively to present a wider range of human experience.[27]

In terms of curriculum and instruction, Postmodernism and constructivism are compatible. Knowledge and subjects are constructed by human beings and are not a set of objective facts, concepts, or laws independent of the knower that is waiting to be discovered. Humans make knowledge rather than discover it. To express our constructions, we use language, which is also a construction.[28] Knowledge is not universal or eternal. As a human construction, it is always in a state of fluidity and is being reconstructed. Human understandings are tentative, incomplete, and imperfect, even though all of them may not be equally imperfect.

An important principle among Idealist, Realist, Essentialist, and Perennialist educators (especially in the humanities, literature, art, and music) is that students can develop new forms of aesthetic expression by first going through the historical and existing forms. In other words, aspiring student writers study the novels of important authors—Wharton, Steinbeck, Hemingway, Mailer, Vidal, and others who have been recognized in their genre—and find in their writing styles models that they can imitate, revise, and extend into their own writing. In the same way, aspiring artists are exposed to and study the important genres of art developed over time in order to imitate and extend them to their own modes of artistic appreciation and creation. This approach—a going through—differs from constructionism. Postmodernists would regard the designation an "important novelist" and "an important period of art" to be a form of privileging art that is similar to privileging knowledge. Some expert in an elite group of literary or art critics has made a determination that a novel or work of art is significant enough to be designated important and to be a model for students in these fields. In contrast, Postmodernists would regard the necessity of going through the models in aesthetics to represent a domination by imposing a standard on the aspiring artist's freedom to create his or her new style and mode of expression. New forms should not be regulated by older forms of artistic expression and aesthetic critique. There are myriad forms and modes of expressing the aesthetic sense. Further, there is no privileged standard for judging it.

Schools and Schooling

Postmodernists would take a critical look at schools, especially how they are organized and controlled. As educational institutions, public schools in the United States are agencies of the official social, political, and economic system. The canons that are part of the public school ideology purport that schools educate the children of all the people, provide for upward social and economic mobility, and are necessary to maintain and continue American democratic society. In deconstructing the public school ideology, Postmodernists contend that schools, especially as part of publicly controlled systems, represent places to represent official knowledge and maintain it by instilling it into the young. However, the schools, like other institutions, are used to reproduce a social order that is patriarchal in that it favors male dominance of women. They are Eurocentric in that what is represented as official knowledge is actually constructed by white people of European stock. They are capitalist in that private property and the corporate attitude are enshrined in the free market ideology. Given these official foundations, the dominance of white, European males is approved, reinforced, and reproduced in institutionalized education. Other groups (e.g., people of color, many women, and gays and lesbians) are excluded from the official narratives. They are placed at the margins of the schools and society.[29]

The organization of public schools typically is hierarchical, with rules, regulations, and procedures coming down from centralized educational bureaucracies to local schools and classrooms. The more schools are centralized and run by top-down bureaucracies the more pervasive are attempts at official control.

Postmodernism argues that schools should be local educational spaces in which local community experience is at the heart of constructing an informed consciousness of the people directly involved. In these local sites, students are to use their own voices and their own situated knowledge to understand and shape their own lives.[30] The educator's role is to help people to learn to use their own voices. Postmodernists want schools to be decentralized, as local educational spaces in which local communities—children, parents, teachers, and neighbors—decide what they want to learn, why they want to learn it, and how they will learn it—without the monitoring of administrators, experts, and consultants to make sure that external standards are being enforced.

Foundations of Education

Especially pernicious, contend Postmodernists, is the claim that scientific objectivity can be extended from the natural and physical sciences to the social sciences and education. Some experts in fields such as psychology, sociology, political science, and education claim that they can approach their areas of inquiry with scientific objectivity and arrive at disinterested knowledge claims. Postmodernists believe that such claims are feigned or false. All knowledge claims and the texts that convey them represent power relationships. Claims to objectivity are used to deflect critical analysis.

Postmodernism questions the possibility of foundations—the bodies of knowledge, usually history, philosophy, psychology, and sociology—that are designated as the theoretical base on which educational practice is derived. The foundations, too, are either metanarratives or the posturing at science, which holds the allegiance of those committed to the method. Rather than explanatory foundations, the real meaning of education is found in the subjective encounters of persons—teachers and students—in the classroom and schools. The foundations of education should be approached genealogically, with attention to the situations that gave rise to them—historically, philosophically, psychologically, and sociologically.

A Controversy over Power in Historical Representation

Throughout this book, I have challenged readers to reflect on their educational experiences to begin the process of constructing their own philosophy of education. As I was writing this chapter about Postmodernism, I recalled an episode in my own teaching that caused me to reflect on historical representations and how history is a source of power. I was teaching a course in the history of Western education and had finished lecturing about the ancient Egyptians and Greeks. My representation was generally following the conventional historical interpretation that ancient Egyptian civilization was a highly static despotism and that its major cultural legacy was its great architectural monuments. My interpretation saw Greek culture, especially Athenian democracy, as the cradle of Western civilization.

At this point, an African American student objected to my interpretation, saying that it had been challenged by the historian Martin Bernal, who claimed that the Greeks had appropriated many of their concepts about government, philosophy, the arts, sciences, and medicine from ancient Egypt.[31] Furthermore, the student said, the Egyptians, geographically located in North Africa, were an African people, and we need to look for the origins of Western culture in Egypt rather than in Greece. Though they recognize the interactions between Egyptians and Greeks, Bernal's critics contend that he greatly overemphasizes Egypt's influence on ancient Greece.[32] The student also

said that how we represent and interpret history is a means of exercising power. Bernal's interpretation would empower those who argue for a broader interpretation of Western history and education and would be a rationale for an Afrocentric curriculum. At this point, I admitted that I knew little about Bernal's interpretation and suggested that the topic was important enough to warrant further investigation. The students and I investigated Bernal's claims. I found a documentary on a video that examined Bernal's thesis and the counterarguments of his critics. We found that the Bernal thesis had generated a heated debate among historians. Some tentative findings indicated that Egyptian–Greek cultural contacts, particularly at Crete, introduced the Greeks to Egyptian mathematics and art. This intriguing historical controversy has important ideological significance. Whoever interprets the past gains the power of illuminating and shaping the present.

This episode, an event in my own interaction with students, brought to mind the Postmodernist argument that there is a relationship between discourse and power. It demonstrated how a discourse leads to related, interlocking, and mutually supporting statements, which define and describe a particular subject. For example, if Bernal is correct then the conventional underpinnings about the origins of Western civilization are put in jeopardy. At question is the issue of who is to construct interpretations and explanations in history.

Conclusion

Postmodernism is a provocative philosophy whose influence pervades contemporary thinking in philosophy, literature, art, the humanities, and education. It has support among some feminist theorists and multicultural educators. Simultaneously, it has sparked a sharp negative reaction by those who argue against its extreme relativism and its often dense and highly repetitive language.

Those who endorse Postmodernism see it as having a liberating power in its questioning of philosophical, political, social, economic, and educational systems that set the boundaries for our social roles. They endorse its challenge to the dominance of the boundaries, definitions, prescriptions, and proscriptions that the systems establish. Postmodernism has opened up and freed our thinking about gender, race, sexual orientation, and ethnicity. Its demands for the recognition and celebration of differences and the acceptance of others in society have shaped multiculturalism in education. In its relativistic pluralistic discourse, it warns against allowing one frame of reference to dominate education.

Critics see Postmodernism leading to a kind of social mitosis in which groups continually split off, go their own way, and construct their own systems of meaning without regard for any social or political commonalities. In such extreme pluralism, it becomes impossible to talk about a common good or a community based on the common good because the idea of a common is a universal that carries with it the repression of those who are uncommon. Because of the fear of domination, it becomes virtually impossible to create common government and a common school system and the means to adjudicate disputes according to some kind of common law. Without a central method of authority for adjudicating disputes, groups are left in isolation, living in their own spaces, and weaving their own conceptions about community and society.

Constructing Your Own Philosophy of Education.   Now that you have read the chapter on Postmodernism, will you use it in constructing your own philosophy of education? Will you use it to deconstruct and critique other philosophies of education? Do you see it as a possibility for infusion in your own philosophy of education?

Questions for Reflection and Discussion

1. Compare and contrast the concepts of "modern" and "postmodern." Are you a modern or a postmodern person?

2. Examine the statement "Some societies are advanced and others are primitive" from a Modernist and Postmodernist perspective.

3. Do you accept or reject the Postmodernist argument that the curriculum is a contested area? Explain your answer.

4. Do you agree with the critics of Postmodernism who regard it as failing to establish the common values that a society needs to function?

5. Reflect on the courses that you are taking or have taken at your college or university,

especially in literature, political science, sociology, and education. Do you find evidence of Postmodernism in how these courses are represented?

6. Reflect on courses dealing with women's education or multicultural education that you are taking or have taken at your college or university. Do you find evidence of Postmodernism in how these courses are represented?

7. Do you accept or reject the Postmodernist argument against claims to have universal truth and values?

Inquiry and Research Projects

1. Using deconstruction, examine a syllabus in a course in teacher education at your college or university.

2. Examine a textbook in world history, at either the secondary or higher level. Is the general interpretation Modernist or Postmodernist?

3. Do some research on No Child Left Behind by going to the text of the law that established it. Using deconstruction, try to determine the genealogy of the law: Who supported it? Why was it passed? What kind of power relationships does it establish?

4. Visit elementary and secondary school classrooms. Observe the kind of teacher representations that are taking place. How might a Postmodernist evaluate these representations?

5. Research the mission statement of the NCATE or another accreditation document relating to the teacher education program at your college or university. Using deconstruction, determine the genealogy of the statement. What kind of power relationships does it express? Does it endorse an "official" or "privileged" knowledge?

6. Watch the same television news station for a week and keep a log of what is covered and how much time is devoted to the particular coverage. Determine what kind of consciousness this representation creates.

Building A Postmodernist Vocabulary

Canon: an official text that has authority in a culture, political order, society, religion, or learned discipline.

Deconstruction: Derrida's method of penetrating and analyzing texts to explore their different shades of meaning to determine why they are officially privileged.

Episteme: according to Foucault, the assumptions that govern the intellectual outlook of a society at a particular time in history.

Eventualization: the distinct, separate, and multiple historical events that we use to define ourselves and organize our relationships.

Eurocentric: official knowledge, constructed by white people of European ancestry, that emphasizes their cultural and social contributions.

False Consciousness: the Marxist concept, appropriated by Postmodernists, of an ideological smoke screen constructed by dominant groups to distract oppressed people from a genuine consciousness about their exploitation.

Logos: the universal principles of rationality that traditional philosophers claim are inherent in the universe.

Metanarratives: the universalizing and legitimizing grand texts of theology, philosophy, science, politics, economics, and education that constitutes "official" knowledge.

Postmodern Condition: the cultural changes generated by the contemporary information and service society and economy.

Representation: the processes individuals and groups use to interpret and give meaning to their experience.

Regimes of Truth: according to Foucault, the ideologies, institutions, and practices by which people control, regulate, govern, and even define each other at different periods of history.

Internet Resources

For a discussion of Postmodernism and philosophy of education, access www.ed.uiuc.edu/EPS/PES-yearbook/95_docs/burbles.html.

For efforts to define Postmodernism, access http://plato.stanford.edu/entries/postmodernism.

For an overview of Postmodernism, access www.allaboutphilosophy.org/postmodernism.htm.

For a perspective on Postmodernism, access http://elab_eserver_org/hFL042.html.

Suggestions for Further Reading

Aronowitz, Stanley, and Henry A. Giroux. *Postmodern Education: Politics, Culture, and Social Criticism.* Minneapolis: University of Minnesota Press, 1991.

Ball, S., ed. *Foucault and Education.* London: Routledge, 1991.

Best, Steven, and Douglas Kellner. *Postmodern Theory.* New York: Guilford, 1991.

Butler, Christopher. *Post-Modernism: A Very Short Introduction.* Oxford, UK: Oxford University Press, 2002.

Cahoone, Lawrence E. *From Modernism to Postmodernism: An Anthology.* Oxford, UK: Blackwell, 1996.

Carr, D., ed. *Education, Knowledge and Truth: Beyond the Postmodern Impasse.* London: Routledge, 1998.

Connor, Steven. *Postmodernist Culture.* Oxford, UK: Blackwell, 1989.

Cooper, David E. *A Companion to the Philosophy of Education.* Malden, MA, and Oxford, UK: Blackwell, 2006.

Cooper, David E. *World Philosophies: An Historical Introduction.* Oxford, UK, and Cambridge, MA: Blackwell, 1996.

Derrida, Jacques. *Of Grammatology.* Baltimore: Johns Hopkins University Press, 1976.

Doll, William E., Jr. *A Post-Modern Perspective on Curriculum.* New York: Teachers College Press, Columbia University, 1993.

Foucault, Michel. *The Archeology of Knowledge and the Discourse of Language.* New York: Pantheon Books, 1972.

Foucault, Michel. *Power Knowledge.* Translated by Colin Gordon, Leo Marschall, John Mepham, and Kate Sopher. New York: Pantheon, 1980.

Giroux, Henry A. *Postmodernism, Feminism, and Cultural Politics: Redrawing Boundaries.* Albany: State University Press of New York, 1991.

Hassan, Ihab. *The Postmodern Turn.* Columbus: Ohio State University Press, 1987.

Jencks, Charles. *The Post-Modern Reader.* London: Academy Editions, 1992.

Kincheloe, Joe L. *Toward a Critical Politics of Teaching Thinking: Mapping the Postmodern.* Westport, CT: Bergin & Garvey, 1993.

Lyotard, Jean-Francois. *The Postmodern Condition: A Report on Knowledge.* Translated by Geoff Bennington and Brian Massumi. Minneapolis: Minnesota University Press, 1984.

Lyotard, Jean-Francois. *Toward the Postmodern.* Edited by Robert Harvey and Mark Roberts. Atlantic Highlands, NJ: Humanities, 1993.

Rose, Margaret. *The Post-Modern and the Post-Industrial: A Critical Analysis.* Cambridge, UK: Cambridge University Press, 1991.

Rosenau, Pauline M. *Post-Modernism and the Social Sciences: Insights, Inroads, and Intrusions.* Princeton, NJ: Princeton University Press, 1992.

Slattery, Patrick. *Curriculum Development in the Postmodern Era.* New York: Garland, 1995.

Endnotes

1. Friedrich Nietzsche, *The Will to Power,* trans. Walter Kaufmann (New York: Vintage, 1967).
2. David E. Cooper, *World Philosophies: An Historical Introduction* (Oxford, UK, and Cambridge, MA: Blackwell, 1996), p. 467.
3. Christopher Butler, *Post-Modernism: A Very Short Introduction* (Oxford, UK: Oxford University Press, 2002), p. 29.
4. P. Sloterdijk, *Critique of Cynical Reason,* trans. M. Eldred (Minneapolis: University of Minnesota Press, 1987), pp. xi, 5.
5. George R. Knight, *Issues and Alternatives in Educational Philosophy* (Berrien Springs, MI: Andrews University Press, 1998), p. 86.
6. Jacques Derrida, *Of Grammatology* (Baltimore: Johns Hopkins University Press, 1976).
7. Cooper, *World Philosophies: An Historical Introduction,* p. 473.
8. Howard A. Ozmon and Samuel M. Craver, *Philosophical Foundations of Education* (Columbus, OH: Merrill/Prentice Hall, 1999), p. 356.
9. Knight, *Issues and Alternatives in Educational Philosophy,* pp. 86–87.
10. Butler, *Post-Modernism: A Very Short Introduction,* p. 45.
11. Jennifer M. Gore, "Enticing Challenges: An Introduction to Foucault and Educational Discourses," in Rebecca A. Martusewicz and William M. Reynolds, *Inside/Out: Contemporary Critical Perspectives in Education* (New York: St. Martin's Press, 1994), p. 110.
12. Gore, "Enticing Challenges: An Introduction to Foucault and Educational Discourses," p. 114.
13. Cooper, *World Philosophies: An Historical Introduction,* p. 476.
14. David E. Cooper, "Postmodernism," in *A Companion to the Philosophy of Education* (Malden, MA, and Oxford, UK: Blackwell, 2006), p. 208.
15. Cooper, *World Philosophies: An Historical Introduction,* p. 476.
16. Cooper, "Postmodernism," p. 210.
17. Rebecca A. Martusewicz and William M. Reynolds, *Inside/Out: Contemporary Critical Perspectives in Education* (New York: St. Martin's Press, 1994), pp. 11–13.

18. Butler, *Post-Modernism: A Very Short Introduction,* pp. 17–18.

19. Edward K. Berggren, "Deconstruction and Nothingness: Some Cross-Cultural Lessons on Teaching Comparative World Civilization," in Rebecca A. Martusewicz and William M. Reynolds, *Inside/Out: Contemporary Critical Perspectives in Education* (New York: St. Martin's Press, 1994), pp. 24–25.

20. Peter Seixas, "Schreiber! Die Kinder! Or, Does Postmodern History Have a Place in the Schools?" in Peter N. Stearns, Peter Seixas, and Sam Wineburg, *Knowing, Teaching and Learning History: National and International Perspectives* (New York: New York University Press, 2000), pp. 19–37.

21. Butler, *Post-Modernism: A Very Short Introduction,* pp. 37–38.

22. Butler, *Post-Modernism: A Very Short Introduction,* p. 3.

23. Butler, *Post-Modernism: A Very Short Introduction,* pp. 110–111.

24. Martusewicz and Reynolds, *Inside/Out: Contemporary Critical Perspectives in Education,* pp. 3–4.

25. Cooper, "Postmodernism," p. 212.

26. Elizabeth Ellsworth, "Representation, Self-Representation, and the Meanings of Difference: Questions for Educators," in Rebecca A. Martusewicz and William M. Reynolds, *Inside/Out: Contemporary Critical Perspectives in Education* (New York: St. Martin's Press, 1994), p. 100.

27. Elizabeth Ellsworth, "Representation, Self-Representation, and the Meanings of Difference: Questions for Educators," pp. 100–101.

28. John A. Zohorik, *Constructivist Teaching* (Bloomington, IN: Phi Delta Kappa Educational Foundation, 1995), p. 11.

29. Angeline Martel and Linda Peterat, "Margins of Exclusion, Margins of Transformation: The Place of Women in Education," in Rebecca A. Martusewicz and William M. Reynolds, *Inside/Out: Contemporary Critical Perspectives in Education* (New York: St. Martin's Press, 1994), p. 152.

30. Michel Foucault, *Power/Knowledge,* trans. Colin Gordon, Leo Marshall, John Mepham, and Kate Soper (New York: Pantheon), 1980, pp. 81–83.

31. Martin Bernal, *Black Athena: The Afroasiatic Roots of Classical Civilization: The Fabrication of Ancient Greece 1785–1985* (New Brunswick, NJ: Rutgers University Press, 1987), pp. 2–3.

32. For the ongoing controversy over ancient Egypt's possible influence on Greece, access "Ancient Egypt—Mathematics and the Liberal Arts," at http://math.truman.edu/~thammond/history/ancient egypt.htm.

7

Ideology and Education

Karl Mannheim (1893–1947), a leading sociologist who analyzed ideology's impact on society.

Chapter Preview

We examine ideology and its impact on education as an introduction for the chapters in which we discuss particular ideologies, their general significance for policy formulation, and their impact on education. Ever since the eighteenth-century Enlightenment, ideologies have been and remain potent forces for shaping and expressing social, political, economic, and educational ideas. The American Revolution in 1776, the French Revolution in 1789, the

Bolshevik Revolution in 1917, and the Chinese Communist Revolution in 1949 were, in large part, caused by ideology. Ideology has significant consequences for education. A particular ideology, for example, Nationalism, Liberalism, Conservatism, or Marxism, carries with it an ideological portrait of the preferred person. In painting this portrait with an ideological brush, the ideologist uses strokes that are historical, sociological, political, and economic. In reproducing the preferred person, the ideologist relies heavily on education. Informal educational agencies, especially the media—the press, motion pictures, radio, and television—are used, as well as the formal educational agency, namely the school, which recreates the prototype through the milieu (hidden curriculum) and the curriculum, the official and explicit program.

Since the rise of the modern nation-state, ideology has influenced policy making and policy implementation in many areas such as economics, science, technology, and education. Educational policies, and the programs and practices that they engender, have a direct impact on schooling.

Ideology serves to give theoretical legitimacy to a group's outlook, aspirations, program, and action. Rather than appearing to be based on personal or group special interests, ideological justification or legitimacy appeals to a higher and seemingly more generalizable, hence more applicable, authority. Often, the appeal to myth or history is used to legitimize policies and actions.

Ideology is also used to justify and determine the power relationships between contending groups. For example, contemporary educational policy in the United States has tended toward inclusiveness rather than exclusiveness; that is, it has worked to make educational opportunities more available to groups, such as African Americans, Native Americans, Hispanics, women, and people with disabilities, who were excluded in the past.

The impact of ideology on modern education is as profound as that of the traditional foundational disciplines of philosophy, psychology, and sociology. Since the eighteenth-century Enlightenment, individuals and societies have inhabited an ideological world. After the sociopolitical theorists of the Enlightenment and the revolutionaries in the American colonies and in France shattered the absolutist status quo, people first in Western nations and then throughout the world experienced a time during which ideologies originated and then competed for the loyalty of individuals, groups, and nations. With the emergence of nationalism and the rise of modern nation-states, schools were organized to function as parts of national systems of organized education. Further, the rise of social-class consciousness, stimulated by industrialization, also engendered competition between socioeconomic and political groups over the control of nation-states and their governmental and educational systems. As a result, much institutionalized education, or schooling, has been shaped by ideological outlooks and programs.

Ideology is so pervasive in our lives, in our group identification and membership, and in shaping our behavior that we are all touched by it. Consciously or unconsciously, we all share and are shaped by ideologies. To introduce our discussion of ideology, we describe and analyze the concept in order to study it and to use it as a guide, a cognitive map, to recognize an ideology and to determine how it functions in society and education. As we study the concept of ideology, we also need to recognize that we have been and are influenced by ideology in general and by specific ones in particular. We need to understand how an ideology originates, functions, and is sustained to appraise it. As teachers, we need to recognize and examine both the conscious and unconscious ideological assumptions that people use to interpret and to guide their social, cultural, political, economic, and educational behavior. The chapter covers the following topics:

- Ideology's ambiguity
- Historical origins of ideology
- Contributors to the study of ideology
- A stipulated definition of ideology
- Ideology, education, and schooling
- Ideology and philosophy

It is very unlikely that you will be constructing an ideology of education. However, you can use the concept of ideology as you construct your own philosophy of education. You might consider how ideology has shaped your ideas about education and how these ideas relate to your thinking about philosophy of education.

Ideology's Ambiguity

Ideology is a slippery and ambiguous term that arouses strong reactions in people. Although some people see ideology as a generally negative term, the same people are likely to be strongly committed to a particular ideology such as Conservatism or Liberalism. For these reasons, a stipulated definition is deferred until the history and background of ideology have been examined. But so that we have some initial terminology for our discussion, we begin with a preliminary working definition of ideology.

Ideology is often defined as the belief system of a group, usually based on a rendition of its past, which carries prescriptions for policy. Group beliefs arise primarily in a historical, social, political, and economic context, however, rather than in a metaphysical system that seeks to transcend such cultural particularities. The ideological interpretation of the past also suggests how this past has created and shaped the individual's and the group's present situation; from this interpretation comes a theory of social change that seeks to predict the course of future social developments. Ideologies are prescriptive in that they recommend policy guidelines for programs to move society in the desired direction.

Action-oriented, rather than merely theoretical, ideology is used to guide political, social, economic, and educational policies. Insofar as institutionalized education, especially schooling, is used as an instrument of achieving these policies, education follows an ideological direction.

Although some ideologists have sought to create a worldview that appears to transcend a particular cultural context, their abstractions are generally historically derived and represent the desire to give worldwide validity to a particular interpretation of the past. Indeed, the particular cultural heritage of the group holding the ideology often brings about a significant reshaping of the ideology. For example, the Chinese version of Marxism and the resulting policies reflect the Chinese cultural heritage and environmental conditions (geographical, political, social, and economic).

Historical Origins of Ideology

In this section, we examine the historical origin of the concept of ideology in the eighteenth-century Enlightenment and the rise of contending ideologies in the nineteenth century. The section includes an analysis of Karl Marx's critique of ideology.

The Origins of Ideology in the Enlightenment

In the eighteenth century, the *philosophes* of the French Enlightenment originally used the term *ideology* as an epistemology to explain how groups generate and use ideas. In contrast to theology and metaphysics, the *philosophes* hoped to create a science of ideas. For example, the French *philosophe* Étienne Bonnot de Condillac (1715–1780), denying that ideas were innately present in the mind as asserted by Plato, claimed that sensation was the source of all human ideas. In relationship to the development of ideology, Condillac and other *philosophes* asserted that human ideas did not originate in a metaphysical realm that was prior to human experience but rather resulted from the human being's sensory experience with the environment.

Antoine Destutt de Tracy (1754–1836) used the word *ideology* to designate his efforts to create a science of ideas that examined how people originated and used ideas to create institutions and to regulate their behavior.[1] Like the other *philosophes,* de Tracy believed that ideology could be an empirical science rather than metaphysical speculation. As they fashioned a nontheological and nonmetaphysical explanation of the origins of human knowledge, the *philosophes* attempted to develop a social science that replicated the scientific investigation of physical phenomena.

In the case of the Enlightenment **ideologues**, ideas about society eventually led to action that changed social and political institutions. If the *ancien régime* of the French Bourbon monarchy rested on scientifically untenable propositions such as the divine right of kings or the theory of absolute monarchy, then the *philosophes* reasoned that these obsolete and erroneous political and social residues should be discarded and replaced by scientific ones. Enlightened persons could use the scientific method to investigate social phenomena in the same way that Isaac Newton and others had investigated physical phenomena. A genuine social science could uncover the natural order of society. Once the natural laws of social, political, and economic life were discovered, they could be used to create a new and scientifically legitimate social and political order. In eighteenth-century America and France, the Enlightenment ideology stimulated two major revolutions that shook the foundations of the Western political order and ushered in republican governments, which, supporters claimed, conformed to natural laws. The theory of natural law applied to government was proposed by the Enlightenment ideologues and had general educational implications. In the past, individuals had been indoctrinated by archaic structures of religious or classical education to accept a static view of society. A new education had to be developed to educate a rising generation of republican citizens who could establish representative institutions and govern themselves by the methods of science and reason.

The Rise of Contending Ideologies in the Nineteenth Century

In the late eighteenth and nineteenth centuries, those who sought to design the ideal social and political order did not reach a single conclusion for creating the "heavenly city" on earth. Social theorists and practicing politicians devised a variety of alternative models for creating the good society. In England, John Locke's notion of the natural rights of life, liberty, and property for all people became the influential doctrine that guided politics in the United Kingdom. In the United States, Jefferson adopted Lockean principles as the ideological guide for the new republic. In France, in the years following the revolution that dethroned the Bourbons, a plethora of political plans were proposed by moderate monarchists, republicans, socialists, and communists. Each of these formulations of the "good political order" had its corresponding educational equivalent.

The late eighteenth and nineteenth centuries experienced not only political revolution but also the economic and social transformation produced by the industrial revolution and then a pervasive technological modernization. The use of mechanical power, the development of the factory system of mass production, and the greater availability of inexpensively manufactured products dramatically transformed economic life in Western Europe and North America. The well-known recital of the growth of large industrial cities, the development of transportation networks, and the urbanization of society has been recounted in many historical works. The industrialization of society had a profound impact on the concept of ideology. The industrial revolution nurtured socioeconomic class antagonisms. In the nineteenth century, the middle class, consisting of factory owners, professionals, merchants, and business people, became the emergent class that challenged the social and political supremacy of the older landed gentry and traditional aristocracy of birth and blood. Those who worked in the factories, mills, and mines—the working class, the future industrial proletariat—would eventually challenge the middle class in the twentieth century.

To the older conceptions of political ideology that arose from political theorizing were added economic class conceptions of ideology. The middle class—the bourgeois—found a congenial and supportive political ideology in the **Liberalism** of Locke and other proponents of individualism. To Lockean individualism was added the laissez-faire theories of Adam Smith, David Ricardo, and Thomas Malthus. A body of social, political, economic, and educational ideas emerged under the aegis of liberal ideology.

In the early nineteenth century, a counterideology emerged to challenge Liberalism. Saint-Simon, Fourier, Owen, Cabet, and others believed that liberal ideology was an erroneous interpretation of socioeconomic realities. Lumped together under the vague term of "Communitarian Socialism," the visionary reformers condemned what they regarded as the dismal theories of classical Liberalism that justified working-class repression and exploitation. Communitarian Socialism argued that the emergent forces of urbanization and technology could be planned and patterned in a rational way to alleviate human misery and suffering.

Socialism took another turn when labor-based political parties were organized, such as the Social Democrats in Germany, the Labour Party in the United Kingdom, and the various Socialist parties in France and Itaty. The United States, too, had a Socialist Party led by Eugene V. Debs and Norman Thomas, which functioned as a third party. The Socialist parties sought to create a welfare state that protected certain rights of the working class: to organize trade unions, to have safe working conditions, and to have access to state-supported educational systems, and guaranteed health and old-age services and pensions. Depending on the particular Socialist party, the degree to which industry, transportation, and other services would be nationalized—run as public agencies—varied.

Still another important variant of Socialism were the Marxist or Communist parties that rejected the parliamentary approach to gaining political power by elections. Communists argued that genuine social change could come only by the overthrow of the capitalist classes who held power by an organized proletariat.

Whereas classical liberal ideology sought to explain, to justify, and to rationalize middle-class supremacy, and whereas Communitarian Socialists challenged these assumptions, the defenders of the old order—the landed gentry, the wealthy establishment, and the traditional aristocracy—developed a counterrevolutionary ideology. This was the ideology of **Conservatism**, ably stated by Edmund Burke, which sought to preserve an older and more settled traditional way of life.

After World War I, totalitarian movements developed on the extreme right and left, namely Fascism in Italy and Spain, National Socialism in Germany, and Communism in the Soviet Union. According to totalitarianism, either of the extreme right or left, all power was organized in the state and its leader. With one monolithic political power in place, the state was to regulate all aspects of social, cultural, economic, and educational institutions and processes. People (e.g., the Fascists in Italy and Nazis in Germany; or the proletariat in the Soviet Union) were willing to give their freedom to the totalitarian state in exchange for the promise of a regenerated and glorious future in which their nation would be triumphant.

Through the twentieth and into the twenty-first centuries, the ideologies that originated in the late eighteenth and nineteenth centuries have worked their way through human life, society, and education. They have become interrelated and interconnected clusters of ideas that have shaped our worldviews, cultural outlooks, political programs, and educational policies. They have also generated political conflicts, hostilities, and world wars.

By the end of the nineteenth and throughout much of the twentieth centuries, ideologies have often been classified on a continuum that ranges from the political and cultural right with Fascism at the far right, then Conservatism, moving to Liberalism at the center, and to Socialism at the left and Communism at the far left. The ideological continuum is useful, but it needs serious and frequent qualifications. **Nationalism**, the ideology that is based on the nation as the focus of group life and on nationality as the primary mode of personal identification, blurs the continuum. (Nationalism is examined in the next chapter.) The various ideologies, throughout their history, have exhibited nationalist impulses. Extreme nationalism, or chauvinism, was a feature of the totalitarian movements. Conservatives regard love of country as a cherished traditional value. Even Liberals and Socialists have not escaped the force of nationalism.

Although general ideological classifications provide a useful cognitive map, they need to be made more specific in terms of the variety of ideologies that have developed as either new or the restructuring of older ones in the twenty-first century. The question is where to locate newer ideologies such as the Green environmentalist movement, feminism, multiculturalism, Libertarianism, the peace movement, and religious fundamentalism.

Consider feminism, for example. Some would argue it is the women's rights movement or an academic area of study rather than ideology. However, others regard it as an ideology that expresses the shared ideas and values of a group of women who want to raise women's consciousness about their situation in a male-dominated society and to construct avenues of greater freedom and choice for women. As ideologists, feminists construct their history by describing the efforts of the suffragettes and other pioneers of women's rights in the nineteenth century and identity such leaders as Elizabeth Cady Stanton and Lucretia Mott. They regard gender as the crucial element and how women have been subjugated or disempowered in a male-dominated patriarchal social, economic, and educational system.[2] One issue in locating and interpreting feminism is whether it is an independent, freestanding ideology or it is connected to larger ideologies.

Multiculturalism raises many of the same issues as feminism. Should it be seen as a movement or an area of study? Or, is it an ideology? Several sets of questions can be raised regarding ideology. Note that many of the major ideologies on the left-to-right continuum, including Marxism, originated in Western Europe. They were then transported to Asia, Africa, and Latin America. Multiculturalism argues that world social reality consists of a pluralism of racial, ethnic, and language groups, each of which is culturally equal to the other. It sees social justice, for instance, as based on pluralistic equality rather than domination. It can be viewed as a counterideology to ideologies that hold that Western cultures are more culturally and technologically advanced and that those in non-Western places need to be raised to the Western standard.

The relationship of religion to ideology raises serious issues, especially in the contemporary world. Religions are based on theologies that examine profound questions about the nature of God and the relationships of God to the universe and to human beings. Theology is much like philosophy, especially those philosophies that are grounded in metaphysics. Unlike philosophies, the major religions, especially those identified as Abrahamic, are based on sacred authoritative texts (holy books), that contain the word of God (the truth), revealed to special agents (the prophets). For Judaism, the book is the Bible; for Christians, too, it is the Bible, but including the Old and New Testaments; for Muslims, it is the Koran revealed to the prophet Mohammed. Because they are based on theology, religions are not ideologies. Nor do specific political activities by members of religion constitute an ideology. For example, actions taken by Roman Catholics to get state aid for parochial schools or by Muslims to challenge discrimination in airport security screening practices are so specific that they do not constitute an ideology.

The major ideologies, with the exception of Conservatism, that developed in the nineteenth century were secular. Liberals generally sought to separate the state from church control and to separate the church from state control. Marxists were antireligious, seeing religion as a smoke screen to distract the workers from their true situation.

The strong currents of religious fundamentalism in the contemporary world represent the mixture of religious and ideological beliefs. Religious fundamentalism seeks to control the general political processes and shape public policy in particular contexts—sometimes an entire country, or sometimes only a region or state. Religious fundamentalists can become heavily politicized and even tied to a particular political party. For example, Christian evangelical organizations support conservative candidates who are generally in the Republican party in the United States. Thus, there is a general ideological alliance between Evangelical Christians and conservatives.

Islamic fundamentalism is a variant of Islam that has ideological overtones. Politicized Islam has a religiously motivated political agenda that blurs distinctions between religion and ideology.[3] It seeks to overthrow or change moderate Islamic or secular states that have a predominately Muslim population and instead establish a strict interpretation of Islamic law. In Iran, for example, a council of clerics has authority to revise or nullify actions by the country's legislative body. The council also can set and enforce cultural norms as to acceptable dress and public behavior.

Marx's Critique of Ideology

In *The German Ideology,* Marx and Engels commenced their critique of Idealism, then the dominant philosophy in German culture. They asserted that the Idealist claim that ideas had a pure and transcendent existence created an illusion.[4] They called this illusionary false consciousness an ideology. Whereas the early French *philosophes,* Condillac and de Tracy, saw ideology as a positive breakthrough in human thinking, Marx condemned it as the source of **false consciousness**, erroneous beliefs about reality, especially social and economic reality. For Marx, **false ideology** was more than misguided fairy tales about society; it was used as a tool by which the dominant economic class controlled social, political, and economic institutions by manipulating subordinate classes into thinking that illusions were reality. The method of manipulation was to claim that ideas about religion, politics, society, law, and morality existed on their own and were detached from the economic base. Schools, controlled by the dominant classes, had a key role in indoctrinating the children of oppressed classes in the ideology that justified and sustained upper-class domination. For instance, teachers were to indoctrinate students to accept the beliefs and values that sustained the status quo.

Despite Marx's critique, the Western nations in the nineteenth century experienced a proliferation of ideologies that sought to explain, justify, rationalize, and enlist adherents. Karl Marx, the genius of what would be termed "Scientific Socialism," hurled his theoretical invective against all of these ideologies and denounced them as theoretical smoke screens designed to cloud the vision of the exploited working class. According to Marx, the various ideologies of Liberalism, Conservatism, and even of Communitarian Socialism merely served to preserve the power of the exploiting classes. In Marx's analysis, such ideological formulations produced a false rather than a genuine consciousness in the minds of people, especially in the outlook of the working-class proletariat.

According to Marx, all social and political phenomena and institutions arose from the economic base of productive means and modes. Roughly defined as raw materials, techniques, and human and mechanical energy, the means and modes of production were the economic bedrock of society. Throughout history, Marx reasoned, the means and modes of production had been controlled by a specific economic class. For instance, in the Roman Empire, the wealthy estate owner had controlled the agricultural base of society and had exploited the slaves who tilled the soil. During the Middle Ages, the manorial feudal lords had replaced the old Roman magnate as the exploiting class, and the victims of exploitation then were the serfs. At the time of Marx's writing of the *Communist Manifesto* and *Das Kapital,* the exploiters were the middle class—the bourgeois capitalists—who owned the factories, the mills, the mines, the railroads, and the banks. The victims of exploitation were the workers. Using a dialectical conception of history, Marx predicted that the working class would eventually arise in armed revolution to displace the capitalists and initiate a new classless society.

In Marx's analysis, then, the foundations of reality are material and are lodged in the economic means and modes of production. Convinced of the scientific accuracy of his historical interpretation, Marx attacked the Liberals, Conservatives, and Communitarian Socialists for creating false ideologies. While the Liberals had deliberately distorted history, the visionary Communitarians had created confused theories that Marx labeled "utopian."

A brief examination of what he regarded as false consciousness illustrates Marx's view of ideology. Although middle-class capitalists exploited their workers, they used ideology to rationalize their action and to confound their opponents. Claiming to be the proponents of representative institutions and popular education, Liberals pretended to defend freedom of speech, press, assembly, and religion. For Marx, these Liberal gestures created an ideological smoke screen to camouflage their true designs. According to Marx, those who controlled the economy ruled society's institutions. The bourgeois slogan of "freedom of the press" disguised the capitalist control of information, which defended the special interests of the capitalists and ignored the system's critics. The exercise of freedom of speech, if it challenged the capitalist system, meant the loss of employment. Schools in a capitalist-controlled society did not educate but indoctrinated students to believe that they lived in the best of all possible worlds. According to Marx, the false ideologies had to be demolished so that the proletariat could become conscious of its destined social and political role.

This brief examination of Marx's conception of ideology is useful in explaining how *ideology* came to take on a negative connotation. In terms of historical development, the Marxist conception of history and of the good society became another ideology that competed for people's hearts and minds. Marx's critics used his arguments against his position, claiming that Marxism was but another ideology, one of many competing for believing adherents.

Contributors to the Study of Ideology

The Marxist critique did not kill the concept of ideology but rather made it a field of greater study. Because ideologies circulated and contended with each other and had important consequences in political, social, economic, and educational life, they need to examined.

Karl Mannheim

Karl Mannheim (1893–1947), a pioneering sociologist, devoted his scholarly attention to analyzing ideology's meaning and functions in society. He resumed the earlier research of the French *philosophes* Condillac and de Tracy in seeking to identify the pattern of ideas that governs society. As a sociologist, Mannheim looked to society for the origins and workings of ideology. He found that ideology was a feature of society and applied to how people identified themselves as group members.[5] Discounting Marx's critique of ideology, Mannheim argued society was not simply a place of two competing ideologies but of many subgroups, each of which had their own ideology. Mannheim's grounding of ideology in society raises important questions for education. What is the general ideology that shapes educational ideas and practices in a particular society? What are the subgroups in a society and what are their ideologies and how do these ideologies influence that group's ideas about education? Is subgroup ideology in congruence or conflict with the general ideology and with other subgroup ideologies?

In his analysis of the relationships of ideology to society, Mannheim observed how a group's beliefs about itself are embodied in its histories, myths, and stories and how its ceremonies, rituals, and observances filter into an ideology. For example, think about the American holiday of Thanksgiving and how its observance carries with it a mytho-history about the relationships of the English settlers and the Native Americans, about how the Puritan religious beliefs were conveyed as an act of thanks given to God, and how the historical event has been replicated and ritualized around the American dinner table on a designated Thursday in late November. This kind of observance affects the person at both the social and psychological levels. There is a socially approved norm for celebrating the event as well as a psychological good feeling about being with family and friends at this celebration.

Mannheim also raised the issue of how an ideology relates to social stasis or maintenance and to social change. The supporters of the dominant ideology who hold power in a society use ideology to justify and rationalize (to conserve) the social, economic, political, and educational institutions that support their position. Depending on the degree of their alienation from the dominant ideology, other groups may develop a counterideology that seeks to change or modify institutional arrangements or to overthrow them. All groups—ranging from conservatives seeking to preserve the status quo, liberals seeking to modify it, or revolutionaries seeking to overthrow it—see their ideology as providing the way to the good life within the good society. Mannheim applied the term **utopian** to ideologies that seek to create a society based on their vision of how things should be.[6]

Mannheim drew inferences from his analysis of ideology to the role of the intelligentsia and to social reconstruction. For him, the intelligentsia was a group who was able to interpret the world to the members of their society. As a society became more mobile and enjoyed greater educational opportunities, the intelligentsia came from broader and more varied social and economic backgrounds.[7] Because of their education, they became more independent of their class origins and were able to present a detached, unbiased interpretation. Mannheim's concept of the intelligentsia can be interpreted as embracing teachers. Teachers, especially in Western nations such as the United States, come from a broad range of socioeconomic classes and cultural backgrounds. Because their work is not directly related to the agencies of production and consumption of goods or dependent on being elected to political offices, they can take a disinterested, unbiased look at society and construct objective interpretations. They can interpret ideological structures for their students.

Mannheim also was an advocate of social reconstruction. He believed that modern societies required a great deal of social, economic, and education planning. This belief was also found in the Social Reconstructionists in education. (See the chapter on Social Reconstruction and Education.)

Antonio Gramsci

Antonio Gramsci (1891–1937), an Italian Marxist and anti-Fascist, analyzed the concept of ideology from a neo-Marxist perspective. He redefined and broadened the meaning of ideology from Marx's original definition of an illusory false consciousness. He also enlarged the scope and meaning of ideology from economics and politics to the larger culture, including the media, art, and education. He developed the concept of **hegemony**—the control and domination of one group over another—that is so important in contemporary Neo-Marxism, Postmodernism, and Critical Theory.

Gramsci saw ideology as signifying a large and complex network of ideas that were cultural as well as economic and political. Ideology shaped group ideas about religion, politics and law, and culture. Ideological influences were present in the family and media as informal educators and particularly in formal educational institutions (schools and colleges). It included the broad network of cultural, ethical, and moral beliefs and expressions that were disseminated through the mass media and educational institutions.

Gramsci revised and broadened Marx's concept of how the bourgeoisie dominated society. According to Marx, the bourgeoisie, because of their control of the economic base, also controlled the state and its military, police, and legal apparatus, using them to enforce its rule and domination of the working class. Gramsci broadened the concept of hegemony to mean the social control of the culture and how culture was expressed. He argued that the culture was consciously manipulated by the dominant class to create a pervasive and permeating climate of opinion in which the oppressed classes, mistakenly thinking they were free, actually were diverted from and remained unconscious of their oppressive situation.[8]

Paulo Freire

Paulo Freire (1921–1997), a Brazilian educator who developed Liberation Pedagogy while working to educate Brazil's impoverished illiterate peasants and urban poor, further developed the concept of ideology. As an educator, his analysis of ideology was more definitely related to education than those of Mannheim and Gramsci. Freire did not skirt the edges of ideology but went right to its heart; he argued that education, schooling, teaching, and learning are never objective, or neutral, but always involve ideological commitment and imposition.

Freire's interpretation of ideology was influenced by Marxism, Existentialism, and Liberation Theology. Although he revised Marx, Freire used Marx's argument that economic conditions shape human relationships. However, unlike Marx, he did not believe that human reactions to these conditions are determined.[9] He rejects the Marxist determinism that our future, like our past, is a product of historical inevitability. Like the Existentialists, he rejects the view that the human being is predefined at birth as to status and condition. Drawing on Existentialism, he sees the person as an incomplete and unfinished presence in the world. Freire's literacy campaigns were supported by Roman Catholic social action groups who worked among the poor. Part of his thinking was shaped by Liberation Theology, a belief popular in Central and South American that Christians should be socially and politically active in working to change conditions of oppression.[10]

Freire sees ideology as being highly contextual in that the cultural, social, political, economic, and educational conditions are historically derived and are the ongoing reality in which people find themselves. As people develop a true consciousness of their social reality, they can interpret their situation and understand the personal and social conditions that either repress or liberate them.

In his discussion of ideology, Freire clearly distinguishes Liberation Pedagogy, as a radicalizing ideology, from other ideologies that distort history and rely on myths to create a sense of false consciousness in the oppressed. Freire, who constructed his ideas in the Latin American context, faced the opposition and repression of right-wing reactionary ideologies that were supported by vested oligarchic economic elites and militarist regimes. He was imprisoned and then exiled by the military regime in Brazil. He criticizes Conservatism as an ideology that fears change and tries to "slow down the historical process" by constructing a protective official history that seeks to legitimize the ruling elite's privileged position in the name of traditional values.

Freire finds Liberalism to be a particularly insidious ideology. Liberalism, especially the Neo-Liberal variant associated with economic globalization, though it promises eventual equality of opportunity and socioeconomic mobility, establishes institutions and procedures that create new elites, usually bureaucratic and corporate ones. Though they portray themselves as working to improve the condition of minorities and the lower socioeconomic classes, Liberals use institutions, including schools, to maintain and reproduce their privileged status. Avoiding transformative reform to change the exploitative economic conditions from which they profit, Liberals offer the poor transactional piecemeal reforms that create the illusion of change, but that, in reality, maintain their own privileged social and economic status. Even the Liberal notion of welfare and assistance, benignly intended to aid the poor, creates dependency that locks the dependents into the system rather than liberating them from it.[11]

Though advocating a radical transformation of society, Freire rejects what he calls doctrinaire left-wing sectarian ideologies. Leftist sectarian ideology justifies its actions, even if violent, in the belief that their end justifies the means to reach it. True to his Existentialist learning, Freire is highly suspicious of radicals who base their actions on inevitably establishing a predetermined perfect state of society, a utopia. For the leftist sectarian, the future is "inexorably pre-ordained" rather than, as Freire argues, existentially indeterminate and arising from immediate contexts.[12]

To think critically means to be empowered to penetrate through the ideological mists of false consciousness—the myths, theories, and rationales that others, especially the oppressors, have constructed to confuse and indoctrinate dominated groups. These rationales, derived from the oppressor's ideology, are designed to indoctrinate the oppressed to accept uncritically the oppressive conditions in the social environment as being "right," "just," "the standard," or "in the nature of things." Thinking critically requires the ability to see these rationales for what they are—the constructions of an oppressive group. For Freire, educational institutions and processes are never free of the conditions and situations—the contexts—of which they are a part. They are never ideologically neutral or scientifically objective. All educational systems, like all social, political, and economic systems, are ideologically conditioned. Education either convinces the younger generation to accept and conform to the power relationships of the existing system or it becomes a pedagogy of liberation. Education, committed to liberation, implies raising people's consciousness, encouraging them to reflect critically on social reality, and empowering them to transform the conditions, the contexts, that shape their lives. Freire's contextualism is similar to that found in Postmodernism, which asserts that all societies exhibit relationships of power that empower some and subjugate others. Freire, like the Postmodernists, is most concerned with the marginalized people of the earth.

A Stipulated Definition of Ideology

As you can see from the preceding discussion, ideology has had a long and somewhat tortuous history. It has had a variety of definitions, meanings, and uses since it was coined by the French *philosophes* who were trying to create a science of ideas. Because its definition is contested, I am stipulating a definition of ideology that we can use in the rest of the chapter. Ideology is defined here as a set of related ideas held by a group that explains its past, examines its present, and gives direction to its future. Based on this definition, we can consider the following ideological elements: (1) an ideology provides an orientation for a group in time and space by interpreting its history; (2) the ideology then explains the group's present social, economic, political, and educational circumstances; (3) the examination of the past contributes to a conception of social change; that is, it attempts to predict that what can be expected to happen in the future is likely to follow patterns that occurred in the past; and (4) the ideology is also policy generating in that it presents a blueprint for the future that indicates to the group what policies are needed to attain certain desired ends or goals; in this way, an ideology becomes programmatic or action-oriented. To attain the group's goals, the ideologue recommends political or educational action.

Ideology As an Interpretation of the Past

First of all, an ideology examines a group's past. The group may be the citizens of a nation, such as the German people or the Russian people; or the group may refer to the members of a socioeconomic class such as the working class or the middle class. The group may consist of a professional or an occupational group such as teachers, clergy, or physicians. The ideologue examines the group's past to develop a historical interpretation that orients the group in time and place and gives meaning to group membership. That is, it creates a sense of group identification and solidarity.

This examination provides the group with a way of arranging historical time in its contexts (its spaces or places). The ordering is selective in that it arranges persons and events into a manageable (often simplified) and metaphorical or allegorical pattern, by merging fact with fiction, especially **myth**. This ordering of the past is presented in narratives, stories that easily engage listeners or readers, such as movie or television audiences or groups of children. The field trip to a historic site is a frequent occasion for school classes. For example, school groups may visit restorations of southern plantations that emphasize the cultural

Ideological Clusters of Ideas

elegance of the great house, or manor, and either ignore or marginalize the slave quarters. (Recently, public historians have revised these representations to also include illustrations of the conditions of African slaves.) Visitors, often a group of schoolchildren, touring a plantation received a selective ordering of plantation culture.

While recently visiting the City Museum in Paris, I was struck by the power of narrative in forming group identity, especially in constructing a collective national identity. I encountered a teacher leading a school field trip through the exhibits on the French Revolution. The teacher—white, well-spoken, and apparently competent—was well versed in the events of the Revolution. Further, the exhibit was artfully illustrated with magnificent large paintings that told the story, especially of how the people had overthrown absolutism to enshrine the values of "liberty, equality, and fraternity." I was struck, however, by the realization that the children, engrossed in viewing the paintings and listening to their teacher, did not resemble the people in the paintings. Most were of African or Arabic ethnic origin and were in the ideological process of becoming members of the French nation.

The view of the group's history or story constructs a collective memory of events that has a deep and profound meaning for the group. Historical narratives through the construction of a group's memory provide identity and locate us in time. Through snapshots that enter the consciousness representing the past, images drawn from history connect us to the group's past. Our own autobiography is joined to the group's history. These historical snapshots, images of our past, always tell only part of the story because they emphasize some aspects of the past while minimizing other aspects. The snapshot is about us and a selected image that sets us apart. For example, the image of George Washington and his troops at Valley Forge and video that shows the collapse of the twin towers of the World Trade Center in New York on September 11, 2001, are part of the collective memory of Americans; the images of police at Selma, Alabama, using dogs and tear gas against civil rights marchers and the voice of Martin Luther King, Jr., giving his "I have a dream" speech in Washington, D.C., form the collective memory of African Americans. These are dramatic events; collective memories are also constructed through many smaller but more personal events such as ethnic celebrations, photograph albums of families, and so on.

The interpretational component, which interprets the past as well as assesses the present situation with the intent of shaping the future, is an important element in an ideology.[13] It influences the shaping of beliefs as well as their application to policy formulation and programmatic action. According to the interpretational component, a correct interpretation of the belief system guides the programmatic implementation.

The ideological interpretation of the past may or may not be historically accurate. The ideologist examines a group's past for a particular interpretation or justification. Such a highly selective search for meaning often leads to a tortured view of history, which frequently confuses myth with history, fiction with fact. Using what historians condemn as "presentism," the ideologist uses the past to create a version of how the group's present came to be. If necessary, past events may be shaped to fit a preconceived thesis that justifies a present or future program. For example, in the Classical Liberal formulation, John Locke referred to the state of nature in which the individual possesses natural rights to life, liberty, and property. Although it is impossible to locate such a state of nature in a definite historical time frame, the mythical state of nature is used as the point of origin and of departure for social, political, and economic doctrines that assert the individual's priority over society.

Another example is that of Marx, who used history to find evidence of one economic class's exploitation of another. Operating from a preconception that asserted that economic factors determined historical events, Marx argued that intellectual, artistic, religious, political, and educational events were secondary to the economic factors that caused them. Through a selective past, Marx explained the existence of two antagonistic economic classes—the bourgeois capitalists and the proletarian workers. By such a highly selective historical interpretation, Marx used the past to orient the proletariat to class consciousness and a sense of meaning and destiny.

Historically Generated Beliefs and Values.   From its interpretation of a group's past, ideology is descriptive: It helps to form and disseminate a set of beliefs to describe and interpret social, political, economic, cultural, and educational reality. The descriptions, which tell the story of how things came to be, argue that the processes that made them such can and should be replicated or changed. What should be done to maintain or change the context—the conditions with which the group lives? To maintain or to change raises the future question of how to maintain or how to change. Many "should" or "ought" value issues emerge. Thus, ideological descriptions and interpretations of the past also generate moral and ethical issues about human action, reaction, or inaction. For example, the concern for social justice issues found in many teacher education programs is hinged on ideological descriptions of a just or unjust society and how schools and teachers should react to these issues. Philosophies raise similar but much more general issues about social justice; ideologies attempt to deal with these issues in a more particular way politically and socially in the contexts in which they arise.

The merging or the blurring of descriptions (explanations of reality), prescriptions (appropriate behavior), and proscriptions (inappropriate behavior) pervades a society's culture, especially its symbols. The symbols are cultural representations of both cultural reality and values. Note how the American flag is a symbol of the United States. When schoolchildren pledge allegiance to the flag, they are affirming loyalty to the republic for which the flag stands; it symbolizes the nation's political processes and that the Union is one. It also symbolizes commitment to the nation's values, "liberty and justice for all." Also, consider the symbolic meaning of a yellow ribbon to show support for troops, of the red cross for aid during disasters, and so on.

The Present Situation and Ideological Interpretation

Once the ideologist has used the past to create a sense of group solidarity and identity, then it is possible to assess the group's contemporary social, political, economic, and educational condition. For example, the liberal middle-class value orientation that emphasizes individualism, competition, property rights, and representative government can be explained and justified in terms of the history of the middle class in its struggle with oppressive aristocratic and monarchial governments that interfered with these values.

Another example of the use of the past to explain a present situation can be seen in the conceptions that certain "oppressed people" have developed. For example, the Basques of Spain reckon themselves to be a people who once had a great and noble history. Historic events have caused this once great culture to be submerged by the Hispanic culture that surrounds it. Thus, part of the movement for Basque freedom, or autonomy, derives from their view of the past. The historically or mythically derived idea that a particular racial or ethnic group has been repressed in the past and is now seeking to secure its lost freedom is an important driving force in the contemporary reassertion of ethnonationalism. An important part of the ideology of ethnonationalism is that the sense of a "lost greatness or grandeur" be nurtured and kept alive in the young until the moment comes for liberation from the oppressors.

In this linking of the past with the present, educational processes acquire a significant importance. Informal sources of education, such as the mass media, become the means for forging the links between what was and what is and what ought to be. Institutionalized education, in the schools, functions to create a sense of group identification in the minds of the children, the immature members of the group, that connects them to the past. In such a linkage, myths, stories, and heroic portrayals are particularly useful. In India, for example, the story of Gandhi's struggle for Indian independence provides a figure of heroic dimension that in a dramatic way links the young Indian with both his or her past and present. Additionally, the figure of Martin Luther King, Jr., becomes a heroic figure who exemplifies values that are worthy of imitation by the young African American. In a more advanced school situation, at either the upper grades of the elementary school or in secondary education, the selection of both historical and literary works cultivates a means of linking the individual with the past in such a way that the present situation acquires an added significance that is meaningful to group identity.

Social Change and Ideology

Ideology represents an interpretation of history and of how institutions change over time. History is interpreted contextually; change, too, is viewed in terms of the need to preserve and maintain or to change existing institutions. The idea of social change itself is screened and interpreted through the lenses of the competing ideologies. For example, think about the following qualifiers that are used with change: *gradual, orderly, radical, transformative, transactional, utopian, revolutionary*, or *planned*. *Gradual* and *orderly*, for a Conservative, are likely to mean slow, natural, or unhurried. *Radical, transformative*, and *revolutionary* is likely to be seen as socially dangerous for a Conservative but socially desirable for a Critical Theorist. *Transactional*, in the sense of being limited, negotiated, and defined is likely to be socially, politically, and educational desirable for Liberals. The word *utopian* can be highly charged. It can mean a vision of the future for some, whereas Conservatives, Liberals, and Marxists tend to view it with suspicion. For Conservatives, it conjures up a dangerously idealized future used to justify any means to reach an end; for Liberals, it may mean ignoring existing contexts and step-by-step methods; and for Marxists, it can mean ignoring the necessity of class conflict and struggle.

How an ideology nuances the meaning of change is a key to how it seeks to socialize the young. The general Conservative suspicion of change encourages seeing existing social institutions as being grounded in some higher source that stands outside of but guides the legitimate principles operating in the context. The assertion that the United States is founded on Christian principles or that the U.S. Constitution should be strictly construed using the original meaning that the founders of the republic gave to it are examples of historically ordained contexts. These principles are to be enshrined in the minds of the young so that they will maintain these governing and guiding principles.

In contrast, the Liberal approach to socializing the young is to build familiarity and to practice democratic methods to use discussion and clarification in regard to issues and even values. Rather than being perceived as immutable givens, values are subject to clarification, discussion, and revision. The revisions are to follow procedures that operate within prescribed channels and don't spill out of them to create "dangerous" situations. The modus operandi is that of constantly reconsidering and revising.

Ideologists are rarely content to have their interpretation of the past and assessment of the contemporary situation remain at the level of academic discussion. The conception of the past and the assessment of the present often imply a desire to fashion values and to shape behavior. In other words, ideologies possess elements that are both descriptive and prescriptive. The descriptive phase of an ideology arises from the explanation of the past and the examination of the present. The view of the past, especially when portrayed by heroic models, is used to reinforce the concept of what constitutes proper behavior in the present. Such behavior is also designed to guide future action. Depending on the particular ideology, the prescriptive element may be a set of simple behaviors that characterize the good member of the group. Or it may become an elaborate social, political, and educational code. A particular approved behavior in ideological terms can be illustrated by a brief examination of Classical Liberal attitudes. (See the chapter on Liberalism.) The child who is being raised in the milieu of Classical Liberalism learns that he or she is an individual who has certain rights and certain responsibilities. For example, he or she learns that it is important and desirable to compete against peers and to win. Competition and winning are defined in personal and individualistic terms. If there are winners, then there are also losers. Winning the spelling bee, the track meet, the essay contest, or the musical competition requires that effort be expended to discipline oneself and to acquire the skills needed to win. It is important to be a winner.

Further, the value of competition is presented as being socially useful as well as personally fulfilling. Competition leads to discovery, invention, and human progress. In fact, the liberal tradition of progress by means of individual effort is a linking device that connects past, present, and future. It becomes a crude linear theory of social change. The progress of humanity depends on individual initiative within a social, political, economic, and educational milieu that emphasizes competition.

The Marxist historical interpretation and assessment of the present offers a very different theory of social change from Classical Liberalism. For Marx, the economic class rather than the individual is important. Personal values are determined by one's relationship to the means and modes of production. In a prerevolutionary situation, members of the working class need to identify with their class and to struggle for its liberation. In a postrevolutionary situation, members of the society are to work to realize Marxist goals by cooperating for the good of the state. Beyond this, Marx developed a theory of social change based on history's dialectical pattern. Throughout history, Marx argued, economic classes struggled to control the means and modes of production. In the course of historical evolution, the proletariat will come to control both the economic base of society and the political, social, and educational superstructure that has been erected on it. The proletariat's coming victory is historically destined and irreversible, Marx and his followers preached.

Ideology As Policy Generating and Programmatic

Although ideologues may use academic devices, they rarely expend their energies in the pursuit of knowledge because of its intrinsic value. Ideologies, embracing as they do theories of social change, become instruments for achieving a desired social goal or even a new social order. The programmatic element in ideology stems from the prescription that arises regarding the contours of the desired social order.

Ideologies are prescriptive in that they make social, political, economic, and educational assessments or judgments. These assessments, identifying what is good or bad, lead to prescriptive policies. If the assessment is favorable to the status quo, then the ideological policy is conservative in that it seeks to preserve it. If unfavorable, then it seeks to bring about change in ways that may range from the evolutionary to the revolutionary. Indeed, ideologies are action oriented or programmatic.

Ideologies are aimed at the public political and educational arena and, in seeking to garner public support for a program, are in conflict with each other. They encompass large (macro) principles and also smaller, more specific (micro) ones. A key challenge for maintaining ideological coherence is to avoid letting specific aims splinter the ideology. For example, consider the related issues of immigration and illegal aliens in the United States. American Conservatives, typically members of the Republican Party, in principle want to maintain a traditional culture core that includes English as the official language and to secure U.S. borders to prevent the entry of terrorists into the country. Consequently, some Conservatives favor restrictions, especially no amnesty, for illegal aliens. The reality, however, is that some businesspeople, who argue that free enterprise and competition is a key Conservative principle, rely on immigrants for plentiful and cheap labor. The issue for Conservatives is how to relate their general principles on American culture and economics with the specific issue of immigration.

The Ideological Continuum and Educational Policy

To illustrate the functioning of ideology and its impact on education, we can use the concept of the ideological continuum. Ideology operates as a continuum that encompasses the following: (1) the origins of the belief system based on a view of the past that may be mythic or historical or a combination of both; (2) an instrumental interpretation of the past intended to make certain aspects of it operational in the present; this attempt to operationalize an ideology results in policy formulation—the design of a plan to bring about some action in the present that will shape the future; and (3) action, based on the policy guidelines, that will bring about the desired results.

The ideological continuum suggested here contains both descriptive and prescriptive elements. For example, we might consider the formulation of educational policy in the United States to illustrate the functioning of the ideological continuum.

A vital and continuing policy issue is how schools are and should be funded. Funding education is always an important political issue in states across the nation as legislatures debate various funding formulas. Boards of education and school administrators frequently engage in campaigns to convince voters to increase taxes for schools. Internal arguments occur among board members over establishing budgets and setting spending priorities for educational programs. The inequality in school funding is well known and extensively documented. For example, in *Savage Inequalities,* Jonathan Kozol, describing inequalities in America's public schools, found wide disparities between facilities and programs in the poorest inner-city communities and schools in the wealthier suburban communities. Kozol examines how the unequal funding of schools relates to social class divisions, institutional and environmental racism, isolation and alienation of students and staff within poor schools, the physical decay of buildings, and the health conditions of students. Funding based on property taxes and property values discriminates against lower socioeconomic classes, and this unequal funding leads to inferior schools and creates a wide disparity between schools in the poorest and wealthiest communities. Isolation of students, staff, and the community is a direct result of the inequities in funding.[14]

The issues of how to spend funds and who should pay the bill for education is obviously a practical fiscal problem. However, behind the problem is ideology. The long-standing traditional pattern is to pay for education through a combination of state aid and revenue generated by property taxes in the local school districts. This pattern has minimal federal support, usually around six percent of the total. The ideology supporting the traditional pattern is that of local and state rather than federal responsibility. It draws from Conservatism as well as, to a more limited extent, from Liberalism. To avoid national control and support, defenders of the traditional pattern are willing to accept disparities in funding. A result is the unequal funding of schools that Kozol decries. Further, the unequal funding works to favor economically advantaged groups and classes. Neo-Marxists and Critical Theorists see inequalities in funding as a deliberate effort by advantaged groups to maintain their privileged status. The tax on property to support schools, however, can be seen from a Liberal perspective as a way to provide some equity in funding without radically tampering with the economic system.

Because revenues generated by the property tax vary considerably from district to district, some analysts have proposed using more revenues from income taxes or from sales taxes. If the income tax is graduated, those in higher brackets would pay more and would be supporting the education of lower income groups. This kind of tax is progressive and so would likely garner support from Liberals, especially when combined with the property tax. It is the kind of policy that Liberals could be expected to endorse. However, a sales tax would be regressive, placing the same burden on all income brackets. Though an equal kind of taxation, a sales tax is not an equitable one in terms of social justice.

Finally, there are those who argue that education should be privately controlled and paid for by those who use the schools and not by the general public. The ideological issue here is whether education is a public or a private good.

National Reports

A Nation at Risk, Action for Excellence, and many national reports on education were based on an interpretation of the U.S. educational present.[15] This perspective expressed such beliefs as: (1) the U.S. preeminence as a leading technological, economic, and military power had been established, at least in part, by the nation's educational system; (2) other nations were threatening to overtake the United States and surpass it as a preeminent technological and economic power; and (3) the U.S. educational system, especially the public schools, was in a state of crisis because of poorly defined goals; a soft, nonacademic curriculum; declining scholastic standards; permissiveness; inadequately prepared teachers; and myriad other causes of educational malaise. Although some educators, including philosophers of education, questioned the accuracy of the analysis, it nevertheless was accepted as accurate by large segments of the public and by policymakers in both the national administration and Congress, and by state governors, legislators, and many local school boards.

The interpretation that came from the analysis of the condition of U.S. education led to a generalized policy that stated: U.S. education was in a state of crisis that could be resolved by strengthening the academic components of schooling, especially mathematics and science, and by restoring discipline to the schools. Various states and local boards developed specific policies to resolve the crisis. Among them were the following proposals: increase the length of the school day and school year; require competency examinations to guarantee that students master basic skills; establish teacher competency examinations to ensure that teachers possess adequate skills and knowledge; reduce expenditures for nonacademic and vocational components of schooling.

The policy proposals were designated as educational reforms by their proponents, who anticipated improvement in mathematics and science teaching and competencies in particular, and higher standards of achievement in other academic subjects. Some proponents of "reform" believed that the restoration of discipline would lead to a decrease in juvenile delinquency and drug abuse, and an affirmation of political and moral values. Ultimately, the proponents of reform believed that schooling, conceived of as the rigorous study of academic subjects, would substantially aid the efforts of the United States to regain its economic and military preeminence as a world power.

Standards Movement.   The criticisms voiced in *A Nation at Risk* further stimulated the standards movement, which endorsed a policy to improve American education by creating high standards, or benchmarks, that can be used to assess students' academic achievement through standardized tests. The standards movement affected schools throughout the United States as states enacted legislation requiring standardized testing to measure student academic achievement and teacher competency. Further, it had a ripple effect as it stimulated professional "learned" organizations such as the American Historical Association to work to establish standards in their disciplines that could guide how subjects were taught in the school curriculum.

The standards movement led to significant policy developments at the federal level, when the Elementary and Secondary Education Act of 2001, the No Child Left Behind Act (NCLB) endorsed by President George W. Bush, passed Congress. The act assumes that there are necessary basic skills, such as reading and mathematics, and that students' academic achievement in these skills can be assessed objectively by standardized tests. Further, the act implies that students' scores on standardized tests indicate how well schools and teachers are doing to meet stated outcomes. To qualify for federal aid under the terms of NCLB, states must establish annual assessments in reading and mathematics for every student in grades 3 through 8. Proponents of NCLB contend that these test results will identify schools in which large numbers of students fail to achieve to the standard.[16] The law holds school districts accountable for improving the performance of disadvantaged students as well as the overall student population. Schools and districts failing to make adequate yearly progress are to be identified and helped. If the schools fail to meet standards for three years, their students may then transfer to a higher-performing public or private school.[17]

My purpose in commenting on the national reports and the standards movement is not to debate the validity of their analyses of American education or to assess their results. Rather, this discussion is intended to illustrate how ideology shapes educational policies and classroom practices.

The Use of Ideology to Create Consensus

Ideology, which gives identity to a group, is used to create a sense of shared ideas, goals, and commitments. It functions to form group identity and to sustain group cohesion by generating a "we-feeling" or sense of group solidarity. Assumptions about the world and the society that are embraced by the particular ideology are publicly expressed and used to develop togetherness, solidarity, and agreement among group members.

As a molder of **consensus**, ideology functions in the society as a whole and also in its informal and formal educational agencies. Informal educational agencies, especially the media, express and reinforce ideological commitments. Formal agencies, such as schools, likewise build a sense of group identification, or a "we-feeling" in the young through the school milieu—the hidden curriculum—and through certain components of the formal or explicit curriculum, such as literature and history. All school systems work to cultivate a sense of national identity and loyalty in the young; they also function to cultivate a sense of social consensus, an adherence to the group's dominant values.

The origins of the public, or common, school system in the United States provides a clear example of how education was used to construct consensus. Horace Mann, Henry Barnard, Catharine Beecher, and other proponents of common schools saw them as agencies to construct a common American society marked by widespread consensus, or agreement on the political processes that should govern the United States and on the ethical values that should govern individuals' public and personal behavior. They wanted to create a system of state-funded and controlled public schools that could be used to mold a society in which ideologically homogeneous citizens shared a commitment to common beliefs and values.[18] They saw public schools, especially their administrators and teachers, as public agents to transmit an official version of American culture.[19]

Once constructed and maintained by dedicated educators, the official consensus was to absorb and Americanize immigrants, reduce class conflicts, and develop a national community, a society united by shared interests, commitments, and values. They especially worked to use the public consensus to guard against ideas and groups, counter ideologies, that might fragment American social, cultural, and political unity. Even as the overarching consensus could be peripherally revised to incorporate new groups, such as European immigrants and African Americans freed from slavery, the consensus would retain its core features.

Ideology and Outlook

As part of the process of forming social consensus, ideology shapes a person's outlook on self and society. The use of *outlook* is deliberately imprecise. It refers to the way in which we intellectually organize or "put together" our ideas about social, political, economic, and educational concepts, events, and trends. It creates a view of the world in which we live and seeks to answer the following questions: Who am I? What are my origins? What is the role of society and my place in the social order? What are the requirements and responsibilities of citizenship? How should I function in the economic system? Outlook, broadly defined, is shaped by formal and informal educational agencies. A major part of the schooling process is devoted to shaping a person's social, political, and economic perspective and to developing skills and knowledge for functioning in the society, in the economy, and in the political process.

Shaped by ideology, a person's outlook not only affects external relationships to social, political, economic, and educational systems, but it also shapes a person's interior sense of being or self-identity and esteem. How one ultimately relates to these systems determines a person's attitude about his or her identity, role, function, aspirations, and destiny. Ideology, through both the hidden curriculum of the educational milieu and the formal curricular components of schooling, serves to organize the various role personalities and role functions of persons both in school and in future social, political, and economic (employment) situations.

In its origins an ideology is contextual, that is, formulated by a group in a society. Many adherents of an ideology are content to keep it in the place and among the people who originated it or to see it as so contextual that it is special to them and cannot and should not be exported elsewhere. This was the case with American isolationists who wanted no involvement with people or situations elsewhere in the world. However, there is a tendency for advocates of an ideology to see it moving from the contexts of origin to a broader field of operations. Ideologies that strive to be transcontextual develop a *Weltanschauung,* an all-encompassing outlook that interprets the world for its adherents. For example, the Marxist ideology has a set of explanations and procedures for socioeconomic and political change that are universally operative. It has also been argued that American democratic institutions and processes can be exported to and implemented in other countries such as Iraq, for example. This policy stance, articulated by neo-Conservative ideologists in the United States, represents a belief that American political institutions are universally applicable.

Ideology's Permeability and Flexibility

Ideologies contain patterns of related and interconnected combinations and clusters of cultural concepts. A key to understanding an ideology lies in recognizing how the concepts are arranged and determining which are at its core and which are adjacent. Core concepts need to be stable whereas adjacent ones can be revised and adjusted. In both Liberal and Progressive educational thinking, respect for the child's individual needs, interests, and differences is a core concept. At the same time, Liberals and Progressives are concerned about children's socialization, their ability to work democratically and collaboratively in groups. The issue for teachers in these perspectives is to develop strategies that maintain the core concept—children's individuality—with related concepts of working in groups. If the group becomes paramount rather than related, it can coerce the individual as in authoritarian situations.

Ideologies are permeable, that is, they can absorb concepts from other ideologies, from philosophies, and from religions and use them to reconstruct their conceptual pattern. This **permeability** is a feature of an ideology's functional flexibility. An illustration is provided by American Conservatism. A core feature of Conservatism is the authority given to tradition as a source of group wisdom and guidance. Conservatives often assert the need to maintain traditional family values. In its contemporary format, American Conservatism has absorbed concepts from Classical Liberalism, especially the emphasis on individualism and the sanctity of private property. Conformity to traditional values remains at the Conservative core but individualism has found its own place there. Critics of Conservative ideology, especially Liberals, contend that conformity to what is defined as traditional values can seriously limit individual freedom and expression. American Conservatism has also absorbed religious beliefs of Evangelical Protestants about what constitutes appropriate family values. What emerges from the relationship of Conservatism with Evangelical Protestantism is a definition of marriage as monogamous, between a man (the husband) and a woman (the wife) who are legally married; and the family as the husband and wife and their children, living in a unit. The concept of family values, so defined, is thus religiously sanctified and culturally justified.

In building consensus and commitment, ideologies vary in their functional flexibility. The efficacy of an ideology in building consensus ranges between those ideologies that encourage or tolerate pluralism and those that are monolithic. Throughout its history, there has been continuous debate in the United States about how new immigrant groups were to function in U.S. society. Antagonists in the debate were divided between those who argued for Americanization of immigrants and those who argued for cultural pluralism.

According to the ideological orientation of the "Americanists," the American past was largely the history of the contributions and achievements of white, English Protestants. The development of institutions of representative government, judicial practices based on the common law, and the nation's rise to an industrial world power were interpreted as achievements of the dominant English-speaking Protestants of the older stock of Americans. The study of history and social studies reinforced the ethos of the dominant group by portraying historic heroic models from the dominant group.

Anticipated results of the Americanization policy were to enculturate immigrants—the great majority of whom were neither English nor Protestant after 1880—into a monolithic national character. For Americanists, this policy would preserve the national character and institutions.

Educational policy conceived according to such a monolithic ideological interpretation shaped both the school's milieu—the hidden curriculum—and the formal or explicit curriculum. The school's milieu—namely the rules, regulations, etiquette, and student–teacher relationships—emphasized the values associated with the Protestant ethic: punctuality, orderliness, frugality, industriousness, and respect for private property. These values were also congenial to training a disciplined workforce for an emerging industrial society.

The educational policy of the Americanization ideology used certain components of the formal curriculum to create a monolithic society. The language of instruction, reading, and literature was English. Non-English-speaking children were to learn English and abandon their own languages to become like the dominant group.

In contrast to a monolithic conception of the American character, those who subscribed to the ideology of cultural pluralism saw the American past in a broader and more varied perspective. Many groups and peoples contributed to the still emerging and evolving American character—Native Americans, African Americans, Hispanics, Asians, and Europeans from both southern and eastern Europe as well as the British Isles and northern Europe. Such a culturally pluralistic interpretation of the American past was multilingual, multisocial, and multiethnic. The consensus-generating power of cultural pluralism, though less specific than the Americanist version, possessed a vitality that had the capacity to unite various groups into a larger American identity that respected and did not jeopardize other group identifications. In other words, the core beliefs of cultural pluralism could be shared without eradicating distinctive characteristics of ethnic or language groups. For example, a policy designed to encourage bilingual education rests on the assumption that the use of English as well as another language enhances a student's development in both the linguistic-ethnic subgroup and the larger society.

Just as a monolithic ideology has implications for the school milieu and the curriculum, so does a cultural pluralistic ideology. In terms of the school milieu, language, ethnic, and racial differences are valued. The school's value orientation would emphasize multicultural understanding. The formal curricular components, especially literature, history, and civic education, includes the contributions of various ethnic and racial groups to the common heritage. It should be noted, however, that the dominant contemporary U.S. public school ideology, while culturally pluralistic, continues to emphasize commonalities related to government, law, and property. The delicate balance in a culturally pluralistic ideology and society is that of maintaining a commonly shared framework of experience and belief in which cultural differences can exist and flourish.

Ideology, Education, and Schooling

Ideology, particularly that of the dominant group, or the official ideology, has a direct impact on education, especially on schooling, in the following areas:

1. It works to shape educational policies, expectations, outcomes, and goals.
2. Through the school milieu or environment, it conveys and reinforces attitudes and values.
3. It emphasizes selected and approved skills and knowledge through the curriculum, which is the formal and explicit program of the school.

Educational Policies, Expectations, Outcomes, and Goals

In studying the shaping influence of ideology on schools, we first need to examine the interplay, or the relationship of ideological ideas about society, politics, and the economy to education. Ideologies typically operate as systems of beliefs that are mutually interdependent.

In any given society, a range of ideologies is likely to exist. If we use the United States as an example, we can identify a variety of ideological perspectives. The two major U.S. political parties—the Democrats and Republicans—operate from ideological bases that include views of the past with their own heroes. Traditionally, these heroes have been Abraham Lincoln for the Republicans and Thomas Jefferson and Andrew Jackson for the Democrats. Every four years, the national convention of each political party approves a platform that identifies its policies. Like the national political parties, other groups—the American Federation of Teachers, the National Education Association, the American Medical Association, the National Farmers Union, the National Association of Manufacturers, and countless others, for example—present an array of ideological shadings. Despite this spectrum of ideologies, the dominant ideology in the United States appears to be based on middle-class conceptions of knowledge, values, and standards of behavior that influence educational policies, attitudes toward schooling, and measures of educational success. This ideology, really the ideology of the dominant class or group, influences education, schools, and the curriculum.

Values Conveyed by the School Milieu

The **school milieu** or environment—the atmosphere in which teaching and learning take place—helps to shape student social and intellectual attitudes and values. In terming the school milieu the "hidden curriculum," Michael Apple refers to the inculcation of "norms, values, and dispositions" that occurs as students experience the school's institutional expectations, incentives, routines, rewards, and punishments.[20] The milieu reflects ideological factors arising both in and out of the school. Power, prestige, and status, as determined by the dominant or official ideology's criterion of success, shape not only educational goals but also teacher and student behavior.

Ideology and Curriculum

In terms of the formal curriculum, ideology seeks to answer the question, What knowledge is of most worth? Most worth to whom? To national policies and priorities? To personal goals and expectations? For participation in the society and the group? For preferred social and economic positions? Does the policy emphasize the mathematical and scientific knowledge needed for technological development? Or does the curriculum reflect the literary and artistic styles and tastes of a leadership elite? As these questions are answered, often in terms of an ideological perspective, the curriculum takes shape.

Ideology and Instruction

In our discussion of ideology in this chapter, the important characteristics of ideology were identified: (1) they are contextual and provide group adherence and allegiance; and (2) they are not disinterested, neutral, or objective and seek to gain adherents and support on behalf of particular programs of political and social action. In other words, they are committed to a version of the past and to the implementation of a particular program of action. The role of ideology in instruction has been controversial, especially to those who claim that ideologically referenced education, especially in terms of what is included and excluded in the curriculum and how it is taught, leads to indoctrination of students.

The charge of indoctrination relates not only to an ideology's selective use of the past and its specific programmatic commitments but also to its persuasive nature. Critics contend that instruction based on ideology is designed to persuade students to accept the teacher's ideological commitments. Critics allege that ideologically based curriculum and instruction (despite its claims to foster commitment to tradition as in the case of Conservatives, open-minded process learning according to Liberals, or critical consciousness with Critical Theorists) is nonetheless the transmission of a set of beliefs intended to enlist individuals to join ideological groups and to accept the ideology's platform and program. Further, ideologies deliberately blur fact and value, the rational and the emotional, in making their case.

Those who defend ideology's role in curriculum and instruction argue that all education by its nature is ideological. For example, George S. Counts, a founder of Social Reconstructionism, argued that all education is contextual and as it is particular to a particular place and time, it imposes the knowledge, beliefs, and values of those who live in a place at a given time in history. There are also defenders of the role of ideology who contend that the argument for objective and disinterested curriculum and teaching is a strategy for those who hold power to endorse the status quo in schools. This guise is used to block consideration of alternative ideologies by claiming that the one already in place represents truth and values.

Ideology and Philosophy

Although it may appear difficult to distinguish between philosophy and ideology, we will attempt to do so. The traditional philosophies discussed earlier, namely Idealism, Realism, and Thomism, were based on a metaphysical view of reality. These philosophies, which explained reality in terms of universal being or essence, are therefore abstract in the sense that they answered the question What is real? in general, abstract, and universal terms. In contrast, ideologies are **contextual** and concrete. By contextual we mean that they are heavily related to time, their historical point of origin, and to place, a geographical, economic, political, sociological situation. Most philosophies, especially the traditional systematic ones, seek to transcend time and place; ideologies are essentially contextual.

Philosophers are concerned with the truth of their claims about reality, the moral and ethical rightness of the values they prescribe, and the coherence, or logical validity of their arguments.[21] Much philosophical writing probes for inconsistencies in other philosophies. Philosophers ask general questions such as: What is reality? What is true? How do we know? What is valuable? What makes this position or set of beliefs or arguments consistent and coherent? They would examine such concepts as "social justice," presently a key concept in many teacher education programs, in terms of: What is the meaning of the terms *social* and *justice*?

Operating at a high level of generality, philosophies seek to explain what is real, how we think, and how we value. In terms of valuing, in ethics and aesthetics, philosophies are also prescriptive. All philosophies, in attempting to explain the most general human concerns, seek to establish meaning. For example, the Experimentalist's analysis of the interaction of a human organism with the environment seeks to explain and make meaningful to us the nature of experience. The Existentialist is more concerned with the private and subjective meaning that we give to ourselves by choosing to act in the most significant situations that we encounter.

Ideologies, while also a quest for meaning, look more to economics, politics, and society for meaning. Meaning in these contexts comes from an interpretation of the past, which is either historical or mythological, or a combination of the two, and from an interpretation of policies and programs. In contrast to the speculative detachment or analytical reflection of philosophy, ideology, oriented to action, is often a rationale for explaining action.

Philosophers, seeking to extend their ideas outside of their own contexts, use language that is much more abstract and general than ideologists, who are more context-related. At times, there are similarities in expression. To make their ideas understandable, philosophers often provide examples that are made concrete by locating them in a context. Ideologists, in seeking to give their ideas greater transference from one context to another, may attempt to universalize their language. However, to enlist group loyalties for a specific program, ideologists, unlike philosophers, need to restore the concreteness that was developed in a context. Ideologies often rely on concepts that carry specific meanings but can enlist broad support, that can be descriptive but also highly emotional, that can be expanded but also simplified. Such concepts are conveyed by terms that are specific and direct but also expansive such as *family, race, gender, ethnicity, language, class, property,* and so forth.

In contrast to philosophy's speculative or analytical quest for meaning, ideology functions to create loyalty to the vision of the group's past and sense of historic destiny and to mobilize resources to achieve desired programmatic goals. In creating loyalty and commitment, ideologists use a variety of persuasive techniques that range from the rational to the emotional. Ideologies also possess a rhetorical or journalistic element, a persuasive means for fostering commitment and bringing about mobilization, that is generally absent from philosophy.

Conclusion

This chapter analyzed ideology as the belief system of a group and the source of group identification. It discussed how groups use a selective interpretation of history to construct their identity, to explain social change, and to formulate policies and programs of action. Because of the ambiguity of the term, a definition of ideology was stipulated that enabled us to examine how ideology is used to create consensus. In schools, ideology operates to shape the school milieu, especially the hidden curriculum. The role of ideology in formulating educational policy such as the current standards movement was discussed. Although similarities exist between philosophies and ideologies, philosophies are more general and abstract whereas ideologies are based more in contexts and are more action-oriented.

Constructing Your Own Philosophy of Education. Now that you have studied ideology, do you believe that your educational ideas have been shaped by ideology? Can you identify this ideology? Do you plan to relate ideology to the construction of your own philosophy of education?

Questions for Reflection and Discussion

1. Reflect on your political and economic beliefs and values. How have they been influenced by ideology?

2. Reflect on the groups of which you are a member. How has your group identity been shaped by ideology?

3. Reflect on your family's beliefs and values and determine whether they have been shaped by ideology.

4. Mannheim believed that intellectuals, including teachers, can be objective enough to act as mediators of different group's beliefs and values. Do you agree?

5. Freire claimed that all education and all schooling are ideological. Do you agree or disagree?

6. Reflect on your own schooling. Did it include ideological symbols?

Inquiry and Research Projects

1. Visit a public school and a private school and compare and contrast how their environments have been shaped by ideology.

2. Access the Web sites of the American Federation of Teachers and the National Education Association. Determine whether these organizations have an ideology.

3. Look through your family's photo albums. Do you think these photographs serve to create a collective family memory? How has this family memory shaped your beliefs and values?

4. In your field studies or teaching at a particular school, can you detect how children are taught the myths and symbols of a particular ideology?

5. In your field studies or teaching at a particular school, can you detect the presence of a hidden curriculum?

6. Research your institution's teacher education program. Do you find evidence of ideological assumptions in the program?

Building an Ideological Vocabulary

Consensus: a feeling of shared goals, aspirations, and commitments that comes from group identification and solidarity.

Conservatism: an ideology that emphasizes the role of the cultural tradition and historically derived institutions and the basis of society.

Contextual: ideology's relationship to specific places and historic periods; the belief that ideas and values arise in contexts, particular places at particular times.

False Ideology: A Marxist term that argues the capitalists who control the superstructure of society manipulate subordinate classes into thinking that cultural illusions are real.

Hegemony: Gramsci's concept of the social control and domination of one group over another.

Ideologues: French Enlightenment theorists who tried to develop an empirical theory of how people formed their ideas.

Ideology: the shared ideas and values that create group identity and meaning, especially in terms of politics, society, economics, culture, and education.

False Consciousness: Marx's description of ideology as a misleading form of consciousness contrived to block true consciousness.

Liberalism: an ideology that emphasizes the rights of individuals and society as a compact of individuals to protect their natural rights of life, liberty, and property.

Myth in Ideology: a legendary story, often concerned with actual, but embellished, or imagined significant events in a group's past.

Nationalism: an ideology identifies the nation as the focus of group life and nationality as the primary mode of personal identification.

Permeability: an ideology's ability to absorb concepts from other ideologies and to rearrange them in terms of its own core beliefs and values.

School Milieu: the atmosphere or environment that pervades a school in terms of rules, regulations, styles, behavior, and relationships.

Utopian Ideology: ideologies that seek to create a society based on their vision of how things should be in the future.

As you begin to read the next chapters on Nationalism, Liberalism, Conservatism, and Marxism, you might wish to refer back to this overview box.

Overview of Ideologies and Education

Ideology	*The Past*	*Present*	*Future*	*Educational Implications*	*Proponents*
Nationalism	Is based on the history and myths of a particular nation.	Is the ongoing historically derived achievements of a particular national group.	Is the extension of the national group in time and place, renewing its national heritage and extending it.	An emphasis on national history, literature, stories, myths, symbols, and ceremonies. The learning of a national language and literature.	Depends on particular nation. In American experience, Webster, and others.
Liberalism	Importance of the Enlightenment— application of reason and science to society. Locke's inalienable rights; parliamentary government.	Application of democratic and scientific processes; continuation of parliamentary processes; separation of church and state.	Directed peaceful and nonviolent incremental change; reform of existing institutions when needed.	Academic freedom; use of scientific method and open processes; objectivity and impartiality. Cultivating commitment to democracy.	Locke Jefferson Mill Dewey
Conservatism	Affirmation of traditional and customary wisdom. Protection of historically evolved institutions and values.	Maintenance and protection of historically evolved institutions from radical change. Restoration of traditional values.	Maintain the cultural heritage and traditional values. Acceptance of only gradual necessary change.	Transmitting the cultural heritage and values; emphasis on patriotism, civility, and tradition.	Burke Reagan
Marxism	Class conflict over control of the means and modes of production. Dialectical and predictable conflict.	Organize to resist economic and political domination. Engage in consciousness raising and oppressed class militancy.	After the proletarian revolution, the coming of a classless society that will be without oppression.	Study of objective economic conditions; exposing false consciousness; developing critical consciousness.	Marx Engels

Internet Resources

For a discussion of ideology, access www.plato.sanford .edu/entries/law-ideology/.

For the origins and characteristics of ideology, access www.culturaleconomics.atfreeweb.com/anno/ cranston%20ideology%20EB%202003.htm.

For an introduction to ideology, access www .academic.regis/jriley/introide.htm.

For sources and resources on ideology, access www.intute.ac.uk/socialsciences.

Suggestions for Further Reading

Balkin, J. M. *Cultural Software: A Theory of Ideology.* New Haven: Yale University Press, 1998.

Ball, T., and R. Dagger. *Political Ideologies and the Democratic Ideal.* New York: Longman, 1999.

Boudon, R. *The Analysis of Ideology.* Oxford, UK: Polity Press, 1989.

Eagleton, T. *Ideology: An Introduction.* London: Verso, 1991.

Freeden, Michael. *Ideologies and Political Theory: A Conceptual Approach.* Oxford, UK: Clarendon Press, 1996.

Freeden, Michael. *Ideology: A Very Short Introduction.* Oxford, UK: Oxford University Press, 2003.

Freire, Paulo. *Letters to Cristina: Reflections on My Life and Work.* London: Routledge, 1996.

Freire, Paulo. *Pedagogy of Freedom: Ethics, Democracy, and Civic Courage.* Lanham, MD: Rowman and Littlefield, 1998.

Freire, Paulo. *Pedagogy of Hope, Reliving Pedagogy of the Oppressed.* New York: Continuum, 1995.

Freire, Paulo. *Pedagogy of the Oppressed.* Translated by Myra Bergman Ramos. New York: Continuum, 1984.

Gadotti, M. *Reading Paulo Freire: His Life and Work.* New York: SUNY Press, 1994.

Gramsci, Antonio. *Selections from Prison Notebooks.* Edited by Q. Hoare and G. Newell-Smith. London: Lawrence & Wishart, 1971.

McLaren, Peter, and Peter Leonard. *Paulo Freire: A Critical Encounter.* New York and London: Routledge, 1993.

Morrow, Raymond A., and Carlos Alberto Torres. *Reading Freire and Habermas: Critical Pedagogy and Transformative Social Change.* New York: Teachers College Press, Columbia University, 2002.

Taylor, P. *The Texts of Paulo Freire.* Buckingham, U.K.: Open University Press, 1993.

Vincent, A. *Modern Political Ideologies.* Oxford: Blackwell, 1995.

Endnotes

1. Michael Freeden, *Ideology: A Very Short Introduction* (Oxford, UK: Oxford University Press, 2003), p. 4.

2. Freeden, *Ideology: A Very Short Introduction,* pp. 99–100.

3. Freeden, *Ideology: A Very Short Introduction,* pp. 101–102.

4. Freeden, *Ideology: A Very Short Introduction,* p. 5.

5. Freeden, *Ideology: A Very Short Introduction,* pp. 12–13.

6. Freeden, *Ideology: A Very Short Introduction,* p. 13.

7. Freeden, *Ideology: A Very Short Introduction,* p. 14–15.

8. Freeden, *Ideology: A Very Short Introduction,* pp. 19–20.

9. Donaldo Macedo, "Foreword," in Paulo Freire, *Pedagogy of Freedom: Ethics, Democracy, and Civic Courage,* trans. Patrick Clarke (Lanham, MD: Rowman & Littlefield, 1998), p. xxiv.

10. Although its origins are in Catholic action groups, the recent popes, John Paul II and Benedict XVI, have condemned what they say are the Marxist orientation and overt politics of Liberation Theology.

11. Donaldo Macedo, "Foreward," in Paulo Freire, *Pedagogy of Freedom, Ethics, Democracy and Civic Courage,* p. xxviii.

12. Paulo Freire, *Pedagogy of the Oppressed,* trans. Myra Bergman Ramos (New York: Continuum, 1984), pp. 21–23.

13. For an analysis of the "interpretational component," see Stanley E. Ballinger, *The Nature and Function of Educational Policy* (Bloomington, IN.: Center for the Study of Educational Policy, Department of History and Philosophy of Education, Indiana University, 1965); also see Richard Pratte, *Ideology and Education* (New York: David McKay, 1977), pp. 49–51.

14. Jonathan Kozol, *Savage Inequalities: Children in America's Schools* (New York: HarperPerennial, 1991), pp. 67–74.

15. Among the national reports are: National Commission on Excellence in Education, *A Nation at Risk: The Imperative for Educational Reform* (Washington, DC: Government Printing Office, 1983); Task Force on Education for Economic Growth, *Action for Excellence* (Denver, CO: Education Commission of the States, 1983).

16. No Child Left Behind (Washington, DC: U.S. Printing Office, 2001), p. 1.

17. Ibid., pp. 8–9.

18. Kathryn Kish Sklar, *Catharine Beecher: A Study in American Domesticity* (New York: W. W. Norton & Co., 1976), p. xii.

19. The concept of "cultural interpreter" is developed by Kathryn Kish Sklar, *Catharine Beecher: A Study in American Domesticity,* p. xiii.

20. Michael W. Apple, *Ideology and Curriculum* (London: Routledge and Kegan Paul, 1979), p. 67

21. Freeden, *Ideology: A Very Short Introduction,* p. 67.

8

Nationalism, American Exceptionalism, Ethnonationalism, and Education

Children pledging allegiance to the American flag and "to the republic for which it stands" which instills a sense of national identity.

Chapter Preview

Nationalism, American Exceptionalism, and ethnonationalism are all variations on the nationalist theme. Nationalism is based on a commitment to the nation as the primary source of identification, commitment, and loyalty. American Exceptionalism, an American variety of nationalism, sees the United States as unique among the countries of the world.

Ethnonationalism focuses on the ethnic group as the source of primary allegiance. The chapter examines how these related ideologies have shaped education, schooling, curriculum, and teaching and learning. The following are the major topics examined in the chapter:

- Definitions of nationalism, American Exceptionalism, and ethnonationalism
- The connections between nationalism, the nation-state, and school systems
- Nationalism's major ideological themes
- Constructing national identity
- Education as cultural transmission
- American Exceptionalism
- Ethnonationalism
- Nationalism, American Exceptionalism, ethnonationalism, and multicultural education

Because Nationalism as an ideology is so pervasive in society and school, you will need to consider how it relates to your philosophy of education. How does nationalism, especially American Exceptionalism, and ethnonationalism relate to your view of education, schooling, teaching, and learning? Will you include elements of nationalism or find ways of excluding them?

Defining Nationalism

This chapter examines nationalism, an ideology that is paradoxically disarmingly simple and direct and also highly complex. We can illustrate the paradoxical nature of nationalism by reviewing a few definitions. The dictionary defines **nationalism** as "national spirit or aspirations" and "as devotion to the interests of one's own nation." That definition seems very direct if we take it to mean that we are devoted to the interests of the United States and possess the American spirit. Then, we look up the root, **nation,** from which nationalism is derived, and find that it means "a body of people, associated with a particular territory, that is sufficiently conscious of its unity to seek or to possess a government peculiarly its own," "the territory or country itself," and "an aggregation of persons of the same ethnic family, often speaking the same language or cognate languages."[1] To complete our definitions, we can also turn to how Steven Grosby, a leading scholar, has defined nationalism. He says it refers to a set of beliefs about the nation, focusing on its value and worth and the desirability of belonging to it. For him, a "nation is a territorial community of nativity," which has evolved through historical processes, into which a person is born or naturalized as a citizen.[2]

Now, our initial discussion of nationalism has become more complex. We are faced with two paradoxes: (1) Although Americans are conscious of their unity and have their own government, they are not of the same racial and ethnic family; (2) Although the majority of Americans speak English, many of them speak other languages.

In examining nationalism, we have an ideology that is simple and emotional in that it evokes love of our country. The nation's symbols, its flag and anthems, stir our emotions. Even if we cannot deconstruct or analyze nationalism, we can feel it because we have been taught from childhood to be inspired by it. Simultaneously, nationalism is highly complex: it is not limited to our emotions only but penetrates into other areas. It can cross over to and override other group identification such as socioeconomic class, gender, ethnicity, and race.

How often have we heard, especially in times of crisis, such phrases as "united we stand; divided we fall," or "we are all Americans"? To begin to unpack the bundle of emotions as well as the complex relationships of nationalism to our lives and institutions, we can focus on several leading questions:[3]

- Why do people separate themselves from other people in nations?
- What does the existence of nations and nationalism tell us about people?
- What role does education and schooling play in this separating of peoples and in creating of nations?

Throughout modern history, nationalism has been a significant ideology in constructing the primary identification in which we distinguish "us from them" and in mobilizing the people of nation-states.[4] In particular, nationalism penetrates the school systems of nation-states. In the United States, nationalism is often expressed as **American Exceptionalism**, the belief that the United States is an exceptional country and that Americans are a special people. Throughout history, the ethnic and racial group has had a profound effect in shaping cultural identity, character, and social commitments. At times, ethnicity and race have promoted nation-state nationalism. At other times, they have weakened the sense of nation-state nationalism. In the twenty-first century, **ethnonationalism**, based on ethnicity or race, is a powerful global force. Ethnonationalism, an old and a new way of viewing one's cultural identity and affiliation and of distinguishing "us from them," raises profound issues for education.

Connecting Nationalism, the Nation-State, and Schooling

A direct connection exists between nationalism, as an ideology, and the school, as an institution of formal education. The connection comes through the nation-state, a country, such as the United States, France, or Japan. A **nation-state** occupies a particular geographical territory over which it has sovereignty, that has its own political, social, economic, and educational institutions. A nation is composed of a group of people, its citizens, who live within its political boundaries and participate in its cultural, political, religious, and educational institutions. Based on the concept of the nation as the primary unit of identification, nationalism manifests the sense of belonging to and sharing common membership in the country. This identification manifests itself further in the group's national ethos or patriotism. The idea of national citizenship in the nation is nationality, that is, being designated an official member by being born in the country or naturalized in it as a citizen.

Historic Origins of Nation-States

Racial, ethnic, and language groups such as the ancient Greeks, Hebrews, and Egyptians identified themselves as a distinct people before the rise of the modern nation-state. However, the modern nation-state, stimulated by nationalism, developed in the late eighteenth and early nineteenth centuries. Key events that generated nationalism's rise were the American

Revolution in 1776 and the French Revolution in 1789. The emerging nationalism of the American rebels against British colonial rule was born of their sense that they were no longer Englishmen and -women connected to the mother country but were becoming a distinct people, living in their own territory, and developing their own American culture. As Jefferson asserted in the Declaration of Independence, Americans had the inalienable right, as a people, to create their own self-governing and sovereign nation-state.

In 1789, the second great revolution occurred in France in a popular insurrection against the monarchy and aristocracy. The revolution proclaimed that the French people, not the Bourbon monarch, constituted the French nation. Napoleon's efforts to conquer Europe and remake it into a system of French satellite states generated a counternationalist tide among the British, Russians, Spanish, Germans, and other national groups. In the nineteenth century, the idea of the country as a nation-state rather than a realm of a dynastic monarch took hold in Europe. Throughout the nineteenth century, the major European powers, especially France, England, and Germany, stimulated by nationalist rivalries, colonized much of Africa and Asia. Two additional ideologies—imperialism and colonialism—both with significant educational implications, developed. Imperialism was based on the belief that powerful nation-states such as the United Kingdom, France, and Germany had the right to occupy foreign territory and control other peoples such as the Indians, the Indo-Chinese, and the Africans and to exploit them in the interest of the imperial nation. Colonialism held that certain people, usually of color in Africa and Asia, were inferior and needed to be controlled and tutored by the imperial nation. Nationalism caused the tensions, armaments races, and military alliances and counteralliances that led to World Wars I and II.

European imperialists unconsciously exported the nation-state model of political organization to South America, Asia, and Africa. When Spain's Central and South American colonies revolted and became independent sovereign states, they adopted the nation-state model of organization. When the British, French, Dutch, and Portuguese colonies gained independence in the twentieth century, they, too, adopted the model of the nation-state organization as independent and sovereign nations.

Nationalism and Nation-States' Structures

As indicated, the nation-state connects with and is the location for the nation. A nation-state, such as the United States, the United Kingdom, or Brazil, creates institutional structures—governments, parliaments and other legislative bodies, courts, police and armed forces, and school systems—designed to preserve and promote the nation's territorial integrity, survival, maintenance, and interests. The nation-state exercises sovereignty over its territory through laws that relate the members, the citizens of the nation-state, to each other.[5] They establish governments with presidents, prime ministers, parliaments, congresses, and courts to manage their internal political affairs. They establish treasuries, banks, and taxation agencies to support the nation-state financially. They maintain police and military forces—armies, navies, air forces—to protect their security and maintain their borders. They create diplomatic services to conduct their international relations with other nation-states. They create educational systems to educate their children and young people, especially to socialize them in the political ideology and processes that sustain the nation-state and reproduce it for future generations.

Nation-States and Schools

In the nineteenth century, nation-states began to establish **national school systems**. In the United Kingdom, Parliament gave financial grants to voluntary school societies in the 1830s to promote primary education. France, under the leadership of François Guizot, established national primary schools. Although not establishing a national or federal system of education, the individual states of the United States established locally controlled common, or public, school systems. Though not an official national system, the fifty state school systems have many characteristics of a national system including that the books and materials they use are similar and that their teachers generally have a similar preparation. In some countries, the national schools either cooperated with or replaced the existing religious schools. In nation-states such as France and Mexico, there were strong and prolonged conflicts between state and religious authorities for control of the schools. Just as nation-states are found throughout the world, so are national school systems. As new nation-states appeared in the twentieth century after winning independence from colonial powers, they, too, established some version of a national school system. National, state-operated schools became key agencies in constructing a sense of national identity and in bringing about political socialization in the young. Often building on nationalist themes, political socialization instills patriotic and civic values in the young. The close relationship between nationalism, nation-states, and national school systems raises serious implications for education. For much of the nineteenth and twentieth centuries, national school systems fostered a patriotism in the young that glorified their own country over all others. Now that we have made a connection between nationalism and schooling, we can turn to a more thorough analysis of nationalism as an ideology.

Nationalism in the Foundations of Education

In the foundations of education, the early studies of nationalism's affect on education were conducted by Isaac Kandel, a comparative educator, and Edward Reisner, a historian of education. Kandel and Reisner studied nationalism within the political context of particular nation-states such as France, Germany, Italy, and Russia. Kandel and Reisner examined nationalism as a force in creating an individual's identity with the nation-state and in mobilizing the people of these nation-states for politically based agendas such as defense, war, imperialism, and modernization. These pioneer educational theorists identified nationalism with modernization as a force that eroded residues of feudalism, localism, and provincialism. Kandel and Reisner concluded that: (1) nationalism was a powerful emotional force for constructing an individual's primary identification with and social cohesion with the nation-state; (2) modern national school systems, supported by nation-states, were educational agencies designed to deliberately cultivate national identity and social and political cohesion; and (3) the modern curriculum, dating from the early nineteenth century, was a medium for instilling national sentiments, loyalties, and values. Kandel's and Reisner's pioneering studies assessed nationalism's power in mobilizing nation-state energies, examined its uses in education, and identified the ideology's nonrational aspects.

A theoretical tension developed in educational theory about nationalism's nature and impact. Whereas nationalism was seen as necessary to the modern nation-state and in schooling for the nation-state, extreme nationalism, especially when chauvinistic, was condemned as generating conflicts between nations that endangered world peace. The educational problem then became how to use nationalism as a constructive force in building nations while reining it in and circumscribing those conflict-generating elements that threatened world peace and security. This tension between nationalism's constructive and destructive potentialities remains an important and unresolved issue in education.

Nationalism's Ideological Themes

In this section, we turn to an analysis of nationalism's most important ideological themes.

History, Myth, and Memory

All nations have historical beginnings and processes of development. For example, the United States' historical beginnings were as thirteen British colonies on the Atlantic coast of North America. The history of the United States taught in schools recounts the story of these colonies' settlement, their struggle for independence, and the creation of a new republic by American heroes such as George Washington, Benjamin Franklin, and Thomas Jefferson. Interwoven with the historical account are images and myths about the Pilgrims, especially the first Thanksgiving, which they celebrated with the Indians. The myth is carried by many symbols—Pilgrim girls in white caps and aprons and Indians in tribal regalia, wearing headbands of brightly colored feathers. Go to any elementary school classroom in the United States in November and you will see pictures of the Thanksgiving feast drawn by children that replicate the scene, which becomes encased as a powerful myth in the individual and national memory. Equally important are the values that the combination of history and myth carry—images of a family, sitting with their heads bowed in prayer at a dinner table laden with turkey, dressing, sweet potatoes, and pumpkin pies. The scene carries the economic values of an American bounty, the social values of family togetherness and sharing, and the religious values of a people thanking God. It creates the very powerful image of the United States as a bountiful nation that has been especially blessed by a providential God.

The blending of history and myth works to create a **collective memory**, one in which the same symbols of the nation get the same response throughout the republic. The history of the settlement of the American west, the movement of the line of settlement from the Atlantic to the Pacific Ocean, is conveyed through the images and stories of the mountain man, the pioneer, the cowboy, the settler, the wagon train, and so on. Instilled in the account are the mixed and unresolved tensions of rugged individuals but also of people traveling in groups and building communities together. To the degree to which history and myths are filtered, so are these memories. The earlier images and memories of a filtered "official history" of a blessed nation under a benevolent God, conveyed by the Thanksgiving story, may be challenged and even shattered by other, often submerged alternative histories about African American slavery, the war with Mexico, and the oppression and forced resettlement of Native Americans. However, the earliest images of the nation, like the earliest images of God, have great staying power in memory and are likely to remain despite contrary evidence. In other words, the facts often do not matter.

Making People Different from Each Other

As our national psyche is shaped through shared or collective memories, history becomes more than facts and events, and myth becomes more than imagined stories and images. It weaves the fabric of a national consciousness that is different from the national consciousness of other peoples.[6] Every nation—Japan, China, Russia, France, and the United States, for example—has its own understanding of its past as a national narrative that is different and distinctive from that of other peoples.

The past, however, is not a completed set of episodes, relegated to history. The past is moving and alive; it flows like a current into the present and helps shape it. It transcends the narratives about historical and mythical episodes and heroes and enters into a group's collective consciousness. It constructs a "we-feeling" that distinguishes and separates us from them. It makes Americans interpret themselves as a people different from the Chinese, French, or Russians.

Schooling for Difference.   Schooling, especially in nation-state school systems, is a powerful force in building the collective national consciousness of being a different people. We preface our discussion of how children are schooled to be different in terms of their national identity by stating what is important but also overtly obvious. Human beings are, with some slight genetic differences, essentially alike; children are born biologically alike. Political socialization, an important part of schooling, is the process that makes them different in their national identification. Children learn to speak, read, write, and listen in the language of their particular nation. The language, in turn, carries the beliefs and values and the laws, rules, and customs particular to the nation. When children begin to perceive of themselves as being like those who share the same history, myth, and memory, they become participants in the common collective national self-consciousness and memory. As these beliefs and values are shared with others in the national community, the individual child becomes socially and politically related to others and acquires the feeling of being an American. The sense of being an American makes the person understand themselves as being different from other people. As they take on this common collective self-consciousness, they construct a political and cultural national identity or "we-feeling." Along with identifying with those who are like us, those who are different are the others, the outsiders.

Space and Time

Two important concepts developed in a child's education are the meaning and relationships of space and time. These two key concepts in interpreting the world are of special significance in developing a child's collective national self-consciousness. We have already discussed how the sense of time, in terms of nationalism, is developed through history and myth. Now, we turn to space, or territoriality, another key component of constructing national identity and consciousness. When it merges with the mythical and historical sense of the past, a national territory is replete with rich and heightened meanings. The lyrics of well-known songs, such as "from sea to shining sea," "this land is your land; this land is my land," "God bless America, my home sweet home," which are all known by children and sung at school ceremonies, designate space, place, and territoriality. The particular people have a land, a place, a space called the homeland. In some countries, the homeland, personified as a parent, is lovingly called the "motherland" or the "fatherland."

The sense that our homeland belongs to us and not to them is important: After the terrorist attacks on the World Trade Center in New York City on September 11, 2001, Americans rallied to the defense of the homeland. The United States Congress, on the recommendation of the president, established a federal Department of Homeland Security.

The national space or homeland is much more than an area on a map; it is a place filled with relationships—between a spatially situated past and a changing present—that creates an almost spiritual sense of being there that is expressed in such phrases as "the indomitable and unconquerable American spirit." Thus, time and space are connected in the spirit of past and present generations in the American homeland.

The nation occupies the space of a territorially distinct people that is formed by its memories and its historically based institutions, and its sense of civic belonging and membership.[7] The nation becomes a set of social, political, and emotional relationships that are temporally interwoven in a collective memory based on history and myth and spatially reinforced by the living place of those who share this consciousness. More important, the nation, when perceived as a territorial space, generates the values of "possession" and "attachment." As conveyed by the lyric, "this land is my land," the member of the nation has a sense of possession or ownership in the nation. Attachment means being connected to the territory across time. The past generations prepared and defended the homeland, as with the celebrated "greatest generation," for the present generation, which, in turn, is responsible for transmitting the cultural inheritance to posterity. Based on the sense of a collective cultural consciousness and memory, developed by history and myth, and a national space, or homeland, the following generalizations can be stated regarding a nation. It has a:

- territory, bounded by borders that keep others out.
- name that designates it as a particular territory, such as the United States or the United Kingdom.
- capital, a center, in which is located its major government institutions and national monuments (e.g., Washington, DC, or London).
- history that expresses its existence over time.
- relatively common culture, institutions, political processes, and laws.[8]

Nationalism and Constructing National Identity

Nationalism, an ideology identified with the nation-state, is used to construct a sense of primary identification, a collective consciousness of being and feeling French, English, Italian, Chinese, or American, for example. The chords of national identity arise through the shared participatory experience of speaking a common language, worshiping in a common religion, and possessing common culture.

A Common Language

A common language is instrumental in instilling national history and myths into the individual's collective consciousness. A common language is a means of everyday communication, and yet its cultural meaning is much more powerful than being a simple tool. Its words express the meaning of time and space and the values of honesty, loyalty, beauty, friendship, politeness, and family in a unique national and cultural context. The language describes a shared version of self and the past and prescribes what should be in the future.

Many countries have an official language that is standard in their schools. By learning a shared language, individuals also become immersed in the nation's cultural context. Speakers of the common language are identified as being like us. A common language unites people by constructing shared meanings and understandings—ideas, beliefs, and values—about themselves as a group and their relationships to others who, not speaking the same language, are different from them. Indeed, the ancient Greeks denigrated non-Greek-speaking people as barbarians.

School curricula, throughout the world, give priority in time and resources to teaching the national language. In the primary or elementary schools, reading instruction as a central activity commands most of the instructional time and resources. A child's academic access to and success at the secondary and higher level of education is often determined by how well she or he masters the national language. As children learn language, their ideas, beliefs, and values become more contextualized and more particular to the national setting.

Nationalism endorses a common language and its teaching in nation-state schools, but language instruction itself is often emotionally and politically charged as is the case with bilingual education in the United States. In earliest childhood, before commencing school, children are socially learning the language of their family and their immediate society. With spoken and heard (listened-to) language already ingrained in their early socialization, they enter school—a social and often national educational agency that devotes much of its time and resources to language learning. As the child begins formal language instruction in school, an important question is: Is the language of instruction the same or different from the language that the child already knows? If the same, the school reinforces the linguistic and cultural traditions the child already has. In monolingual and monocultural nation-states such as Iceland and Japan, the educational issues relating to language instruction are much simpler and basically pedagogical than in multilingual and multicultural countries. It focuses on devising and implementing methods to teach the national language more effectively, easily, and efficiently. In multiethnic, multiracial, and multilingual nation-states, especially in India and Nigeria but also to a degree in the United States, language learning is much more complicated because it involves political decision-making and power relationships as well as pedagogical concerns. The basic political issue is that of having or not having an official language. If there is an official language, what is that language? The inclination in nation-states has been to have an official language and to impose that language of those who do not speak it.

Patriotism

Instilling patriotism, love of country and the nation, is an important goal of education in national or state-operated school systems throughout the world. **Patriotism** means a primary identification with the nation and a commitment to its territory, the homeland. Schools instill it by bringing children into the national consciousness by transmitting an official language and history, a literature that exemplifies the national story and character, and through ritual ceremonies that celebrate the nation and the significant events in its history. In the United States, Independence Day, the Fourth of July, is commemorated with parades, speeches, and fireworks that engage the young. In France, on Bastille Day, July 14, the posting of the tricolor flag, the singing of "La Marseillaise" and parades invoke historic national memories. In Israel, Holocaust Remembrance Day commemorates the genocide of six million Jews by the Nazis during World War II. Each nation has these ceremonial events, its heroes and heroines, its days of commemoration. In schools, these ceremonial events, with their songs, stories, and patriotic reenactments, are part of the process of political socialization and identification of students in nationality and the nation-state. Similar to religious rituals, these patriotic ceremonies and symbols elicit an almost automatic response in the person.

Whereas most educators have little problem with patriotism as an educational goal, they debate its meaning and how it should be cultivated in schools. Some conservatives have argued that too many public schools in the United States emphasize cultural relativism and ignore the importance of instilling patriotic values. They point to countries that are splintered by racial and ethnic hatreds and warn that it could happen here if public schools do not require solid patriotic core subjects in the curriculum that promote patriotic values. In contrast, Liberals and Critical Theorists argue that narrow patriotism can become chauvinistic and that patriotism should be redefined in more pluralistic, multicultural, and international terms. They do not want schools to encourage a monolithic view of America or to generate prejudice against people of other countries.

Nationalism and Religion

Another element in constructing national identification in many countries is a common religion, often an "official church." The relationship between religion and nationalism is historically very complex. Where the observance of a particular religion is territorial, religion and nationality coincide. When it is the religion of the land, religion helps to give spiritual support to nationalism and nationalism gives political and economic support to religion. In eastern Europe—Russia, Serbia, Romania, and Bulgaria—and in Greece, for example, Orthodox Christianity was an important historical force in the emergence, unification, and cohesion of nationality and is a force for cultural homogeneity.[9] In Italy, Poland, Ireland, Portugal, and Spain, Roman Catholicism provides a religious and cultural sense of belonging. In Israel, Judaism is the religious and cultural link. In Egypt, Pakistan, Malaysia, Afghanistan, Iraq, and Iran, Islam is deeply embedded in the culture. In Thailand, Buddhism is embedded in the culture.

Historically, the origin of formal education, or schooling, can be traced to temples, churches, mosques, and synagogues. In all countries, churches and religious institutions remain powerful informal educational forces. In many countries, the teaching of religion, especially that of the official church, takes place in the state-operated schools. In the United States, where church and state are separated constitutionally, the government does not sponsor or sanction religion, nor does it interfere with the free exercise of religion. Religiously as well as culturally pluralistic, the United States is home to a variety of Protestant denominations as well as to Roman Catholics, Orthodox Christians, Jews, Moslems, and other religious denominations.

The role of religion in American national life and education, however, has really never been settled. There have been religious issues in American education since the establishment of the common or public schools. Although the Enlightenment influence in the American tradition, especially in Jeffersonianism, emphasized separation of church and state and correspondingly separation of public schools from religious control, evangelical Protestantism identified American institutions with a generalized Protestant cultural ethos. Today, there are concerted campaigns, especially on the part of cultural conservatives allied with fundamentalist Christians, to fashion American institutions, especially schools, on Christian beliefs and values. These groups define the United States as "a Christian nation," founded on Christian principles.

Common Culture

Nationalism, manifested in identification with a common cultural heritage, finds expression in the art, history, literature, poetry, drama, music, and architecture that exemplifies a national ethos. As far back as the ancient Greeks, cultural symbols and artifacts were used to construct ethnic and cultural identity in the young. Homer's epic poems, the *Iliad* and *Odyssey,* gave the young Greeks a sense of what it meant to be a Greek hero. The Parthenon on the Acropolis in Athens was a visible monument to Greek culture, religion, and architecture. Writing about the Greeks, the historian Herodotus wrote, "We are one in blood and one in language; those shrines of the gods belong to us . . . all in common, and the sacrifices in common, and there are our habits, bred of a common upbringing."[10]

Certain cultural works and artifacts convey the sense of nationalism. In the United States, the novels of James Fenimore Cooper, Henry James, Herman Melville, Edith Wharton, Ernest Hemingway, and F. Scott Fitzgerald and the essays of Ralph Waldo Emerson, Henry David Thoreau, and Mark Twain exemplify American literature. The poetry of Emily Dickinson, Walt Whitman, and Robert Frost portrays the American mood in verse. The architecture of Louis Sullivan and Frank Lloyd Wright expresses American design. The White House, the Washington Monument, the Statue of Liberty, Mount Rushmore, the Lincoln Memorial, all evoke American consciousness.

For Germans, the literary masterpieces of Johann Wolfgang von Goethe and Friedrich Schiller and the music of Ludwig van Beethoven and Richard Wagner evoke the sense of being a German. Wagner, who composed some of the world's greatest operas, was also a strident nationalist. In France, nationalist themes were conveyed by Alexander Dumas and Victor Hugo, especially the latter's literary masterpiece, *Les Misérables.* The epic murals in the Louvre and the Chamber of Deputies portray glorious events in French history. The stirring strains of "La Marseillaise" and vistas of the Eiffel Tower and Arc de Triomphe elicit vivid images of France. For Italians, Giuseppe Verdi's dramatic operas portray Italia. Frederic Chopin's stirring Polonaise inspired Polish patriots to rally for their country's freedom. In China, the Great Wall, the Forbidden City, Tiananmen Square, and Mao's tomb tell the story of that country's cultural heritage. In India, the Red Fort, the statue of Gandhi in Bombay, and the Taj Mahal are physical symbols of the Indian past.

These works of art, literature, music, and architecture are aesthetic references in the psyches of those who share a common national consciousness. In the school curriculum, these great works are used to bring the young into contact with their national heritage.

Courses in literature, music, art, and drama as well as field trips are used to introduce the young to the monuments of their national culture so that they will recognize, participate in, and appreciate it.

Education as Cultural Transmission

Formal education and schooling for nationalism, particularly curriculum and instruction, takes the form of transmission of the national cultural heritage, developing patriotism and loyalty to the nation, instilling the proper performance of national ceremonies and rituals, and creating a national collective consciousness.

As indicated, nationalism rests on the shared collective consciousness that the individual shares membership with other nationals or citizens of the nation-state. The cultural consciousness is constructed through shared memories based on history and myth. In constructing cultural consciousness, the schools' primary role is to transmit the elements of the national culture to the young.

An important political issue that has strong educational implications regards the questions—What is the culture? Who determines what it is? Is the culture a completed or an ongoing project? In answering these questions, the different educational philosophies, ideologies, and theories line up on opposing sides. Conservatives and Essentialists see the national culture as already existing and construe **cultural transmission** as having the goal of molding people to fit into the existing culture. Liberals, Pragmatists, Social Reconstructionists, and Critical Theorists, in varying degrees, see American culture as an unfinished project, and argue that education is more than merely transmitting what is claimed to exist; it is designed to reshape and reconstruct American culture. Conservatives and Essentialists reply, in rebuttal, that an American cultural tradition exists and that to be sustained it needs to be transmitted to the young. Otherwise, they contend, the cultural relativism that they see their opponents proposing will erode core knowledge and values. They argue that an American cultural core belongs at the vital center of curriculum and instruction. An American cultural core would consist of the following:

- English as the language of instruction
- American history and government
- American literature

American History

Transmitting a national history plays a critical role in developing a national consciousness. This is particularly true in the United States where American Exceptionalism, the belief that the United States is a special nation populated by an exceptional people, had exercised a powerful influence on the national consciousness. In transmitting a national history, an official version is generally used to construct a sense of American nationality and identity. Such an official history is often highly generalized, emphasizing American progress, achievements, and victories. According to the historian Gary Gerstle, "nationalism demands that boundaries against outsiders be drawn, that a dominant national culture be created or reinvigorated, and that internal and external opponents of the national project be subdued, nationalized, vanquished, and even excluded or repelled."[11]

The content and interpretations of the history taught in schools have been continually contested. What is the official history? Who decides what it is? There are alternative interpretations of versions of the past and alternative versions of the culture. The issue becomes, What is the preferred version? A preferred version raises the further question of, preferred by whom? For nationalists, culture and history are raw materials used to mold and create the myths that vivify and sustain the preferred interpretation. The construction of an official culture and version of history requires decisions about what is to be consciously remembered and what is to be repressed or excised from the official version of the national memory.[12] Alternative histories develop under the surface and at the margins of the official history and struggle to replace or revise the official version of the past.

American Exceptionalism

The belief that the United States is a "shining city on a hill," "a beacon to the world," a special country blessed by Providence, and a country with a Manifest Destiny expresses an American version of nationalism called American Exceptionalism. Proclaiming that the United States is an extraordinary, unique land that is very different from and, indeed, better than other countries, American Exceptionalism is embedded in both American history and culture and in the public school philosophy.

Alexis de Tocqueville, a young French intellectual, spent 1831 and 1832 traveling throughout what was then the United States. In his insightful account of his experiences, *Democracy in America* (1835), Tocqueville detected the origins of American Exceptionalism in the young country. He wrote, "Everything about the Americans, from their social condition to their laws, is extraordinary; but the most extraordinary thing of all is the land that supports

Nationalism as an Ideology

Ideology	View of the Past	Present Program	Curriculum	Instruction	Issues
Nationalism	Uses history and myth to construct a shared national consciousness or memory.	To reinforce national identity through education, commemorative events, and definitions of citizenship.	National themes reflected in an official history, language arts, and literature. Patriotic events commemorated in school programs and activities.	Education as cultural transmission.	Should there be a national cultural core? An official language? Bilingual-bicultural education? Multicultural education?

them."[13] He observed that Americans "have an immensely high opinion of themselves and are not far from believing that they form a species apart from the rest of the human race."[14]

As the U.S. frontier moved westward to occupy the vast territory lying between the Atlantic and Pacific Oceans in the nineteenth century, many Americans believed they had a **Manifest Destiny** to occupy the North American continent. The term *manifest destiny* was coined by publicist John Sullivan, who wrote an article, "The Great Nation of Futurity." Sullivan wrote that,

> our national birth was the beginning of a new history, the formation and progress of an untried political system, which separates us from the past and connects us with the future only; and so far as regards the entire development of the natural rights of man, in moral, political, and national life, we may confidently assume that our country is destined to be the great nation of futurity.

Using the theme that the United States is a nation blessed by Providence, Sullivan wrote, "We are the nation of human progress, and who will, what can, set limits to our onward march? Providence is with us, and no earthly power can."[15]

Resting on the ideology of American Exceptionalism, Manifest Destiny proclaimed that Divine Providence, in bestowing a vast continent with immense expanses of land and an abundance of natural resources on Americans, had favored them above all other peoples. Protected from hostile and less deserving nations by the great Atlantic and Pacific Oceans, God had given Americans a bountiful land of vast expanses and natural resources to settle and exploit. In their protected homeland, Americans had created the best of all possible political systems—a republican government, democratic institutions, and a free enterprise economy. As the recipients of Providence's blessings, Americans had a mission to perform in the world. The United States, an exemplary and exceptional nation, was to be a beacon light of freedom and democracy for people in less favored lands.

Influencing American culture and politics, American Exceptionalism shaped American beliefs and attitudes about education. The public schools Americans established were agencies for constructing a sense of identification with and loyalty to the United States. The public schools, like the country they served, were unique institutions established to educate the sons and daughters of an exceptional people. Originally called common schools, they differed from the class-based educational institutions of Europe. Unlike old Europe's schools, American public schools were the great social equalizers that were open to all children of all people. While European schools reflected a socioeconomic class organization that benefited the children of aristocrats, American public schools brought children from all classes into one egalitarian institution. Whereas Europe's schools reproduced the socioeconomic status quo, American public schools gave students the gift of upward social and economic mobility. In the public education ideology, common schools are held to be special, unique institutions, created by an exceptional people.

Ethnonationalism

We now turn to ethnonationalism, an important contemporary ideology that is generating major changes in the relationships between people, especially in multiethnic nation-states.

Nationalism generates a sense of identification with the nation state; ethnonationalism unites the members of the same racial, ethnic, or tribal group in a sense of ethnic identity with their group.

At first glance, nationalism and ethnonationalism may seem to be very similar. In the nation-states where there is a single racial or ethnic group such as Japan and Iceland, nationalism and ethnicity converge and are mutually reinforcing. In multiethnic, multi-tribal, or multiracial nation-states, however, ethnonationalism may cause groups within the nation-state to diverge and often oppose each other.

Whereas Nationalism constructs primary identification and cohesion with the nation-state, ethnonationalism instead focuses primary identification and loyalty to one's particular racial and ethnic group. Ethnonationalism rests on the belief, often embodied in a powerful myth, that an individual is a member of a unique group because of descent from common ancestors and a blood relationship shared only with those similarly descended, as is the case of Serbs, Croats, Quebecois, Ibos, or Basques, for example.[16] Those sharing their perceived common ancestry may address each other as brothers or sisters. Ethno-nationalism sees the members of the group as related through kinship. Not dependent on genetic verification, the belief in common ancestry is mythic and emotional. Myth, as used here, refers to a powerful sense of meaning that may be partially historical or pseudohistor-ical but nonetheless is the reference point for belief in a common ancestral identity. Although the mythic ideology supporting ethnonationalism is emotional and subconscious, it creates ethnic group self-identification. For ethnonationalist identity, the scientifically correct description of ethnic group membership is not paramount; what the group believes to be historically and contemporaneously true is of utmost significance.

The various enthnonational groups have strong traditions and narratives, often epics, about the particular group's origins, history, triumphs, and adversities. Many ethnonational groups trace their origins to a creation story or epic. For example, the ancient Israelites believed they were descended from Abraham and the Romanians from the ancient Latinized Dacians.[17] The collective memory of Serbs is stirred by commemorations of their defeat at the Battle of Kosovo in 1389, when they were led by the heroic Prince Lazar. The transmission of the group's language and heritage from the older generation to the younger takes place through informal as well as formal education. In situations in which the partic-ular ethnic group is suppressed by a more dominant group, its ethnic heritage may be passed on informally or even secretly. Whereas nationalism seeks to focus on the nation as a larger and more encompassing entity, ethnonationalism, especially in multiethnic and multiracial nation-states, may erode larger commitments and replace them with more par-ticular racial or ethnic identification.

In Africa, ethnonationalism takes the form of tribalism. In countries such as Nigeria, Burundi, Rwanda, the Sudan and others, the primary identification is to the tribe rather than to the nation-state. In Nigeria, for example, the political and educational situation has been tortured by attempts of Yorubas, Hausas, and Ibos to gain hegemony over each other. In the Sudan, the dominant group, supported by the state, has repressed and conducted a cam-paign to remove the African minority.

In the Western world, ethnonationalism has asserted itself in political and educa-tional conflicts in Canada where the French-speaking Quebecois energetically seek to maintain their language and culture against Anglicization; in Belgium, where the Flemish resist Walloons; and in Spain, where the Basques seek greater autonomy. For international education, especially peace and conflict-resolution education and multicultural education, the contemporary rise of ethnonationalism poses immense challenges.

Nationalism, resting in the nation-state or country, and ethnonationalism, resting in the ethnic group, poses a contemporary world dilemma. In some instances, the nation-state and the ethnonational group are in violent confrontation and conflict. Some subordinated ethnic groups such as the Kurds in Iraq, Iran, and Turkey; the Chechens in Russia; and the Albanians in Kosovo have resorted to armed conflict to win independence. Some Basques in Spain have used terrorist tactics to win greater autonomy or independence. As an emergent or reemergent international trend, ethnonationalism is a significant force in multiethnic nation-states that range from technologically developed countries such as Canada and Belgium; to former Soviet-bloc countries in eastern Europe such as the constituent republics of the former USSR and the former Yugoslavia; to less technologically developed nations such as Somalia, Nigeria, Rwanda, and Sri Lanka. Ethnonationalism is a worldwide trend as the preponderant number of nation-states are multiethnic, and ethnic consciousness has been rising rather than diminishing.

Throughout the world, there are signs of ethnonationalist conflict and a recognition that political and ethnic boundaries rarely coincide. A list of conflict areas illustrates this point: Russia and the other republics of the former Soviet Union; Northern Ireland; the successor states of the former Yugoslavia; tribal conflict in Nigeria, Burundi, Uganda, and Somalia; ethnic and racial conflict in Tibet and other border regions of the People's Republic of China; communal strife in India, especially between Muslims, Hindus, and Sikhs; language conflict in Belgium between Flemings and Walloons; conflict in Mexico between mestizos and Indians; ethnic and language conflict in Canada between English- and French-speaking groups, particularly in Quebec. The issue among the Quebecois, the French-speaking people of Quebec, is whether they consider themselves to be Canadians or to be a different people. The issue illustrates ethnonationalism in a multiethnic country such as Canada. What is the language? What is the history? What is the culture? The list of conflict areas where ethnonationalism is the root cause is a long one.

Ethnonationalism and Education

As indicated, education, especially schooling, is a process that creates group identity and the sense of "we-feeling." Informal education—living in a particular ethnocultural milieu of family, church, and community—socializes children into that particular ethnic group. In instances in which the particular ethnic group is dominant, schools, too, continue the process of ethnic socialization. In instances in which the particular ethnic group is subordinate, however, its children may attend schools where the language of instruction and the curriculum reflects the dominant group's culture rather than its own. Historically, the process of Americanization in the United States represented the use of schooling to impose the dominant white, English-speaking, Protestant culture on subordinate groups. The process, if successful, erodes the subordinate culture and assimilates its members into the dominant culture. Some of the controversies over bilingual, bicultural, and multicultural education in the United States reflect ethnonational issues.

In some countries, ethnonational issues are interwoven with language issues. Is there to be an official language or are there to be several languages used in government and education? When ethnonational issues come to the surface in education, they involve: (1) using the ethnic group's language rather than the dominant group's official language; (2) including the ethnic group's traditions, literature, and history in the curriculum; and (3) constructing a school milieu that celebrates and reinforces ethnic group membership and identity. Defenders of the nation-state as the central focus of identity contend that using several languages and literatures rather than the dominant national one is divisive and weakens the nation-state. Those who seek ethnonational recognition, autonomy, or independence, in contrast, argue that each group has the right to ensure its ongoing existence. In education, conflicts between multiethnic state and subgroup ethnonational identity occur over control of schools, curriculum, and language of instruction. Cases of such conflict have occurred in Canada, where the Quebecois have resisted Anglicization; in Belgium, where the Flemish have resisted imposition of French; and in India, where non-Hindi speakers have opposed imposition of Hindi. Ethnonationalism creates resistance to cultural and educational imposition by other groups, but it also uses education positively to preserve and extend the particular ethnic group's identifying characteristics. Among these characteristics are: (1) the use of the ethnic mother tongue as the medium of instruction rather than the official national language; (2) inclusion of the ethnic group's literature, history, and traditions in the curriculum to create a sense of group identity; and (3) use of the hidden curriculum to reinforce a sense of "we-feeling" by cultivating a group response to ethnonational symbols.

In educational policy studies, the concept and force of ethnonationalism is one that needs analysis. Education, in its organized form as schooling, has traditionally: (1) transmitted the cultural heritage from the adult members of the particular society to the children; and (2) since the late eighteenth century, been a force for creating national identity through the teaching of a national language, literature, and history in the school curriculum. Although they involve some degree of imposition, these two large goals have shaped educational programs in modern nation-states. American educators have debated the degree to which the school and the curriculum should transmit and cultivate both a common cultural identity and also encourage recognition and cultivation of more particular racial, ethnic, and language identities. Multiculturalism has been an American educational response to cultural, racial, ethnic, and language diversities. However, there are many features of the American situation that differ from the ethnonational resurgence taking place throughout the world. One particular area of difference is the absence or slight degree of communication and assimilation between peoples of different ethnic backgrounds throughout the world. Further, the American educational experience with its manifestations of assimilation and multiculturalism fails to adequately correspond to the international phenomenon. Unlike immigrant and racial groups in the United States, the ethnonational groups throughout the world tend to be located in particular regions within nation-states that they consider their traditional ancestral cultural preserve and homeland.

Nationalism, Ethnonationalism, and Multicultural Education

Throughout history, nationalism has posed serious challenges to education for international understanding. Today, the resurgence of ethnonationalism has made these challenges even more pressing. The dilemma for educators is the tension that nationalism and ethnonationalism can lead to positive personal identification and group solidarity but also to destructive rivalries. Today, education in the United States and other countries is infused with multicultural programs that seek to cultivate the positive aspects of ethnicity without accentuating the negative aspects of rivalry, antagonism and conflict. Multicultural education emphasizes that although human beings belong to diverse racial, ethnic, and language groups they all share a common humanity with the same needs, hopes, and fears. Multicultural education seeks to expose and examine racial and ethnic stereotyping and bigotry.

The history of life on earth is one of magnificent cultural achievements but also of the gross inhumanity of people to each other. Throughout the world, this inhumanity has taken the form of violence by one national, racial, ethnic, or religious group against another. From the time of the great Oriental empires of Egypt, Mesopotamia, India, and China, purges and extermination of people who were different have occurred.

Violence of group against group reached its extreme form during World War II when the Nazis operated concentration camps in which millions of Jews, Slavs, gypsies, and others were systematically exterminated. The Nazi racial ideology regarded those who were being exterminated as subhumans who were to be eliminated so that the favored "Aryans" would rule the earth. Part of the process of extermination involved deliberate efforts to dehumanize the victims, as occurred in the infamous Warsaw ghetto. When one group looks at another as so different that they are not members of the same human family, the danger of violence and genocide occurs.

Since the end of World War II, multiculturalism and its inclusion in the school curriculum has become a worldwide educational movement. Internationally, it is possible to identify several cases in which multicultural education is either being implemented or needs to be implemented. Although some nations may appear to be homogeneous at first glance, on closer examination they are likely to have multicultural populations. Nations that have been settled by large-scale immigrations invariably exhibit multicultural situations. Among such nations are the United States, Australia, Canada, New Zealand, South Africa, Chile, Argentina, and other Latin American nations. In addition to the immigrant population in these nations, there is also the indigenous population that was present at the time of immigration. In the United States, the indigenous people is the Native American population. In Australia, it is the native Austroloid peoples, and in New Zealand, the Maoris. In these nations, multicultural education examines immigrant–indigenous cultures and relationships.

A second kind of multicultural issue arises in nations, often former colonial countries, that have a large number of ethnic, language, and perhaps racial groups. In Asia, India presents an example of a nation with 17 major languages, several large ethnic divisions, particularly those of Aryan and Dravidian stock, and major religions such as Hinduism, Islam, and Sikhism. Nigeria in sub-Saharan Africa, with its more than 400 languages and dialects, is still another example of a nation in this category.

A third type of multicultural issue can be found in eastern and central Europe, including the former Soviet Union, where different ethnic and language groups are included in the same nation-state. In these nations, ethnic and language tensions have a long history. Since the end of Soviet control, many supposedly dormant ethnic tensions have been rekindled. For example, the former Yugoslavia, especially Bosnia and Kosovo, composed of Serbians, Croatians, Slavic Muslims, is a region of ethnic, language, and religious hostilities. Ethnic and language tensions are also present in Slovakia between Slovaks and Roma, in Bulgaria between the Bulgar majority and the Turkish minority, and in Romania between the Romanian majority and the Hungarian minority. In addition to ethnic rivalries in central and eastern Europe, the region has a long history of anti-Semitism, especially in the former Soviet Union and Poland.

In western Europe, the former homogeneity that characterized nations such as the Netherlands, France, Germany, and the United Kingdom has been eclipsed by immigration to these countries. In the United Kingdom, there has been immigration of peoples from Britain's former colonies in Asia, such as Pakistan and India, in Africa, and in the Caribbean. In France, immigrants have come from Indochina and North Africa. In the Netherlands, there has been immigration from Indonesia. These former colonial rulers are experiencing the need for multicultural education. The United Kingdom, for example, had made concerted efforts at multicultural education, especially in its larger cities, where there is significant cultural, ethnic, racial, and religious diversity. Still another kind of immigration in western Europe has been that of workers and their families from countries such as Turkey who have settled in technologically developed nations such as Germany, Switzerland, and Sweden. With the implementation of the European Economic Community in 1992, Europe is becoming increasingly multinational and cross-cultural as persons from the participatory nations freely move across borders for economic, professional, and cultural reasons.

School administrators and teachers throughout the world are now experiencing the need to develop multicultural sensitivity and pedagogical skills to educate diverse groups. The awareness of the need for multicultural education has become so significant that James A. Banks, a leading authority on the subject, has called it "an international reform movement."[18]

Today, the world is full of ethnic, religious, and racial violence and atrocities. In India, the Muslims struggle against Hindus; in the Sudan, Arab fights against African. The list of ethnic, racial, and religious intolerance and violence goes on and on. This violence takes the form of terrorism, repression, and at its extreme, genocide.

Conclusion

This chapter examined the ideology of nationalism and the related ideologies of American Exceptionalism and ethnonationalism and their implications for education. It explored how national identity and collective consciousness is constructed from history and myth. It then considered how school systems are related to nation-states and are agencies for developing primary identification with the nation. National school systems were examined as agencies to deliberately instill the sense of nationalism in the young as a means of their political socialization in the nation-state. American Exceptionalism was examined as an ideology that has given Americans a belief that they are a unique, indeed, an exceptional people. Ethnonationalism was examined as a revival of an old but submerged ideology that makes the racial or ethnic group the focus of an individual's primary identification.

The world is organized into nation-states, independent, sovereign countries, each of which uses nationalism to create and maintain a sense of national identity. National school systems socialize that nation's children into its citizens. How this socialization takes place is vital for our future. It can involve both identification with one's own country but also respect for the people of other countries. Or, it can take the form of chauvinism, which exalts one's country over all others. Extreme nationalism has led to world wars and conflicts. Ethnic identification too can be a force of group pride and self-esteem. It can be a positive celebration of one's ethnic heritage that also respects the racial and ethnic heritages of other people. If, however, ethnic identification becomes a strident assertion of one group's superiority over others it can lead to suspicion of and violence toward other groups. Strident ethnonationalism can degenerate into ethnocentrism, the belief in the inherent superiority of one's group and seeing members of other groups as inferior.

Constructing Your Own Philosophy of Education.   At the beginning of the chapter, you were asked how nationalism, as an ideology, might relate to your own philosophy of education. Now that you have read the chapter and discussed it with your colleagues, will nationalism, especially American Exceptionalism, have an influence in shaping your ideas of education, schooling, teaching, and learning?

Building a Nationalist Vocabulary

American Exceptionalism: the belief that the United States is an exceptional country and that Americans are a special people.

Collective Memory: the shared consciousness of a nation's past constructed by history and myth.

Cultural Transmission: deliberately passing on the culture, through informal education and schooling, from the adults to the children of the society or nation.

Ethnonationalism: an ideology that asserts the primacy of the ethnic group in an individual's identification.

Manifest Destiny: the belief that it was the God-given right of Americans to occupy the North American continent.

Nation: a body of people, living in a particular territory, that is sufficiently conscious of its unity to seek or to possess a government of its own.

National School System: a system of schools organized, supported, maintained, and governed by the government of a nation-state.

Nationalism: an ideology that asserts the importance, value, and worth of belonging to a nation.

Nation-State: an independent country that occupies and is sovereign over particular geographical territory and has its own political, social, economic, and educational institutions.

Patriotism: a love, commitment, and desire for the well-being of the nation and its territory.

Questions for Inquiry and Discussion

1. What is a collective consciousness? Do you believe you share a collective consciousness? If so, how did your upbringing and schooling help to form this consciousness?

2. Think about the relationship of history and myth in forming a collective national memory. Did you encounter this relationship in your education? Do you find examples of it in schools today?

3. Do you find examples of American Exceptionalism in your own educational experience? Do you find it operating in schools and society today?

4. Reflect on the idea that schools should transmit the American cultural heritage. What does this mean for curriculum and instruction? Do you favor or oppose the concept of transmitting the cultural heritage?

5. In your own education, did you encounter special activities related to a national commemorative holiday or observation? What did you learn? Has this learning had an impact on your national consciousness?

Topics for Reflection and Inquiry

1. Reflect on your national identity. How did you become conscious of being an American? Write a short autobiography that focuses on your national identity, especially the role played by your community, schools, and teachers.

2. Begin a clippings file of newspaper and magazine articles that deal with the contemporary debate over immigration. After you have collected a number of articles, analyze them for elements of nationalism, American Exceptionalism, ethnonationalism, and multiculturalism.

3. Interview international students from various countries who are studying at your college or university. Invite them to discuss education, schooling, and the forming of national character from their own perspectives. Then, write a short paper that analyzes your findings.

4. If you are teaching or planning to teach in the primary and intermediate grade levels, examine the books and materials used in the language arts. See whether you detect elements relating to constructing a national identity.

5. If you are teaching or planning to teach at the secondary level, examine the books and materials used to teach history and literature. See whether you detect elements relating to constructing a national identity.

6. Begin a clippings file of newspaper and magazine articles that deal with the contemporary debate over bilingual and bicultural education. After you have collected a number of articles, analyze them for elements of nationalism, American Exceptionalism, ethnonationalism, and multiculturalism.

7. Debate the topic: "Resolved, the United States should have one official language."

8. Visit a cultural center or heritage museum of a racial or ethnic group. Determine whether the exhibits at the center or museum have ethnonationalist elements.

Internet Resources

For the theory of nationalism, access www.dmoz.org/Society/Politics/Nationalism/Theory.

    For a discussion of nationalism, access www.soc.ucsb.edu/Faculty/scheff/36-html.

For a discussion of the Nationalism project, access www.nationalismproject.org.

Suggestions for Further Reading

Alter, Peter. *Nationalism.* New York: Edward Arnold, 1994.

Banks, James A., and James Lynch, eds. *Multicultural Education in Western Societies.* New York: Praeger, 1986.

Branson, Margaret Stimmann, and Judith Torney-Purta. *International Human Rights, Society, and the Schools.* Washington, DC: National Council for the Social Studies, 1982.

Brass, Paul R. *Ethnicity and Nationalism: Theory and Comparison.* Newbury Park, CA: Sage, 1991.

Charny, Israel W. *Genocide: The Human Cancer.* Boulder, CO: Westview Press, 1982.

Connor, Walker. *Ethnonationalism: The Quest for Understanding.* Princeton, NJ: Princeton University Press, 1994.

Diamond, Larry, and Marc F. Plattner. *Nationalism, Ethnic Conflict, and Democracy.* Baltimore: Johns Hopkins University Press, 1994.

Edwards, John R. *Language, Society, and Identity.* New York: B. Blackwell, 1985.

Eriksen, Thomas H. *Ethnicity and Nationalism: Anthropological Perspectives.* London, UK, and Boulder, CO: Pluto Press, 1993.

Farnen, Russell F., ed. *Nationalism, Ethnicity, and Identity: Cross National and Comparative Perspectives.* New Brunswick, NJ: Transaction, 1994.

Gates, Henry L., Jr. *Loose Canons: Notes on the Culture Wars.* New York: Oxford University Press, 1992.

Gellner, Ernest. *Encounters with Nationalism.* Oxford, UK, and Cambridge, MA: Blackwell, 1994.

Gillis, John R., ed. *Commemorations: The Politics of National Identity.* Princeton, NJ: Princeton University Press, 1993.

Grosby, Steven. *Nationalism: A Very Short Introduction.* Oxford, UK: Oxford University Press, 2005.

Hutchinson, John, and Anthony D. Smith, eds. *Nationalism.* New York: Oxford University Press, 1994.

Ignatieff, Michael. *Blood and Belonging: Journeys into the New Nationalism.* New York: Farrar, Straus, and Giroux, 1994.

Kammen, Michael. *Contested Values: Democracy and Diversity in American Culture.* New York: St. Martin's Press, 1995.

Kellas, James G. *The Politics of Nationalism and Ethnicity.* New York: St. Martin's Press, 1991.

Nieto, Sonia. *Affirming Diversity: The Sociopolitical Context of Multicultural Education.* New York: Longman, 1992.

Reimers, Fernando, and Noel McGinn. *Informed Dialogue: Using Research to Shape Education Policy around the World.* Westport, CT: Praeger, 1997.

Smith, Anthony D. *National Identity.* Reno: University of Nevada Press, 1991.

Synder, Louis L. *Global Mini-Nationalisms: Autonomy or Independence.* Westport, CT: Greenwood Press, 1982.

Takaki, Ronald. *A Different Mirror: A History of Multicultural America.* Boston: Little, Brown and Co., 1993.

Watson, Michael, ed. *Contemporary Minority Nationalism.* New York: Routledge, 1990.

Williams, Colin H., and Eleonore Kofman, eds. *Community Conflict, Partition and Nationalism.* New York: Routledge, 1989.

Endnotes

1. *The Random House Dictionary of the English Language* (New York: Random House, 1968), p. 886.
2. Steven Grosby, *Nationalism: A Very Short Introduction* (Oxford, UK: Oxford University Press, 2005), p. 7.
3. Grosby, *Nationalism: A Very Short Introduction,* pp. 4–5.
4. In introducing his subject, Steven Grosby uses the phrase "us and them" as a basic feature of nationalism. See Grosby, *Nationalism: A Very Short Introduction,* p. 1.
5. Grosby, *Nationalism: A Very Short Introduction,* p. 22.
6. Grosby, *Nationalism: A Very Short Introduction,* p. 8.
7. Grosby, *Nationalism: A Very Short Introduction,* pp. 10–11.
8. Grosby, *Nationalism: A Very Short Introduction,* p. 26.
9. Grosby, *Nationalism: A Very Short Introduction,* p. 83.
10. Herodotus, *The History,* quoted in Steven Grosby, *Nationalism: A Very Short Introduction* (Oxford, UK: Oxford University Press, 2005), p. 2.
11. Gary Gerstle, "Liberty, Coercion, and the Making of Americans," *Journal of American History,* 84 (2) (1997), pp. 524–588; quote from p. 555.
12. Linda S. Levstik, Chapter 17: "Articulating the Silences: Teachers' and Adolescents' Conceptions of Historical Significance," in Peter N. Stearns, Peter Seixas, and Sam Wineburg, eds. *Knowing, Teaching, and Learning History: National and International Perspectives* (New York: New York University Press, 2000), p. 284.
13. Alexis de Tocqueville, *Democracy in America,* J. P. Lawrence, ed. (New York: Perennial Classics//Harper Collins, 2000), p. 280.
14. De Tocqueville, p. 374.
15. John L. Sullivan, "The Great Nation of Futurity," *The United States Democratic Review,* 6 (23), pp. 426–430.
16. My definition of ethnonationalism relies heavily on Walker Connor, *Ethnonationalism: The Quest for Understanding* (Princeton, NJ: Princeton University Press, 1994), p. xi.
17. Grosby, *Nationalism: A Very Short Introduction,* p. 12.
18. James A. Banks, *Multiethnic Education: Theory and Practice,* 2nd ed. (Boston: Allyn & Bacon, 1988), pp. 3–4.

9

Liberalism and Education

John Stuart Mill (1806–1873), English Utilitarian and Liberal philisopher who argued for individual liberty and freedom.

Chapter Preview

Liberalism, an important Western and American ideology, as an "ism" is derived from the word *liberal.* Liberals are open to change, believe in progress, and oppose restrictions on individual liberties. Opposing repressive political regimes, liberals support representative, parliamentary, democratic government. They believe that people should enjoy the greatest possible individual freedom and that this freedom should be guaranteed by the due process of law and the protection of civil liberties. In education, liberals are not bound by tradition but believe in the free flow of ideas and the testing of human experience. Liberalism, based on its Enlightenment origins, is optimistic about the possibility of the progressive improvement of human culture and society.

At the beginning of our discussion, we examine the concept of "liberal education." In its ancient Greek origins, a liberal education was an education for free persons (almost always men) in contrast to training for slaves. As the concept developed in Western education, liberal education came to mean a grounding in the arts and sciences. While Liberals may see education as liberal in the sense of the arts and sciences, Conservatives, too, endorse this kind of education. Liberalism in education means more than the arts and science curriculum—it also describes certain beliefs, attitudes, values, and especially procedures. The chapter discusses the following major topics:

- Historical antecedents of Liberalism
- John Locke as a founder of Liberalism
- Jeremy Bentham's and John Stuart Mill's Utilitarianism
- Modern American Liberalism
- The key elements of Liberal ideology
- Liberalism's educational implications

Historical Antecedents of Liberalism

Liberalism originated in the late sixteenth and early seventeenth centuries when medieval feudalism was disintegrating as a political system. The new commercial classes of shopkeepers, bankers, lawyers, and other professionals began to challenge the old landed aristocracy for social and political power. The established class structure at the time of the liberal challenge in Western Europe consisted of the feudal aristocracy and the peasantry. Aristocrats held land and with it, political power and social status. Membership in the aristocracy was ascribed because a person had to be born into aristocratic families. The same was true of the peasants who tilled the soil—their situation was largely ascribed. **Ascription** means that a person's role is defined at birth; a person typically stayed in the class into which he or she was born. Educationally, if a person's role is known at birth, educational decision-making is already done for the person. The son of an aristocrat will be educated to exercise his father's role as a landowner; the daughter will be educated to be the wife of an aristocrat. Children of peasants will be trained, largely by doing tasks, to be farmers. Although this socioeconomic condition prevailed during much of the Middle Ages, it began to erode as new classes emerged that were neither aristocrats nor peasants. Occupying a position on the social ladder between the aristocrats and the peasantry, these new middle classes were called the **bourgeoisie**. The middle classes came to their position through their use of economic power; they earned or merited their status. In the early eighteenth century, their political role was still being shaped—largely through their own efforts. Their educational situation, too, was ambiguous because they needed to create their own kinds of schools.[1]

By the eighteenth century, liberals had constructed an evolving ideology that challenged the absolutism of divine right of kings and lords. The rationalism of the Enlightenment, or Age of Reason, nourished liberal ideology. French *philosophes* such as de Tracy and Condillac, who had initially articulated the concept of ideology, sought to replace the dogmas of the church and the traditional authority of absolutism with what they believed were the empirically grounded truths supporting a new society. The *philosophes* believed they could construct a social science, an empirical way of studying society and politics, that replicated how scientists investigated natural and physical reality. Once they had discovered the natural laws of human growth and social development, they could begin a twofold mission of guided reform. First, existing ideas, especially those supporting institutions such as the absolutist monarchy, could be either removed or reconstructed; next, new, more rational and scientifically based institutions could be created. If this were done, humankind's future, unlike its past, would be better and more progressive. In this project for a progressive future, existing educational institutions—schools and universities—needed to be reappraised and transformed. Existing schools served their aristocratic and clerical masters in that they taught blind tradition and superstition as unquestioned "truths." Using dogmatic catechetical rote learning in schools and prescientific scholasticism at the higher levels, educational institutions maintained the old order's intellectual stagnation rather than the new progressive scientific outlook.

Liberalism was very much an ideology that came out of the intellectual, social, political, economic, and educational change spawned by the Enlightenment, the Age of Reason. It inspired the middle classes to throw off domination by absolute monarchs and privileged aristocrats. Culturally, Liberals looked to individual initiative and innovation to develop new social and educational structures and processes. An interesting feature of the Liberal cultural agenda is that it is always unfinished and remains incomplete.

John Locke: A Founder of Liberalism

In this section, we examine the contribution of the English philosopher John Locke (1632–1704) to Liberal ideology. Our treatment of Locke is divided into three parts: (1) a short biographical sketch, (2) a discussion of his work on epistemology and education, and (3) an analysis of his *Two Treatises on Civil Government* (1690), which established Liberalism's essential principles.

Locke's Biographical Sketch

Locke was the son of John Locke, an attorney and small landowner. Locke's family were Puritans who dissented from the Church of England. For the first fourteen years of his life, Locke was tutored by his father.[2] From 1646 to 1651, John Locke attended Westminster School. At this famous preparatory institution, he studied traditional Latin and Greek classics to prepare for entry into Oxford University. In 1652, at the age of twenty, Locke received a junior studentship at Christ Church College in Oxford. He was awarded the bachelor of arts degree in 1656 and earned his master's degree in 1658. In 1660, he became a lecturer in Greek, rhetoric, and moral philosophy. He then studied medicine. Although he did not complete a medical degree, he became a respected physician.

Locke's great attraction was to political philosophy rather than medicine. An appointment as secretary and personal physician to Lord Ashley, Earl of Shaftesbury, in 1667 brought Locke into contact with the world of politics. Among his duties, Locke served as the tutor of Ashley's son.

While Ashley was Lord Chancellor, from 1672 to 1674, Locke was close to political power and held several government appointments. When Shaftesbury fell from power during the Stuart restoration, Locke went into exile as an expatriate in Holland. While in exile, Locke completed his *Treatises on Government*. With the Glorious Revolution of 1688 and William and Mary's accession to the English throne, Locke returned to England where he was appointed Commissioner of Appeals. In ailing health, Locke retired from government service in 1700 and died four years later.

Locke made important contributions to Liberal ideology in his *Two Treatises of Government* (1689) and *A Letter Concerning Toleration* (1689). His works on philosophy, *An Essay Concerning Human Understanding* (1690) and *Of the Conduct of the Understanding* (1706), contributed directly to empiricist epistemology and indirectly to sense-based process learning. Locke's *Some Thoughts Concerning Education* (1693) dealt specifically with issues of teaching and learning.

Locke on Epistemology and Education

Locke's *An Essay Concerning Human Understanding* (1690) became a classic statement of empiricist epistemology.[3] Locke began his analysis by attacking the Platonic theory of innate ideas, which asserted that knowledge originated in fundamental concepts present in the mind at birth and prior to sensory experience. In attacking Platonic assumptions, Locke sought to establish the empiricist view that human knowledge originates in sense perception. At birth the mind is a **tabula rasa**, a clean slate, a white paper, on which the data of experience are impressed. These ideas are either simple or complex. If complex, they are relational and arise from mental faculties that enable us to compare, contrast, abstract, and remember them.

Locke's theory denied the exclusive reliance on tradition, custom, and authority based on immutable first principles. His **empiricism** emphasized the use of the scientific method. Locke's rejection of innate ideas and his *tabula rasa* concept of mind suggest that human character is shaped by experience. However, while there are no innate ideas in the mind, individuals have different mental potentialities.

Locke's epistemology argues that we construct our concepts of knowledge through the cognitive process of building ideas from our sense experience. Every human being possesses this power of generating ideas through experience; therefore, knowing is an individual matter. It is not limited to a group or class of people, such as an aristocracy or a gifted elite, who have an innate power of knowing more than others. Locke's epistemology individualized and equalized the process of knowing. Individuals have the freedom to act on their ideas and to accept the consequences for their actions.

Locke's *Conduct of the Understanding* reiterated the empirical epistemological arguments made earlier in *An Essay Concerning Human Understanding* and applied them to education. He argued strongly against the Platonic epistemology of innate ideas, which he felt impeded genuine empirically based reasoning. Locke warned that the belief in innate ideas gave an unwarranted credence to those who set themselves as authorities who had a special insight into the truth and whose pronouncements were to be accepted uncritically. Critical thinking, Locke argued, required a careful examination of how one's ideas had originated in sensation and how through analysis and reflection the products of sensation became clear and distinct ideas. Language was a construction to express our ideas with as much clarity and precision as possible. Discussion of ideas was to be done with civility, avoiding traditional biases and prejudices. Locke also introduced the concept of "indifferancy," which would be further developed by John Stuart Mill. Indifferancy meant being indifferent to partiality and striving for impartiality in weighing the evidence.[4] Recall that Postmodernists reject this concept of impartiality and objectivity, associated with Locke, that is a key Liberal principle.

Locke's *Some Thoughts Concerning Education* (1693) was not a philosophical treatise but rather a guide to an English gentleman's education.[5] Locke identified four major educational aims. The first is virtue, the practice of self-denial, which inhibits impulsive behavior and resists temptation. The cultivation of virtuous habits facilitates leading a life governed by reason. Education's second aim is wisdom, the shrewd and practical skill that enables a person to manage affairs and property successfully and to be prudent in human affairs. The third aim, good breeding, guides one in fulfilling life's social obligations. Learning, the fourth aim, is concerned with studying morality, politics, civil society, government, law, and history. Education is to develop the habits of reasonable thinking in children's minds and to develop their bodies physically. Locke's ideas about education followed themes that became part of Liberal pedagogy. Reinforcing the Liberal emphasis on individualism, Locke advised teachers to be cognizant and respectful of children's individual differences and to use a child's individual interests to motivate learning. Emphasizing the middle-class preference for utilitarian and practical rather than classical and ornamental studies, Locke recommended such useful subjects as reading, arithmetic, writing, accounting, geography, geometry, science, and history. Following the Liberal propensity for orderly procedures, Locke made a strong case that education should cultivate civility, which meant having personal self-esteem while encouraging the self-esteem of other persons and taking care to use power responsibly so as not to dominate others.[6]

Locke on Government

Locke's *Two Treatises of Government* had the greatest significance for the development of Liberal ideology. His concepts of representative government and the inalienable rights of the person expressed Liberalism's germinal concepts. In this section, we examine these concepts and their educational implications.

Locke's social contract theory contributed to a new conception of the polity—a commonwealth of self-governing individuals. While both Rousseau and Locke wrote about the social contract, Locke's **natural rights theory** and contract form of government had the greatest impact on the American Liberal theorists, especially Thomas Jefferson and the framers of the Declaration of Independence.

Locke and Human Rights

In 1690, Locke's *Two Treatises of Government* not only justified Britain's Glorious Revolution of 1688 but also elaborated a new ideological perspective. Finding the general principles governing human association in the original state of nature, Locke claimed that "no one ought to harm another in his life, health, liberty or possession." Each person, like every other individual, equally possessed inherent natural rights to life, liberty, and property. When these natural rights were in jeopardy, individuals in common association formed a social contract in mutual defense against those who transgressed these natural rights. Individuals entered into political society and formed a government to protect these natural rights. According to Locke, individuals who unite in one civil body have agreed to "a common established law" and can appeal to a judiciary to which they have given "authority" to settle "controversies between them" and to punish offenders.[7]

For Locke, individuals are free, equal, and independent and no one can deprive them of property or subject them to another's political power without their consent. Arising from the mutual agreement of those who form the civil society, government relies on majority rule, the fairest way of formulating policy and making political decisions. According to Locke, every person, by agreeing to form a government, enters "an obligation to everyone of that society to submit to majority rule."[8] While all the members of the society agree to the general processes of the social contract, some will agree and others will disagree on specific legislation. Majorities and minorities that arise over specifics are temporary and shifting. Based on the mutual respect of the individuals who comprise the civil society, the rights of both the majority and the minority are to be respected.

In Locke's version of civil society, the three branches of government—legislative, judicial, and executive—are calculated to achieve a balance of power. This threefold division of powers is clearly apparent in U.S. political institutions. In Locke's social compact, a known common law arises from common consent through elected representatives in the legislature. The executive of the commonwealth enforces the common law; the judiciary renders objective decisions based on its interpretation of the common law.

The legislature is created by the individuals who enter into the social contract; its power to enact laws is given to it by the members of society. The elected members of the legislature are subject, as are other individuals, to the laws they enact. Whereas the enacted legislation grows into a cumulative body of law that is subject to revision, the composition of the legislature itself is temporary, its members serving fixed terms. When its work is done in a particular session, the members of the legislature return to their various constituencies.

For Locke, and for Liberals in general, the legislature was the basis of representative government. Members of the legislature, coming from the ranks of the people who have joined in the social contract, represent these people. Crucial to the principle of a representative government was the process of election by which citizens elect their representatives to the legislature.

In addition to its political prescriptions, Locke's Liberalism held significant implications for education. First of all, Locke's prescription of representative institutions directly challenged the doctrine of the "divine right of kings," which held that authority descended from God to the king, then downward to a hereditary aristocracy, and then further downward until it reached the masses of the population. In the theory of the divine right of kings, no check existed on the sovereign except that which came from God.

In the class structure based on the divine right of kings theory of government, three political castes existed: (1) the reigning monarch and aristocracy of birth, (2) the clergy, and (3) the so-called third estate, which included all other people. Members of all three classes were educated according to the doctrine of social class appropriateness. Because the social roles of both the members of the aristocracy and the masses were ascribed at birth, the type of education that they were to receive depended on, or was appropriate to, their membership in a hereditary social class. Each hereditary socioeconomic class had political and economic duties that were also ascribed on the basis of birth. For the prince who was expected to succeed his father to the throne, there were instructions in statecraft, diplomacy, and royal etiquette. The prince's education was to prepare him to rule and to exercise authority. The aristocracy received the appropriate education to serve as the monarch's subordinates, magistrates, and officers. They were prepared to be generals in the army, administrators, or diplomats. The hereditary aristocrats were educated in the rubrics of court ceremony. Conversely, the masses of the population were trained as toilers, workers, and soldiers. Their civic duties were to hear and obey the commands of hereditary superiors.

The education of the hereditary aristocracy was based on ascribed political and economic roles. Leaders were born to rule and then prepared to exercise their authority. Likewise, followers were born to follow and then conditioned by their training to follow with docile obedience. Because a person's political role was ascribed, civic education was based on performing a specifically defined role rather than participating in the general political process.

In contrast to the theory of the divine right of kings, Locke's **contract theory** of government and the resultant Liberal ideology created a change in politics and education. To be sure, the political implications were evident much earlier than were the educational ones. Representative government meant that any citizen could be elected to serve in the commonwealth's legislature. The flow of political authority was no longer downward through a hierarchical pattern as in the model of the divine right of kings; rather, it arose from the people—from the governed—who, in forming the social contract, created the government. Because service in the legislature was not hereditary and was temporary, civic education was no longer appropriate to membership in a particular class. Instead, education was necessary for all citizens of the commonwealth so that they might participate in elections and serve in one of the three branches of Liberal government: the legislature, executive, or judiciary.

Of greatest significance in Lockean ideology was the need for members of society to be political generalists rather than specialists. An individual's civic destiny was not specifically defined at birth but was influenced by many factors, one of which might be election to office. The elective process also meant that every citizen would be a voter and a decision maker. Because Locke's ideology called for civic generalists, it also implied that a person's civic education should be general and include the following: (1) the theory of contract government based on the recognition of fundamental human rights, (2) knowledge about the organization and functions of government based on the divisions of power, (3) knowledge of the procedures of representative institutions, and (4) cultivation of civic attitudes and values that sustain representative institutions and processes. The educational implications of Locke's political theory were of immense significance in the United Kingdom and the United States. What was required was a new conception of civic education.

Locke and the Right of Revolution

In his *Two Treatises of Government,* Locke argued that the purpose of government was to protect the rights of its citizens. Whenever a government violates that trust, the people may replace it with a new one. Locke's treatise sought to justify the revolt of 1688 against the Stuart monarchy and the establishment of William and Mary as constitutional monarchs, subject to parliamentary rule, on the English throne. When a government—such as that of the Stuarts—sought to subvert basic human freedoms, then the people had the right to revolt to regain their original liberty and to establish a new government, thus renewing the social contract.

Thomas Jefferson, in writing the Declaration of Independence, used Locke's arguments to justify the American Revolution against King George III and English rule. Accusing the British monarch of violating the social contract and of depriving the American colonists of their natural rights, the Americans, Jefferson argued, had a right to overthrow and replace English monarchical rule with a new republican government. In appealing to the theory of natural rights, Jefferson proclaimed the self-evident truths that "all men are created equal, that they are endowed by their Creator with certain unalienable rights, that among these are life, liberty, and the pursuit of happiness."

By ignoring these self-evident truths, George III had violated the contract between the governed and the government. Jefferson affirmed the colonists' right to revolt and to establish a new government to fulfill the social contract and to secure the people's unalienable rights:

> Whenever any form of government becomes destructive to these ends, it is the right of the people to deter or abolish it, and to institute a new government, allying its foundation on such principles, and organizing its powers in such form as to them shall seem most likely to effect their safety and happiness.

Both Locke and Jefferson identified liberty as one of the three unalienable human rights. Liberty meant freedom to frame alternatives, to choose between them, and to fulfill them through political, social, economic, religious, intellectual, and educational action.

Classical Economic Liberalism

In the nineteenth century, the United Kingdom and the United States experienced the industrial revolution with the factory system of production. Along with Locke's political ideas, a group of economists, called the Manchester school, added a strong economic rationale to the Liberal ideas on politics and society. This economic rationale became know as **Classical Liberalism**.[9] Classical Liberals emphasize the right of individuals to possess property and engage in free trade with little or no interference from government.

Adam Smith, the foremost theorist of the Manchester school, endorsed a completely free trade or laissez-faire economic and political position. Smith argued that society prospered when its economy was free from government interference and regulations. A free market is the the most efficient mechanism in satisying human needs and in using natural and human resources most productively. He argued that a natural law of **supply and demand** works on its own to regulate the economy. When there is a need (a demand) for a particular product, enterprising entrepreneurs will establish businesses (factories) to manufacture and sell that item. After a time, the need for that item will be satisfied and a surplus will result. As the demand for the item falls, so will the price; factories manufacturing the item will either close or be converted to other areas of production; workers making the item will be laid off, become unemployed, and need to be retrained to make other items. According to Smith, political attempts to interfere with the natural functioning of the economy are doomed to fail and are economically and socially useless and counterproductive. Individuals should be encouraged to enter into business and compete with other individuals to make profits. To maximize their profits, they will invent new processes of making products more efficiently and more cheaply. These profits will result in investments in business expansion that employs more people and will trickle down to benefit the entire society. Government interference in trying to regulate the economy, supervise working conditions, or interfere with the natural law of supply and demand will result in bureaucracy that stifles economic innovation and growth.

Giving support to Smith's ideas were David Ricardo and Thomas Malthus. Ricardo, the proponent of the iron law of wages, provided industrialists with an economic rationale for low wages and long hours of work.[10] If wages rose above the subsistence level, workers would use the increased income to have more children. More children meant a labor surplus in which workers would be forced to work for reduced wages. A far better use of profits was more capital investment in more factories and machinery. Reverend Malthus, in his influential *Essay on the Principle of Population as it Affects the Future Improvement of Society,* in 1798, argued that population has a constant tendency to increase beyond the supply of food. If war or disease did not check population growth, famine would reduce it to manageable levels that could subsist on the food available.

In Classical Liberalism, individuals are the foremost actors in society, economics, and politics. In terms of social justice, Classical Liberals believe that the matter is an individual one because the formal equality of individuals remains as the paramount operating principle.[11] They would oppose what they would call "unwarranted and unnecessary meddling" to engineer some kind of social equality. Human relationships, like market relationships, are exchanges to satisfy individual interests.

Although laissez-faire economic policy became a standard feature of Liberalism, Liberal political theorists continued to stress freedoms of speech, press, assembly, and religion against a powerful state's interference. Economically, socially, politically, and educationally, Liberals sought to fashion and bring to power an ideology that asserted the rights of individuals and safeguarded the property rights, free markets, freedom of contract, and other interests of the rising middle classes.[12]

Dissatisfied with inherited traditional political, religious, social, and educational systems, Liberals argued for reforms. How to bring about that change was a major issue that divided Liberals into two camps: the laissez-faire classical liberals and those who advocated a limited government role in bringing about social and political reforms.

Utilitarianism

Liberals could agree on Locke's premises that individuals and their natural rights of life, liberty, and property precede and exist independent of society; however, they began to experience an internal tension about the nature of social change and reform, especially government's role. For the Classical Liberals—the followers of Smith, Malthus, and Ricardo—people could not legislate change, especially economic change, as it was governed by natural not enacted laws. They did, however, believe that certain kinds of political change could be legislated to protect free trade. For example, government could remove the tariffs, bounties, and taxes that the old aristocratic rulers had used to limit free trade. Other Liberals, especially the Utilitarians, the followers of Jeremy Bentham, believed that government legitimately could legislate limited incremental reforms that brought about gradual change.[13]

Jeremy Bentham (1748–1832), the son of a wealthy London lawyer and an intellectually gifted child, was called "the philosopher." He was educated at Westminster, a venerable English public school, and Oxford University. Although educated to be a lawyer, he did not practice law but committed himself to philosophy. He believed that England's judicial system needed to be reformed according to rational principles. Bentham's *Rationale of Judicial Evidence* (1827) proposed to replace Britain's cumbersome legal system based on precedent with a new legal code of easily applied basic regulations.

Bentham's *Introduction to the Principles of Morals and Legislation* articulated his Utilitarian philosophy. He called his philosophy **Utilitarianism** because it rested on the principle of utility, which meant, for him, maximizing pleasure and minimizing pain. He believed that an individual could calculate, or estimate, the likely degree of pleasure or pain that a particular action would produce. Social actions, too, could be evaluated by the principle of "the greatest good for the greatest number of people."

Bentham's Utilitarianism shifted the Liberal focus from inalienable natural rights to individual self-interest. His emphasis on an action's usefulness in bringing about predicted consequences came to guide Liberal policymakers. Bentham's method of calculating a law's or program's anticipated consequences and then measuring these expectations against actual results was a forerunner of the proposition that everything that exists can be measured. It anticipated using opinion polls to measure public opinion and approval.

Bentham's Utilitarianism retained but broadened the central Liberal concept of individualism. Though individuals still acted in their own self-interest, they could relate their individual self-interest with those of others. This uniting of interests had the social benefit of bringing about the good of those who had conjoined their interests. This broadened concept of individualism marked Liberalism's transition from an exclusive concern for the individual to broader social issues. Existing institutions, laws, customs, traditions, and conventions could be reevaluated. If they did not produce the greatest good for the greatest number, they could be reformed.

Liberals, in general, both Classical Liberals and Benthamite social reformers, were active politically. True to Locke's original Liberalism, they both believed in elected representative government and in checks and balances. Classical Liberals wanted policies that would establish free trade policies, protect private property, and ensure competition. They were adamantly opposed, however, to government social programs. Utilitarians, in contrast, believed a limited government role was needed in areas such as education, police, and sanitation.

Advocating moderate, measured, gradual, and nonviolent reform, Utilitarianism relied heavily on education to cultivate an informed public opinion. Bentham saw popular education as the means by which individuals would know their true self-interests and could participate in forming the public interest. Under the leadership of Bentham and other Utilitarians, the University of London was established in 1828 to emphasize social philosophy and social science to educate people about the process of reform.

John Stuart Mill

John Stuart Mill (1806–1873) was a proponent of Liberalism in philosophy, social policy, and education.[14] Mill's reconceptualization of Liberal ideology, based on a revision of Jeremy Bentham's Utilitarianism, moved Liberalism in the direction of humanitarian social reform.

For Mill, personal freedom and the free expression and circulation of ideas were necessary conditions for a life and society of quality. In *On Liberty,* Mill expressed his belief in human progress through the exercise of freedom of thought. According to Mill, "the only purpose for which power can be rightfully exercised over any member of a civilized community, against his will, is to prevent harm to others. His own good, either physical or moral, is not a sufficient warrant."[15]

Mill based his emphasis on individual liberty on his belief that a society benefited from the presence of critically minded individuals who challenged conventional wisdom and originated new ideas. Liberty and criticism were utilitarian or useful to a society because they made it possible to express divergent opinions and test new ideas. Mill obviously opposed authoritarian and despotic government that used overt power to censor ideas. However, equally dangerous to intellectual freedom was the power of conventional thinking, tradition, and customs that impeded free expression. Intellectual freedom meant freedom of expression—the freedom to communicate ideas in speech, in print, and in the classroom. This meant that the school should not be an agency to impress conventional wisdom and the status quo on the young but rather an agency to foster individual intellectual initiative, especially the power of critical thinking.

Mill's political philosophy rested on the Liberal ideological commitment to an elected representative government in which legislators are responsible to those who had voted them into office. Mill believed that civil liberties are best secured and defended by political conditions of self-government. Representative government required that the people, the electorate, have a civic education that made them conscious of the need to maintain their liberties and to elect legislatures that would act in the name of liberty.

Mill prophetically anticipated what he feared was the construction of a mass mind, a generalized and pervasive mentality that might be generated through mass communications that catered to sensationalism rather than to critical thinking. In the nineteenth century, the best-selling newspapers appealed to the largest readership. To attract this readership, the reporting of news and human interest features was geared to the widest possible audience, a mass audience. To capture the largest possible audience, the media geared their reporting of information and presenting of entertainment to what the majority wanted. Although he favored a free press, he feared the power of a press that thrived on sensationalism and catered to the puerile readers. If he were alive today, Mill would fear the power of the mass media and mass entertainment—television, motion pictures, and even the Internet—to orient their presentations to the appetites of the largest possible audience. Instead of providing choices, the mass media creates a sameness in which most programs, geared to the average audience, end up being the same in a kind of self-induced censorship that generates its own pervasive conformity. (Also, see the chapter on Existentialism.)

Just as Mill feared the **tyranny of the majority** might reduce standards to the average, he feared that representative institutions might be subverted when special interest groups (lobbies) promote legislation to advance their causes rather than those of the greatest number of persons. Mill looked to education, especially the education of a disinterested group of citizens, who could resolve the dilemma of special interests.

For Mill, a group of well-educated persons, or **disinterested participants**, might be able to stem the tide of the tyranny of the majority as well as reconcile the contentions of conflicting special interest groups. A disinterested person was one who was neither biased by personal interests nor motivated by the desire for personal profit. Although the disinterested person was unprejudiced, he or she was nonetheless a participant in the social and political processes and not aloof from them. Unlike the member of the special interest group, the disinterested person would not be motivated to seek special privileges or advantages. The quality of disinterestedness implied having an educated perspective that made it possible to evaluate an issue objectively. Educated people, Mill reasoned, would be concerned with the general good rather than special class interests. Note that Postmodernists, Marxists, and Critical Theorists dispute the possibility of the disinterested observer.

Mill argued in *On Liberty* that new ideas that express human inventiveness and creativity advance individual and social progress. In a social and political climate of freedom of thought and opinion, alternative ideas will be expressed and compete with each other. From the competition of ideas, truth will emerge and new policies will be formulated.

The Utilitarianism of Bentham, James Mill, and John Stuart Mill moved Liberalism into a new direction. Not only was it an ideology that sought to safeguard individual and civil liberties but now it was to be an instrument of social, political, economic, and educational reform. The new social reformist strain in Liberalism split the Liberal ranks. Some Liberals remained loyal to the Classical Liberal doctrines of noninterference by government and laissez-faire in the economy. In the United States, these Classical Liberal doctrines became part of the Conservative ideology (which is examined in the following chapter). Other Liberals saw the government as a necessary agent of social reform. It needs to be pointed out that the new social reformist Liberals were not revolutionary. They believed that reform should take place incrementally and bring a gradual improvement that restored existing institutions to an efficient and good working order instead of overturning them. This moderate and incremental concept of reform became a central feature of American Progressivism.

Based on our survey of Utilitarianism, we can speculate about how a Utilitarian would reform schools. They would accept schools as necessary and beneficial institutions. However, over time, schools, like other institutions, become overly formal and too traditional. The curriculum and methods of teaching might become irrelevant to socioeconomic change. They might not reflect scientific discoveries and technological innovations. When this happens, the schools themselves need to be reformed. The curriculum and teaching methods can be reformed to incorporate new areas of knowledge. Indeed, some new subjects and skills might need to be added and obsolete ones removed. Such a process of reform would make schools more utilitarian, more relevant, and more efficient. This kind of reform would work for the good of the greatest number of students and teachers.

American Reform or Modern Liberalism

In this section, we examine American Liberalism, which is sometimes called **Modern Liberalism** or Reform Liberalism to distinguish it from Classical Liberalism. It is also sometimes referred to as social welfare liberalism. To simplify terminology, we shall refer to the American version of modern liberalism as Reform Liberalism.

In the United States, Liberalism was infused by the reform impulses of the Progressive movement. Occurring from the late 1890s through the early 1920s, the Progressive movement attempted to reform American politics, society, economics, and education. Progressive reform was stimulated by the work of investigative journalists such as Upton Sinclair, who wrote an exposé of the meatpacking industry in *The Jungle* and Ida Tarbell, in her exposé of the Standard Oil Company. Progressive investigative journalists wrote for popular journals such as *McClure's Magazine* that had a large readership. Progressive politicians such as President Theodore Roosevelt, President Woodrow Wilson, and Senator Robert LaFollette supported legislation to reform government, curb the powers of economic monopolies, and conserve natural resources. Like the Utilitarians, Progressives believed in bringing about reform through essentially liberal processes that involved: (1) identifying an area that was not functioning in the service of the general public because it was being manipulated or controlled to the advantage of special economic interests, protected by corrupt politicians; (2) raising the public's consciousness about the malfunctioning problem area through investigative journalism; (3) having experts conduct empirical, often statistical, research into the problem; (4) structuring possible ways to remedy the situation and fix the malfunctioning sector; and (5) passing laws to reform the problem and to regulate the area to ensure that it functioned efficiently and that those who were responsible for operating the area were held accountable to the general public.

Progressivism transformed American Reform Liberalism. It gave a large role to education—both through informal agencies such as the media and press and through formal ones such as schools and universities. The expert advice of academics, especially professors who were authorities in economics and sociology, often aided in drafting legislation. It also gave the government, or state, a regulatory power to ensure that things were functioning in the public interest. For example, federal inspectors were to make periodic checks to ensure that food and drugs were being processed safely and hygienically. It gave inspectors the authority to inspect mines and factories to ensure that working conditions were safe. Reform Liberalism's regulatory power had moved American Liberalism far from the classical laissez-faire position of little or no interference with the economy. It was at this point that the Classical Liberal ideas of the free marketplace and a limited government role in the economy was appropriated by American Conservatism.

Progressive reformist Liberals initiated legislation to restrict child labor and to make schooling compulsory for certain age groups. Their argument was that such actions improve the quality of people's lives and also enhance economic well-being in the long run. The movement to restrict child labor and require compulsory school attendance in the United States represented the tension between Classical and Reformist Liberalism. For example, Jane Addams and other American reformist liberals organized the National Child Labor Committee in 1904 to work to remove children from the workforce. Compulsory school attendance laws, enacted in many states, required children's mandatory attendance in school to age fourteen. In 1916, Congress passed the Keating-Owen Child Labor Act, a federal law to restrict child labor. However, in 1918, the U.S. Supreme Court, relying on Classical Liberal precedents, ruled that the law was unconstitutional because it violated freedom of trade in interstate commerce.[16]

In the 1930s, President Franklin Roosevelt's New Deal sought to bring the country out of the Great Depression. Roosevelt used the federal government to provide relief to millions of unemployed people and their families, by establishing programs to stimulate recovery and enacting laws that would reform the system. Roosevelt's New Deal, like the earlier Progressive movement, was an effort at internal reforms that would save the American political and economic system by incremental changes rather than radically transforming or overthrowing it. The important point in both the New Deal and the earlier Progressivism is that it relied on government (especially the federal government) to be the major agency of reform. This change was almost diametrically opposed to the Classical Liberalism of the nineteenth century that wanted the government to stay out of society and the economy.

Along with the new Liberal politicians and journalists, several leading educators, too, called for the development of a new Liberalism that saw government providing needed social services in the new industrial, corporate society. Foremost among these educators was the prominent Pragmatist philosopher, John Dewey, who urged that Liberalism become an active ideology that promoted a cooperative society that provided for the social welfare and education of all of the people. George S. Counts, a Reconstructionist educator, called on teachers to join with other Progressive groups in working for a more planning, collaborating, and sharing society. Harold Rugg called on the schools to prepare people to use the new technology for social betterment.

President Johnson's Great Society Program

President Lyndon B. Johnson's Great Society and War on Poverty programs enacted in 1965 provide a clear illustration of the working premises of American Reform Liberalism. It is especially informative for the role Johnson, who wanted to be known as the "Education President," gave to education. Johnson, whose ideological formation took place as a National Youth Administrator during Roosevelt's New Deal, took a broad view of the federal government's socioeconomic and educational role.[17] A former teacher and school principal, he was earnestly committed to a larger federal role in education.

Johnson saw education in broad socioeconomic terms that connected it to progress in society. Federal aid proposals would be key elements in a comprehensive program of broad socioeconomic change. He envisioned education as an important component in a comprehensive federal policy to eliminate poverty and promote social welfare and economic growth. Federal programs would be used to stimulate and diffuse innovations throughout the nation's schools.[18]

Johnson relied on the Liberal-Progressive strategy of expert opinion, often from social scientists, to provide evidence that supported his proposed legislation. Liberal scholars argued that America's big cities, particularly their urban ghettoes, and some rural areas, such as Appalachia, were blighted by poverty issues, especially high unemployment and little economic investment. John Galbraith, the liberal economist, in his *Affluent Society* had called attention to the existence of pockets of poverty, a residual problem in an otherwise seemingly prosperous economy. Liberal economists linked poverty to two conditions: the residual factor, identified by Galbraith, and structural adjustment, unemployment due to low or inappropriate workers' skills in a technological economy. Johnson's War on Poverty sought to correct both of these deficiencies by eliminating poverty in its residual pockets and by training and educational programs to help the workforce adapt to structural changes in the economy. Liberals, taking a view that human beings are essentially good, attributed higher crime rates and drug abuse in urban ghettoes to structural weaknesses in the urban environment that could be corrected. If the social environment, the communities in which people lived, was improved, individual behavior also would improve. At this point in our analysis, we can detect Liberal ideology at work in several ways.

Johnson's War on Poverty programs required community participation on advisory and other kinds of boards and committees. These requirements were designed as community-building, consensus-generating strategies. Events in the late 1960s, however, would replace his ideas of consensus with conflicts as angry students demonstrated on campuses against the war in Vietnam and the inner cities exploded in urban disorders.

Liberalism's Transformation

As a result of Progressivism, the New Deal, and the Great Society, Liberalism was transformed into modern or social welfare Liberalism. Liberals still prized the freedom of the individual and civil rights and liberties, but they now extended their ideological perspective to give government a greater role. The government, especially the federal government, was to improve the general welfare by providing old-age pensions, health care, social security, and aid to hitherto disadvantaged groups; ending racial segregation; and promoting integration, affirmative action programs, protection for persons with disabilities, and aid to people at the poverty level. As importantly, liberals believed that education was about more than learning basic skills and subjects. Public schools were redefined as agencies to promote gradual social change. They were to provide compensatory education to help economically disadvantaged children; to devise means of ending racial segregation and creating racial integration; to mainstream children with disabilities into regular classrooms; to provide early childhood education; to develop programs addressing sex education, drug

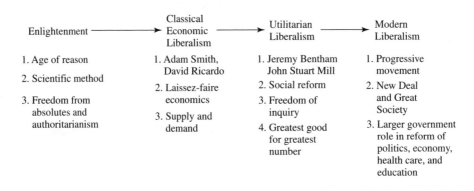

Development of Liberalism

and alcohol abuse, and AIDS education; and to create a climate of multiculturalism. In other words, the new Liberal agenda made schools into much more than academic institutions—they were to act as multipurpose institutions that were involved in treating social ills and solving social problems. Modern American Liberalism emphasizes equal protection and treatment of individuals. It also has worked to equalize economic and gender opportunities and to promote respect for cultural and religious diversity within a framework of shared operational procedures.

Liberalism's Core Elements

In the following sections, we identify and examine certain key elements in Liberal ideology. Among them are the Liberal conception of property and the economy, the Liberal view of human nature and reason, secular orientation, the emphasis on the individual, the propensity for progress, the reliance on representative institutions, the programmatic nature of Liberalism, and the view of social change. These concepts provide the framework for Liberal views of schooling.

The Liberal Conception of Property and the Economy

In its historical origins, Liberalism appealed to the property-owning professional and business middle classes. Note that Locke asserted that the possession of property was an inherent individual right. Liberal policy and legislation sought to safeguard the individual's economic freedom to compete and acquire property. Economic initiative and competition emphasized an effective means of satisfying needs arising from self-interest as well as bringing about general economic prosperity.

The Liberal rights of property involve the freedom of contract—that employers have the right to hire, employ, and dismiss employees; and that investors have the right to earn income, decide how to invest their money, and to make a profit, a financial dividend. (They also face the prospect of losing their investment because of poor investment strategies, or to the vicissitudes of the market.) This self-motivated economic interest stimulates people to invest their time and money in education, hoping to learn saleable skills to enter and advance through the corporate economic ranks.

Although agreeing on the basic core right of individuals to hold private property, Liberals disagreed on the extent to which the economy should be regulated. Laissez-faire Classical Liberals, insisting that government should keep its hands off the economy as much as possible, would restrict the role of government to guaranteeing a free enterprise climate and a competitive marketplace, governed only by the laws of supply and demand. Conversely, Reform Liberals see the government functioning as a regulating agency to prevent restraint of trade, to ensure the health and safety of workers and consumers, to protect the environment, and to regulate the hours and conditions of work.

When Reform Liberals moved toward social welfare policies, they revised the principle relating to the right of property. While still asserting the right to own property as a fundamental individual right, they used the "greatest good for the greatest number" mechanism to argue that the government needs to assist individuals in the lowest socioeconomic levels, especially at the poverty level, with the resources—food, health care, low-cost housing, and job training—needed to help them improve their condition. Government needs to encourage affirmative action programs that give preference in college and university admissions and in jobs to members of underrepresented minority groups. To support this assistance, those in higher income groups should pay a higher rate of taxation, a progressive tax, to generate the needed revenues for social, health, and educational services. For modern Liberals, property, though still an individual right, should not be permitted to overturn the right of a person to the necessities of a decent life—health care, housing, and education. It was on this point that Classical Liberalism, now part of American Conservatism, and Reform Liberalism diverged. Today, Conservatives argue that excessive taxation associated with the Liberal welfare state is taking away the right to own property.

Liberal economic theory has an impact on educational policymaking. In economic policymaking, education is an input, an investment that relates to productivity and to careers and occupations. It leads to debate over how funds for education should be used. Should they be directed to training in saleable skills, to develop technological competency, to enhance American competition in the global economy, for social programs, or other kinds of programs? Liberals, both Classical and Reformist, insist on freedom to choose one's occupation or profession. Liberals argue that attending school and completing high school and college leads to higher-paying jobs. However, the choices made in education have consequences because they may or may not lead to employment. Classical Liberals seek to predict employment needs based on supply and demand. Reformist Liberals weigh educational policies in terms of social and health as well as economic needs.

Ideologies are permeable in that concepts from one ideology may be appropriated and used by another ideology. In the United States, this has occurred with Neo-Conservatism, which appropriated some key provisions of Classical Liberalism. It is an interesting ideological twist that contemporary U.S. Neo-Conservatives have annexed key economic principles of Classical Liberalism as part of their agenda. They seek to deregulate the economy by removing or reducing Reformist Liberal regulatory controls over business and the corporate sector. They also seek to eliminate affirmative action guidelines designed to provide reserved proportionate educational places and jobs for underrepresented members of minority groups, on the grounds that it unfairly circumscribes individual initiative and merit. Some Neo-Conservatives would privatize schooling by issuing vouchers that parents could use to select educational alternatives to public schooling. (For a further discussion of the Neo-Conservative appropriation of Classical Liberal economic theory, see Chapter 12, Conservatism and Education.)

A fuller discussion of globalization follows in later chapters, but at this point the term *Neo-Liberalism* is introduced as it relates to Liberalism and its critics. Some Postmodernists, Critical Theorists, and Neo-Marxists have attacked what they refer to as Neo-Liberalism, or the role of corporate capitalism in the global economy. These critics contend that Neo-Liberalism represents the linking of corporate capitalism with the pretense of establishing democratic institutions throughout the world for exploitative profit-making purposes. Like the nineteenth-century Classical Liberals, contemporary proponents of globalization argue that countries, especially less technologically developed ones in Latin America, eastern Europe, and Africa, need to restructure their governments to reduce regulations and subsidies to inefficient economic sectors such as small farmers, to eliminate trade barriers and restrictions on free trade, and to create democratic institutions. The proponents of a worldwide free market economy argue that globalization's long-term benefits will reduce production costs and make goods available to more buyers in an expanding global marketplace. Similar to the arguments of laissez-faire economic theorists in the nineteenth and early twentieth centuries, the proponents of free trade globalization contend that the elimination of tariffs and other trade barriers, erected by individual nation-states, will make production more efficient and bring jobs to more people, especially in less technologically developed countries. Globalization's critics see it as a strategy to exploit the world's poor by turning the earth into a global factory, whose engines are driven to give wealth and power to corporate elites. Given their criticisms directed against Liberalism, especially what they have coined as "Neo-Liberalism," Postmodernists and Critical Theorists need to restudy the history of Liberalism, noting its complexity and the tension between Classical and Reformist Liberals. They also need to note the permeability of ideologies and how Conservatives have appropriated many Classical Liberal ideas and accommodated their ideology to them.

Rationality and the Power of Reason

Liberalism's origins began in the eighteenth century with the Enlightenment, the Age of Reason, a powerful intellectual movement that eventually reshaped the European and American worldview. The key ideas of the Enlightenment were voiced by the *philosophes,* a group of French intellectuals that included Denis Diderot, Etienne Condillac, and Jean-Jacques Rousseau. They believed that human beings, by their nature, possessed the power to reason. For them, reasoning took an empirical direction. By using the scientific method, people could observe and examine natural and physical phenomena. They also sought to create a social science in which individuals could examine society, politics, and education in much the same way that they did the physical world. Social science would enable them to discover the natural laws that were meant to apply to social, political, economic, and educational institutions. If these natural laws were permitted to function, human life and society could be reformed, improved, and perfected. However, powerful special interests and institutions were entrenched, blocking the needed inquiry and the projected reforms. Among the institutions that blocked reform were the monarchy, in which a king ruled with unquestioned authority by the grace of God; an aristocracy who occupied the places of influence and privilege, not by merit, but simply by their birth into noble families; a Church that emphasized the unquestioning acceptance of its dogma; a society and economy based on rigid social class divisions and the proposition that the "poor would always with us"; and schools and teachers who told students that "they lived in the best of all possible worlds." The *philosophes'* questioning of the institutions of the old order worked to undermine them and contributed to the republican ideas of the American Revolution of 1776 and the French Revolution of 1789.

Liberalism asserts the human power of using reason to solve problems and improve life and society. What interfered with the free exercise of reason were the residues of superstition and ignorance. Once the channels of free inquiry were cleared of the debris of an unenlightened past, human intelligence could take its course. James Mill, the father of John Stuart Mill and a committed Utilitarian Liberal, argued that reasonable individuals could "weigh evidence" to make their decisions. Believing in the power of the majority to make correct decisions, he claimed that the greatest number of such reasonable persons would "judge right."[19] John Dewey, a modern Reformist Liberal, moved the cause of freed intelligence further when he argued that the scientific method of inquiry could be applied to life's myriad social, political, economic, and educational problems.

The Liberal assumption that human beings are rational and that most people can be reasonable have enormous educational implications. In informal education, especially in the media and in publishing, there needs to be freedom to access and disseminate information. As John Stuart Mill argued, freedom of speech, press, and assembly encourages competition in the marketplace of ideas.[20] School libraries and computer programs need to be free of censorship. Teachers need to use methods, especially the scientific method, that liberates and uses intelligence.

John Dewey, in *How We Think,* provides a useful examination of how thinking, or reasoning, occurs. His discussion of epistemology illustrates the Liberal emphasis on the efficacy of human reasoning and its application in schools. Like Mill and earlier Liberals, Dewey identified the conditions that interfere with critical and problematic thought, or reasoning. Existing conditions, especially customary beliefs, may block inquiry. In resisting change in society and schools, the belief that something should remain as it has always been has a staying power that blocks inquiry into new patterns of thought and action. To establish the conditions that encourage reflective thought in school, it is necessary to challenge customary with scientific thinking.[21] Dogmatic beliefs that compel students to follow established rules handed down by some authority are based on maintaining the status quo. For example, staying with the existing curriculum because it is already in place or using the same teaching methods because they are comfortable when alternatives might produce better results represent the power of unexamined traditions to block inquiry and innovation.[22]

For Dewey, as well as for many Liberals, reflective thought requires research into the facts, collecting and weighing evidence, developing tentative hypotheses for action, conjecturing the likely consequences of acting on these hypotheses, and selecting a particular hypothesis, reaching a reasoned conclusion.[23] In Dewey's discussion of reflective thinking there is a similarity to what James Mills referred to as "weighing the evidence." Reflecting on or weighing the evidence is characterized by a tentative attitude, a time to pause and think about its validity. It involves a conscious inquiry into the nature, conditions, and bearings of the evidence. While this process is going on, the reflective inquirer needs to suspend judgment. Suspending judgment means that conclusions are tentative and subject to further revision.[24]

Secularism

Although they might be religious in their personal lives and be members of churches, Liberals generally oppose state efforts to enforce religious conformity and support officially established churches. In France and Mexico, Liberals worked to disestablish the Roman Catholic Church as the official religion. In England, Liberals, often members of dissenting or nonconformist churches, wanted to free both political and educational life from domination by the official Anglican Church.

Thomas Jefferson, a founding father of the American republic, sought to separate church and state.[25] In particular, he wanted to disestablish the Church of England as Virginia's official church. Jefferson believed that officially established churches denied citizens liberty in the free exercise of religion as well as the objective pursuit of knowledge. Jefferson's "Bill for Establishing Religious Freedom" in 1779 stated that ". . . God . . . created the mind free, and manifested his supreme will that free it shall remain by making it altogether insusceptible of restraint." Arguing against religious tests as a basis for citizenship and for public office, Jefferson asserted that "civil rights" do not depend "on our religious opinions."[26] The Constitution of the United States prohibits the establishment of religion by the government, guarantees the free exercise of religion to its citizens, and prohibits a religious test to vote and to hold public office.

The role of religion in American politics, society, and education is still controversial and divides Liberals and Conservatives. Although many of the republic's founders shared Jefferson's belief in **separation of church and state**, others such as Benjamin Rush believed that the nation's origins and purpose reflected Christianity. In the nineteenth and twentieth centuries, the U.S. Supreme Court generally upheld separation of church and state and religion from public education. In the twenty-first century, most American liberals argue for maintaining separation of church and state. However, the strict separation of church and state is questioned by Neo-Conservatives and Christian fundamentalists, who want prayers in public schools, publicly funded vouchers for their children to attend religious schools, and the teaching of Creationism in the science curriculum.

Liberals believe that religious identification and church membership is a personal rather than a public matter. Individuals should be free to practice their religion but are not to impose their beliefs on others through state-ordered observances, ceremonies, or financial aid. There should be no religious test for citizenship or to seek and hold public office. For Liberals, church and state should be separate and public schools should be separate as well. Believing that religious dogmas can block freedom of inquiry, Liberals contend that public schools need to be free from religious controls. They oppose religious instruction, religious observances and prayer, posting the Ten Commandments, and the teaching of Creationism in public schools.

The Liberal principle of separation of church and state has generated some strong opposition in the United States. The chief opposition comes from Christian Evangelical Fundamentalists, often associated with the Neo-Conservative ideology. Many Roman Catholics, too, believe that the doctrine of separation of church and state has been overextended from the founders' original intent and want state aid for Roman Catholic parochial schools.

Christian Evangelical Fundamentalists base their opposition on two lines of argument. First, they say that the United States was established as a Christian nation and that the ideas of the founders of the republic were based on Christian ideals. Second, they contend that Liberals, while denying the right of others to religious observance and instruction, have imposed their own secular humanist creed in public schools. They see Secular Humanism as a relativistic ideology, derived from Liberalism, which sees all truth and values as human constructions rather than commandments coming from God. They also oppose Secular Humanism's claims that human behavior, especially values regarding right and wrong, are culturally based and relative to different cultures and not universal. This moral relativism has weakened values and created an "anything goes" kind of attitude. Fundamentalists believe the restoration of religious values in schools will remedy what they see as the decline in moral values and behavior caused by relativism.

Individualism

A key Liberal core concept is that individuals possess inherent human rights that society cannot give or take away. Rather, society exists to promote and protect these individual rights. For example, Locke proclaimed and Jefferson reiterated that the individual person possesses unalienable natural rights of "life, liberty, and property" that government is created to protect and maintain. The "Declaration of the Rights of Man and the Citizen" proclaimed in the French Revolution asserted that "all men are born and remain free and equal in rights." In these early statements of Liberal individualism, the person's rights exist prior to society and remain regardless of the particular social and political order in which he or she lives. The thoughts and activities of individuals are to be private and as free as possible from government interference or regulation.

By the early nineteenth century, Classical Liberals interpreted the priority of the individual as the person's right to unrestricted economic competition. The Social Darwinist Herbert Spencer asserted that individual competition was nature's means of selecting the fittest for survival. Even in the reformed Darwinism of John Dewey, the individual was still prior to the group. While social intelligence came from group interaction and participation, the group, composed of separate individuals, depended for its existence on its individual members.

Clearly, the Liberal impulse sought to advance the freedom and development of the individual person. In education, Liberals, concerned with the individual student and his or her progress, did not sacrifice individual needs to group or social needs. Some Liberals, such as Herbert Spencer, saw education as preparing individuals for a competitive world; others, such as John Dewey, stressed cooperative group participation. What was common to educational Liberals was their emphasis on individuals, their needs and development.

In its development, Liberals, though agreeing on individualism as a necessary core concept, differed on the individual's relationship to society. This tension still affects how Liberals relate to society and to education. Reform Liberalism reaffirms individual rights and freedoms, often framed as human rights and civil liberties, but simultaneously emphasizes the importance of human association in government, society, and education. For Liberal principles to function in society, there needs to be a commonly held social **consensus** to use agreed-on political and educational processes. This kind of procedural or process consensus relies on a social contract to uphold certain working premises and to follow agreed-on methods.

In the historical origins of the American common schools, Horace Mann, Henry Barnard, and other leaders saw public education as constructing a broad consensus that embraced democratic institutions, private property, a strong work ethic, and patriotic values. Public schools in their mission statements still reflect this commitment to consensus building.

In American public schools, there is a simultaneous, but not always realized, emphasis on both the individual and the group. This emphasis arises from two basic and simple classroom realities: individual children are educated in group settings. From these realities, teachers face two equally compelling premises: (1) they are to identify and respect the needs and interests of each child as an individual; (2) they are also advised that social success requires individuals to function well in groups and that group activities, especially collaborative learning, are an effective and socially enriching way to learn. For example, the Reform Liberal attitude to the individual and the group is reflected in group activities. As members of a group, students are encouraged to express and share their ideas with the group; they are then expected to cooperate with other students in reaching an agreement or consensus in a collaborative way that will enable the group to meet its goals, solve its problem, or complete its project.

Further, the tension between Classical and Reform Liberalism surfaces over competition and cooperation in schools. Children are encouraged to be creative, even competitive; to do their own work; and to respect private property and the property of others. At the same time, they are also encouraged to be good group members, to take turns and to share, to use collaborative learning to solve group problems, and to be team players.

These ideological paradoxes in schools mirror those in the larger society of the tensions between the individual and the group. Individual competition and initiative is prized but so is being a team player and an effective member in business corporations and an active joiner and participant in community projects.

Progress

Since the Enlightenment, Liberals have believed that the liberation of human intelligence will lead to progress. Although not defining **progress** specifically, Liberals were committed to the possibility of improving the human condition. Because Liberalism arose in the context of the rapidly changing society and economy of the industrial revolution, Liberals saw science and technology as instruments to improve the conditions of life. Unlike traditionalists or conservatives, followers of Liberalism did not look backward to a "golden age" in the past.

As Liberalism developed ideologically, Classical and Reformist Liberals began to differ on how progress would occur. Both Liberal camps agreed that it was necessary to remove obstacles such as political absolutism and religious establishment that interfered with progress. Once these obstacles were removed, Classical Liberals believed that natural laws of supply and demand and individual competition would lead to scientific discoveries and technological innovations. Government should ensure freedom of competition but otherwise limit its scope of operations. Reformist Liberals, however, believed that progress needed to be stimulated.

Utilitarian Liberals such as Jeremy Bentham and James Mill believed it possible to calculate and to achieve good for the greatest number of people. U.S. Progressives believed it possible to create a "Great Society" in which all Americans could share in the good things of life. Woodrow Wilson could design plans for the ending of World War I by means of an international parliamentary body such as the League of Nations. In general, Liberals believed that society was dynamically changing for the better and human intelligence could create a good society by means of reform.

Running throughout Liberalism, from its view of the past to its present policies, programs, and projects, is the concept of progress—the belief that the future can be better than the past through liberating human energy and creativity, using the methods of science, and exercising freedom to inquire and to act. The Liberal outlook has been progressive and directed to the present and future rather than to the past. Liberals eschew utopianism and do not envision the establishment of a perfect society. Rather, their view of social reform is limited and relative in that if a social or institutional imbalance or strain appears, then reform is needed to apply the necessary remediation or regulation so that the institution will function more effectively and efficiently.[27]

Representative Political Institutions

Liberalism brought change in western Europe and in the United States about the concept of the state and government's role and functions. Historically, Liberalism grew out of the protest, and in some cases the revolt, of the middle classes against states that ruled them but in which they had either no voice or only a very limited one. In England, liberals challenged the Stuart monarchs' attempts to rule by divine right. In Britain's thirteen American colonies, the colonists rebelled against British colonialism and established their own republic. In France, the revolutionaries overthrew the Bourbon monarchy and the aristocracy.

Although these political actions differed somewhat because of the contexts in which they occurred, they had a common thread running through them—the desire to establish political institutions and processes that would give the middle classes the right to govern themselves. The revolutionaries, now in positions of power, established legislative bodies that would represent the citizens who elected their members. In the United Kingdom, the legislative body was the House of Commons, in the United States the Congress, and in France the Chamber of Deputies. Eligible voters would elect the members of these legislative bodies for fixed terms. After serving in Congress, for example, its members would return to the people. An important point was that the terms of these members were for a fixed duration and not for life. Further, they were elected and did not gain their seats by ascription—by inheritance because they were from noble families. The Liberal formula of **representative institutions** recognizes that the state needs power to effect the decisions of the majority. However, it requires that the exercise of power be done through approved procedures, through due process, and that it be as limited and restrained as possible. Those who exercise power are accountable for its use and for following representative political processes.

Liberalism's emphasis on process, gradual reform, and change contributed to a conception of the state that functions by means of elected legislative bodies. The interests of the people are identified with the power of the state through a representative government in which elected representatives are responsible to the electorate. Liberalism's political processes, especially in England and in the United States, emphasized the power of numbers and the roles of majorities and minorities in the process. With the creation of parliamentary government, revolution left the street and entered the legislative chamber where it became institutionalized in peaceful parliamentary processes. In such a system, the majority is not to abuse its power; the minority has the right to work for change through legislative processes. Further, majorities and minorities are temporary and will change as their members shift their positions on specific issues.

Further, within the Liberal state, constitutional guarantees of civil rights protect the individual against arbitrary action by the government. The U.S. Constitution, adopted in 1788, illustrates the constitutional process. According to the U.S. Constitution, the state machinery is based on the principle of popular sovereignty; the Bill of Rights protects and guarantees civil liberties, and the Constitution may be amended peacefully.

Liberal political processes emphasize the freedom of individuals to make their own choices about electing candidates for public office. Hopefully, the choice is an informed one; however, if not informed, it is nonetheless the right of the individual to make his or her choice and to be responsible for the consequences that come from that decision. This freedom of choice applies to voting for candidates for public office; choosing a college or university; choosing a career; and a range of life options.

Education for General Citizenship

The Liberal emphasis on representative political institutions has profound educational implications. As noted, in an absolutist political state or in one ruled by hereditary aristocrats, the person or persons who will govern the state are well known in advance of their actual taking of power. They can be given the prescribed and specific education that prepares them to rule. For example, the education for a prince is appropriate to his being king; for a princess to be queen; for an aristocrat to be a member of a ruling elite. In these situations, there is no need for aptitude tests or for career guidance. What is in place is the doctrine of education that is appropriate to a known future. In a system of representative institutions, however, it is not known in advance who will be president, a governor, or a member of Congress, for example. The often cited adage, "A student in this class may become President of the United States," is true.

The proposition that citizens of the country elect their leaders and legislators carries with it a need for general citizenship education that will: (1) provide a general knowledge base and understanding of how the political system works; (2) provide citizens with the skills to make informed decisions about those they will elect to office: (3) provide future elected officials with the knowledge and skills they need to be responsible and responsive representatives of the citizens who elected them; and (4) build a value commitment to respect and use the system. Note that these four points apply to all citizens generally—voters and elected officials.

The Need for a Generally Educated Public. Liberal societies and governments have established systems of popular education designed to cultivate a generally educated public. While particular career, occupational, and professional training are also provided, schools cultivate a general education in the belief that the performance of responsibilities, such as voting in elections, requires a literate and generally educated citizenry. The assumption underlying general educational policies and programs is that citizens will be called on to make decisions in areas other than the specialties related to their occupations or professions.

Still another argument for general education arises from the need to have educated persons who can be disinterested decision makers. John Stuart Mill believed that disinterested decision making was needed to maintain the sense of objectivity that Liberals see arising from the application of reason to the political, social, economic, or educational situation.

Liberals believe that an educated citizenry should have a general interest in the problems and issues of the society and also have a methodological commitment to the representative and parliamentary processes designed to resolve these issues. In addition to this general interest, individuals and groups have special interests. For example, teachers may have a special interest in the support given to schools but a general interest in trade or energy policies. In dealing with general interests, individuals can be disinterested (not having a special interest) in resolving them. On any given issue, a body of disinterested citizens can be expected to deal with the issue objectively.

Civic Education.   In addition to general education, Liberalism emphasizes a particular kind of civic education that is specific to both the cognitive and affective development of future citizens. In the cognitive dimension, civic education seeks to develop knowledge of the institutions and structures related to government. This would include a historical perspective on the organization and development of these institutions and an analysis of their functions in contemporary society. For example, the civic education of a U.S. student would involve an examination of federal, state, and local government and of the executive, legislative, and judicial branches of government. Civic education also seeks to cultivate values that encourage a commitment to participate in the political process.

The affective dimension of civic education, according to Liberalism, is public accountability. All those who hold public office are expected not only to fulfill the requirements of the position but also to maintain the integrity of the process. Public service, though renewable, is temporary in that elected officials come from the public and return to it on completing their terms of office.

An important cognitive and attitudinal blending is found in the Liberal notion of civility. As indicated, Liberals tend to stress process or procedures both in politics and in education. They assume that individuals need to know what the process is, how it came to be, and how it works. Raising issues, then defining, discussing, and resolving them are to take place in a reasonable, nonviolent, procedural fashion in which the participants agree to the process, follow it, and exercise civility. For Liberals, civility means to have a respect for but not necessarily an agreement with the opinions of others and to follow the rules of orderly decision making. Obviously, Liberals in education would stress learning and playing by the rules.

Constitutional Literacy

Similar to the Liberal emphasis on civic education, Toni Marie Massaro recommends constructing a core curriculum around the theme of the U.S. Constitution and cases related to its interpretation, especially those concerned with rights and due process. Massaro argues that (1) there is an "American paideia," a concept of formative education, that brings persons into civic understanding and participation; (2) schooling is a powerful force of cultural transmission and formation; (3) a curricular core that emphasizes constitutional literacy can revitalize schooling's central mission in U.S. society; and (4) such a constitutional curricular core can develop a consensus to accommodate both political and procedural commonalities and cultural conflicts.[28] Massaro's emphasis on constitutional literacy reiterates Liberal arguments that in order to maintain and renew itself, a society needs agreed-on processes that can keep conflict within a communal framework. When the framework does not exist or has eroded to the degree that it is ineffective, disagreements may become noncommunal to the extent that the society can no longer maintain and renew itself in a peaceful, nonviolent way. Necessary to agreed-on processes is the building and creation of a consensus—a shared commitment to accept and to use the processes. Liberals, historically, have been consensus builders. They seek to create a middle, moderate, or centrist position in politics, society, and education that can accommodate pluralisms within a shared framework of processes or procedures.

Massaro's argument for constitutional literacy takes a middle position in debates over multiculturalism and a cultural core. Proponents of a national core curriculum, such as E. D. Hirsch, Jr., Allan Bloom, Arthur M. Schlesinger, Jr., and others, argue that cultural commonality, its consensual core, is disintegrating and needs restoration. Proponents of a national core curriculum attribute this cultural disintegration to both a declining historical and political public literacy and to a deliberate disuniting of the strands of U.S. cultural identity by extremist multiculturalists. Critics of a national core curriculum, preferring cultural diversity and multicultural pluralism, counter that the public school curriculum should no longer transmit a monocultural version of U.S. cultural identity as it did in its assimilationist past. Rather, it should encourage racial, religious, gender, and ethnic pluralism.[29]

Seeking to build consensus, Massaro proposes a synthesis to unite contentious factions in a procedural framework. She argues that (1) a national core curriculum is needed; (2) such a curriculum can embrace both the commonality that unites Americans as well as the diversity and pluralism that enriches their society; and (3) the U.S. Constitution, its rights and processes, provides the context for constructing the curricular core and for cultivating a sense of constitutional processes. Massaro contends that the Constitution and its legal interpretation offer a coherent framework for a core curriculum that can be used to educate a constitutionally literate populace that is sensitive to the issues of freedom of religion and expression, and equal protection of the law. Her analysis confronts what she regards as Liberal democracy's essential educational paradox—promoting "neutrality among competing versions of the good life while trying to instill . . . the principles of the liberal democratic state, among them the nonneutral preference for critical deliberation."[30]

Meaningful conversation, informed by constitutional literacy and undertaken within a consensual framework of shared processes, will encourage productive explorations about religious, racial, ethnic, gender, class, and other differences. With a constitutional core in place, teachers and students then can critically examine the U.S. continuing multicultural issues—its racial, religious, ethnic, gender, and class conflicts.

Process-Oriented Change

Once it had evolved from its revolutionary origins in the early nineteenth century, Liberalism came to emphasize a cautious, moderate, and balanced approach to solving social, economic, and political problems. Liberal methodology was one of limited objectives in which problems were solved one by one. Liberals avoided developing utopian grand designs that promised to solve all social problems in one broad sweep. Liberals, including modern

Social Welfare Liberals such as John Dewey, were suspicious of large-scale hypotheses for social transformation. Large transformative agendas broke the continuity of testable experience by making often utopian leaps into untested, uncharted, and remote waters.

Although they shared some basic common assumptions, Liberals eventually divided into two camps. Classical Liberals, such as Herbert Spencer, continued to believe that government was best which governed least. Classical Liberals, who preferred that government maintain its role of passive watchdog and avoid entering into social reform, regarded any such ameliorative legislation as social tampering that would only confuse and worsen the condition that it sought to remedy.

On the other hand, modern Liberalism—originating with the British Utilitarians and continuing down to the reformist progressives—believed that government should exercise regulatory and ameliorative functions. Where social abuses or injustices existed, the government should correct them. Furthermore, only government could provide needed social services in such areas as sanitation, factory regulation, water supply, and education, among others. In approaching problems, however, modern Liberals usually deal with specific issues rather than general social reconstruction.

Theories such as Social Reconstructionism and Critical Theory, discussed in later chapters, have attacked Liberal incremental reforms as being piecemeal and lacking the power to transform society. Liberals would counter that sweeping transformative agendas, generally more polemical than substantive, fail to arise from existing conditions and neglect the necessity to constantly relate means and ends. They would contend that supposedly transformative, good-intentioned proposals have often had tragic consequences, unanticipated by utopian reformers, such as the reign of terror in Robespierre's revolutionary France or the massive purges of Stalin in the Soviet Union.

Liberalism encourages an intellectual outlook that recognized change as part of an evolutionary process. Change could be encouraged by nonrevolutionary and gradual legislative reforms. The traditional Liberal process of legislating change was to investigate a problem; collect statistics, data, and evidence; and then recommend reform legislation.

Gradualism, moderation, balance, and the absence of a sweeping grand design all characterize the Liberal temperament. Liberals are process oriented in their devotion to the scientific method or the method of legislative reform. The efficacy of the process requires that its users respect it. It was not the end result that was important in the long run; it was, rather, a willingness to use process and to implement its results.

In school curriculum and instruction, Liberal educators, especially in the United States, emphasized process-centered education. Both John Dewey and William Kilpatrick exalted democratic processes in education. Kilpatrick's "project method" was designed so that children would work in groups to solve specific problems. Learners would not only solve the specific problems, but also concomitantly acquire experience in using group-centered democratic procedures. Collaborative learning, a contemporary revival of the project method, sees learning enriched by the sharing of information and the participatory use of skills. Collaborative learning, in some respects, is a pedagogical counterpart to Reformist Liberal participatory democracy. (See the chapter on Progressivism.)

Liberals emphasized process and opposed ideologies in which the ends justified the means. As life, society, politics, and education changed, the processes of the scientific method or of democratic procedures gave individuals some control over their destinies.

Human intelligence could chart the course of the future. Not bound by long-standing traditions nor mired in abstract theoretical dogmas, Liberals could deal with present problems in an unencumbered and relativistic way.

Liberalism's Educational Implications

In this section, we examine several of Liberalism's educational implications. Among them are Liberalism's promotion of universal education, process-oriented teaching and learning, and the defense of academic freedom.

Universal Education

When Liberal political parties in the United Kingdom, the United States, France, and Mexico won power in the nineteenth century, they gradually established universal education systems. A universal system of education provides formal schooling, usually government mandated and supported, to a broad section of the population, typically children and adolescents. These school systems transformed Liberal knowledge beliefs, political processes, and values into educational content and processes. In particular, they came to emphasize civic (citizenship) education. Often, they were directed to constructing children's identification with the nation-state and in cultivating a political socialization that features Liberal processes and values. School climates came to reflect the Liberal emphasis on the value of literacy and training, commitment to republican civic processes, and the need to maintain public order and practice scientific processes. The Liberal interpretation of civic sensibilities and productive economic individualism replaced more traditional religious beliefs and values. For example, anticlerical Liberals in France and Mexico ended the Catholic Church's special privileges in education.

In the United States, common school leaders such as Horace Mann and Henry Barnard followed the American Whig party's general Liberal orientation. They saw public education as a necessary corollary of republican civic institutions and political processes. Universal public education provided an investment against misinformed mobs that might be manipulated by demagogues. For example, Horace Mann's emphasis on property and individual initiative reflected the developing merchant and industrialist capitalism in the United States in the nineteenth century. Mann believed that business leaders had the social and educational responsibility to be the stewards of wealth and society. The taxes they paid to support schools were an investment in the future of their community and their country that would be repaid in the dividends of social stability, political order, and economic productivity.

In addition to the arguments cited by Liberals on the relationship of universal education to government, business interests saw organized education as a means to train future generations to be industrious workers and efficient managers. Industrial intelligence could be diffused throughout the population through the schools. Thus, Liberals in Western Europe and in the United States could be counted among the friends of organized systems of education. While some Liberals were altruistic, others saw schools to be instruments of social control of unruly elements in society.

Educational Policy in a Liberal System

In a Liberal system, policy development and implementation are often slow and uneven. This is especially true if one considers two Liberal prescriptions, namely (1) that power should be diffused through a system of checks and balances, and (2) the need to maintain a vital center, or sense of balance. Although U.S. education is constitutionally a state responsibility, educational policymaking is also done by the federal government and local school boards. In particular, the U.S. historical tradition supports locally controlled school policies. The process of making educational policies, then, is slow and uneven, depending on a variety of policy-making authorities. This diffusion of power protects schools from monolithically imposed policies and also from rapid reform.

In public education, various individuals, groups, and associations have agendas for policy formulation. These organizations include such diverse groups as the National Education Association, the American Federation of Teachers, parent–teacher associations, the National Association of Manufacturers, the American Legion, and many others. The result of these often conflicting educational agendas has been that policy tends to be centrist, not moving in radically different directions, as least in the public sector.

Modern Reformist Liberals have moved increasingly toward a larger federal educational role. State and local control and funding of schools has created inequalities in education. For example, in *Savage Inequalities,* Jonathan Kozol documented wide disparities between facilities and programs in the poorest inner-city communities and schools in the wealthier suburban communities. Liberals, though not endorsing a national school system, have supported federal initiatives to reduce these inequities.[31]

Process-Oriented Instruction

The Liberal conception that life should be lived, especially socially and politically, according to well-defined and mutually accepted procedures has a particular relevance for teaching and learning in schools. Both early childhood education and primary education can establish and reinforce procedural habits such as respecting other children's property and of taking turns and waiting to use certain items or playthings.

The concept that the group should establish its own rules of governance and conduct is also a Liberal derivation found in some classrooms. The assumption underlying this kind of discipline is that such rules will be more readily accepted and adhered to by members of the group if they arise out of common consent and consensus. In U.S. secondary schools, a wide variety of student organizations, clubs, and associations exist, each having its own elected officers who conduct meetings according to parliamentary processes.

It is anticipated that these procedural behaviors, learned by participating in the school milieu, will become habitualized standards of behavior that will be transferred to the larger out-of-school society. Membership in school clubs or associations provides experience and may lead to the skill of working well with others, which can contribute to success in business. Participation in school activities is expected to reinforce a civic outlook that sees voting in elections, running for office, and serving on juries as an ethical responsibility. These predispositions arising in the school milieu are also designed to create an attitude that disputes and conflicts should be settled according to nonviolent and fair procedures.

The distinction between schools as separate from explicit political ideology and yet reflective of and encouraging of attitudes, values, and methods supportive of a Liberal civic outlook is a difficult and delicate one. In the Liberal orientation, the methodology associated with decision making in the broader society is also compatible with academic freedom within the school. Critics, especially Critical Theorists, however, allege that the school in a liberal democracy is a servant of the reigning political ideology.

Liberalism and Academic Freedom

In this section, we examine Liberalism and academic freedom—the freedom to teach and the freedom to learn. First we consider how the Liberal view of **negative freedoms** has shaped academic freedom. By negative, we mean those situations that interfere with education and need to be eliminated. We then examine how Liberalism has positively defined academic freedom.

Negative Freedom and Education

Historically, Liberalism, as a largely middle-class ideology, opposed the absolutism and traditionalism of the old aristocratic political order, especially its limitations on individual freedom. It sought to remove restrictions on freedom by limiting government's authority. For example, among these liberal negative freedoms are: there shall be no restrictions on freedom of speech, press, and assembly; there shall be no taxation without representation; there shall be no interference with free exercise of religion. The concept of negative freedoms can be extended to education, schooling, and teaching and learning in the classroom.

Freedom from a Restrictive Past.   Liberalism does not ignore the past but rather wants it to be instructive for interpreting the present and planning for the future. History can be instructive; it can also be limiting when the past is seen as the source of customs, traditions, and practices that need to be followed in the present and safeguarded for the future. Everyone has had educational experiences and almost everyone has attended school; therefore, there are concepts of education that come from this past experience. The important premise for Liberals is that this past be revisited and revised but not be used as an ironclad straitjacket on thinking. A restrictive sense of the past is one that does not allow traditions to be questioned. For example, the past-based traditional view that schools should limit their curriculum to basic skills such as reading, writing, and arithmetic limits curricular innovation, reconstruction, and change. In societies worldwide, there are many traditional prohibitions and prescriptions on women and their education—on what they can or cannot be taught.

Freedom from Indoctrination.   Historically, Liberals sought to separate church and state. In doing so, they ran into the reality that historically schools were organized and supported by churches. Church-supported schools taught the religious doctrines, beliefs, rituals, and values to the young so that they were brought into church memberships and could defend their denominational beliefs against other churches. Today, church-related schools still perform this role, which includes defending believers against secularism which they believe dominates public schooling. Many church-related schools perform the function of bringing the young, immature members of the church into its doctrines. In this sense, *indoctrinate* means to lead to and instill doctrines.

Liberals, such as Jefferson and Mill, opposed religious indoctrination as closing the mind to considering alternatives to the church-sanctioned doctrines. For example, evolution was regarded as contrary to Biblical authority, to church doctrine, and so should not be taught.

In the twentieth century, the Liberal view of indoctrination broadened to include prescriptions against what they regarded as closed political totalitarian ideologies, namely Fascism, Nazism, and Communism. These ideologies insisted that they possessed political truth and that other political alternatives should be eliminated. Students according to these totalitarian ideologies were to be instilled with their political truths. Now, Liberals faced a dilemma—should teachers who were members of totalitarian political parties be allowed to teach?

Freedom from Censorship.   For Liberals, among the negative freedoms of individuals is that there shall be no restriction on the free and open exchange of ideas. In schools, this means the freedom of teachers to teach within their area of academic competence; it also means the freedom of students to learn, even if it means questioning tradition. The Liberal view of **academic freedom** is that critical thinking is valued and encouraged in schools. However, there are many times when academic freedom is threatened even in a Liberal society. There are those—both individuals and organizations—that do not want some things taught, discussed, and studied in schools.

A Positive Statement of Academic Freedom.   From a negative statement that opposed limitations on academic freedom, Liberals developed a positive conception of academic freedom. Schools should be places of academic freedom, where teachers are free to teach and where students are free to learn, without having their freedom curtailed by censorship or arbitrary controls. The curriculum should be open to new ideas and to methods of inquiry in which students are free to ask questions that may challenge the status quo. Libraries should not be censored but should include on their shelves controversial books. Teachers should encourage critical exploration and discussion of ideas in which students can question and share ideas.

Academic Freedom as Process.   In their approach to politics, society, and education, Liberals value the processes of using appropriate methods or procedures to do things fairly, effectively, and efficiently. Their devotion to process originated in their Enlightenment ideas of using the scientific method, observing due process in law, and using parliamentary procedures in enacting laws.

In schools, academic freedom means that teachers and students: (1) are free to examine and discuss issues, even controversial ones; (2) apply the same procedures to all participants; and (3) accept decisions but also are open to changing them by using the same process by which they were established. What is important is the tentativeness of knowledge and values; they are reached by examination and discussion and are not imposed by an authority figure or by being derived from some a priori principles. For the process to work, those who use it need to be committed to it and know how to use or work it. All members of a class have the right to participate and be listened to so long as they follow the rules that apply equally to all of them.

Conclusion

This chapter examined Liberalism as an ideology and discussed its social, political, economic, and educational implications. It treated Liberalism as historically evolving ideology that developed from its origins in John Locke's contract theory, through Classical economic theory and Utilitarian reform, to modern Social Reformist Liberalism. Liberalism's affinity for process, procedures, and gradual, moderate, incremental change was discussed and how this tendency relates to education as a process was examined. Particular emphasis was devoted to a discussion of Liberalism and academic freedom.

Constructing Your Own Philosophy of Education. Now that you have read about Liberalism, reflect on how this ideology has either influenced or not influenced your thinking about politics, society, change, reform, and education. Determine whether you find Liberalism compatible with your educational experiences and efforts to construct your own philosophy of education. Are there elements of Liberalism that you plan to include in your philosophy?

Questions for Reflection and Discussion

1. Do you believe that Liberalism is a relevant ideology in American politics, society, and education? Explain your answer.

2. Critics contend that the Liberal claims of objectivity and fairness are false and cover up special interests. Do you agree or disagree?

3. Consider how Liberals define academic freedom. In your educational experience, is this how education was treated in schools that you attended?

4. Reflect on your experiences in schools as a student and a teacher. Did you find that academic freedom was encouraged or discouraged by your teachers and other students?

5. Reflect on John Stuart Mill's fear of the "tyranny of the majority." Do you believe that there is a tyranny of the majority operating in contemporary American life and education?

6. Do you believe that the idea of moderate incremental change is adequate for the problems facing American society and education?

Topics for Inquiry and Research

1. In a survey of the students in this class, determine whether they agree or disagree with the major liberal principles.

2. Examine the syllabi and textbooks in several courses in teacher education at your college or university. Do you find a tendency to Liberalism in your analysis of this material?

3. Examine the procedures at your college or university that deal with students' rights and due process. Do these procedures reflect a Liberal orientation?

4. Interview several experienced teachers about the innovations or reforms that they have experienced in schools. Determine what kind of change these reforms or innovations have generated.

5. Research the policies of a particular high school regarding co- or extracurricular student

organizations or activities. Are these policies compatible with Liberal principles?

6. Research the guidelines that apply to the student newspaper at a high school or college. Are there limitations on what the newspaper may cover?

Building a Liberal Vocabulary

Academic Freedom: the freedom of teachers to teach and students to learn, without having their freedom curtailed by censorship or arbitrary controls.

Ascription: a term meaning that a person's social and economic role is defined at birth by the class into which they are born.

Bourgeoisie: the French word for members of the middle class.

Classical Liberalism: the economic theory developed by Adam Smith and others of the Manchester school that government should not interfere with commerce and should encourage free trade in an open market.

Consensus: for Liberals, a pervasive social agreement to uphold certain processes and to follow agreed-on methods.

Contract Theory: Locke's concept that government is a contract between the government and the governed.

Disinterested Participant: Mill's concept of a participant in politics and society who is unbiased and not motivated by the desire for personal profit and can evaluate an issue objectively.

Empiricism: an epistemology that holds that human ideas and hence knowledge is based on sensory experience.

Modern Liberalism: a transformation in Liberalism in which the government became responsible for social welfare and health programs and ending racial segregation and promoting integration, affirmative action, protection for persons with disabilities, and aid to people at the poverty level.

Natural Rights Theory: the belief that individuals possess inherent rights; for Locke, these were life, liberty, and property; for Jefferson, life, liberty, and pursuit of happiness.

Negative Freedoms: laws that restrict government from interfering with speech, press, assembly, and religion, in which the government should make no interference with or of.

Progress: the belief that society can be reformed and improved.

Representative Institutions: institutions, usually political ones, that are governed by elected officials who represent the people.

Separation of Church and State: the liberal proposition that the church and state should be separate, that is, the state should not establish a religion or interfere with its free exercise.

Supply and Demand: the classical Liberal argument that the economy is self-regulating by supply and demand; when goods are scarce there is a demand for them in the market; when plentiful, a declining market.

Tabula Rasa: a Latin phrase meaning a blank or clear slate. In Locke's epistemology, the mind, too, is blank, or clear of ideas, prior to sensory experience.

Tyranny of the Majority: Mill's fear that in a mass society, the majority may impose prevailing opinions on the minority.

Utilitarianism: Bentham's philosophy of utility based on calculating pleasure and pain.

Internet Resources

For Liberalism as a theory, access http://plato.stanford.edu/entries/liberalism/.

For the Liberal theory of the state, access www.ourcivilisation.com/cooray/btof/chap.162.htm.

For a Liberal theory of freedom of expression for children, access http://lawreview.kentlaw.edu/articles/79-1/Macleod.pdf.

Suggestions for Further Reading

Carlisle, Janice. *John Stuart Mill and the Writing of Character.* Athens: University of Georgia Press, 1991.

Donner, Wendy. *The Liberal Self: John Stuart Mill's Moral and Political Philosophy.* Ithaca, NY: Cornell University Press, 1991.

Garforth, Francis W. *Educative Democracy: John Stuart Mill on Education in Society.* Oxford: Oxford University Press, 1980.

Grote, John. *An Examination of the Utilitarian Philosophy.* Bristol, UK: Thoemmes, 1990.

Holmes, Stephen. *Passions & Constraint: On the Theory of Liberal Democracy.* Chicago: University of Chicago Press, 1995.

Jackson, Julius. *A Guided Tour of John Stuart Mill's Utilitarianism.* Mountain View, CA: Mayfield, 1993.

Johnston, David. *The Idea of a Liberal Theory: A Critique and Reconstruction.* Princeton, NJ: Princeton University Press, 1996.

Kerner, George C. *Three Philosophical Moralists: Mill, Kant, and Sartre.* New York: Oxford University Press, 1990.

Kurer, Oskar. *John Stuart Mill: The Politics of Progress.* New York: Garland, 1991.

Massaro, Toni Marie. *Constitutional Literacy: A Core Curriculum for a Multicultural Nation.* Durham, NC: Duke University Press, 1993.

Rawls, John. *Political Liberalism.* New York: Columbia University Press, 1993.

Strasser, Mark P. *The Moral Philosophy of John Stuart Mill: Toward Modifications of Contemporary Utilitarianism.* Wakefield, NH: Longwood Academic, 1991.

Endnotes

1. This historical account is deliberately simplified to indicate the early differences between a society based on ascription and one based on merit. The social structure during the Medieval period was complex if one considers the role and power of the clergy.
2. Richard I. Aaron, *John Locke* (London: Clarendon Press, 1963), p. 2; M. V. C. Jeffreys, *John Locke: Prophet of Common Sense* (London: Methuen, 1967), p. 21.
3. John Locke, *An Essay Concerning Human Understanding,* ed. Raymond Wilbur (New York: E. P. Dutton, 1947), pp. 8, 65, 106, 145, 253.
4. Amy M. Schmitter, Nathan Tarcov, and Wendy Donner, "Enlightenment Liberalism," in Randall Curren, ed., *A Companion to the Philosophy of Education* (Malden, MA: Blackwell, 2006), pp. 83–85.
5. John Locke, *Some Thoughts Concerning Education* (Cambridge: Cambridge University Press, 1902), p. 419.
6. Schmitter et al., "Enlightenment Liberalism," pp. 82–83.
7. John Locke, *Two Treatises of Government, 1690,* from the 1823 edition of Locke's works published in London by Thomas Tegg and others, in *Communism, Fascism and Democracy: The Theoretical Foundations,* ed., Carl Cohen (New York: Random House, 1972), p. 399.
8. Locke, *Two Treatises of Government, in Communism, Fascism and Democracy: The Theoretical Foundations,* ed., Cohen, p. 399.
9. Brad Stetson, *Human Dignity and Contemporary Liberalism* (New York: Praeger/Greenwood, 1998), p. 26.
10. Michael J. Gootzeit, *David Ricardo* (New York: Columbia University Press, 1975).
11. Michael Freeden, *Ideology: A Very Short Introduction* (Oxford: Oxford University Press, 2003), pp. 68–69.
12. Ian Adams, *Political Ideology Today* (Manchester, UK: Manchester University Press, 2001), p. 20.
13. J. Salwyn Schapiro, *Liberalism and the Challenge of Fascism: Social Forces in England and France* (New York: McGraw-Hill Book Co., 1949), pp. 43–59.
14. For his autobiography, see John Stuart Mill, *The Autobiography of John Stuart Mill* (New York: Columbia University Press, 1944). Among biographies of Mill are: Alan Ryan, *John Stuart Mill* (New York: Pantheon Books, 1970); Peter J. Glassman, *J. S. Mill: The Evolution of a Genius* (Gainesville: University of Florida Press, 1985); and Richard J. Halliday, *John Stuart Mill* (London: Allen and Unwin, 1976).
15. Schapiro, *Liberalism and the Challenge of Fascism,* p. 281.

16. Michael McGeer, *A Fierce Discontent: The Rise and Fall of the Progressive Movement in America: 1870–1920* (New York: Free Press/Simon & Schuster, 2003), pp. 108–109.

17. For Johnson's programs, see James MacGregor Burns, *To Heal and to Build: The Programs of President Lyndon B. Johnson* (New York: McGraw-Hill Book Co., 1968).

18. Hugh Davis Graham, *The Uncertain Triumph: Federal Education Policy in the Kennedy and Johnson Years* (Chapel Hill: University of North Carolina Press, 1984), pp. 60–61.

19. J. Salwyn Schapiro, *Liberalism: Its Meaning and History* (New York: D. Van Nostrand Co., 1958), p. 44.

20. Schapiro, *Liberalism: Its Meaning and History,* pp. 44–45.

21. John Dewey, *How We Think* (Mineola, NY: Dover, 1997), p. 45.

22. Dewey, *How We Think,* pp. 20–21.

23. Dewey, *How We Think,* pp. 5–6.

24. Dewey, *How We Think,* pp. 12–13.

25. Gordon C. Lee, ed. *Crusade Against Ignorance: Thomas Jefferson on Education* (New York: Bureau of Publications, Teachers College, Columbia University, 1961), pp. 10–11.

26. Jefferson, "A Bill for Establishing Religious Freedom," in Julian P. Boyd et al., eds., *The Papers of Thomas Jefferson,* II (Princeton, NJ: Princeton University Press, 1950), pp. 545–547.

27. D. J. Manning, *Liberalism* (New York: St. Martin's Press, 1976), pp. 20–23.

28. Toni Marie Massaro, *Constitutional Literacy: A Core Curriculum for a Multicultural Nation* (Durham, NC: Duke University Press, 1993).

29. For examples of the debate, see Henry L. Gates, *Loose Canons: Notes on the Cultural Wars* (New York: Oxford University Press, 1992); Dinesh D'Souza, *Illiberal Education: The Politics of Race and Sex on Campus* (New York: Free Press, 1991); Arthur M. Schlesinger, Jr., *The Disuniting of America: Reflections on a Multicultural Society* (Knoxville, TN: Whittle Direct Books, 1991); and James A. Banks, *Multiethnic Education: Theory and Practice* (Boston: Allyn and Bacon, 1994).

30. Massaro, *Constitutional Literacy: A Core Curriculum for a Multicultural Nation,* p. 73.

31. Jonathan Kozol, *Savage Inequalities: Children in America's Schools* (New York: HarperPerennial, 1991), pp. 67–74.

10

Conservatism and Education

Ronald Reagan (1911–2004), the 40th president of the U. S., led a Conservative revival, emphasizing limited government and free market economics.

Chapter Preview

Conservatism, as an ideology, has experienced a significant revival in the United States and in Europe. The word's root, *conserve,* means to keep, maintain, preserve, to prevent loss or decay. Conservatism originated as a reaction of the landed gentry and religious establishment in Europe against what they considered to be the excesses of the French Revolution. Conservatism both reacts against rapid change and also accommodates to it by incorporating certain new features and rendering them safe for the culture. Like Liberalism, Conservatism has changed over time; though it retains its key core principles, it has appropriated some specific items from other ideologies. For example, it has appropriated much of Classical Liberal economics. American Neo-Conservatism has had a significant impact on contemporary education, especially in the restoration of the teaching of basic skills and subjects and in its endorsement of academic standards. The following topics are discussed in the chapter:

- Edmund Burke as a proponent of cultural civility
- The principles of Classic Euro-American Conservatism
- Contemporary American Neo-Conservatism
- Conservatism's implications for education, schooling, curriculum, and teaching and learning
- Neo-Essentialism and Neo-Perennialism

As you have read the chapter on Conservatism, think back on your own educational experiences. Determine whether you experienced Conservatism in your own education. Conservatism is also an important cultural ideology; consider its impact on American society generally. As you read and discuss this chapter, see whether you agree or disagree with Conservatism.

Edmund Burke: Conservative Proponent of Cultural Civility

Edmund Burke (1729–1797), a graduate of Trinity College in Dublin, was a distinguished British statesman and writer on political philosophy. Elected to the House of Commons in 1765, Burke became a leader of the Whig party. Opposing the royal policies that he believed were forcing the thirteen American colonies into rebellion, Burke urged conciliation. Although he supported moderate reform policies, Burke believed that traditional political, social, and religious institutions manifested the historically evolved wisdom of the human race.

Burke wrote on philosophical and political themes. His *Vindication of Natural Society* (1756) was a satire against political rationalism and religious skepticism. Burke's *Philosophical Enquiry into the Origin of Our Ideas of the Sublime and Beautiful* (1756) examined aesthetics from a romanticist perspective. His antagonism toward the violence and excesses of the French Revolution was expressed in *Reflections on the Revolution in France* (1790), which became a classic statement of Conservative ideology.

Reacting against the excesses and violence of the French Revolution, Burke saw the revolutionaries as sacrificing the bulwark of tradition to a utopian end that justified any action, no matter how reprehensible, on the pretext that it would create a better, more progressive future. The trial and execution of the king and queen, decimation of the aristocracy, and attack on the church had undermined France's primary institutions that had once given a core stability to French society. Without these traditional institutions to channel change, the Revolution had been taken over by a dictatorial gang of conspirators who had usurped the legitimate natural elite of birth and breeding. The conspiratorial elite, led by Robespierre, had embarked on a "reign of terror," with mass trials and purges, which anticipated the crimes that other totalitarian despots such as Hitler and Stalin would commit in the twentieth century in the name of a utopian future. Robespierre and other zealots of the French Revolution believed that the end justified the means as they attempted to create a perfect society on earth. Their orders for mass executions were justified by the Revolution's true believers as the necessary steps in eliminating those who stood in the way of creating a perfect republic. Burke warned that such counsels of perfection and revolutionary excesses were doomed to fail. Human beings, who themselves are imperfect, cannot possibly create a perfect society. Burke's *Reflections* warned against revolutionary change and social engineering that undermined civilization and civility.

For Burke, the traditional cultural heritage was a repository of the time-tested achievements of humankind. He saw the social, political, religious, and educational institutions—the family, state, church, and school—as cultural achievements that had evolved over centuries of human experience. Standards of civility and discourse, of ethics and values represented the wisdom of the human race.[1] An educational ideology derived from Burke would stress the need to cultivate in the young a sense of awe and respect for cultural institutions. Education would involve the inculcation of traditional standards of behavior and civility in the young. Such an ideological orientation would be suspicious of radical change, seeing it as a threat to both civilization and civility.

The following tenets constitute Burke's major contributions to Conservative ideology: (1) institutions form a complex framework of customary practices and historically evolved rights and duties; (2) human behavior evolves within the conditioning influence of the institutional system, and it is a cultural inheritance to be transmitted from one generation to the next; (3) human culture and institutions represent a continuum of tested experience that should not be broken by untested innovation or revolutionary action; and (4) tradition is the repository of a collective social intelligence. To be educated according to these Burkean principles meant that the young were to be encultured in the traditions of their parents, who in turn had been nurtured in the traditions of their parents. Thus, the heritage was passed on and kept alive.

Burke, who distrusted Locke's reliance on government by majorities, believed in decision making by an elite of well-educated persons, an aristocracy of culture and civility. He did not believe that the genuine interests of a nation and a people could be determined by taking polls or adding up numbers. Further, he feared that Liberalism would lead to a society of selfishness where decision making would fall to narrow special-interest groups. Burke believed that Conservative leadership and decision making should come from a public-spirited elite, who, steeped in tradition, would represent the enduring interests of the entire nation.

The assumption that every society should be governed by the elite is an important Conservative principle that has serious educational implications. Throughout history, the belief in rule by an elite has had many proponents, the most prominent of whom was Plato, who argued that the philosopher-kings, an aristocracy of intellectuals, should rule. Differences in human potentiality result from the social milieus into which people are born and reared; as a result, being a member of a "good family" and having a proper upbringing become important social credentials. A contemporary example of an elite governing class is that of the graduates of England's famous public schools (really private preparatory schools) such as Eton, Rugby, Winchester, and Harrow, who, after completing university studies at either Oxford or Cambridge, become the nation's ruling class. This British elite, generally deriving from the gentry, was, by birth and breeding, destined to rule. Their education in the classics, languages, and history, in addition to learning sportsmanship, was designed to make them the bearers of traditional outlooks and values.

Elitism in the Burkean sense rejected both Locke's and Rousseau's ideas of equality in the state of nature as fiction. If attempts were made to implement equality in society, the results would be a disastrous leveling or mob rule. The good society, in Burkean terms, recognized and prized uniqueness or differences. The better-educated, the more prudent, and the more expert were to protect and guide the less-educated, the weaker, and the inexpert. Educationally, the Conservative society would prepare the culturally gifted to rule and prepare those of lesser ability to respect and follow their rule.

Burke's vision of society, like Plato's, was not one in which the ruled were suspicious of or tending to rebel against the rulers. Manifesting a great deal of paternalism, the society governed by Conservative ideological principles was like a family, where love and loyalty emanated from a respect for the past and engulfed all in a single community. This community was deeply rooted in a sense of identity, membership, and duty. Burke's expression of Conservatism moved the Conservative attitude from a sentiment or feeling to the level of a consciously articulated ideology.

The Principles of Classical Euro-American Conservatism

In this section, we examine some principles of classical European and American Conservatism derived from Burke's classic statement of Conservatism. In the early American republic, Conservatism found a home in the Federalist Party, especially in the political outlook of Alexander Hamilton and John Adams, who believed that there was a natural elite to whom government should be entrusted. It also was expressed academically by some influential interpreters of the liberal arts tradition such as Russell Kirk. Although certain elements of Classical Conservatism are preserved in modern Neo-Conservatism, the new Conservatism has modified and revised some of its themes, especially in its American expression.

An Imperfect and Flawed Human Nature

Classical Conservatism, approximating the doctrine of humankind's fallen and sinful nature due to original sin, sees the human being as imperfect, flawed, and weak. Because of this inherent imperfection, individuals are inclined toward egotism, selfishness, idleness, and incivility. We become civilized when we learn to control our instincts and channel them into constructive rather than destructive behavior. A good human character can be formed by the correct kind of upbringing as a member of a family, by attendance at church, and by being educated in an effective academic school. The family is the setting in which traditional values are transmitted in an intimate, personal, and nurturing way from parents to their children. The church, intertwined in the culture, promotes and interprets moral and ethical values in a religiously charged context. Schools, emphasizing an academic curriculum and traditional values, build on and extend the value formation begun in the family and the church. These primary institutions transmit the traditional core of knowledge and values, protecting against individual alienation and social instability.

In a later chapter on Progressivism, we examine the educational ideas of Jean-Jacques Rousseau, who developed a view of human nature that is exactly contrary to the Classical Conservative view. Rousseau argued that the child at birth is innately good and that the natural human instincts are to be encouraged to develop freely. Just as Burke had opposed the excesses of the French Revolution, Classical Conservatives opposed Rousseau's ideas as harmful romantic utopianism. Because of humankind's flawed nature, it is impossible to create a perfect society on earth. Those who promise to do so mislead people into a false utopianism in which the ends justify the means.

Conservatism and the Past

For Conservatives, the past is the source of the traditions that shape social institutions and human relationships. From the past, people acquire a sense of cultural identity and belonging as members of a distinct community, a nation, that is rooted in a given place at a particular time in history. A moment in human history, a person's present, is not transitory but rather is part of a continuum that binds the past and the future. From the past, a people, a particular society, inherits a collective wisdom based on lessons learned over time.

The Conservative reverence for the past and the historic sense is to be cultivated through education. Today, the incessant mobility and social change associated with modern life has produced a sense of rootlessness in which people find themselves without a sense of place or belonging. Conservatives argue that education should create a sense of cultural identity in the young by emphasizing a literature and a history that build connections with a great and vital past. Language, literature, and history should celebrate the achievements of the past, the major events in the collective life of the group, and the heroes and heroines who best exemplify the group's values and aspirations. Indeed, when such a heritage and its values are reinforced by religious observance and ritual, they are encased in dramatic form in the psyches of the young.

Tradition, Historically Evolved Institutions, and Change

The Conservative worldview emphasizes a reliance on tradition as a source of cultural and moral authority, the need to maintain and fortify historically evolved institutions, and a cautious and limited approach to change.[2] Conservatism emphasizes the civilizing power of **tradition** in providing sociocultural cohesion and stability. Tradition is the legacy, the repository, of humankind's collective and tested wisdom, that maintains social stability and continuity from one generation to the next. Tradition builds a sense of identity and meaning that gives people a sense of belonging to a culture, to a nation.

Historically Evolved Institutions

Conservatives believe that institutions are historically evolved and perform necessary primary roles in society. Human institutions, each having a primary purpose in the whole of society, have been shaped by a continuum of historical experience. A primary role is original, basic, or essential to an institution. Basic institutions—the home, family, school, state, and the church, for example—have evolved over time. This continuum, this historical continuity, should not be broken by revolutionary actions or untested innovations and social experimentation. Social experimentation will only cause moral confusion, weaken the safeguards provided by civility, and bring about social disequilibrium and cultural disarray. For example, marriage is the primary institution for a man (a husband) and a women (a wife) to live together in wedlock. Conservatives believe that the primary function of marriage is sacred and that other relationships such as a man and woman living together without wedlock or a same-sex "marriage" distorts and violates the high purpose of this institution. The family has the primary purpose of providing the home environment in which a married man and woman raise their children. For Conservatives, so-called alternative family styles distort the family's primary role and function as an institution.

Schools have the primary purpose of providing an academic education to students. Conservatives dispute what Progressives claim is the residual function of the school. The residual function means that when a institution no longer performs its function then another institution can assume it. If families, for example, do not perform their function of properly bringing up children, then the school is to assume that neglected function. If families do not inform their children about sex, then the school is to take on the function of sex education. Conservatives disagree. When schools assume nonacademic custodial, therapeutic, and social functions, they dilute, weaken, and distort their **primary role**. When different institutions are not clear about their primary role or try to usurp the roles of other institutions, the process of historical evolution is disrupted. For example, Conservatives believe that schools as historically evolved educational institutions have the primary role of transmitting the cultural heritage, often prescribed as academic skills and subjects and the values of civility to the young. When schools cross over and assume the roles of other institutions, they dilute their primary role. Conservatives want to keep institutions functioning according to their primary and traditional purpose.

Ideologically, Conservatism functions in two ways regarding institutions: (1) to maintain and preserve those institutions that are functioning according to their intended original or primary purpose; (2) to restore those institutions that have been altered or changed so that they no longer function according to their original, primary, and traditional purpose. If schools have taken on nonacademic custodial, social, and therapeutic functions, these functions should be removed so that schools can perform their original, traditional, and historic academic functions. Teachers are to teach academic skills and subjects to students and not dilute or distort their traditional roles by trying to be babysitters, therapists, counselors, or social workers. Time spent on nonacademic functions takes away time and energy from the primary academic purpose for which schools were established.

Conservatism's Alliance with Organized Religion

Conservatives, historically, are allied with religion, especially with established churches. In Europe, Conservatives favored an establishment of religion by the state. For example, the Church of England, or Anglican Church, is the official state church in England and the monarch is the titular head of the church. The Russian Orthodox Church was the official religion in Tsarist Russia. In Norway and Sweden, the Lutheran Church is the official state church. For European Conservatives, an officially sanctioned and state-supported church was another means of relating individuals to an integrating cultural heritage.

Contemporary Conservatives build alliances with religion to give a supernatural sanction to their political, social, economic, and educational beliefs.[3] When the cultural core is seen as coming from a higher supernatural source, it is more than a human construction. Rather, it represents a kind of covenant between humankind and God. This covenant is usually not generalized to the whole human race but is presented as a particular and special relationship between God and a particular group of believers—those who have the true faith. For example, Christian fundamentalists in the religious right see the covenant in terms of Evangelical Protestantism. Orthodox Jews see it in terms of Judaism. Fundamentalist Moslems see it in terms of Islam.

Change

The Conservative worldview emphasizes a decided preference, indeed, a longing, to maintain **historically evolved institutions** in a way that is true to their original primary purposes. Relying on tradition as a source of authority, Conservatives take a cautious and moderate disposition to change. They endorse the saying, "The more things change, the more they stay the same." Conservatives recognize the reality and importance of scientific and technological change; however, their point is that these kinds of changes in the material realm—that of science and technology—be subordinated to and put into historical perspective by traditional cultural controls. Changes will inevitably occur, and they need to be accommodated and incorporated into the traditional cultural heritage rather than changing the heritage to fit the areas of change.

Conservatives recognize that societies change but it is important that this change be correctly channeled so that basic institutions and values are preserved. Conservatives often appear anxious when faced with massive change, such as the countercultural movement of the 1960s. Conservatives, for example, use the concept of a cultural core that needs to be maintained regardless of technologically generated change. The core is typically presented as consisting of the knowledge and values of Western civilization and of the American heritage. Conservatives distinguish between gradual or natural change as changes that they prefer, often indicating that this kind of change is really a return to older, established values.[4] Natural change is a kind of gradual organic change that is regarded as growth. This kind of slow change is not as disruptive to society as is rapid change. Changes that they oppose are labeled radical, revolutionary, and utopian. For example, the supposed radical change of the French and Russian revolutions was utopian and destined to fail. What resulted from this kind of change was perversely all-powerful states, ruled by conspiratorial revolutionary elites that repressed personal and religious freedom. Conservatives are particularly opposed to attempts to engineer social change through the schools, unlike Liberals and Reconstructionists. Social engineering programs are disruptive, disjointed, and disconnected from the true purposes of schools. Schools should be agencies devoted to preserving the cultural core that gives balance and ballast to society.

It is obvious that schools that function according to a Conservative ideology would not be centers of social change or cultural reconstruction. Rather, their foremost goal would be to cultivate a social stasis and continuity. Conservative educators seek to preserve the traditional curriculum and would be suspicious of educational innovations. They would use the history of education to illustrate the fleeting insignificance of many highly publicized educational innovations such as team-teaching, competency-based learning, the discovery method, the "new mathematics," collaborative learning, and whole language reading. What persists over time, they would argue, are the essential skills and subjects, especially those that exemplify cultural roots, such as literature and history.

Despite their reservations about educational innovations, Conservatives recognize that from time to time certain mechanical or technological changes occur that have an impact on culture and society. When such an innovation occurs, it is important that it is linked to and connected with the heritage so that it is not socially or culturally disruptive. An example of such a technological innovation is the computer. Conservatives would see computers as an instrument to make instruction in the traditional subjects efficient rather than to transform or radically alter the curriculum.

The Conservative Fear of Alienation

Conservatives regard community as coming from historically evolved institutions and the integration of individuals in such institutions as the family, church, and school. The church, especially established churches that are intertwined in the culture, promote interpretive moral and ethical values in a religiously charged context. The family is the setting in which traditional values are transmitted in an intimate and personal way from the old to the young. The school, as a social agency, builds on and extends familial and religious values. These primary institutions—family, church, and school—are encouraged by the state to transmit the traditional core of knowledge and value so that the society and its institutions can be perpetuated and protected against change that would weaken or jeopardize cultural and social stability.

Conservatives contend that the Liberal emphasis on individualism will lead to an atomistic society in which people will act on their self-interests without regard to historically evolved cultural traditions. Just as undesirable to the Conservative is the mass society with its mass culture and mass-produced tastes that result in social leveling rather than in a hierarchy that recognizes quality, good taste, and talent.

Conservatives want individuals to be integrated into the culture and society and not feel separated or alienated from it. They are especially opposed to those, such as the Postmodernists and Critical Theorists, who view society through the Marxist lens of alienation. For Marx, human alienation from the existing society and economy is caused by the capitalist lust for profits at the expense of workers. Alienation means that the workers' time and the products made are taken from them and sold for a profit that they do not enjoy. For Marxists, the institutional superstructure in a capitalist society—school, church, state, and

European Classic → Conservatism	Classic Liberal → Economic Theory	Modern Neo-Conservatism
1. Tradition	1. Supply and demand	1. Traditional patriotic values
2. Religion	2. Competition	2. Christian fundamentalism
3. Historically derived institutions	3. Free market	3. Free trade and economic competition
	4. Limited government	4. Individualism

American Neo-Conservatism

media—are economically controlled by the dominant class. Institutions are dependent on the owners of property. They are not historically evolved as Conservatives claim. Marxists and Critical Theorists argue that education should raise the consciousness of exploited people so that they understand the basis of their alienation and the forces that cause it. Conservatives believe that what is called *consciousness-raising* is another word for indoctrinating people in a false reading of history. The purpose of education, for Conservatives, is to bring people into the culture by transmitting it to them.

Contemporary American Neo-Conservatism

Although our discussion of Conservatism is more concerned with its ideology as a cultural and educational movement, a brief discussion of American politics serves to provide the context for the ascendancy of **Neo-Conservatism**. From the Roosevelt New Deal in the 1930s until the late 1960s, Liberalism was the dominant political ideology in the United States. Conservatism was the minority ideology, espoused by some traditional Republicans, such as Robert Taft, who wanted to curb what they considered to be the excessive growth of the federal government. In academe and journalism, Conservatism had articulate spokespersons such as Russell Kirk and William Buckley, but they were in the minority. In 1964, Barry Goldwater, the Republican senator for Arizona and presidential candidate, in his book, *The Conscience of a Conservative,* launched a more popular and less academic Conservative movement. With the election of Ronald Reagan as president in 1980, Conservatism in the United States was on the political ascendancy. It enjoyed a strong revival as Neo-Conservatism, the new Conservatism. In the election of 1988, the victorious Republican candidate for president, George H. Bush, continued the policies of Neo-Conservatism. In the elections of 2000 and 2004, George W. Bush was elected and reelected as a "compassionate Conservative."

A Neo-Conservative Interpretation of the American Past

Our discussion of general Conservative principles emphasized that Conservatives look to the past, to history, as the source of cultural and moral authority. Contemporary American Neo-Conservatives, too, look to American history as the source of American traditional beliefs and values. As is true of ideologies, they have constructed their own interpretation of the past. Like all ideologies, the American Conservative history is a selective interpretation. Their interpretation highlights the theme of American Exceptionalism, the belief that Americans are a unique and special people, living in a land providentially blessed with natural resources and abundant land. Eliciting sentiments of patriotism and loyalty to the nation, it presents a nationalist story of American greatness and rightness. (See the discussion of American Exceptionalism in the chapter on Nationalism, American Exceptionalism, and Ethnonationalism.) Americans are a good people, ordained by Divine Providence to settle in a new world, to tame the wilderness, and to establish a republic, governed by law and civility. Of course, many historians would seriously question the accuracy of this version of the past. However, for an ideology, that is not the point. In creating a preferred interpretation of the past, myth becomes entwined with history. (For a discussion of the ideological use of the past, see the chapter on Ideology and Education.)

The thirteen colonies were settled by people from Great Britain and northern Europe who came to the new world to create a better life in which they were free to govern themselves and to practice their religion. The Pilgrim and Puritan founding fathers, seeing their new country as the fulfillment of the Biblical "city on a hill," formed a special covenant with God. This special covenant made the United States a Christian nation. The War for American Independence marked the beginnings of American patriotism in fighting for a just cause. The founding fathers at the Constitutional Convention established a government based on the original Christian principles that had inspired the Puritans. As in the days of the ancient Hebrews, when Mosaic Law was regarded as a covenant between the Jews and God, Neo-Conservatives see American government, too, as a covenant in which the people adopted a constitution as their instrument of self-government. For them, the Constitution rests on the tradition of essential Christian principles and precedents from Anglo-American common law. The Neo-Conservative interpretation of American history emphasizes the United States as a faith-based and religiously inspired nation. Believing in the importance of choosing one's founding fathers, it does not emphasize the Deist beliefs of some leaders of the early republic such as Thomas Jefferson, who urged separation of church and state.

The Neo-Conservative interpretation of American educational history emphasizes how public schools, in the past, functioned to create a common American identity. For example, Noah Webster (1758–1843), a leading educator and lexicographer in the early national period, is seen as working to create a distinctive, but standardized, version of the English language.[5] Public schools, like the common schools, should resist bilingual and bicultural programs that seek to maintain languages other than English as languages of instruction. While these programs might be used to transition non-English-speaking students into using the English language, they should be temporary and not permanent.

Catharine Beecher, a pioneer teacher educator, held ideas that contemporary Conservatives would endorse. Endorsing Evangelical Christianity as a part of teacher education, Beecher saw teachers, especially women, as missionaries of Western culture and civility.[6] Women teachers, serving as moral exemplars, were to use their "sensibility" to teach a common language and curriculum that brought literacy and civility to the western frontier.

Still another Neo-Conservative educational hero is William Holmes McGuffey (1800–1873), the author of the widely used McGuffey readers, which affirmed the values of literacy, hard work, diligence, punctuality, patriotism, and civility.[7] McGuffey readers emphasized the moral values of white middle-class Protestant Americans.

The westward-moving American frontier brought historically based institutions—the home, town, church, school, farm, and small business—to the wilderness. These institutions gave the growing nation a sense of stability, marked by political order and economic prosperity. In the frontier settlement of the western territories that became the United States, the settlers were community builders. As soon as they had constructed their crude cabins, the next structures to be created were the town meeting place, the church, and the school. These institutions were the transplanted agencies of civility. However, along with community building, there is a unique interpretation that has entered American Conservatism about the winning of the west. The American west was settled by rugged individuals, who through their own courage and initiative, conquered a hostile environment. They and their families stood on their own two feet and did so without government handouts. The rifle and the gun were the necessary instruments that they used to protect themselves against hostile Indians and outlaws. For some American Conservatives, an important part of their version of the past is "rugged individualism," which differs greatly from the European version of Conservatism. Also emphasized is the right to keep and to bear arms as an important safeguard provided by the Constitution.

The United States became a modern industrial nation because individual creativity and inventiveness were not shackled by an intrusive government. Inventors such as Alexander Graham Bell and Thomas Edison and industrialists such as Andrew Carnegie and Henry Ford built a great nation. Today, it is still possible for enterprising individuals such as Bill Gates and Warren Buffett to amass wealth. The economic development of the United States is presented, not as exploitative, but as representing an opportunity for those who have the ingenuity and energy to compete. All have a chance to earn and to learn and through their own merit to share in the prosperity of a great nation. The Neo-Conservative interpretation of American economic history appropriates a good deal from the Adam Smith school of free market economics in which individuals are free to compete in producing and selling goods and services without government regulation.

Conservatives see the United States as a country of immigrants, of people who came to America to find the personal freedom and economic opportunity that the country's original settlers found in the settlement of the new world. When the immigrants arrived, they found an American cultural and political tradition already in place. Established by the nation's founders, the characteristics of this tradition were: (1) English as the "official" language in government, business, and education; (2) a willingness to work hard and be thrifty and industrious as a reflection of the generalized Puritan or Calvinist ethic; and (3) respect for the Constitution and obedience to the law. But for immigrants to succeed, they needed to be **Americanized**, that is, learn to speak the English language, practice civility, and be law-abiding and industrious contributors to American culture. Their role was to join the American national community and not try to change it into a version of the countries that they left behind. Conservatives would argue today's new immigrants from Asia, the Middle East, and South America should emulate the patterns of the earlier European immigrants and Americanize themselves to function in the society of their adopted country.

The Conservative version of how immigrants were successfully assimilated into American life, politics, and society has immense educational implications. First of all, there is the notion that there already exists a completed model of American culture that was defined in the early decades of the republic. New generations, be they native born or immigrants, are to absorb and be assimilated into this model. The model is not open-ended and changing—it is rooted in the American cultural heritage and tradition. Education, then, is to further the process of assimilation into the model. Schools are to transmit an American cultural core to students so that they adopt and adapt to the model. This means that the English language should be the language of instruction rather than other languages as in bilingual programs. Schools should impart a solid cultural core that is based on American history and literature rather than multiculturalism. The values inculcated by the school focus on respect for legitimate authority, hard work, diligence, and civic responsibility.

Immigration has been a persistent area of controversy in the United States since the Know-Nothings of the 1850s sought to restrict immigration to the United States. Today, immigration is a highly controversial political, cultural, and national security issue. The debate, shaped by contrasting versions of history, carries ideological overtones. Contending that immigrants, especially illegal aliens, are an expensive burden on the country's educational, health care, and social services, Neo-Conservatives want laws to restrict immigration and stop illegal immigration. They argue that the movement of illegal immigrants across U.S. borders threatens national security, especially in the war on terrorism.[8]

In terms of foreign policy, Conservatives think of the United States as a good country, inhabited by morally good people, who do the right thing internationally. The United States represents a model of democratic government and human rights that other countries should emulate. Some Conservatives, in the past, were isolationists, believing that the United States, as a democratic fortress protected by two great oceans, should, as George Washington advised, avoid entangling alliances with other countries. Two world wars, the Cold War, and the war against terrorism have eroded the older isolationist view. Neo-Conservative foreign policy is driven heavily by an ideology that sees world issues in terms of moral right and wrong. For example, in the Cold War, President Reagan saw the Soviet Union as "an evil empire." President George W. Bush has called the governments of Iran, North Korea, and Iraq (before the fall of Saddam Hussein) "an axis of evil." Neo-Conservative ideology argues that when other countries refuse to take the moral high ground, the United States has the right to make unilateral decisions in world affairs.

The Neo-Conservative Christian Fundamentalist Alliance

Christian fundamentalists, often referred to as the "religious right," are often strongly affiliated with the Conservative ideology. The morally good society builds its institutions and values on religious foundations. For them, the United States, as a nation, rests on a generalized Christian ethic, which is summed up nicely by "in God we trust." Though some **Christian Conservatives** would challenge the doctrine of separation of church and state, many would argue that the doctrine has been incorrectly interpreted by the courts. According to strict construction of the Constitution, the government is not to establish an official religion. Other faith-based initiatives such as government support of churches that provide child care, education, health care, and other social services do not violate the Constitution. Neo-Conservatives want a conscious affirmation by government and educational authorities that America's institutions rest on a religious, a Christian, core of values.

Christian Conservatives are fearful that some trends in modern society are undermining fundamental values. They assert a need to restore "family values." Religious Conservatives—Christian Fundamentalists and Roman Catholics—are especially opposed to the Supreme Court's decision in *Roe v. Wade,* which gave a legal right to abortions. Conservatives say that abortion denies the unborn child's right to life.

Christian Conservatives have an educational agenda that they see as needed to restore religious values to schools. They contend that many public schools subscribe to secular humanism, a kind of secular religion based on Pragmatism and Liberalism, that sees truth values as relative and situational. Neo-Conservatives want the public schools to reflect what they believe are the country's abiding traditional Christian values. They favor moments of silence for quiet reflection, the posting of the Ten Commandments, and permission for student groups to meet for prayer in public schools. Sex education programs need to be carefully monitored so that they emphasize abstinence from sexual relations before marriage and do not encourage other kinds of birth control such as the use of condoms.

A long-running issue between Christian Conservatives and their Pragmatist, Liberal, and Progressive opponents is the teaching of Darwin's theory of evolution in the science curriculum. In 1859, Charles Darwin (1809–1882) in *The Origin of Species by Means of Natural Selection* established the theory that all existing plants and animals had evolved by gradual modifications that, if they contributed to survival, were passed on to their offspring as inherited characteristics.[9]

Darwin's theory of evolution provoked deep controversies in religion, philosophy, and education. For many Christians, evolution challenged the Biblical account of Creation, in Genesis, that God created all species as they now exist.[10] Although some theologians interpret Genesis allegorically, Christian Fundamentalists, taking a literal view of the Bible, reject Darwinian evolution.

The Scopes Trial in 1925 in Dayton, Tennessee, dramatically illustrated the tension generated by the teaching of evolution in the schools. John Scopes, a high school science and mathematics teacher, was tried for violating the Butler Act, which prohibited teaching evolution in Tennessee's public schools.[11] Although Scopes was convicted and fined a minimal one hundred dollars, the prosecution case was more of a symbolic than a real victory.[12]

Today, the issue is framed as the teaching of Evolution versus Creationism or Intelligent Design in the science curriculum. Christian Fundamentalists, who argue that evolution is a theory rather than a factual account, want equal attention given to Creation Science or Intelligent Design. Creation Science argues that there is sufficient scientific evidence to support the Biblical account of Creation. **Intelligent Design** argues that life is too complex to have developed without the intervention of an intelligent outside power.[13] Neo-Conservative Christian Fundamentalists seek to have these alternative views included in the curriculum.

Although Christian Conservatives continue their struggle for an alternative to Darwinian evolution in the science curriculum, they have been unsuccessful in the courts. The U.S. Supreme Court has ruled that local school boards and state legislatures cannot legally prohibit the teaching of evolution, nor require the teaching of Creationism, either alongside evolutionary theory or in place of it. For example, the Supreme Court ruled (in 1968) that a 1928 Arkansas law that made it a crime to teach evolution in a public school or state university violated the First Amendment's Establishment Clause in that it had a religious purpose to prevent students from being instructed in a position opposed by fundamentalist Christians.[14]

In 1982, Federal District Court Judge William Overton, in *McLean v. Arkansas Board of Education,* ruled against the "Balanced Treatment for Creation-Science and Evolution-Science Act," which required creation science to be taught alongside evolution. Overton ruled that Arkansas law violated the Establishment Clause and that creation science was not science, but based wholly on the biblical account of Creation. Therefore, the teaching of creation science clearly advances religion and entangles it with the government. In a similar case, the Supreme Court in *Edwards v. Aguillard* (1987) struck down a Louisiana law that forbade the teaching of the theory of evolution in public schools unless it was accompanied by instruction in creation science.[15] In *Kitzmiller v. Dover Area School District* (2005), Federal Judge John E. Jones III ruled that the board's decision to include Intelligent Design in the town's high school science curriculum violated the Establishment Clause.

These court rulings apply to the teaching of Creationism in science courses but not in other courses such as in literature or world religions classes. The Supreme Court has ruled that "the Bible may constitutionally be used in an appropriate study of history, civilization, ethics, comparative religion or the like."[16]

Neo-Conservatives hope that judges in the future will be appointed to the Supreme Court and other federal courts on their concurrence that the Constitution should be strictly interpreted. They believe that strict constructionists will not interpret the law liberally and that the decisions on abortion and evolution may yet be overturned.

Neo-Conservative Economic Beliefs

In considering the economic beliefs of Neo-Conservatives, it is necessary to return to the concept of **ideological permeability**, which means that ideologies often appropriate the ideas of other ideologies.[17] Neo-Conservatism has appropriated the Classical Liberal laissez-faire economic theories of Adam Smith and David Ricardo, of the Manchester school of economics, which were developed in the early nineteenth century. Classical Liberal economic theory argued that: (1) government should not interfere with the operations of the free and open market; (2) the law of supply and demand, a natural economic law, operates on its own to make needed adjustments to the economy, without the need for external regulation; and (3) economic growth results from competition that brings about new inventions and innovations. Neo-Conservatives have applied Classical economic theory to contemporary economic globalization specifying that trade barriers between countries should be removed, economies should be deregulated, and as many government services as possible should be deregulated.

Other commentators in the educational foundations have called this revival of Smith's and Ricardo's economic theories Neo-Liberalism, which means the new Liberalism. I think that the term *Neo-Liberalism* causes confusion in trying to disentangle the nuances of various ideologies. For example, Modern Liberalism, or New Liberalism, is a long-used term for Dewey's Experimentalist-influenced Liberalism and for social welfare Liberalism, shaped by the economists John Maynard Keynes and John Kenneth Galbraith, which continues to infuse contemporary Liberalism. The term *Classical Liberalism* is more useful in that it identifies key ideas in early-nineteenth-century Liberalism that are being applied today in Neo-Conservatism.

The American and European Neo-Conservative appropriation of Classical Liberal economics has been very influential in domestic as well as in global economies. Ideas that were once directed to business entrepreneurs and industry are now applied to the larger and more interconnected corporate economy. Recall that in the previous chapter, it was emphasized that Modern Liberals have profoundly revised these ideas and prefer a larger government role to provide more social services. In opposition to the Modern Liberal social welfare state, American Conservatives advocate an open market, free trade, supply and demand, competitiveness, and the deregulation and privatization of social and some educational services. A free and competitive marketplace, they argue, will encourage the most industrious and able individuals to achieve and produce without having to fear the weight of carrying the less productive on their economic shoulders. Neo-Conservatives believe that government intervention in regulating the economy leads to higher taxes and inefficient bureaucracy. It is important to restore the economy to its free-flowing condition by deregulating it, that is, by removing the controls of government regulatory agencies.

Though Neo-Conservatives have appropriated **Classical Liberal economic theory**, they have abandoned the older Conservative sense of economic paternalism, in which the upper classes were responsible for the well-being of the poorer socioeconomic classes. For Neo-Conservatives, the modern Liberal social welfare state relegates the poor to a dependent underclass. Conservatives charged that the social welfare assistance programs, enacted by Liberals, especially in Roosevelt's New Deal and Johnson's Great Society, created and perpetuated an underclass dependent on government-sponsored welfare. For Neo-Conservatives, the poor need the training that will enable them to compete in an increasingly technological society. The older Conservative paternalism has been redefined as private voluntarism in which individuals, by their private philanthropy, aid educational institutions. The idea of private philanthropy and voluntarism can be combined into faith-based religious programs to uplift the poor.

For Neo-Conservatives, modern welfare Liberals have enacted bureaucratic regulations that have weakened American economic productivity. For example, administrators and teachers in public schools have to spend far too much time in meeting bureaucratic requirements and filling out countless forms that take them away from their real job—teaching basic skills and academic subjects. It is these skills and subjects that are vitally needed to revive American economic productivity. They have replaced the tried-and-true traditional values of hard work, diligence, respect for authority, and patriotism with Progressive and Liberal so-called innovative tinkering and experimentation with the curriculum. Rather than preparing the well-trained workforce and managers needed in an increasingly technological global economy, public schools, too often controlled by misguided Liberal educationists, have miseducated children.

In addition to reforming public schools by restoring their primary academic role, some Neo-Conservatives argue that the public school system is a tax-supported educational monopoly. As in a monopoly, it resists competition among schools. Competition between schools would stimulate the more academic schools to be identified and attract students. Conservatives believe there should be greater educational freedom of choice. A program of government-subsidized vouchers would enable parents to choose their preferred public or private school. In such a competitive educational arena, it will be possible to distinguish the most effective and efficient schools from mediocre ones. Effective schools will attract academically inclined and motivated students. Thus, the voucher system, a form of educational privatization, would make schooling an arena of challenging competition.

Neo-Conservativism's Response to Confrontations

Neo-Conservatism is a protective ideology that reacts against attacks on its core beliefs and values especially from a counter ideology such as Liberalism or a countertheory such as Critical Theory. The Conservative strategy is to assemble a defensive array of counter concepts, a conceptual "circle of the wagons," directed against whatever appears to be threatening its version of the good society.[18] For example, in the abortion controversy, a "woman's right to choose" is countered by "the right to life." In health care, federal medical insurance is countered with the freedom and privacy between doctor and patient. The teaching of Darwin's theory of evolution in the science curriculum is countered with the teaching of Intelligent Design. A multicultural curriculum is countered with a core curriculum based on Western culture.

Conservatism's Implications for Education, Schooling, Curriculum, and Teaching and Learning

We have commented on Conservatism's and Neo-Conservativism's ideas about education throughout the chapter; we now turn to a more specific commentary on their implications for education, schooling, curriculum, and teaching and learning.

American Neo-Conservatives have a definite educational agenda. They want to restore the school to what they argue is its primary function—the transmission of the cultural heritage by deliberately organized instruction in academic skills and subjects in a climate of traditional moral values. For them, restoration is needed because decades of miseducation by Dewey's Pragmatists, Liberals, Progressives, cultural relativists, and secular humanists have disrupted the school's academic mission and eroded its cultivation of moral values.

Education

For Conservatives, education is the transmission of the cultural heritage, the essential aspects of the culture, from generation to generation so that the culture is preserved or saved. The cultural heritage means the important elements in the culture—historically tested traditional knowledge and values, as well as historically evolved institutions—that comprise a culture. **Cultural transmission**, which avoids social disruption, provides the young with the correct idea of how institutions function and informs them that each institution has a primary function. Education, both informally and formally, through schooling, should create a sense of time that is transgenerational and of place, as constituting a homeland.

Schools

Schools, as historically evolved social and cultural institutions, have the primary role of introducing and transmitting the cultural heritage to the young by educating children and adolescents in academic skills and knowledge. They promote cultural continuity through language, history, literature, and the arts. Educators are to safeguard and protect the traditional curriculum from those who want to experiment with, add nonacademic frills to, and impose nonacademic functions on schools and teachers. They warn against being deluded by panacea-like promises that the introduction of a new subject or method will make teaching and learning easy and effective. From time to time, certain changes occur such as the introduction of computers and electronic information technologies. The educational challenge is to use these technologies so that they are linked to and reinforce the cultural heritage. Computers can be used to transmit the cultural heritage in a more dynamic and efficient way. In *A Nation at Risk,* computer literacy was now identified as a new basic, along with the traditional language, mathematics, science, and history. Computer literacy is a necessary skill in the global economy.

Order and Civility.   Conservatives argue that schools have been moving in the wrong direction regarding values and character education. Misguided by Dewey's Pragmatism, Liberalism, and Progressivism, the moral climate of schools has been eroded by hedonism, permissiveness, irresponsibility, and inappropriate dress and behavior. In the past, teachers were respected persons in society and schools were respected institutions. This kind of respect was earned by emphasizing the tried-and-true historically validated moral values—patriotism, diligence, hard work, respect for private property, and the practice of manners and civility—that made the United States into a great and prosperous nation. It is time to reassert these core values in schools so that they have clear and unambiguous educational and moral purposes. Schools should be places in which students learn to respect their country, their teachers, and each other.

Curriculum

For Conservatives, the **curriculum** is historically derived and validated. It consists of skills and knowledge that contribute to cultural survival, have met the test of time, and remain necessary and useful in the culture. The tool skills of reading, writing, and composition contribute to a literacy that is important in reaffirming, maintaining, and reproducing the cultural heritage. Arithmetic is important for its generative power in higher mathematics and the sciences. Geography, a subject neglected in contemporary education, needs to be reestablished so that Americans are no longer geographically illiterate. It is useful in creating knowledge about location and place. The secondary curriculum is organized as subjects, each of which has clearly defined boundaries, and which should be taught by teachers who have knowledge of what they are teaching. Knowledge of the liberal arts and sciences is necessary for teaching competency. Too often, it has been sacrificed in teacher education programs for courses in methods—on how to teach but not on what to teach. Science, mathematics, history, language, and literature should be taught in an orderly and sequential way.

A Cultural Core.   Conservatives believe that schools need to transmit a **cultural core** that is rooted in Western civilization and American culture. The heritage of Western civilization, as Conservatives define it, is based on the great ideas of Plato, Aristotle, Jesus, Aquinas, Luther, Calvin, Locke, Burke, and others and the major events of European history such as the Renaissance, Reformation, and Enlightenment.

In addition to the core of Western civilization, Conservatives want the schools to emphasize what they identify as the core knowledge and values of American culture. This means that students should be taught American history and literature and should be expected to know the important persons and events that shaped the country. It should not be taught in a way that downgrades American patriotism and minimizes the great achievements Americans made in creating their nation. It should emphasize knowledge of the Constitution, and respect for law and duly constituted authorities. Conservatives would oppose what they regard as an extreme multiculturalism that minimizes American core values and represents the United States as a nation of unassimilated racial and ethnic groups.

Language, literature, and history should celebrate the achievements of the past, the major events in the group's collective life, and the heroes and heroines who best exemplify the group's values and aspirations. History is presented in terms of a tradition that is the basis of culture and a defensive rationale to be used against opponents. It is presented as a cumulative wisdom of the past that present students need to inherit to remain stable and law-abiding citizens. Economics is interpreted in laissez-faire, free market terms.

Restoring Academic Standards.   The contemporary standards movement and the federal No Child Left Behind Act mark a Neo-Conservative effort to restore academic standards to the school. The standards movement was inaugurated by the Reagan administration with *A Nation at Risk* (1983), which sought to reverse the nonacademic undermining of the schools. This national report called for a curriculum of academic basics—the English language, mathematics, science, language, social studies and history, and computer literacy. The Reagan administration developed a strategy that encouraged the states to enact legislation that added requirements in the basics, especially in English, mathematics, and science. It also encouraged them to use standardized testing to determine students' academic competency at specific grade levels. The initiative stimulated by *A Nation at Risk* led to the standards movement in education that asserts that schools need to be held accountable for the academic instruction that they are supposed to provide. The only way to really determine academic competency is to require standardized testing that measures students' academic achievement, especially in the key areas of reading and mathematics at specific grade levels. The Education Act of 2001, the No Child Left Behind Act, sponsored by the George W. Bush administration, requires states to implement standardized testing in reading and mathematics, in grades three through eight, in order to receive federal funds.

The Conservative Teacher

The teacher in the Conservative educational setting is an agent of transmitting the cultural heritage to children and youth so that they can incorporate it into their intellectual outlooks and characters. Such teachers should be people who cherish the cultural heritage, who know it well, and who reflect in their personalities and behavior the culture's traditional values. Like the Idealist teacher, they are character models that students can imitate. Although they may use educational technology to transmit the tradition more effectively, Conservative teachers are not agents seeking to change or reconstruct society. Nor do such teachers encourage cultural alternatives and diversity. In a world that has grown increasingly unstable because of social and technological change, incessant mobility, and moral relativism, Conservative teachers use the school as a stabilizing agency. Their task is to maintain the cultural heritage as a repository of the enduring achievements of the human race by introducing it to the young so that they can absorb it and perpetuate it.

Neo-Essentialism and Neo-Perennialism

For many Neo-Conservatives, U.S. public schooling has been moving in the wrong direction. They believe that Dewey's Pragmatism, Progressive education, and Critical Theory are philosophies and theories that have contributed to the schools' miseducative problems. These philosophies and theories have brought about a decline of academic standards, an increase of indiscipline and incivility in both schools and society, an erosion of traditional ethical values, and a decline in U.S. economic productivity. To remedy these perceived defects, Neo-Conservatives have called for educational reforms. Although the theories of Perennialism and Essentialism are discussed elsewhere, we will treat them briefly here in relationship to the Neo-Conservative educational agenda.

Many of the reforms of the 1980s that were stimulated by *A Nation at Risk* were designed to correct what Neo-Conservatives regarded as declining academic skills and subjects. Similar to Idealists and Realists, they argue that schools have a primary function: to foster basic skills and competency in traditional academic subjects, namely, mathematics, science, language, and history. To return to fundamental skills and subjects, the curricular residues of Liberalism and Progressivism need to be removed. For example, they challenge the Liberal concept that the school is a multifunctional community service institution. Multi-functionalism, Neo-Conservatives assert, weakens the schools' primary role.

Neo-Conservatives, especially those inclined toward Perennialism, see the schools as transmitting a knowledge and value core derived from the Western cultural experience. They see the classical Greco-Roman, Medieval, Renaissance, Reformation, and Enlightenment eras as presenting a needed cultural frame of reference that orients the young to the cultural heritage. Within this framework are the languages, literatures, history, and arts that were developed in Western civilization. Encased within the larger Western heritage is the American experience in which European settlement is highlighted. Also, for many Neo-Conservatives, the issue of the language of instruction in the schools is highly significant. Some would end bilingual and bicultural programs, claiming they erode an English-language-based cultural core.

Neo-Conservatives, similar to Essentialists, also argue that schools are tied to the country's economic growth and productivity. Using studies that compare the academic achievements of U.S. students in mathematics and science with those of other countries, Neo-Conservatives claim that U.S. productivity has been declining in the face of foreign competition. Neo-Conservatives have supported reforms in the state legislatures to mandate increased requirements in mathematics and science.

It is interesting to note that the Neo-Conservative agenda in education has included both Perennialist and Essentialist arguments. From Perennialism it takes the position that schools must identify and transmit a stable cultural core that links generations in an inherited tradition. From the Essentialist position, it argues that the efficient and effective teaching of key skills and subjects has a positive impact on economic productivity.

Neo-Conservatives decry what they perceive to be declining standards of morality and civility in society. The failure of schools to impart a stable cultural core and universal ethical standards to the young has resulted in violence, immorality, and mediocrity, which are all symptomatic of cultural rootlessness. Further, the failure of schools to hold up worthy personal models that young people can emulate further compounds the moral malaise besetting a relativist society. Some Neo-Conservatives, especially those who identify with religious orthodoxy and fundamentalism, look to a revival of traditional religious values to remedy what they see is moral decline. They advocate prayer in the schools, religious observances, and religious education. Other Neo-Conservatives see moral and ethical decline to be the result of cultural relativism and situational ethics in education. For them, the remedy is to turn to the Western heritage, especially those aspects of it that assert universal, eternal truths and values.

Conclusion

This chapter examined Conservatism as an ideology. It discussed its origins with Edmund Burke, as a reaction against the French Revolution. It then identified and analyzed Conservatism's key principles, which focus on the preservation, maintenance, and reproduction of the cultural heritage. Contemporary American Neo-Conservatism was examined as an ideology that has influenced the revival of the academic subject-matter curriculum and the standards movement, especially the testing of competency in basic skills and subjects. The chapter examined Conservatism's implications for education, schools, curriculum, and instruction.

Constructing your own philosophy of education.   Now that you have read the chapter on Conservatism, reflect on your own educational experiences. Did you experience Conservatism in your own education? Conservatism is also an important cultural ideology, with significant political implications; consider how it has shaped educational policy in the United States. Do you agree or disagree with Conservatism? Do you plan to include Conservatism in your own philosophy of education?

Questions for Reflection and Discussion

1. Do you consider Conservatism to be a relevant ideology in American society, politics, and education?

2. Do you find a pro-Conservative or anti-Conservative orientation in the courses that you have taken or are taking for your degree?

3. Think back on the various courses that you took in American history in high school and college. Were these courses ideologically neutral or were they influenced by a Conservative or Liberal bias?

4. Critics of American Neo-Conservatism contend that it misrepresents American culture in order to use it as a rationale for its policies. Do you agree or disagree? Do you think this charge can be leveled against other ideologies as well?

5. Reflect on the concept of alienation. You have encountered it in the chapter on Existentialism and will encounter it in the next chapter on Marxism. What is alienation? Do you consider yourself alienated? How might a Conservative react to your considerations about alienation?

Topics for Inquiry and Research _____

1. In class discussion, identify the leading contemporary contributors to Conservative thinking.

2. Read a leading newspaper for a week. Make a reference file of the articles and frequency in which Conservatism is mentioned.

3. In class discussion, examine the meaning of the term *traditional cultural values*. What are traditional values? What impact do traditional values have on teaching?

4. Debate the immigration issue in contemporary American politics and society. Assign students to argue from a Liberal and Conservative position.

5. Do an analysis of several high school texts in American history on the chapters that deal with recent history from the 1960s to the present. Do you find these texts to have an ideological bias? How do they treat the Neo-Conservative revival?

Building a Conservative Vocabulary _____

Americanization: the educational policy by which immigrants are to learn the English language and to take on American ideas and values about government, work, and education.

Christian Conservatives: Christians, often Evangelical Protestants, who believe that Conservatism is most compatible with their religious values.

Classical Liberal Economic Theory: also called Neo-Liberalism; the ideas of the free market and limited government interference in the economy that originated with Liberals but are now part of Neo-Conservatism.

Cultural Core in the Curriculum: knowledge areas, or subjects, that transmits the heritage of Western civilization and American culture.

Cultural Transmission: passing the cultural heritage, the essential aspects of the culture, from generation to generation so that the culture is preserved and reproduced.

Curriculum: for Conservatives, historically derived skills and subjects that are transmitted to the young to reproduce cultural heritage and values.

Historically Evolved Institutions: institutions that have evolved over time and have developed a specific role and function.

Ideological Permeability: when one ideology accommodates to and appropriates the ideas of another ideology.

Intelligent Design: a theory that argues that life is too complex to have developed without the intervention of an intelligent outside power.

Neo-Conservatism: the revival of Conservative political, social, cultural, and educational principles in contemporary America.

Primary Function of Schools: the transmission of the cultural heritage by deliberately organized instruction in academic skills and subjects in a climate of traditional moral values.

School: for Conservatives, a historically evolved educational institution that transmits cultural heritage identified in prescribed academic skills, subjects, and values.

Tradition: the knowledge, beliefs, and values of the past that as a cultural authority influence the present.

Internet Resources _____

For a discussion of the ideas of Russell Kirk, a leading American Conservative theorist, access www.townhall.com/hall_of_fame/Kirk/Kirkhome.html.

For an essay on Conservatism, access www.xrefer.com/entry/522667.html.

For a short history of Conservatism, access www.freecongress.org/centers/cc/history.asp.

For Conservatism as a political theory, access www.library_Vanderbilt.edu/romans/polsci/polthought.html.

Suggestions for Further Reading

Abbott, Pamela, and Claire Wallace. *The Family and the New Right.* London and Boulder, CO: Pluto Press, 1992.

Bennett, William J. *The De-Valuing of America: The Fight for Our Culture and Our Children.* New York: Simon & Schuster, 1992.

Cheney, Lynne V. *Telling the Truth: Why Our Culture and Our Country Have Stopped Making Sense—and What We Can Do About It.* New York: Simon & Schuster, 1995.

Frohnen, Bruce. *Virtue and the Promise of Conservatism: The Legacy of Burke and Tocqueville.* Lawrence: University Press of Kansas, 1993.

Goldwater, Barry M. *The Conscience of a Conservative.* Princeton, NJ: Princeton University Press, 2007.

Gottfried, Paul. *The Conservative Movement.* New York: Twayne, 1993.

Kekes, John. *A Case for Conservatism.* Ithaca, NY: Cornell University Press, 2001.

Kirk, Russell. *Academic Freedom.* Chicago: Henry Regnery Co., 1995.

Mullen, Jerry Z. *Conservatism: An Anthology of Social and Political Thought From David Hume to the Present.* Princeton, NJ: Princeton University Press, 1997.

Stanlis, Peter J. *The Best of Burke: Selected Writings and Speeches.* Chicago: Regnery, 1999.

Endnotes

1. Edmund Burke, *Writings and Speeches,* vol. VII (London: Bickers & Sons, 1865), pp. 93–95.

2. Glenn D. Wilson, ed., *The Psychology of Conservatism* (New York: Academic Press, 1973), p. 13.

3. Michael Freeden, *Ideology: A Very Short Introduction* (Oxford, UK: Oxford University Press, 2003), p. 88.

4. Freeden, *Ideology: A Very Short Introduction,* pp. 50, 88.

5. Harlow Giles Unger, *Noah Webster: The Life and Times of an American Patriot* (New York: Wiley, 1998).

6. Catharine E. Beecher, *An Essay on the Education of Female Teachers,* (New York: Van Nostrand & Dwight, 1835), p. 19.

7. John H. Westerhoff, *McGuffey and His Readers: Piety, Morality, and Education in Nineteenth-Century America* (Nashville, TN.: Abingdon, 1978). See also James M. Lower, "William Holmes McGuffey: A Book or a Man? Or More?" *Vitae Scholasticae* (Fall 1984), pp. 311–320.

8. Close Up Foundation Civics Education/U.S. Immigration Policy, www.closeup.org/immigration.htm. (1-1-2007).

9. Jonathan Howard, *Darwin* (New York: Oxford University Press, 1982). Also, see Michael Ruse, *The Darwinian Revolution* (Chicago: University of Chicago Press, 1979).

10. Neil C. Gillespie, *Charles Darwin and the Problem of Creation* (Chicago: University of Chicago Press, 1979).

11. The Scopes Trial continues to fascinate Americans. *Inherit the Wind,* a drama about the trial, was a popular play and motion picture.

12. *The Scopes Trial: A Photographic History,* introduction by Edward Caudill (Knoxville: University of Tennessee Press, 2000), pp. 1–20. Also, see Edward J. Larson, *Summer for the Gods: The Scopes Trial and America's Continuing Debate over Science and Religion* (New York: Basic Books, 1997).

13. David Masci, "From Darwin to Dover: An Overview of Important Cases in the Evolution Debate," Pew Forum on Religion & Public Life (September 22, 2005).

14. Masci, "From Darwin to Dover."

15. Masci, "From Darwin to Dover."

16. Masci, "From Darwin to Dover."

17. Freeden, *Ideology: A Very Short Introduction,* pp. 63–64.

18. Freeden, *Ideology: A Very Short Introduction,* p. 89.

11

Marxism and Education

Karl Marx, a 19th century philosopher, who developed Marxism, an ideological and political movement that emphasizes economically-generated class conflict.

Chapter Preview

Marxism, an ideology named for its founder, German philosopher Karl Marx (1818–1883), has been and continues to be an important mode of economic, social, political, and educational critique and analysis. We now discuss its basic doctrines, and their implications for education, schooling, curriculum, and teaching and learning. Whether or not we reject Marxism as an ideology, we need to recognize that the power that Marx gave to economic factors is a force in shaping society, politics, and education. In education, especially the foundations of education, Marxism and Neo-Marxism exert a significant influence on educational analysis. The designation **Neo-Marxist** refers to new or contemporary Marxists, who, while keeping Marx's basic doctrines, have revised them in terms of the modern situation. Marxist themes also can be found in Postmodern philosophy and in Critical Theory. The following major topics are examined in the chapter:

- Karl Marx as a revolutionary ideologist
- Marxism's basic doctrines: Dialectical and historical materialism
- Marx's analysis of Capitalism
- The proletariat as the revolutionary destined class
- Between philosophy and ideology: Marxism's philosophical and ideological relationships
- Marxism's educational implications
- Schools in a capitalist society

Karl Marx: Revolutionary Educator

Karl Marx, the son of a prominent lawyer, was born in 1818 in Trier, Germany, into a middle-class family of Jewish ancestry. Marx, who was educated at home until age twelve, was heavily influenced by his father, who believed in the ideas of the Enlightenment philosophers.[1] The young Marx was also influenced by Baron von Westphalen, his future father-in-law, who encouraged him to read the history, philosophy, and literature that filled the shelves of his library.

Marx's formal schooling began in Trier, where he attended the local *gymnasium,* or academic secondary school. He received a classical humanistic education, studying Latin, Greek, French, religion, mathematics, and history.

Intending to become a lawyer like his father, Marx entered the university at Bonn in 1835, where he studied philosophy and literature as well as law. After spending a year at Bonn, he transferred to the more prestigious University of Berlin. There Marx studied Hegelian Idealism, the philosophy that dominated German intellectual life at the time. Although he would reject Hegelianism's nonmaterialism and spiritualism, Marx did retain Hegel's dialectical process, which he incorporated into his philosophy of dialectical materialism.

In addition to Hegel, Marx was also influenced by Ludwig Feuerbach, author of *Theses on the Hegelian Philosophy.* Like other nineteenth-century German intellectuals, Feuerbach was reacting to Hegelian Idealism. Rejecting the Hegelian concept that historical events were caused by the unfolding of a spiritual force, the Absolute Idea, Feuerbach asserted that human history was a product of material conditions, the economic factors that existed at a particular time. Nonmaterial elements such as art, literature, and other cultural forms were not independent entities but reflected the underlying economic reality. Impressed by Feuerbach's arguments, Marx later united the concept of materialism to the Hegelian dialectical process, his synthesis of dialectical materialism.

Marx later studied at the University of Jena, where he completed his doctorate in philosophy in 1841. Unable to find a position in higher education, he accepted a job as editor of a liberal Rhineland newspaper, the *Rheinische Zeitung.*

Marx's evolving ideology was influenced by Moses Hess, the publisher of the *Rheinische Zeitung,* who combined traditional Judaism and humanitarianism with Hegelian Idealism. From Hess, Marx came to see private property as the source of all human ills. As a humanitarian, Hess wanted to organize an international society based on a collective economy. As a result of his association with Hess, Marx came to emphasize economic influences in shaping historical and social forces. He also stressed the need for an international revolutionary organization.

As editor of the *Rheinische Zeitung,* Marx attacked the conservative policies of the Prussian government. In 1843, the government suppressed the journal's publication. Now unemployed, Marx, who had married Jenny von Westphalen in 1843, emigrated to France. He went to Paris with his young wife to write for the German-language periodical, *Deutsch-Französische Jahrbücher.* He had already formulated some basic ideas that would be expressed in his synthesis of scientific socialism, such as the premise of a material universe, dialectical processes of social change, and the coming class struggle.

As an exile in France from 1843 to 1845, Marx completed his ideological transformation and became a convinced socialist. During his French exile, Marx encountered Saint-Simon and other Utopian Socialist theorists. He agreed with Saint-Simon that economic relationships determined the course of history, which was largely the record of the conflict of competing economic classes. Saint-Simon's belief that the government should be in the hands of a small group of expert scientists and technicians contributed to Marx's emphasis that the coming revolutions should be led by an elite vanguard of the proletariat. However, he rejected what he regarded as the naive view of Fourier, Owen, and other Utopians that social and political change could be attained without revolutionary violence.

While in Paris, Marx became a lifelong collaborator with the wealthy German radical Friedrich Engels. Devoting himself to theory and writing, Marx and his family lived in near poverty. Engels provided the economic support that enabled Marx to do his work.

The years between 1847 and 1848 found Marx still in exile from his native Germany, living in Brussels, Belgium. He now developed his basic ideological themes, especially on economic determinism and historical inevitability. Marx believed that economic forces, the means and modes of production, were at the base of society. Historical processes and events were caused by history's inevitable and inexorable course. These economically directed historical forces would lead to the inevitable triumph of the proletariat, the working class.

Marx's theorizing was broken by the momentous revolutions that swept Europe in 1848. This revolutionary situation stimulated Marx and Engels to write their famous *Communist Manifesto,* which begins: "A specter is haunting Europe—the specter of Communism," and concludes:

> The Communists disdain to conceal their views and aims. They openly declare that their ends can be attained only by the forcible overthrow of all existing social conditions. Let the ruling classes tremble at a Communist revolution. The proletarians have nothing to lose but their chains. They have a world to win. Workingmen of all countries, unite![2]

When the uprisings of 1848 failed to overthrow the reactionary Prussian government, Marx spent the rest of his life in London, researching and writing his monumental work, *Das Kapital,* an extensive analysis of economics.

Marxism's Basic Doctrines

In this section, we examine the basic doctrines of Marx's ideology. Among them are **dialectical materialism** and his theory of economically determined history. Particularly significant is the concept of economic control and class conflict.

Dialectical Materialism

Marx sees the basic force in the universe as matter in motion. Philosophically, he took the concept of matter, found in materialism and realism, and combined it with the Hegelian Idealist idea of dialectical change. Marx enlarged the meaning of materialism from the physical, concrete objects found in nature, to include observable human activity, especially human beings' practical interactions with their environment.[3]

The Human Being. Marx defined human beings as natural, social, economic, and historical individuals. They differ from animals in that they use the material conditions in their environment to produce their own economic means of subsistence. The **human being** is a material physical creature, with physiological needs and drives, who possesses a brain that enables thought. Living in a material world, humans work to produce goods or commodities that they need. How and what they produce determines how they organize themselves politically, socially, and economically and how they use education.[4]

Society

Marx challenges the traditional Idealist and Realist view of society in which human beings are what they are because they share a common essence, human nature, and that human societies arise as organizations of individuals who share in this essential common humanity. Marx challenges the Liberal view of society, more closely associated with capitalism, that a society is atomistic and composed of discrete individuals, social atoms, who join associations for self-protection, either in the literal Darwinism sense of self-preservation or to defend their inalienable rights as asserted by John Locke.

Marx sees **society** as a developing, expanding, and changing network of human relationships that have economic consequences. The means and modes of production connect the biological, sociological, political, and educational aspects of group life with its economic foundation.[5] Group life and social cooperation has a material or economic base that rests on production of commodities. Social events are caused by the need to keep expanding and further developing the means of production, the industry, machinery, and technology that makes production possible.

A Marxist analysis of the social, philosophical, and cultural foundations of education focuses first on the material or economic conditions in a society.[6] If the analyst begins with the social composition of students attending a particular school, for example, she or he is soon led to the students' socioeconomic class. If the issue is the difference in resources between schools in inner cities and suburbs, the difference will have an economic cause such as disparities in revenues generated for education. If the issue is differences between groups in high school completion or college attendance rates, the cause will be economic and related to socioeconomic class.

The Dialectic

Marx, who had studied Hegelian Idealism as a university student, continued to rely on Hegel's principle of the dialectic. (For a discussion of Hegel, see the chapter on Idealism.) When he abandoned Idealism, Marx retained the idea of the dialectic but transferred it from the realm of ideas, where Hegel had located it, to material reality—to the means and modes of production. For Hegel, all ideas came forth from the mind of the Absolute Idea, the universal idea that contained all other subordinate ideas. History, for Hegel, was the unfolding of these ideas on earth over time and historical change was the result of the resolution, the creation of new syntheses, in this realm of ideas. Every idea stated a thesis that, while it embodied a partial truth, also held its contradiction. From the conflict of thesis and antithesis emerged a newer and higher idea, a synthesis, a new and more integrated idea that, as a new thesis, generated a new conflict and continued the dialectical process. Borrowing Hegel's dialectical process, Marx transferred it to his own version of reality that was strictly material or physical. Instead of a conflict of ideas, Marx saw human history as a ceaseless struggle between conflicting economic classes for control of the material economic conditions of society. History is a process of conflict and resolution between opposing economic classes for power and control in society.

Dialectical Epistemology. Marx's dialectical way of thinking, or **dialectical epistemology**, portrays the human situation as immersion in a process of continuing class conflict and struggle. In **dialectical thought**, there are always two opposing sides and two sets of arguments. These opposites are contradictory stages that eventually will be reconciled in a synthesis, a new thesis. Neo-Marxists continue to use dialectical reasoning to analyze social, political, and education issues in terms of contradictions or conflicts to be resolved by the struggle for power. Though they are less certain that history is determined than are orthodox Marxists, they continue to find the dialectic a useful form of social and educational analysis.

   The change from one stage of economic development to another involves taking elements for the new stage from the older one that preceded it. The dialectical process works in history by eliminating something in the old stage but also transforming some parts of it in the new stage.

Marx's Philosophy of History: Historical Materialism

Marx constructed a detailed interpretation of history, termed **historical materialism**. An account of the major events of the past, it is primarily a historically derived theory of economically generated social, political, and educational change. Marx saw history unfolding according to dialectical materialism. For Marx, history's forward course is inevitable and inexorable. In an ideological form of predestination, past, present, and future are the products of the dialectical process—the struggle of contending classes to control the means and modes of production. The dialectical process follows a predetermined pattern that relentlessly builds new syntheses from the clash of thesis and antithesis. Marx argued that historically identifiable developments in economic production such as feudalism and the emergence of capitalism made the future predictable.

   History begins when human beings begin to produce the goods, the commodities, the food, clothing, and other products, needed to sustain life. The first major historical event, in the broad sense, is the human construction of material life—what they do and how they organize to satisfy their needs. Each satisfaction of needs generates additional needs in an ongoing continuum of production of goods. Throughout much of history, land was the material condition on which social control was based. People were agricultural, tilling the soil, planting and harvesting crops, and raising livestock during the Greek and Roman classical and the Western European medieval periods. A strong group of warriors, the medieval knights, created the European feudal system, in which they owned the land and forced others, the serfs, to work it for them. In addition to their brute physical force, which directly oppressed the agricultural workers, the knightly landlords used the church as an agency of social control to convince the oppressed that life on earth was fated to be this way and life in heaven would be better. The social and religious patterns of medieval culture created a false consciousness in the serfs that deluded many of them from understanding their true condition and the sources of their oppression.

Agricultural production eventually created a surplus of wealth. This surplus led to the formation of a new class, the bourgeoisie, or the middle class, which left agricultural and took up other economic pursuits such as trade, banking, and the professions. In the industrial revolution of the early nineteenth century, machines were invented that produced goods on a mass scale. Some of the middle class invested their capital in the new industries to create the factory system of mass production and the economy of mass consumption.

For Marx, modern industrial society is composed of two classes: the **capitalists**, who own the factories—the means and modes of production—and the **proletariat**, the workers who produce goods but who do not own the machines on which they work. For Marx, economic class is our primary identification. Our social relationships are based on our relationship to the economy—the means and modes of production. The economic class that controls the economy, the means and modes of production, also controls society's institutional superstructure. Among these institutions are the state (the government), the church (organized religion), the courts (the legal system), the police and military (the arms of state power), the media (agencies of information), and the school (the agency of organized education). The exploiting class also constructs a highly usable false ideology, designed to mislead and miseducate the workers so they are not conscious of their true situation as exploited victims.

At this point in our discussion, we turn to Marx's analysis of capitalism, the historical stage at which he wrote in the nineteenth century. It is Marx's analysis of capitalism that engages most of his interpreters today. Then, we return to Marx's prediction of the inevitable proletarian revolution and the creation of a classless society.

Marx's Analysis of Capitalism

Marx devoted much of his life to an analysis of capitalism, an economic system he believed was doomed to fail because of its own internal contradictions. Capitalism is the system of private ownership and production. (See the chapters on Liberalism and Conservatism for the Classical Liberal rationale for capitalism.) Marx's detailed critical analysis identified capitalism's key elements: commodities and production, private ownership of property, money, capital, labor, surplus value, accumulation, and crisis. He saw capitalism as an expansive force, much like globalization today, that, in seeking new markets and larger profits, would move beyond its place of origin in western Europe and North America to universalize itself and to spread across the earth.

For Marx, society is organized into classes that, in turn, are based on what they own or do not own. Capitalism was based on the bourgeoisie, the middle class, emphasis on the right of individuals to own private property. The middle classes, as Marx understood them in the nineteenth century, were the business, commercial, and professional classes, who stood in the middle of the old social order between the aristocracy and the peasantry. For the middle classes, their right to hold their own property was, as John Locke stated, an inalienable natural right. The industrial revolution of the late nineteenth and early twentieth centuries had generated new forms of property and ownership that had changed the economy and society. Industrialism, especially the factory system of production, had generated a new class—the proletariat, the industrial workers. According to his conflict theory, modern history had reached the stage where the middle-class industrial capitalists, the thesis in the historical dialectic, were locked in conflict with the proletariat, their antithetical adversaries.

Producing Commodities

Under capitalism, as well as the earlier agricultural modes of production, a **commodity** is something material produced by human labor to satisfy human needs. In a capitalist economy, commodities are produced by workers who are paid wages for their labor. Every commodity has both a "use" and an "exchange" value. How something is used satisfies a human need so that a customer wants to buy it. Exchange value determines the value of a particular commodity, such as a computer or an iPod, in relationship to other commodities.[7] Commodity production (e.g., manufacturing automobiles) is geared to exchange value. Work or the labor needed to produce a commodity is analyzed as "concrete labor" and "abstract labor." **Concrete labor** refers to the skills needed to produce a particular commodity. **Abstract labor** refers to the general expenditure of human labor in producing commodities. Concrete labor can be measured and paid for by an employer and the worker is paid wages; also the products made can be sold, again for money. Concrete labor is the source of abstract labor. What is the socially average time needed to produce a commodity becomes Marx's labor theory of value.[8] When exchange value is greater than the other factors of production, surplus value is created, which is expropriated by capitalists as profits.

Illusion in Marketing Commodities. In the capitalist economy, marketing and advertising are used to stimulate the consumers' desire to purchase commodities. Illusions are used to sell commodities by appealing to the sensual or the emotional rather than to real needs. In capitalism, these marketing illusions are beauty, empowerment, and sexual attraction. For example, think about the marketing of shampoo to young women. Television commercials tell them that buying and using a particular shampoo will improve their appearance and make their hair lustrous. This, in turn, will attract the glances and attention of males and lead to relationships between a beautiful young woman and a handsome young man. Or, for young men, owning a luxury car will make them the envy of their male rivals and attractive to beautiful women.

Maintaining and Extending the System

The capitalist strategy for power and profit has both conservative and innovative dimensions. The two-pronged strategy requires: (1) maintaining, defending, and reproducing the social, political, and educational orders that they have constructed to ensure their domination; and (2) seeking to develop new productive technologies that will increase their profits, extend their property holdings, and enlarge their power. In both of these strategy strands, education, both formal and informal, plays a key role in creating false consciousness that dulls the sense of oppression of the exploited classes.

Maintaining, Defending, and Reproducing the Capitalist Social Order.   Marx calls the social, political, and educational agencies in capitalism the **superstructure** of society. It can be compared to the upper stories of a building that are most evident to a person's view. However, the crucial element in holding the upper stories in place securely is the foundation on which it rests. The upper stories depend on their foundation. For Marx, the necessary foundation of society was the economic means and modes of production. He reasoned that whoever controlled the means and modes of production also controlled and determined the contours and purposes of the superstructure. In a capitalist society, the capitalists owned the means and modes of production as their private property. They constructed the superstructure to cover and protect the economic foundation that they owned. Social institutions are not independent entities; they depend for their existence on the economic foundation or base on which they are erected. The class that controls the material conditions, the economy, will also control the superstructure.

The modern nation-state is the principal agency in the social superstructure. The nation-state, under capitalist control, has military and police forces, a legal system, and prisons to protect it, especially from dissenters and, of course, from Marxist revolutionaries. The church, an agency in the superstructure, gives supernatural sanction to the status quo that protects capitalism. Further, national school systems are agencies that indoctrinate the young to accept the status quo by transmitting a false ideology to them.

In both informal education, via the media, and in schooling, the role played by false ideology is crucial in defending a capitalist society. Although the dominant classes will

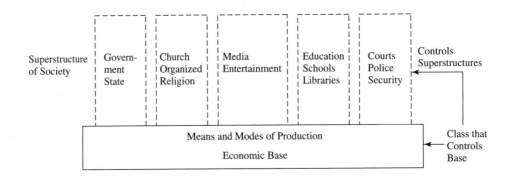

Marxist Means and Modes of Production: Economic Base

proclaim their ideology to be true, Marxists label it false. A false ideology is one that purports that the agencies in the superstructure have a life of their own and are independent of those who control the economic base. For example, religion, dealing with the human relationship to God, seeks to create a separate realm of thought, theology, to explain this relationship. The religious emphasis on a supernatural heaven and an afterlife, Marx felt, was the "opiate of the masses" that deluded them from understanding their true economic condition. Another example of false ideology can be found in education, especially among Liberals, who claim that they can be objective and not take a position on social and political issues. The claim to objectivity is another example of falsity. (For an example of disinterested objectivity, see the section on John Stuart Mill in the chapter on Liberalism.) For the Marxist, there is no neutral position in which to hide. You are either on the side of the oppressors or on the side of the oppressed.

Contemporary Neo-Marxist educators continue to pay great attention to who controls the superstructure. They point out that the schools are controlled by the capitalists and often serve the interests of the modern business corporation. For them, it is necessary to examine the actual economic conditions in which an institution functions. If you want to cut through the sentimental fog of the false ideology that proclaims the public school to be the agency of equality of opportunity, you have to go to schools and to their neighborhoods. You have to study the material conditions of schools in the inner cities and analyze the impact that poverty, homelessness, unemployment, gang violence, and drugs have on education. This kind of analysis cuts through the fog of false ideology and replaces it with true ideological consciousness.

The superstructure consists of the government institutions and agencies: government (a president and legislature); security agencies (military and police forces); courts or legal system; and the prison system. Although the government may appear to be democratic and elected, in reality, the various political parties differ in name only and stand for the same thing—enacting and enforcing the laws that protect and benefit the capitalists. The security agencies enforce and arrest those who threaten the continuation of the system. The courts try them and the prisons incarcerate them.

The superstructure also consists of informal educational agencies—the media, newspapers, television, radio—that mold what is called "public opinion" and formal educational agencies such as schools, colleges, and universities. These agencies play the role of "informing and educating the public," which Marxist would say is deluding the public by generating disinformation and diffusing miseducation. Media programs include an incessant marketing and advertising of the commodities, the products, produced by the system, which enhances capitalist profits. The news of the day is reduced to sensational stories about prominent entertainers rather than important national and international issues. The news is programmed as quick, colorful, and superficial items that blur the distinctions between entertainment and information.

Schools, colleges, and universities, in a capitalist society, play the role of creating a mind-set, a mentality, that is favorable to and exalts the inventions, discoveries, and innovations of capitalism as human progress. At the same time, the schools are so structured and organized that they reproduce the class structure. Although there is a public school system in the United States, there are schools that the children of the economically affluent attend and those that the poor attend. There are schools whose enrollment consists largely of students from the same class and race. The end result is to reproduce the class structure.

Developing New Productive Technologies.   Despite the maintenance and reproduction of the capitalist economy and society, capitalism is not static but is a dynamic force of production in which technological change is driven by the need to increase the profits that sustain and expand the system. The capitalist classes constantly encourage technological innovations that will increase production and sale of commodities, which in turn increases their profits. But more profits stimulate more innovation and technological development. These technological developments, however, do not stay lodged in the economic realm but infect and reshape social, political, and educational relationships. It should be pointed out that Marx and the Marxists do not opposed technological innovation and development. What they oppose is the expropriation of technology for the profits of one group and the exploitation and alienation of another.

An example of technological innovation that generates more technological innovation is the computer, the Internet, the World Wide Web, and e-mail. As soon as a new computer program is developed, it becomes technologically obsolete and is rapidly replaced by another, which is sold through intensive marketing. The computer and electronic data information is used by national and international airlines, banks, business firms, and other enterprises worldwide. The Web and Internet become tools to sell products and disseminate information, often disinformation. Electronic surveillance becomes an instrument of police and security forces. Computer and electronic data messaging and retrieval enhance the capitalist economic dominance; they also produce social, political, and educational changes that impact societal relations, nationally and globally. They give groups opposed to capitalism, especially globalization, a means of networking and organizing. The Internet and e-mail provide people a means of communication outside of the capitalist-controlled media. In schools, computer-assisted instruction, like most technologies, by itself is pedagogically neutral. It may enhance instruction, be used to indoctrinate, or provide an opening for students beyond the control of school officials.

Colonialism, Imperialism, and Globalization

When Marx constructed his ideology in the nineteenth century, the major European nations—Great Britain, France, Germany—and even the smaller ones—the Netherlands and Belgium—were in a race to build far-flung worldwide empires. They established colonies in Africa and Asia. The United States, too, claimed overseas colonies in Hawaii and the Philippines. They were locked in a race for colonies that led to the armaments buildup that was one cause of World War I. Marx viewed imperialism and colonialism as consequences of the capitalist race for new markets and profits. The capitalist nations would seize and occupy other nations, and turn them into colonies that would supply raw materials—minerals, foodstuffs, rubber, fibers, and oil—that would be used to produce commodities in the capitalist nation, which were then exported back for sale in the colony and on the world market. Marx predicted that the capitalist nations would clash and destroy themselves in a struggle of their own making. The Bolshevik, or Communist, Revolution in Russia in 1917 was viewed by Marxists as the beginning of the proletariat revolution. The worldwide revolution did not occur. After World War II, nationalist movements in Africa and Asia led to independence of the former colonies.

Globalization.   Contemporary Marxists see the globalization and global economy of the twenty-first century as a new imperialism and colonialism that is relevant to Marxist analysis. For them, globalization is a worldwide economic process that is turning the earth into a global factory. Multinational business corporations, rather than nation-states, are the agents of globalization. Raw materials are extracted from some countries, processed in others, and used to produce commodities in still others. The owners and managers of the corporations seek the countries with the cheapest workforce, where wages and benefits are low and working conditions poor or unregulated and where environmental protections are not enforced, in which to locate their factories. Workers in countries where wages and benefits are higher often are displaced and lose their jobs. The advocates of globalization claim that its economic benefits will eventually trickle down to all people; Marxists and other opponents see globalization in its capitalist form, as another more advanced and technologically driven force for profits. However, the multinational corporations, like the imperialists before them, obsessed by profits, fail to understand that they are actually creating new productive relationships that will lead to their destined and inevitable demise.

Alienation

For Marx, human alienation is economically produced by the capitalist insatiable greed for more profits made at the expense of workers. Remember, however, that capitalist avarice is caused not only by personal greed but also by the fact that the capitalist is being pushed by impersonal economic forces that will lead to his or her inevitable destruction. **Alienation** means that the worker's time and the products of her or his labor are owned and sold for a profit that the worker does not enjoy. At the root of this estrangement is the capitalist money system, private property, exchange and competition that separates the workers, the producers, from the product they make. The worker is trapped in an inevitable repetitive economic cycle.

The factory system of the nineteenth century, when Marx penned his ideology, marked the origin of mass production. The aesthetic sense of craftsmanship, enjoyed by the artisans of earlier history, was now a thing of the past. The repetitive work of the assembly line, in which the worker performed the same task over and over, had destroyed it. The wholeness of creating an object of which the craftsman felt ownership had been torn apart by the repetition, minuteness, and staccato of the assembly line. The harder the laborers worked and the more commodities they produced, the poorer they became. In the process of production, the worker was reduced to a commodity to be bought and sold. As the capitalist exploited his labor, the worker became separated, disenchanted, or alienated from his work. Marx's argument struck home for all those who felt exploited, unappreciated, and alienated in their jobs.

The Futility of Trying to Be Part of the System.   In capitalist economies, the capitalists use a variety of strategies to defuse workers' alienation by trying to delude them into believing that they are part of the system. Parliamentary government, democratic elections, and representative institutions, including educational ones, in a capitalist society and economy are a chimera, a false siren or image, that distracts workers from their true interests and the revolutionary measures needed to end them. The primary purpose of government, the state, in a capitalist society is to justify the existing economy and patterns of the ownership of private property. The rationales for private ownership in the capitalist system find their way into the school curriculum in courses in civics, government, social studies, and consumer education. All politics, all government, like all society, originates in the material conditions of life. Educational institutions, like governmental ones, too, originate in the economic base of society. Whoever controls the economic base—the means and modes of production—controls institutional life. Schooling in a capitalist society provides a sedative that lulls the workers and their children into believing that political change can end economic alienation through piecemeal palliatives; for example, student loans, with support of the federal government, can provide workers' children with access to higher education, leading to better-paying jobs and higher social status. This palliative mechanism really won't change anything but will perpetuate the system that requires student loans.

Alienation and Resistance in Schools

Marx's analysis of alienation can be applied to schools, teaching, and learning. When the results of schooling are defined as products or commodities to be attained by students, such as learning saleable skills or academic subjects that contribute to economic production and consumption, then the educational process is commoditized. A more direct feature of commoditization occurs when skills and subjects are defined as necessary to the economy and measured by standards imposed by others that are external to the educational process. Like the factory system, the teachers and students, although responsible for meeting quantity standards, have not determined these standards. They do not have ownership in the educational product that they are expected to produce. Not only are they alienated from the product but they also are alienated from the process—from schooling and from instruction. The process, like the product, is imposed on them much like the routine of the assembly line. The goals and ends of instruction have been determined outside of the classroom and imposed on those within it. Schooling takes on more features of the industrial factory system in that what is supposed to be the educational process—teaching and learning—is monitored or supervised by a set of managers, school bureaucrats, who make certain that approved processes are being followed by teachers and students. This kind of alienation has several consequences for teachers and students. First, they accept the system and enter into it by competing with other schools, teachers, and students for higher test scores. In other words, they work to exceed the anticipated outcome much like factory workers seek to exceed production quotas. In their acceptance, however, they have shifted learning from something that is internal to something that is external. Second, they become more and more passive, trying to meet set production goals, without enthusiasm or interest. The educational process sinks into deadening routine. Third, they begin to understand what is happening to them and grow in consciousness of their true situation and find ways to resist it. They engage in activities that are not mandated or standardized. Teachers, in particular, may organize themselves in unions to resist commoditization of education. In this stage, the Marxist educator plays a significant role in exposing false consciousness, arousing true consciousness, and organizing for resistance and change.

The Proletariat as the Revolutionary Destined Class

At this point, we turn to an examination of the proletariat, the working class, which Marx predicted was destined to revolt against and overthrow capitalism. Without property and without true representation, the proletariat is a universally suffering class, exploited and victimized. The proletariat is the destined revolutionary class that because of its exploitation and repression, will organize, arise, revolt, and overthrow its capitalist exploiters.

Capitalism, with its insatiable appetite for profits, is destined to sow the seeds of its own destruction. Its demands for more markets and more consumer goods will lead to spirals of overproduction, which, in turn, lead to recurring economic crises of inflation, recession, and depression. Capitalists will be forced to reinvest profits to increase production without being able to guarantee the consumption of commodities produced. As the ranks of unemployed grow because of "economic restructuring," more people will need goods and services but will be unable to purchase them. Imperialist wars will result between capitalist nations that seek mastery over colonial sources of raw material and markets. Unemployment, once periodic, will become chronic, and conditions will grow ripe for revolution.

After the revolution, all instruments of production will be centralized in the proletarian state created by the victorious workers. The dictatorship of the proletariat will be established to bring about the reforms needed in a classless society. The state apparatus will be taken over and redirected to ensure the working-class consolidation of power and control. After the remnants of the old capitalist regime have been obliterated, a classless society will appear, in utopian fashion, in which there is no repression. When everyone is a member of one class, the working class, the state, as an instrument of the domination of one class over another, will wither away.

Contemporary Neo-Marxists are most likely to reject or to seriously revise Marx's original premise of historical inevitability. They may still think in dialectical terms that involve the clash of opposing classes and see society as an arena of competing class interests, yet they are unlikely to accept the idea that victory is inevitable. Events are not just going to take place because of the fated dialectical process. The struggle will be long, with many temporary setbacks along the way.

When the Revolution is Accomplished and Institutionalized

Marx saw history moving in a predetermined and inexorable way to eventual revolution, the overthrow of capitalism, and the establishment of the communist society. For Marx, history was moving toward a specific goal and future. This future was inevitable and once realized, irreversible. Whereas orthodox Marxists hold to this view of predestined change that leads to an end, neo-Marxists and those whose ideas are influenced by Marxism such as Postmodernists and Critical Theorists downplay or dismiss Marx's historical inevitability. Conservatives and Liberals can agree that the perfect society promised by Marx is dangerously utopian and provided a cause, a justification, for Communist zealots to take any action, any means, they thought justified by the end of a promised perfect society. The leaders of the Soviet Union, especially Lenin and Stalin, justified their massive repressions, gulags, concentration camps, and purging and execution of perceived opponents to be necessary steps, justified by the utopia at the end. Pragmatists, especially Dewey, regarded Marx's claim that he had constructed a "scientific socialism" as a most unscientific method that closed rather than opened the process of scientific inquiry because it had a predestined end or goal.

To examine more thoroughly Marx's end of the revolutionary road, the Communist society of the predestined future, we need to look at how Marx conceived of this new world. After it had eliminated the vestiges of feudalism and the state apparatus that protected and maintained the capitalists in power, the proletarian revolution would bring about a total transformation of society as humanity reached a higher state of development. The means and modes of production underlying the industrial-technological base of capitalism would now be possessed by the people as a whole rather than just the capitalist class. With the elimination of the private ownership of property, the new society of the future would be without classes and without alienation. Importantly, because the new communist society was without classes, class conflict would end. The old history of class warfare would end and a new history would begin.[9]

Between Philosophy and Ideology: Marxism's Philosophical and Ideological Relationships

Marx was a philosopher who constructed an ideology and Marxism lies between being a philosophy and an ideology. In its generalizations, it appears, like other philosophies, to offer universal explanations. However, its origins, lodged in western European nineteenth-century capitalism, are contextual. Marx sought to analyze capitalism as a universal global force and his alternative, Marxism, leading to the inevitable classless society, too, was described in universal terms.

Speculative philosophies such as Idealism and Thomism, like religion, contributed to the false consciousness of the proletariat, according to Marx. Realism, especially its scientific variety, could be used to gain an accurate picture of reality when incorporated with Marxist dialectical materialism. Ideologies such as Liberalism and Conservatism were also part of the defensive armor of dominant groups to control subordinate ones. Certain aspects of Utopian Socialism, Marx believed, provided a useful analysis but a muddle-headed strategy for social change. Thus, Marx saw part of his task as consigning the philosophies and ideologies that contributed to false consciousness to the trash heap of history.

Like the Reconstructionists, Marx redefined philosophy and its purpose. Philosophers such as Plato, Aristotle, and even Hegel had attempted to speculate about the nature of reality and to describe it in metaphysical terms. Because their description is metaphysical, the reality of their speculations cannot be tested empirically. The universality found in the traditional philosophies came from the a priori definition of the human being as endowed with a defining human nature that was part of a universal architecture. For example, the Idealist would argue that the Universal Mind, or God, is a spiritual idea and that the human's identity as a human being comes from sharing in this spirituality or intellectuality. The Aristotelian Realist would argue that in a purposeful and rationally organized universe human beings are what they are because they are reasonable. Marx challenged this traditional view of universality and sought to replace it with another kind of universality, labor as its source. Human beings are universal, not because of their nature, but by their activity as producers. Human beings everywhere are producers; therefore, it is possible to look to a universal interpretation of history to see how production changed and socioeconomic classes developed.[10]

Marx retained the idea that the philosopher's task was to interpret reality. But the reality he described and interpreted was material—the means and modes of production: It was not metaphysical. However, Marx gave the philosopher a new and added role—to change reality by acting on it. Unlike the Pragmatist who saw action as the person's interaction with a changing environment, the Marxist view of change and action meant that the person was able to identify and join with the movement of history.

Marx's view of philosophy as taking action to change society is revolutionary. The revolutionary use of philosophy is "practical-critical activity" that is directed to a goal—to changing society.[11] It is philosophy with an agenda, to make a revolution, which more traditional philosophical critics would say moves it from philosophy to ideology.

Marxism and Communist States and Parties

Communism is the political face of Marxism that moves it further in the direction of ideology. *The Communist Manifesto* in 1848 moved Marx's theory from a dialectical materialism drawn from philosophy and history to revolutionary political organization and action. During Marx's life, there were Communist political parties but there was no actual country or state where it had been implemented. However, Marx's ideas about Communism became mixed with political parties calling themselves Communist.

In the twentieth century, Marxism was implemented as the official state ideology in the Soviet Union, the Soviet satellite nations in eastern and central Europe, the People's Republic of China, Vietnam, Cuba, and North Korea. Although Marxism was supposed to transcend and move through varying national and social contexts, it became contextualized in the nations and societies where it was implemented. In these countries, Marxism was codified into the reigning political and educational system and reinforced by monolithic repressive police states. From 1917 to 1989, Marxist-Leninism, or Communism, was redefined by Nikolai Lenin and Josef Stalin as the official ideology of the Soviet Union and the Soviet-controlled nations of eastern Europe. With the collapse of the Soviet system, Marxist-Leninism lost its official status and fell into disrepute in the former Soviet Union and in eastern Europe. The People's Republic of China (PRC) was established as a Communist nation in 1949. Chairman Mao Ze-dong, reinterpreting Communism as a peasant-based revolutionary movement, conducted the failed "great leap forward" and the cultural and educational purges of the Cultural Revolution. Although Communism formally remains as the PRC's official ideology, state and private capitalism is practiced as the country experiences unprecedented economic growth. In Cuba, Fidel Castro revised Marxism into an ideology that mixed Communism with the Latin American style of the personalist "great leader" dictatorship. Castro's Cuba remains a nation in which Marxism is the official state ideology.[12]

Marxism's critics contend that it has led to dictatorship and authoritarian repression wherever it has been implemented and see it as a failed and discredited ideology. Marxism's defenders say that it was never really implemented as Marx had designed it and that the Soviet version of Communism was really authoritarian statism rather than true Communism.

Marxist Educational Implications

Marx was more directly concerned with economic and political themes rather than with education. When he wrote about education in the formal sense, as schooling, he saw it as the content and methods that contributed to the person's intellectual and physical development.

He emphasized **polytechnic education** that related his theory of scientific socialism to the knowledge and skills need for production in modern industrial society. The foremost values in polytechnic education related to socially useful labor—work done to benefit the entire society and not just a few. Polytechnic education, Marx argued, was a genuine education, as opposed to capitalist indoctrination, which developed a critical consciousness that eradicated false consciousness.

More than formal education, much of Marx's writings dealt with informal education as the raising of mass consciousness, especially that of the proletariat, and about the real economic power relationships that exploited them. As informal educators, Marxists were to write pamphlets and tracts, organize protests and demonstrations, and inform the public in any way possible about the causes of exploitation.

Marx's interpreters, especially in the foundations of education, have developed many of the ideology's educational implications, especially analyzing schooling in a capitalist society.[13] They call for an education that creates a critical consciousness in students. They argue that the dominant class controls schools, as well as other social institutions, and uses them to socially control the oppressed classes.[14] Many Marxist-influenced contemporary educators take a broader and more comprehensive examination of the causes of class domination that extends beyond Marx's original economic factors. They see capitalism as a cultural as well as an economic system. Capitalist culture, reflected and reproduced in schools and other institutions, is hegemonic as the dominant group imposes its ideological beliefs and values on subordinate groups. In addition to analyzing the economic factors that impact schools, they examine how schools reproduce ideological, social, and political relationships that reflect dominant group interests.[15] Marxist teachers are to work at raising their students' **critical consciousness** by examining the real economic, political, and social conditions that impact their lives. Much of the examination focuses on **classism**, the control of one class by another; on racism, discrimination and oppression because of one's race; and sexism, the oppression of women in a male-dominated patriarchal society. They call on teachers to examine critically the material conditions in which schools function—the surrounding neighborhood and its conditions of unemployment, lack of health care, and lack of hope. This kind of critical examination helps to expose and combat the false ideology of consumerism, promoted by capitalists, and raise the consciousness of students about the true nature of the exploitative conditions in which they live. Teachers are to undertake a critical examination that reveals who owns much of the economy. They are to examine how large, modern business corporations, the capitalist successors of the older industrialists, control politicians through campaign contributions, manipulate the media through paid advertising, and use the courts to legitimate their exploitation. Modern society, for them, remains an arena of conflicting economic interests. They would broaden the contours of class struggle to enlarge Marx's proletariat to include oppressed racial and ethnic groups, women, the homeless, and the poor. It is the ownership and exploitation of the economy, the material conditions of society, that cause racism, sexism, and other forms of discrimination. Neo-Marxist educators would call for a thorough and critical examination of economic control.

Space and Time

In terms of developmental constructs, Marxism provides insights on space and time, two major constructs people develop and use to order their living, working, and social relationships.

Much of informal education and formal education in schools is concerned with developing children's concepts of space and time. The discussion of space and time refers to how these two constructs are organized in capitalist society and schooling.

Space.   Private property is given highest priority in the middle-class capitalist value schema. In Locke's liberalism, property is an inalienable natural right of the individual that cannot be taken away by government. In capitalism, the ownership of private property makes the middle classes who and what they are. The capitalist school strives to instill in children respect for and the value of private property. The little child's unwillingness to share a toy, for example, often expressed as "This is mine," means "I possess it and it is not yours." The concept of space is developed through the hidden curriculum, the values found in the school's milieu. Children have their own chair at the table in the nursery school, their own desk in the elementary grades, and their own locker in the high school. Personal space is delineated and is something that others should not invade.

Time.   One of the most frequent clichés in the capitalist lexicon is "time is money." Like most clichés, it is very true. The workers are selling their time to the employer and, indeed, the employer owns the workers' time, which means they do not own their own lives during their working hours. In a time-driven workplace, the stress on increasing unit production turns into human stress. Unit production, in the modern technological workforce, needs to be seen in quantitative terms. For the physician and the nurse it means the number of patients seen and treated; for teachers, it is the number of students instructed. Being "stressed out" or "burned out" refers to the physiological and psychological consequences of meeting quotas and deadlines on one's health.

Schooling, which is heavily scheduled and programmed, prepares individuals to lead time-programmed lives. It accentuates the Calvinist origins of honored school values such as being on time, using time wisely, and not wasting time. It also reduces instruction to time on task. Efficient teachers are those who can teach basic skills to large numbers of students who in turn receive high scores on standardized tests.

Vanguard of the Proletariat

Although they might be styled as academic or educational workers, teachers typically are identified with the proletariat, or the working class. In Europe, teachers, especially those who teach in secondary school and universities, are often identified with the intelligentsia, the intellectuals. How then are teachers part of the revolutionary class, which according to Marx is the proletariat?

Karl Marx and his chief collaborator, Friedrich Engels, were not members of the proletariat; they were not factory workers. A university graduate from a middle-class family, Marx had earned a doctorate in philosophy and was a journalist. If one is defined by her or his economic class, how could Marx, himself, have escaped the thinking and values associated with being middle class? Marx reasoned that a small intellectual elite of dedicated revolutionaries, knowing history's true course, would raise the consciousness of the working class, help to organize them, and lead the coming proletarian revolution. Because they were removed from the actual means of production, this group of intellectual ideologists could escape their economically determined class position. The **vanguard of the proletariat** plays an educational as well as an action-oriented mission. It is to: (1) study the true course of history as a dialectical process generated by economic class conflict; (2) organize the workers and raise their consciousness about the true conditions of their exploitation; (3) lead the revolution at the correct revolutionary moment; and (4) organize the new classless society destined to replace the capitalist economic order.

In orthodox Marxist ideology, especially Leninism, the vanguard, a secretive conspiratorial group following a rigid strategy, was the revolutionary elite. Marxism influences current educational movements such as Neo-Marxism, Liberation Pedagogy, and Critical Theory, which include some university professors, teachers, and other intellectuals. (Critical Theory is discussed in a later chapter.) Contemporary Marxist-influenced ideologists resemble a vanguard movement in education. They have revised Marx's original concept of the vanguard of the proletariat as an elite group into broad-based popular organizations and activism working for change.

Contemporary Neo-Marxist educators oppose such new forms of modern capitalism as the multinational business corporation, economic globalism, and the ethics of a consumer-driven society. For them, the multinational business corporation, an extension of the national corporation, is a new global economic force. Multinational corporations, knowing no national limitations, have located factories in third world countries in Africa, South America, and Asia, where workers, often including child laborers, work at a near poverty level. Agribusinesses, too, have displaced small family-run farms with huge single-crop agricultural estates that produce food for export while many residents of the country in which they operate are ill-nourished.

False Ideology.   An important goal of Marxist-inspired education is to expose the **false ideology** constructed to support and defend capitalism and to replace it with the true ideology of Marxism. In a capitalist society and educational system, children of oppressed groups are indoctrinated into a false ideology that denies them the opportunity to study and critically examine the social, political, and economic conditions that contribute to their subjugation. The imposition of the official ideology denies students a critical understanding of their reality. Marxist educators, in the position of the vanguard of the proletariat, have the task of raising the revolutionary consciousness of the masses of people, the proletariat, through formal and informal education.

Contemporary Neo-Marxist educators would seek to develop critical consciousness among students. Such critical consciousness requires: (1) a realistic examination of the economic factors that lead to exploitation in modern society; (2) an exposure of the "false ideology" into which students are indoctrinated in a capitalist consumer-driven society; (3) a discussion of what can be done to organize oppressed groups to improve their economic, political, and social situation; and (4) development and implementation of strategies of revolutionary action.

Marxism as Critique

Marxism has appealed to some scholars in the foundations of education in its various forms. It, of course, appeals to orthodox Marxists who are guided by the original ideology and to Neo-Marxists who reinterpret it in light of the contemporary situation. It also appeals to educational theorists who find the writings of Antonio Gramsci and the Frankfurt School to be cogent analyses of society, politics, and education. It has a new currency, especially with some Postmodernists and Critical Theorists, who use some of its ideas in constructing their own theories. A relevant question is why does Marxism, a nineteenth-century ideology linked with failed state systems such as the Soviet Union, continue to exert this attraction? Why does it continue to resurface, especially in the foundations of education?

Perhaps, the answer lies in Marxism's power to critique existing systems. Marx's writings were detailed critiques of the western European nineteenth-century world in which he lived, particularly industrial capitalism. He once wrote that "we have to accomplish" a "ruthless criticism of all that exists" without fearing where this will take us or whom it might offend, regardless of their power over us.[16] Marxism lends itself to the idea that education involves social and cultural criticism.

The idea that education should exercise a critical function is not new, however, nor is it unique to Marxists and those scholars influenced by Marxism. Renaissance humanists such as Erasmus asserted education's critical role. Other, more contemporary scholars in the educational foundations—Pragmatists, Progressives, Liberals, and Conservatives—accept the role of social and educational critics. However, the criteria for criticism is non- and often anti-Marxist. What is at issue is the criteria for criticism. For Realists and Perennialists, for example, criticism is an exercise of reason, a power inherent by nature in the person. For the Pragmatist, criticism is experimental and necessary to executing scientific method and is methodological rather than based on antecedent definitions. There is a further distinction of criticism between academic and Marxist-action–oriented criticism. Educational critique as academic criticism is much like literary, artistic, and cinematic criticism, which evaluates an author, actor, or director in terms of genre, style, effect, and performance. Educational critique as academic criticism is an activity educators do as peer reviewers of colleagues in the field.

Unlike academic criticism, Marxism analyzes social, economic, political, and educational conditions in terms of a criterion based on analytical concepts such as commodity, property, labor, ownership, class conflict, and alienation. As a method of criticism, Marxism specifically focuses on concepts such as class, gender, race, and ethnicity when they are interpreted as sources of oppression by dominant groups, generally economically favored ones, over marginalized economically disadvantaged ones. Unlike the temperamental coolness of dispassionate academic criticism summed up by "don't let your emotions cloud your judgment," Marxist criticism is meant deliberately to raise consciousness and a sense of oppression, indignation, and resistance in those who are exploited and marginalized.

Neo-Marxists and those influenced by Marxism have selected aspects of Marx's theory as analytical tools. They have broadened Marx's concept of the proletariat, the working class, as the original dispossessed and oppressed class to include other marginalized groups in American society such as women, African and Latino Americans, homosexuals and lesbians, the homeless, and others. Drawing on Marx's themes of capitalist imperialism and colonialism, Marxist critique is also applied to globalization and global economics. Critiques based on Marxist analysis are to raise the consciousness of the dispossessed groups and inspire resistance to the exploiting ideology and bring about transformative social, economic, political, and educational change.

Conflict Theory in Education

In Marxism, the origin of socioeconomic classes and inevitable class conflicts are economically determined by the class's relationship to the means, modes, and ownership of production. According to Marx, the capitalists and the proletariat are modern society's major conflicting classes. Subgroups that appear, at first glance, to be outside of these classes in socioeconomic reality are satellites or appendages of the two major conflicting contenders for power. The lower middle class—small-business owners, self-employed craftspeople, and even adjunct professors—is destined to sink gradually into the proletariat because they cannot resist the force of globalization. The idea of class conflict, refined into conflict theory, is an important concept of Marxist-influenced education. It interprets the school, curriculum, and the relationship between teachers and administrators in terms of conflict theory.

In **conflict theory**, based on Marx's idea of class conflict, Marxist-influenced educators argue that schools, like other social institutions, are places where contending groups struggle for power and control.[17] The essential struggle is between the dominant groups—the white upper and middle class who enjoy a favored economic status—and the dominated, oppressed groups—racial and ethnic minorities, the unemployed and underemployed, and women. To understand group dominance and subordination and to raise students' critical consciousness, Neo-Marxist educators seek to: (1) examine the nature of class and class culture; (2) determine how power is distributed between the classes; (3) examine the social control mechanisms that the dominant class has developed to subordinate the dominated class; and (4) examine how the dominant class uses schools as agencies of social reproduction and control.

Marxist educators see schools in a capitalist society as agencies used by the dominant class to reproduce the existing class structure that favors their interests. Schooling reproduces the ideological, social, political, and economic relationships based on dominant class interests. The school's location reflects the material conditions of the society. If it is located in a predominately white, affluent, upper-middle-class district, with a high tax base and a low crime rate, the climate within the school will reflect these material conditions of the larger society. However, if it is located in a predominately African American, lower income district, with a high rate of unemployment, the school, too, will reflect these material conditions. The school's curriculum will reflect how the dominant class conceives of and uses knowledge. What is selected in the curriculum will reinforce existing beliefs and values for the children of the dominant class and will be used to convince children of subordinate classes that this curriculum is also valid for them. Within the school, administrators employed by the dominant group will claim that they are using standardized tests as an objective measure of students' academic achievement. However, Marxists will allege that these so-called objective instruments are framed in class-referenced ways that work for the benefit of the dominant class. Students then will be grouped according to test results. What really is happening, however, is that the tests are used as a sorting device to arrange groups in the school that mirror and reproduce the class situation that exists outside of the school.

Rather than being the institutions that they claim to be in a capitalist society, schools are agencies designed to reproduce, ensure, and perpetuate the control by the dominant group. They do not implement equality of opportunity and social justice but rather reinforce and reproduce existing inequalities. They educate those who are in a favored position to stay in that position by preparing them for prestigious colleges and universities so that they can take their fathers' places in the corporate sector. Simultaneously, the children of the less favored dominated classes are also prepared to stay in their places at the bottom of the social and economic scale.

Schools in a Capitalist Society

Neo-Marxist educational theorists have analyzed the role of schools in culturally reproducing the dominant capitalist culture. They see the curriculum, both overt and hidden, methodology, and testing as representing the dominance of one group over another. Neo-Marxists see a deliberate connection between the curriculum and instruction and the larger society. They believe that the symbols and meanings filtered into the capitalist schools' curricula shape, confirm, and maintain the dominant class ideology. In a capitalist society such as the United States, the very location of the school, whether it is in an affluent suburb or in the economically depressed inner city, reflects and reproduces the attitudes and values of the surrounding locality. Within a school setting, the grouping and instructing of students reproduce the social, political, and economic status quo. The school mirrors the essential class divisions of the larger society, and rather than changing them, hardens these divisions by perpetuating them in the young.[18]

Because Marxists define class on the basis of people's relationships to the means and modes of economic production, class is an economically derived social phenomenon. Schooling in a capitalist society, argue the Marxists, reflects the outlook and values of the dominant or privileged class. Again, it perpetuates these dominant class values by transmitting and inculcating them in the young.

The interests and values of the dominant class will be framed in a context of the common good. For example, the values of respect for private property, the sanctity of contracts, and respect for law and order have long been traditional public school values. According to the Neo-Marxist critique, these traditional values are designed to protect the property of the dominant monied class. By encasing these class-centered values in a framework that extols the common good, the school is bending the minds of the young to accept their society as being the best of all possible worlds.

When a privileged and dominant class has managed to establish its thought-ways and values among subordinate or suppressed classes, it has established ideological control over them.[19] Rather than being a place where ideas contend in an open market, as Liberal apologists assert, the school in a capitalist society is closed to alternative viewpoints that may threaten the hegemony that the dominant class enjoys over the lower class, argue the Neo-Marxists. Such hegemony is truly established when members of the lower or subordinate class begin to express the views and to share the values of the dominant class.

Contemporary Neo-Marxists, such as Michael Apple, have revised the bipolar model of class conflict of the more orthodox Marxists, who see class conflict as historically destined to occur between two incompatible classes—the capitalists and the proletariat. Apple contends that the class structure within modern capitalism is more complex than that suggested by orthodox Marxists in the nineteenth century.

Class structure refers to "the organization of social relations" based on class interests. Class formation, which refers to the "organized collectivities" within the structure, is related to economic forces and also to cultural, political, and social patterns and trends.[20] The formation of class cultures is further complicated in racially and ethnically diverse nations such as the United States. In addition to economic conditions, class cultures also reflect racial, ethnic, and gender histories, relationships, and conflicts.[21] Apple argues that seventy percent of working-class occupational positions are filled by women and members of minority groups. Thus, an analysis of class formation needs to consider patriarchal and racial dominance themes.[22]

The middle class, with its interest in acquiring technical and managerial information and skills, holds an important place in an advanced capitalist society.[23] The middle-class situation rests more on control of cultural reproduction as well as economic exploitation. In educational policy, the middle class has its own general ideological orientation but it tends to be fractionalized into those who favor subject-matter competency and economic efficiency, such as the Essentialists, and those who are more progressively inclined to child-centered schooling.

Through their formal curricula and instructional programs, schools prepare the future workforce.[24] In establishing and maintaining these programs, a determining element is exercised by those who hold economic power. The school's economic function is to identify and select those who will occupy the various rungs in the corporate ladder of the capitalist society. It trains people for the specialties that make the division of labor possible. It prepares people to be consumers of the products of a capitalist economy. Based on premises of economic inequality, such schooling is a determinant, albeit a partial one, of the rewards and penalties that its graduates will receive. In effect, it perpetuates the economic inequalities of the society and maintains the status quo.

In a capitalist society, schools reproduce the educational sorting that precedes and accompanies the functional division of labor. Further, they condition the dominated group to accept as legitimate the testing, grouping, and selecting processes that will make them into subordinate cogs in the corporate–industrial machinery. For example, homogeneous grouping in a capitalist society reproduces socioeconomic phenomena. The reproduction of social strata in the school, allegedly based on academic ability, implies that membership in a particular group or track is determined by an objective and competitive meritocratic system. In reality, Marxists would argue that the identification of a student with a particular track is economically based. Schools reproduce the existing socioeconomic structure and condition students to accept the legitimacy of that structure.

In addition to the overt economic programming done by schools, Neo-Marxist interpreters of education often refer to the hidden curriculum, or the concomitant learning that goes on in a school. According to Michael Apple, the hidden curriculum "reinforces basic rules" regarding conflict and its uses. It establishes a "network of assumptions" that reinforces legitimacy and authority.[25] The hidden curriculum underscores the norms and values of the dominant group in such a pervasive way that challenges to it are rendered illegitimate.

For example, the emphasis on the sanctity of private property can be reinforced as a value by assigning certain school spaces to particular individuals. Punctuality and the efficient use of time are also values reinforced by the school process. These attitudes and values, which are held to be characteristics of the effective school, are also conducive to the functioning of a capitalist economy.

Conclusion

This chapter discussed Karl Marx and Marxism as an ideology. It examined Marxism's essential tenets such as dialectical materialism, the means and modes of production, production of commodities and alienation, class struggle between the capitalists and the proletariat, false consciousness, and role of the vanguard of the proletariat. It then considered the educational implications of Marxism. It considered the Marxist critique of education and schools in a capitalist society and Neo-Marxism's view of schools as contested sites in the class struggle.

Constructing Your Own Philosophy of Education. Now that you have read and discussed the chapter on Marxism, you may wish to consider its relevance for your philosophy of education. Marxism has been and continues to be an important mode of economic, social, political, and educational critique and analysis. Do you plan to use Marxism in constructing your own philosophy of education?

Questions for Reflection and Discussion

1. Critics of Marxism contend that it exaggerates the economic factor in society and aggravates class conflicts. Do you agree or disagree with these critics?

2. Do you agree with Marx that the superstructure of society—the government, church, press, and school, for example—rests on an economic base and is controlled by those who own this base?

3. Why do you think that Marxism has influenced theories in the foundations of education?

4. Do you agree with Marxists who say that the school is a contested site between those who have and do not have power?

5. Do you agree with Marxists who claim that the capitalist economic system creates consumer desires through the manipulation of illusions in marketing? Defend your answer.

6. From a Marxist perspective, what is the role of teachers in the class struggle?

7. Have you taken courses in which the instructor has used such terms as *hegemony, power, marginalization,* and *empowerment?* How would a Marxist analyze these terms?

Topics for Inquiry and Research

1. In your classroom observations, identify aspects of the hidden curriculum and describe how they function to establish patterns of behavior and control.

2. Analyze several textbooks that are used in the teacher education program at your college or university. Do you find comments about

the impact of social economic class on education expectations and academic achievement? Would a Marxist agree or disagree with these comments?

3. Reread either the chapter on Liberalism or on Conservatism. Apply a Marxist critique to that chapter.

4. In your classroom observation, look for and determine whether the learning situation reproduces the culture and class relations in the culture.

5. Visit several schools and determine whether the economic situation of the neighborhood in which the school is located has an impact on the curriculum and on teaching and learning.

Building a Marxist Vocabulary

Abstract Labor: the general expenditure of human labor in producing commodities.

Alienation: that which in a capitalist system separates workers from the work of their labor; the workers' time and the products of their labor is owned and sold for a profit that they do not enjoy.

Capitalists: in a modern society, the ruling class who owns the means and modes of production.

Classism: the control of one class by another.

Commodity: a product produced by human labor to satisfy human needs.

Concrete Labor: the skills needed to produce a particular commodity.

Conflict Theory: Marx's idea of class conflict in which contending groups struggle for power and control.

Critical Consciousness: a realistic understanding of the conditions in society that are either exploitative or liberating.

Dialectical Epistemology: Marx's dialectical way of thinking in which the human being is immersed in a process of continuing class conflict and struggle.

Dialectical Materialism: Marx's concept of reality that the basic element in the universe is matter in motion.

Dialectical Thought: for Marx, thought in which there are two opposing and contradictory arguments that eventually will be reconciled in a synthesis, a new thesis, stage.

False Ideology: an unexamined acceptance of the beliefs of dominant groups that purports to be the truth.

Historical Materialism: Marx's philosophy of history in which history unfolds according to dialectical materialism to a determined end.

Human Being: in Marxism, a physical creature, with physiological needs and drives, who possesses a brain that enables consciousness and is a producer of commodities and services.

Neo-Marxist: new or contemporary Marxists who revised Marx's ideology in terms of the contemporary situation.

Polytechnic Education: education that relates to socially useful labor, to the skills and knowledge needed for production in modern industrial economy that benefit the entire society.

Proletariat: the industrial working class which is economically determined to revolt and seize power from the capitalists.

Society: for Marx, a developing, expanding, and changing network of human relationships that are economically generated.

Superstructure: institutions, resting on the economic base of society, such as the state, church, schools, courts, and so on, that are controlled by the dominant class.

Vanguard of the Proletariat: the enlightened people who work to create the Marxist society.

Internet Resources

For discussions of Marx and education, access www.marxists.org/subject/education/index.htm.

For Marx and informal education, access www.ifed.org/Thinkers/et-marx.htm.

For Marx on cultural institutions, access www.sociology.org.uk/marxism.doc.

Suggestions for Further Reading

Apple, Michael W. *Ideology and Curriculum.* London: Routledge, 1990.

Blumberg, Werner. *Karl Marx.* New York: Verso, 2000.

Bowles, Samuel, and Herbert Gintis. *Schooling in Capitalist America.* New York: Basic Books, 1975.

Brosio, Richard M. *A Radical Democratic Critique of Capitalist Education.* New York: Peter Lang, 1994.

Churchich, Nicholas. *Marxism and Morality: A Critical Examination of Marxist Ethics.* Cambridge: James Clarke, 1994.

Cole, Mike. *Marxism, Postmodernism, and Education.* New York: Routledge, 2007.

Green, Anthony, et al., eds. *Renewing Dialogues in Marxism and Education: Openings.* New York: Palgrave Macmillan, 2007.

Gottlieb, Roger S. *Marxism, 1844–1990: Origins, Betrayal, Rebirth.* New York: Routledge, 1992.

Lefort, Claude. *Complications: Communism and the Dilemmas of Democracy.* Translated by Julian Bourg. New York: Columbia University Press, 2007.

Levi, Margaret, ed. *Marxism.* Brookfield, VT: E. Elgar, 1991.

McLellan, David. *Karl Marx: Selected Writings.* Oxford, UK: Oxford University Press, 2000.

Osborne, Peter. *How to Read Marx.* New York: W. W. Norton & Co., 2006.

Strike, Kenneth. *Liberal Justice and the Marxist Critique of Education: A Study of Conflicting Research Programs.* New York: Routledge and Kegan Paul, 1988.

Torrance, John. *Karl Marx's Theory of Ideas.* New York: Cambridge University Press, 1995.

Van Parijs, Philippe. *Marxism Recycled.* New York: Cambridge University Press, 1993.

Wheen, Francis. *Karl Marx: A Life.* New York: W. W. Norton & Co., 2001.

Wood, Ellen M. *Democracy Against Capitalism: Renewing Historical Materialism.* New York: Cambridge University Press, 1995.

Endnotes

1. David McLellan, *Karl Marx: His Life and Thought* (New York: Harper & Row, 1973), pp. 2–6.
2. Karl Marx and Friedrich Engels, "Manifesto of the Communist Party," in Carl Cohen, ed., *Communism, Fascism, and Democracy: The Theoretical Foundations* (New York: Random House, 1972), pp. 80, 89.
3. Peter Osborne, *How to Read Marx* (New York: W. W. Norton & Co., 2006), pp. 22, 24.
4. Osborne, *How to Read Marx,* pp. 33–34.
5. Osborne, *How to Read Marx,* p. 37.
6. Kenneth Strike, *Liberal Justice and the Marxist Critique of Education: A Study of Conflicting Research Programs* (New York: Routledge and Kegan Paul, 1988), p. 23.
7. Osborne, *How to Read Marx,* pp. 11–12.
8. Osborne, *How to Read Marx,* p. 13.
9. Osborne, *How to Read Marx,* p. 79.
10. Osborne, *How to Read Marx,* p. 54.
11. Osborne, *How to Read Marx,* p. 31.
12. Samuel Farber, *The Origins of the Cuban Revolution Reconsidered* (Chapel Hill: University of North Carolina Press, 2006).
13. Frank Margonis, "Marxism, Liberalism, and Educational Theory," *Educational Theory,* 43, no. 4 (Fall 1993), p. 449.
14. Michael Apple, "Education, Culture, and Class Power: Basil Bernstein and the Neo-Marxist Sociology of Education," *Educational Theory,* 42, no. 2 (Spring 1992), p. 127.
15. Apple, "Education, Culture, and Class Power: Basil Bernstein and the Neo-Marxist Sociology of Education," p. 128.
16. Osborne, *How to Read Marx,* p. 59.
17. Walter Feinberg and Jonas Soltis, *School and Society* (New York: Teachers College Press, 1985), pp. 43–44.
18. Feinberg and Soltis, *School and Society,* p. 49.
19. Feinberg and Soltis, *School and Society,* pp. 50–52.
20. Apple, "Education, Culture, and Class Power: Basil Bernstein and the Neo-Marxist Sociology of Education," p. 137.
21. Apple, "Education, Culture, and Class Power: Basil Bernstein and the Neo-Marxist Sociology of Education," p. 139.
22. Apple, "Education, Culture, and Class Power: Basil Bernstein and the Neo-Marxist Sociology of Education," p. 143.
23. Apple, "Education, Culture, and Class Power: Basil Bernstein and the Neo-Marxist Sociology of Education," pp. 134–135.
24. Samuel Bowles and Herbert Gintis, *Schooling in Capitalist America* (New York: Basic Books, 1975).
25. Michael Apple, *Ideology and Curriculum* (London: Routledge & Kegan Paul, 1979), p. 87.

12

Theory and Education

Theory based on practice, illustrated by a still from the motion picture, Freedom Writers, *in which students' autobiographical writings generate shared experience.*

Chapter Preview

In this chapter, we consider the relationships between theory and education. *Theory* is an often used but elusive term. In our everyday speech, we use it to mean that we have constructed some ideas that explain something, or that we have a hypothesis about something, or that we have conjectured some cause-and-effect relationships (e.g., if I diet and exercise, I am going to lose weight). A theory represents a cluster of ideas that we can generalize about and apply to other situations. For example, if other people diet and exercise, they, too, can be expected to lose weight. You can test this kind of theory empirically, or scientifically, by standing on a scale and weighing yourself before and after you have completed your regimen of diet and exercise. However, there are other kinds of theories that we cannot verify empirically, such as the Realist theory that the study of the liberal arts and sciences cultivates a person's power of reasoning. In education, we find instances of both kinds of theory—the empirically verifiable ones and those that cannot be verified scientifically. The word *theory,* however, is used constantly in education, and as we move through this chapter, we shall attempt to examine the various uses of the word. The chapter includes the following topics:

- Defining theory
- Studying theory
- Theory as a bridge between philosophy and ideology and practice
- Theory as derivation
- Theory as reaction
- Theory arising from practice

Constructing your philosophy of education inevitably brings you to theorizing about education, school, curriculum, and institution. The act of constructing means that you are intellectually engaged in and generalizing about education. As you read the chapter, reflect on how theory relates to your philosophy of education.

Defining Theory

The word *theory* is derived from the ancient Greek word, **theoria**, which means intellectually contemplating, considering, or conjecturing something. It could mean comparing and contrasting objects and relating them to each other, as Aristotle did in his system of classifications. Or it might be thinking about how change occurred, as he did in his theory of the four causes. The ancient Greeks often dichotomize theory from practice. For example, Plato and Aristotle regarded theory—abstract thought about the nature of things—to be a higher, more elevated, and more rational activity of the mind than actual practice, or doing something or making something. (See the chapters on Idealism and Realism for Plato and Aristotle.) Also, note that John Dewey, in his Experimentalist philosophy, challenged the Greek dualistic way of thinking and argued against separating theory from practice. (See the chapter on Pragmatism.)

At this point, we can consider several meanings of theory, each of which has implications for education. As a hypothetical set of ideas or principles that can guide practice, theories can be turned into "if–then" statements: If I do this or act in this way, then the following is likely to happen. Theorizing can refer to the act of forming generalizations—plans that we can replicate in varying situations—based on how something is done successfully in a given field such as medicine, law, or education, for example. In this instance, theory arises from observing or performing similar actions that cause results that can be anticipated. Here, the process of forming the generalizations is inductive; the reasoning and logic used goes from the specific instance to the general case. For example, a football coach, who has had experience in the sport, can frame a number of plays or strategies that the team can use successfully in certain situations in a series of games. In education, especially in instruction, a teacher, who has had experience in teaching reading or mathematics, can identify those exercises and activities that have succeeded and those that have failed to bring about the desired outcomes. The teacher can generalize about those that work and arrive at a set of principles that guide instruction. The guiding principles, derived from a particular experience, can be generalized and applied to other teaching situations. Further, a group of teachers can collaboratively share their experiences in teaching a particular skill or subject or dealing with a particular issue and problem and generalize to a set of operating principles—how to do something, what methods to use, in a given teaching situation.

Theory can refer to a general abstract conceptual frame of reference that can be used to guide practice. Such a frame of reference includes: (1) a set of generalizations, or explanations, about the subject or field; (2) strategies on how to apply the generalizations as guiding principles in action; and (3) hypotheses, conjectures, or expectations about what is likely to happen when the generalization is applied in a specific instance. Such a frame of reference can be created in at least two ways: (1) based on experience that arises from practice, as discussed earlier; or (2) deduced from another set of generalizations as in the case of putting a philosophy or an ideology into practice. In the later instance, the theory is formed by deductive reasoning in which the guiding principles are extracted from the broader and more comprehensive body of thought and applied to given situations. For example, a lawyer, using the common law, will look for precedents, earlier decisions, that can be used to support her or his argument in a particular case. A teacher can look to a philosophy such as Idealism or Realism or an ideology such as Liberalism or Conservatism to draw forth for them goals to be implemented in the classroom. Here, the problem is taking the abstractions, provided by the philosophy or ideology, and rendering them into a format or strategy by which they can be implemented in practice.

Still another meaning of theory is our beliefs, ideas, and concepts about phenomena— the objects, people, and situations—that we observe and with which we interact. Kerlinger, for example, defines a theory as "a set of interrelated constructs (concepts), definitions, and propositions that present a systematic view of phenomena by specifying relations among variables, with the purpose of explaining and predicting the phenomena."[1] It is what we attribute to be the origin and nature of something and the actions and reactions that take place. This kind of theorizing occurs when we try to make sense and give meaning to our situations and the actors, objects, and happenings in these situations. It is a way of generalizing about our experience so that we construct some explanations about it. An important characteristic of a theory is the interrelationship of its parts and how it is possible to deduce one proposition from another.

In the case of all of these meanings of theory, the important point is that theory is a guide to practice. However, further questions remain—Are the assumptions in the theory valid? If the assumptions are valid, can they be successfully transferred and applied to other situations? Will implementation confirm or invalidate the theory's working generalizations? Or is the failure to transfer the theory due to faulty implementation rather than to inadequacies in the theory? For example, consider the following assumptions given as a rationale for the No Child Left Behind Act:

We know from business practices that if we want to boost performance, we must set clear, measurable goals and align our systems to them. In education, academic standards is the foundation of a performance-based system. High standards do not just help teachers; they also encourage children, because children tend to perform to meet the expectations of adults. If these expectations are low, children can miss their true potential. When expectations are high, progress can be amazing. . . .

Creating clear and rigorous academic standards is an important first step in improving our schools. We will never know, however, if we are reaching those standards unless we measure student performance.[2]

Studying Theory

Individuals find themselves in constantly changing concrete situations or events. Each of these situations is unique in that the setting and the actors, the other people, and the issue or problem may be different. However, in these situations, there are some common elements. It is the recognition and the clustering together of these common elements that are the foundations of theorizing. For example, at the beginning of each school year, a teacher will find that she or he has a class of new and unfamiliar students. However, with experience, the teacher will have built up a repertoire of strategies in engaging her or his students. It relates to the question that all teachers have—what do I do on the first day of school? The teacher can recognize that students' needs and abilities fit into patterns that are found in each class of students each new year. From this recognition, the teacher can generalize about the similarities found in different groups of students and create plans of action—strategies—that can be used in instruction. Further, teachers can collaborate with each other and discuss common successes, weaknesses, and issues and formulate some generalizations about teaching. These generalizations, when clustered and organized together, are the basis of a theory of teaching. Such theoretical underpinnings are the basis of methods.

Theory also relates to the larger issue of teacher professionalization. In contrast to a trade, which consists of the mastery of a set of techniques, a profession rests on a theoretical foundation—informed hypotheses, based on knowledge, about why as well as how something is done. For example, in the first chapter in this book, we discussed the theory of reflective teaching in which teachers construct a conceptual framework for teaching. In other words, they construct a philosophy of education. While there are certain techniques that are followed in teaching, teaching itself implies more than using these techniques. It is informed by concepts from learned disciplines such as philosophy, history, sociology, and psychology that provide a theoretical foundation—an examination of why something is done in its larger contexts.

Theory as a Bridge between Philosophy and Ideology and Practice

This chapter on theory and education can be thought of as a bridge that carries the reader from the more abstract chapters on philosophies and ideologies to four selected theories of education: Essentialism, Progressivism, Social Reconstructionism, and Critical Theory. (Perennialism, as a theory, is discussed in the chapter on Realism.) As indicated in our definition of theory, these four theories: (1) operate from a coherent set of generalizations and explanations about the purpose of education, the organization and structure of schools, and processes of teaching and learning; (2) contain guiding hypotheses or working principles about how curriculum and instruction should be organized and conducted; and (3) indicate projected outcomes that will follow if the theoretical assumptions are applied in practice. In the next sections, we examine theories (1) as derived from or deduced from other larger and more abstract bodies of thought such as philosophies and ideologies; (2) those that develop as educational, or school-centered responses to larger social, economic, cultural, or political problems and issues; and (3) those that arise as generalizations or hypotheses from practices within schools and classrooms. It should be pointed out that in some cases a theory may include all three elements: derivations, responses, and generalizations from practice.

Theory as Derivation

In this section, we consider how education is derived from another area, discipline, or field of inquiry. Specifically, we examine theory that is derived from philosophy and from ideology.

Philosophical Derivation

Part I of this book examined the philosophies of Idealism, Realism, Theistic Realism, Pragmatism, Existentialism, and Postmodernism. Of these, Idealism, Realism, and Theistic Realism are based on a grand, large, metaphysical structure that provides a kind of architecture of the universe and the human being's place in it. These older, more traditional philosophies are systematic in that they expound on what is real (metaphysics), how we know (epistemology), and what is right and beautiful (ethics and aesthetics). Education—especially schooling, curriculum, and instruction—is dealt with in these larger systems and subsumed as areas that are included and explained by the larger and more comprehensive worldview. Throughout history, these metaphysically based philosophies have attracted adherents who sought to apply their principles to society, politics, and education. Educators, who look to eternal and universal truths, seek to apply them to education and to base a curriculum on what they believe is always good, true, and beautiful. For example, Essentialism exhibits strong elements of Idealism and Realism and Perennialism draws heavily from the Realism of Aristotle and Aquinas.

More modern philosophies such as Pragmatism, Existentialism, and Postmodernism reject the metaphysical base of the older philosophies as unverifiable speculation and turned their attention to epistemology, meaning, and other issues. Dewey's Experimentalism, a variety of Pragmatism, influenced Progressivism, which sought to apply the concepts of democracy, community, and the scientific method to education, schooling, and instruction. Postmodernism, which borrowed some Existentialist and Marxist themes, has a strong influence on Critical Theory.

Ideological Derivation

Educational theories are also derived from ideologies such as Nationalism, Liberalism, Conservatism, and Marxism. Schools in countries throughout the world are organized into national systems of education. In these systems, strong elements of Nationalism are used in children's political socialization and are designed to construct a person's primary identification. For example, public schools in the United States seek to create a sense of American identity and citizenship in students. The content of the school curriculum is often a contested area on a number of grounds—some political, some cultural, and others methodological. Liberals, Conservatives, and Marxists differ on the goals of education, the purpose and function of schools, curriculum content, and styles of teaching and learning. Conservatism, with its emphasis on traditional knowledge and values, has influenced Essentialism and Perennialism. Liberalism, with its emphasis on flexibility and innovation, has influenced Progressivism. Themes from Marxism and Liberation Pedagogy such as class domination, control, and conflict are evident in Critical Theory.

Theory as Reaction

Theory can also be developed as a reaction to social, political, economic, and educational situations, issues, problems, and crises. For example, there is growing concern about global warming and the degradation of the environment because of industrial and fossil-fuel emissions, depletion of the rain forests, and the hunting of endangered animal species. Environmental concerns contributed to the establishing of courses in environmental education that emphasize conservation of natural resources, learning to use alternative energy sources, and recycling of items—paper, glass, and plastic—that could be collected and reused. These courses also emphasize the personal and social ethical responsibilities regarding protection and respect for conserving the natural environment. They also emphasize the aesthetic sense of natural beauty that comes from a healthy planet. When environmental issues are scrutinized and taken to their global implications, they can be generalized to include questions about the role of industrialized nations such as the United States as a major pollutant, about the socioeconomic disparities between the wealthy nations of the Northern and the poorer ones of the Southern Hemispheres, about the negative effects of economic globalization by multinational corporations, and about strategies for sustainable development. At this juncture, the theory of environmental education, which originated as a response, was juxtaposed with other philosophies, ideologies, and educational theories and reformulated. For example, Marxists see the multinational business corporation as a modern form of capitalism that exploits the poor of the less technologically developed nations. Freire and Illich argued that literacy programs tied to small-scale, grassroots, and sustainable development projects will empower the poverty-ridden classes in these countries. These themes of empowerment are also embraced and voiced by Critical Theorists.

Incidences of violence have increased in schools in the United States. Some students, in locations across the country, smuggled guns into schools, shooting and killing

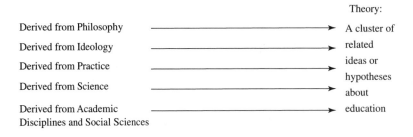

Derivation of Theories

their classmates and teachers. One of the most tragic cases of in-school violence took place at Columbine High School near Littleton, Colorado, when two male students, using guns and bombs, killed twelve of their classmates and two teachers. These incidents clearly signaled that the nation faced a major problem. Educators responded with programs to create safe schools with zero tolerance for those who endangered the lives of others. Part of the response included programs in conflict resolution and in identifying and providing therapy to bullies, social isolates, and other students with social and psychological problems. As a result, a theory of nonviolent safe schools developed. Once again, this theory that arose as a response soon was juxtaposed to other ideological positions. Conservatives claimed that the problem of violence in schools mirrored the moral breakdown in the larger society. Rap music, videos, and games that used violence as a theme had eroded and weakened traditional social morals and engendered a climate that was prone to violence. Permissiveness and values clarification programs in schools had created a climate of ethical relativism that lacked universal moral standards. Perennialists called for a reaffirmation of universal values found in the Judeo-Christian religious tradition and in the Aristotelian philosophical tradition. Conservatives called for a return to strict discipline and moral standards along with zero tolerance school management. Religious Conservatives called for the posting of the Ten Commandments in the schools as a reminder of universal moral values and responsibility. However, at the same time, many Conservatives oppose gun control as violating what they consider to be the Constitution's right of citizens to keep and bear arms.

Theory Arising from Practice

In many instances (e.g., in medicine, nursing, and education), theory arises from practice. In this scenario, the practitioner in a field has the experience of dealing with a number of similar instances. For example, a pediatrician may have dealt with a number of ear infections in children and as a result can form generalizations about their cause and treatment. These generalizations provide the physician with a set of hypotheses about the prevention and treatment of these cases. Or a foreign-language teacher, who has taught a course in Italian for several years to secondary school students, may have identified the situations that facilitate or impede learning the language for most students. She or he then reflects on these situations and arrives at some generalization to guide instruction. These generalizations then form a theory that can guide a method of teaching the language.

An example of theory being generated from practice can be found in the "effective" schools movement. Certain schools, their principals, and teachers, are identified as especially competent educators whose students have demonstrated high levels of academic achievement. After analyzing specific practices that contributed to effective schools, the U.S. Department of Education in *What Works: Research About Teaching and Learning* arrived at the following generalizations:

- Belief in the value of hard work, the importance of personal responsibility, and the importance of education itself contribute to success in school.
- Children learn science best when they are able to do experiments, so they can witness "science in action."
- Teachers who set and communicate high expectations to all their students obtain greater academic performance from those students than do teachers who set low expectations.
- The most important characteristics of effective schools are strong instructional leadership, a safe and orderly climate, schoolwide emphasis on basic skills, high teacher expectations for student achievement, and continuous assessment of pupil progress.[3]

The effective schools theory consists of a cluster of related generalizations about school organization and administration, the role of the principal and teachers, the climate of the school, methods of teaching, and student assessment. It is assumed that these generalizations validly describe an effective school and that they can be replicated in other schools. The anticipated result is that if these practices are implemented they will result in an increased number of effective schools.

An E-mail Discussion about Theory

I received an interesting e-mail from a student who was using my book on philosophy of education. The student raised some questions about my use of the term *theory*. He indicated that he was a major in one of the natural sciences and had learned that a theory is a hypothesis that can be tested empirically and either proved or disproved through experimentation. I wrote this reply to the student in an e-mail:

Thank you for your email. You make important points about scientific theories and their verification. I hope that you will share your ideas with the other students in the course. If my book should have another edition, I'll make every effort to emphasize scientific theory in the chapter.

I am not sure if your class is reading the entire book or just the chapter on theory. The book is divided into essentially three parts: philosophies, ideologies, and theories. I try to show relationships between the three areas. My intention in the chapter on theory was to give a descriptive sample of the term "theory" and its importance and use in educational philosophy and policy. Education in the United States is a public concern, vested in the states, and therefore, non-specialists—legislators, parents, students—will be propounding theories as well as teachers and professionals.

Textbook writing is difficult in that authors are always pressed by publishers to include more

(Continued)

An E-mail Discussion about Theory   *(Continued)*

items but to use fewer pages. In my chapter, I tried to highlight theories as they are often used in education—arising from experience, especially classroom experience, or coming from, being derived from, a more speculative philosophy or ideology. Some theories used in education, such as that supporting *No Child Left Behind,* can be verified, if you accept standardized tests scores as validation or lack of verification. However, other educators would hold that such empirical tests are incomplete in that you cannot test empirically for affect. An interesting exercise might be to contrast how the two theories of Evolution and Intelligent Design are debated in education and politics. Theory is a slippery, varied, much used term. It can be used as Plato used it as speculation and application of the insights from speculation. Or as Aquinas used it as a plan of action derived from higher theological and metaphysical truths or doctrines. In education, a much used word is policy—a theory of actions that will achieve desired results—as in effective schools theory. Then there is the very important kind of theory that you emphasize in your email—

scientific theories that are subject to empirical verification.

Your definition of theory is the standard one used in the physical and natural sciences—predictability based on testable data and applied or replicated in legitimate situations. Today, however, in the philosophy of science, the standard model of scientific theory is regarded as problematic. There is the contention the very observations we wish to account for are themselves "givens" in the assumptions of the theory; there is the issue of under-determination in which contradictory data can be equally well explained by the extant theory. These issues are explained in the excellent work on scientific theory by Larry Laudan, *Science and Relativism: Some Key Controversies in the Philosophy of Science,* University of Chicago Press, 1990. You may want to read Laudan's arguments about theory.

I want to thank you for your intelligent and well-crafted statements in your email. I'll try to do a more complete job if I have the opportunity to do another edition of the book. Best wishes on your career in education. Gerald Gutek

Conclusion

This chapter examined the relationships between theory and education. Theory was defined as a set of ideas or principles that are derived from a larger body of thought such as a philosophy or an ideology, are responses to issues, or generalized from experience. It was emphasized that teachers, as they reflect on their experiences and use them to create teaching strategies, are theory builders.

A theory can be seen as a guide or a map that leads us through the educational terrain. It can take us from a set of ideas that point to action to the various dimensions of education such as schools, curriculum, instruction, teaching, and learning. It may arise from practice in these areas and lead to transferable generalizations about them.

Constructing Your Own Philosophy of Education.   Now that you have read and discussed the chapter on theory, do you plan to use the ideas expressed about theory in your philosophy of education?

Questions for Reflection and Discussion

1. How would you define an educational theory? Do you have any theories about effective education?

2. What expectations do you have about teaching as a career? How do these expectations form a theory?

3. In your opinion, what constitutes a competent teacher? Do your ideas about teacher competency constitute a theory of education?

Topics for Inquiry and Research

1. Examine the requirements for your degree as presented in your institution's catalogue. Are these requirements based on a theory of education?

2. Interview several experienced teachers. As a result of your interviews, see whether there are some common features in their experiences that can be generalized into a theory of teaching and learning.

3. Obtain a copy of your state's guidelines for the approval of teacher education programs. Analyze the guidelines and determine whether they reflect an underlying theory of education.

4. Do some research on a recent movement in education such as the standards movement, authentic assessment, or constructivism. Determine whether these movements rest on a theory of education.

Building a Theoretical Vocabulary

Theoria: the Greek word for intellectually contemplating, considering, or conjecturing something.
Educational Theory Derived from Ideology: deducing or extrapolating a theory of education—ideas about education—from an ideology.
Educational Theory Derived from Philosophy: deducing a theory of education—ideas about education—from a more general philosophy.

Educational Theory as Reactive: a theory of education—ideas about education—that are based on a reaction to social, political, economic, and educational situations, issues, problems, and crises.
Educational Theory Arising from Practice: an educational theory—ideas about education—that are generated from classroom practices.

Internet Resources

For educational systems theory, consult http://education.indiana.edu/frick/edusys.html.

For links to philosophy, theories, and education, consult Educational Policy Studies at the University of Illinois, Urbana, at http://w3.eduiuc.edu/EPS/category.asp?-token-phil-n-phil-of-ed&site=Res.

As you begin to read the next chapters on Essentialism, Progressivism, Social Reconstructionism, Critical Theory, and Globalization, you might wish to refer back to this overview box.

Overview of Theories of Education

Theory	Aim	Curriculum	Educational Implications	Proponents
Essentialism (rooted in Idealism and Realism)	To educate the useful and competent person	Basic education: reading, writing, arithmetic, history, English, science, foreign languages, mathematics	Cultural maintenance and subjects that transmit the cultural heritage and contribute to socio-economic efficiency	Kandel Bagley Bestor
Progressivism (rooted in Pragmatism and Liberalism)	To educate the individual according to his or her interests and needs	Activities and projects	Instruction that features problem solving and group activities; teacher acts as a facilitator	Dewey Kilpatrick Johnson
Social Reconstruction (rooted in Pragmatism, Liberalism, Socialism)	To engage schools, teachers, and students in building a new society	A curriculum infused with social, political, economic, and environmental issues	To raise consciousness about the issues society faces and to bring about engagement in solving these issues	Counts Brameld Rugg
Critical Theory (rooted in Neo-Marxism and Postmodernism)	To raise consciousness about issues of marginalization and empowerment	Autobiographies about oppressed people; issues about marginalization and exploitation	Focus on local, site-based learning—that examines the real conditions impacting a school and its community	Freire Illich McLaren Giroux
Globalization (rooted in capitalism, Neo-Liberalism)	To integrate the world economically and in communications	Marketing, language skills, management, international skills	To prepare people to live and function in an increasingly interdependent global society and economy	

Suggestions for Further Reading

Archer, Margaret S. *Realist Social Theory: The Morpho-netic Approach.* New York: Cambridge University Press, 1995.

Chambliss, J. J. *Educational Theory as Theory of Conduct.* Albany: State University of New York Press, 1987.

Collins, Randall. *The Sociology of Philosophies: A Global Theory of Intellectual Change.* Cambridge, MA: Harvard University Press, 1998.

Feinberg, Walter. *Understanding Education: Toward a Reconstruction of Educational Inquiry.* New York: Cambridge University Press, 1983.

Hare, William. *What Makes a Good Teacher: Reflections on Some Characteristics Central to the Educational Enterprise.* Ontario, Canada: Althouse Press, 1993.

Jackson, Philip. *Life in Classrooms.* New York: Teachers College Press, 1993.

Phillips, D. C. *Philosophy, Science, and Social Inquiry.* New York: Pergamon Press, 1987.

Silver, Harold. *Good Schools, Effective Schools: Judgments and Their Histories.* New York: Cassell, 1995.

Endnotes

1. Fred N. Kerlinger, *Foundations of Behavioral Research* (New York: Holt, Rinehart, and Winston, 1973), p. 9.
2. U.S. Department of Education, Office of the Secretary, *Back to School, Moving Forward: What "No Child Left Behind" Means for America's Communities* (Washington, DC: U.S. Department of Education, 2001), pp. 6–7.
3. *What Works: Research About Teaching and Learning* (Washington, DC: U.S. Department of Education, 1986), pp. 7, 17, 23, 45.

13

Essentialism and Education

William C. Bagley (1874–1946), a professor of education, who articulated the Essentialist position.

Chapter Preview

Essentialism as a significant educational theory has had remarkable staying power in American schooling. Here, we discuss Essentialism's philosophical and historical relationships, the ideas of its prominent leaders, and its implications for education, schooling, curriculum, and teaching and learning. Essentialism, sometimes called basic education, is a rather straightforward theory that argues that schools are academic institutions and that their curriculum should consist of fundamental generative skills and subject-matter disciplines. It sees the school's primary function to be the preservation and academic transmission of the basic elements of human civilization. It emphasizes (1) a curriculum of basic skills and subjects; (2) learning as the mastery of these skills and subjects that is monitored by consistently high verifiable standards; (3) schools as places of order, discipline, and efficient and effective instruction; and (4) the goal of organized education to prepare people to be productive, civil, and patriotic individuals. Currently, the standards movement, the use of standardized tests to measure student academic achievement, and the No Child Left Behind education law reflect the continuing influence of Essentialism on American education and schooling. The chapter examines the following major topics:

- Essentialism's historical and philosophical rationale
- William C. Bagley and Arthur E. Bestor, leading Essentialist theorists
- The relationships between Neo-Conservatism and Neo-Essentialism
- Essentialism's implications for education, schools, curriculum, and teaching and learning
- Philosophies and ideologies that either support or oppose Essentialism

As you read the chapter and think about constructing your own philosophy of education, does Essentialism appeal to you as a teacher? Do you find evidence of Essentialism in your own education? Do you plan to use it in constructing your own philosophy of education?

Essentialism's Historical and Philosophical Rationale

Essentialism asserts that education properly involves learning the basic skills, arts, and sciences that have been useful in the past and will remain useful in the future.

Essentialism forcefully argues that a genuine education requires learning the basic literary and mathematical skills needed to function in civilized society and studying the liberal arts and sciences needed to understand the cultural heritage. Historian Diane Ravitch attributed the term **essentialism** to Michael Demiashkevich, who contrasted two competing theories, Essentialism and individual-pragmatism, or Progressivism, in his *Introduction to the Philosophy of Education* (1935). Essentialism, which Demiashkevich endorses, aims to transmit the social and cultural heritage by teaching students subject-matter disciplines such as mathematics, natural sciences, and history and forming their moral and ethical character. Progressivism, in contrast, sought to guide students to develop their own interests into what was useful at the moment. For Demiashkevich, the Progressive goal of individual "growth" disconnected education from the cultural heritage's reservoir of the humanities and sciences.[1]

Although it has been identified by names other than Essentialism, the theory that education and schools should emphasize a curriculum of basic skills of literacy and mathematical computation and subject matter derived from the liberal arts and sciences has had a long history and continuing support in American education. Clifton Fadiman has stated the case for **basic education**, another name for Essentialism. Basic education, he says, is concerned with subjects that have "generative power," which means the potency to endow students "with the ability to learn the higher, more complex developments of these master subjects as well as the minor or self-terminating" ones. Such generative subjects deal with "language, whether or not one's own; forms, figures, and numbers; the laws of nature; the past; and the shape and behavior of our common home, the earth."[2]

The common Essentialist themes are: (1) the elementary curriculum should emphasize basic tool skills that contribute to literacy and numeracy; (2) the secondary curriculum should include history, mathematics, science, literature, and language; (3) discipline is necessary for systematic learning in school situations; (4) respect for legitimate authority, both in school and in society, should be cultivated in students; (5) the mastering of a skill or a subject requires effort and diligence on the part of the learner; and (6) the teaching of these necessary skills and subjects requires mature and well-educated teachers who know their subjects and are able to transmit them to students.

Essentialism's Historical and Philosophical Roots

In this section, we position Essentialism within a generalized interpretation of the back-and-forth movement, the pendulum, in the history of curriculum in American schooling. Then, we look at how Essentialists constructed their own history of curriculum. After discussing its historical roots, we turn to Essentialism's philosophical roots.

In the history of the American school curriculum, two long-standing polar positions are evident on curriculum construction. The metaphor of the pendulum, much like that of a clock, can be used to illustrate these positions. At one pole of the pendulum are the educational theorists who argue that schools are primarily a place for students to learn academic skills and subjects. The view that the school is primarily an academic institution, endorsed by Essentialists, sees the curriculum as consisting of organized academic skills such as reading, writing, arithmetic, and civility and basic subjects such as history, mathematics, science, and English and foreign languages. At the other pole are theorists who counter that schools are multifunctional rather than strictly academic sites where children should be encouraged to grow and develop through experiences such as activities and projects. The view that schools are multifunctional institutions, endorsed by Progressives, contends that schools are places for children's and adolescents' socialization through a variety of activities such as projects, "hands-on learning," activities, collaboration, and constructivism. Schools in the United States, historically, have incorporated elements from both poles of the curricular pendulum and now have both academic and the multifunctional aspects in their programs. As the curriculum pendulum swings to and fro, however, either the primarily academic view or the multifunctional socialization orientation has been dominant at different times.

Essentialism and Public Education

Historically, Essentialists root their theory in the European liberal arts and science tradition that was brought to the United States and implemented in secondary schools such as the Latin grammar schools, the academies, and in academic high schools. They envision the origins of public education in the nineteenth-century common schools, which, for them, emphasized literacy—reading, writing, listening, spelling, and basic mathematical computation—as the essential version of elementary schooling that should continue today. In addition to cultivating essential skills, the common schools, through the teaching of American history, literature, natural science, music, and art, served to provide children with an essential cultural foundation. This foundation, commonly shared, was a necessary factor in constructing an American identity and understanding the origins and processes of political democracy. The common cultural foundation also served as a shared source of morals and ethics that, in public schools, was manifested by civility. The curricular orientation that supported Essentialism also related education and schooling to economic productivity and, at times, to the ability of the United States to compete successfully in the world economy.

In the more recent history of American education, Essentialism appears, if challenged, to retreat, to readjust to change, and then to reappear, as in the case of the basic education and standards movements. Although the name may vary, the Essentialist message remains fundamentally consistent. There are, however, variations on the theme. Essentialism has been a highly persistent theory in education. Despite many challenges from various reformers— Pragmatists, Postmodernists, Liberals, Progressives, Constructivists, and Critical Theorists— Essentialism, in its various forms, remains and exerts a significant influence over schools. In the nineteenth century, Essentialism took the form of the "three R's" (reading, writing, and 'rithmetic) and mental discipline (the theory that certain subjects trained or disciplined the mind). In the 1930s, a group of educators opposed to Progressive education, led by William Chandler Bagley, spearheaded the Essentialist movement. In the 1950s, Essentialism was voiced by educational theorists such as Arthur E. Bestor, Jr., who called for a return to the teaching of fundamental intellectual disciplines. In the 1970s and 1980s, the Council for Basic Education stimulated a revival of basic education. In the 1980s, the U.S. Commission on Excellence in Education's *A Nation at Risk* asserted Essentialist themes. In the early twenty-first century, the **standards movement**, based on identifying benchmarks that measured academic progress, exerted a profound impact on schools, curriculum, and instruction. Scholarly organizations such as the American Historical Association and the National Council for the Teaching of English, for example, established commissions to identify the standards that signify a knowledge base in their fields for students. States mandated standardized testing in basic subjects. In 2001, the education act No Child Left Behind mandated standardized testing in reading as a requirement for federal aid to local school districts.

Essentialism's Philosophical Roots

Although Essentialism operates primarily from a historical perspective of education, it can be examined philosophically. Though we examine it philosophically, it is a theory of education that is heavily influenced by a history of education that emphasizes the importance of the liberal arts and sciences in Western education and by a history of curriculum that sees a valid curriculum organized into skills and subjects and valid instruction as largely the transmission of the cultural heritage to the young.

In examining Essentialism philosophically, we can consider its root in the term *essence,* a concept found in the metaphysical positions of the traditional philosophies of Idealism and Realism. Essence means that which is necessary to and indispensable about something—an object, a discipline, or a subject, for example. Essence relates to the intrinsic, fundamental, or basic character of something rather than its accidental, temporary, or incidental features. Related to education, what is there about an education that is necessary to having an education and being educated? Essentialists such as Bagley and Bestor have framed their answer to the question more historically than philosophically—finding what is essential to education in the liberal arts and science tradition in the Western educational experience. Essentialism asserts that certain basic ideas, skills, and bodies of knowledge, over the course of history, have proved essential to human culture and civilization and need to be transmitted to oncoming generations. Basic skills and certain bodies of knowledge can be formulated and organized into subjects that can and should be taught by adults to the young. Deliberate instruction as the **transmission** of basic skills and knowledge areas from one generation to the next guarantees civilization's perpetuation and survival. These fundamentals or essentials are the skills of literacy (reading and writing) and computation (arithmetic) and the subjects of history, mathematics, science, languages, and literature. (A more extended discussion of the Essentialist curriculum follows later in the chapter.) To disengage from this necessary and essential cultural transmission as suggested by Progressives, Reconstructionists, and Critical Theorists places civilization in peril. Essentialists further insist that this transmission takes place more efficiently and effectively through methods that have stood the test of time. Because there is much to learn and a limited time in which to learn it, instruction should be planned, deliberate, and efficient. It is important to learn from the past rather than trying to keep reinventing the wheel. Schools, then, are academic agencies established by society to transmit basic skills and knowledge to its children and youth.

Philosophically, Essentialism's argument that there is an existing body of knowledge, the arts and sciences, rests on a concept of antecedent reality. That means that there is something there before we come on the scene that is of vital importance to us. In other words, the bodies of knowledge, organized into skills and subjects, exist before the students enter the school in kindergarten. The curriculum is about this **antecedent knowledge** and the school's purpose is to transmit it. It does not depend on whether students are interested in learning it; it is important for them to learn it, just as it was for the students who preceded them in school and in society. Though teachers can motivate students to study this antecedent knowledge, they cannot ethically abandon their historical mission when the going gets tough.

Essentialists encounter considerable opposition from an array of adversaries who decry their theory as traditionalism. Experimentalists associated with Dewey's Pragmatism, Progressives, Postmodernists, and Critical Theorists all attack the Essentialist curriculum that rests on antecedent knowledge. For Experimentalists, antecedent knowledge does not arise in the learner's experience. Progressives contend that it does not arise in the child's interest or needs. Postmodernists and Critical Theorists see it as an imposition of the powerful over the marginalized. We shall return to the discussion of Essentialism's philosophical and ideological relationships later in the chapter. At this point, our discussion is to examine Essentialism's historical and philosophical origins in general. Now, we turn to a discussion of the educational ideas of two leading Essentialists: William Chandler Bagley and Arthur E. Bestor, Jr.

William Chandler Bagley

In his definitive biography of William Chandler Bagley, J. Wesley Null calls him "one of the most invisible of the truly prominent educators of the twentieth century."[3] Because of his commitment to social progress, Null positions Bagley within Progressivism as a broad movement but qualifies him as a "disciplined progressive" for his insistence that teaching and learning academic disciplines were central to education and schooling. Bagley opposed what he considered to be extreme Progressives, such as William H. Kilpatrick, who sought to substitute projects for academic subjects and Reconstructionists, such as George S. Counts, who wanted schools and teachers to build a new social order.

Bagley, who devoted his career to teacher education, was a professor of education at Montana State College, Oswego Normal School, the University of Illinois, and Teachers College, Columbia University. Educational theory at Teachers College was dominated by Progressives such as Kilpatrick and Reconstructionists such as Counts and Harold Rugg; Bagley, in the company of the comparative educator Isaac Kandel, found himself in the minority.[4] Bagley and Kandel shared a vision of teacher education that integrated a knowledge core in the liberal arts and sciences and professional education studies in the historical, philosophical, comparative, and psychological foundations of education. Teaching methods, for them, integrated a knowledge base, the content of subjects such as science, English, and history with methods that organized them for teaching by relating them to the readiness and prior learning of students.

Bagley was the spokesman for a like-minded group of Essentialist educators who met at the convention of the American Association of School Administrators (AASA) in February 1938. In outlining the "Essentialist Platform," Bagley stated that (1) U.S. elementary school students were failing to meet the "standards of achievement in the fundamentals of education" attained in other countries; (2) U.S. secondary school students lagged academically behind the eighteen-year-olds of other countries; (3) increasingly large numbers of high school students were essentially illiterate and could not read effectively, and because of deficiencies at the primary and intermediate levels, remedial reading programs had to be instituted in many high schools; (4) in addition to declining literacy, notable deficiencies existed in mathematics and grammar; and (5) despite increased educational expenditures in the United States, there was a noticeable increase in the rates of serious crime.

Bagley identified two specific causes of the United States' educational malaise: (1) dominant educational theories, such as extreme Progressivism, were "essentially enfeebling," and (2) the relaxation of academic standards in many school systems had led to the policy of widespread "social promotion." Bagley chastised Progressives who overemphasized the child's freedom, interests, and play, and sacrificed discipline, effort, and work. For Bagley, Progressive education had contributed to the "complete abandonment in many school systems of rigorous standards of scholastic achievement for promotion from grade to grade, and the passing of all pupils 'on schedule.'"[5] Instead of a curriculum based on systematic and sequential learning and consecutive, cumulative, and orderly academic development, the Progressives had substituted an undifferentiated program of activities, projects, and incidental learning. Bagley's condemnation of social promotion was similar to today's arguments that students should master minimal competencies before being promoted to a higher grade or being awarded a diploma.

Bagley was joined by other professional educators such as Michael Demiashkevich, Walter H. Ryle, M. L. Shane, and Gary M. Whipple, who, calling themselves Essentialists, urged U.S. schools, teachers, and administrators to return to the basic skills of recording, computing, measuring, U.S. history, health instruction, natural science, and the fine and industrial arts. In taking their stance, the Essentialists asked:

> Should not our public schools prepare boys and girls for adult responsibility through systematic training in such subjects as reading, writing, arithmetic, history, and English, requiring mastery of such subjects, and, when necessary, stressing discipline and obedience?[6]

Arguing that Progressive education had created discontinuity between the generations, Bagley urged U.S. educators and schools to provide each generation with "possession of a common core of ideas, meanings, understandings, and ideals representing the most precious elements of the human heritage."[7]

Bagley as an Educational Theorist

Bagley's theory of education needs to be examined from two related perspectives: (1) the elementary and secondary school curriculum and (2) teacher education. In both of these perspectives, Bagley was an educator who deliberately sought to avoid what he regarded as extremist positions. For Bagley, the vital center of education was based on the liberal arts and sciences, which traditionally formed the core of undergraduate study in higher education. Bagley, and especially his colleague Kandel, saw the liberal arts and sciences as education's vital core. Bagley, similar to the Perennialists, distinguished between a general education (the education that everyone should have) and vocational education (the education that some people need for a specific occupation).[8] The two kinds of education should be distinguished from each other and not confused. A general education for all rested on the liberal arts and sciences. The elementary curriculum with generative skills of language—reading, writing, listening, and composition—were the necessary processes that had to be learned for students to approach the academic subjects—mathematics, history, sciences, languages and literature, geography, and civics—at the secondary level. These subjects were based on the liberal arts and sciences and led to their advanced study in colleges and universities.

At the vital center of education, the liberal arts core needed to be maintained and transmitted as a body of indispensable and necessary skills and subjects. Further, the schools' primary function as an academic institution that transmitted the core had to be protected against what Bagley regarded as extremist positions. During his life the extremist positions were associated with extreme child-centered Progressivism, which he believed would have sacrificed the necessary skills and subjects to the child's interests as interpreted by well-meaning or misguided educational sentimentalists and romantics. For Bagley, teachers should not ignore children's interests but should be guided by what they really needed to know—the essential skills and subjects. Reconstructionism constituted another extremist camp among educators. Reconstructionists, such as Counts and Rugg, would politicize schools by indoctrinating children in a utopian ideology that sought to remake society. (Reconstructionism is discussed in a later chapter.) Bagley reasoned that although students should study history and government, politically ambitious theorists should not distort these subjects into ideological pieces to accomplish goals that were external to education. Bagley's arguments against extreme educational positions did not make him popular among the Progressive and Reconstructionist professors at Teachers College. If Bagley were alive today, he would most likely find Postmodernism and Critical Theory to be another extremist assault on the liberal arts core that he saw at the vital center of education.

Throughout his professional career, Bagley was a teacher educator. His approach to teacher education was based on: (1) the school as the transmitter of the liberal arts and science heritage; and (2) educating teachers who knew how to prepare students to learn this heritage and who could effectively transmit it to students. Teachers then prepare students to learn by motivating them and creating a readiness and desire to learn. Children learn many things in their daily experiences both in and out of school; a teacher's primary function in the school is to stay focused on essential skills and subjects. Teachers must know the essential skills and subjects, before they attempt to teach them—how they developed, their key concepts and vocabularies, and their structural logic as intrinsic bodies of knowledge. They need to know how the arts and sciences, as the repository of civilized knowledge, inform and contribute to society, economy, and culture. Then, they need to know how to teach them effectively and efficiently. This means that teachers need to develop methods that enable them to transmit the skills and subjects in an orderly and cumulative **sequence** to students. Bagley believed that methods of instruction needed to be integrated with the skill and subject and not be separated from it as some Progressives insisted. As a teacher educator, Bagley believed that teachers should study the history, philosophy, and psychology of education as a necessary foundational base for their profession.

The Crux of the Conflict between Essentialists and Progressives. The highly articulate Bagley, using an almost Hegelian format of thesis and antithesis, analyzed the "crux of the conflict" between Progressives and Essentialists.[9] Whereas Progressives emphasized children's interests in learning, Essentialists stressed the need for effort in mastering lessons; whereas Progressives stressed freedom to learn, Essentialists argued that discipline was needed; whereas Progressives exalted individual experience, Essentialists prized the experience of the human race over time. Further, Progressives emphasized the psychological organization of the curriculum in contrast to the Essentialists' emphasis on the logical and chronological organization of subjects. Finally, Progressives emphasized learning through activities whereas Essentialists maintained the need for subject-matter organization. After outlining the polar opposites, Bagley then sought to reconcile them with a Hegelian-like synthesis. He argued that interest may lead children to problems, but they need effort to pursue them to their solution. Further, not all interests were equally important. Some were more important than others because they led to matters of permanent concern. The view that some areas of the curriculum are related to permanent cultural matters was a real point of difference between Progressives and Essentialists. Still another serious difference centered on the role of teachers. Bagley argued that the teacher, as an adult representative of the culture, is to guide learners to a definite goal in contrast to the Progressives' ambiguous concept of "open-endedness."[10]

Essentialism's Revival in Neo-Essentialism

For many years, Essentialism was either dismissed or relegated to a footnote in most books on history and philosophy of education. It enjoys a revival in Null's biographies of Bagley and Kandel and in Diane Ravitch's historical analysis of recent American educational history.[11]

Bagley and his Essentialist conferees' identification of educational deficiencies in late 1930s America would be reiterated several times in the history that followed them. Bestor and other critics in the 1950s and the proponents of *A Nation at Risk* in the 1980s would mount similar arguments. Later subject-matter proponents had an even more definite view of the curriculum than the Essentialists, yet their arguments followed a similar logic. They would make comparisons between the achievement of American students with those of other countries; find defects in the educational system, usually attributable to Progressive education; and then call for a uniform subject-matter curriculum for all students. Among these educational deficits, identified by the Essentialists and echoed by Bestor, the basic educational movement, and the standards movement were:

- American students had lower academic achievement rates than those in other industrialized countries.
- The de-emphasis on logic, chronology, system, and sequence in the curriculum caused a decline of academic standards in the United States.
- Social promotion policies have promoted students who were often functionally illiterate and unprepared for the next higher levels of education.

The Development of Life Adjustment Education

To continue the discussion of the continuing appearances of Essentialism in American educational history, we need to move forward to the period from the late 1940s and early 1950s, the period after World War II and before the Cold War. A key issue that caused the recurring debate between Progressives and Essentialists was generated by the life adjustment movement. As we proceed in this discussion, it should be noted that some Progressives, especially those associated with Dewey's Experimentalists, did not regard life adjustment as a genuine assertion of Progressive education.

Life Adjustment Education

In 1945, with United States' education readjusting to peacetime after World War II, Charles Prosser, a leader in vocational education, inaugurated the life adjustment movement. Arguing that sixty percent of American secondary school students were underserved by existing academic college preparatory and vocational education programs, Prosser called for a new approach, which he called **life adjustment education**. For Prosser and his like-minded colleagues, the time was ripe to restructure the high school into a broad-based institution where adolescent growth and development was related to saleable vocational work skills that would lead to a socially satisfying and economically productive adulthood. For the life adjustment educators, the emphasis on academic subjects would be replaced by different curricular linchpins—students' personal, social, and economic needs.

Prosser and the other life adjustment educators did not intend that a new course called life adjustment was to be merely added to the traditional curriculum. They wanted life adjustment at the heart, at the vital center, of the secondary school curriculum. This of course would raise the ire of Essentialists who placed the liberal arts and sciences at the curriculum core. Life adjustment educators often used the term *infusion*. Infuse life adjustment into the entire curriculum, they said. To get the new curriculum in place required seriously modifying existing courses and creating new ones. All existing courses, including language, mathematics, science, and history, would need to be revised to deal with the real problems of living rather than academic preparation for college. With the curriculum so broadened to include all areas of life, then the nature of the school itself, and the teacher, would need to be expansively reconceptualized. The school was to be a multifunctional agency that addressed all areas of human life, including, but not exclusively limited to, academic ones. The school of the future would deal with education in very broad terms that were social, personal, civic, and economic, as well as academic. Further, because the concept of adjustment involved much that was psychological and emotional as well as intellectual, the life adjustment school had to become completely multifunctional. It had to deal with the students' total adjustment, especially the psychology of adjustment.

The Reaction against Life Adjustment

The 1950s and early 1960s saw a strong and concerted reaction against life adjustment. Unlike the earlier Essentialist reaction against Progressivism that came primarily from a group of professors of education led by Bagley, the reaction against life adjustment came primarily from critics outside of professional education. For example, Hyman Rickover, a leading critic, was an admiral in the U.S. Navy, and Arthur E. Bestor, Jr. was a college professor of history.

Admiral Hyman G. Rickover

Admiral Hyman G. Rickover, a U.S. Navy officer, was a persistent national critic of American education. Known as the "father of the atomic submarine," Rickover had supervised the scientists and engineers who developed the first U.S. nuclear-powered submarine, the Nautilus.[12] Because of his interest in national defense and military technology during the Cold War, Rickover was especially concerned with the academic preparation of mathematicians, scientists, and engineers. This interest led him to mathematics and science and their teaching in American secondary schools. Reiterating some of the earlier Essentialist criticisms, Rickover found American secondary schools were failing in mathematics and science. Like the earlier Essentialists, Rickover, comparing U.S. schools to those in other countries such as Switzerland, Germany, and the Soviet Union, found American students lacking the mathematical and scientific knowledge needed in a technological era. While American high school students were being taught life adjustment courses, European secondary students were studying history, mathematics, and the sciences. By the end of their secondary schooling, many European students, in contrast to American students, had mastered not only their own native language but also knew one or two foreign languages.[13] He also criticized the public education system for failing to provide curricula that challenged gifted students.[14] Rickover proposed that model schools be established for the top twenty percent of academically talented students.

Arthur E. Bestor, Jr.

A leading critic of life adjustment education was historian Arthur E. Bestor, Jr. The son of Arthur E. Bestor, Sr., the director of the famed Chautauqua Institution in New York, Bestor was a scion of a distinguished academic family. At the time of his major critiques of American education, Bestor was a history professor at the University of Illinois in Urbana, where he taught courses in American history, historical methods, and U.S. constitutional history. Though advocating a new approach to Essentialism, Bestor, like Bagley, was not a political conservative. He was a liberal in matters of academic freedom and civil rights. A member of the American Civil Liberties Union, he served on its Illinois board of directors. Bestor was also a member of the National Association for the Advancement of Colored People. Bestor was a major figure in the Council for Basic Education, serving as its first president in 1956–57. His most important books on education were *Educational Wastelands* (1953) and *The Restoration of Learning* (1955).[15]

In *The Restoration of Learning,* Bestor, like Bagley, argued the school has a primary purpose; it is an academic institution, a place of thorough and disciplined intellectual development. He argued that life adjustment education had spawned an anti-intellectual ideology that diverted schools from their primary academic purpose to "trivial" aims that separated the curriculum from "the disciplines of science and scholarship."[16]

According to Bestor: (1) academic standards in U.S. public schools had declined because of an anti-intellectual educational ideology that separated schools from the scientific and scholarly disciplines; and (2) a narrowly educated group of professional educators, administrators, and department of education bureaucrats at the state level controlled entry into the teaching profession by manipulating certification requirements. Bestor urged that the trend to anti-intellectualism be reversed and that the public school curriculum be based on the intellectual disciplines of English, foreign languages, history, mathematics, and science.

In *The Restoration of Learning,* Bestor established a criterion of education based on intellectual disciplines. Strongly implied in Bestor's educational theory is a conception of U.S. democracy based on the rule of reasonable and intelligent citizens. An intelligently functioning democracy is a government of law, orderly parliamentary processes, and democratic guarantees for all citizens. Bestor expressed a definite Essentialist theory of education that provides

> sound training in the fundamental ways of thinking represented by history, science, mathematics, literature, language, art and other disciplines evolved in the course of mankind's long quest for usable knowledge, cultural understanding, and intellectual power.[17]

These intellectual disciplines should be fundamental in the school curriculum for they are basic in modern life. In the elementary school, reading, writing, and arithmetic provide indispensable generative skills. The essentials of the secondary school curriculum are science, mathematics, history, English, and foreign languages. These intellectual disciplines, the core of a liberal education, are humankind's most reliable tools in solving personal, social, political, and economic problems.

Bestor sought to achieve his educational ideal through an essential subject-matter curriculum based on history, mathematics, science, foreign languages, and English. Indeed, the years devoted to the pursuit of formal learning are based on these five essential intellectual disciplines. During the first four, five, or six years of schooling, reading, writing, and arithmetic are the necessary generative tool skills. The elementary school student should also be introduced to the structures and methods of the natural sciences, geography, and history.[18]

Junior high school, the grades from seven to nine, marks the beginning of organized and systematic study. A transition is made from arithmetic to the more abstract forms of mathematical reasoning, beginning with elementary algebra. History is organized as a recognized chronological structure. From the generalized natural science studied earlier, a transition is made as the student is introduced to sciences such as biology, physics, or chemistry. Instruction in foreign languages moves forward to grammatical analysis.

Students in the senior high school are to pursue a subject systematically and to use abstract reasoning. Specifically, mathematics is continued through advanced algebra, plane geometry, trigonometry, analytical geometry, and calculus. Systematic work in chemistry, physics, and biology furnishes the needed scientific knowledge. History's chronological pattern and structure are emphasized. English is employed with accuracy, lucidity, and grace. One foreign language is mastered and another begun.[19]

Bestor's proposed curriculum is prescribed for all students. Once he or she has mastered these essentials, the student can begin vocational or college education. Training in the liberating disciplines prepares a person for intellectual life, citizenship, a vocation, and for a profession.

Bestor feared that U.S. schools were failing to provide the needed intellectual discipline. He charged that some professional educators postulated an erroneous view of a democratic education. Because the intellectual disciplines were once reserved to aristocratic elites, these educators failed to realize that the progress of the modern age now made an intellectual education the democratic right of all.

Bestor charged that professional educators, no longer content with methodology, had usurped curriculum making. Curriculum construction, he argued, is best exercised by the scholars and scientists who are expert in their academic disciplines. Some professional educators had distorted Progressive education into a "regressive education," according to Bestor. They had watered down the great intellectual disciplines and introduced vocational and life-adjustment courses into the general curriculum to the detriment of the academic subjects. By weakening liberal education, too much of public education had become anti-democratic and anti-intellectual.

Bestor's educational agenda emphasized two fundamental principles: (1) ensuring disciplined intellectual education to every future citizen, and (2) providing opportunity for advanced study to all who possess genuine intellectual capacity and a willingness to develop their intellectual powers.[20] These two principles serve as the basis of the school's primary responsibilities, which are outlined as follows: (1) the school should provide a standard program of intellectual training in the fundamental disciplines geared to the needs of serious students and to the capacities of the upper two-thirds of the school population; (2) the school should provide special opportunities for exceptionally able students; (3) programs designed for the highest third of the school population should be balanced with adequate remedial programs for the lowest third, the slow learners; (4) a program of physical education for all children should be provided that is distinguished from interschool athletics; and (5) the school should diversify its offerings to include certain areas of vocational training.[21]

Neo-Essentialism, Basic Education, and Neo-Conservatism

In the 1980s, Essentialism, in the form of the basic education movement, made an important comeback that had significant implications for American education at the end of the twentieth and into the twenty-first centuries. Basic education became closely related to the Neo-Conservative ideology. It set the stage for *A Nation at Risk,* which, in turn, led to the standards movement and to No Child Left Behind. Neo-Conservatism had been gathering momentum since the turbulent 1960s and was victorious with the election of Ronald Reagan as president. Conservatism and Neo-Conservatism are discussed in detail in an earlier chapter; the discussion here emphasizes its relationship to Neo-Essentialism. The Neo-Essentialism that began in the 1980s differed somewhat from the educational ideas of Bagley and Bestor. Although Bagley's Essentialists in the 1930s were concerned with the effects of the Depression and with the rise of totalitarianism in Europe on American democracy, they argued that schools should not be politicized. Also, Bestor, himself a liberal, saw his version of basic education as advancing democracy, in the general sense, rather than a particular political ideology.

The basic education revival began as a rather amorphous movement that attracted people from outside of schools rather than from professional educators. The slogan "back-to-the-basics" covered a wide-ranging set of criticisms about public education, such as:

- Overly permissive Progressive educators, by neglecting the basics, had weakened American education, causing functional illiteracy and ethical indifference.
- Values clarification and secular humanism in public schools had undermined traditional values of industriousness, honesty, and patriotism.
- Schools and teachers need to be held accountable not only for students' academic success but also for their failure.
- A plethora of so-called curricular innovations such as the "new math," "new science," and "new social studies," process-learning, and constructivism have replaced the necessary basics.
- Social promotion policies move children and adolescents through the public schools without adequate assessments to determine their academic competencies.
- Using schools for social engineering rather than teaching academic skills and subjects had confused the purposes of education, especially at the high school level.

Supporters of the revival of basic education often had mixed motives in that they knew what they were against but not always what they were for. For example, some business organizations claimed that academically deficient public schools were not training students in the skills and competencies needed in a technologically changing economy. Some organizations, decrying increasing property taxes for schools, wanted school budgets trimmed by eliminating what they called "unnecessary frills and fads." Of growing ideological importance were individuals who wanted to return to an idealized version of schooling, when public schools instilled clearly defined skills and subjects and instilled traditional values of patriotism, telling the truth, hard work, competition, and abstinence from sex until persons married. They charged that Liberals, Progressives, and radicals who supported values clarification, cultural relativism, and secular humanism had deliberately confused the meaning of knowledge and values. The United States, with its rising rates of teen pregnancy, violence, crime, and drug addiction, desperately needed a return to traditional values.

The values issue generated major criticisms of public schools from what became known as the "religious right," a group largely made up of fundamentalist Protestants but also including members of other religions. The ascendancy of faith-based politics saw demands for prayer in the public schools, the teaching of Creationism and Intelligent Design in science parallel to Darwin's theory of evolution, and the freedom of educational choice through state-paid vouchers that could be used in private and parochial schools as well as public schools.

Educational issues took center stage in American politics. Some conservative politicians campaigned for office as champions of basic education. They attacked declining academic standards, lack of discipline in the schools, and the need to restore academic quality in public schools. Some also drew support from the religious right by urging prayer in the schools and an emphasis on teaching "sound moral values." Ronald Reagan became keenly aware of the power of education as a national issue and kept it in the forefront of his administration, from 1981 to 1989.

A Nation at Risk

Reagan, guided by his effective Secretary of Education, Terrel Bell, advanced an educational agenda that integrated themes from Essentialism and basic education with Neo-Conservatism. Essentially, the Reagan administration sought to: (1) improve the academic quality of schools by emphasizing a basic subject curriculum; (2) encourage effective schools with strong principals and high teacher expectations; (3) relate education to national economic productivity; and (4) reduce indiscipline and violence in schools by insisting on high standards of behavior and performance.

In August 1981, Bell appointed a National Commission on Excellence in Education, chaired by David L. Gardner, president of the University of California. The commission was to conduct a comprehensive review of the quality of education in the country's schools and colleges, do a comparative study of academic outcomes of U.S. and other countries' school systems, examine the relationships between college admission requirements and the high school curriculum, and make recommendations to restore excellence to American education. In 1983, the commission issued *A Nation at Risk*.

Like other reports calling for a return to rigorous academic standards, *A Nation at Risk* warned that "the educational foundations of our society are presently being eroded by a rising tide of mediocrity that threatens our very future as a Nation and a people."[22] Echoing the criticisms of Bagley and Bestor, the National Commission on Excellence reported its findings. Among them were the following:

> Secondary school curricula have been homogenized, diluted and diffused to the point that they no longer have a central purpose.[23]

In many other industrialized nations, courses in mathematics (other than arithmetic or general mathematics), biology, chemistry, physics, and geography start in grade 6 and are required of all students. The time spent on these subjects, based on class hours, is about three times that spent by even the most science-oriented U.S. students, i.e., those who select 4 years of science and mathematics in secondary school.[24]

In many schools, the time spent learning how to cook and drive counts as much toward a high school diploma as the time spent studying mathematics, English, chemistry, U.S. history, or biology.[25]

Leaning heavily in the direction of a content-oriented and subject-matter curriculum, the Commission on Excellence recommended

that State and local high school graduation requirements be strengthened and that, at a minimum, all students seeking a diploma be required to lay the foundations in the Five New Basics by taking the following curriculum during their 4 years of high school: (a) 4 years of English; (b) 3 years of mathematics; (c) 3 years of science; (d) 3 years of social studies; and (e) one-half year of computer science. For the college-bound, 2 years of foreign language in high school are strongly recommended in addition to those taken earlier.[26]

The Commission also recommended

that schools, colleges, and universities adopt more rigorous and measurable standards, and higher expectations, for academic performance and student conduct, and that 4-year colleges and universities raise their requirements for admission. This will help students do their best educationally with challenging materials in an environment that supports learning and authentic accomplishment.[27]

A Nation at Risk stimulated other national reports and educational recommendations that urged emphasis on basic skills and subjects. For example, the Task Force on Education for Economic Growth, in *Action for Excellence,* stressed basic skills and competencies for productive employment in a structurally and technologically changing society. The College Board in *Academic Preparation for College* identified the basic academic competencies or "broad intellectual skills essential to effective work" in college as reading, speaking and listening, writing, mathematics, reasoning, and studying. Added to this conventional list of tool skills was a basic knowledge of computer processes, terminology, and application.[28] The College Board identified the basic academic subjects that provide "the detailed knowledge and skills" for effective college work as English, the arts, mathematics, science, social studies, and foreign languages.[29]

The Standards Movement

The essential theme of the standards movement is that American education will be improved by creating high academic standards, or benchmarks, to measure students' academic achievement. For example, an empirical measurable goal should be predetermined to indicate whether a student is reading at grade level or has reached a specific level of achievement in mathematics and science. Students are assessed by using standardized tests to determine whether they are achieving at the set standard in the subject, or below or above it. Using statistics based on the performance of students in a given school, that school could be judged to be performing at, above, or below the set standard. Advocates of setting standards and measuring them by standardized tests argue that student performance in a particular school could be used to determine the competency of the teachers and administrators in that school. Progressives and Critical Theorists contend that using standardized tests forces teachers to "teach for the test" rather than to genuinely educate students. Though the debate over standards rages among teachers, the standards movement gained a strong footing in the various states. A very pronounced endorsement of standards came with the enactment of the federal Education Act of 2001, No Child Left Behind.

No Child Left Behind

The No Child Left Behind Act, promoted by President George W. Bush, rested on the premise running through the standards movement—students' academic achievement could be measured by using standardized tests. Schools in which large numbers of students failed to perform at the set standard of achievement could be identified and given remediation designed to improve performance. If this comparative identification of school performance was left undone, children in low-performing schools would be left behind academically. The rationale for the act followed the usual Essentialist–basic education strategy of identifying deficiencies and prescribing measures to correct them. Among the deficiencies identified were:

> Today, nearly 70 percent of inner city fourth graders are unable to read at a basic level on national reading tests. Our high school seniors trail students in Cyprus and South Africa in international math tests. And nearly a third of our college freshmen find they must take a remedial course before they are able to even begin regular college level courses.[30]

Although the act is comprehensive legislation that deals with many areas of education, certain key features, reflecting the standards movement, reinforce a Neo-Essentialist–basic education approach. It identifies the key basics as reading and mathematics and requires that standardized tests be used to determine students' achievement in these essential subjects. The act mandates that school districts, to qualify for federal aid, establish annual assessments in reading and mathematics for every student in grades three through eight. It holds school districts accountable for improving the performance of disadvantaged students as well as the overall student population. Schools and districts failing to make adequate yearly progress are to be identified and remediated. If the schools fail to meet standards for three years, their students may then transfer to a higher performing public or private school.[31]

Essentialism reappeared in the arguments of E. D. Hirsch, Jr., Chester Finn, and Diane Ravitch, who contend that public schools are failing to impart the knowledge needed for cultural and political literacy. For example, E. D. Hirsch, Jr. argues that the average American's declining cultural literacy, the lack of a shared body of common knowledge, is negatively impacting a sense of a national cultural identity and ability to communicate effectively with other Americans. Because the contemporary school curriculum does not deliberately transmit a core to develop cultural literacy, many students complete their formal education without the necessary contextual background that enables them to reference and interpret materials crucial for public communication and for effective functioning in the workplace. A core curriculum designed to promote cultural literacy, Hirsch contends, is needed if citizens are to participate in the institutions and processes of political democracy.[32]

Ravitch argues that schools and teacher education should be intellectual and academic. She contends that some strains of Progressivism contributed to anti-intellectualism in education. In *Left Back,* Ravitch argues that the failure of many educational reforms of the twentieth century can be attributed to Progressive educators who weakened the schools' primary academic function. As they created different curricular tracks for different students, Progressives jeopardized and weakened the schools' mission to provide all students with academic skills and subjects. For her, the true leaders in American education were often-neglected Essentialist educators such as William C. Bagley and Isaac Kandel, rather than Progressives such as William H. Kilpatrick and George S. Counts.[33]

Essentialism and Education, Schooling, Curriculum, and Teaching and Learning

Essentialists share some generalizations about education, schooling, curriculum, and teaching and learning; there are also shades of difference between the various manifestations of the theory in American education. In the next section, we examine some of these general features of Essentialism and basic education.

Education

Although connections can be made between Essentialism and the traditional philosophies of Idealism and Realism, Essentialism's view of the purpose of education is primarily historically based. For Bagley and Bestor, in particular, education is to transmit the liberal arts and sciences from one generation to the next. Beginning with the ancient Greeks and Romans and developed and refined during the Medieval, Renaissance, Reformation, and Enlightenment periods, the liberal arts and sciences represents humankind's repository of humanistic and scientific knowledge. This knowledge has a past and a tradition but it continues to grow as scholars and scientists continue to add to it, refine it, and enlarge it. To enlarge this corpus of knowledge, it is first necessary to know it. This knowledge base is antecedent to us, as the Idealists and Realists argue. It is there for us to learn. It has an intrinsic value that makes it worth knowing. It also, however, has a use or instrumental value in that it can be applied to practice in engineering, medicine and health care, the economy, and technology. It is important that the intrinsic and instrumental values be kept in perspective. We must first learn it before we can apply it. We do not have to keep reinventing it but can use the inheritance that comes from the past. The past, however, is not static but is dynamic. Change in education and society comes through the core of knowledge and not by ignoring or circumventing it.

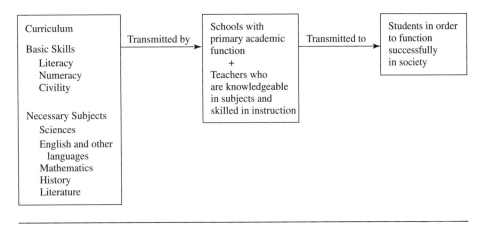

Essentialist Education

The School

Essentialism defines the school as an educational institution whose primary role is to instruct students in well-defined prescribed academic skills and subjects. Essentialists are wedded to two views of the school that Pragmatists and Progressives oppose: transmission and preparation. The school, in particular, is an agency of cultural transmission that passes these essential skills and subjects on as a cultural inheritance from one generation to the next, thereby maintaining the cultural heritage needed in civilized society. It rejects the Liberal and Progressive orientation that the school is a multifunctional institution that performs a variety of social, political, economic, and psychologically therapeutic roles. Essentialists oppose diverting the school's time, resources, and energy away from its academic function.

Essentialists see schooling as an upward movement through institutions beginning with preschool and kindergarten, moving upward through the primary and intermediate grades of the elementary school, through the secondary education of the middle and high school, to the college and university. Each stage is to provide the skills, competencies, and academic subjects—the preparation needed for the next stage. Thus, educational institutions are linked to, or articulated by, each other. Because schooling leads a person to another institution and another set of goals, it is important that the network of institutions, the educational ladder, be articulated in terms of its core, the essential curriculum. In such an arrangement, the higher institution sets many of the goals of the lower ones through it expectations and entry requirements.

Curriculum

Essentialists firmly endorse the subject-matter curriculum in which subjects, also referred to as academic disciplines, are differentiated and organized according to their own internal logical or chronological principles. They are highly suspicious of so-called innovative or process learning approaches such as Constructivism in which students construct or create their own knowledge in a collaborative fashion. Essentialists argue that civilized people learn effectively and efficiently by using the knowledge that has been developed and organized by scientists, scholars, and other experts. There is no need to waste time and resources by "discovering" what is already known. There is no need to continually reinvent the wheel. Curriculum that ignores the past, is interdisciplinary or transdisciplinary, crossing subject-matter boundaries as recommended by Experimentalists, Progressives, and Critical Theorists, results in superficiality: it may purport to be knowledge, yet blurs expertise. Based on the concept that the school has a primary function to perform, the curriculum, too, is very specific to instruction in what is termed the basic skills and subjects. The curriculum's skills and subjects should be well-defined as to scope, have a sequence, be cumulative, and be designed to prepare students for the future. When subjects are related such as in the history of science, it is necessary to be competent first in both history and science.

Scope.   Essentialists are suspicious of education that knows no borders or boundaries. For them, reading and arithmetic are specific skills to be taught in a specific way at a definite time in a child's life. History as an academic subject is defined as a chronological description and interpretation of the human past. Essentialists are suspicious of interdisciplinary methods such as whole language learning, Constructivism, and broad area studies such as language arts and social studies. They believe that for something to be learned it has to be taught. Children will not simply acquire knowledge of arithmetic, history, and geography as concomitant learnings as some Progressives (e.g., Kilpatrick) claimed.

Sequence.   Essentialists believe that instruction in particular skills and subjects is determined largely by the internal logic of that skill or subject. There is an order to be observed in teaching something. For example, the teaching of American history follows a definite chronological order such as (1) encounters between the Native Americans and Europeans; (2) European settlement; (3) the Revolutionary War and struggle for independence; (4) the early national period; (5) the westward-moving frontier; (6) the Civil War and Reconstruction, (7) industrialization and immigration; (8) the Progressive movement; (9) World War I; (10) the Great Depression; (11) World War II; (12) the Cold War; and (13) the new world order characterized by economic globalization and terrorist threats to American security. Sequence also means that instruction in a particular subject area is organized according to its order of complexity, abstraction, and difficulty. For example, mathematics instruction begins with basic arithmetical computation and operations, moves to algebra, then to geometry, and on to calculus and trigonometry. The principle of sequence means that skills and subjects are to be taught according to a definite procedure and not necessarily according to what may currently interest students.

Each subject has its own chronology or logic; it also has a method that is appropriate to it. For example, history uses the historical method. Essentialists are suspicious of the Experimentalist argument that the scientific method can be applied to all experiences. Though they favor critical thinking, they are suspicious of methods that claim that critical thinking is a process that can be separated from subject matter. It is impossible, they say, to think without thinking about something. If we think about something, that something is located in a subject matter.

Cumulative.   For Essentialists, the curriculum is a series of building blocks in which one level is cumulative, that is, it builds on the preceding level and supports the next level. The emphasis on the cumulative is especially important at the skill level. Skills such as reading, writing, and computation are generative; they generate a process that can be used as preparation for the next higher academic level but also can be used throughout life because they transfer to a variety of situations. When related to preparation for the next higher level of education, literary and computation skills are necessary for the learning of content—the subject-matter disciplines. Based on these foundations, students advance onward to other subjects that have a greater complexity and require higher order thinking. The end result is a cumulative effect in which the student attains a repertoire of skills and a body of knowledge that is needed for both further education, for work, and for life.

Teaching and Learning

Going back to Bagley's early Essentialism, we find that teachers are to have a general education in the liberal arts and sciences and a professional education in the foundations of education and in methods of instruction. For example, the teacher of history is to have a content knowledge in history. At the high school level, teachers of history would have had a major in history. Methods of instruction would be geared to how to organize American history, for example, into teachable and learnable units based on the students' prior academic background and readiness. Students might not be interested at first in the subject; however, the teaching of the subject does not depend on students' interest. Hopefully, through their efforts, they will become interested in the subject.

Essentialists such as Bestor (though not Bagley) were much more concerned with knowledge of the content of a subject as sufficient to teach it. If a person knew the subject thoroughly, he or she would deduce how to teach it. Students, regardless of their background and interests, according to Essentialists, all have the same right to learn the necessary skills that will lead them to the liberal arts and sciences.

For both teachers and students it is important to stay on task and to learn the skill and the subject. It is important that they not be diverted into areas that are trivial and anti-intellectual. Although Essentialists recognize that teachers and students have their own political and economic beliefs, they believe that instruction can objectively present contending points of view. Political, economic, and social issues can be explored in terms of subjects that are relevant to them, and yet schools should not endorse particular political, social, and economic ideologies and agendas. They should not be used as agencies of political indoctrination. Further, Essentialists do not believe that schools have it in their power to solve society's problems and ills. What schools can do is to teach students the basic skills and subjects that will prepare them to deal with social, political, and economic problems in the future.

Essentialists are highly suspicious of so-called innovative or process learning approaches, such as Constructivism, in which students construct or create their own knowledge in a collaborative fashion, and in so-called authentic assessment, in which students evaluate their own progress. Essentialists, in contrast, argue that civilized people learn effectively and efficiently by using the knowledge base developed and organized by scientists, scholars, and other experts. We need not continually reinvent the wheel, wasting time and resources by "discovering" what is already known.

Competent teachers always try to stimulate a student's interest, but curriculum content should be based on time-tested experience of the human race. Genuine freedom comes from internalizing the discipline of learning what is needed and staying with the task. Emphasizing teacher-directed instruction, Bagley, for example, argued that children have the right to expect teachers, as trained professionals, to guide and direct their learning.[34] Similar to the Scientific Realists, Essentialists argue that students need to learn about the objective real world rather than misguidedly following the Constructivist view that they should create their own version of reality.

Essentialism's Philosophical and Ideological Relationships

Because Essentialism emphasizes traditional education, it has few friends but many philosophical and ideological adversaries. In this section, we identify and discuss its philosophical and ideological allies and adversaries.

Essentialism's Philosophical and Ideological Allies

Earlier in this book, we encountered the term *essence* in our discussions about the metaphysics of Idealism, Realism, and Thomism, which assert the existence of an underlying ultimate and universal being or nature in reality. They also contend that human beings, by their nature, possess the power to be intelligent, as the Idealists claim, or rational, as the Realists assert. Essentialism, too, as its name indicates, is based on the idea that education has an essence, or essential characteristics. Essentialists agree that the human being, as an intelligent and rational being, is capable of being and, indeed, needs to be educated. For Essentialists, education is to bring the human being into contact with knowledge. Metaphysically, Idealists and Realists assert the existence of an antecedent reality that exists prior to each individual person. However, every person can approach and know this reality, which the Realists assert is the best guide to human conduct. Essentialists, such as Bagley and Bestor, argue that historically there is a corpus of antecedent knowledge, found in the liberal arts and sciences, that constitutes what people need to know to be intelligent and rational. For the traditional philosophies as well as the Essentialists, this knowledge base is organized into subjects, which Bestor called **intellectual disciplines**.

While competent teachers always try to stimulate a student's interest, curriculum content should be based on time-tested experience of the human race. Genuine freedom comes from internalizing the discipline of learning what is needed and staying with the task. Emphasizing teacher-directed instruction, Bagley, for example, argued that children have the right to expect teachers, as trained professionals, to guide and direct their learning.[35] Similar to the Scientific Realists, Essentialists argue that students need to learn about the objective real world rather than misguidedly following the Constructivist view that they should create their own version of reality.

There are similarities and some important differences between Essentialism and Perennialism. (Perennialism is examined in the chapter on Realism.) Associated with Robert Hutchins, Mortimer Adler, and Jacques Maritain, Perennialism is heavily rooted in Realism, especially the philosophies of Aristotle and Thomas Aquinas. Whereas Essentialism is historically based, Perennialism has a metaphysical, or philosophical foundation. Perennialists, like the Realists from which they originate, argue that there is an objective reality that is antecedent to us, but that we can come to know. It further asserts that as rational beings we can use our power of reason to understand, to know, this reality and to base our ethical conduct on its natural laws. Religious Perennialists such as Maritain, guided by Thomas Aquinas, see this reality as spiritual and having natural dimensions that human beings can approach through faith and reason. Because reality is objective, truth about it is also objective; because reality is eternal, truths about it are eternal; and because it is universal, truth, too, is universal and does not depend on contexts and circumstances of time and place. Essentialists and Perennialists agree on the importance of the liberal arts and sciences, but their reasons are somewhat different. For the Essentialists, the liberal arts and sciences have been developed over time, historically, as the best, or most civilized body of thought in Western civilization. For Perennialists, the liberal arts and sciences speak to human beings about a truth that is universal and unchanging. Both Essentialism and Perennialism assert the school's primary function is academic and intellectual and that the curriculum should focus on basic skills and subjects. An important difference, however, is that Perennialists base their arguments on the Aristotelian-Thomistic concept of a rational human nature, whereas Essentialism is more historically than metaphysically grounded. It looks to the past, rather than to human nature, to identify the skills and subjects that have contributed to human survival and civilization.

Contemporary Essentialism, especially the basic education and standards aspects, is closely aligned with the Neo-Conservative ideology. This alignment was not present in the earlier versions developed by Bagley and Bestor, who sought to keep education clear of ideology. Neo-Conservatives and Neo-Essentialists agree that schools should be academic institutions with a well-defined curriculum of basic skills and subjects and that they should cultivate traditional values of patriotism, hard work, effort, punctuality, respect for authority, and civility. They argue that schools and colleges should stress the required core based on Western civilization and traditional American values. Members of the religious right, especially evangelical Protestant fundamentalists, argue that Western and American traditional values are based on Christianity and that the United States is essentially a Christian nation. In addition to the congruence of Neo-Essentialism and Neo-Conservatism on traditional educational principles, they also concur that schools have an important economic role in enhancing U.S. economic productivity in a highly competitive global economy.

Essentialism's Philosophical and Ideological Adversaries

Essentialism meets strong opposition from philosophies such as Pragmatism, Existentialism, and Postmodernism, from ideologies such as Marxism, and from theories such as Progressivism and Critical Theory. Liberals, depending on their type, are somewhat critical of Neo-Essentialism, particularly when it is associated with religious fundamentalism.

Pragmatists, such as Dewey's Experimentalists, find much to oppose in Essentialism, especially its emphasis on antecedent knowledge, on the school as an exclusively academic institution, on subjects as knowledge, and on teaching methods embedded in subject matter. Experimentalists reject the concept that knowledge is antecedent and exists prior to the learner's experience. This conception of knowledge rests on the idea that it is a finished and completed body of knowledge that can be transmitted and learned. Experimentalists see knowledge arising as individuals and groups interact with their environment, necessarily as they solve problems that arise in experience. Experimentalists reject the notion that the school is primarily an academic institution. Like the Essentialist conception of knowledge, they consider the academic definition of a school as too inflexible. Rather, schools are community agencies and, like communities, frequently redefine their functions. Nor do some subjects have an academic character whereas others do not. For the Experimentalist, a subject is a body of tentative findings about an area of human experience such as history, chemistry, or biology that can be approached instrumentally and redefined. It is not necessary to master an entire subject; rather, we can take what we need from it to solve a current problem. Pragmatists oppose the Essentialist assumption that the curriculum can be defined as a priori subjects to which students are led. To them, the curriculum is open-ended, like experience, and grows out of students' needs and interests. An important disagreement relates to methods of instruction. For Essentialists, methods are plural in that they are embedded in and specialized to subjects, such as the historical method or the scientific method. Experimentalists believe that the scientific method is applicable to all areas of problem solving.

Progressives, echoing many of the Pragmatist objections to Essentialism, oppose Essentialism's emphasis on tradition and its neglect of students' needs and interests. Essentialists, such as Bagley and Ravitch, argue that education is based on a traditional historical conception of the liberal arts and sciences and that the school's primary function is academic and intellectual. Progressives resist the authority of tradition, the past, over the changing needs of the present. Kilpatrick, for example, attacked what he called bookish education as ignoring the interests and needs of learners. Whereas Essentialists like Bagley argued that students needed to expend effort to learn what was not immediately interesting or might be difficult, Progressives counter that children's interests are immensely educative in that they might lead anywhere, into new and uncharted expanses of human experience. Essentialists see the teacher as an adult authority figure who teaches skills and transmits subjects to students; Progressives redefine the role of the teacher as a facilitator who guides rather than controls students' learning. Essentialists assert the necessity of a curriculum organized into subjects; Progressives, decrying it as inert information, argue for experience-based learning, especially projects.

Existentialists find much to oppose in Essentialism, which they believe imposes an externally defined rather than a self-constructed education on students. Like Experimentalists, they oppose the Essentialist reliance on a prior or antecedent knowledge as a necessary condition of education. A *necessary condition* for an education means that there is no choice about the matter. Teachers and students need to be free, Existentialists would say, to take what they want from a subject and appropriate it by making it their own. Whereas Essentialists would argue that there are correct or incorrect answers in replying to questions about subjects, Existentialists would not look to external authorities to ascertain the rightness or wrongness of an answer. It is up to students to pose their own questions and construct their own answers. The contemporary Neo-Conservative and Neo-Essentialist emphasis on academic standards and academic testing would raise the ire of Existentialists. For them, standardization reduces the uniqueness of personal experience.

Postmodernists see Essentialism's claims to transmitting civilization via a required curriculum, based on the liberal arts and sciences, to be a dated historical rationale that once ensured the education of favored socioeconomic groups and classes. Indeed, they contend that Essentialists are elevating the scientific, historical, and literary works that compromise the liberal arts and sciences to the status of metanarratives—representations of human culture that are taken out of context and given a totalizing prominence. The liberal arts and sciences are Eurocentric and patriarchal and designed to give educational legitimacy to some ideas but not to others.

Critical Theorists, similar to Postmodernists, find the Essentialist mandate for basic skills and subjects to actually be a guise for reproducing the socioeconomic status quo and locking students into predetermined class-based situations. Although Essentialists such as Bagley and Bestor assumed that what they were advocating was non ideological, Critical Theorists contend that their subject-matter curriculum is based on a Eurocentric and patriarchal ideology that presents knowledge as constructed by white males of European ancestry and ignores the experiences of marginalized groups such as African, Latino, and Native Americans and women. It presents knowledge as something completed by scholars among the elite groups (Bestor's intellectual disciplines), that are to be mastered by students, and that reproduce the status quo. Especially repugnant to Critical Theorists is the contemporary linkage between Neo-Conservatives and Neo-Essentialists, who, in the name of objectivity, impose the standards of the dominant group on all others.

Liberal Neutrality

So far, we have discussed philosophies and ideologies that either support or oppose Essentialism. We now consider Liberalism, which approaches Essentialism, especially its affirmation of the liberal arts and sciences, with some neutrality. The liberal arts and sciences have an important but not exclusive place in education; they form part but not all of the curriculum. There also needs to be room for less-structured, experimental, and process-oriented learning. Is it not possible to have a curriculum with various components? On the other hand, Liberals would reject the contemporary alliance of Neo-Conservatism and Neo-Essentialism as imposing what is too much of a closed rather than an open view of knowledge. They would oppose school prayer and the teaching of Creationism as serious breaches of separation of church and state.

A Reminiscence of Professor Bestor as a Teacher

In my own education, I have had teachers who were Traditionalists and Essentialists and those who were Progressive and Reconstructionists. To illustrate Essentialism, I draw on my memory of Professor Arthur E. Bestor, Jr., as a teacher.[36] As a graduate student in history at the University of Illinois in the late 1950s and early 1960s, I enrolled in two courses offered by Professor Bestor: Historical Methods and American Constitutional History. My memory of Professor Bestor as a teacher illustrates, I think, his theory of education as intellectual disciplines.

Professor Bestor consistently came to these courses meticulously prepared with an antecedent view of what he would teach. The syllabi for the courses were precise and specific and clearly told students his expectations for their work. There were no open spaces in the course where we would put aside the planned sequence to discuss a current event. As a teacher, Professor Bestor stayed on course and expected us to stay with him.

The course on historical methods was designed to prepare us to be historians; it dealt with primary sources and documents and how these sources were to be read, analyzed, and interpreted. Bestor was not a presentist who read the past in terms of the present. Rather, the past needed to be seen as human experience that had occurred in which people were in an actual situation in the
(Continued)

A Reminiscence of Professor Bestor as a Teacher   **(Continued)**

human experience. Part of the course was lectures but another part of it consisted of individual work with primary sources. We were to interpret a set of documents that dealt with the controversy between Robert Owen and William McClure at New Harmony, Indiana, in the early nineteenth century over their financial obligations. Bestor, at the time, was writing what would be an award-winning book, *Backwoods Utopias,* about Robert Owen's community at New Harmony. Later, as I was doing my own research on the educators at New Harmony, I found out that Bestor had undertaken the challenging work of organizing the documents at the site into an archive that he and other scholars could use. Later in my career, I was grateful that he had done his work so well.

Another individual exercise required me to prepare a thesis proposal, with a projected outline and a tentative bibliography. I wrote a proposal for a thesis on George E. Brennan, a rather obscure Illinois Democratic leader in the 1920s. Each student had an individual conference with Dr. Bestor. He critiqued my proposal as not being historically significant (Brennan was a very minor figure) and advised me that the sources were too few to do solid historical analysis. In providing this critique, there was no exchange of pleasantries—no real questions about why I wanted to do this study. The professor stayed on task and criticized the project as a senior experienced historian advising a novice. I dropped my plan. I would later write my doctoral dissertation on George S. Counts, a highly significant educator. I later revised my dissertation into two books on Counts.

While Bestor used lecturing and individual critiques, there was also a field trip in the course.

We went to Springfield, Illinois, the state capital, to visit the state historical archives, where the staff led a tour of the building and the collections. I was excited to see actual documents related to the events of the past, especially to Abraham Lincoln.

Bestor's course on American Constitutional History was done entirely by lecture. He was always meticulously prepared and well organized. The main points of the lecture were consistently clear and presented with sufficient supporting background to establish the context for a particular judicial decision and a perspective on its significance in American law. I do not recall students asking questions or there being discussions. There was a body of knowledge, defined as a subject, that the professor was expert in and transmitted to us.

Professor Bestor left the University of Illinois and I went on to study the history and philosophy of education. Maybe coincidently or perhaps because of my work on the New Harmony project that Bestor had given us, I found myself interested in education at New Harmony. I discovered an educational pioneer by the name of Joseph Neef, who had studied with Pestalozzi and wrote one of the first books on teaching methods to be published in the United States in the early nineteenth century. Early in my career as a historian and philosopher of education, I decided to write a biography of Neef but needed support for travel expenses to use the archive at New Harmony that Bestor had been instrumental in organizing. With some trepidation, I wrote to Dr. Bestor, requesting that he write a letter of support for a grant that I was applying for from the National Humanities Foundation. Bestor wrote the letter of support, I received the grant, and I wrote a book about Joseph Neef.

Conclusion

During its various appearances and under such titles as "the three R's," the Essentialist platform, intellectual disciplines, basic education, the structure of disciplines, and the standards movement, Essentialists have been consistent in defining schools as primarily academic institutions. They have been equally consistent in defining the curriculum as basic skills and subjects. It is important to recognize the core features of this recurring educational theory that has remained rather constant. It is equally important to recognize that Essentialists, in their educational constancy and commitment, see this approach to education as being the most certain path to human survival and civility. Although the social, economic, and political problems may change, the best response for schools, say Essentialists, is to reaffirm and rely on the tried, true, and tested curriculum of basic skills and subjects.

Constructing Your Own Philosophy of Education. As you reflect on constructing your own philosophy of education, what elements of Essentialism appeal to you as a teacher? Which appeal least? Why? Are there elements of Essentialism that you plan to incorporate into your philosophy?

Questions for Reflection and Discussion

1. Define Essentialism and indicate how it applies to the contemporary school and curriculum.

2. Does the standards movement reflect an Essentialist or basic education point of view?

3. Reflect on your own educational experience. Do you find evidence of an Essentialist or basic education orientation?

4. Of the philosophies and ideologies examined in this book, which is most compatible and which is least compatible with Essentialism?

5. How much of your formal education has been based on the doctrine of preparation?

6. Do you think that the contemporary standards movement and the use of standardized tests resonates well with Essentialism?

7. Do you find much evidence of Essentialism in your teacher education program?

8. Essentialists often claim that teacher education programs are biased against their view of the purpose of the school and curriculum content and organization. Do you agree or disagree with this Essentialist contention? Why?

Topics for Inquiry and Research

1. In the classrooms and teachers observed in your clinical experience, do you find evidence of Essentialism?

2. Make a list of the skills and subjects that you think are essential or necessary to a sound education. Does your list agree with the Essentialist position?

3. Debate the proposition: True equality requires all students to enroll in the same curriculum.

4. Review several textbooks used in your teacher education program. Do they support or reject Essentialist educational principles?

5. If you have taken a course in educational methods, reflect on the course and conjecture how an Essentialist might react to it.

6. Identify several innovative approaches to education that are emphasized in your teacher education program. Critique them from an Essentialist perspective.

Building an Essentialist Vocabulary

Antecedent Knowledge: subjects that exist prior to a student's learning of them; knowledge is already there to be learned and not constructed.

Basic Education: a revived form of Essentialism that calls for a return to the basic skills and subjects.

Essentialism: a term coined by the educational philosopher, Michael Demiashkevich, that asserts education's primary mission is transmitting the civilized cultural heritage by teaching essential subjects such as mathematics, natural sciences, and history.

Essentialist Curriculum: reading, writing, listening, and composition in elementary schools; academic subjects—mathematics, history, sciences, languages and literature, geography, and civics—at the secondary level.

Intellectual Discipline: Arthur Bestor's argument that the curriculum should consist of the fundamental disciplines, historically developed in Western culture.

Life Adjustment Education: curriculum that is based on students' practical and immediate interests, needs, issues, and problems that leads to a satisfactory adjustment to living and working.

Scope: the boundaries that mark off one subject from another.

Sequence: instruction largely by the internal logic of a skill or subject that is taught in an orderly fashion.

Standards Movement: creating high academic standards, or benchmarks, to measure students' academic achievement.

Transmission: instruction that deliberately transmits, passes along, essential skills and subjects from one generation to the next, thereby maintaining civilized and literate society.

Internet Resources

Consult the Council for Basic Education Web site at www.c-b-e.org and examine the council's educational philosophy.

For standards and accountability in the No Child Left Behind Act, consult the U.S. Department of Education at www.ed.gov/inits/nclb/part3.html.

Suggestions for Further Reading

Bagley, William C. *Education and Emergent Man: A Theory of Education With Particular Application to Public Education in the United States.* New York: Thomas Nelson, 1934.

Bestor, Arthur E., Jr. *Educational Wastelands: Retreat from Learning in Our Public Schools.* Urbana: University of Illinois Press, 1953.

Bestor, Arthur E., Jr. *The Restoration of Learning: A Program for Redeeming the Unfulfilled Promise of American Education.* New York: Alfred A. Knopf, 1956.

Bunzel, John H., ed. *Challenge to American Schools: The Case for Standards and Values.* New York: Oxford University Press, 1985.

Gutek, Gerald L. *Basic Education: A Historical Perspective.* Bloomington, IN: Phi Delta Kappa Educational Foundation, 1981.

Hirsch, E. D., Jr. *Cultural Literacy: What Every American Needs to Know.* Boston: Houghton Mifflin, 1987.

Hirsch, E. D. *The Schools We Need.* New York: Anchor, 1996.

Kandel, Isaac L. *The Cult of Uncertainty.* New York: Macmillan, 1934.

Kandel, Isaac L. *William Chandler Bagley: Stalwart Educator.* New York: Teachers College Press, 1961.

National Commission on Excellence in Education. *A Nation at Risk: The Imperative for Educational Reform.* Washington, DC: U.S. Government Printing Office, 1983.

Null, J. Wesley. *A Disciplined Progressive Educator: The Life and Career of William Chandler Bagley.* New York: Peter Lang, 2003.

Null, J. Wesley. *Peerless Educator: The Life and Work of Isaac Leon Kandel.* New York: Peter Lang, 2007.

Null, J. Wesley, and Diane Ravitch, eds. *Forgotten Heroes of American Education: The Great Tradition of Teaching Teachers.* Greenwich: Information Age, 2006.

Ravitch, Diane. *Left Back: A Century of Failed School Reform.* New York: Simon and Schuster, 2000.

Ravitch, Diane, and Chester E. Finn, Jr. *What Do Our 17-Year-Olds Know? A Report on the First National Assessment of History and Literature.* New York: Harper & Row, 1987.

Ravitch, Diane, and Joseph P. Viteritti. *Making Good Citizens: Education and Civil Society.* New Haven, CT: Yale University Press, 2001.

Rickover, H. G. *American Education—A National Failure.* New York: E. P. Dutton and Co., 1963.

Rickover, H. G. *Education and Freedom.* New York: E. P. Dutton and Co., 1959.

Rickover, H. G. *Swiss Schools and Ours: Why Theirs Are Better.* Boston: Atlantic-Little, Brown and Co., 1962.

Endnotes

1. Diane Ravitch, *Left Back: A Century of Failed School Reforms* (New York: Simon and Schuster, 2000), pp. 293–294.

2. Clifton Fadiman, "The Case for Basic Education," in James D. Koerner, ed., *The Case for Basic Education* (Boston: Little, Brown, 1959), pp. 5–6.

3. J. Wesley Null, *A Disciplined Progressive Educator: The Life and Career of William Chandler Bagley* (New York: Peter Lang, 2003), p. xi.

4. For a biography of Kandel, see J. Wesley Null, *Peerless Educator: The Life and Work of Isaac Leon Kandel* (New York: Peter Lang, 2007).

5. William C. Bagley, "An Essentialist Platform for the Advancement of American Education," *Educational Administration and Supervision,* (April 1938), pp. 241–256.

6. Adolphe E. Meyer, *The Development of Education in the Twentieth Century* (Englewood Cliffs, NJ: Prentice Hall, 1949), p. 149.

7. Bagley, "Essentialist Platform," p. 254.

8. Diane Ravitch, *Left Back: A Century of Failed School Reforms* (New York: Simon and Schuster, 2000), p. 121.

9. William C. Bagley, "What is the Crux of the Conflict Between the Progressives and Essentialists?" *Educational Administration and Supervision,* 26 (1940), pp. 508–511.

10. Bagley, "What is the Crux of the Conflict Between the Progressives and Essentialists?", pp. 508–509.

11. See J. Wesley Null and Diane Ravitch, *Forgotten Heroes of American Education: The Great Tradition of Teaching Teachers* (Greenwich, CT: Information Age, 2006) and Diane Ravitch, *Left Back: A Century of Failed School Reforms* (New York: Simon and Schuster, 2000).

12. Clay Blair, Jr., *The Atomic Submarine and Admiral Rickover* (New York: Henry Holt and Co., 1954).

13. Hyman G. Rickover, *Education and Freedom* (New York: E. P. Dutton and Co., 1959), p. 131.

14. Hyman G. Rickover, *American Education—A National Failure* (New York: E. P. Dutton and Co., 1963).

15. Arthur E. Bestor, Jr., *Educational Wastelands: The Retreat from Learning in Our Public Schools* (Urbana: University of Illinois Press, 1953) and *The Restoration of Learning: A Program for Redeeming the Unfulfilled Promise of American Education* (New York: Alfred A. Knopf, 1955).

16. Bestor, *The Restoration of Learning,* pp. 3–4.

17. Bestor, *The Restoration of Learning,* p. 7.

18. Bestor, *The Restoration of Learning,* pp. 50–51.

19. Bestor, *The Restoration of Learning,* pp. 50–51.

20. Bestor, *The Restoration of Learning,* p. 358.

21. Bestor, *The Restoration of Learning,* pp. 364–365.

22. National Commission on Excellence in Education, *A Nation at Risk: The Imperative for Educational Reform* (Washington, DC: U.S. Department of Education, 1983), p. 5.

23. National Commission on Excellence in Education, *A Nation at Risk,* p. 18.

24. National Commission on Excellence in Education, *A Nation at Risk,* p. 20.

25. National Commission on Excellence in Education, *A Nation at Risk,* p. 22.

26. National Commission on Excellence in Education, *A Nation at Risk,* p. 24.

27. National Commission on Excellence in Education, *A Nation at Risk,* p. 27.

28. The College Board, *Academic Preparation for College: What Students Need to Know and Be Able to Do* (New York: The College Board, 1983), pp. 7–11.

29. The College Board, *Academic Preparation for College,* p. 13.

30. No Child Left Behind (Washington, DC: U.S. Printing Office, 2001), p. 1.

31. No Child Left Behind, pp. 8–9.

32. E. D. Hirsch, Jr., *Cultural Literacy: What Every American Needs to Know* (Boston: Houghton Mifflin, 1987).

33. Ravitch, *Left Back: A Century of Failed School Reforms,* pp. 15–18, 465–467.

34. J. Wesley Null, "Social Reconstruction with a Purpose: The Forgotten Tradition of William Bagley," in Karen Riley, ed., *Social Reconstruction: People, Politics, Perspectives* (Greenwich, CN: Information Age, 2006), pp. 27–44.

35. Null, "Social Reconstruction with a Purpose," pp. 27–44.

36. My memories of Arthur E. Bestor, Jr., as a teacher were stimulated by Dr. J. Wesley Null, the biographer of William Bagley, who asked me in a conversation at a meeting of the Midwest History of Education, in October 2007, about my classes with Bestor at the University of Illinois.

14

Progressivism and Education

Students with Marietta Johnson (1864–1938), a leading Progressive, at the School of Organic Education at Fairhope, Alabama.

Chapter Preview

Progressivism is a significant ideology, especially in the American experience, that promotes social and educational change and reform. Progressivism affirms the belief in "Progress," the possibility that human life and social institutions can be improved. We discuss Progressive education's origins in the Enlightenment, especially with the ideas of Jean-Jacques Rousseau, and then position Progressive education in the context of the Progressive movement in the American experience. After describing William H. Kilpatrick's project method as an expression of Progressive education, we identify and analyze Progressivism's implications for education, schooling, curriculum, and teaching and learning. The following topics are examined in the chapter:

- The origins of Progressivism in Rousseau's naturalism and in the Progressive movement in the American experience
- The Progressive education movement and internal divisions within Progressive education
- William H. Kilpatrick's project method
- Progressivism's implications for education, schools, curriculum, and teaching and learning
- Progressivism's philosophical and ideological relationships

As you read the chapter and reflect on constructing your own philosophy of education, does Progressivism appeal to you as a teacher? Do you find evidence of Progressivism in your own education? Do you plan to use it in constructing your own philosophy of education?

Origins of Progressivism

In this section, we trace the origins of Progressivism and Progressive education. First, we examine the European origins of Progressive education by analyzing the ideas of Jean-Jacques Rousseau and then consider how the Progressive movement shaped the context of American Progressive education.

Rousseau and Progressivism's European Origins

Progressive education's origins can be traced back to the **Enlightenment**, know as the Age of Reason. Enlightenment philosophers, known as the *philosophes* in France, challenged the theological doctrines of Christianity that saw children, because of Adam and Eve's original sin, as born as either spiritually depraved or deprived. The *philosophes* challenged the idea that schooling was seen as a remedy to exorcise children's instinctive inclinations to disorderliness, disobedience, and incivility.

Naturalism. Although the *philosophes* challenged such Christian theological doctrines as original sin, they continued to look to a Higher Power that set the universe in operation. They generally subscribed to a Deist rather than a theist view of the origin of life. For them, God created human beings with the power to reason and left it to them to work out their own destiny. In place of supernaturalism, the Enlightenment philosophers set forth ideas about nature and the natural workings of the universe. They developed what could be called a naturalist concept of the universe's design that also explained how the world worked. The Enlightenment era saw theorists looking to nature to find clues on how life should be lived.

Education was important because, in the minds of the Enlightenment philosophers, it prepared people to live according to nature's principles.

The concept of the scientific method held by the *philosophes* was not that of modern evolutionary and relativistic science; in fact, they did not move far away from Aristotle's ideas about science. However, the *philosophes* rejected learning about science by reading the ancient Greek and Roman texts about it. For them, the scientific method was an objective, systematic, and careful way of observing natural phenomena. Through careful and consistent observation, it was possible to discern the laws or principles that made the universe work, such as the patterns of the revolution of the planets around the sun, the rotation of the earth, the growth of plants, and the circulation of the blood in the body. The idea that children learned by observing and reflecting on the natural and social environments in which they lived, rather than from books, became a consistent theme in child-centered American Progressive education. American Progressive educators would emphasize the role of the senses in learning. Children would learn most effectively and efficiently by using their senses in observing and experiencing the natural objects of their environment.

French *philosophes* such as Rousseau saw children as inherently good, not evil, at birth and possessing instincts that needed to be followed so that they could grow and develop. Their strategy to improve the human situation was to use science to discover the natural laws, the general operating principles about how the universe functioned, and to use them to reform social, political, economic, and educational institutions. Embracing the ideal of **Progress**, the Enlightenment thinkers projected a better future if the human power to reason and to use science was liberated and used for reform. Freedom of thought meant that human beings needed to be liberated from arbitrary, authoritarian, and absolutist restrictions placed on their minds by the church and the state. From the Enlightenment theorists came four important principles that influenced the later Progressives: (1) children are naturally good and their instincts and needs should guide education; (2) human growth and development is a natural process; (3) people can use their intelligence, especially the scientific method, to solve problems and reform society; and (4) humankind's future can be progressively better than its past.

Jean-Jacques Rousseau's Naturalism

Jean-Jacques Rousseau's (1712–1778) writings generated a major change in thinking about childhood and education that helped to shape child-centered Progressive education. Rousseau's ideas were an amalgamation of naturalism, romanticism, and science that, though not always integrated, provided a point of departure for later American Progressive educators.[1] Rousseau's didactic novel, *Emile*, became a guidebook for many child-centered Progressives.[2]

Rousseau's own childhood experiences shaped many of his ideas on education, which, in turn, he integrated into the Enlightenment's general ideology. The son of Suzanne Bernard and Isaac Rousseau, a watchmaker, Jean-Jacques was born in Geneva, Switzerland, the city where John Calvin once preached the doctrines of the Protestant Reformation. Rousseau's mother died when he was nine days old. Like him, his fictional character, Emile, was also an orphan, but a wealthy boy, not poor like Rousseau. In reflecting on his own childhood, Rousseau claimed that he was overindulged by his highly emotional, impulsive aunt and his irresponsible, pleasure-loving father.[3] Rousseau recalled his father, his first tutor, read books to him that he did not understand or that filled his mind with vague mystical thoughts. In *Emile,* Rousseau warned against introducing books too early in the child's life. It is better for children to enjoy direct experiences of their immediate environment before reading about abstract concepts about which they know little or nothing. Rousseau's admonitions about the importance of direct experience and interaction with the environment and delaying reading were important themes that influenced American Progressive educators.

In 1739, when he was twenty-seven, Rousseau served as a tutor to the two sons of M. de Mably. He wrote about his experience as tutor in his first treatise on education, the *Project of the Education of M. de Sainte-Marie.* In 1741, Rousseau went to Paris, the intellectual center of Europe's Enlightenment. In Paris, Rousseau entered into a relationship with Therese Levasseur, an illiterate maid. They had five children, all of whom Rousseau, their father, placed in orphanages shortly after their births. Readers of Rousseau's *Emile* find it ironic that Rousseau, an early proponent of child permissiveness, abandoned his own children.[4]

In 1749, Rousseau established himself as a *philosophe* with his award-winning essay, "Has the Progress of the Arts and Sciences Contributed More to the Corruption or Purification of Morals?"[5] Rousseau attacked the traditional view, still endorsed by Essentialists and Perennialists, that the arts and sciences as the repository of Western wisdom should be transmitted in schools. In contrast, Rousseau argued the arts and sciences tended to corrupt rather than liberate. His attack on the arts and sciences as the corpus of education differed from the view of Essentialists such as William C. Bagley and Arthur Bestor, Jr.

Rousseau's major political work, *The Social Contract,* was published in 1762, the same year that *Emile* appeared. On July 2, 1778, Rousseau died of uremia at Ermenonville, some thirty miles from Paris. He was buried on the Girardin estate. On October 11, 1794, his remains were transferred to the Pantheon in Paris.

Emile

Rousseau's *Emile, or* On *Education,* begins with "Everything is good as it comes from the hands of the Maker of the world but degenerates once it gets into the hands of man." For Rousseau, children are not born evil but rather are intrinsically good by their nature. It is an artificial miseducation that harms them. Children are not born as cheats, thieves, and liars but rather learn these vices from corruptive adults. Children's intrinsic natural goodness is spoiled by corrupting adults and their social institutions, including schools.

For Rousseau, the educational challenge is to educate Emile in a natural environment where his naturally benevolent instincts can develop freely without being intruded on by the outside corruptive society. In an environment where he is free to develop, Emile can construct his self-identity through self-esteem, or **amour de soi**. Rousseau contrasts **amour de soi** with **amour propre**, or selfishness, by which a person learns to manipulate others for his or her own purposes.

Child-centered Progressives, influenced by Rousseau, encourage children to follow their own instincts and to construct their own strategies for exploring the environment. This natural process is far better, they assert, than using schools to impose adult standards and behaviors on them—which usually means curbing their own inclinations so that they can be taught to play adult-designed roles.

Rousseau's novel recounts how a tutor educates a well-to-do orphan, Emile, in a natural setting, a rural estate. This natural environment contrasts with conventional schools where the preestablished curriculum focuses on reading, writing, arithmetic and subjects such as history, geography, and science, taught from reading books and memorizing and reciting their contents. Drawing on Rousseau, child-centered Progressives sought to replace the traditional school classroom with a more open, flexible, unhurried, and unscheduled environment.

Rousseau's Stages of Development.   In this natural environment, the tutor is determined to guide Emile to the experiences that are appropriate to his interests and readiness at a particular stage of development. Rousseau's concept of human beings proceeding through natural **stages of development** is particularly important for Progressives. Rather than preparing children to learn the socioeconomic roles for their adult life, Rousseau turned to nature, especially child nature, to identify the stages of development through which children pass as they move from infancy to adulthood. In the human life span, individuals are born, proceed through infancy and childhood, come to maturity, reach old age, and eventually die. For each stage of development, there are appropriate experiences and activities based on the particular development stage.

Rousseau identifies infancy as the earliest stage of human life. The period is a long one, starting at birth and extending until the child is five years old. Diet, exercise, and freedom to explore the environment are important so that Emile can grow into a physically healthy and mentally curious child. During infancy, the child, like an unspoiled primitive person, is very close to the state of nature. The child's behavior is simple, unaffected, and natural. It is important to preserve these simple and honest early behaviors so that they can grow into a natural adult character.[6]

Rousseau's elongated period of childhood is markedly different from the contemporary pushing and rushing of young children into academic activities as early as preschool and kindergarten. Progressive educators, especially Marietta Johnson, warned against the hurried and premature forcing of children into studies for which they were unready.

Rousseau's second stage is boyhood, from age six through twelve. Increasingly conscious that some activities cause pleasure and others pain, Emile now constructs his own self-identity and develops his earliest moral feelings. Rousseau develops two concepts of moral development: ***amour de soi*** and ***amour propre***. Arising from a person's natural instinctive self-interests, *amour de soi* is the basis of healthy natural values. *Amour propre,* in contrast, is socially rather than naturally derived and causes the person to play roles and manipulate other people for self-aggrandizement.[7]

In arguing that values arise naturally rather than being forced on children, Rousseau warns against the futility of preaching to children about what is right or wrong. It is more important that Emile learn that his actions have consequences. Some actions bring pleasure and others pain. Again, Rousseau's ideas on moral education have influenced Progressive education. For example, Dewey saw genuine's thinking and valuing taking place when the child begins to step back and reflect on the consequences of action. Other Progressives warned that talking about morality or taking a paper-and-pencil test about ethics are very different from being a moral and ethical person.

Rousseau warns of the "youthful sage," the highly verbal and seemingly precocious child who can spout off bits of memorized information without really understanding it. Such children adjust their behavior to earn adult praise. Their behavior is artificial rather than natural.

Rousseau continues to advise against introducing books too early in the child's life. Children should not be pressured into reading. Emile will read when he is ready and wants to read. Emile, like a young scientist, uses and strengthens his powers of observation as he observes the objects in the environment and learns to estimate their size, shape, and dimensions.

Rousseau's second stage corresponds to the years when many children attend elementary schools. Several of Rousseau's ideas are present in how Progressive teachers organize instruction. Rousseau's admonitions that children should engage in **sensory learning**, actively using their senses in direct explorations and observations of the environment, are an early version of Constructivism. Marietta Johnson featured nature walks, unstructured field trips in which the teacher did not have a set agenda but was free to discuss anything that interested the children. Progressives believe that the most effective learning takes place when children learn directly by constructing their knowledge about reality. Still another Progressive strategy of extending the child's environment is the field trip—to arboretums, zoos, botanical gardens, museums, and other sites—where children can learn through exploration.

Rousseau's third stage, from age twelve through fifteen, is when education focuses on learning about the instrumental aspects of experience and cause–effect relationships.[8] Continuing his explorations of the natural environment, Emile, still the young natural scientist, asks the tutor questions about what he observes, wanting to know why something happens and how one event causes another. Why does the sun rise and set? Why do trees lose their leaves in the fall and sprout new ones in the spring? Why does water run downhill rather than uphill? It is important that the questions be Emile's and not the tutor's. Emile creates his own maps to make his own guide to his surroundings. He also learns a manual skill, such as carpentry, to learn the correct combination of mental and physical labor. Emile, now interested in reading, breaks into the skill. His first book, *Robinson Crusoe,* tells how Crusoe, marooned on a tropical island, learns to survive by living off the land. Emile learns about the concept of mutual dependence that arises between Crusoe and Friday, another person who comes to the island.

Emile's next stage is the years between fifteen and eighteen.[9] Emile is now interested in sex and has many questions that the tutor answers directly, without embarrassment, coarseness, or mystery. Emile is also developing a social awareness about the needs of other people. In developing a sense of social justice, Emile builds on the early natural instincts of his childhood. Moral education, for Rousseau, does not come from preaching about avoiding what is evil or from speculating in an abstract sense about ethical dilemmas. It is acquired naturally through interactions with the environment, especially learning that what one does will have an effect.

Rousseau calls the next stage, from eighteen to twenty, the "age of humanity." Having enjoyed a natural childhood and adolescence, Emile is ready to explore the broader world of culture, art, music, and literature. When he is twenty, Emile has reached adulthood. He meets and falls in love with his future bride, Sophie, the future mother of a natural family. Emile and

Sophie's family will begin a new natural society. At the book's conclusion, Emile promises that he will educate his children according to nature, just as he was educated.

Child-centered Progressives, inspired by Rousseau, see childhood as a very important phase of human growth and development. Rousseau's *Emile* inspired child-centered Progressives with a strong commitment to permissiveness that encouraged children to follow their needs and interests as far as possible.

Rousseau made a very clear statement about the importance of education being appropriate to a child's stage of development and readiness. Readiness became a major theme in Progressive education. It was an admonition against shortening childhood by pushing children into academic learning for which they were not developmentally ready. For example, Progressive educator Marietta Johnson argued that prolonging childhood is necessary for human progress, especially as society becomes more technologically complex.[10] Using this premise, she saw children as growing individuals who needed to follow their own internal timetables rather than adults' scheduling.

The Progressive Movement and Progressive Education

In addition to European antecedents, especially Rousseau's educational ideas, Progressive education was part of a broad social and political movement in the United States from 1880 to 1920. Focused on reforming American society, its aims were social, political, economic, and educational. This period simply sets the stage for the appearance of Progressivism, whose influence continues in American society and education today.

Progressivism was rooted in the spirit of social reform that gripped the early twentieth-century **Progressive movement** in U.S. politics. As a sociopolitical movement, Progressivism held that human society could be refashioned by political reforms. Such U.S. political programs as Woodrow Wilson's "New Freedom," Theodore Roosevelt's "New Nationalism," and Robert LaFollette's "Wisconsin Idea," although varied in particulars, shared the common concern that the emerging corporate society should be ordered to function democratically for the benefit of all Americans. The leaders in Progressive politics represented what was essentially the middle-class orientation to reform characterized by gradual change through legislation and peaceful social innovation through education.

In education, Progressive educators redefined the concepts of childhood and adolescence in ways that contributed to the reforming of education and schools. Reacting against the prim and proper Victorian dictum that "children should be seen but not heard," Progressive educators wanted children to have more open, free, and liberating educational experiences than they themselves had had. They viewed with disdain how the childhoods of working-class children in the cities and farm children in rural areas had been shortened by abruptly putting them to work as soon as they could legally leave school. Like Rousseau, they wanted to enlarge the time and experiences of childhood.

Progressive educators developed an American version of adolescence, the teenage years. Using the concept of stages of development, Progressives constructed an interval of growth that allowed time between childhood and entry into the adult workforce. Progressive educators, constructing a scientific rationale for adolescence, looked to the educational psychologist G. Stanley Hall, who had researched and published his findings and opinions in *Adolescence* (1904). Hall identified adolescence as a crucial period of human development, in which adolescents recapitulated the movement of the human race from primitive to civilized life. Progressive educators sought to restructure the traditional academic high school into a new kind of institution that reflected the research on adolescence.

Along with child and adolescent psychology, Progressive educators eagerly used the philosophical rationale provided by John Dewey's Experimentalism. (Dewey's Experimentalism is discussed elsewhere in the book; attention here is given to its impact on Progressivism). From 1896 to 1904, Dewey conducted an experimental "Laboratory" school at the University of Chicago, where he tested his Experimentalist ideas on education by putting them into practice. Progressive educators eagerly accepted the idea that a school should be like a laboratory where ideas about education could be tried. Dewey's other books of the Progressive era, *The School and Society* and *The Child and the Curriculum*, were widely read by Progressive educators. From Dewey, Progressives believed that the schools of the future should be multifunctional community centers, where the curriculum originated with children's direct experiences and then extended into society's larger issues and concerns. Opposing the imposition of adult aims on education, Progressives were keen to accept Dewey's view that education's sole aim was human growth, an ever broadening human experience.

Progressive Education Association

In 1919, Progressive private and public school educators and professors of education organized the **Progressive Education Association** (PEA), with John Dewey as the association's honorary president. The association's journal, *Progressive Education,* disseminated articles about educational reforms and innovative programs across the country.[11]

The association stressed the following principles: (1) Progressive education should provide the freedom to encourage the child's natural development and growth through activities that cultivated his or her initiative, creativity, and self-expression; (2) all instruction should be guided by the child's own interest, stimulated by contact with the real world; (3) the Progressive teacher is to guide the child's learning as a director of research activities, rather than as a taskmaster; (4) student achievement is to be measured in terms of mental, physical, moral, and social development; (5) there should be greater cooperation among the teacher, the school, and the home and family in meeting the child's needs for growth and development; (6) the truly Progressive school should be a laboratory in innovative practices.

Although they came in many varieties and had multiple goals, Progressives united in opposing traditional book-centered, teacher-dominated instruction. For them, the child should be the focus of classroom activity with instruction arising from children's interests and needs rather than externally imposed goals. Teachers, in such situations, should be directors of research and inquiry, who established learning environments conducive to children's growth and development. Though Progressives agreed in their opposition to traditional school practices, they disagreed on the nature of and degree of children's freedom.

Dewey himself, in *Experience and Education,* challenged the notion of making children's freedom into an educational absolute divorced from society.[12]

Progressive educators generally had a three-pronged agenda: (1) to remove the formalism, routine, and bureaucracy that devitalized learning in many schools; (2) to devise and implement innovative methods of instruction that focused on children's needs and interests; and (3) to professionalize teaching and school administration to make it more competent, efficient, and scientific. Progressive educators pioneered new methods of education such as "learning by doing," activity-based learning, group projects, and problem solving. Contemporary innovations such as Constructivism and process-based learning are latter-day versions of Progressive education.

Internal Divisions within Progressive Education

Though united in opposing traditional schooling, Progressive educators split into two factions: child-centered and Social Reconstructionist educators. Child-centered Progressives saw the child as education's vital focus. For them, the curriculum grew out of the individual child's interests and needs rather than being imposed as the prescribed, preestablished skills and subjects of the traditional curriculum. Child-centered Progressives, such as Marietta Johnson (1864–1938), the founder of **Organic Philosophy of Education**, epitomized child-centered Progressive education in which learning revolved around children's needs and interests. They believed that children, free from arbitrary rules, should be at liberty to pursue their own interests. Through their own self-initiated activity, children, guided by permissive and encouraging teachers, were to explore their environment and thereby enlarge their horizons of space and time.

Like the child-centered Progressives, the **Social Reconstructionists** opposed traditional schooling's formalism, routines, and authoritarian tendencies. Seeing education as a politically charged process, Reconstructionists wanted schools used as agencies for deliberately directed social, political, and economic reform.[13] Reconstructionists such as George Counts, Harold Rugg, and Theodore Brameld sought to forge Progressive education into an ideological weapon to create a new society.[14] (The discussion of Social Reconstruction is condensed here as it is examined in the next chapter.)

The child-centered and Reconstructionist Progressives disagreed on the degree to which schools and teachers should deliberately attempt to direct social and political change. Some child-centered educators feared the Reconstructionist agenda was so politically motivated that it would lead to students' indoctrination. The Reconstructionists, in contrast, argued that Progressive educators, by not taking a stand on the major political and economic issues, were reinforcing the status quo. These variations among the Progressives gave the movement vitality; it also contained the seeds of internal divisions and conflicts. Though Progressives could agree on what they opposed, they sometimes disagreed on what they proposed.

Dewey's Critique of Progressive Education

Although John Dewey's Experimentalism has been discussed elsewhere in this book, his Progressive educational position is made clear by Dewey's critique of the movement in *Experience and Education.*

Sources   Tensions

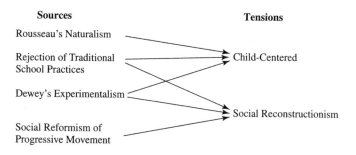

Sources and Tensions in Progressive Education

___

Dewey warned that the controversy between traditional and Progressive educators had degenerated into an assertion of either/or positions. Although sympathetic to Progressivism, Dewey believed that many Progressives were merely reacting against traditional school practices and had failed to formulate an educational philosophy capable of serving as a plan of pragmatic operations.

Dewey's analysis of the traditional and the Progressive school highlights the contrasts between these two institutions. The traditional school, he said, is a formal institution that emphasizes a subject-matter curriculum composed of discretely organized disciplines, such as language, history, mathematics, and science. Traditionalists, such as Perennialists and Essentialists, hold that the source of wisdom is located in humanity's cultural heritage. Morals, standards, and conduct are derived from tradition and are not subject to the test of the scientific method. The traditional teacher regards the written word as the font of wisdom and relies on the textbook as the source of knowledge and the recitation as the means of eliciting it from students. Traditionalists isolate the school from social controversies. Holding to their belief that learning is the transmission and mastery of bodies of knowledge inherited from the past, the traditionalists ignore the learner's own needs and interests and neglect urgent social and political issues. The products of conventional education (namely, the students) are expected to be receptive to the traditional wisdom, have habits and attitudes conducive to conformity, and be respectful of and obedient to authority.

Although Dewey shared the Progressive antagonism toward the traditional school, he feared that many Progressives were merely reacting against it. Too many Progressives had ignored the past and were concerned only with the present. In their opposition to the traditional school's passivity, some Progressives had come to emphasize any kind of activity, even purposeless activity. Many Progressives had become so antagonistic to education imposed by adults that they had begun to cater to childish whims, many of which were devoid of social and intellectual value.

After urging that Progressive educators avoid the polarization of an either/or educational position, Dewey outlined the philosophy that he believed was suited for the genuinely Progressive school. Progressive education needed a philosophy based on experience, the interaction of the person with the environment. Such an experiential philosophy was to have no set of external goals. Rather, the end product of education is growth—that ongoing experience that leads to the direction and control of subsequent experience.

Truly Progressive education should not ignore the past but rather should use it to reconstruct experience in the present and direct future experiences. For Dewey, education should be based on a continuum of ongoing experience that unites the past and the present and leads to the shaping of the future.

Dewey also warned that Progressive education should not become so absorbed in activity that it misconstrued the nature of activity. Mere movement is without value. Activity should be directed to solving problems; it should be purposeful and should contain social and intellectual possibilities that contribute to the learner's growth.

The true Progressive educator is a teacher skilled in relating the learner's internal conditions of experience—that is, the student's needs, interests, purposes, capacities, and desires—with the objective conditions of experience—the environmental factors that are historical, physical, economic, and sociological.

Dewey asserted that Progressivism should be free from a naive romanticization of child nature. Although children's interests and needs are always at the beginning of learning, they are not its end. The child's instincts and impulses need to be refined and developed into reflective social intelligence. Some impulses contain possibilities for growth and development; other impulses have the opposite result in that their consequences impede growth. Impulse became reflective when the learner is able to estimate the consequences of acting on it. By developing an "end-in-view," the learner could conjecture the consequences that would result from action. Understanding the purpose of a particular act involves estimating the consequences that had occurred in similar situations in the past and forming a tentative judgment about the likely consequences of acting in the present. Thus, Progressive education should encourage the cultivation of purposeful, reflective patterns of inquiry in the learner.

Challenging Essentialism and Perennialism, Dewey warned educators against trying to "return to the intellectual methods and ideals that arose centuries before scientific method was developed." Truly Progressive educators would seek systematically to utilize the "scientific method as the pattern and ideal of intelligent exploration and exploitation of the potentialities inherent in experience."

William Heard Kilpatrick and the Project Method

As a teacher and school principal in rural Georgia, William Heard Kilpatrick (1871–1965) had devised his own version of Progressive education as a reaction against traditional school practices. Kilpatrick's efforts to construct his own philosophy of education illustrate how theory is constructed from practice. (Refer to the chapter on theory, especially the section that discusses theory arising from experience.) Kilpatrick believed that genuine learning came from children's own interests in a relaxed and informal educational environment. Rather than sitting quietly at their desks as they waited for the teacher to call on them to recite a memorized lesson, students should be free to move about the classroom and collaboratively share their ideas. He replaced traditional report cards with monthly written progress reports.[15] He emphasized internal rather than external discipline.

Determined to make the study of education his career, Kilpatrick entered Teachers College at Columbia University in New York City for his doctoral study. Here he encountered

John Dewey and his Experimentalist philosophy. Kilpatrick was open to Dewey's emphasis on learning as problem solving according to the scientific method and his rejection of a priori absolutes that limited thinking. His study with Dewey, Kilpatrick said, "remade my philosophy of life and education." Dewey, in turn, praised Kilpatrick as his best student.[16]

In 1909, Kilpatrick joined the Teachers College faculty as a part-time lecturer in the history of education. In 1910, he received a full-time appointment and on January 11, 1911, successfully defended his doctoral dissertation on the Dutch schools of early New York. Until his retirement, Kilpatrick taught at Teachers College, earning the title of the "million dollar professor" because of the revenue his well-attended courses generated for the college.

As a professor of education at Teachers College, Kilpatrick became a noted interpreter of Dewey. His writings and lectures, which espoused themes associated with Experimentalist philosophy and Progressive education, attracted a large and receptive audience. A gifted lecturer, Kilpatrick clarified many of Dewey's more difficult theoretical concepts. He was not, however, merely an interpreter. He also advanced his own educational philosophy, which synthesized Progressivism and Experimentalism into the "purposeful act." or the "project method." Because he reached a large number of teachers in his classes, Kilpatrick exerted a shaping influence over U.S. educational theory and practice.

The Project Method

Kilpatrick's "The Project Method: The Use of the Purposeful Act in the Educative Process" appeared in *The Teachers College Record* in July 1918.[17] Kilpatrick designed the **project method** to integrate Dewey's scientific method of problem solving, the "Complete Act of Thought," with Progressive educational practices. Today, the project method is used by teachers in schools throughout the world.

Kilpatrick opposed traditional subject matter–dominated and teacher-controlled school practices. He criticized the traditional school curriculum for its rationale that skills and subjects should be taught how adults conceived of them rather than as children actually experienced them. In traditional schools, teachers transmitted a finished, prepackaged, secondhand subjects to students. Instead of learning by transmission, Kilpatrick argued that real learning occurred when children solved a problem or satisfied a curiosity that explored and explained their environment and added to their experience.

Kilpatrick's project method rejected traditional education's reliance on a book-centered instruction. Kilpatrick asserted that books are not a substitute for learning through living. The most pernicious form of bookishness is the textbook's domination of conventional teaching. Too frequently, teachers rely exclusively on information in textbooks. This often leads to mechanically organized, secondhand experiences. The student who succeeds in the traditional school is frequently successful in memorizing but not always in understanding what was read. Because of its stress on memorization, conventional schooling had degenerated into devitalized mechanical routines in which teachers assign lessons from textbooks, drill their students on the assignments, hear recitations of memorized responses, and then evaluate them on their recall of the material. Such schooling, in Kilpatrick's view, stifled individual creativity, led to boredom, and lacked collaborative social purposes.

Following Dewey's lead in emphasizing education's social nature, Kilpatrick stressed the social significance of transforming classrooms into collaborative, democratic, learning communities. The project method incorporated several principles that Kilpatrick had developed over his years as a teacher and a teacher educator. Among them were "wholehearted purposeful activity," "primary responses," "associate responses," and "concomitant responses." To engage in wholehearted purposeful activity meant that students were motivated by their own interests, committed to do the work necessary to complete a project, and wanted to collaborate with their peers in mutually sharing the information and the skills needed in the process. A primary response was what students had to do to begin and complete a project. Associate responses were ideas, skills, and information generated by the primary response. For example, in setting up a balanced aquarium, the primary task, students might need to use library and research skills to read about fish and aquatic plants. Concomitant responses might be social, ethical, and political attitudes such as learning to cooperate with others—to share information and ideas, to take turns in using tools—and, more important, coming to understand that actions had consequences. Unlike the closed nature of the prestructured curriculum, Kilpatrick's process was open-ended in that the exact nature of the outcomes and responses could not be specified in advance.[18]

In contrast to the rote nature of traditional book-centered education, Kilpatrick's project method was designed to elaborate a constructive Progressivism along Experimentalist lines. In the project method, students are to choose, plan, direct, and execute their work in activities, or projects, that stimulate purposeful efforts. In its theoretical formulation, the project is a mode of problem solving. Students, either individually or in groups, would define problems that arose in their own experiences. Learning would be task centered in that success would come by solving the problem and testing the solution by acting on it. Action from purposeful planning would meet the pragmatic test and be judged by its consequences.

Kilpatrick recommended that the school curriculum be organized into four major classes of projects. First, the creative, or "construction," project involves concretizing a theoretical plan in external form. For example, the students might decide to write and then present a drama. They would write the script, assign the roles, and actually act out the play. Or, the creative project might actually involve the design of a blueprint for a library. The test would come in the construction of the library from the plan devised by the students. Second, the appreciation, or "enjoyment," project is designed to contribute to aesthetic enjoyment. Reading a novel, seeing a film, or hearing a symphony are examples of projects that would lead to aesthetic appreciation. Third, the "problem" project is one in which the students would be involved in resolving an intellectual problem. Such problems as the resolution of racial discrimination, the improvement of the quality of the environment, or the organization of recreational facilities are social problems that call for disciplined intellectual inquiry. Finally, the "specific learning" project involves acquiring a skill or an area of knowledge. Learning to type, swim, dance, read, or write are examples of the acquisition of a specific skill.

Kilpatrick's project method should be interpreted both in terms of its suggested social consequences and its strictly educational aims. To be sure, the project method had educational objectives, such as improvement in creative, constructive, appreciative, intellectual, and skill competencies. However, acquiring these competencies is only a part of Kilpatrick's plan for educational reform. Kilpatrick believed, as did Dewey, that education as a social activity is a product of human association and collaboration. In a free society, democratic discussion, debate, decision, and action depend on the willingness of individuals to use the methods of open and uncoerced inquiry. Kilpatrick believed that the project method lent itself to group work, in which students could collaboratively pursue common problems and share in associative inquiry. Such was the essence of the democratic processes. Even more important than the acquiring of specific skills is the student's need to acquire attitudes appropriate to a democratic society.

The Progressive Teacher in the Project Method

Compared to instruction through transmission in traditional schools, Kilpatrick's Progressive teacher appears to play a secondary or supplemental role in the project method. However, the Progressive teacher's role is different rather than supplemental. The Progressive teacher needs to make the child her or his primary subject and to be knowledgeable about other kinds of subjects, information and knowledge areas that might be needed in accomplishing a project's goals. The teacher needs to know her or his students as persons, considering their family and ethnic backgrounds, prior experiences, and interests. The teacher is to guide but not control students' learning. The Progressive teacher exercises an important role in structuring the environment so that it is rich with opportunities for learning. The teacher is to guide students to new activities, new projects, new problems, and thus enlarge and broaden their social and cultural relationships.

The person whom Kilpatrick envisioned as a result of education based on purposeful collaboration is the democratic man or woman. Such a person would possess an experimental attitude and would be willing to test inherited traditions, values, and beliefs. Through the project method, students would learn to use democratic methods of open discussion, carefully reasoned deliberation, decision making that respected both the rights of the majority and the minority, and action that resulted in peaceful social change.

Kilpatrick's model of the democratic citizen was much like that envisioned by middle-class Progressives in politics and in education. This person would use a democratic methodology and would expect opponents to use the same procedure. As a reconstructive person, this Progressively educated man or woman would believe that social institutions were creations of human intelligence and could be periodically renovated when the situation required it. The democratic citizen would be open to using the scientific method and would discard theological, metaphysical, political, and economic absolutes as dogmatic impediments that blocked human inquiry into the conditions of life. Above all, Kilpatrick wanted to educate individuals who shared a common framework of democratic values. Such men and women would be wholehearted and willing participants in the democratic community.

Progressivism's Implications for Education, Schools, Curriculum, and Teaching and Learning

As a theory of education, Progressivism was shaped by general ideas of educational reform such as Rousseau's naturalism; Pragmatism, especially John Dewey's Experimentalism; Liberal reformist ideology; and reactions against Victorian-era prescriptions and traditional school practices. Progressivism's implications can be considered in terms of education, schools, curriculum, and teaching and learning.

Education

Given the variety of Progressives within the main body of Progressivism, they more easily agreed on what they opposed than what they proposed in education. Reactively, they agreed that education was not the transmission of doctrines or dogma. Progressives saw education as requiring an openness and flexibility to change. For child-centered Progressives, inspired by Rousseau, education was highly subjective and personal. It was a way in which children expressed themselves, free of the constraints from the Victorian past. For Dewey and the Pragmatically inclined Progressives, education meant an openness to experience in which learners solved problems arising in their environment by using the scientific method. Progressives who were influenced by Liberalism saw education as a way of informing people about what had gone wrong with representative political, economic, and social institutions and how life could be improved by reforming these institutions so that they functioned in the popular interests. For Liberal Progressivism, an educated public could devise the regulatory strategies in which democratic government could regulate the economy, guarantee pure food and drugs, protect the environment, and end political corruption. Through these strategies, education was an instrument to bring about progress and improve life and society.

Schools

The Progressive construction of the school was both reactive against traditional schools and proactive in envisioning a variety of new educational prototypes. The Progressive view of the school ranged from reforming the existing school to creating a new school. Those who wanted to reform existing schools were educators who were already in the established system. They believed that they could reform school structure through incremental changes, deletions, and additions. For example, recitations of memorized materials could be deleted and field trips could be added. Progressives reactively sought to replace the more formal traditional skill and subject-focused and teacher-dominated school with learning spaces where teaching and learning was informal and child-centered. Others, like Dewey, saw the school in a new form as an educational laboratory to test new ideas about teaching and learning.

Naturalism, especially Rousseau's version, inspired the child-centered Progressives to view children as naturally good, or at least morally neutral, in their early years. Johnson, like Rousseau, contended that children's nurturing and education should be free of artificial restraints. She as well as Kilpatrick accentuated the educational efficacy of activities and excursions that connected the school and classroom to the natural environment and the neighborhood and community.

Curriculum

The Progressive concept of curriculum, like most of their beliefs, ranged from making small incremental alterations in the existing curriculum to constructing something that was completely new. Generally, Progressives rejected the Essentialist curriculum that was organized into separate skills and subjects. Liberal Progressives believed that skills and subjects could be correlated with each other and taught in a more unified and integrated way. For example, reading, writing, spelling, and composition would be reorganized and integrated as the language arts. In similar fashion, history, geography, civics, and government could be reorganized and taught in an integrated way as the social studies. In this move toward fusion and integration, skills and subjects were still being taught but in a more integrated way that reflected both students' interests and society's needs.

Other Progressives wanted a completely new form of curriculum. Child-centered Progressives, inspired by Rousseau, argued that the curriculum could not be specified in advance; the curriculum was actually an unfinished and ongoing act of construction that came from children's needs and interests.

Dewey-inspired Progressives saw the curriculum being organized around children's interest and needs in relationship to humankind's past experience and current problems. They did not separate curriculum and methods but saw them in a process-based interface. Using the scientific method to solve problems would arise in the present situation, take students into the past to gain its insights, and bring them from the present into a future that they could shape.

Opposition to External Standards. Most Progressives would be opposed to standards that are externally imposed on teachers and students. For example, the child-centered Progressive Marietta Johnson condemned standards as "absolutely unnecessary." Johnson argued that external standards, such as those found in the contemporary standards movement, force children to do what adults determine they should do rather than what is appropriate to their own growth and interests. Because a genuine education arises out of a child's own stage of development and readiness, teachers can develop flexible guidelines for children's instruction based on child development and child and adolescent psychology but still reject external standards. She argued that because "every individual is unique there can be no other reasonable standard of accomplishment." Johnson charged that basing curriculum and instruction on what was examined on standardized tests geared education to a mythical average child who did not exist in reality. Rather than following expectations based on the achievement of the "average child" who did not exist in classroom reality, the teacher "should develop a keen and definite judgment of individual ability and endeavor to keep each pupil up to this standard."[19]

If Kilpatrick were alive today, he would probably join Johnson in opposing externally imposed standards. Both the reliance on tests and the use of standards imposed external authorities on children that jeopardized their following of their own interests to solve problems. Just as today there is a basic inconsistency between using portfolios and standardized tests, there was an inconsistency in Kilpatrick's day between standardized testing and the project method. He fought against what he regarded as the domination of tests over education. Tests, he argued, assessed facts that could be easily looked up and ignored the true results of learning such as the ethical values of sharing, responsibility, and respect of others, and neglected aesthetic values of appreciating art and music. Tests could be used to diagnose, and yet were of little use in measuring genuine learning. Kilpatrick believed that the growing emphasis on testing and measuring was confining teachers and students in an educational straitjacket that gave them few options. An increasing emphasis on standardized testing was driving the curriculum and forcing teachers to teach for the test.

Teaching and Learning

Progressives agreed that teaching and learning was not the transmission of existing subjects by teachers to learners. Neither was it the memorization and recitation by students of what was transmitted to them by teachers and textbooks. For Progressives, inspired by Rousseau's naturalism, teaching meant guiding learning by arranging a rich environment that excited children's curiosity and interests. It meant refraining from being intrusive in children's learning by encouraging them without forcing them.

For **Dewey-inspired Progressives**, teaching and learning was highly procedural, or process-based. Dewey's belief that the sole purpose of education was growth for the sake of further growth corresponded nicely to the Progressives' call for children's freedom to explore and learn from activities in the environment. His concept of experience as the interaction of the person with the environment corresponded well with the Progressive emphasis on process, "learning by doing," projects, and activities. Dewey's Complete Act of Thought, or problem-solving according to the scientific method, corresponded to the Progressive orientation that children learned best by reflecting on future actions and validating these actions in terms of the consequences they produced. His emphasis on shared human experience, or associative living and learning, corresponded well with Kilpatrick's emphasis on collaborative group projects. Children would solve problems by using the scientific method. For example, Kilpatrick's project method saw children and adolescents learning to be democratic members of society by sharing ideas, participating in mutual endeavors, and concretizing their ideas in completed projects. Conclusions, however, are not final but rather are constructions that are capable of being revised through further research, experimentation, and reinterpretation.

Constructionism.   Progressivism would find the contemporary Constructivist approach to instruction to be highly compatible. Constructionism is a psychology of learning that argues that human beings, through their interactions with the environment, construct their own meanings of experience rather than appropriate those that are given to them by others. Especially in early education, children, in constructionist settings, are engaged in exploring and in defining their own environment. Through these interactions, they acquire a framework of meaningful ideas that is their own network for sorting out, cataloguing, and interpreting subsequent experiences. Progressives would find much to endorse in Constructionism, which in some ways approximates the Progressive theory (especially Dewey's version) of learning through problems that occur in environmental interactions.

Progressivism's Philosophical and Ideological Relationships

As a theory of education, Progressivism draws heavily from Rousseau's Naturalism and Dewey's Pragmatism. From Naturalists, such as Rousseau, Progressives took the idea that children should be free to develop according to their interests and needs.

The child-centered Progressives' emphasis on children's needs and interests led them to conclude that the curriculum should develop from the child and that the most effective school environment was a permissive one in which children were free to explore and act on their interests. From the origins of Progressivism to the present, Progressives have stressed children's directly expressed needs and interests over academic subject matter.

Progressives drew their educational rationale from the Pragmatism or Experimentalism of John Dewey. Progressivism, like Pragmatism, rejects traditional philosophy's metaphysical assertion that reality is antecedent to and exists prior to human experience and that education is to aid human reason in knowing, or intellectually grasping or discovering prior knowledge. For Progressives, knowing is a human construction, arising from experience and not antecedent to experience.

Although they could agree that children should be liberated from repressive schooling, they disagreed on the extent to which education was a social force or involved some degree of social imposition. Believing that human intelligence was shaped by social interaction, Deweyan Progressives emphasize the group, social issues and problems, and the power of the scientific method in complete and reflective thought.

Progressivism rejects the more traditional philosophies of Idealism, Realism, and Thomism and their emphasis on antecedent reality, hierarchical categories, and subject matter. Though sympathetic to improving working conditions, ensuring just wages, and eliminating child labor, Progressives feared the radical left, especially Marxism, as a dogmatic threat to individual freedom. Marx's preaching of inevitable class struggle and revolutionary warfare contrasted with the Liberal Progressive method of using democratic parliamentary processes to bring about reform. Progressives, by choosing their middle way, sought to redefine individualism into persons with a social conscience.

Ideologically, Progressivism is more compatible with Liberalism than with other ideologies. Liberalism's concern for individual rights and freedom finds an educational corollary in Progressivism's emphasis on the individual child. The freedom to inquire and test ideas, exemplified by Liberal theorists such as John Stuart Mill, is also stressed by Progressives.

The Progressive inclination toward change rather than stasis is much like the Liberal orientation. Progressivism is seen by Conservatives as threatening cultural continuity, eroding the power of tradition as a stabilizing factor, and jeopardizing legitimate authority. Conservatives fear that Progressive permissiveness, like Liberal individualism, will weaken standards.

The Liberal emphasis on representative institutions and gradual incremental reform rather than Marxist revolution is compatible with Progressive social reform. Progressive social reformers worked within the social and political system. Their efforts at reform were designed to improve the system by using representative institutions and processes to remedy its internal weaknesses. Progressive reformers, like Liberals in general, prefer open-ended reform, which has limited ends-in-view rather than preconceived ends.

Progressivism and Liberalism share many common themes: the Liberal commitment to reform through gradual processes of change; the following of shared procedures to adjudicate differences of opinion; open discussion and debate; and the freedom to express ideas are all viewed favorably by Progressives. Progressives, like Liberals, seek to be consensus builders. Democracy, for both Progressives and Liberals, requires the construction of a broad, general consensus or agreement on the procedures by which we govern ourselves, compromise our differences, and adjudicate our disputes. Education is seen as a consensus builder in which people learn the procedures, practice them, and are committed to using them.

Progressivism, as a theory of education, opposes many principles of Essentialism and Perennialism. Whereas Essentialists and Perennialists take an academic view of the school, Progressives see schools as multipurpose and flexible institutions, and learning communities that serves a broad range of individual and social needs. Concerned with the education of the whole person, the school's aims are intellectual, psychological, moral, social, civic, and economic. Progressives warn against the Essentialist and Perennialist "four walls" philosophy of education that separates schools from their society and the community they serve.

Based on education's multiple goals, Progressive curriculum and instruction rejects the more traditional emphasis on predetermined discrete skills and subjects that are prior to children's experience. Rather, Progressives contend that the curriculum should come from children's interests and needs and their exploration of the environment to stimulate creativity through expressive activities. It also presents occasions in which children can encounter problem-solving situations, work out solutions, and construct their concepts of reality. Just as the goals of the Progressive school are multifunctional, the instructional repertoire of Progressive teachers needs to be highly versatile. They need to have informed insight into children's cognitive and emotional growth and development; they need to have a large range of skill and subject knowledge as a background for teaching; and they need to be skilled in using group dynamics for cooperative learning.

The contemporary standards movement is contrary to the ideas of the Progressive educators. A child-centered Progressive would reject the contemporary emphasis on standardized tests to measure achievement and basing instruction on external standards as misdirected neotraditional education. External standards, coming from legislators and learned academic societies, force children to do what adults determine they should do rather than what is appropriate to their own growth and interests. Genuine education arises out of a child's own stage of development and readiness; teachers should be free of external interference so they can create flexible guidelines for children's instruction based on child development and child and adolescent psychology. Externally imposed standards not only adversely affect students but they also constrain teachers into teaching for the test rather than for the child.

An important point of conflict between Progressive educators and Essentialists and Perennialists is values education. While Progressives see values as arising in cultural contexts and changing with these contexts, Essentialists see values as more stable and arising in humankind's historical experience. Perennialists see values as based on an unchanging human nature. Progressives see values arising, not from absolute and universal standards, but as human reactions to a changing environment. Arising in the particular environmental situations in which they occur, the times and places in which people live, values are relative to these particular cultural situations. Valuing is the result of estimating and judging how behaviors contribute to human growth, development, culture, and satisfaction.

Relating Progressivism to Postmodernism and Critical Theory reveals some interesting similarities but also differences. (Postmodernism is treated in an earlier chapter and Critical Theory in a later one.) As indicated, Progressivism rests on the concept of progress that originated in the Enlightenment. It embraces the belief that humankind can construct a better future by using the scientific method, which to Deweyan Experimentalists is the method of problem-solving. Postmodernists and Critical Theorists are hostile to the Enlightenment's privileged and powerful interpretation in Western history. For them, the Enlightenment's doctrine of progress in just another historical metanarrative used to rationalize and justify domination by a ruling group. The objectivity claimed for the scientific method is but a mask for its use by powerful and domineering elites.

Still another point of contention would be the Progressive inclination to use transactional reform in which parts of the school and parts of the curriculum are changed, generally by adding to it. Critical Theorists believe that this kind of change preserves more of the status quo than it changes; instead of transactional and piecemeal change, they argue for transformational change to radically reform schools and society.

Critical Theorists would find the Progressive concept that the school can be an agency of community building to be a useful site-based strategy in constructing a new version of community-based democracy. They would also applaud the Progressive tendency to remove the barriers between subjects and to include more integrated interdisciplinary processes in curriculum and instruction.

Critical Theorists would find much more compatibility with the Social Reconstructionist Progressives who argued that the school should create a new social order. Critical Theorists would likely agree with the Reconstructionists, who believe that following children's interests as the sole criterion of curriculum and instruction retreats into laissez-faire romanticism that reinforces the status quo rather than reforms society. Reconstructionist Progressives, like the Critical Theorists, want to use schools as agencies for social reform by emphasizing controversial issues that examine social, political, and economic problems and that seek to solve them.

My Experience with the Project Method

As I wrote this chapter, I reflected on my own educational experience and sought to identify instances of Progressive education. I thought back to my high school experience. I was attending Streator Township High School, in Streator, Illinois, a town of about 15,000 inhabitants. When I was a senior in high school, I was enrolled in a course in American Problems. My teacher, Miss Dorothy Bash, used the project method. The course examined issues in American society and government. Miss Bash was a Progressive teacher, who frequently related the topics in the course—the organization of the federal government, state and federal powers, and foreign policy—to current events. It was 1952 and there was a presidential election. The two major candidates were Dwight Eisenhower, the Republican nominee, and Adlai Stevenson, the Democratic nominee. It was inevitable that in a class like Miss Bash's we should discuss the election. However, we decided to do more than discuss; Miss Bash got us involved directly in the election. The class devised a schoolwide project to "Get out the vote." We were going to make sure that the citizens in Streator exercised their right to vote.

Because I was very interested in politics, I was chosen to have a leading role in the project. Most planning for the project was done by student committees. We decided that we would encourage a large voter turnout in the community with a

My Experience with the Project Method   *(Continued)*

contest. Local businesses were solicited by students and asked to contribute prizes that would be given to the elementary-age students who collected the greatest number of voters' tags. Most of the town's businesses were pleased to join in the project. High school students involved in the project would be stationed at the polls, the various voting places, and would give each voter a tag, indicating that they had voted. After the polls had closed, the elementary students who wished to would collect the tags, and those with the highest number of tags would receive the prizes. In this way, we got the community and the younger students involved in our project.

Miss Bash made sure that we had the approval of the high school administration to carry out the project. Students met with the principal, who reviewed and agreed to our proposal. I also remember that Miss Bash said that we needed to inform the community about what we were planning to do. I remember that I went with her to meet with the editor and publisher of the local newspaper. The editor was interested in our project and agreed to give it extensive coverage in the paper. At this point, the project was becoming a community-wide project.

Although we were all too young to vote, the students in the project decided that we could organize some events in the high school related to the national election. We arranged some presentations by students, who played the roles of the leading candidates. Though we did not have a debate, there was a school assembly in which the student playing General Eisenhower gave a campaign speech. I played the part of Governor Stevenson, the Democratic candidate. We then conducted a mock election with all the high school students eligible to vote. At that time, voting was done with paper ballots and we had paper ballots printed by the school print shop. Students in the course on American Problems acted as election officials. The local election board allowed us to use the voting booths that would be used on election day. I don't know whether it was because of my speech but Stevenson carried the student vote. He would lose the actual election to Eisenhower.

The project worked in many ways. The students in the American Problems course got to see how an election worked at the local level. The larger community became involved with the high school and its students in a community-wide project. For me, there were many of what Kilpatrick would call concomitant learnings. I learned how to work with other students on committees. I learned the process of discussion and of working out the inevitable issues and conflicts that arise in working with a group. I also made many friends that I would not normally have made.

Conclusion

Progressive education's influence is found in teacher education programs that emphasize such process-oriented learning strategies as "educating the whole child," "learning by doing," the project and activity methods, cooperative and collaborative learning, constructivism, use of portfolios, and site-based management. Progressives contributed to reshaping the traditional elementary school curriculum from specifically defined skills and subjects into broad fields. For example, reading, writing, and arithmetic were reorganized into the integrated language arts; history and geography were restructured into the multidisciplinary social studies.

Progressivism continues to exert an ongoing influence on contemporary American education. It operates from an orientation that education is to help us learn to interact intelligently with our natural and social, and our national and global environments. It is to give us the intellectual tools to work out our social, political, economic, and cultural relationships in ways that are most satisfying for human growth and development. Indeed, our social knowledge and values are relational in that they are constructed through satisfying mutual interactions with our peers.

Constructing Your Own Philosophy of Education. Now that you have read and discussed the chapter on Progressive education, reflect on how it might influence your philosophy of education. Did you experience Progressivism in your own educational experiences? Do you plan to use Progressivism in constructing your philosophy of education?

Questions for Reflection and Discussion

1. Do you believe that most Americans believe in the concept of Progress; that the future will be better than the past? If so, how does that belief shape their social, political, and educational expectations?

2. Do you agree or disagree with critics of Progressive education who allege that it has weakened the academic quality of public education by inserting nonintellectual activities into the curriculum?

3. Reflect on Rousseau's ideas about stages of human development. Do you find an emphasis on stages of development in contemporary education?

4. If you have been involved in project-based learning as part of your own education or your teaching, reflect on Kilpatrick's rationale for the project method. Do you think he was right or wrong about the outcomes of project-based learning?

5. Do you agree with the broad Progressive view of the school as a multifunctional institution or with the Essentialists, who see it as an academic institution?

6. Do you think that the ethical relativism associated with Progressive education is compatible with the current moral climate in the United States?

Topics for Inquiry and Research

1. Do you observe evidence of Progressivism in classroom situations that are part of your professional clinical experience?

2. Write a position paper in which you describe how Progressives might react to the standards movement and the use of standardized tests to measure student achievement.

3. Visit some kindergartens or preschool situations. Do you find evidence of what child-

centered Progressives would call the premature, or too early, introduction of academic activities?

4. If you have been involved in assessment by portfolios and standardized testing, compare and contract your reactions. How might Progressives react to your reflections?

5. In a group discussion, consider whether the contemporary situation is congenial or adversarial to Progressive principles of education.

Building a Progressive Vocabulary

Amour de soi, or **Self-esteem:**   values that arise from a person's natural and instinctive self-interests.

Amour propre, or **Selfishness:**   the process by which a person learns to manipulate others for his or her own purposes.

Child-centered Progressives: Progressive educators who base curriculum and instruction on children's freedom and their interests and needs.

Dewey-inspired Progressives: Progressive educators who emphasizes the importance of experience in education, which often means activity-based instruction and process-oriented problem solving by the scientific method.

Emile: Rousseau's educational novel about the education of a child in a natural environment.

Enlightenment: The eighteenth-century Age of Reason that emphasized rationalism and the scientific method as agents in creating a more progressive society.

Naturalism: the set of beliefs that argue that Nature should be the source of principles about human development and education.

Organic Philosophy of Education: a version of child-centered Progressive education developed by Marietta Johnson at the Organic School in Fairhope, Alabama.

Philosophes: French theorists of the eighteenth-century Enlightenment.

Progress: the concept, originating in the Enlightenment, that people can use their intelligence to create a better future.

Progressive Education Association: an organization of Progressive private and public educators established in 1919.

Progressive Movement: in American history, from 1890 to 1920, when there was a concerted effort for reform of government, society, the economy, and education.

Progressive School: a multifunctional institution that serves a broad range of individual and social needs.

Project Method: Kilpatrick's method of education in which students work in groups engaged in activities related to a project.

Sensory Learning: using the senses to observe objects found in the environment.

Social Reconstructionist Progressives: Progressive educators who want schools to be used as agencies for deliberately directed social, political, and economic reform.

Stages of Development: the concept that human beings go through stages, periods of growth and development, during the life cycle.

Internet Resources

For recent developments and an active voice for Progressive education, contact the John Dewey Project on Progressive Education at the University of Vermont at www.uvm.edu/dewey/.

For an overview of Progressive education, access www.uvm.edu/~/dewey/articles/proed/html.

Suggestions for Further Reading

Beineke, John A. *And There Were Giants in the Land: The Life of William Heard Kilpatrick.* New York: Peter Lang, 1998.

Boyd, William, ed. *The Emile of Jean-Jacques Rousseau.* New York: Teachers College Press, Columbia University, 1966.

Boyd, William, ed. *The Minor Educational Writings of Jean-Jacques Rousseau.* New York: Teachers Press, 1962.

Carlson, Dennis. *Making Progress: Education and Culture in New Times.* New York: Teachers College Press, 1996.

Cremin, Lawrence A. *The Transformation of the School: Progressivism in American Education, 1876–1957.* New York: Alfred A. Knopf, 1961.

Cranston, Maurice W. *The Noble Savage: Jean-Jacques Rousseau, 1754–1762.* Chicago: University of Chicago Press, 1991.

Cranston, Maurice W. *Jean-Jacques: The Early Life and Work of Jean-Jacques Rousseau, 1712–1754.* Chicago: University of Chicago Press, 1991.

Cullen, Daniel. *Freedom in Rousseau's Political Philosophy.* DeKalb: Northern Illinois University Press, 1993.

Dewey, John. *Experience and Education: The 60th Anniversary Edition.* West Lafayette, IN: Kappa Delta Pi, 1998.

Graham, Patricia A. *Progressive Education: From Arcady to Academe—A History of the Progressive Education Association, 1919–1955.* New York: Teachers College Press, 1967.

Hayes, William. *The Progressive Education Movement: Is It Still a Factor in Today's Schools?* Boulder, CO: Rowman & Littlefield, 2006.

Kliebard, Herbert M. *The Struggle for the American Curriculum, 1893–1958.* Boston: Routledge & Kegan Paul, 1986.

Melzer, Arthur M. *The Natural Goodness of Man: On the System of Rousseau's Thoughts.* Chicago: University of Chicago Press, 1990.

Norris, Norman D. *The Promise and Failure of Progressive Education.* New York: Scarecrow Education, 2004.

Rousseau, Jean-Jacques. *Discourses on the Sciences and Arts: First Discourse and Polemics.* Hanover; NH: University Press of New England, 1992.

Rousseau, Jean-Jacques. *Emile: or On Education.* Translated by Allan Bloom. New York: Basic Books, 1979.

Tanner, Daniel. *Crusade for Democracy: Progressive Education at the Crossroads.* Albany: State University of New York Press, 1991.

Trachtenberg, Zev M. *Making Citizens: Rousseau's Political Theory of Culture.* London and New York: Routledge, 1992.

Zilversmit, Arthur. *Changing Schools: Progressive Education Theory and Practice, 1930–1960.* Chicago: University of Chicago Press, 1993.

Weiss, Penny A. *Gendered Community: Rousseau, Sex, and Politics.* New York: New York University Press, 1993.

Endnotes

1. For his autobiography, see Jean-Jacques Rousseau, *The Confessions,* trans. J. M. Cohen (Baltimore: Penguin Books, 1954). Biographies of Rousseau are Jakob H. Huizinga, *Rousseau: The Self-Made Saint* (New York: Grossman, 1976); George R. Havens, *Jean-Jacques Rousseau* (Boston: Twayne, 1978); and Gavin R. De Beer, *Jean-Jacques Rousseau and His World* (London: Thames and Hudson, 1972).

2. Gerald L. Gutek, *A History of the Western Educational Experience* (Prospect Heights, IL: Waveland Press, 1995), pp. 164–167.

3. William Boyd, ed., *The Minor Educational Writings of Jean Jacques Rousseau* (New York: Teachers College, Columbia University, 1962), pp. 7–23.

4. William Kessen, "Rousseau's Children," *Daedalus* 107 (Summer 1978), 155–164.

5. Jean-Jacques Rousseau, *The First and Second Discourses,* ed. Roger D. Masters (New York: St. Martin's Press, 1964).

6. Jean-Jacques Rousseau, *Emile: or On Education,* trans. Allan Bloom (New York: Basic Books, 1979), pp. 37–74.

7. Rousseau, *Emile: or On Education,* pp. 77–163.

8. Rousseau, *Emile: or On Education,* pp. 165–208.

9. Rousseau, *Emile: or On Education,* pp. 211–355.

10. Marietta Johnson, *Thirty Years with an Idea* (University, Alabama: University of Alabama Press, 1974), pp. 20–21.

11. The definitive history of the Progressive Education Association is Patricia Albjerg Graham, *Progressive Education: From Arcady to Academe—A History of the Progressive Education Association, 1919–1955* (New York: Teachers College Press, Columbia University, 1967).

12. John Dewey, *Experience and Education: The 60th Anniversary Edition* (West Lafayette, IN: Kappa Delta Phi, 1998).

13. For the history of Social Reconstructionism, see Michael E. James, *Social Reconstructionism Through Education: The Philosophy, History, and Curricula of a Radical Ideal* (Norwood, NJ: Ablex, 1995).

14. George S. Counts, *Dare the School Build a New Social Order?* (New York: John Day, 1932), pp. 17–18.

15. John A. Beineke, *And There Were Giants in the Land: The Life of William Heard Kilpatrick* (New York: Peter Lang, 1998), pp. 22–23.

16. Beineke, *And There Were Giants in the Land: The Life of William Heard Kilpatrick,* pp. 59–61.

17. William H. Kilpatrick, "The Project Method: The Use of the Purposeful Act in the Educative Process," *Teachers College Record* (September 1918).

18. Beineke, *And There Were Giants in the Land: The Life of William Heard Kilpatrick,* pp. 106–107.

19. Johnson, *Thirty Years with an Idea,* p. 106.

15

Social Reconstructionism and Education

George S. Counts (1889–1974), whose question, "Dare the school build a new social order?,"
sparked Social Reconstructionism.

Chapter Preview

By analyzing the ideas of George Counts, Harold Rugg, and Theodore Brameld, we can
examine the origins, development, and influence of Social Reconstruction on education.
Reconstructionism argues that teachers and schools should act as agents of directed change
in creating a new social order rather than mirroring and reproducing the status quo. George
Counts inaugurated **Social Reconstructionism** with his *Dare the School Build a New Social*

Order? Theodore Brameld then enlarged its foundations by including educational anthropology as an agency of socioeducational interpretation, change, and reform. Social Reconstructionism, also known as Reconstructionism, raised important issues for education such as can schools and teachers attempt to bring about directed social change or should they mirror existing knowledge and values? The chapter includes the following topics:

- Introducing Social Reconstructionism
- George Counts and Theodore Brameld as leading Reconstructionists
- Reconstructionist themes
- Educational implications
- Reconstructionism's ideological and philosophical relationships

Introducing Social Reconstructionism

Social Reconstructionism argues that education can and should be used to create a new, more democratic, more humane, and more equitable society. This process of educational reconstruction involves integrating selected cultural elements with new and emerging ones, such as technology, to create a new social order.

It is not easy to position Social Reconstructionism as a philosophy, ideology, or theory because it connects with and overlaps these divisions. It has strong philosophical connections to Pragmatism and its leading figures often referred to it as a philosophy. It shades quickly into an ideology in that Social Reconstructionists, such as George S. Counts, like most ideologists had an interpretation of the past, an analysis of the present, and an action program for the future. However, it was a theory of its times and still remains relevant.[1]

Karen Riley, an historian of education, sees an examination of Social Reconstruction as an intellectual and educational challenge "to understanding the American mind and what makes us tick."[2] Educational theorist William B. Stanley calls it "an influential school of thought in the current education reform dialogue."[3]

Contemporary Relevance

Wayne Urban, a distinguished historian of education, finds Social Reconstructionism relevant to what he identifies as attacks on the idea of the public schools. Among these attacks are the contemporary movement for standardized testing that "threatens to rob the pedagogical process of any flexibility," and the efforts of fundamentalist religious groups, who advocate homeschooling as an alternative to what they perceive to be public schools' secular values.[4] William B. Stanley, a social studies educator and student of Reconstructionism, finds relevance in the Reconstructionist insights that:

- Social change outdistances the capacity of existing institutions, including schools, to make the needed adaptations.
- Social criticism is necessary in education.

- Futurist thinking—conjecturing how society might be improved—is a fruitful educational exercise.
- The groups who dominate society, politics, and education will use schools to reinforce and reproduce their control.[5]

George S. Counts and Theodore Brameld as Leading Reconstructionists

Although there were many Social Reconstructionists, we examine the ideas of two leading theorists: George S. Counts, who was an originator of the concept, and Theodore Brameld, who developed it further as a theory of education.

George S. Counts

When George S. Counts (1889–1974) asked the question—Dare the school build a new social order?—he sparked the movement that developed into Social Reconstructionism. A pioneer in the social foundations of education, Counts used interdisciplinary lenses to examine education. He moved back and forth, crossing the boundaries of academic fields such as history, political science, economics, sociology, and comparative education to examine educational issues.[6] For almost all of his career, Counts was a professor of education at Columbia University's Teachers College, where from 1927 until 1955 he worked with other Progressives such as William H. Kilpatrick, Harold Rugg, and John Childs. This group, followers of John Dewey's Pragmatic Instrumentalist philosophy and self-styled "frontier thinkers," in their frequent meetings shaped early Social Reconstructionism. Of them, Counts was also a political activist, who helped found the American Labor Party and then the Liberal Party in New York State.[7] Always supportive of organized labor, Counts was the American Federation of Teachers' president from 1939 to 1942.

Before he launched the early Reconstructionist movement, Counts, as a professor, had been examining American education's broad social, political, economic, and cultural contexts. His *Secondary Education and Industrialism* (1929) analyzed industrialization's impact on education and *The American Road to Culture* (1930) examined the school's role in transmitting and shaping American culture.[8] The crucial years for the origins of Social Reconstruction, however, coincided with the great and devastating economic depression of the 1930s, when Counts in 1932 startled the members of the Progressive Education Association at their annual convention by asking, "Dare Progressive Education be Progressive?" He then repeated his challenge to the educators of the United States, asking them, "Dare the School Build a New Social Order?"[9]

The Mentoring Relationship Between Charles Beard and Counts

An unusual combination of academic thinker and political activist, Counts pursued his own question, seeking to enlist teachers in the cause of social reconstruction. As he pursued his cause, his ideas were further developed by his association with the distinguished historian Charles A. Beard, who being older than Counts served as his mentor in shaping and tempering his ideas. Counts often seemed to be too radical, too polemical in his expressions, and the more experienced Beard would tone him down. At other times, Beard pointed Counts in new directions of research and analysis. The Beard–Counts relationship points out the importance of mentoring when applied to teaching, especially when a new, relatively inexperienced teacher works cooperatively with an older, more experienced teacher. Just as the experienced Beard provided Counts with suggestions and feedback, a mentor teacher can suggest strategies and methods based on experience.

Beard had some key ideas about history, the social sciences, and education that stimulated Counts in his own thinking. Counts and Beard were both members of the American Historical Association's Commission on the Social Studies and frequently worked as a team. Beard was a leader in writing what was called the "new history," a Progressive interpretation of America's past. Beard argued that economics had been a powerful force in American history, even to the point that economic factors had shaped decisions made at the Constitutional Convention at the country's founding. Beard claimed that history and the social sciences, constructed and functioning in a context of time and place, could never be completely objective, or even neutral, but were "organized around some central philosophy."[10] Instruction in the social sciences could and should not be isolated from social issues but needed to respond to social change.[11] Important for their influence on Counts, Beard argued that teachers needed to have a frame of reference that recognized that American society: (1) was in profound change; (2) was an industrial economy, based on science and technology; (3) needed rational planning and intelligent cooperation in all its sectors, and (4) that democracy requires informed public discussion, debate, and criticism.[12] Spurred by Beard and his frontier colleagues, Counts proceeded to construct the needed frame of reference that became Social Reconstructionism.

Counts's Frame of Reference

In developing his frame of reference, Counts first prefaced it on **contextual relativism**, that is, the importance that living in a particular place at a particular time has on culture and education. Taking a cue from Beard, Counts stated that history was not objective but was the story of a people struggling to solve their real problems.

The Importance of Context.   Arguing that education, like history, happened in a context, Counts wrote:

> . . . education is always a function of time, place, and circumstance. In its basic philosophy, its social objectives, and its program of instruction, it inevitably reflects . . . the experiences, the conditions, and the hopes, fears, and aspirations of a particular people or cultural group at a particular point in history. . . . Education . . . is always relative, at least in its fundamental parts, to some concrete and evolving social situation.[13]

Counts's argument that education is always based on a context raises important philosophical issues. Philosophical critics, especially Idealists and Realists, would argue that Counts, by tying education to a specific context, moved the discussion out of philosophy because it is no longer general or transferable but is limited to one place at one time. These critics, as well as their educational allies, the Perennialists and Essentialists, would argue further that Counts confused and blurred the distinctions and relationships between education and schooling. They would contend that education is a general and universal process found in all cultures and societies that transcends particular places; it is schooling that is particular to a particular culture. For example, people worldwide are educated to use a language; they are schooled by their context to use a particular language such as English or Russian. In rebuttal, Counts would likely reply that these philosophical generalities dodge the real issues of economics and politics that people face in their daily life that should be at the heart of the school program.

A Particular Interpretation of History.   The first plank in Counts's frame of reference was to interpret the American past historically. To do this, he relied on Beard's Progressive version of history. Counts saw American history in terms of two conflicting traditions: one based on the popular, democratic, and egalitarian ideas of Thomas Jefferson and the other on the elitism and special economic interests of Alexander Hamilton. When he told Americans that they needed to choose between these rival traditions, Counts urged them to choose the Jeffersonian version, which he believed provided the democratic and egalitarian heritage that needed to be reconstructed into the new social order.[14] Counts asserted that the Jeffersonian heritage of democracy and equality could be reasserted against the special economic interests, the big business corporations, and their conservative political allies.

In his analysis of American history, Counts did not take a neutral or objective position. He believed, like the contemporary Critical Theorists, that teachers could not be neutral but had to take a side. Protestations of neutrality meant that those who held power in an inequitable status quo would prevail. To build a new society, the vested interests had to be challenged. Counts based his historical interpretation on a point of view deliberately committed to a particular version of social change. His critics charged him with **presentism**, the selective writing and teaching of history based on a political agenda in the present rather than for an accurate understanding of the past.

Cultural Crisis in an Industrial-Technological Society

After identifying the Jeffersonian democratic heritage as the historical element in his frame of reference, Counts next turned to the cultural crisis confronting Americans. While the economic catastrophe of the Great Depression seemed the most obvious problem facing Americans, Counts diagnosed it as a symptom rather than the underlying cause of the great cultural crisis. The crisis, he reasoned, was caused by Americans' inability to reconstruct their institutions and values in terms of the emergent industrial-technological reality. The cultural crisis was aggravated by a **cultural lag** between the rate of technological inventions and innovations and the society's ability to construct the necessary processes to harness technological change for the public good. In developing this part of his frame of reference, Counts relied on William F. Ogburn's theory of cultural lag. According to Ogburn:

> The inventions occur first, and only later do the institutions of society change in conformity. Material culture and social institutions are not independent of each other, for civilization is

highly articulated like a piece of machinery, so that a change in one part tends to effect changes in other parts—but only after a delay. Men with habits and society with patterns of action are slow to change to meet the new material conditions.[15]

A contemporary example of cultural lag is global warming. The mass use of automobiles, powered by gasoline made from petroleum, a fossil fuel, in technologically developed and developing countries has resulted in massive emissions of carbon dioxide and other pollutants into the atmosphere, resulting in global warming. This has caused the melting of the polar ice caps, and climate change that threatens the planet's health, the survival of species, and growing desertification. The lag occurs when a nation, such as the United States in particular, is unwilling to develop alternatives and strategies to check global warming.

For Counts, education needs to close the lag between technological development and its control by an informed society. In the example of global warming, schools need to include this issue as an important part of their curriculum. Students, guided by teachers, (1) need to analyze the meaning and causes of global warming; (2) develop alternatives to control, limit, and hopefully end the emissions of the by-products of fossil fuels that cause global warming; and (3) actively work for the enactment of legislation to halt global warming.

In his thinking, Counts went beyond merely narrowing the cultural lag. It was necessary to develop bold strategies to harness technology as an instrument to improve society— to construct a new social order based on equality and justice. Counts argued that: "The growth of science and technology has carried us into a new age where ignorance must be replaced by knowledge, competition by cooperation, trust in providence by careful planning, and private capitalism by some form of socialized economy."[16]

Counts was not against technology. He defined technology as the application of science to material culture, especially industry. Identifying technology with the scientific method, he saw its operations as functional, planful, dynamic, efficient, practical, purposeful, precise, and orderly.[17] He recommended the infusion of the study of technology throughout the school curriculum to create the planning attitudes needed to reconstruct society. He believed that technology had the power to improve the human condition if it was integrated with the Jeffersonian democratic heritage.

Individualism versus Collectivism

Counts identified what he believed was a powerful and serious obstacle to reconstructing society—the embedded concept of individualism. He argued that the American ideal of the individual, part historical and part myth, conjured up an image in the American psyche of the solitary person who conquered life's obstacles alone.[18] The semiofficial pervasive tale of American individualism had a grip on the collective American memory that blocked the forming of the spirit of cooperation needed to reconstruct democracy in a technological world. Counts argued that special economic and political interests used individualism as an ideological smoke screen to block needed reform, regulation, and reconstruction.

Counts called for a new concept, **democratic collectivism**, to replace the old and obstructive idea of individualism. Using democratic collectivism, the people, through representative institutions, could seize the initiative and redirect the industrial-technological economy away from selfish special interests to meet common needs. Educators should join with other Progressive forces in a great coalition to construct the new collective but also democratic society. The school curriculum would be reconstructed to prepare the upcoming generation to understand the dynamics of technological change, to engage in social planning, and to build a new social order.

Counts's use of the term *democratic collectivism* was highly controversial. His Conservative opponents called him a Communist and alleged that Counts was endorsing Soviet-style planning for the United States. Whereas the Conservative response was expected, democratic collectivism also generated a negative reaction from some Liberals and Progressives who saw it as advocating a closed rather than an experimental approach to social change.

A Social Reconstructionist Educational Strategy

Counts developed three key elements in his frame of reference for Social Reconstruction: (1) a Progressive interpretation of the American past that exalted the Jeffersonian democratic heritage; (2) reducing and perhaps eradicating the cultural lag by integrating the new elements of an industrial-technological economy with the democratic heritage; and (3) an educational and politically action-oriented program to reconstruct American institutions.[19]

In particular, the school curriculum should: (1) provide a social history about ordinary people and how they developed democratic institutions and processes; (2) examine the development of an industrial and technological economy and society; (3) examine the major conflicts and issues in America; and (4) develop the skills in making critical appraisals and intelligence choices to reconstruct society.[20]

Although Counts was an originator of Social Reconstructionism, he did not stay with it but turned to other educational interests. During the Cold War between the United States and the Soviet Union, Counts, an expert of Soviet education, turned to critical analyses of the Soviet system.

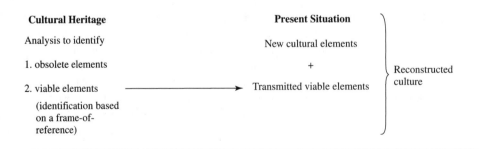

Reconstructionist Strategy for Directed Change

Theodore Brameld

Theodore Brameld (1904–1987) assumed the leading role of energizing and reformulating Social Reconstructionism after World War II and reconceptualized it as a major philosophy of education that moved beyond its Depression-based origins. Brameld recognized that technological change, rapid communication, and transportation were creating an increasingly interdependent global society. He enlarged Counts's concept of context-based education to embrace a global community of people. Whereas Counts developed a historically based analysis of American society, Brameld took an anthropological and human relationships approach to education and redefined Reconstructionism to include a more future-oriented vision of a new world order that would improve the health care, economic condition, and security of the great masses of people. The educational historian and biographer Craig Kridel portrays Brameld as a theorist who addressed and analyzed such major educational issues as "democracy in the schools," curriculum integration, "reconciling free inquiry with the inculcation of values," and encouraging "broader cultural and international awareness."[21]

Connecting Philosophy or Ideology of Education to Other Fields

Like the contemporary Postmodernists and Critical Theorists, Brameld moved across academic disciplines. He developed an interdisciplinary or transdisciplinary approach that moved educational philosophy into anthropology and human relations. He coined new terms in educational theory such as:

- **anthropological philosophy**, which integrated philosophy and anthropology
- **educology**, which studied education as distinct field of inquiry
- **anthropotherapy**, the directed course of human cultural evolution by the planned improvement of life by integrating cultural analysis with values and ethical actions
- **culturology**, the examination of philosophy on culture.[22]

Role of Anthropology

Whereas Counts focused on the American context and had relied heavily on history to construct his theory, Brameld moved beyond particular contexts to construct a theory with global implications. To enlarge his scope, Brameld moved from particular country contexts such as the United States, Japan, and Puerto Rico, where he had worked, to a larger, bolder global theater of operations. As Counts used American history to formulate his strategy for Social Reconstruction, Brameld relied on anthropology to analyze relationships between culture and education. Brameld states that all cultures practice education, which he defined as the "entire range of practices by which a culture perpetuates and improves itself through acquainting each successive generation with its most important traditions, habits, and experiences."[23]

Influenced by the anthropologist Edward B. Tylor, Brameld used Tylor's definition of culture as the "whole complex—the knowledge, belief, art, morals, law, custom, and any other capabilities and habits—that human beings acquire as members of society."[24] Important for education is the word *acquire,* in which each generation has to teach its culture to the next in order to transmit it. Through the informal and formal educational process of **enculturation**, a culture transmits and modifies its institutions, beliefs, and values by passing it from one generation to the next.[25] Essential components of a culture that education needs to transmit, examine, and reconstruct are:

- Order, the patterns of relationships in family, class, politics, economics, and religion.
- Process, the dynamics by which individuals move in cultural institutions.
- Goals, values that give direction and purpose to culture.

Again, relying on anthropology, Brameld borrowed the concept of "cultural blowups."[26] Somewhat like Ogburn's "cultural lag" theory, Brameld saw human history proceeding through a series of major cultural events, or "blowups," that generate pervasive social change. Education has the role of helping society to rebalance itself. However, rebalancing is not the restoration of the old order that existed before the blowup; rather, it requires harmonizing what remains viable in the old order with the new dynamic that caused the cultural blowup. One can think of atomic and nuclear power as generating a cultural blowup that needs to be reconstructed into the viable elements of the old culture. A key term is *viable,* or what is useful to renewing a culture. Viability does not mean neutrality for Brameld; rather, it means being partial to achieving particular goals that liberate human beings.

Defensible Partiality.   Determining cultural viability called for the making of important political and educational choices. In determining what these choices should be Brameld called on educators to exercise **defensible partiality**. Like the Critical Theorists, he believed that educational decision-making always occurred against and within an ideological backdrop. (Critical Theory is examined in the next chapter.) Teachers needed to recognize and detect operating ideologies, especially those that justified maintaining the status quo, and to construct their own defensible and partial ideology. Defensible partiality involved: (1) ensuring that the preferred goals and means used to obtain them can be defended and sustained in light of rigorous and critical examination and analysis; and (2) partiality in that goals and means could be sustained and definitely and positively defended by those who hold them.[27]

Human Relations and Conflict Resolution

In addition to the rational scientific activities of human beings, Brameld considered nonrational, volitional, and emotional aspects of human behavior, especially as they affected cooperative group activities. Found in all human behavior, irrationality causes ethnocentric and stereotypic thinking and conflicts at the personal, ethnic, racial, and religious levels. To deal with the irrational, it is important, he argues, to identify and analyze the nonrational forces that impede needed reconstruction.

When Brameld was constructing his theory, there had been significant developments in the field of human relations that included social psychology, counseling, and group and intercultural relations. Brameld wanted the design and implementation of Reconstruction-ism to democratically arrive at the broadest possible consensus. Simple voting at elections, although necessary, was not sufficient in building consensus. It was necessary that people reach a pervasive agreement, a consensus, on aims and ends. Educators needed to under-stand the dynamics of group relationships and the methods of bringing individuals into a comprehensive consensus. Human relations skills would be useful in resolving misunder-standing, tension, prejudice, hatred, and conflict. Teachers, he reasoned, needed to have human relationships knowledge and strategies as these kinds of tensions and conflicts among students interfered with more academic education. Brameld devised several stages or phases for consensus building and conflict resolution:

1. When a conflict developed, it needed to be defined, refined, and diagnosed; any emerging hypothesis for resolution of the conflict needed to be tentative and subject to further restatement.
2. Several hypotheses, possible solutions, had to be constructed and considered before selecting the most promising one; it was important to conjecture likely consequences of acting on the particular hypothesis.
3. The selected hypothesis needed to be acted on and tested to determine whether it successfully resolved the conflict.[28]

From Contextualism to Generalizations about One Human Race

Both Counts and Brameld were part of the Pragmatist, Experimentalist, and Progressive orientation. Counts emphasized the importance of a particular context—a given time and place—on education. As he was developing his Reconstructionist theory, Brameld increasingly moved out of a particular context to the larger global community. Neither Counts nor Brameld philosophically were attuned to the more traditional philosophies such as Idealism and Realism or to Perennialism, which emphasized a universal human nature and universal education. Whereas Counts stayed in the contextual framework, Brameld, seeking to develop a global theory, needed to devise a means for discussing human commonalities (what is the same about people worldwide) without lapsing into a universalizing metaphysics. Brameld believed he found a solution to the problem in anthropology, which examined human culture as all people everywhere had some form of culture.

While recognizing cultural differences, Brameld sought to identify human common-alities. The emphasis on commonalities was needed to deal with the issue of cultural diver-sity within world unity and to construct Reconstruction's international dimension of Reconstructionist philosophy. Much the same question applies to multicultural education and education for human rights: People are culturally different but do they share common-alities, especially a shared idea of human rights and social justice? In answering the ques-tion, Brameld sought to recognize and encourage the diverse contributions of different races, ethnic groups, and religions while embracing all people in a global cultural whole. In making the case for a global association of people, Brameld looked to the commonalities that different cultures shared, the common denominators that made for one human race.

Identifying common denominators that were functional, based on what people do, Brameld stated that people:

> . . . make love; they nourish themselves; they take care of their bodies; they play; they work; they learn; they worship; they create aesthetically; they make rules; they sorrow; they communicate; they govern; they shelter and clothe themselves; they protect one another; they count; they possess; they visit and trade; they cooperate and organize.[29]

According to Brameld, the needed philosophy of education should express values based on interests and needs of human beings as determined by the anthropological study of earth's cultures. It should identify the common values that races, ethnic and language groups, religious denominations, and socioeconomic classes share as well as those that are different and separate them. The emergent Reconstructionism, as an educational theory, should attempt to establish, by discussion and consensus, the institutional patterns needed so that human beings could achieve those values they share worldwide.[30]

Brameld's Reconstructive Design for American Education

Brameld argued that the "great imperative confronting American schools" is to "transform them into powerful institutions of cultural change toward the goal of a planet-wide democratic order." Education should devote itself to reconstructing the culture, which was in peril of collapsing if not revitalized.[31] For him, the needed reconstruction was no longer limited to the United States but required a far-reaching remaking of world culture in which technology is used for the healthy economic security of the masses of people. Brameld's list of areas that needed to be included in a broadened curriculum were:

- Examining controversial political, social, economic, moral, scientific, religious issues often closed to educational analysis.
- Analyzing middle-class psychocultural patterns for their weaknesses and strengths.
- Examining technologically generated cultural and social change.
- Examining sexual relationships for their moral as well as biological aspects.
- Analyzing emotional and psychological problems.
- Studying the problems generated by nuclear energy, proliferation of nuclear weapons, and the implications of space exploration in the science curriculum.[32]
- Examining the global problems of population explosion, environmental degradation, and the disparity between the technologically developed and less technologically developed areas of the world.[33]

A Reconstructionist School and Curriculum. To illustrate how Reconstructionism would function in a school setting, Brameld described it in a community college, with students ranging in age from seventeen to twenty. The curriculum would be organized around one central question: "What kind of world can we have and do we want?" The question would be pursued in a committed way by both students and teachers; however, there would be no attempt at indoctrination. The students' and teachers' beliefs and values would be clearly stated, according to Brameld's concept of defensible partiality, so that those who held them could articulate them to others and invite critical awareness, discussion, and even dissent. Students would examine the question from an interdisciplinary and multidisciplinary approach in its historical, political, economic, scientific, philosophical, and religious perspectives. A wide array of resources would be used from original research, journals and books, community experience, and expert authorities. Students and teachers would also approach the question from a discipline, from the sciences or humanities.[34]

Brameld structured the curriculum over four years. The first year would be devoted to economics—to the processes needed for producing, consuming, and distributing goods and services. In true Reconstructionist style, planning was emphasized and the focusing questions related to the equitable and environmentally safe use of energy, economic security, and full employment. The second year examined redesigning democratic political structures to safeguard majority rule and minority rights. The third year was devoted to the broad cultural sphere where students examined how human culture, especially health care, education, art, and religion are affected by economic and political change and reconstruction. The fourth year is subdivided into examining the psychological sphere and the interrelations of the economic, political, cultural, and psychological dimensions of human experience.[35]

Reconstructionist Teaching

In 1944, Brameld designed a school program, "Design for America," which was implemented, as an experiment, at Floodwood High School in Minnesota. The overriding goal of the project was to "build by cooperative thinking and exploration a blueprint of our future society."[36] The focusing questions that guided the project were: (1) Is it important to construct a plan for America's future? and (2) Is it possible to state the plan's goals so precisely that they will be clearly indicate their implementation? Using cooperative learning and problem-solving, the students recommended: a national public works program; full employment; fair treatment of minorities, especially African Americans; and international and intercultural respect and social justice for all races and peoples.[37]

Brameld's Vision of Reconstructed Society

Brameld's Reconstructionism pointed to a vision of a reconstructed America and a reconstructed world. Though originating with Dewey's Instrumentalism, Brameld's vision of a new world appeared to some to be utopian and too separated from the reality of the here and now. Brameld made no apologies for being visionary, if not utopian. A vision of the possibilities of humanity would guide humankind to a new and better future. The promised good life would encourage individuals to release and share their ideas and values and to share them with others. The reconstructed society of the future would be free of barriers that kept people apart, segregated, or confined to sexist, racist, and classist enclaves. In the new global world order, people of all nations would have unlimited freedom to meet each other through travel and open communication. The world's economic resources would not be monopolized by the wealthy but would be shared by an international democratic government subject to the will of the majority of the world's people. Education in the new world would have a large place for the arts and humanities as well as for the sciences.[38]

Reconstructionist Themes

Although the Reconstructionists saw themselves as philosophers of education, their ideas did not fit the more traditional definition of philosophy. Though it was a better fit with Pragmatism, the fit was inexact. Unlike the Idealists and Realists, the Reconstructionists, like the Pragmatists, did not undertake to explain truth, knowledge, and values in universal metaphysical terms. Such speculation for them was unscientific speculation. Their use of the scientific method, a basic ingredient of Pragmatism, too, had to be reconstructed and tied to the culture in some way. They also typically related and anchored their philosophy or ideology to another area or discipline. Calling his approach a "civilizational" philosophy of education, Counts anchored it to American history, especially to Beard's Progressive interpretation. Brameld, too, anchored his philosophy to anthropology, calling it an "Anthropological Philosophy of Education."

Of the Reconstructionists, Brameld, unlike Counts, had earned a doctorate in philosophy. While Counts was an educator who veered into philosophy, Brameld took the other route and was a philosopher who entered the field of education. To make Reconstructionism a philosophy, Brameld needed to stipulate his own definition of philosophy. He did so by redefining philosophy in terms of Reconstructionism rather than determining how Reconstructionism corresponded with the definition of philosophy. Brameld defined philosophy not as metaphysics, epistemology, and axiology but rather said it is "the persistent effort of both ordinary and sophisticated people to make life as intelligible and meaningful as possible." It offered a means "to analyze and organize the premises" on which people conduct their "political, scientific, aesthetic, religious, and educational practices."[39] Anticipating Postmodernism and Critical Theory, Brameld used the term *operationalist* to describe Reconstructionist philosophy in that laws and morals were human constructions based on humankind's "ever changing transactions with nature and culture."[40]

In constructing a new definition of philosophy, the Reconstructionists met with criticism. More-traditional philosophers, especially those associated with Aristotle and Realism, claimed that the Reconstructionists were not genuine philosophers but were really politicians or ideologues in the guise of philosophers. Even some of their Experimentalist conferees claimed that the Reconstructionists had imposed political ends on education, which should be an open-ended process of free inquiry.

Broadening the Meaning of Philosophy of Education

Just as they redefined philosophy, the Reconstructionists also reconstructed the meaning of philosophy of education and of education itself. They took a very broad view of education that went well beyond formal education in the school. Philosophy of education should be interdisciplinary and incorporate the most significant new research and findings of the physical, biological, and social sciences as well as the innovative creations of the arts, literature, and architecture.

The Reconstructionist educators fashioned a broad definition of education that includes schooling but also encompasses a full range of informal and nonformal institutions and agencies such as the media, churches, clubs, museums, and galleries, and today would include the World Wide Web and the Internet. In particular, a Reconstructionist philosophy of education is oriented to the future and is visionary. Its purpose is not only to analyze and deconstruct knowledge but to use it as building blocks in creating the desired society of the future.[41]

Further, the Reconstructionist sees education in political, economic, and social terms. Brameld, for example, argues that education should become the "copartner of politics—the politics of comprehending and implementing popular government on a worldwide scale." In this sense, philosophy of education is concerned with the necessary foundations for such a partnership. For him, these foundations should be global and oriented to the public welfare. Internationally, they should encompass people and their institutions on a functional continuum from localities, states, and regions to the nation. They should be oriented to guaranteeing the general social and economic welfare of people—a welfare state of public service.[42] The public service state establishes and implements standards safeguarding human welfare in work, education, and health care.

Here, the Reconstructionists encountered the opposition of the Essentialists, such as William C. Bagley and Isaac Kandel, who argued that the Reconstructionists were creating impossible demands on schools that could never be realized. If education included everything, what was special about schools? The Essentialists, countering the Reconstructionist argument, insisted that schools had the primary function of being places of academic learning that transmitted necessary skills and subjects that were based on the liberal arts and sciences and that led students to this cultural heritage.

Relating Ideology to Education

Although Counts called his version of Social Reconstructionism a "civilizational philosophy" of education, it more closely resembles an ideology rather than a philosophy. Although concerned with moral and ethical considerations, Counts, unlike a philosopher, did not deal with broad metaphysical and epistemological issues. Rather, he developed a highly contextual ideology with its own version of the past and a program for deliberate social change. Counts was developing an educational ideology to be used as an instrument to mobilize the nation's Progressive and Liberal educators to join with like-minded allies in the struggle against vested special economic interests and the forces of Conservatism and reaction. Teachers were to be partisan, not neutral, and committed, not aloof, from the momentous issues facing the nation and, indeed, the world.

Contextualism and the Identification of Contemporary Issues

Social Reconstructionism emphasizes the examination of the cultural-social-political-economic contexts in which education and schooling occur. They look at particular places in which schools are located to find the issues that need to be addressed. In doing this, however, they were not localists who argued for the local control of schools. Nor did they necessarily favor site-based administration and curriculum. For Counts, the context was the United States; for Brameld, the world. In closely analyzing schools in relation to context, Reconstructionist analysis is geared to locate socioeconomic and political strains, inconsistencies, and tensions that can be defined and addressed as problems and issues. When educational problems are traced back sociologically, historically, economically, and politically to contexts in which they are situated, the analysis becomes multidisciplinary.[43] The educational policies, too, become inter- or multidisciplinary. The contemporary issues that would attract the most attention from Reconstructionists are those that relate to social justice and equality. Reconstructionists, much like contemporary Critical Theorists, would seek to expose, examine, and end what they define as antidemocratic trends, such as hedonistic individualism and consumerism, profit-driven global economics, and disparities in the distribution of wealth.[44]

Cultural or Contextual Relativism

The Reconstructionists were relativists who looked to particular cultures as their fields of inquiry. As proponents of **cultural relativism**, they held that beliefs and values varied with different groups, living in specific places, at particular times in history. As the group's cultural situation changed, so did their belief and value systems.

Counts, Brameld, and the other Reconstructionists rejected the Idealist, Realist, and Perennialist view that as truth was universal and eternal so was education. They rejected the Platonic and Aristotelian philosophies in which education was a universal process, as Robert Hutchins and Mortimer Adler claimed, in which unchanging truths were the same at every time and place. The relativistic impulse was easily translated into an educational principle—that education, too, especially when organized as schooling, expressed a particular culture and society at a given period of history in a given geographical setting.

Cultural relativism is a major issue that sets Conservative ideology and Perennialist educational theory apart from Pragmatism, Reconstructionism, Postmodernism, and Critical Theory. The simple but highly charged question is: Are people essentially the same or are they different? If they are the same, then they should have the same education; however, if they are different, then they should have an education based on these differences.

The older and more traditional philosophies such as Plato's Idealism and Aristotle's Realism asserted that human beings shared a common human nature that defined them as human beings. Christianity, too, asserted the reality of a universal human nature and a God-created and ordained world of universal and eternal truths and values. Educational theories based on this universality emphasize that truth is universal and timeless and the education should be based on this truth.

Pragmatists, such as John Dewey, challenged the doctrine of an unchanging human nature and emphasized that human beings live in, adapt to, and respond to a changing natural and social environment. Dewey and the Pragmatists looked to the process of the scientific method as the means by which human beings successfully interacted with an ever changing natural and social reality. Rather than looking to a universal human nature, Dewey and his Experimentalist and Progressive followers sought to find a process that could be applied to solving problems of an ever changing environment. The Reconstructionists, emphasizing contexts of the field of culture and education, looked to people dealing with problems in particular situations for the cues about education rather than to an unchanging human nature.

Contextual or Cultural Relativism versus Universal Truth and Values

Contextual or Cultural Relativism	*Universal Truth and Values*
1. Claims to truth and expressions of values are relative to contexts—particular places and times.	1. Truth and values are universal and are the same throughout the world.
2. Education and schooling reflect the cultural contexts in which they occur.	2. Education is the universal process of how people acquire learning; schooling is the particular process in which the culture is transmitted from adults to children.
3. Because values are relative to times and places, they are changing and reflect responses to environmental situations.	3. Values are eternal and universal and need to be transmitted deliberately by schools and teachers.
4. Human freedom is enhanced by providing people with the cultural and educational tools to reexamine, redefine, and reconstruct their values.	4. Human freedom is safeguarded by recognizing that people, by their human nature, have universal human rights.

Educational Implications

Fascinated by social analysis and criticism and concerned about the future of American and world culture, the Reconstructionists see the school as a transformative agent, an agency for deliberate social change. The school should not only dare to build a new social order but it is imperative that it do so. The school's curriculum should not be a mirror that reflects back the existing society. The image reflected back contained the injustices, inequalities—the unresolved issues and conflicts—of the status quo. It reflects the image of the powerful and how they think and what they value. No, the Reconstructionists argue, the school should do much more than reflect the existing society; it needs to change the society. The Reconstructionists believe that the school could and should take a leading role in building a new society.[45]

Reconstructionists challenge the Conservative and Essentialist idea that education and schooling should transmit the existing culture and society; for them, transmission is largely a process in which the school acts to preserve the status quo and its inequities. For Reconstructionists the educational process is to reconstruct, reform, and renew the existing society.

Role of the Social Studies

Because of their emphasis on social, political, and economic analysis, the key Reconstructionist curriculum area is the **social studies**. The social studies, as a curriculum area, spans both elementary and secondary schools. Unlike the older subjects of history, mathematics, and science, the social studies were developed in the twentieth century. Social studies represent a fusion and integration of information and generalizations from history, geography, anthropology, sociology, economics, and political science. This integrated study is especially amenable for the Reconstructionists, who in their theory building use an interdisciplinary approach for a range of subject-matter disciplines. The social studies, which are frequently reexamined and revised, meet the Reconstructionist demand that education and the curriculum not be set in stone as monuments to the past but instead experience constant reappraisal and reconstruction in the light of social, political, economic, and cultural change.

The social studies were shaped by historical and cultural relativists such as Charles Beard and George S. Counts, who believed that there were no universal laws of history but rather that historical trends were shaped or conditioned by the social, political, and—most important—economic forces and trends of a given time and place—a context. The past is written and interpreted in terms of the present's problems and the future's possibilities.[46]

Interdisciplinary social studies were opposed at the time of their origin and today face Conservative and Essentialist critics who see them as free-floating and ill-defined. These critics contend that the social studies are unsystematic and unstructured and to blame for American students' ineptitude in history and geography.

Harold Rugg and the Social Studies Controversy

The relationship of the social studies to Social Reconstructionism is nicely illustrated in the history of curriculum by the Rugg textbook controversy. Harold Rugg (1886–1960), a colleague of Counts at Teachers College, was a national leader in the social studies as well as a prominent Reconstructionist.[47]

Conceiving of the social studies as an multidisciplinary issues-focused area, Rugg wrote a social studies textbook series, titled *Man and His Changing Society,* that sold more than a million copies and enjoyed nationwide school adoptions in the 1920s and 1930s.[48] Rugg's texts were designed to involve students in critical thinking on controversial social, political, and economic issues. Most texts at the time reflected the prevailing attitudes and were used to cultivate patriotism; Rugg's texts often criticized inequities and disparities in American society.[49] Rugg's issue-oriented books were deliberately intended to raise provocative, controversial questions such as, "Is the United States a land of opportunity for all our people?" The series' instructional guide advised teachers that the United States is not a land of opportunity for all and there were differences in living standards, income, and security between different socioeconomic classes.[50] Rugg was challenging celebrationist school histories that pictured the country as a seamless community, united by American patriotism, and enjoying political freedom and the competitive opportunities of an unbridled free market economy.

During the depression years of the 1930s, Rugg joined other Reconstructionists such as George Counts in arguing that the schools should construct a new social order. Rugg's vision for America was that of a great society created by "large-scale social and economic planning" and by a reconstructed education that would "cultivate integrated and creative" persons.[51]

In the early 1940s, Rugg encountered staunch opposition from conservative business and political groups who launched a national investigation of his textbooks, claiming they were subversive to the American tradition and the free enterprise system. In 1941, for example, the American Legion distributed pamphlets, entitled *The Complete Rugg Philosophy,* that charged Rugg with undermining Americanism and seeking to indoctrinate students in socialism.[52] Under relentless attack, Rugg's books were withdrawn in many school districts and virtually disappeared from the schools.[53]

The episode regarding Rugg's textbooks signaled that the social studies would be a consistently controversial area. The social studies deal with citizenship education—the teaching and learning of civic knowledge and values. R. W. Evans, a nationally recognized social studies educator, identifies the key questions as: "What kind of citizens and citizen education do we want? How far can and should schools go in providing opportunities for social criticism?" Social studies are often redefined and reorganized to incorporate developments in the parent social sciences on which they are based; they are also redesigned periodically to reflect contemporary social, political, and economic issues and trends. They come under attack from more traditional educators, especially Conservatives and Essentialists, who argue that history and geography provide a more stable and structured introduction to social knowledge about time and place.

The Rugg textbook episode remains highly instructive for teachers. There is always a risk in teaching controversial issues that deal with race, religion, ethnicity, language, class, feminism, and human sexuality. For example, sex education is controversial between those who argue that it should prescribe abstinence from sexual relationships outside of marriage and those who argue that it should inform students about method of contraception. Teaching about war and peace can be controversial, especially in the current sharp divisions over the war in Iraq. Even the issue of teaching about Darwin's theory of evolution of species remains highly contentious. The Social Reconstructionists urged teachers to risk being committed to a new vision of America and the world. What do you think?

Natural and Physical Sciences

Coming out of Pragmatism and Progressivism, the Social Reconstructionists saw science and the scientific method as part of the strategy to be used in creating a new social order. Although they generally subscribed to Dewey's Experimentalism or Instrumentalism, they did not see the scientific method as a neutral process but saw it being used to reach defined goals such as social and economic equality. The social studies, or social sciences, most directly conveyed Reconstructionist themes in the curriculum, but the Reconstructionists also were proponents of science and the use of the scientific method. Indeed, they most likely viewed political science, anthropology, economics, sociology, and social psychology as evolving sciences. They generally aligned themselves with Dewey's emphasis on the scientific method and saw it as being encapsulated into solving social, political, economic, and educational problems. Some of their Pragmatist critics contended that their end of a reconstructed society involved slapping a preconceived nonscientific end on the process that closed rather than opened it. Nevertheless, Reconstructionists championed their version of the scientific method, as they conceived of it.

Counts and other Reconstructionists gave great importance to technology, which they saw as the application of science to industry and communications. They welcomed technology and in their penchant for planning adopted a kind of social engineering. For all of these reasons, science is an important subject in the curriculum.

Reconstructionist Philosophy of Science Education

An important issue was: Is science objective, neutral, and divorced from social, political, and economic issues? Does the scientist need to be a neutral observer who does not allow the intrusion of extraneous variables to jeopardize the experiment? As he took on the issue of teaching about religion, Brameld sought to answer the question. He related philosophy of science to philosophy in general and to the social sciences. Scientists needed to become conscious of the social and cultural consequences of their discoveries and inventions. What happened in the laboratory soon found its way outside. For example, the splitting of the atom changed society and culture. The atomic bomb could end human life on earth. But then again, nuclear energy might be a new, less polluting way of running the engines of an increasingly technological society. The teaching of the natural and physical sciences—biology, botany, zoology, chemistry, and physics—needed to be reconstructed. Like the social studies, they should not be taught in departmentalized fashion, isolated from their interdisciplinary connections. The pervasive interconnections between science, the social sciences, the humanities, and the arts need to be made intrinsic to teaching and learning. The pressing issues were how can science improve health care, protect the environment, and improve the quality of all life—plant, animal, and human—on earth.

Religion in the Public Schools

In the twenty-first century, the issue of the role of religion in American society and education has again come to the surface. It is not the first time, however, that religious issues have been discussed and debated in the United States. For some, the various Supreme Court decisions have mandated Jefferson's idea of the separation of church and state: Government should not support the establishment of the religion, nor should it interfere with its free exercise. For others, especially some cultural conservatives and fundamentalist Christians, the U.S. Constitution does not specifically prohibit commemorative religious observances in public spaces, including schools. They also contend that the United States is a nation founded on Christian principles.

Religion and its influence are historically significant in global and American history. How should this influence be examined in schools? The Supreme Court has stated that teachers can teach about religion but not teach a religion. What does it mean to teach about religion? Most Reconstructionists, because of their contextualism, were cultural relativists. They were also heirs of the Enlightenment who saw the interpretation of the world in scientific terms. Closely affiliated with secular humanism, they considered religious beliefs and practices private, definitely not public, matters.

Brameld, who spoke to so many issues that others feared to broach, addressed teaching about religion. He concluded that, historically, human beings worldwide have had some kind of religious experience and that experience, like any other experience, should be studied in the public schools. He carefully distinguished teaching *about* religious experience from teaching religion. The key word was *about*. His position differed from teaching religion, which meant instructing students in the doctrines of a particular church or denomination. Brameld also did not hesitate to discuss spirituality and spiritual values, which he believed to be part of any discussion of human values. For him, spiritual values, though they might be related to religion, were not necessarily religious.

Brameld believed the religious dimension of human cultural experience should be studied, as with any dimension, by using his principle of defensible partiality. Applying defensible partiality to the study of religious experience meant students should be exposed to a consideration of beliefs as they are expressed by those who hold them. However, all beliefs, including religious ones, are subject to searching comparative analysis in which their adherents are compelled to defend them openly and publicly in the face of all possible evidence for and against their religious commitment.[54] The presentation and discussion of religious beliefs is to take place in an atmosphere of mutual respect.

The Indoctrination or Imposition Issue

The Reconstructionists urged schools, teachers, and students to go beyond the neutral discussion of topics in which the teacher presented both sides of an issue and left it to students to make up their own mind. Typically, solutions were to be deferred until a later date, when the student completed school and was an adult voter. The Reconstructionists believed that this kind of neutrality was not really neutral at all but in reality preserved the socio-economic and political status quo and left power in the control of dominant economically favored individuals and groups. Believing that claims of neutrality and objectivity were either phony or an attempt to step away from social responsibility and justice, the Reconstructionists called on teachers and students not only to examine issues but to structure promising solutions and work for their implementation.

The Reconstructionist emphasis on commitment to agreed-on goals and strategies raised the issue of academic freedom. Should instruction be objective and neutral or should it be committed to a specific point of view? Reconstructionists, like the Critical Theorists, believed ideological neutrality was impossible. Critics of the Reconstructionists, who included some Progressives and Pragmatists as well as the more traditional Essentialists and Perennialists, argued that the Reconstructionists, in pursuing their goal of creating a new social order, would indoctrinate students. They would use schools and teachers to impose their blueprint for the future society on students. Essentialists and Perennialists argued that the role of teachers was to transmit academic skills and subjects and not to act as political activists in the classroom. Although many Reconstructionists came out of the Pragmatist philosophical tradition, some Pragmatists argued that the Reconstructionists were distorting the use of the scientific method because the Reconstructionist new social order did not come from open-ended inquiry but involved adding their own antecedent plan to the process. Progressives, especially child-centered ones, felt that the Reconstructionists were imposing a political agenda on children that would interfere with their own individual creativity and exploration of the environment.

The Reconstructions, however, maintaining their position, replied that education, or schooling, always involves choosing some elements of human culture, some skills or subjects over others, and that this choice imposes a particular version of culture on children. Schooling, they contended, is never neutral but always committed to some ideological perspective.

Brameld, who argued for defensible partiality, claimed that the Reconstructionist position was not indoctrination. He argued that indoctrination is instruction that proceeds in only one direction—from the teacher to the student—to establish in the student's mind a firm acceptance of some doctrine without critical discussion and comparison to alternative doctrines.[55] He argued that what the Reconstructionist teacher advocated had to stand up to rigorous and open criticism and comparison and contrast to alternative positions.

Educational Leadership

Reconstructionism enlarges the social, political, and economic dimensions of school administration and teaching beyond pedagogy. Counts and others talked about preparing a new kind of leader in education, an educational statesperson, who went beyond curriculum construction and instruction to operate from a larger, broader, more politically and culturally charged vision of the future that included hypothesizing about a culture's promises, purposes, and problems. This visionary leader would work to adapt or reconstruct educational institutions to society's changing needs.

Reconstructionism's Ideological and Philosophical Relationships

Philosophically, Social Reconstructionism grew out of American Pragmatism, especially John Dewey's Instrumentalism. Although he associated with the Reconstructionists at Teachers College, Dewey did not identify specifically with Reconstructionism as an ideology or theory. However, the concept of the reconstruction of personal and social experience, which permeated Dewey's Instrumentalism, was a Reconstructionist theme. For Dewey, socially intelligent persons continually reconstructed their ideas and values as they used their previous experiences as instruments to solve new problems. Intelligent societies, like intelligent persons, too, reconstructed their social, political, and economic experience when they faced problems. As individuals joined in communities and used open-ended experimental and democratic processes to solve their shared and mutual problems, they were on the way to creating the "great society," the great democratic community. Dewey's books *Individualism Old and New* and *Liberalism and Social Action* addressed issues raised by Counts, Brameld, and other Reconstructionist educators.[56] Like Counts, Dewey called for a reconstruction of individualism and Liberalism that moved them from their laissez-faire origins to a more cooperative, associative, and revitalized process of thinking and acting. A revitalized and socially charged Liberalism could be an instrument in solving the problems of an increasingly corporate industrial and technological society.

The curriculum historian Gerald Podner identifies three significant ideas from Pragmatism, especially Dewey's Experimentalism, that shaped Reconstructionist theory: (1) the method of experimental science; (2) the concept of democracy; and (3) the concept of interdependence.[57] Reconstructionists believed that the scientific method needed to be applied to political decision-making and, in turn, schools could cultivate the public use of the scientific method. Education could develop social intelligence as a democratic means of decision-making. Reconstructionists endorsed Dewey's concept of democracy as an open-ended society, free from absolutes that restricted freedom of inquiry, but gave it their own more particular political and economic interpretation. They also emphasized, like Dewey, that American society was rapidly moving beyond individualism and voluntarism to a growingly interdependent society and economy.

Liberalism

Reconstructionists shared many of the principles of Liberalism, especially freedom of speech, press, and assembly; government through popularly elected legislative bodies; a fair and independent judiciary; public education; and academic freedom. They embraced the welfare-state version of Liberalism, especially the need for government to secure the common good through social security and health care programs.

There were significant differences, however, in how Liberals and Reconstructionists viewed social planning and directed social change. As incremental transactionists, Liberals responded to particular issues and problems by implementing specific solutions that they believed were pertinent to how the problem had been defined. Their concept of social and educational change was incremental—in small pieces or additions —rather than sweeping and transformative. Further, Liberal motivations were to preserve and maintain the basic social and educational structure by reforming or improving it rather than radically transforming it.

Progressivism

The Progressive movement in education and the Progressive Education Association (PEA) were highly porous, large umbrella-like groupings that attracted like-minded people who had wide-ranging educational views. The movement was big and broad enough to include both the child-centered and the Social Reconstructionist educators. Child-centered Progressives believed that the curriculum should be based on children's interest and needs, which would grow into social intelligence. For the child-centered Progressives, Progressive schools would be indirect agencies of social change. The focus of education, for them, was the individual child. Free of coercion, the Progressive school would liberate children, who, in turn, would liberate society. The child-centered Progressives emphasized education that liberated children from unnecessary restraints on their curiosity and creativity. They opposed the Reconstructionist goal of creating a new society as another form of imposition on children that limited their creativity and freedom.

Like their child-centered conferees, Social Reconstructionism came from Progressivism but it was Progressivism with a socioeconomic and political agenda. Social Reconstructionists saw the school as an agency to create deliberately a new social order. It was to be a social order that was democratic, cooperative, and egalitarian. The Reconstructionist school would follow an agenda and have a program designed to create a new society. It was at this juncture that Progressive child-centered educators and Social Reconstructionist educators clashed.

Marxism

Marxism's influence on Reconstructionism is often debated. Counts, the catalyst for Reconstructionism, was a scholar in comparative and international education. He conducted on-site research in the Soviet Union, where the official ideology was Marxist-Leninism, in the late 1920s and early 1930s. Although he initially admired Soviet centralized planning in Stalin's first Five-Year Plan, he had grown disenchanted and become a decided anti-Communist by the late 1930s. Counts opposed international and American Communism throughout the rest of his career. He apparently heeded the advice of the historian Charles A. Beard, his friend and mentor, who advised him to base his educational theory on American rather than foreign sources. Counts, influenced by Beard, saw the economy as a largely conditioning but not necessarily determining cause in social and political change and control. Here Beard's and Counts's orientation departed from the Marxist insistence that all history, politics, and society are economically determined and subject to the universal laws of dialectical materialism.[58] Taking care to refer to the shaping power of economic forces as a conditioning rather than determining process, Counts stated: "It is contended here that man in history is neither wholly bound nor wholly free, that his life, though always conditioned, is never fated. . . . Within the bounds of the possible human preference operates."[59]

Brameld had studied Marxism while a doctoral student at the University of Chicago, where he researched Lenin's writings for his dissertation, "The Role of Acquiescence in Leninism." Brameld's dissertation was revised and published as *A Philosophic Approach to Communism* (1933). Brameld would later find Marxism to be an inadequate dogmatic doctrine.

Critical Theory

In many respects, Social Reconstruction theoretically anticipated Critical Theory. (For Critical Theory see the next chapter.) Both theories argue for a rigorous critique of American society and education, argue against educational objectivity and neutrality, and are committed to a program of action to change society and schools.

There is a similarity between Counts's emphasis on the relativism of history and the Postmodernist emphasis on history as a construction of the record of the past by contending groups and classes. In his argument that history is contingent on those who interpret it and that their interpretation, in turn, reflects time, place, and circumstances, Counts argued that history is a construction. Critical Theorists would find Counts's and Brameld's contextual and multidisciplinary approaches of education congenial with their own theoretical position. Critical Theorists would likely praise the Reconstructionists' concern for the nation's unemployed and underrepresented masses and their argument that education should be a transformative force for popular change. Both Postmodernists and Critical Theorists would agree with the Reconstructionists that education is never completely objective, unbiased, and neutral. They would commend the Reconstructionist call for teachers to be committed to an interpretation of history and to an analysis of social, economic, and political issues that would empower the dispossessed and downtrodden groups and classes.

Although there are similarities between the Reconstructionists and the Critical Theorists, there are also distinct differences. Drawing from their Progressive origins, the

Reconstructionists embraced the Enlightenment belief in progress, that the future, if intelligently guided, would be better than the past. For them, modernity, deriving from the Enlightenment, was a positive force to improve the human situation. They had faith in the power of science, social science, engineering, technology, and planning to promote social and economic progress.[60]

The Reconstructionists were modernists, not antimodernists; they were in the Enlightenment tradition in that they believed in progress through the application of inquiry and science to society. They were not affected by a Luddite mentality of opposition to technology but saw technology instead as a force of liberation. For example, Reconstructionist educators would see global warming and the degradation of the environment as a major planetary issue. They likely would look to technology to find alternatives to the use of fossil fuels and not adopt a back-to-nature solution. They would see rampant capitalism and runaway consumerism as the forces causing global warming.

In their attachment to the Enlightenment, progress, science, and modernity, the Reconstructionists differed from the Postmodernists and Critical Theorists who see the Enlightenment as the source of many of humankind's ills. Rather than being a necessarily liberating force, science, when bound up with progress and modernity, became a source of power by which scientific elites dominated the oppressed. The whole Enlightenment rationale that ushered in the Age of Reason was an ideological smoke screen, an ideological pabulum, fed to the uncritical masses to keep them waiting for the illusory promised land that was forever on the horizon but never in reach.

However, Postmodernists and Critical Theorists would find Counts overly impressed and overly committed to technology, which he saw as emanating from Enlightenment theory. Indeed, he was developing the concept of technology into a metanarrative—a transforming force that was working throughout the world. Counts was clearly preaching the merits of modernity and modernization. It was not modernity that he feared but rather that the engines of modernization would be controlled by special interests. For Postmodernists, modernity itself is a historical construct that originated in and still sustains oppressive power relationships.

Reconstructionists and Critical Theorists also disagreed on the degree of centralization and localism in social, political, and educational agencies. A difference between Critical Theorists and Reconstructionists is the degree of centralization and localism in the new society. The Reconstructionists believed that only a centralized authority could accomplish the creation of the new society; Critical theorists emphasize the local site. Brameld, however, called for a working synthesis that integrated centralized authority with decentralized administration.[61]

Conservatism, Essentialism, and Perennialism.   The Conservatives, Essentialists, and Perennialists would find very little to support and much to condemn in Reconstructionism. These schools of educational ideology and theory would condemn the Reconstructionist view of the school as an agency of deliberate social change as a serious attack on the school's primary purpose as an academic institution. To them, the school's primary mission is to transmit the cultural heritage as knowledge, organized into skills and subjects, from one generation to the next. Perennialists, in particular, would contend that the Reconstructionists used terminology carelessly, confusing the distinctions between education, in the general sense, and schooling, in the particular sense. Schooling might be contextual; education itself, however, is transcontextual and is a universal process of human growth and development. Essentialists would contend that Reconstructionists were foisting an ideology on the students and indoctrinating them in a particular version of history and the social studies. Further, their cultural relativism would lead to ethical relativism that would erode ethical and moral standards. For Diane Ravitch, Counts's ideological platform was another of the "failed reforms" of the Progressives and Reconstructionists that attempted to divert schools from their academic purposes.[62]

A Reconstructionist Educational Scenario

The scenario for the illustration of Reconstructionist instruction takes place in a charter high school that emphasizes interdisciplinary teaching and learning.[63] Ms. Martha Seward is teaching a social studies class. In a graduate course in philosophy of education that she is taking for her master's degree, she read the works of Harold Rugg and Theodore Brameld and decides to try their ideas in her class. Because she teaches at a magnet school, geared to interdisciplinary teaching, she decides to introduce an issue-oriented approach that would lead to some change.

Ms. Seward met her class of twenty-five sophomore students in early September and introduced the idea that they would be working on an issue in the social studies. Unlike the more laissez-faire Progressive teacher, Ms. Seward was more directive—she would introduce the approach but also encourage students to indentify the particular problem.

Stage One: Identifying the Issue

In a large group discussion, Ms. Seward asked the students to think about the most important issues facing the United States and the world. She also told them that they would be asked to identify an issue that would be the class project for the entire semester. She asked them to watch the news on television and to read the newpapers and to return the next day to identify the issues that they had discovered in their reading and watching. Also, she encouraged them to talk to their parents, family members, and friends about these issues.

Over several classes, the students identified the issues. They came up with a whole range of issues: the war in Iraq, the tribal and religious conflict in Dafur in Sudan, the high cost of attending colleges and universities, terrorism, school violence, and global warming and climate change. Ms. Seward led the class discussion. The class decided that all the problems were important. Several students who had older brothers and sisters in the armed services in Iraq made the case that the war should be the topic. Others agreed but contended that global warming was crucial. If the environment of the planet was in jeopardy, all life would also be in jeopardy. Ms. Seward did not have the students vote on the issue that they preferred. Rather, the students put forth their viewpoints and reached a consensus in which all agreed to pursue the topic. (Ms. Seward used Brameld's ideas about using human relations skills to arrive at agreement.)

Stage 2: Defining Terms and the Problem

Once the problem had been identified, Ms. Seward wrote the term *global warming* on the chalkboard. Now, she decided to see what the students would do with the term. She asked them to define *global warming*. Martin Swift, a student, volunteered, "It's obvious that it means that the temperature of the earth is getting higher and the climate is getting warmer." Mina Patel, whose grandparents had immigrated to the United States from India, volunteered, "When I visited India last year, the temperatures were much higher than in the United States and I had some problems adjusting to them." She asked, "Does global warming mean that the temperatures everywhere are getting higher, or is it something that is happening in specific countries?" Several students said they didn't know enough about the problem. Ms. Seward said that the class needed to define their terms and do some initial basic research on global warming. At this point, the class divided into teams to do preliminary research: Team A would do research in the library, trying to identify books and articles about global warming; Team B would access the Web and explore sites dealing with the topic. Anthony Cizek volunteered, "I'm taking Mr. Kleminski's class on the integrated natural sciences and he has discussed global warming. I'd like to invite him to visit our class and share some information with us." Ms. Seward agreed that would be a good idea. Students met in their research groups, shared their information, and prepared to report their findings to the class.

The students found out that global warming is a specific example of a more general term, *climate change*. Although there are natural causes for climate change, they found that much scientific evidence points to human factors that are contributing to it. The class stipulated a definition of global warming as the increase in the average temperature of the earth's atmosphere and oceans in recent decades and in an open-ended way raised questions about its projected rise in the future. Mr. Kleminski, the science teacher, made a presentation in class. He had developed a PowerPoint program that included charts and graphs about patterns of global temperatures and carbon dioxide emissions in the atmosphere over the past one hundred years that showed a rise in the last decade. He said that many scientists, but not all of them, concluded that the increase in global temperatures since the mid-twentieth century is very likely caused by increases in "greenhouse gas emissions." At this point, Anthony Cizek raised his hand and asked Mr. Kleminski, "What are greenhouse gas emissions?" Mr. Kleminski replied, "They are caused by human beings who use fossil fuels such as oil, gas, and coal for energy; the emissions from these fuels rise in the earth's atmosphere and create a cover of pollutants that keep the temperatures close to the earth and over time caused them to rise." Mike Carbone, a student, asked "What difference does global warming make to us, why should we worry about it?" Mr. Kleminski said that the increase in global temperatures is expected to produce changes such as glacial melting at the North and South poles that will cause the oceans to rise and flood coastal areas and cities; it may cause serious weather changes, especially rainfall, that may spur the growth of deserts and reduce food production; it may lead to the extinction of certain species, such as polar bears and walruses, that cannot adapt to drastic climate change. The class thanked Mr. Kleminski, who as he was leaving turned to Ms. Seward and said, "Why don't we have a teacher's meeting on this subject?" Mr. Kleminski, who was very interested in global warming, also had an ulterior motive. He wanted to get to know Ms. Seward, whom he found to be an attractive and intelligent young woman.

Interdisciplinary Cooperation.   Later, Ms. Seward and Mr. Kleminski met over coffee in the teachers' lounge. Ms. Seward further explained that she was experimenting with Social Reconstruction in her social studies class and that her class had chosen to examine global warming as its problem. Mr. Kleminski said that his science class was also dealing with global warming as an issue in the sciences. At this point, they decided to work collaboratively on global warming. At certain times in the semester, they would bring their classes together to share findings and discussion. They also decided to set up a student steering committee composed of members of both classes to plan and arrange interdisciplinary research and activity. The proposed cooperation was facilitated by the fact that a number of students were enrolled simultaneously by the fact both courses.

Stage 3: Formulating the Problem

At the next class meetings, Ms. Seward decided to pull things together and refocus the issue on the social studies. She pointed out that the issue was a political, social, and economic one as well as a scientific one. Many countries, especially in the United Nations and the European Union, had expressed concerns and many of them had signed the Kyoto Protocol, aimed at reducing greenhouse gas emissions. The United States, however, had not signed, mainly because of economic reasons. Further, she added that China and India were experiencing rapid industrialization and were likely to add more emissions to the atmosphere. In class discussions, the students, guided by their teacher, developed some focusing points. Chief among them was that, although a great deal of scientific evidence supported the thesis of global warming, the issue included some further questions: (1) What would be the level of global warming in the future? (2) Were the arguments of those who discredited global warming valid? (3) Would there be changes around the world and especially in their own region in the Midwest? (4) The debate over what to do about global warming was more than a problem in science and the environment, it was also a political, social, and economic one. What position should the United States take on global warming? (5) What could they do as high school students?

Stage Four: Reporting Findings

Various student research committees reported their findings about global warming.

 • Committee A: The science students reported their findings that the major greenhouse gases are water vapor, causing between 36 and 70 percent of the greenhouse effect; carbon dioxide (CO_2), which causes 9–26 percent; methane (CH_4), which causes 4–9 percent; and ozone, which causes 3–7 percent. Concentrations of CO_2 and methane have increased by 31 percent and 149 percent, respectively, above preindustrial levels since 1750. These levels are considerably higher than at any time during the last 650,000 years. Emissions from fossil fuels have produced about three-quarters of the increase in CO_2 from human activity over the past 20 years.[64]

 • Committee B: Planetary Changes Due to Global Warming: A rise in global temperatures may in turn cause such planetary changes as the melting of the polar ice caps, melting of glaciers, and the rise of sea levels. Changes in rainfall may cause flooding in some areas and drought in others. There may also be changes in the frequency and intensity of extreme weather events. Other effects may include changes in agricultural production, extinction of threatened species, and desertification.

- Committee C: Political and Economic Effects of Global Warming: Global warming has had a mixed impact on countries, business corporations, and individuals. Environmental groups, especially Green political parties and organizations, have organized demonstrations and protests to alert people to global warming. There has been some movement by business corporations, especially automobile manufacturers, toward increased energy efficiency. The world's primary international agreement on combating global warming is the Kyoto Protocal, designed to decrease greenhouse gas emissions. The Kyoto Protocol has been signed by 160 countries but not the United States, which is allegedly the world's largest source of emissions.

Stage Five: Structuring Possible Solutions

At this point, the class met to consider possible solutions. The point was raised that the large number of automobiles in the United States is an important factor in producing emissions. When a student asked about the number of cars owned by students' families, many responded that their family owned two vehicles and that they expected to drive and have their own car. A student volunteered that personal change was needed as well as that by government agencies. Tentatively, the students agreed to write letters to their U.S. senators and members of the House of Representatives in support of signing the Kyoto Protocol. They also concluded that more research was needed into the role of local and state business firms regarding their actions to curb emissions. The students agreed to continue working on the issue.

Conclusion

Reconstructionism has a continuing relevance for educators. The school curriculum is based on the selection and emphasis of some skills and subjects over others. What is selected and rejected depends on the frame of reference of those who construct the curriculum. The Reconstructionist sought to identify the cultural elements that were viable or obsolete in terms of contemporary issues. For them, the selective lenses of viability and obsolescence were changeable and relative to changing contexts. Curriculum construction involved locating the obstacles to social justice and equality and removing them. The culture's viable elements could be reconstructed in light of new elements and forces.

Constructing Your Own Philosophy of Education. As you reflect on constructing your own philosophy of education, what themes or elements of Reconstructionism appeal to you as a teacher? Which appeal least? Why? Are there elements of Reconstructionism that you would like to incorporate into your philosophy?

Summary Chart on Social Reconstructionism

Theory	Purpose of Education	Curriculum	Method	Philosophical and Ideological Relationships	Leading Theorists
Social Reconstructionism	To deliberately bring about social change and create a more equitable and democratic society.	Pressing social, political, and economic issues.	Applying group-centered discussion and problem solving on social, political, and economic issues.	Liberalism Marxism Critical Theory Progressivism Pragmatism	Counts Brameld Rugg

Questions for Reflection and Discussion

1. Assume you are a Reconstructionist teacher. How would you respond to a student who says, "I don't care about social, political, and economic issues. I'm more interested in music, sports, and hanging out with my friends. Anyway, I can't do anything about these issues."

2. Assume you are a Reconstructionist teacher. How would you respond to a student who says, "We hear a lot about social justice and multiculturalism in this class. Why?"

3. Have you ever reconstructed a belief or value? How did you do this?

4. What is the difference between subject-matter, disciplinary-based, and interdisciplinary curriculum and instruction? Have you encountered these approaches in your own education or in your teaching? What are the strengths and weaknesses of both approaches?

5. At a parent–teacher conference, a parent accuses you of indoctrinating students in your political beliefs and threatens to take her complaint to the board of education. How would you respond?

Projects for Reflection and Inquiry

1. Arrange a classroom debate on the question: "Dare the school build a new social order?"

2. Watch and listen to the news on television and radio for a week. List the issues reported and bring them to the class for further discussion.

3. In class discussion, identify the major political, social, and economic problems facing the United States and the world. What might be an educational response to these problems?

4. Analyze some of your textbooks in education courses. Do you find any hints of Reconstructionism in them?

5. Reflect on recent trends in education such as standards, process learning, Constructivism, collaborative learning, and authentic assessment. How might Reconstructionists react to these trends?

6. Reflect on Brameld's theory of defensible partiality and then consider how it might operate in a debate between advocates of evolution and Intelligent Design.

Building a Reconstructionist Vocabulary

Anthropological Philosophy: Brameld's reconstructed philosophy that integrated anthropology and philosophy.

Anthropotherapy: Brameld's theory that human evolution can be planned and improved by integrating cultural analysis with ethical actions.

Contextual Relativism: the concept that cultural contexts, the particular places and times in which people live, are the most important influence in shaping education and schooling.

Cultural Lag: the belief that technological changes moves at a faster rate than social change or social adaptation.

Cultural Relativism: similar to contextual relativism, the assumption that a group's beliefs and values are determined by their particular culture, especially their place and time.

Culturology: Brameld's theory of examining the impact of philosophy on culture.

Defensible Partiality: Brameld's theory in which persons holding a particular view can defend them in light of rigorous critical examination.

Democratic Collectivism: a term coined by George Counts that argued that the new social order would be cooperative and planned rather than individualistic.

Educology: Brameld's view of education as a distinct field of academic inquiry.

Enculturation: the informal and formal educational processes by which a culture transmits and modifies its institutions, beliefs, and values by passing them from generation to generation.

Imposition: the Reconstructionist view that education and the school curriculum is never ideologically neutral but always involves choosing some cultural elements over others to impose a particular version of culture on students.

Presentism: an argument that opposes a selective interpretation of history based on a contemporary political agenda rather than a historically accurate understanding of the past.

Reflective Theory of Curriculum: the idea, opposed by Reconstructionists, that the school curriculum should reflect, like the image in a mirror, the knowledge and values of the existing society.

Social Reconstructionism: an educational ideology or theory that argues that education and schools should be agencies to create a new and more equitable and democratic society.

Social Studies: a curriculum for social education that fuses and integrates generalizations and information from history, geography, anthropology, sociology, economics, and political science.

Internet Resources

For Reconstructionism and curriculum, access www.oregonstate.edu/instruct/ed416/pp3.html.

For Reconstructionism as a philosophy, access www.vancouver.wsu.edu/Fac/walkerT/philosophies.html.

For a discussion of Theodore Brameld, access www.newfoundations.com/GALLERY/Brameld.html.

Suggestions for Further Reading

Beard, Charles A. *A Charter for the Social Sciences in the Schools.* New York: Charles Scribner's Sons, 1932.

Brameld, Theodore. *Education for the Emerging Age: Newer Ends and Stronger Means.* New York: Harper and Row, 1965.

Counts, George S. *The American Road to Culture: A Social Interpretation of Education in the United States.* New York: John Day Co., 1930.

Counts, George S. *Dare the School Build a New Social Order?* New York: John Day Co., 1932.

Counts, George S. *The Social Foundations of Education.* New York: Charles Scribner's Sons, 1934.

Dennis, Lawrence J. *George S. Counts and Charles A. Beard: Collaborators for Change.* Albany: State University of New York Press, 1989.

Dennis, Lawrence J., and William E. Eaton. *George S. Counts: Educator for a New Age.* Carbondale: Southern Illinois University Press, 1980.

Evans, Ronald W. *The Social Studies Wars: What Should We Teach the Children.* New York: Teachers College Press, 2004.

Evans, Ronald W. *This Happened in America: Harold Rugg and the Censure of Social Studies.* Greenwich: Information Age, 2007.

Gutek, Gerald L. *George S. Counts and American Civilization: The Educator as Social Theorist.* Macon, GA: Mercer University Press, 1984.

Gutek, Gerald L. *The Educational Theory of George S. Counts.* Columbus: Ohio State University Press, 1970.

Ravitch, Diane. *Left Back: A Century of Failed School Reforms.* New York: Simon & Schuster, 2000.

Riley, Karen, ed. *Social Reconstruction: People, Politics, Perspectives.* Greenwich: Information Age, 2006.

Stanley, William B. *Curriculum for Utopia: Social Reconstructionism and Critical Pedagogy in the Postmodern Era.* Albany: SUNY Press, 1992.

Stone, Frank A. *Theodore Brameld's Educational Reconstructionism: An Intellectual Biography.* San Francisco: Caddo Gap Press, 2003.

Endnotes

1. When I began writing this book, I thought carefully about whether or not to include a chapter on Reconstructionism. My own initial doctoral research and dissertation was about George S. Counts, an originator of Social Reconstructionism, but I wondered whether it was still relevant to contemporary American education. I knew it was especially relevant in the history of American education but at first it seemed to me that Critical Theory had replaced Social Reconstructionism by appropriating many of its themes and issues. I have observed a considerable revival of interest in Social Reconstructionism stimulated by the work of Karen Riley and her colleagues and I decided that the book needed a chapter on Reconstructionism.

2. Karen L. Riley, ed., *Social Reconstruction: People, Politics, Perspectives* (Greenwich, CT: Information Age, 2006). p. xi.

3. William B. Stanley, "Education for Social Reconstruction in Critical Context," in Karen Riley, ed., *Social Reconstruction: People, Politics, Perspectives,* p. 89.

4. Wayne J. Urban, "Social Reconstructionism and Educational Policy: The Educational Policy Commission, 1936–1941," in Karen Riley, ed., *Social Reconstruction: People, Politics, Perspectives,* p. 162.

5. William B. Stanley, "Education for Social Reconstruction in Critical Context," p. 108.

6. George S. Counts, "A Humble Autobiography," in Robert J. Havighurst, ed., *Leaders in American Education: The Seventieth Yearbook of the National Society for the Study of Education* (Chicago: University of Chicago Press, 1971),

pp. 151–174. Also see Gerald L. Gutek, "George Sylvester Counts (1889–1974): A Biographical Memoir," in *Proceedings of the National Academy of Education,* 3 (Stanford, CA: National Academy of Education, 1976), pp. 333–353.

7. Counts was chairman of the American Labor Party, from 1942 to 1944, and a founder of the Liberal Party, serving as its chairman from 1954 to 1959 and as its candidate for U.S. Senator in New York in 1952.

8. George S. Counts, *The American Road to Culture: A Social Interpretation of Education in the United States* (New York: John Day Co., 1930).

9. George S. Counts, "Dare Progressive Education Be Progressive?" *Progressive Education* 9 (April 1932), pp. 257–263 and Counts, *Dare the School Build a New Social Order?* (New York: John Day Co., 1932).

10. Charles A. Beard, *A Charter for the Social Sciences in the Schools* (New York: Charles Scribner's Sons, 1932), p. 34.

11. Beard, *A Charter for the Social Sciences in the Schools,* p. 24.

12. Beard, *A Charter for the Social Sciences in the Schools,* pp. 34–51.

13. George S. Counts, *The Social Foundations of Education* (New York: Charles Scribner's Sons, 1934), p. 1.

14. Committee of the Progressive Education Association on Social and Economic Problems, *A Call to the Teachers of the Nation* (New York: John Day Co., 1933), p. 12.

15. William F. Ogburn, *Recent Social Trends in the United States* (New York: McGraw-Hill Book Co., 1933), p. 166.

16. Counts, *Dare the School Build a New Social Order?* p. 48.

17. Counts, *The Social Foundations of Education,* p. 55.

18. George S. Counts, "Present-day Reasons for Requiring a Longer Period of Pre-Service Preparation for Teachers," *National Education Association Proceedings* 73 (1935), p. 697.

19. George S. Counts, *The Prospects of American Democracy* (New York: John Day Co., 1938), pp. 176–194.

20. Counts, *Social Foundations of Education,* p. 548–558.

21. Craig Kridel, "Theodore Brameld: Reconstructionism for Our Emerging Age," in Karen Riley, ed., *Social Reconstruction: People, Politics, Perspectives,* p. 70.

22. Kridel, "Theodore Brameld: Reconstructionism for Our Emerging Age," p. 71.

23. Theodore Brameld, *Education for the Emerging Age: Newer Ends and Stronger Means* (New York: Harper and Row, 1965), p. 99.

24. Brameld, *Education for the Emerging Age: Newer Ends and Stronger Means,* p. 114.

25. Brameld, *Education for the Emerging Age: Newer Ends and Stronger Means,* p. 115.

26. Brameld, *Education for the Emerging Age: Newer Ends and Stronger Means,* pp. 112–113.

27. Kridel, "Theodore Brameld: Reconstructionism for Our Emerging Age," p. 76.

28. Brameld, *Education for the Emerging Age: Newer Ends and Stronger Means,* pp. 132–133.

29. Brameld, *Education for the Emerging Age: Newer Ends and Stronger Means,* p. 128.

30. Brameld, *Education for the Emerging Age: Newer Ends and Stronger Means,* p. 139.

31. Brameld, *Education for the Emerging Age: Newer Ends and Stronger Means,* p. 1.

32. Brameld, *Education for the Emerging Age: Newer Ends and Stronger Means,* p. 12.

33. Brameld, *Education for the Emerging Age: Newer Ends and Stronger Means,* p. 17.

34. Brameld, *Education for the Emerging Age: Newer Ends and Stronger Means,* pp. 34–35.

35. Brameld, *Education for the Emerging Age: Newer Ends and Stronger Means,* pp. 184–187.

36. Theodore Brameld, *Design for America: An Educational Exploration of the Future of Democracy for Senior High Schools and Junior Colleges* (New York: Hinds, Hayden, and Eldredge, 1945), p. 3.

37. Kridel, "Theodore Brameld: Reconstructionism for Our Emerging Age," p. 78.

38. Brameld, *Education for the Emerging Age: Newer Ends and Stronger Means,* pp. 140–141.

39. Brameld, *Education for the Emerging Age: Newer Ends and Stronger Means,* p. 21.

40. Brameld, *Education for the Emerging Age: Newer Ends and Stronger Means,* p. 78.

41. Brameld, *Education for the Emerging Age: Newer Ends and Stronger Means,* p. 76.

42. Brameld, *Education for the Emerging Age: Newer Ends and Stronger Means,* pp. 80, 85.

43. Urban, "Social Reconstructionism and Educational Policy: The Educational Policy Commission, 1936–1941," p. 153.

44. Stanley, "Education for Social Reconstruction in Critical Context," p. 94.

45. Gerald Podner, "Social Reconstructionist Curriculum Impulses: Pragmatism, Collectivism and 'The American Problem,'" in Karen Riley, ed., *Social Reconstruction: People, Politics, Perspectives,* pp. 241–242.

46. Lawrence J. Dennis, *George S. Counts and Charles A. Beard: Collaborators for Change* (Albany: State University of New York Press, 1989), p. 19.

47. In the 1930s, Rugg wrote three major books on Reconstructionist themes: *Culture and Education in America* (1931), *The Great Technology* (1933), and *American Life and the School Curriculum* (1936). He later wrote *Now Is the Moment* (1943), *Foundations of American Education* (1947), *The Teacher of Teachers* (1952), *Social Foundations of Education,* with William Withers (1955), and *Imagination* (1963), which was published posthumously.

48. R. W. Evans, "Social Studies vs. the United States of America: Harold Rugg and Teaching for Social Justice," in Karen L. Riley, ed., *Social Reconstruction: People, Politics, Perspectives,* pp. 46, 51.

49. Peter F. Carbone, Jr., *The Social and Educational Thought of Harold Rugg* (Durham, NC: Duke University Press, 1977), pp. 24–25.

50. The quotation from Rugg and the paraphrasing from the teacher's guide is from Karen L. Riley, "The Triumph of Americanism: The American Legion vs. Harold Rugg", in Karen L. Riley, ed., *Social Reconstruction: People, Politics, Perspectives,* p. 115.

51. R. W. Evans, "Social Studies vs. the United States of America: Harold Rugg and Teaching for Social Justice," p. 52.

52. Riley, "The Triumph of Americanism: The American Legion vs. Harold Rugg," p. 111.

53. R. W. Evans, "Social Studies vs. the United States of America: Harold Rugg and Teaching for Social Justice," pp. 46–47.

54. Brameld, *Education for the Emerging Age: Newer Ends and Stronger Means,* p. 167.

55. Brameld, *Education for the Emerging Age: Newer Ends and Stronger Means,* pp. 152–153.

56. John Dewey, *Individualism Old and New* (1929). Reprint, New York: Capricorn, 1962; and Dewey, *Liberalism and Social Action* (1935). Reprint, New York: Capricorn, 1963.

57. Podner, "Social Reconstructionist Curriculum Impulses: Pragmatism, Collectivism and 'The American Problem,'" pp. 242–243.

58. Dennis, *George S. Counts and Charles A. Beard: Collaborators for Change,* pp. 2–4.

59. Counts, *The Prospects of American Democracy,* p. 76.

60. Podner, "Social Reconstructionist Curriculum Impulses: Pragmatism, Collectivism and 'The American Problem,'" p. 241.

61. Brameld, *Education for the Emerging Age: Newer Ends and Stronger Means,* p. 150.

62. Diane Ravitch, *Left Back: A Century of Failed School Reforms* (New York: Simon & Schuster, 2000), pp. 465–66.

63. The scenario was created by the author, who relied for background information on Wikipedia.

64. "Earth's Annual Global Mean Energy Budget" (PDF). *Bulletin of the American Meteorological Society* 78 (2): 197–208, and Water vapour: Feedback or Forcing; RealClimate (6 Apr 2005).

16

Critical Theory and Education

A still from the motion picture, Freedom writers, *in which the teacher challenges students to critically examine their lives by writing their own autobiographies.*

Chapter Preview

Critical Theory is a complex of assumptions about society, education, and schooling that analyzes aims, institutions, organization, curriculum, and instruction in terms of power relationships. It seeks to raise consciousness and bring about transformative change in the society and education. It has been influenced by Marxism, Freire's Liberation pedagogy, Postmodernism, and multiculturalism. The word *critical* means to engage in a rigorous probing and analytical investigation of social and educational conditions, in schools and society, in order to expose exploitative power relationships such as domination and marginalization and bring about transformative change. The anticipated consequence of this analysis is to empower subordinate classes and groups to self-determine their own futures in an equitable society.

Critical Theorists believe that many institutions, especially political, economic, and educational ones, maintain and reproduce inequitable and exploitative conditions that favor one group or class, the dominant one, over subordinate groups and classes. Self-determination is possible if people become conscious of and overthrow these exploitive forces.

The following major topics are examined here:
- Critical Theory's historical, philosophical, and ideological contexts
- Paulo Freire and Henry Giroux as leading contributors to Critical Theory
- Critical Theory as an educational theory
- Critical Theory's implications for schools, curriculum, and teaching and learning
- Critical Theory's opposition to ideologies such as Conservatism and Liberalism

As you read the chapter and think about constructing your own philosophy of education, consider whether Critical Theory appeals to you as a teacher. Do you plan to use it in constructing your own philosophy of education?

Putting Critical Theory in Context

The Critical Theorists emphasize contexts—the places and times in which education occurs. Because of this emphasis, we examine the historical and philosophical context in which Critical Theory developed as an educational theory.

Historical Context

Critical Theory, as a movement in education, originally gained impetus in the United States during the 1960s, a time of intense social change that was marked by the civil rights movement led by Dr. Martin Luther King, Jr., and by the antiwar movement in opposition to the war in Vietnam. The period saw the concerted effort by African, Hispanic, and Native Americans to organize for increased political, economic, and educational representation and opportunities. During the 1960s, the women's rights movement began a renewed effort to secure equal rights and employment opportunities and compensation for women. Environmentalist groups began the Green movement, campaigning against the degradation of the natural environment and for greater conservation of natural resources. Gays and lesbians, too, went public in their demands for recognition of their right to an alternative lifestyle and against discriminatory practices in education and employment. The period was also a time of concerted protests, demonstrations, and teach-ins, often sparked by disaffected students and intellectuals, against the American corporate structure and its political allies.

Although some philosophers of education were taking a more radical and leftist stand, a new Conservativism was also growing in the United States and in some countries in western Europe, especially the United Kingdom. In the 1980s, the election of Ronald Reagan as president of the United States marked the ascendancy of Neo-Conservatives to power and the decline of Liberalism. Neo-Conservative forces in the Republican Party, supported by the Moral Majority and Christian fundamentalists, succeeded in electing George H. Bush in 1988 and George W. Bush as president in 2000 and 2004. At the same time that there was a Neo-Conservative ascendancy in the United States, Margaret Thatcher led the Conservative Party to victory in the United Kingdom.

By the end of the 1980s, the Soviet Union and its Communist satellites collapsed in central and eastern Europe and the Cold War ended after more than fifty years. With the Soviet Union's demise, state socialism or Communism, Marxist-Leninism, was discredited as an ideology, which posed a serious dilemma for Marxists. Some Marxists had already declared their ideological independence from the Soviet version because of the Soviet regime's oppressive policies in what were police states in the USSR and its satellites. Nevertheless, academic Marxists looked for ways to revitalize the ideology, stating that Soviet Communism did not represent true Marxism and was a grossly distorted version of what Marx had said.

With Communism gone as an adversary, the United States and other technologically developed countries commenced on a policy of globalization that emphasized free market economics, reduced government controls, and deregulation. In American education, the Neo-Conservative political ascendancy was marked by the resurgence of a new Essentialism, called basic education, the emergence of the standards movement, a greater association of schooling with economic training, mandated achievement testing, and the enactment of the No Child Left Behind Act.

Philosophical and Ideological Context

In educational philosophy and theory, the convergence of several trends paved the way for the emergence of Critical Theory as a force in the foundations of education, an area that includes philosophy of education. Liberals, who had dominated American politics since the 1930s, were losing the support of some intellectuals, especially university professors and students who accused them of abetting and contributing to the growth of the military-industrial complex and to economic globalization. As the influence of Philosophical or Language Analysis declined in philosophy of education, more radical theorists in the Foundations were drawn to the Frankfurt school and to the Liberation education of Ivan Illich and Paulo Freire. Postmodernism also exerted a strong influence as educators encountered and adopted the ideas of prominent French philosophers Jacques Derrida and Michel Foucault. Critical Theorists, already subscribing to Postmodernism and Liberation ideology, became an oppositional force against the Neo-Conservative and Neo-Essentialist ascendancy in education.

Marxism. Marxism is a potent ideological force in Critical Theory. (Marxism is discussed in another chapter; the discussion here emphasizes only those aspects that relate most directly to Critical Theory.) Marxist analytical concepts such as economic control of society, the class struggle for control of the means and modes of production, and alienation have influenced Critical Theorists. Critical Theorists have reduced the ideological rigidity of these concepts and used them in a more flexible social and educational analysis. They use these concepts as tools to analyze society, education, and schools rather than as specific dialectical recipes for creating a revolutionary society. For example, Critical Theorists agree with Marx that those who control the economic base, the means and modes of production, also control social, political, and educational institutions in a particular society, especially a capitalist one. Seeing history as a determined inflexible process, Marx said that control of the economy would lead to an inevitable war between the capitalist exploiting class and the working class, the proletariat, with the inevitable victory going to the workers. Although Critical Theorists use the Marxist concept of class conflict, they have broadened it from economic classes to other oppressed groups such as African, Latino, and Native Americans; women; the poor; and gays and lesbians. Critical Theorists also discount the idea of an inevitable revolution and give a much greater role to education to raise consciousness about social, economic, and political realities. Focusing on schools as social institutions, Critical Theorists contend that, in contemporary America, educational institutions are controlled by the powerful economic classes—the wealthy who are invested in the corporate economy. The educational needs of less-favored economic groups are subordinated to those of the rich and powerful. The struggle for control, in schools, takes the form of domination of the curriculum. It is through the control of governance of schools and the curriculum that the upper classes subordinate and **marginalize** the lower classes.

The Critical Theorists also use the Marxist concept of alienation. In a capitalist society, the workers are exploited by those who control the means and modes of production—the industries, businesses, and corporations. They do not receive the benefits of their labor; instead, the value that they create through work is expropriated, seized by the capitalists as profits. As a consequence, work in a capitalist society results in social and psychological alienation of workers from their labor and from the products, the commodities, they make. Critical Theorists use the concept of alienation in broader terms to refer to the social and psychological states of people who have been marginalized, driven to the peripheries, of society—the homeless and those who live in poverty. In addition to the economically destitute, others also have been alienated, or marginalized, in modern society—African Americans, Hispanics, women, and gays and lesbians, for example. The educational struggle for Critical Theorists takes places in the immediate situation and condition of schools, the sites where education takes place. The struggle takes the form of raising the consciousness of the alienated so that they can empower themselves to take their rightful place in society.[1]

The Frankfurt School.   The Frankfurt School—a group of social and cultural theorists that included Max Horkheimer, Theodor Adorno, and Herbert Marcuse at the Institute of Social Research at University of Frankfurt in Germany—also influenced Critical Theory.[2] The Frankfurt theorists developed several themes significant in Critical Theory analysis such as: (1) ideology exerts a powerful impact on human consciousness; (2) more than academic skills and subjects, education is an agency of political, social, and economic socialization; and (3) broadly construed, education includes informal educational agencies, especially the media, as well as the more formal schools. Socialization, the acquiring of the culture, is not a neutral process but is always ideologically charged. There is not one culture, but several cultures in competition in a given society. In a capitalist society and economy, political and ideological socialization is intended to indoctrinate children in the officially mandated beliefs and values of the dominant class and to marginalize competing cultures, especially those of powerless people. The analysis of socialization, according to the Frankfurt School, requires a transdisciplinary method that examines the texts and representations used by the media and in schools and in politics and economics.[3]

The Frankfurt School theorists developed the idea of "culture studies" to examine the impact of technology and consumerism on the mass culture. The culture industries—the media, television, and radio programs—exhibit features that are similar to industrial production: both are geared to produce mass tastes in a mass audience that is a mass market. The culture industries, with their approved story lines, act to legitimize existing capitalist societies and to socialize a mass audience by instilling a false consciousness into the mass audience.[4]

Postmodernism. (Postmodernism is treated in another chapter; the discussion here emphasizes only those aspects that relate most directly to Critical Theory.) Critical Theory has been influenced by Postmodernism and shares its antipathy to metaphysics in the older Idealist and Realist philosophies. Like Postmodernism, it sees what is exalted as the great works of philosophers such as Plato, Aristotle, Aquinas, and Hegel to be metanarratives used as rationales for the established way of thinking. Critical Theory, like Postmodernism, rejects the prominent role given to the eighteenth-century Enlightenment as a historical and scientific rationale for modernism. It is especially antagonistic to the Enlightenment's claims that reason, especially the scientific method, is an objective means of solving problems.

Critical Theory shares Postmodernism's focus on language, especially its use in constructing and deconstructing texts and canons. It finds language to be a construction that arises in specific contexts and not a reflection of a generalized reality. For both Critical Theorists and Postmodernists, the claims and interpretations of knowledge are never neutral or objective but are statements of power and ideology. They reject the compartmentalization of knowledge into areas with boundaries, claiming that the elites have constructed canons or texts that establish arbitrary definitions, illustrations, and cases that mark off one subject from another. By deconstructing the canon or text, it is possible to get to the motives and purposes of those who constructed them.

Liberation Pedagogy and Deschooling. Critical Theory has also been influenced by deschooling and Liberation Pedagogy, especially the ideas of Ivan Illich and Paulo Freire, two educators who worked in Latin America. Both of these educators, though concerned with education worldwide, developed many of their ideas by working with the economically disadvantaged people in less technologically developed societies. Illich worked largely in Mexico and Freire in Brazil. Illich, in *Deschooling Society,* argued that Westernized schooling is the instruction of neocolonialist exploitation and repression of the people in less technologically developed societies in Asia, Africa, and South America. Schooling had become a great "sales pitch" that imposed capitalist consumerist ideas on working-class and peasant children, conditioning them to want commodities they did not need. It also conditioned people to believe that all learning had to be in schools rather than in informal voluntary associations. Although Critical Theorists find much of Illich's analysis congenial to their ideological orientation, particularly their opposition to capitalist globalization, they do not call for the elimination of schools. Rather, they believe that it is possible to change schools into agencies of human liberation. Illich's work, however, influenced Critical Theorists to think of the struggle to empower the dispossessed in global terms in which the marginalized groups in the United States are connected to the oppressed in less technologically developed societies.

Paulo Freire has been an inspiration for many Critical Theorists. In *Pedagogy of the Oppressed,* Freire called for education that would raise peoples' consciousness about the reality of their economic and social condition and encourage them to take the steps needed for their own **empowerment**. Since Freire is such an important voice for Critical Theorists, we discuss his Liberation Pedagogy in some detail and then turn to Giroux as a leader of the contemporary movement.

Paulo Freire and Liberation Pedagogy

Paulo Freire (1921–1997) developed **Liberation Pedagogy** while working in a literacy campaign among Brazil's impoverished peasants and workers. (Freire's contribution to Ideology is discussed in the chapter on Ideology.) Realizing that literacy meant more than learning to read and write, Freirie saw it as a tool for **consciousness-raising**, for people to become aware of the conditions of their lives and work. Informed by their own consciousness, people, empowered by literacy, could identify and change the economic, social, and political conditions that caused their exploitation.[5]

At the time of Freire's literary campaign, Brazil's society and economy was unevenly developed between a small ruling elite and a large impoverished underclass. The peasants in its rural agricultural regions were poverty-ridden and exploited by landlords. Rio de Janeiro and Sao Paulo, Brazil's largest cities, with their avant-garde architectural centers, were ringed by sprawling urban slums with grossly inadequate sanitation, health care, educational, and social services. A powerful ruling elite of landlords and industrialists, backed by the military, controlled Brazil's government and economy.[6]

Freire, associated with the Catholic Action Movement, organized literacy circles to improve the situation of Brazil's impoverished classes. Freire's literacy teams taught the peasants to read by focusing their attention on the immediate social and economic conditions that shaped the contexts of their daily struggle to earn a living. Freire had learned, himself, that literacy had political as well as educational implications. Brazilian landowners and military saw Freire's literacy campaign as a threat to their privileged positions. In 1964, a military coup, overturning a reformist government, seized control of Brazil, and ruled for the next twenty-one years until 1985.[7] Freire was arrested, imprisoned, and then deported from Brazil. During his exile, Freirie worked on literacy programs in Chile, and was a visiting professor at Harvard University, where he was also a Fellow at the Center for the Study of Development and Social Change. While at Harvard, Freirie wrote his well-known and influential *Pedagogy of the Oppressed,* which became an important text for Critical Theorists. He next served as an assistant secretary of education for the World Council of Churches. When military rule ended in Brazil, Freire returned to his home country, where he served on the faculty at the University of Sao Paulo and then as the minister of education for the City of Sao Paulo. He died at the age of seventy-five on May 2, 1997.

Philosophically, Freire was influenced by Existentialism, which also found its way into Critical Theory. Similar to the Existentialists, Freire rejected the traditional positions of Idealism and Realism in which the human being is antecedently defined as a predetermined general category. In contrast, Freire sees invididuals as incomplete presences in the world who can construct their own projects for making the world into a better place for humanity. Consciousness-raising, in Existentalist terms, means that people, regardless of their socioeconomic status, can become aware that they have the power to take the actions needed to complete themselves.[8]

Ideologically, Freire was influenced by Marxism but, from his Existentialist perspective, rejected its historical determinism. He employs Marxist analysis when he urges that dispossessed and marginalized people raise their consciousness by examining the material conditions that have an impact on their lives.[9] These cultural, social, political, economic, and educational conditions, though historically derived, can be changed when people understand the conditions and the agents that repress them.

Religiously, Freire was a Roman Catholic who joined Catholic Action, an organization committed to improving the conditions of the poor and to promoting social reform. Thomas Aquinas, who shaped Maritain's ideas and probably some of Freire's, saw teaching as a vocation in which teachers led students to knowledge through their love of humankind. Freire, too, seeing teaching as inspired by persons with teachable hearts, maintained that "Love is the basis of an education that seeks justice, equality, and genius."[10] Paradoxically, Freire was familiar with the spiritually oriented philosophy of such Catholic philosophers as Jacques Maritain as well as with Marx's dialectical materialism.[11]

Freire's Liberation Pedagogy

Key terms in Freire's educational theory are "liberation" and "pedagogy." *Liberation* means freedom from the exploiting social, economic, political, and educational conditions that give a ruling group power over others, especially those who are impoverished materially and culturally. *Pedagogy,* a Greek word that means leading a person to knowledge, is an education that raises consciousness about the conditions of life and work and suggests strategies to improve them.

Raising consciousness is a major Freirean educational goal. It relates to the Portuguese word *conscientizacao,* which for Freire meant constructing a critical awareness of social, political, and economic conditions and contradictions under which people live and work. "Critical awareness" is an important concept in Critical Theory. More than intellectual knowledge, it is action-oriented as it generates a desire to act as an agent of change to replace oppression with freedom.

Similar to Marx, Freire sees history as a vital critical study in raising consciousness. Differing with Marx, Freire rejects the interpretation that history is determined by inexorable laws that make it beyond human control. Further, Freire, like the Social Reconstructionists, emphasizes the importance of concrete contexts in shaping our reality. Here, he disagrees with both Marx, a materialist, and Hegel, an Idealist, who see history as the working out of universal laws. Born in and living in concrete contexts, we have had a limited control over the persons and events that have shaped us. However, we have not had control over other persons who have controlled the events, primarily the economic and educational ones, that play a role in our lives. This lack of control is most pernicious when it is exercised by those who want to exploit us and minimalize us by telling us who we are rather than permitting us to define ourselves. These exploiters might be the landlord of a vast agricultural estate in Brazil, who exploits the peasants who work for him. It might be the more impersonal, but more powerful, multinational corporation, which exploits workers by paying subsistence wages and having them work in unsafe conditions. Though others have been in control, this does not mean that we need to abandon our choices to them. Becoming conscious of our historical situation means that we no longer accept the status quo and see embedded institutions and practices as something to which we must adjust. We are not merely inheritors of history but we have the power to make history. To begin, it is necessary to dispel the history that masks reality by justifying the status quo as a celebration of great achievements by the exploiting class. The critical study of history reveals that some groups or classes have seized control of natural resources and exploited them for their own aggrandizement without concern for the health of the planet and the welfare of its people. For Freire, our history is exactly that—it belongs to us as the authors of a narrative that is personal and social. If we are willing to empower ourselves and shoulder the responsibility that empowerment carries, we have the power to construct our own autobiographies.

The Program of Action

Again, much like Counts, Rugg, Brameld, and the Reconstructionists, Freire sees all education, schooling, and teaching and learning as taking place in an ideologically charged situation. He distinguishes Liberation Pedagogy, as a radicalizing ideology, from extreme right- and left-wing political ideologies that misuse and distort history to build myths that create a sense of false consciousness. Like them, Freire argues that teachers who claim to be neutral are hiding behind a veil of objectivity that ignores human suffering, manipulation, and exploitation. Pretending to be neutral to avoid controversy actually allies teachers with the exploiters. Teachers need to recognize that what they do or fail to do in the classroom relates to issues of social justice. Freire urged critically-minded teachers to make a stand that advances social justice.[12] Again, like Social Reconstructionism, Liberation Pedagogy is an educational theory to create a new, more open, social order.

Epistemology

Freire draws an intimate connection between thinking (being conscious) and practice (acting on our thoughts) or in his terminology, *praxis*. Having a critical consciousness means that we have seen through the ideological fog of false consciousness—the myths, theories, and rationales—the oppressors have constructed to confuse and indoctrinate dominated groups. These rationales, derived from the oppressor's ideology, serve to indoctrinate the oppressed into believing that their oppression is "right," "just," "the standard," or "the way it is supposed to be." To see this process at work in American history, one can go back in time, and read school textbooks that described Andrew Carnegie and John D. Rockefeller as "captains of industry" who were giants of innovation that developed the American economy. Or, you can find textbooks that claimed that the slaves actually benefited from slavery and the slave owners were paternalistic and benevolent protectors of those they enslaved.

Thinking critically means that one breaks through these rationales of oppression to see them for what they really are—the constructions used by exploiters to indoctrinate those whom they exploit. Critique, while necessary, is not enough for critical thinking. It requires an engagement in liberating dialogues that are alternatives to the status quo. In these dialogues, the oppressed get a voice to tell the truths that they have experienced. Through liberating dialogues, it is possible to construct a genuine consciousness of social reality.

Axiology

For Freire, the major conflict in values are in choices to be made about the conditions that either humanize or dehumanize persons. A truly ethical person, motivated by social justice, becomes conscious of the conditions in which she or he lives and works and deliberately seeks to change those that are unjust or pernicious to human freedom. The ethical person consciously accepts this responsibility to create a future filled with promises and possibilities.[13]

The most important issue in valuation is, are values freely made and chosen by the person who embraces and is guided by them or are they prescriptions imposed on the oppressed by their oppressors? *Prescription* refers to the injunctions about what a person should do, whereas *proscription* is that which he or she should not do. We all know that traditional schooling, indeed most schooling, is replete with prescriptions and proscriptions. Freire opposes prescription, which imposes "one man's choice on another." In a class-based society, prescriptions about the sanctity of private property over human needs imposes the dominant group's values on those who are powerless and marginalized. Prescriptions of oppression—imposed as the "right way" to act or as socially sanctioned behaviors—are often indoctrinated into the oppressed and reinforced by sanctions and threats or actual punishments.[14]

To create values freely, individuals, in true Existentialist fashion, need to know that their choices are theirs alone. They need to liberate themselves from automatically accepting the prescriptions and proscriptions that others, especially those with power, impose on them. Again, like an Existentialist, Freire tells people that they are "unfinished" agents, who can give themselves the power to bring themselves to self-definition.

Freirean Education

For Freire, schools, curriculum, and instruction reflect the contexts, the communities and sites, of which they are a part. Like all social, political, and economic systems, educational ones are conditioned and shaped by ideology of those who control the social structure. Schools, when controlled by the dominant groups, adjust or condition students to accept the official knowledge, the beliefs, of the power-holders and to play the roles assigned them in the economic, political, and social relationships of the existing system. In contrast, when infused with Liberation Pedagogy, schools, curriculum, and teaching and learning can raise students' consciousness, encouraging them to reflect critically on social reality, and empowering them to transform the conditions, the contexts, that shape their lives.

Education for consciousness-raising involves exposing those actors, the administrators and teachers who, often because of their own ignorance, miseducate students. A leading cause of miseducation is imposing false consciousness, a Marxist concept, on students by transmitting a version of history and beliefs, often masked as objective subject matter, on students. False consciousness comes from an uncritical belief in the rhetoric of those who hold power and control institutions. An education that defines a person's values in terms of wealth and power and sees schooling as a ticket to a place in the corporate system misses the mark of being truly humanizing.[15]

Freire attacks education that indoctrinates the young with false consciousness, which in schools comes in the transmission of alleged knowledge, really putting the words of the privileged class into the pages of textbooks and the mouths of teachers. Transmission relies on "teacher talk" in which a teacher plays the role of a "talking text" who describes and interprets reality for students. Teacher talk is backed by the classroom prescription that students should be attentive listeners who, fixing on each word spoken by the teacher, take it in, and store it in their minds for recall on a test. Freire calls the teaching-listening-testing regimen "educational banking."[16] Each bit of information is deposited in the mind, a mental bank, where it is stored and cashed in when needed. The current standards movement that emphasizes standardized testing is an example of assessment based on the banking model of education. The elaborate testing mechanisms constructed to determine student's academic achievement in mastering externally imposed curricula is used to sort students into groups, reproducing the inequalities of the existing social and economic system.[17]

Teaching as Committed Partiality

Freire completely rejects the proposition that teachers can and should be neutral or impartial on social, political, and economic issues.[18] Freire is especially critical of educators who claim to be ideologically unbiased and open-minded in their teaching. For Liberation Pedagogy, claims to objectivity mean the teacher is not conscious of the true conditions that affect education or is engaged in a pretense that masks hidden ideological commitments.

For Freire, genuine learning occurs when both teachers and students engage in a shared, ongoing dialogue that constructs rather than transmits knowledge. The construction of knowledge results when teachers and students share, reflect on, and critically evaluate their experiences.[19] According to Macedo, a close friend and interpreter of Freire, genuine teaching:

- recognizes that all social and educational situations are ideological.
- is ethically committed to fight racial, sexual, and class discrimination.
- requires a critical capacity, tempered by humility and reflection.[20]

For Freire, teaching is not transmitting information; nor is learning memorizing information to be retrieved in the future. Genuine teaching and learning requires teachers and students to be mutually engaged in constructing knowledge through critical dialogue. Freirean-inspired teachers take a rigorous critical attitude in examining society, politics, and economics. Although they are tough-minded in their analyses, they are motivated by love, respect, and humility for their students. This critical but loving attitude means that teachers need to challenge the status quo and what passes for the system's "best practices" as they confront the power structure both inside and outside of schools. Humility means that teachers need to recognize that as human beings they are limited in what they know and need to be open to learning from the community, especially its disempowered groups, and from students. Both participants in the educational dialogue—teacher and students—are reforming themselves. Freire's concept of teaching and learning as mutual reforming of the selves reflects his reliance on the Existentialist theme that the human condition is one of incompleteness in which we act to bring our lives, through our own actions, to wholeness.

Henry Giroux

Henry Giroux, a leading contemporary educational and cultural critic, is an important voice in Critical Theory. He sees education as a "principal feature of politics" by which individuals acquire "the capacities, knowledge, skills, and social relations" to see themselves as social and political agents.[21] Education includes schooling, yet it is much broader than the school and can take place on multiple sites. Education can be either an agency of social and political control or it can be a process of social and political transformation and liberation. Although schools are used by dominant classes to reproduce themselves and their control, they also can be liberated to become an alternative to reproducing domination. When liberated, they can be used as an agencies to examine the institutions and processes of repression and to construct an alternative future. Giroux has constructed a broad cultural and educational theory that includes: (1) a critical analysis of existing institutions; (2) resistance to the imposition of the dominant ideology; and (3) creation of a more egalitarian, democratic, and multicultural society and education.[22]

Giroux argues for education that is reflective and critical and that teachers, among others, act as public intellectuals. Like other Critical Theorists, Giroux works to expose the ways in which power pervades educational institutions to marginalize people, especially dispossessed groups. Like Freire, Giroux opposes the traditional view that instruction is the transmission of selected information by teachers to students. The transmission of official knowledge legitimizes an authoritarian view of knowledge in that it is prescribed by those who hold power as prepackaged content, safe methods of instruction, and controlled mechanisms of assessment.[23]

Giroux sees teachers as transformative intellectuals who are cultural workers and border crossers. As transformative intellectuals, teachers are much more than transmitters of the approved "official knowledge" that is prescribed in lists of standards and state mandates. Official knowledge is that which has been filtered and approved by power holders and the educational bureaucrats who serve them. Teachers need to devise strategies to bring "unofficial knowledge" into their classrooms. Especially in economically disadvantaged school attendance areas, the unofficial knowledge comes from the lives, the stories, of the members of the community and from the autobiographies of the students who live there. Teachers who follow the approved teachers' guides and manuals find themselves relegated as mouthpieces who speak the lines in a script that has been handed to them by those who are in charge. As transmitters, teachers are go-betweens, the transactive agents of those who hold power. To risk being transformative means that the teacher no longer serves to perpetuate the status quo but works to change the culture, politics, and economy of the local community in which she or he works and of the larger community of which it is a part.

Giroux's concept of the teacher as a cultural worker combines elements of the new cultural studies as well as earlier elements from Marxism and Social Reconstructionism. As persons who use their efforts to transform society, teachers are workers. As transformative intellectuals, teachers are not only academicians but are engaged in expending their efforts and energies on changing the schools, culture, and society. Teachers need to involve themselves with social and political movements and groups that work in oppositional public spheres outside of schools and in broader educational arenas. When they recognize themselves as cultural workers, teachers can proceed to break down the divisions between intellectual and manual labor that separate theory and practice in schools.[24]

Marx's concept of socially useful labor gave work a social instead of a profit-making purpose. The Social Reconstructionists urged teachers to join with other Progressive groups and organizations to build a new social order. Giroux and other Critical Theorists urges teachers, as public intellectuals, to join in social and political movements and groups that work in opposition to power holders both in schools and in other public spheres in the larger society.

In addition to enlarging the idea of the teacher as a cultural worker, Giroux also broadened the concept of the culture. His idea of culture is shaped by the emerging field of cultural studies that examines the role of mass culture, especially the media, in creating a new dominant class hegemony. No longer seen as interpretations of the fine arts and literature, cultural studies examine how ideology and culture intersect and how culture is used to reproduce ideology. Dominant groups use mass cultural agencies—media, motion pictures, television, and entertainment—to reproduce the dominant culture. These vehicles of mass culture meet and coincide with formal education, schooling, to shape the thought, especially the consumer needs, to support the economy of the dominant culture. Giroux argues that culture must be analyzed within the social, political, economic, and educational systems through which it is reproduced.[25]

Giroux encourages teachers and students to be "border crossers." A person who crosses a border is one who moves from the boundaries of a delimited territory, often those of a country, to another. The curriculum of secondary and higher education is territorialized; the academic provinces, the subjects, are marked by boundaries. Teaching and learning in traditional schools are to stay within departmentalized boundaries. The academic territory within the boundary has been mined, explained, described, and interpreted, or exploited, by the academic authorities, the experts in the field. For example, the expert authority about the past is the historian; about the natural and physical world, the scientist; about the political world, the political scientist; and so forth. These authorities construct an academically defined official knowledge that is found in the "definitive" texts that constitute the approved reading list. The division of the curriculum into academic fields or subjects leads to a departmentalization of the mind in which some areas belong to a particular field and not to another field.

Giroux's advocacy of **border crossings** means that teachers and students should be free to cross subject boundaries and borders to find and use the information, the knowledge, and methods that they need. The idea of border crossings is not new but can be found in the educational method of John Dewey and other Experimentalists who argued that a genuine problem, as distinct from an academic problem, is not restricted to one subject but required interdisciplinary research in a variety of disciplines. For example, the problem of global warming transcends science and also relates to political science and economics. For Giroux, the issues that marginalize people today—racism, sexism, and class—are not explained by a single academic subject but cross many of them. As they investigate the cultural and social

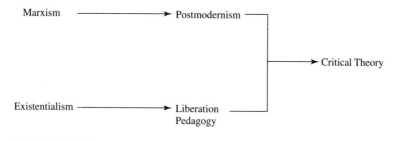

Influences on Critical Theory

terrain in which they work, teachers will face complex issues that are not confined within disciplinary limits. They will gain insights that cultural, race, class, and gender forces have shaped all elements of teaching and instruction. The educational process is complex and not a simple matter of teaching the basics as Conservatives and Essentialists contend. Complexity means that something is composed of interrelated parts or elements that make up a system. An educational system and the educational process cannot be explained one-dimensionally from the viewpoint of a single subject matter or discipline. It needs to be approached from the multidisciplinary, interdisciplinary, even transdisciplinary way, that border crossing suggests. Education and schooling cannot be understood outside of the sociological, historical, philosophical, cultural, economic, political, and psychological contexts that shape it.[26]

Critical Theory as a Theory of Education

In this section, we examine Critical Theory as a theory of education. Attention is given to identifying and commenting on the constructs that guide Critical Theorists' social and educational analysis.

Social Contol

Dominant classes, particularly in a capitalist society, control institutions, including schools. They use their control to maintain, or reproduce, their favored position and to subordinate socially and economically disadvantaged classes. Schools, especially through the official and hidden curriculum, are used by the dominant class to reproduce the status quo that ensures their dominance.

An individual's socioeconomic status, including educational expectations and opportunities, are largely conditioned by race, ethnicity, gender, and class. In the United States, the historically subordinated marginalized groups are the urban and rural poor; African, Hispanic, and Native Americans; women; and gays and lesbians. These groups are pushed to the periphery, to the margins, of society and schooling. The conditions of marginality in the larger society are reinforced by the school's organization and curriculum.[27] Their history is either neglected or added to the margins of the official history. It is possible, through a critical education, for subordinated classes and groups to become conscious of their exploitation, resist domination, overthrow the pattern of domination, and empower them-selves to determine their own future.

Institutions, including educational ones, are centers of contention, or conflict, between the dominant and other less-favored classes. Educational policy and practice, informed by Critical Theory, can empower marginalized groups to gain greater equity, fairness, and justice throughout the United States and in other countries as well.

The Critique

Much of the work of Critical Theorists is a critique, a critical analysis, of existing society and institutions. The critique is both at the microlevel, which examines the forces and con-ditions operating on-site in schools, and at the broader macrolevel, which enlarges the immediate community context to examine the historical, social, political, and economic conditions in the larger society.[28] The Critical Theorist analysis is guided by such focusing questions as:

- Who really controls society and schools and what are their motives?
- How are educational resources allocated and who benefits from this allocation?
- Who makes the policies that govern schools and who benefits from these policies?
- Who determines the goals and expectations of schools?
- Who establishes the curriculum and does the curriculum relate to race, ethnicity, lan-guage, class, and gender?
- What power do teachers and students really have in schools and over the educational process?
- How is student academic achievement assessed and measured?

Critical Theorists begin to answer these questions on-site—in the immediate context of a particular community and school. They begin their critique using **microanalysis**, by assembling and interpreting the demographic information, the case studies, and the life sto-ries, the autobiographies of teachers and students. Typically, schools in economically disad-vantaged urban and declining rural areas are attended predominately by the poor, by African, Hispanic, and Appalachian Americans. The buildings are generally poorly maintained and the programs are underfinanced and lack adequate resources.

Still using microanalysis, the Critical Theorist examines the conditions on-site—in the school. They are likely to find that the typical inner-city urban school is enmeshed in a large weblike bureaucracy that operates in a hierarchical, top-down style. With orders coming down from the top, there is little opportunity for local governance or teacher decision-making. The curriculum, too, is determined, prepackaged, and handed down from higher-level administra-tors, with little room for local initiatives that relate to the life experiences of students in the school or people in the local community. Teachers, within the school, are isolated from each other, teaching in self-contained insulated classrooms. They have little or no power in setting goals or in making decisions about curriculum and instruction. Further, parents and others in the local community are kept at a distance, with little involvement or interaction with the school.

Then, the critique is broadened from the school to the community, the neighbor-hood, where the students live. The inner city or isolated rural community, like the school, is beleaguered by endemic social, economic, political, and educational problems. It is often physically and socially isolated from the health, recreational, and cultural resources of the larger society. There is a higher unemployment rate among adults in the community. The community is likely to be ineffectively organized to secure greater political representation. There is likely to be a high incidence of street gangs and drug and alcohol abuse.

Next, the immediate, microcritique of the local context is connected to the larger social, political, and economic macroanalysis. The immediate problems faced by local schools mirror those of the larger state, regional, and national context. The larger society is controlled by the economically affluent, who influence politicians and the media. The economically affluent—often living in gated residential areas in the large cities or comfortable wealthy suburbs—have isolated themselves from the problems in the inner cities and declining rural areas. Nevertheless, they control institutions, including schools, throughout the country.

Following a Neo-Marxist mode of analysis, Critical Theorists contend that the power of the affluent governing class comes from its control of the capitalist corporate economy. The members of the favored class use schools to maintain their power by educating their children in well-financed schools that prepare them for entry to prestigious colleges and universities and for positions of importance within the corporate and government structures. Invested in maintaining the status quo, they use their power and influence to reproduce the system that gives them control. Children of the less economically favored classes, indoctrinated in the approved official curriculum, constructed by the powerful class, are conditioned to accept subordinate roles at the margins of the existing society.

For Critical Theorists, their critique of society and schools is not a mere academic exercise but is a necessary step in constructing a better future. Influenced by Freire's Liberation Pedagogy, they argue that the purpose of a genuine education is to raise the consciousness of dispossessed marginalized groups. As they learn who and what are causing their subordination, members of marginalized groups will gain the knowledge needed to work out their own self-empowerment. With this background into the constructs and strategies of Critical Theory, we turn our discussion to its educational implications.

Critical Theory's Implications for Schools, Curriculum, and Teachers

In this section, we consider Critical Theory's more direct implications for education. We consider how Critical Theorists conceive of the aims of education, the school, curriculum, and instruction.

Aims of Education

Critical Theorists believe that the aims of education are related to the larger and more inclusive social, political, and economic goals of social justice. As indicated, education should aim to raise the consciousness of those who are forced into lesser, marginal, and subordinate positions in society because of race, ethnicity, language, class, or gender. Such consciousness-raising is necessary if people are to empower themselves.

Schools as They Are and as They Might Be

Critical Theory offers a two-dimenional appraisal of schools: as they now exist in a capitalist society and how they might be in the future. Now and in the future, schools need to be interpreted as having historical origins and reflecting particular ideologies that support sociological, economic, and political interests. Schools are highly ideological and political sites in which conflict groups struggle for power and control. Often relying on interpretations from revisionist history, Critical Theorists argue that schools have been controlled and used by the economically, politically, and socially dominant classes for purposes of social maintenance and control. To maintain the status quo that gives them a commanding position, the children of the dominant classes are given the kind of education that enables them to attend prestigious educational institutions that groom them for high-level careers in business, industry, and government. Children of socially and economically subordinate groups are indoctrinated to accept the conditions that disempower them as being economically and political correct.

Schools are presently state-regulated institutions that power-holding elites use to transmit official knowledge and values that confirm and support their socioeconomic and political interests. The state, through mandates and standards, establishes curriculum based on the dominant ideology and teachers, as state employees, are expected to transmit its contents to students.[29]

Schools in a capitalist economy and society serve to train the workforce to meet the demands of production and consumption. They sort students into various sectors such as management, industry, and service that relate to the economy. Upper socioeconomic class students are groomed for schools that prepare them to take their places in the dominant elite. Lower socioeconomic class students, especially those from marginalized minorities, are trained as the workforce. Proponents of maintaining the status quo will use clichés about objectivity, neutrality as fairness, accountability, standards, and saleable skills to mask the sorting processes actually taking place in schools.

While the powerful classes have dominated schools historically, Critical Theorists do not believe that this domination is inevitable. The schools of the future do not have to be like those of the past and the present. By challenging the dominant class and their ideological rationales, Critical Theorists hope to break the cycle of domination. It is possible to raise the consciousness of the exploited, to deconstruct the texts that support domination, to expose the conditions of domination, and to organize to empower the dispossessed. Schools can become truly democratic public spheres in which young people learn to live the ethics of equality.

By recognizing and resisting the dominant ideology, schools can be sites for liberating students and society. To begin the process of creating an alternative future, it is important to understand schools not as ideologically neutral sites but as places of struggle and contestation between competing ideologies. Rather than accepting and transmitting the dominant ideology, teachers can guide students to construct their own social and political meanings. Teachers and students can explore their own backgrounds, write their own autobiographies, and advance their own liberation.[30]

Curriculum and Instruction

As with the other areas of education and schooling, the Critical Theorists analyze curriculum as it now is and how it might be in the future. They see the curriculum as existing in two dimensions or layers: the overt formal **official curriculum** of skills and subjects and the **hidden curriculum** that is below the surface and penetrates the school milieu. The prescribed curriculum of academic skills and subjects is the officially approved program that teachers are to transmit to students. Recall Freire's warning about prescription as that which imposes one person's choice on another. The hidden curriculum refers to those values, behaviors, and attitudes that are conveyed and imposed on students through the milieu and practices of the school in a capitalist consumer-oriented society. Both the overt official and the hidden curriculum represent the knowledge claims and value preferences of the dominant group or class that controls the school system.

The dominant classes use the official curriculum to reinforce the status quo that gives them power, wealth, and status. They use it to transmit their particular beliefs and values as the legitimate version of knowledge for all students. For example, it has constructed a version of history that portrays the American experience as a largely European-American series of triumphs in settling and industrializing the nation. The heroes in this version of history are typically white males of northern European ethnicity. African, Hispanic, and Native Americans are relegated to the margins of narratives about the American past. The portrayal of industrial capitalism is presented in favorable terms with little discussion about the exploitation of workers or the pollution of the environment. The American role in foreign affairs is generally presented as altruistic. Bilingual and multicultural education is viewed with suspicion as challenging the dominance of English as the semiofficial national language.

The favored method of instruction uses officially sanctioned textbooks to transmit information to students. The process of transmission, instead of critical thinking and analysis, usually reproduces the approved text—the officially constructed version of knowledge.

A key element in social control via the school is lodged in the hidden curriculum. It is called "hidden" because it does not appear in published state mandates or local school policies. It rather permeates the ideology and milieu of the public school. The early emphasis on "this is mine and that is yours" developed in early childhood education begins to build an attitude supportive of a capitalist consumer-driven mentality. In a class-biased society, prescriptions about the sanctity of private property imposes the dominant group's values. The sexist attitude that males are better in mathematics and science courses than females builds a gender-specific attitude to ongoing education and careers.

Educational expectations based on race, gender, and ethnicity contribute to stereotyping and the prediction that some groups are bound to fail in school. Part of the ideology of dominant group interests is manifested in having low academic expectations for students from marginalized, especially minority, groups. The argument that certain groups lack either the native intelligence or the social motivation to succeed in school shifts the educational process from a limited transmission of official knowledge to managing, controlling, and disciplining students from educationally suspect groups. It is expected that they will dislike schooling, disrupt classrooms, score low on standardized tests, and eventually drop out of the system. When these things occur, the anticipation of low expectations is fulfilled.[31]

How students are arranged, scheduled, and grouped in school organizations streams similar students together. Homogeneous grouping, though justified in terms of academic ability, actually perpetuates socioeconomic stratification in schools and reproduces the classism, racism, and sexism of the larger society.

Similar to Postmodernists, Critical Theorists endorse the use of deconstruction in examining language, especially educational representations found in texts, curriculum, and instruction. Language is not a verbal reflection of reality but is a human construction that is contextual and changes as contexts change. If it is constructed, then it can also be deconstructed. Like all contextual elements, language is shifting and changeable and its meaning depends on the contexts in which it is used. Definitions, too, are constructed and subject to revision. Critical Theorists challenge the Realist, Conservative, Perennialist, and Essentialist belief that a definition represents an unchanging reality such as truth, human nature, marriage, and family, for example. Consider the social and educational implications of the question: What is a family? While Realists and others are likely to answer that a family is a man (a husband) and a woman (a wife) and their children, Critical Theorists are likely to answer by referring to extended, single parent, same sex, and other kinds of family arrangements. Consider the implication of these two kinds of definitions for society and schools.

Still another issue relating to language that has an impact on curriculum and instruction is whether there is a standard language or there are many variations in language. If there is a standard language such as standard English, then there also is a correct grammar, syntax, and usage. If there are many variations in language, then each of these has its own grammar, syntax, and usage, which is appropriate to its speakers. Just as the metanarratives proporting to stand for universal knowledge are deconstructed, so are the texts that support the traditional curriculum. The subjects, the areas that reinforce the beliefs of the dominant group, can be broken apart, analyzed, and deconstructed. Just as these fields were constructed by the dominant group, they can be deconstructed by those who are disempowered. The purpose of this analysis is to raise the consciousness of both teachers and students about claims to legitimate knowledge.

After critiquing how the dominant class uses the curriculum to reproduce itself, Critical Theorists then turn to developing transformative strategies to create the schools they envision for the future. For them, knowledge and values that are truly legitimate in the curriculum arise in the local context, the immediate situation, the community in which students live and in the school they attend. The curriculum would begin with the students' own life stories, their autobiographies, as they tell them to each other. In the multicultural society that the United States truly is, there would be many versions of the story of the American experience rather than an officially approved one. Members of each race, ethnic, and language groups would give voice to their own story. A convergence of life stories is likely to take place as similarities and differences are found. It is from these autobiographical beginnings that a historical mosaic of the United States as a multicultural society arises.

The students' community, the place in which the school is located, is a microcosm of the larger society. The place to begin the study of science, social studies, the career world, and the environment is the context in which students live. For Critical Theorists, the purpose of instruction through dialogue is to create rather than to transmit or digest knowledge. Students' autobiographies, images, reflections, and interactions create their own knowledge and values rather than having other-constructed versions imposed on them through the official curriculum.

Given the kind of far-ranging dialogue that Critical Theorists advocate, the boundaries that separate one subject from another are deliberately dissolved. They regard subject-matter boundaries to be human constructions, often defined by academic elites. This approach to curriculum organization is diametrically opposed to the Aristotelian concept that the concepts found in a particular subjects are naturally related. Rather than being subject-specific as advocated by Essentialists and Perennialists, the curriculum is interdisciplinary and transdisciplinary. Critical Theorists also reject the concept of a hierarchy of knowledge that judges some subjects to be more important than others. Dialogue is not limited by location in literature, science, and history, for example, but uses all these disciplines and crosses, as Giroux argues, from one boundary to another, from one subject to another, depending on what needs to be said and examined and what issue needs to be examined. The very crossing from one discipline to another leads to education that cuts across them all and becomes transdisciplinary.

Science in the Curriculum: Philosophical Considerations

Critical Theorists, like Postmodernists, are suspicious about the Enlightenment's lingering effects on Western culture and education. An important continuing effect of the Enlightenment is the belief in the efficacy of science as an objective and disinterested method of finding the truth. Although their definitions of the scientific method may differ, Scientific Realists, Experimentalists, and many Progressives all extol its use not only in the natural and physical sciences but in the social sciences and in education. Critical Theorists argue that those who proclaim science's objectivity either misunderstand or ignore that science can be used as a political force to control and regulate people. The social, behavioral, and educational sciences, constructed in the nineteenth century but shaped by the Enlightenment—sociology, psychology, economics, political science, and anthropology—were used to manage and control the growing urban populations of an industrialized society. The creation of state-managed and controlled school systems, too, needs to be seen as an educational means of social control.

Critical Theorists dispute the power and objectivity of scientific predictability. Similar to Existentialists, Critical Theorists, especially those who take a Freirean perspective, see the world as so complex that it is not possible to have scientific predictability in social, political, and economic realms. Those who claim to be operating from an objective science with objective predictability are either deluded or agents of the dominant power holders. Philosophically, Critical Theorists part company from the Marxists, who claim that change is caused by universal forces generated from the class conflict to control the means and modes of production. They also disagree with the Idealists, especially the Hegelians, who see history as the unfolding of the Universal Mind in an ordered and systematically functioning universe. Critical Theorists also challenge the Realists, including the Scientific Realists, who contend that we discover reality. Like the Social Reconstructionists, the Critical Theorists assert that human beings construct their own meaning by living in concrete historical, social, political, and economic contexts and not from outside of them.

Critical Theorists dispute the idea that education, even when it borrows from the behaviorial and social sciences, can ever be scientific. Education, teaching, and learning are multidimensional and are located on school sites, which in turn are contexts. These community and school contexts are highly complex, dynamic, and so unstable that they resist neat scientific predictions or even statistical probability.[32]

Although Critical Theorists recognize the contributions of science in improving the quality of life, especially in working to eradicate certain diseases, and appreciate the informative power of the social sciences, they see science as another human construction that needs to be related to historical and social contexts. They are suspicious of those who, feigning objectivity, use science to sell commodities and regulate people. Critical Theorists raise questions about how science is used, especially to create new weapons of destruction or to promote economic globalization. They ask, how is science being used and who does it profit?[33]

Constructing Values

Unlike the Idealists, Realists, Thomists, and Perennialists, who see values arising from universal rational or spiritual principles, Critical Theorists see values—ethics and aesthetics—as resulting from informed public discourse and from putting equity and equality into practice. Using their own autobiography, as Freire argued, every person can enter into the discourse about what is right and wrong or beautiful or ugly. Values are not the products of imposition from those in power but are the results of the interface and sharing of people, whose voices have an equal right to be heard.

Teachers should encourage students to voice their beliefs and concerns about their own values. From hearing different voices raised in open and shared discourse, they will come to understand that official standards and values are not truly theirs but have been imposed on them. Rather than one standard for all, there is a multiplicity of values. Critical Theorists emphasize a multicultural process of valuation that includes cultural differences and inclusion. Emphasis on dialogue is inclusive of cultural differences, not to erode them in a bland moral consensus, but to celebrate them as expressions of diversity. Ethical discourse seeks to encourage students to find and use their voices, to articulate their beliefs and feelings, to value the opinion of others, and to become aware of those people and situations that interfere with the free exchange of ideas and values and try to close the dialogue. Teachers are to guide the ethical discussion so that it gradually enlarges to see as injustice the silencing of those who are at the margins and to include them in the dialogue.

Empowering Teachers

As with education and schooling, Critical Theorists critique the contemporary situation of teachers in the United States and present an agenda for their empowerment. Historically, they find that elementary and secondary school teachers have had a severely limited role in determining their own professional life. The majority of elementary school teachers, since the late-nineteenth century, have been women who were underpaid and oversupervised in contrast to males in the general workforce. Although professionals, their generally lower salaries place them in the lower middle classes. Entry requirements for teaching are established by state authorities rather than by teacher professional organizatons. The schools are governed by boards of education that typically represent the favored socioeconomic classes. The administration of schools is controlled by educational bureaucrats.

Along with the long-standing historical features that have disempowered teachers, several more contemporary trends add to their disadvantaged situation. School effectiveness, as determined by the Conservative Neo-Essentialist agenda, is defined in terms of students' performance on standardized academic achievement tests. Teachers and schools are judged by how well their students score on these tests mandated by state legislators and prepared by "experts" outside of the particular school. Thus, an external system has been imposed on teachers that orients instruction to the tests rather than to teachers' educational aims.

Critical Theorists see the contemporary standards movement as resting on a major misconception, a false ideology, in which students are members of one huge homogeneous group in which everyone has the same white, English-speaking, upper-middle-class socioeconomic background.[34] This false ideology contributes to the idea that standardized tests can be administered to all students, without concern for their socioeconomic class, racial, language, and ethnic background. It has the effect of attempting to homogenize a multicultural society.

Idealists, Realists, Essentialists, and Perennialists argue that teachers should prepare lessons based on their research into academic texts in history, science, mathematics, and literature. After researching these texts, teachers are then to construct lesson plans based on the information that they find in them. Teachers are to reorganize this information and transmit it to students. Experimentalists and Progressives challenge this traditional view of preparing lessons as a pre-packaged exercise that ignores students' real interest and needs and limits opportunities for creativity.

Critical Theorists accept but enlarge the Progressive concept that teacher research focuses on students and moves it from an individual analysis of students to a larger social, economic, and political one. Viewing students as socially constructed persons, teachers need to examine students in their lived-in situations.[35]

Critical Theorists urge teachers to begin their consciousness-raising with the students in their classes and with an examination of the conditions in their neighborhood communities. Each student has her or his own life story to share; these life stories can form a collective autobiography that tells about what they are experiencing in school, in their homes, and in their neighborhood. These life stories can be connected with the larger histories of the economic classes and racial, ethnic, and language groups of which they are members. After exploring their own identities and meanings, students, guided by teachers, can work at developing ways to recognize stereotyping and misrepresentation and to resist indoctrination both in and out of school. They can learn how to take control of their own lives and shape their own futures. This kind of microlevel change can be the base from which larger reforms can take place. Endorsing consciousness-raising by critical dialogue, Critical Theorists urge teachers to engage in a profound and far-reaching examination of the conditions in and out of schools that cause their disempowerment and the miseducation of their students. In addition to bureaucratically controlled schools, teachers need to be aware of the broader socioeconomic and political factors that disempower the poor, racial and ethnic minorities, and women in the United States. Rather than simply reacting to change from above, teachers need to take on the role of transformative agents for real and significant social and educational change. They need to:

- find out who their true allies are in the struggle for school control.
- learn who their students are by helping them to work toward their own self-identity and self-empowerment.
- interact and work with the people in local communities for community improvement.

- join with like-minded teachers in collegial organizations that are controlled by teachers and work for real educational reform.
- engage in a larger critical dialogue about the political, social, economic, and educational issues that confront American society.

Ideological Opposition to Neo-Liberalism and Conservativism

Seeing all education and schooling as ideologically contested areas, Critical Theorists oppose countervailing ideologies such as Conservativism and Liberalism. Conservatism, which has been on the ascendancy in the late twentieth and early twenty-first centuries, is opposed as an ideology that argues for traditional academic and moral standards as a way to maintain the status quo. Freire, for example, saw Conservatism as an ideology that seeks to block or at least slow down the pace of social change by constructing an ideological interpretation of history and society that defends the ruling class's privileged position.

Critical Theorists see American Neo-Conservatism as an amalgamation of special interest groups and lobbies on the right such as corporate business interests and Christian religious fundamentalists, who generally support conservative Republican candidates and have an ideological agenda for society and schools. Included in this agenda are:

- Restoring fundamental and traditional values in schools, school prayer, and the teaching of Creationism or Intelligent Design in the curriculum.
- Sex education programs that encourage abstinence and do not include other forms of contraception.
- Efforts to keep the curriculum focused on basic skills and academic subjects by encouraging mandated standardized testing.
- Opposition to curricular and instructional innovations such as process learning, Constructivism, and values clarification.
- Encouraging federal and state aid for private and religious schools and for vouchers enabling students to attend these schools.

Critical Theorists seen the Neo-Conservative agenda for schools as maintaining them as sites of marginalization and reproduction of the dominant power structure. To enact their own agenda, described earlier in the chapter, Critical Theorists oppose the Conservative efforts to control schools.

A contested battleground between Critical Theorists and Neo-Conservatives is the cultural war over what should be included in and excluded from the curriculum. Conservatives, Essentialists, and Perennialists argue that there should be a cultural core, based on the Western heritage, required of all students. The Western cultural core would consist of the great works of history, literature, and philosophy written by Europeans such as Plato, Aristotle, Augustine, Aquinas, Erasmas, Locke, and Rousseau. Critical Theorists resist the imposition of the Western cultural core as a kind of patriarchal Eurocentric educational imperialism that denies the importance of Asian, African, and South American literature.

They argue for a core that is infused with multicultural and feminist history, philosophy, and literature that gives voice to hitherto marginalized and indigenous peoples who have traditionally been silenced in traditional education.[36]

Critical Theorists are also disenchanted with Liberalism. Although it promises equality of opportunity for minority members, Liberalism is transactional and piecemeal in its approach to educational change, usually adding something new to the curriculum and not really eliminating those things that contribute to repression and marginalization in schools. Liberals are so focued on means rather than ends that they are educational tinkerers who keep adding new procedures and creating new bureaucracies that bog down administrators and teachers in a maze of paperwork instead of bringing real transformative change. Liberals display a presumed benevolence toward subordinated groups but do not acknowledge that they, too, are enjoying a privileged position in gated communities and affluent suburbs. Rather than acting directly to end the repression of marginalized people, Liberals skirt the main issues and instead are content with piecemeal reforms that often secure their own position rather than improve the situation of those they pretend to help. Even the Liberal notion of welfare and assistance, benignly intended to aid the poor, can create dependency that locks the dependents into the system rather than liberating them from it.[37]

An important difference between Critical Theory and Liberalism concerns the issues of a vital center and margins. Liberals see the creation of a vital center, marking a vast consensus, on knowledge, values, and especially processes as a desirable education goal. In contrast, Critical Theorists see consensus on what Liberals call a vital center as a subterfuge to construct a core of domination, but to mask it with benign characteristics. Critical Theorists are concerned with groups that have been relegated to the periphery, the margins, of society. They want education that does not blur and obscure differences in the name of consensus but that encourages multicultural differences.

Still another point of contention between Critical Theorists and Neo-Conservatives and Liberals is globalization. Critical Theorists refer to globalization as a form of Neo-Liberalism that is based on the Classical Liberal ideas of Adam Smith and David Ricardo and reiterated by contemporary economists such as Milton Friedman who argue for free trade, little government interference with international commerce, and deregulation. It needs to be pointed out that the market economy, associated historically, has been appropriated by Neo-Conservatives. Liberals argue that globalization is a modern and pervasive economic force but that it should be regulated to protect the environment, eliminate child labor and the exploitation of workers, and provide higher wages and benefits. Critical Theorists question globalization as a new form of international capitalism that is causing economic exploitation and political repression worldwide.[38]

Conclusion

This chapter examined the philosophical and ideological influences of Marxism, Liberation Pedagogy, and Postmodernism on Critical Theory. The chapter discussed the Critical Theorist argument that political, economic, and educational institutions, including schools, maintain and reproduce inequitable and exploitative conditions that favor one group or

A Critical Theorist Scenario

Critical Theorists contend that all students, but especially those who are marginalized by the dominant society, need to be given the opportunity to find and use their voice. The official curriculum, especially the approved version of history, denies them the use of their own voices, their experiences, and the opportunities to express their needs and expectations. Critical Theorists argue that students need to be offered the opportunity to engage in a variety of activities that allow them to speak for themselves and to their peers. One of these opportunities is to think about their lives and to write their own autobiographies.

A possibility for getting the autobiographical process started is to have students view the motion picture *Freedom Writers,* in which a high school English class actually write their own autobiographies. The movie is based on *The Freedom Writers Diary,* a compelling narrative of how Erin Gruwell, an English teacher at the Woodrow Wilson High School in Long Beach, California, used autobiographical writing as an educational method. Gruwell's students, categorized as "at risk," who were expected to drop out of school, kept diaries and then used their accounts to write their own autobiographies. They wrote about the conditions that they were experiencing in their own lived-in situations—street violence, gang warfare, drug abuse, and poverty. As they came to know themselves, they began to know each other. Their writing became a means of raising consciousness and self-empowerment. Contrary to the educational establishment's prediction, these students all completed high school.[39] After viewing the movie, students can discuss it. They can then read *The Freedom Writers Diary.* It might be possible that the students will want to begin writing their own autobiographies. These individual autobiographies might be shared and discussed and, more ambitiously form the basis of a larger **collective autobiography**.

Students can share their life stories to create a collaborative group autobiography that recounts experiences at home, in school, and in the community. They can further connect this group autobiography to the larger histories of their respective economic classes and racial, ethnic, and language groups. The United States' multicultural society provides many more versions of the American experience story than an officially approved one. Members of each racial, ethnic, and language group can tell their own story rather than having it told for them. After exploring their own identities, students can develop ways to recognize stereotyping and misrepresentation and to resist indoctrination both in and out of school. They can learn how to take control of their own lives and shape their own futures.[40]

class, the dominant one, over subordinate groups and classes. It described strategies for liberating schools from the control of dominant groups and making them into agencies of human liberation. Informed by the educational ideas of Paulo Freire, Henry Giroux, and other theorists, Critical Theory seeks to raise consciousness and bring about transformative change in society and education. The social and educational agenda of Critical Theory is to empower marginalized groups to determine their own futures in an equitable society.

Constructing Your Own Philosophy of Education.   Now that you have read and discussed this chapter, reflect on how Critical Theory may or may not inform your ideas about education and schooling. As you construct your own philosophy of education, consider whether Critical Theory appeals to you as a teacher. Do you plan to use it in constructing your own philosophy of education?

Questions for Reflection and Discussion

1. Reflect on the concept of marginality. Have you ever felt that you were at the margin rather than in the center of your school experiences? Identify groups that you believe are marginalized in existing school situations.

2. Identify the key knowledge areas and values that were considered important by teachers in your school experience. Do you believe that these knowledge areas and values were genuinely important to you as a person?

3. Critics of Critical Theory contend that it indoctrinates students in a particular political ideology rather than in an open-ended discussion of various political positions. Do you agree or disagree with these critics?

4. Do you agree or disagree with the Critical Theorist view that objectivity is not really possible in teaching?

5. Reflect on your education. Do you recall events or situations that raised your critical consciousness? If so, describe and analyze them.

Topics for Inquiry and Research

1. Do an analysis of your teacher education program from a Critical Theorist perspective. Do you find any evidence of class or gender bias?

2. In a dialogue with other students, reflect on how they learned to think about race, class, ethnicity and gender.

3. In your class, work with other students to engage in a consciousness-raising dialogue on a common issue at your college or university.

4. In a class discussion, identify what it means to have ideas based on false consciousness.

During your discussion, develop a list of the factors that contribute to false consciousness in American society.

5. In a class discussion, identify those who are empowered and disempowered in American society, in general, and in your educational context, your school or college, in particular.

6. Organize a dialogue that uses Critical Theory to examine what it means to be a teacher and a student.

Building a Critical Theorist Vocabulary

Border Crossings: Giroux's interdisciplinary strategy of moving across the boundaries that set off one subject from another in the traditional curriculum.

Collective Autobiography: when students put their individual autobiographies together as an explanation of who they are as a group.

Consciousness-Raising: an examination that leads to a recognition of the people and conditions that cause exploition and devising strategies to end that exploitation.

Critical Theory: a theory that analyzes control and power in institutions and schools and seeks to empower those who are marginalized in a capitalist society and economy.

Dominant Classes and Groups: those who hold power and use that power to control other groups and classes, especially marginalized ones.

Empowerment: when an oppressed group becomes conscious of the conditions of their exploitation and takes power over their own lives.

Hidden Curriculum: values, behaviors and attitudes that are conveyed and imposed on students through the milieu, or the school environment.

Liberation Pedagogy: Freire's concept of education to liberate people from oppression and to guide them in their own self-empowerment.

Marginalize: to exclude from power and the means of achieving power.

Microanalysis: an investigation of the forces operating internally in an institution such as a school.

Official Curriculum: the prescribed approved program and courses transmitted and imposed on students.

Internet Resources

For a discussion of issues related to Freirean education and a glossary of Freire's terms, consult http://nlu.nl .edu/ace/Resources/Documents/FreireIssues.html.

The home of informal education, www.infed.org, provides a short biography and discussion of Freire's work.

Suggestions for Further Reading

Doyle, Clar and Singh, Amarjit Singh. *Reading and Teaching Henry Giroux*. New York: Peter Lang, 2006.

Freire, Paulo. *Letters to Cristina. Reflections on My Life and Work*. London: Routledge, 1996.

Freire, Paulo. *Pedagogy of Freedom: Ethics, Democracy, and Civic Courage*. Lanham, MD: Rowman and Littlefield, 1998.

Freire, Paulo. *Pedagogy of Hope, Reliving Pedagogy of the Oppressed*. New York: Continuum, 1995.

Freire, Paulo. *Pedagogy of the Oppressed*. Translated by Myra Bergman Ramos. New York: Continuum, 1984.

Gadotti, M. *Reading Paulo Freire: His Life and Work*. New York: SUNY Press, 1994.

Giroux, H. A. *Ideology, Culture, and the Process of Schooling*. Philadelphia, PA: Temple University Press, 1981.

Giroux, H. A. *Teachers as Intellectuals: Toward a Critical Pedagogy of Learning*. Granby, MA: Bergin & Garvey, 1988.

Gore, J. M. *The Struggle for Pedagogies: Critical and Feminist Discourses as Regimes of Truth*. New York: Routledge, 1993.

Held, David. *Introduction to Critical Theory: Horkheimer to Habermas*. Berkeley: University of California Press, 1980.

Kinchloe, Joe L. *Critical Pedagogy Primer*. New York: Peter Lang, 2005.

Martusewicz, Rebecca A., and William M. Reynolds, eds. *Inside/Out: Contemporary Critical Perspectives in Education*. New York: St. Martin's Press, 1994.

McLaren, Peter, and Peter Leonard. *Paulo Freire: A Critical Encounter*. New York and London: Routledge, 1993.

Morrow, Raymond A., and Carlos Alberto Torres. *Reading Freire and Habermas: Critical Pedagogy and Transformative Social Change*. New York: Teachers College Press, Columbia University, 2002.

Endnotes

1. Joe L. Kincheloe, *Critical Pedagogy Primer* (New York: Peter Lang, 2005), p. 51.

2. Kincheloe, *Critical Pedagogy Primer,* p. 46.

3. Douglas Kellner, "Critical Theory," in Randall Curren, ed., *A Companion to the Philosophy of Education* (Malden, MA: Blackwell, 2006), p. 165.

4. Kellner, "Critical Theory," p. 166.

5. Richard Shaull, "Preface," in Paulo Freire, *Pedagogy of the Oppressed* (New York: Continuum, 1984), pp. 9–11.

6. Philip L. Ralph, Robert E. Lerner, Standish Meacham, and Edward McNall Burns, *World Civilizations: Their History and Their Culture,* Vol. II, 8e (New York: W. W. Norton, 1991), p. 785.

7. Ralph et al., *World Civilizations: Their History and Their Culture,* p. 785.

8. Paulo Freire, *Pedagogy of Freedom, Ethics, Democracy and Civic Courage*, translated by Patrick Clarke (Lanham, MD: Rowman and Littlefield, 1998), pp. 25–26, 54.

9. Donaldo Macedo, "Foreword," in Freire, *Pedagogy of Freedom: Ethics, Democracy, and Civic Courage,* p. xxiv.

10. Freire, quoted in Joe L. Kincheloe, *Critical Pedagogy Primer,* p. 3.

11. "People You Should Know: Freire," http://nlu.nl.edu/ ace/Resources/Freire.html (August 11, 2003), 1.

12. Stanley Aronowitz, "Introduction," in Paulo Freire, *Pedagogy of Freedom: Ethics, Democracy, and Civic Courage,* p. 11.

13. Freire, *Pedagogy of Freedom, Ethics, Democracy and Civic Courage,* pp. 25–26, 54.

14. Paulo Freire, *Pedagogy of the Oppressed,* trans. Myra Bergman Ramos (New York: Continuum, 1984), p. 31.

15. Aronowitz, "Introduction," p. 4.

16. Freire, *Pedagogy of the Oppressed,* pp. 57–59.

17. Aronowitz, "Introduction," pp. 4–5.

18. Freire, *Pedagogy of Freedom, Ethics, Democracy and Civic Courage,* p. 22.

19. Aronowitz, "Introduction," pp. 8–9.

20. Macedo, "Foreword," p. xiii.

21. Clar Doyle and Amarjit Singh, *Reading and Teaching Henry Giroux* (New York: Peter Lang, 2006), p. 13.

22. Kellner, "Critical Theory," pp. 171–172.

23. Doyle and Singh, *Reading and Teaching Henry Giroux,* p. 5.

24. Doyle and Singh, *Reading and Teaching Henry Giroux,* p. 26.

25. Kellner, "Critical Theory," pp. 168–169.

26. Kincheloe, *Critical Pedagogy Primer,* pp. 2, 16.

27. Angeline Martel and Linda Peterat, "Margins of Exclusion, Margins of Transformation: The Place of Women in Education," in Rebecca A. Martusewicz and William Reynold, eds., *Inside/Out: Contemporary Critical Perspectives in Education* (New York: St. Martin's Press, 1994), pp. 151–154.

28. Rebecca A. Martusewicz and William Reynold, eds., *Inside/Out: Contemporary Critical Perspectives in Education,* p. v.

29. Doyle and Singh, *Reading and Teaching Henry Giroux,* pp. 16–18.

30. Doyle and Singh, *Reading and Teaching Henry Giroux,* p. 18.

31. Kincheloe, *Critical Pedagogy Primer,* pp. 7–8.

32. Kincheloe, *Critical Pedagogy Primer,* p. 32.

33. Kincheloe, *Critical Pedagogy Primer,* p. 30.

34. Kincheloe, *Critical Pedagogy Primer,* p. 23.

35. Kincheloe, *Critical Pedagogy Primer,* p. 19.

36. Kincheloe, *Critical Pedagogy Primer,* p. 26.

37. Macedo, "Foreword," p. xxviii.

38. Doyle and Singh, *Reading and Teaching Henry Giroux,* p. 7.

39. The Freedom Writers, with Erin Gruwell, *The Freedom Writers Diary: How a Teacher and 150 Teens Used Writing to Change Themselves and the World Around Them* (New York: Doubleday/ Random House, 1999). The story of the Freedom Writers was portrayed in a motion picture in 2007. Also see: the Freedom Writers Foundation at www .freedomwritersfoundation.org.

40. Christine E. Sleeter and Peter L. McLaren, eds., *Multicultural Education, Critical Pedagogy, and the Politics of Difference* (Albany: State University of New York Press, 1995).

17

Globalization and Education

Demonstrators protesting against international banking and financial agencies that promote globalization and structural adjustment policies.

Chapter Preview

We now examine the complex phenomenon of globalization. In writing this chapter, I gave some thought to its appropriateness to a book on philosophy, ideology, and theory of education. Is the topic more appropriate to economics and to sociology? As I attend conferences on the foundations of education, I find more professors addressing and analyzing globalization's educational implications. The topic is frequently addressed by Neo-Marxists and

Critical Theorists who oppose it as a form of neocapitalism. For these reasons, I decided to close the book with a final chapter on globalization. I believe that as educators we will encounter globalization increasingly in our teaching. In this chapter, I have located globalization with the theories of education. However, globalization also has many ideological relationships in that Liberals, Conservatives, and Marxists have reacted to it as an economic phenomenon that affects politics, society, and education. In particular, Critical Theorists have developed a largely negative critique about globalization and its effect on power relationships in societies in both technologically and less technologically developed countries. This chapter moves our discussion of educational theory to the international or global dimension; it is also increasingly apparent that globalization affects us nationally and locally. For example, the recent issue over the importation of toys produced in China that contained unsafe levels of lead has focused attention on the global economy.

In focusing our attention on globalization, we are examining a contemporary phenomenon that has multifaceted and interconnected economic, political, social, and educational consequences. It has implications for a wide range of areas such as international trade and finance, information technology, environmental policy, the transnational business corporation, and international educational exchange and schools.[1] Globalization has had a pronounced impact on education, especially colleges and universities, which have study programs abroad, centers in other countries, and myriad programs of educational exchange of professors and students. The following topics are examined in this chapter:

- Defining globalization
- Processes of globalization
- Economic change and controversy
- Global theory of education
- Ideological perspectives and interpretations of globalization

As you read the chapter, reflect on how globalization has had an impact on your life, on your community, and on the future work that you may do. Consider whether globalization needs to be considered in constructing a philosophy of education. Determine whether you will address globalization and global issues in your philosophy of education.

Defining Globalization

Some commentators argue that globalization is an unprecedented new dynamic world force; others say that it is a new name for an old process. We will look at both sides of the question and look at it as both old and new. Because globalization is so wide-ranging, multifaceted, and controversial, experts disagree on its definition. Academic experts have engaged in long, complicated, and unresolved discussion about globalization's meaning and impact on the world.

Roland Robertson defines **globalization** as an "accelerated compression of the contemporary world and the intensification of consciousness of the world as a singular entity." This compression, Robertson says, is "reducing social and ethnic uniqueness."[2]

Political scientist Manfred Steger defines *globalization* as a "multidimensional set of social processes that create, multiply, stretch, and intensify worldwide social interdependencies and exchanges while [simultaneously] fostering . . . a growing awareness of deepening connections between the local and the distant."[3] In constructing his definition of globalization, Steger uses the term **globality**, the social conditions characterized by worldwide economic, political, cultural, and environmental interconnections that cross borders and boundaries. Globalization refers to these processes that are transforming the contemporary situation into one of increasing globality.[4] Globalization requires people to rethink their conceptions of time and space as communications become electronically instantaneous and distances are diminished by innovations in transportation.

Steger sees globalization as a highly complex "hybridized" concept that mixes, but does not always integrate, a range of cultural forms and educational styles.[5] In his analysis, Steger sees globalization working as a process that multiplies existing social networks and activities and creates new ones that increasingly cross and transform traditional geographical, political, economic, cultural, and educational boundaries.[6] In his consideration of globalization, Steger raises some serious questions that we can think about in this chapter. Among them are: (1) How does globalization occur? (2) Is it caused by one or several factors? (3) Is it part of the process of modernization, or is a new phenomenon?[7]

Stipulating a Definition of Globalization

When experts disagree on definitions as they do with globalization, it becomes necessary to construct or stipulate a definition to begin a discussion of a disputed term. To stipulate a definition of globalization, I begin by extracting and defining its root, **global**. *Global* refers to a system or a process that relates to, involves, includes, or is adapted to the entire world such as climatic, environmental, and health conditions, for example. It includes human engineered systems such as economics, communication, travel, and transportation that encompass the entire world. Then, I add "ization" which combines the suffix *-ize,* meaning to follow a line of action, with the root, *global,* arriving at the word *globalization.* Globalization, then, can be defined as the processes that take a course of action to promote the worldwide involvement, relationships, adaptations, and connections between peoples of different countries, cultures, and languages. As a worldwide process, globalization needs to be considered in terms of those characteristics that are transnational and worldwide but that also affect people in their own local and national spaces.

The Processes of Globalization

In this section, we examine some of the processes of globalization that have accelerated, particularly in economics and communications, to generate worldwide interconnections between peoples across nations and cultures. In the twenty-first century, globalization, as a transformative process, transcends nation-states and involves multinational economic interests and relationships. In the development of communications, especially via electronic and computer technologies, the international relationships between nation-states have been superseded by global contacts between individuals. The most significant forces in contemporary globalization are global communications systems and multinational business corporations.

Global Communications Processes

The rapid changes in communications are a feature of globalization that touches all of us. It is probably the process of globalization with which teachers and students are most familiar. One of the twenty-first century's major transformative innovations is the development of worldwide communications systems in reporting news, providing international entertainment, diffusing information, and making it possible for people to interact with each other via e-mail, the Internet, and the World Wide Web. As very powerful agencies of informal and nonformal education, these systems are influencing how people view themselves, other peoples, and the world. Worldwide news agencies, ranging from CNN, based in the United States, to Al Jazeera, serving the Arab world, provide almost immediate satellite television coverage of and commentary on events occurring around the world. As a result, people are instantaneously and dynamically informed about events in other countries. With this instantaneous reportage, television programming has outdistanced the printed page, newspapers, magazines, and books as a source of information. People within and across countries can communicate and share opinions with an ease and rapidity unknown in the past. While the Internet and e-mail make it possible for people to communicate quickly with each across national boundaries, they also make it possible for global terrorist groups, such as al Qaeda, to plan and coordinate their attacks.

The rapidity of global communications raises serious educational issues. Although schools, too, are electronically connected to the World Wide Web, the most important consequences of the communications revolution relate to informal education and take place outside of schools. By watching television or accessing sites on the Web, students can construct a view of the world that may either relate to or diverge from what is being transmitted by teachers and textbooks. The school curriculum, especially in the social sciences and sciences, is always dated because conveying information by the printed page takes time. Now, the dynamics of the communications revolution challenges the less dynamic portrayal of social studies and scientific information by teachers and books. An important difference is that the materials in the curriculum have been refereed to an extent, have been digested, interpreted, and presented in an organized way. The information from television and the Internet comes more like an avalanche of data that depends on the source and coverage. It is not digested and organized. Neither is it refereed in that timeliness takes priority over scholarly and scientific expertise. Teachers have the challenging task of trying to relate the formal curriculum with the informal sources of information or disinformation. In meeting this challenge, teachers have to ask themselves the philosophical questions: What is truth? Who is constructing the statements that claim to be true? They need to ask themselves: What is the ideology that is behind the programming of information on the media?

Global Economic Processes

Just as we are all touched by the accelerated development of global communications, we also feel the impact of global economic processes. The food we eat, the clothes we wear, and the electronic instruments we use most likely are made in countries other than the United States. Indeed, the parts of some of these products may be made in several countries. All one has to do is to look at the labels on clothing to quickly get the sense of the immediate reality of economic globalization. In addition to affecting us as consumers, the economic processes of globalization exert a strong influence on us as producers. They affect jobs, training, and education. What work will we do in the future? How should our education prepare us for the global economy?

The most powerful agency that has accelerated global economic processes is the **multinational or transnational business corporation**. These transnational corporations (TNCs) may have headquarters and ownership in several countries and have factories and production centers located throughout the world. TNCs operate across national borders and their capital comes from investors from all over the world; components of their products are made in different countries, and assembled in others; marketing may be organized from headquarters in still another country. The final products are sold in still other countries.[8] TNCs range from agribusinesses, to automobile manufacturing companies, to information-generating ones. The extent to which and the rapidity by which the TNCs can transfer financial and personnel resources from nation to nation or region to region exerts a new unprecedented force on the world economy.

Economic globalization, the process of integrating national economies worldwide, involves capital, investments, production, marketing, and distribution of goods and services. These economic processes raise important educational questions that relate to curriculum construction and whether schooling should emphasize the arts and humanities or technological and vocational training. They relate to the formulating of educational policies about resource investment in education, especially to the funding of particular sectors in the school system. Finally, they relate to the role of educating individuals to understand and prepare them to function competently in the global economy.

In the older, industrial nations, such as the United States and the United Kingdom, heavy industries such as iron, steel, and coal have downsized seriously, resulting in unemployment of workers in these sectors. Steel production, for example, has shifted to other countries, such as South Korea, where production costs are lower. Clothing manufacturing has shifted to Southeast Asian and Central American countries for the same reason. The defenders of market-driven globalization argue that this kind of technologically caused unemployment is temporary and requires the retraining of workers in the older industries for different kinds of jobs in the postindustrial high-tech information age. Opponents, especially in the United States, argue that high-paying jobs, with health care and pension benefits, are being outsourced by corporations to other countries that do not meet safety standards for working conditions, nor enforce environmental protection requirements.

Global Political Processes

Globalization's communications and economic processes have the most immediate, direct, and visible effects on us; its more subtle and less overt political and social processes also exert considerable change on us. The change in political processes is largely generated by economic ones that move nation-states to develop policies to attract investment, create new industries, and market their products. Nation-states make themselves attractive to foreign investors by maintaining civil order, reducing incidences of violence, offering tax breaks and other incentives, and reducing tariff and customs duties to encourage corporations to locate in the country. They enact laws that protect foreign investment from seizure, expropriation, labor conflicts, or nationalization.[9]

Loans for economic development from the World Bank and other international financial agencies require less technologically developed countries, primarily in Africa and eastern Europe, to implement structural adjustment policies. The structural adjustment rationale is based on the Classical Liberal, also called the Neo-Liberal, assumptions that free market capitalism produces greater efficiency and productivity. According to this rationale, government interference in the economy impedes the operations of the free market. It results in higher production costs for goods and services and produces large, top-heavy, and inefficient government bureaucracies that stifle economic development. Structural adjustment policies require countries seeking loans to: (1) reduce government bureaucracies; (2) reduce government subsidies for housing, food, social services, and health care; (3) eliminate protective tariffs, price controls, and support for domestic products; (4) devalue currency when necessary; (5) shift production toward export goods for sale on the world market; (6) privatize health, social welfare, and some education programs; and (7) place state-owned industries in private ownership.[10]

Structural adjustment policies have caused reductions in funding social services related to education. As governments reduce educational subsidies, certain costs such as textbooks, material, and activity fees are passed on to students and their families. These user fees, which fall heaviest on the poor in urban and rural areas, may cause lower-income students to leave school for financial reasons.

In many countries, school administrators and teachers are part of the national administrative structure and may be civil servants. Although the number of teachers and the essential conditions of teaching may not be directly affected, the role and function of national educational bureaucracies are being altered. Structural-adjustment advocates view large government bureaucracies as having vested interest in maintaining the status quo and perceive them as fostering "red tape," resistance to change, and inefficiency. Rather than maintaining centralized national agencies to control education, structural adjustment policies encourage greater devolution of authority to local levels.

Globalization introduces new variables into the political context, often creating new economic class divisions or exacerbating existing ones. It may increase economic disparities between groups and generate new social divisions, movements, and conflicts in the nation-state. There is likely to be class-based political realignments or conflicts. For example, the control of the economy may generate conflicts between old and new elites for political power. If there is a market-dominant ethnic group, such as the Chinese minority in Southeast Asia, it may cause ethnic tensions that spill over into the political arena.

Globalization has eroded many of the cultural and social distances between people. Sometimes this change has generated greater global cooperation as in the response to aid the victims of the 2004 Asian tsunami. They can also generate conflicts between racial, ethnic, and language groups, especially in situations in which one group appears to be benefiting economically at the expense of other groups. Some critics fear that globalization is eliminating the uniqueness of local cultures and creating a consumer-generated conformism, a kind of worldwide strip mall, of uniformity and sameness.[11]

Global Educational Processes

Globalization is having an effect on the administration, organization, and funding of educational systems throughout the world. For example, structural adjustment policies in **less technologically developed countries** (LTDCs) imposed by the World Bank and international financial agencies typically reduce the social service aspects of educational funding. Globalization generates conflicting demands in LTDCs—to reduce expenditures but also to expand the system to meet rising educational expectations, especially in the new middle-class sectors.

Globalization generates new educational priorities and the restructuring of the curriculum. It calls for training an industrially skilled labor force in countries that were hitherto primarily agricultural and in developing managerial and technological skills in the middle occupational rungs. It also requires retraining from industrial to service areas in the older industrial countries such as the United States and the United Kingdom as these nations readjust their economies.

Some advocates of globalization, especially those who identify with its private market-driven orientation, contend that administrators and teachers need to be made accountable for students' academic performance. They argue that students' performance can be measured by using standardized achievement tests. This assumption accentuates using standardized testing to measure students' academic progress and statistical analysis to compare and rank academic achievement in different countries. When American students score lower in mathematics and sciences than their counterparts in other countries, this reinforces Essentialist arguments for improved instruction and accountability in instruction in these subjects.

Some educators argue that schools need to include knowledge about globalization in the curriculum that is both conceptual and applied.[12] The curriculum, they contend, needs to be infused with conceptual knowledge about globalization as a process and an analysis of its social and economic implications. Schools also need to include applied knowledge, such as developing competencies in needed technological skills, especially how to acquire and interpret information via computers, the Internet, and the World Wide Web. They also need to learn how to authenticate and interpret this generally unreferenced and unrefereed information.

Globalization has also had a direct impact on education in that many secondary schools and most colleges and universities in the United States have international programs and courses. Colleges and universities have branches in other countries. For example, Loyola University, in Chicago, has long had a campus in Rome, Italy, where students can spend a year studying abroad. Other institutions have campuses throughout the world. There are regular exchanges of professors from the United States to other countries and, in turn, professors from other countries come to teach in the United States. There are large numbers of international students on most college and university campuses.

Economic Change and Controversy

Globalization has generated considerable controversy between those who see it as a process that has the possibility for improving economic conditions and raising living standards for people throughout the world and those who see it as a force that exploits the world's poor.

Though lauded by privatization and free market advocates, globalization has sparked counterreactions. The proponents of a worldwide free market economy argue that globalization's long-term benefits will reduce production costs and make goods available to more buyers in an expanding global marketplace. Similar to the arguments of laissez-faire economic theorists in the nineteenth and early twentieth centuries, the proponents of free trade globalization contend that the elimination of tariffs and other trade barriers, erected by individual nation-states, will make production more efficient and bring jobs to more people, especially in LTDCs. Specifically, the proponents of globalization contend that: (1) its export-driven growth has improved Asian economies; (2) it reduced the isolation of the LTDCs, giving them greater access to the world economy; and (3) it generated social and educational programs that have improved rural education and health projects to treat the victims of diseases such as AIDS.

Opponents of globalization include members of trade unions in TDCs, who see it as causing the movement of jobs to other countries where pay and benefits are low; environmentalists, who see the spread of huge agribusinesses as producing environmental damage; and social activists, who see it as another means of exploiting the poor in LTDCs. The opponents contend that globalization benefits the few at the expense of the many. They claim that poverty has actually increased in some countries, particularly those in sub-Saharan Africa. Meetings of the World Trade Organization, the International Monetary Fund, and other organizations promoting a global economy have been met by protest demonstrations. The opponents see globalization as creating a more stratified world society, with greater disparities between the haves and have-nots, and increasing economic inequalities. In some LTDCs, especially in South America and Africa, agribusinesses, in which multinational corporations own most of the land, engage in the large-scale production of a single crop, such as sugar, pineapples, palm oil, or bananas, for example. This has caused a change in land occupancy as the large agribusinesses gain control of vast acreages. Often, local farmers with small tracts of land are displaced to make way for the large agricultural units. Advocates of market-driven globalization argue that such single-crop large-scale agriculture is more efficient, produces more food at less cost, and employs local people. Critics argue that the dispossessed farmers become an impoverished, landless, lower class; a rural poor; or migrants to urban slums.

Globalization Theory and Education

In the next section, we examine globalization theory and its relationship to education. Scholars began to analyze globalization as a theory in the 1980s. In some respects, globalization theory was constructed on the earlier ideas of modernization and development advanced by C. E. Black and others. Modernization sought to explain how the introduction of modern ideas and technologies transformed traditional societies, typically rural, local, and agricultural ones, into modern nations. Modernization was largely associated with the idea that development could be a force for nation-building—the transformation of traditional societies into modern nation-states. Contemporary globalization, however, appears to be much more extensive and dynamic than modernization as a world force. Though it operates in particular nation-state contexts, it is, as its name suggests, a worldwide phenomenon.

Similarities and Differences between Modernization and Globalization

Some similarities appear to exist between modernization theory that was dominant in sociology, economics, and education during the 1960s and 1970s and contemporary globalization. For example, a copious literature on modernization and nation-building appeared at that time in comparative and international education. **Modernization** was defined as the process by which traditional, rural, and agricultural societies became modern ones. Modern societies, located in nation-states, were defined as: (1) being predominately industrial and urban; (2) having technological, engineering, and scientific elites; (3) having loyalty and primary identification centered on the nation-state rather than on the locality, ethnicity, language group, or tribe; and (4) placing more emphasis on scientific rationality over custom and tradition. Modernization was construed to be a worldwide process destined to reshape traditional societies into modern nation-states. It can be seen that several characteristics of modernization, such as urbanization, industrialization, and scientific thinking, are also characteristics of globalization. Later in this section, some distinctions will be made between modernization and globalization.

Modernization was often identified with nation-building, a frequently used concept in foreign policy, foreign assistance, international development, and in comparative and international education. In the 1950s and 1960s, the Asian and African colonies of the western European nations had either won or been granted independence. In some of these former colonies, especially those that had been created as convenient administrative units by the imperial powers, social cohesion based on national identity was often absent. The former colonial rulers had either temporarily submerged latent ethnic and tribal conflicts or had played off one group against another to maintain their rule. The designations "underdeveloped" or "third world" were used to characterize these newly independent nation-states (e.g., Nigeria). The development strategy used in the 1960s and 1970s assumed that modernization would reduce these internal divisions, promote social and national cohesion, and would improve the economy by introducing industrial and large-scale agriculture. The projected end result, the modernizers predicted, would be strong, modern, nation-states with growing economies.

Education was seen as a necessary force in the process of the nation-state building strategy. Nation-building educators used the following assumptions: (1) more schools and adult literacy programs would reduce illiteracy; (2) more emphasis on vocational education would train a skilled workforce; and (3) a nationally designed curriculum focused on constructing national identity, unity, and social cohesion would reduce ethnic and tribal tensions. (For more detail on nation building and ethnonational tensions, see the chapter on nationalism and ethnonationalism.)

Modernization relied on the nation-state and industrial model that had originated in the United States and western Europe. Some critics in Asia and Africa opposed modernization as Westernization, a new form of cultural and economic imperialism. International development also relied on large-scale, top-down, and government-to-government projects of modernization that minimized more limited local or grassroots efforts. Rather than reducing ethnic, language, and tribal conflicts as was predicted, the incidences of such conflicts increased. By the late 1970s, the once lauded modernization theory was being criticized in economic, sociological, and educational circles. These critics of modernization called it a simplistic theory of top-down linear development that had minimized the importance of key social, economic, cultural, political, and other variables. For example, Erwin Epstein criticizes modernization theory for its "focus on changes within societies or nations and comparisons between them—with Western societies as their main reference. . . ." He also argues that modernization theory neglected the themes of interconnectedness and interdependence between nations and societies.[13]

Some theorists see globalization as a much broader theory than modernization in that it involves economic, technological, cultural, political, and educational dimensions.[14] For example, Roger Dale argues that "globalization is distinct from" earlier processes because it refers to "a global economy that includes all nations of the world."[15] Globalization affects educational systems, the labor market, migration and immigration patterns, the mass media and international communications systems, international finance and banking, and issues of gender, ethnicity, language, and social class.[16]

Other theorists place globalization on a continuum in which it flows out of economic and social trends initiated by modernization. Globalization can be seen in historical perspective as a development that grew out of, redefined, and extended the earlier modernization theory. For example, both modernization and globalization are forces that move economic, social, and educational interactions and relationships out of local contexts and place them in world settings, interactions, and relationships.[17] Both modernization and globalization: (1) are worldwide processes that affect nation-states, especially their economies and societies; (2) are highly attuned to the role of economic forces in shaping the world's social and political order; (3) subordinate the contextual features of given countries, societies, and cultures to what is regarded as worldwide process; and (4) have generated wide interest among academic historians, economists, sociologists, and comparative educators. An important difference between modernization and globalization is that the latter gives much more emphasis to the role of nongovernmental actors, especially multinational corporations, in the process. Globalization also gives more attention to the nation-state context, especially its institutions, in reshaping or redirecting the effects of the process. At the same time, however, it sees the process as having worldwide, regional, and national implications. It is also less certain, less deterministic, about possible outcomes than modernization theory.

The history of modernization theory can be instructive for both the proponents and critics of globalization as a theory and process. During the zenith of modernization studies in the 1960s and 1970s, there was an emphasis on modernization as a worldwide process that worked almost as if it were some kind of universal mechanism regardless of the locale in which the mechanism was placed. In other words, the experts on modernization de-emphasized the importance of the context in which the process operated. Modernization theory accentuated the transforming power of science and technology and downgraded the importance of the context. Modernization theory emphasized the technical, economic, and scientific aspects but often ignored or rejected the importance of the cultural setting—the history, religion, cultural, ideological, and philosophical settings—in which the process was to work.

Today, some interpreters of globalization seem to be repeating the same mistake made by the earlier advocates of modernization. They seem to be minimizing the reality that a process always occurs in a context—somewhere, at some time, and in some place. Processes, such as modernization and globalization, are conditioned and often reshaped by the context in which they are placed. In turn, the processes work to restructure the context. It is important to recognize that there is an interaction between the context, the nation-state's culture and society, and the process of globalization.

Ideological Perspectives and Interpretations of Globalization

Globalization is receiving increasing attention in the foundations of education, especially from commentators on philosophy and ideology. In this section, we analyze globalization from three major ideological perspectives that are placed on a continuum moving from the political and educational right to the left. At the right of the continuum are Conservatism and Essentialism, in the center are Liberalism, Pragmatism, and Progressivism, and at the left are Postmodernism and Critical Theory. We look at globalization as it would be seen from these three perspectives.

As we move into our ideological analysis, there are several questions to think about. Is globalization an old or a new process? Are we examining a contemporary phenomenon or one with historical roots? Because we are living in the period that we are trying to interpret, our view of world history is likely to be influenced by the ideology that we embrace. Important questions raised in this interpretation are: Is globalization an extension of the modern period, beginning with the Enlightenment, or is it something new, a postmodern trend? How we answer this question determines to a large extent how we view globalization. In our earlier discussion of ideology, two characteristics of an ideology were identified as (1) an interpretation of the past that often combined history and myth; and (2) an action-oriented agenda to mobilize the group holding the ideology and to attract new members.

A Conservative Interpretation

As noted in the chapter on Conservatism, Conservatives emphasize the importance of and the need to maintain historically evolved institutions and processes because they give stability and continuity to the present. Globalization is interpreted as contemporary phenomenon but with origins that go back to the ancient world and the dissemination of ideas across civilization. Conservatives interpret globalization as the continuation of a historical process that involved cultural interaction and the borrowing of ideas, processes, and institutions. In the ancient world, there was the interchange of ideas and models, often in religion and art, between such great civilizations as the Indian, the Chinese, the Egyptian, the Mesopotamian, and the Greek. Cultural elements from one civilization were adapted by another, reconfigured to fit the host culture, and then incorporated into recipient culture.

Sometimes cultural borrowing resulted from the peaceful interaction of peoples through trade and economic exchange, and other times it came from war and conquest. For example, Rome's military conquest of the Greek city-states and their incorporation into the Roman empire introduced the Greek language and its cultural and educational elements of philosophy, rhetoric, and the arts and sciences into Roman culture. This Greco-Roman cultural heritage, originally transcultural, became the foundation of Western civilization and education. The crusades of the twelfth and thirteenth centuries, although a bloody era in history, nevertheless generated cultural interchange between Europeans and Arabs. Arabic mathematics, medicine, and architecture were carried into and incorporated into Western culture. Conservative, Essentialist, and Perennialist educators see Western philosophy and education originating in this Greco-Roman cultural period. The beginning of Western philosophy with Plato and Aristotle, the origins of Idealism and Realism, begin here. Thomas Aquinas, who constructed the synthesis of Aristotelian and Christian doctrine, also used this Western cultural heritage, which is prized by Perennialists.

The Beginnings of Globalization in Westernization

How one views Westernization, the movement of ideas and processes from Western Europe and North America through the world, has a significant affect on interpreting globalization. If Westernization is seen as bringing Christianity and science to Africa, Asia, and Central and South America, then it is regarded as a positive cultural force that was antecedent to globalization. If it is interpreted as an exploitation of indigenous peoples by European colonialists and imperialists, then globalization is seen as the continuation of these exploitative policies.

The European Renaissance, often identified as the beginning of the modern period in Western history, signaled the beginnings of exploration and colonization by Western nations with a high degree of central government such as Portugal, Spain, England, and France. Bordering on the Atlantic Ocean, these nations subsidized voyages of exploration by Christopher Columbus, Vasco da Gama, and others. To illustrate the contemporary controversy in interpreting Columbus, think about how Columbus Day is celebrated or denigrated in the United States. Some celebrate it as the discovery of America; others see it as the beginning of European conquest, exploitation, and in some cases the genocide of Native Americans. Conservatives would most likely celebrate the day whereas Critical Theorists would see it as being no cause for celebration.

According to Conservative interpreters, the European explorations that began in the fifteenth century and continued until the end of the nineteenth century introduced Western religion, Christianity, and Western culture to South America, Africa, and parts of Asia. Despite the often violent clashes between Western explorers and colonists, the imperial period needs to be seen as part of the early continuum of cultural interactions between people of different civilizations. The Europeans brought Western science and education to the indigenous people. In contrast, Critical Theorists interpret Western exploration and colonization very differently. For example, they would see the Spanish conquest of Central and South America as a record of Western exploitation, marked by the conquistador's search for gold and silver; the forced conversion of Indians—the Mayas, Incas, Aztecs, and others—to Catholicism; and the effort to eradicate indigenous cultures and replace them with Spanish culture and language.

The empires of the European nations—the British, French, German, Spanish, Portuguese, Dutch, and others—repeated the process of Westernization. For the Conservative interpreter, Westernization brought the European language, such as English in India, as a link language between indigenous peoples who had difficulty in communication because of a multiplicity of languages in even small areas. The schools established by the European powers educated future civil servants who would become leaders of their people in Western law, philosophy, and science. Western medical doctors eradicated endemic diseases. Again, the Critical Theorist interpretation would be markedly different. Despite the achievements of Asians, Africans, and Native Americans in literature, art, and architecture, Europeans regarded indigenous peoples as culturally inferior.

In the Conservative interpretation of the origins of globalization, the next important interaction in the cultural continuum was the nineteenth-century industrial revolution that began in Europe and North America and then was transported around the world. Industrialization, applying science and engineering to energy and machinery, made it possible to produce goods abundantly and cheaply and to make them available to more people than ever before. Although there were periods of economic distress, marked by inflation and recession and periodic unemployment, these were temporary and best resolved on their own without government interference. Industrialization made it possible to mass-produce commodities and make them available to more people; its prosperity contributed to population growth and to the rise of large cities that made art, literature, and music available to more people through museums, galleries, and concert halls. It transformed the petite bourgeoisie into a large middle class that gave balance and stability to the social and political orders. Marxism and Critical Theory have a much different interpretation of industrialism, which they see as introducing domination by the capitalists and exploitation of the working class.

From this very brief interpretation of the historical antecedents of globalization, we move quickly to what Conservatives see as the crucial period for globalization—the end of the Cold War, the collapse of the Communist system in the Soviet Union and its central and eastern European satellites, and the triumph of free market economics and representative political democracy. After the end of World War II, the world entered the decades-long Cold War from 1948 to 1990, when there were two drastically contrasting economic-political-military paradigms competing for dominance. The democratic and free enterprise paradigm was represented by the United States and its allies in western Europe. In contrast, the authoritarian, collectivist, and Communist model was represented by the Soviet Union and its satellites in central and eastern Europe.

In 1990, the Soviet Union, plagued by state bureaucracy and centralized control, collapsed under the weight of its Marxist statist inertia. With its demise, the restive satellites in central and eastern Europe freed themselves from Marxist rule and began to restore free market economies and democratic governments. The great hero, according to the Conservative interpretation of what brought about the victory of democracy and the free market, was President Ronald Reagan, who at the Berlin Wall, challenged the Soviet leader, saying, "Mr. Gorbachev, tear down this wall." The demise of the Soviet bloc ended Communist Party rule and its economic policy of centralized state economic planning, ownership, and control in this region. With the collapse of the Communist system in the USSR and its satellites, the Marxist model of state-centralized control was discredited. Important causes of the collapse of the Soviet system were military spending that exceeded resources and the stagnation and gross inefficiency of state-run industries. At the same time that the Soviet Union was in its death throes, there was a decided political shift in both the United States and the United Kingdom from social welfare state economic policies to the free enterprise capitalist system with the Reagan-Bush administrations in the United States and the Thatcher-Major governments in the United Kingdom. The lessons of history that demonstrated the superiority of the free market and democracy were used as the framework for advancing globalization, further spreading economic prosperity and political freedom.

Conservative Appropriation of Classical or Neo-Liberalism

Political parties associated with welfare-state Liberalism and Socialism have tended to lose elections in the twenty-first century. Conservative political parties have appropriated a "neoliberal" approach to economic and social policy. (See the discussion of the appropriation of Classical Liberal economic theory by Conservatives in the chapter on Conservatism.) What is often called Neo-Liberalism, or the new Liberalism, should be called Classical Liberalism to distinguish it from modern Liberalism. When you read other accounts, you are likely to encounter the term Neo-Liberalism, so it helps to use my term Classical Liberalism to cut down on confusion in terminology.

Classical Liberal economic theory is based on the ideas of Adam Smith (1723–1790) and David Ricardo (1772–1823), who argued that commerce should be based on self-regulating markets, free from government interference. Supply and demand is the mechanism that regulates the market. They advocated the elimination of trade barriers, such as tariffs, that impeded the free flow of commerce. Modern or social welfare state Liberalism, in contrast, abandoned classical economic theory in the twentieth century, and argues that some government regulation of the economy is needed to improve living and working conditions and provide education, social security, and health care to the general population. This kind of regulation is also used to alleviate the economic distress, especially unemployment, caused by economic recessions and depressions. The modern liberal social welfare state still upholds the right to own private property, in contrast to some versions of Socialism that nationalize key sections of the economy such as energy and transportation as public enterprises.

In terms of policies, Conservative governments, using Classical Liberal or Neo-Liberal economic theory, endorse policies to: (1) privatize public enterprises; (2) deregulate the economy; (3) eliminate barriers to trade and industry; (4) provide massive tax cuts; (5) reduce the power of unions and organized labor; (5) reduce public expenditures on social services; (6) downsize government; (7) expand international markets; and (8) remove controls on the global flow of capital.[18]

A Liberal Interpretation of Globalization as Modernization

In this section, we present an interpretation of globalization from the perspective of modern Liberalism, which is philosophically linked to John Dewey's Experimentalism and Progressive educational theory. In extrapolating how Liberals would interpret globalization, we turn to an examination of a more limited period of history than we did with the larger historical overview of Conservatism. My reason for doing so is based on the Liberal's tendency to view history more incrementally and in smaller units of time and Dewey's instrumental use of history to illuminate a present problem—in this case, globalization. An analysis of the concept of modernization, in the period from the 1950s to the present, provides this instrumental view of what contributed to globalization.

Liberals, more than Conservatives, draw inspiration and insights from the Enlightenment, the Age of Science and Reason. They see the Enlightenment as ushering in two major currents that shaped modern history: (1) human beings could use their reason to improve life progressively on earth in all ways, but especially politically, socially, and economically; enlightened education, freed from traditional absolutist religious and political restraints, would be an important instrument in this process of Progressive reformation; and (2) science, as the objective and empirical method of examining the environment, would discover how nature functioned; the scientific method and knowledge, incorporated into education, would be a tool of liberalization and, indeed, of modernization. It is the modern era and the process of modernization that led to the contemporary phenomenon of globalization.

According to the historian C. E. Black, modernization is "the process by which historically evolved institutions are adapted to the rapidly changing functions that reflect the unprecedented increase in man's knowledge, permitting control over environment, which accompanied the scientific revolution."[19] Institutions are modernized when they readapt their traditional functions in order to perform more efficiently. Modernization, like the globalization that followed it, was seen as a worldwide process that operated regardless of cultural, political, and social contexts. Liberals recognized that these contexts existed; they also believed that modernization, like the scientific method on which it was based, would reshape them. In other words, the force of modernization was irresistable and would alter traditional contexts into modern ones. At this point, Conservatives would object to what they regard as the breaking of historical continuity, in this case, tradition. For them, change must be gradual and not disruptive. Even when unexpected or unanticipated results of technological change cause disruption, they can be mitigated by traditional values, often religious ones. Critical Theorists would point to a major inconsistency in the Liberal theory of modernization; it subscribes to cultural relativism but, now minimizing the importance of context, also universalizes modernization as a method of change.

Liberal theorists subscribed to a structural-functionalism theory that related the institutional structures of society to the functions they performed. Based on structural-functionalism, political, social, economic, and educational structures were seen as interrelated and an alteration in one of these structures would produce changes in the other structures.[20] A change in one institution's functions would result in changes in other institutions and their functions. Based on this idea, it would be possible to initiate directed change. By introducing a new function in a given institution, the change would spiral through other institutions.

Latham, who examines modernization in terms of ideology, identified its key assumptions as: (1) "traditional" and "modern" societies are sharply different; (2) economic, social, and political changes are interrelated and interdependent; (3) the movement from traditional to modern is linear—moving in a unilateral direction; and (4) the modernization of traditional societies can be accelerated by their contact with developed ones.[21] These assumptions can also be applied to education in that educational changes are related to and dependent on socioeconomic and political change.

In the 1960s and 1970s, modernization, like globalization, was described as a multidimensional phenomenon that had political, economic, social, intellectual, and educational processes. Liberal proponents of modernization saw themselves as nation builders who were constructing modern nations out of developing societies. The term *developed* was widely used to distinguish technologically developed modern nations, such as the United States, the United Kingdom, and France, from the less technologically developed newly independent nations in Africa such as Nigeria, Ghana, and Chad. The thrust of modernization was also part of the Cold War in that the United States and its western European allies, competing with the Soviet Union, sought to introduce a democratic version of the phenomenon.[22]

The Liberal interpretation of globalization contains large amounts of modernization theory that seeks to bring technological, medical, and educational change and innovation to less technologically developed countries. The educational models that they use feature professional development, specialization, democratic processes, and social and political integration. Specialization in production and services is part of the industrial-corporate pattern. Local markets are replaced by mass markets linked by mass transportation systems. The process of economic modernization affects educational institutions by generating a demand for larger numbers of trained engineers, managers, technicians, and clerical workers. This demand causes tensions between those who want a new-styled, more modern scientific and technological education and those who resist it in favor of the older educational patterns.

The creation of a modern economy requires a particular kind of education system. First, a basic change is required of secondary and higher education from an orientation toward the classics and literature, to technical, engineering, and managerial specializations. Second, secondary schools need to be more diversified and offer a range of options such as those provided by the American comprehensive high school. Third, attitudes and behaviors need to be changed from inefficient but stable patterns of customary behavior to emphases on the efficient use of time and resources. Schools and teachers are regarded as change agents.

For Liberals, knowledge is regarded as something obtained by scientific experimentation and research rather than from the wisdom of the past found in religious or philosophical texts, or in the sanctity of custom. Modern knowledge is tentative, dynamic, and evolving rather than certain or static. One looks not to the past but to the future by manipulating and controlling the environment. Rather than feared, change is welcomed as an opportunity for a better life. A better life, however, is generally defined in quantitative, material, and economic terms rather than qualitatively. The modern intellectual outlook sees the system as creating more things, more goods, and more commodities.

Educators, motivated by Liberalism, in the 1960s and 1970s often used the term *nation building*. Nation building implies that a nation may not exist in the Western sense and needs to be created. They used models derived from their experiences in western Europe and North America, where national governments rather than local ones are the overriding authority. Policy-making, planning, and administration are done centrally. The national or central government extends its authority and power outward, from the center, throughout the country on a functional basis that extends to such areas as education, transportation, communication, health, defense, and social security.

Schools, at the primary level, seek to infuse the curriculum with a sense of nationhood. Civic education seeks to create and use national history, national heroic personages, and common national symbols to build loyalties. If the country was once ruled by a colonial power, a national freedom ideology may also be stressed. National systems, like those of many developed Western countries, favor homogeneity, eroding local customs, traditions, and sensibilities.

In contrast to the traditional society's social stability, Liberals see the modern society as one of continuing, dynamic, and pervasive change. This change, while threatening, also multiplies role and occupational alternatives. As the pace of industrialization quickens, a significant migration of people, especially from rural to urban settings, occurs. Indeed, a phenomenon in many developing countries has been the rapid growth of sprawling urban centers such as Bangkok, Calcutta, and Mexico City. Frequently, the central business core with its modern office buildings is surrounded by slums that duplicate but also multiply and intensify the conditions of rural poverty. Because of restrictions on space and a different kind of occupational structure in urban settings, the extended family begins to erode, to be replaced by the nuclear family.

The changing social relationships of a modern society also shape educational arrangements. Modern societies are characterized by much higher rates of literacy, indeed almost universal literacy, in comparison with traditional ones. Primary schooling also tends to be universal, and more individuals participate in secondary and higher education, which exhibits differentiation from strictly academic to vocational and technical programs. Further, educational opportunities in modern society are less restricted by gender. As the family structure changes, greater numbers of women have increased educational opportunities and enter the workforce. Liberals, influenced by progressive social science and psychology, tend to divide the human life span into stages of growth. They identify the stages of early childhood, childhood, early adolescence, adolescence, and youth as requiring educational institutions that are stage appropriate such as preschools, primary, middle, and high schools. Then, they further construct administrative systems to link, or articulate, the various schools in the stage-specific hierarchy. In contrast, people in a traditional society are likely to move from childhood to adulthood without an extended transitional period of social adolescence. The more modern and the more affluent the society, the longer the years of social adolescence. In modern societies, marriages are deferred to later dates than in traditional societies in which they are often arranged and can take place at a very early age.

The educational system that serves a modern society simultaneously exhibits signs of specialization and standardization. Schools offer more career education options and provide more technical programs. At the same time, a standardized curriculum emerges in which teacher training follows a national pattern as mass-produced textbooks are graded and standardized behavioral responses become the norm for successful academic completion.

Neo-Marxist, Postmodernist, and Critical Theorist Critique of Globalization

In this section, we provide a critique of globalization from the perspective of Neo-Marxism, Postmodernism, and Critical Theory. This perspective takes a view that is almost a polar opposite from that of Conservatism and Liberalism. Neo-Marxist theoreticians developed what was called a "dependency theory" in which the technologically developed capitalist nations such as the United States and those in western Europe (usually countries in the Northern Hemisphere) followed economic policies that deliberately kept the less technologically developed nations (usually in the Southern Hemisphere) in a state of dependency.[23] They identified the new forms of capitalism, such as multinational corporations, as key agencies in developing and maintaining these exploitative economic relationships.

A number of Neo-Marxist–inspired social and educational critics challenged the long-accepted version of the benefits of modern industrial society and the educational systems that served it. In western Europe there arose a critical philosophy based on the works of Antonio Gramsci and Jürgen Habermas. In the United States, some revisionist historians of education challenged the celebrationist historiography associated with Ellwood P. Cubberley that extolled the virtues of schooling as an instrument of the modern industrial state. Revisionist critics also challenged the moderate liberal, middle-of-the-road version of educational history associated with Lawrence Cremin, Bernard Bailyn, and others who had broadened their interpretation of education to include agencies other than the school. The Liberal educational historians, they contended, continued to interpret formal educational processes, especially schooling, in generally positive terms. Revisionists such as Joel Spring, Clarence Karier, Michael Katz, and others constructed an interpretation of schooling that emphasized the concept of social control in which the upper and middle classes use formal education to empower themselves in the dominant political and economic position and to disempower lower socioeconomic classes and minority groups.[24] Neo-Marxist writers on curriculum, such as Michael Apple, analyzed the power of the hidden curriculum as a covert agency used to indoctrinate suppressed groups to accept the values imposed by the dominant groups.[25]

Illich and Deinstitutionalization

Ivan Illich, a cofounder of the Center for Intercultural Documentation in Mexico, articulated a forceful argument against modernization and globalization that anticipated the Postmodernist and Critical Theorist critique. In contrast to Liberal institution building, or nation building, Illich proposed that society's coercive institutions, especially schools, be deinstitutionalized. In *Deschooling Society,* Illich argued for the abolition of the formal school and the deschooling of society as a first step in eliminating other coercive social institutions.[26]

Illich contends that the values of a modern society are deeply embedded in institutions. Further, institutionalized values, especially when viewed from the perspective of globalization, are measured largely as the outputs or products of particular institutions such as corporations, hospitals, or schools. People are conditioned, often by schooling, to accept the false consciousness that it is right to be defined as producers, consumers, and suppliers rather than as human beings. Recall that for Marxists, false consciousness is an ideological construction used by the dominant classes to convince subordinate ones to accept the economic and political conditions that exploit them. Consciousness-raising requires the exposure of false consciousness so that exploited classes understand the socio-economic situation in which they live. (See the chapters on Marxism and Critical Theory.) According to Illich, "When values have been institutionalized in planned and engineered processes, members of modern society believe that the good life consists in having institutions which define the values that both they and their society believe they need."[27] Illich argues that schools play an insidious role because they indoctrinate the young to abandon their own value-creating potentialities to institutions and to become consumers who crave institutionally produced goods and services.

In the global economy, universities, especially schools of management and engineering, train cadres of specialists who perform the specific functions required to produce and market goods and services. According to Illich, the modern global system is driven by the false ideology of the "myth of unending consumption," which proclaims to consumers, often members of marginalized groups, that they need and should purchase the products that sustain the very system that exploits them.

The school, in modern Western societies, Illich says, indoctrinates the young in the false ideology of unending consumption, and prepares and certifies specialists to fit into institutionally defined roles. Schooling, the initial exposure to institutions, conditions people to depend on institutionalized life. Once their institutionalized dependency is created, it is transferred from schools to other institutions. By using graded promotions, the school sustains and calibrates the system. By merging the completion of courses with certification, schools confuse learning with specialization. In an institutionalized society, promotion within institutions and within the economic structure depends on holding the appropriate certification.

The school's educational monopoly is the same throughout the world. Having the same structure, curriculum, and consequences, as described by Illich schooling is a universally coercive "age-specific, teacher-related process requiring full-time attendance at an obligatory curriculum."[28] It shapes a consumer mentality that values institutional commodities and services over the friendly assistance of concerned but uncertificated neighbors. Schooling brainwashes students into believing that the bureaucracies of coercive institutions are truly scientific, efficient, and progressive.

Illich's arguments for deschooling society are directed toward liberating learning from the schools' domination. Free from institutionalized constraints, education could become a form of skill or drill learning in which a person learns a particular skill, from reading, writing, swimming, and sewing to computer programming. Much of skill learning would occur informally or nonformally in specific or on-the-job training. What Illich calls "liberal education" is a general open-ended learning about ideas, literature, history, art, and any subject about which people have an interest. Here, interested individuals meet in voluntary discussion groups to share ideas and opinions for as long as they are interested in the topic.[29]

Illich proposed an early antiglobalization strategy when he devised a plan for "outwitting developed countries."[30] He argues that in modernized Western societies the quality of life is confused with the quantitative dimension of life; it is defined almost exclusively in quantitative terms—more products, more schooling, and more consumer goods. Industries, the media, and government and educational agencies are defined as producers of commodities that are packaged to reflect the Western modernization and domination. Progress is defined as continually expanding these agencies and exporting them to the

LTDCs.[31] Illich contends, "rich nations benevolently impose a straight jacket of traffic jams, hospital confinements, and classrooms on the poor nations and by international agreement call this development." In reality, the poor, not the wealthy, bear the cost of globalization. According to Illich:

> Every dollar spent in Latin America on doctors and hospitals costs a hundred lives. . . . Had each dollar been spent on providing safe drinking water, a hundred lives could have been saved. Each dollar spent on schooling means more privileges for the few at the cost of the many; at best it increases the number of those who, before dropping out, have been taught that those who stay longer have earned the right to more power, wealth, and prestige.[32]

Globalization creates a mass demand and market for consumer goods produced by TDCs. The consumerization of the population of LTDCs creates a demand for packaged solutions that are not only beyond the reach of the masses but are also undesirable for them. Dependency results from rising aspirations caused by intensive marketing and schooling. In contrast, genuine education awakens "awareness of new levels of human potential and the use of one's creative powers to foster human life."[33]

Freire's Liberation Pedagogy Applied to Globalization

Paulo Freire, in *Pedagogy of the Oppressed,* advocates an education that will raise the consciousness of oppressed peoples in LTDCs.[34] Oppressors, according to Freire, use their monopoly of science and technology for economic exploitation and political repression of the poor. Freire insists that Liberation Pedagogy will inaugurate a critical dialogue among oppressed peoples that will lead to the creation of grassroots political, social, and educational organizations that will empower their creators. (For Freire's Liberation Pedagogy, see the chapter on Critical Theory.) Critical dialogue involves identifying and seeking ways to eliminate the conditions supporting oppression. It encourages suppressed people to develop their own political and educational alternatives to end exploitation and oppression. Liberation Pedagogy sees popular self-development as being initiated by poor people at the local level, rather than outside elites. It seeks to raise the self-consciousness of oppressed people that they are in an historical situation they can define for themselves.[35]

Freire's conception of local site development contrasts with globalization as a world-wide process. True development, he argues, involves a direct encounter in which people, at the grassroots level, come together to identify, define, discuss, and determine ways to solve their mutual problems. Through direct dialogue, trust and mutual understanding develops in the group. The direct involvement of local people is designed to foster a critical consciousness of the situation and the particular problem facing people in the community. Dialogue then leads to agreed-on action to solve the problem.[36] Important elements of Freire's theory that contributed to the strategy of grassroots sustainable development are: (1) genuine development should originate locally; (2) locally initiated development should focus on problems or projects significant to those who initiated them, rather than being imposed by outside experts; (3) the initial stage in development projects involves a raising of consciousness so that people know they can change their living conditions; (4) development should encourage a broader humanization or empowerment of people; and (5) grassroots development leads to new political and educational configurations that will challenge and alter the oppressive conditions of the status quo.

Freire's advocacy of sustainable development that begins in the local community resonates well with the Critical Theorist arguments that genuine school reform is site-based at the local school and community that it serves. This kind of grassroots reform between members of the local community and the local school does not depend on outside experts or educational bureaucrats. When the experts leave the local school site, the supposed reform often goes with them. In contrast, local site-based school reform is sustainable because it is constructed by those who are directly involved in improving their own education and in empowering themselves.

Postmodern Critique

A philosophical critique of globalization comes from Postmodernist philosophers. Indeed, Postmodernism is antithetical to the theory of modernization found in Liberal ideology. Postmodernists who assert that we are now living in the postmodern era, a time after modernity, are obviously antagonistic to proposals to intensify modernization by way of globalization. Proponents of modernization argue that it is a globally applicable and scientifically objective theory; Postmodernists challenge the very possibilities of universalism and objectivity. For them, theories such as globalization and modernism are not descriptions of universal phenomenon but are the constructions of particular groups, seeking dominance, especially economic power, over others, at specific times in history. These constructions are the rationales that one group uses to give them power over others. The theory of globalization is a construction of those who want to impose their version of Western for-profit capitalism on others, especially those living in what are labeled less developed societies and countries.[37]

As its name suggests, Postmodernism is a reaction against and a rejection of modernism, especially its emphasis that development, as progress, can be measured quantitatively by economic indicators. It also rejects the concept that societies can be ranked according to economic measures of their level of development. What is proclaimed as scientific objectivity and its use in determining the degree to which a society is modern or not is, in reality, a construction used to rationalize the domination of one group, or class, which is alleged to be developed, over another, alleged to be underdeveloped. Postmodernists contend that what is needed is a liberating, or opposing discourse, such as that suggested by Freire, to raise the consciousness of exploited groups so that they can begin to empower themselves. Real consciousness about the agents and agencies of oppression, such as an exploitative capitalism, marks the beginning of true self-development. Locally designed, grassroots projects of sustainable development are the means that oppressed groups can use to empower themselves. As Illich argued, schools have traditionally functioned as agencies that reproduce the power and control of dominant groups and classes by manipulating what is claimed to be knowledge. A liberating kind of education can deconstruct the rationales of oppression, one of them being the ideology of modernization.

Reflections on Modernization

As has occurred throughout my writing of this book, I have reflected on my own educational experiences as a means of thinking about philosophy of education. I have also encouraged you to do so.

In 1969, I participated in a project designed to study the process of modernization in a traditional and developing country. At that time, "modernization" was the dominant theory in sociology and had made strong inroads into the educational foundations. Many leading figures in the foundations were arguing that the road to world peace, development, and security would be through modernization. Several educators had endorsed the idea of modernization as a form of nation building in which education had a large role to play.

I was selected by Loyola University to be a member of a team of professors from Midwestern colleges and universities who would go to India to study modernization. The project was under the auspices of the Foreign Policy Association and funded by the Agency for International Development (AID). We were to make on-site visits to schools, colleges, and universities and to industries and farms to find how India was moving toward modernization. We were to collect materials and interview politicians, educators, and industrialists. Our goal was to return to the United States with our ideas and materials and to develop curriculum materials for American schools and to design courses on modernization at our home institutions.

We visited small villages and large cities. We went to the states in northern India such as Rajasthan, spent time in the capital, New Delhi, traveled to Bombay, and to the southern states such as Mysore. We went to many schools, some just one room in tiny villages, and others large ones in urban areas. We attended meetings of Indian educators. It was my first real foreign trip and was an exciting and challenging experience. We heard presentations by Indian economic and educational planners. Although some Indian educators supported centralized programs of national modernization, others challenged it, arguing that this version of modernization was in reality a strategy of neocolonial Westernization. While wanting to eliminate the economic and social stagnation and illiteracy that beset much of rural village India, the critics wanted to avoid the problems beginning to appear in modern Western industrial societies, such as environmental pollution, an increase in violent crime, disintegration of family life, and increasing alcoholism and drug abuse. They wanted, they said, an India in which modernity arose from and within the values of the indigenous cultural context. They often pointed to Japan as a modern but not Western society.

This experience has stayed with me throughout my career. I learned several important things. One, to be suspicious of whatever is the current "in fad" in education. Modernization was supposed to remake the world. By the late 1970s, I heard highly critical attacks on modernization theory that took the exact opposite approach from its proponents. Two, I learned that while it is important to study a process, it is equally and perhaps even more important to put that process in its context. What we all needed on that educational venture in 1969 was a better understanding of the Indian context—its history, culture, politics, religion, and society. Over time, I worked at trying to bring context and process together.

Conclusion

The chapter examined globalization as a potent multidimensional force that has a wide range of implications for the economy, society, politics, and education. Because of the complexity and fluidity of the process, the chapter developed a stipulated definition of globalization.

Because of their apparent relationships, the chapter compared and contrasted modernization and globalization. It examined such globally related trends as economic regionalization and structural adjustment policies and their impact on nation-states. The chapter concluded with a discussion of the implications of globalization, specifically on informal education, alterations in curriculum, and the reconfiguration of educational systems.

Constructing Your Own Philosophy of Education.   Now that you have read and discussed the chapter on globalization, you can determine for yourself whether this discussion should or should not be part of a book on philosophy of education. You can determine whether globalization and modernization have had an effect on your life and are present in your educational experiences. You can decide whether you want to make globalization a part of your educational philosophy.

Questions for Reflection and Discussion

1. Examine the various definitions of globalization; then construct your own definition.

2. Compare and contrast modernization and globalization.

3. Do you believe that globalization's effects have improved or reduced the quality of life for most people? Defend your answer.

4. Why has globalization generated controversy?

5. Consider how Conservatives, Liberals, and Neo-Marxists and Postmodernists interpret globalization. What interpretation do you support? Why?

6. Do you agree or disagree with the statement: "Globalization is necessarily related to free market capitalism and democratic political institutions."

7. How has globalization affected your local community in terms of employment opportunities?

8. How has globalization affected the products that are sold in your community?

Topics for Research and Inquiry

1. Consider the impact of e-mail and the Internet on how you communicate and acquire information. How often have your contacts been international or global?

2. Do a survey of businesses in your community. Identify which of them are international corporations.

3. Examine some items in your possession, such as clothing. Determine which of them have been produced in another country.

4. Research the most highly enrolled programs at your college or university. Try to analyze these programs in terms of their relationships to globalization.

5. Examine your college or university catalogue. Identify the courses that are related to globalization.

6. Identify specific ways in which globalization has had an impact on your family, friends, and yourself.

7. Conduct a survey in class that examines the students' opinions on free trade and outsourcing of jobs to other countries.

Building a Globalization Vocabulary

Globalization: the processes that promote worldwide involvement, relationships, adaptations, and connections between peoples of different countries, cultures, and languages.

Globality: social conditions characterized by worldwide economic, political, cultural, and environmental interconnections that cross borders and boundaries.

Global: a system or process that relates to the entire world.

Less Technologically Developed Countries: countries that have a lower level of technology than those ranked higher on the development scale.

Modernization: the process by which traditional, rural, and agricultural societies became modern ones.

Multinational or Transnational Business Corporations: corporations and firms that produce commodities, market, and sell them worldwide.

Structural Adjustment: policies that promote privatization and deregulation.

Internet Resources

For an introduction to globalization, access www.globalization101.org.

For globalization from the perspective of the World Bank, access www.worldbank.org/globalization.

For a policy discussion of globalization, access www.globalpolicy.org/globalization/index.htm.

Suggestions for Further Reading

Appadurai, Arjun. *Modernity at Large: Cultural Dimensions of Globalization.* Minneapolis: University of Minnesota Press, 1996.

Bhagwati, Jagdish. *In Defense of Globalization.* New York: Oxford University Press, 2004.

Blumberg, Rae Lesser. *Women, Development, and the Wealth of Nations: Making the Case for the Gender Variable.* Boulder, CO: Westview Press, 1991.

Burbules, Nicholas C., and Carlos A. Torres, eds. *Globalization and Education: Critical Perspectives.* New York: Routledge, 2000.

Clarke, Ian. *Globalization and Fragmentation: International Relations in the Twentieth Century.* Oxford: Oxford University Press, 1997.

Daun, Holger. *Educational Restructuring in the Context of Globalization and National Policy.* New York: Garland, 2001.

Escobar, Arturo. *Encountering Development: The Making and Unmaking of the Third World.* Princeton, NJ: Princeton University Press, 1995.

Freire, Paulo. *Pedagogy of the Oppressed.* New York: Continuum, 1984.

Hamilton, John Maxwell. *Entangling Alliances: How the Third World Shapes Our Lives.* Cabin John, MD: Seven Locks Press, 1990.

Hoogvelt, Ankie. *Globalization and the Post-Colonial World: The New Political Economy of Development.* Basingstoke, UK: Macmillan, 1997.

Irwin, Douglas A. *Free Trade Under Fire.* Princeton, NJ: Princeton University Press, 2002.

Illich, Ivan D. *Celebration of Awareness: A Call for Institutional Revolution.* New York: Doubleday, 1970.

Illich, Ivan D. *Deschooling Society.* New York: Harper and Row, 1970.

Knippers, Jan. *Development in Theory and Practice: Bridging the Gap.* Boulder, CO: Westview Press, 1991.

Latham, Michael E. *Modernization as Ideology: American Social Science and "Nation Building" in the Kennedy Era.* Chapel Hill: University of North Carolina Press, 2000.

Lingard, Bob, and Fazal Rizvi, eds. "A Symposium on Globalization and Education," *Educational Theory,* Vol. 50, No. 4 (Fall 2000) Urbana: University of Illinois, 2000.

Mansfield, Edward O., and Helen V. Milner. *The Political Economy of Regionalism.* New York: Columbia University Press, 1997.

Popkewitz, Thomas S., ed. *Educational Knowledge: Changing Relationships between the State, Civil Society and the Educational Community.* Albany: State University of New York Press, 2000.

Samoff, Joel. *Coping with Crisis: Austerity, Adjustment, and Human Resources.* London, UK: Cassell, 1994.

Stiglitz, Joseph. *Globalization and its Discontents.* New York: W. W. Norton, 2002.

Wolf, Martin. *Why Globalization Works.* New Haven, CT: Yale University Press, 2004.

Endnotes

1. Peter J. Dougherty, "The Wealth of Nations: A Publisher Considers the Literature of Globalization," *The Chronicle of Higher Education* (July 16, 2004), p. B6.

2. Erwin Epstein, "Globalization of Education," in James W. Guthrie, ed., *Encyclopedia of Education,* 2nd ed. (New York: Thomson Gale, Macmillan, vol. 3, 2003), p. 936.

3. Manfred B. Steger, *Globalization: A Very Short Introduction* (Oxford, UK: Oxford University Press, 2003), p. 13.

4. Steger, *Globalization: A Very Short Introduction,* pp. 7–8.

5. Steger, *Globalization: A Very Short Introduction,* p. 5.

6. Steger, *Globalization: A Very Short Introduction,* pp. 9–12. I have modified Steger's account of globalization's characteristics by adding educational ones.

7. Steger, *Globalization: A Very Short Introduction,* p. 8.

8. Paige Porter and Lesley Vidovich, "Globalization and Higher Education Policy," *Educational Theory,* Vol. 50, No. 4 (Fall 2000), p. 460.

9. Martin Carnoy and Diana Rhoten, "What Does Globalization Mean for Educational Change? A Comparative Approach," *Comparative Education Review,* Vol. 46, No. 1 (February 2002), p. 5.

10. Epstein, p. 937.

11. Fazal Rizi and Bob Lingard, "Globalization and Education: Complexities and Contingencies," *Educational Theory*, Vol. 50, No. 4 (Fall 2000), pp. 419– 420.

12. Epstein, *"Globalization of Education,"* p. 938.

13. Epstein, p. 937.

14. John Hinkson, "Globalization: Political Economy and Beyond," *Arena Journal* 12 (1998), pp. 67–81.

15. Roger Dale and Susan L. Robertson, "The Varying Effects of Regional Organizations as Subjects of Globalization of Education," *Comparative Education Review,* Vol. 46, No. 1 (February 2002), pp. 15–32 and Roger Dale, "Globalization and Education: Demonstrating a 'Common World Educational Culture' or Locating a 'Globally Structured Educational Agenda'?" *Educational Theory*, Vol. 50, No 4 (Fall 2000), p. 435.

16. Nelly P. Stromquist, "Preface," *Comparative Education Review,* Vol. 46, No. 1 (February 2002), p. iii.

17. Stuart Hall, David Held, and Tony McGrew, *Modernity and its Futures* (Cambridge: Polity Press/The Open University, 1992), pp. 66–67.

18. Steger, *Globalization: A Very Short Introduction,* p. 47.

19. C. E. Black, *The Dynamics of Modernization: A Study in Comparative History* (New York: Harper and Row, 1966), pp. 1–34.

20. Michael E. Latham, *Modernization as Ideology: American Social Science and "Nation Building" in the Kennedy Era* (Chapel Hill, NC: University of North Carolina Press, 2000), p. 34.

21. Latham, *Modernization as Ideology,* p. 4.

22. My discussion of these dimensions of modernizations borrows heavily from the discussion in Black in *The Dynamics of Modernization,* pp. 1–34.

23. Latham, *Modernization as Ideology,* p. 5.

24. For example, see Joel Spring, *The Sorting Machine: National Educational Policy Since 1945* (New York: Longman, 1976); Samuel Bowles and Herbert Gintis, *Schooling in Capitalist America: Educational Reform and the Contradictions of Economic Life* (New York: Basic Books, 1976); Michael B. Katz, *Class, Bureaucracy, and Schools: The Illusion of Educational Change in America* (New York: Praeger, 1971).

25. Michael W. Apple, *Ideology and Curriculum* (London: Routledge and Kegan Paul, 1979), pp. 82–104.

26. Ivan Illich, *Deschooling Society* (New York: Harper and Row, 1971).

27. Illich, *Deschooling Society,* pp. 113–114.

28. Illich, *Deschooling Society,* pp. 25–26.

29. Illich, *Deschooling Society,* p. 76.

30. Ivan Illich, "Outwitting Developed Countries," *New York Review of Books,* Nov. 6, 1969, pp. 20–24.

31. Illich, "Outwitting Developed Countries," pp. 20–24.

32. Illich, "Outwitting Developed Countries," p. 20.

33. Illich, "Outwitting Developed Countries," p. 22.

34. Paulo Freire, *Pedagogy of the Oppressed,* trans. Myra Bergman Ramos (New York: Continuum, 1984).

35. Freire, *Pedagogy of the Oppressed,* pp. 72–73.

36. Freire, *Pedagogy of the Oppressed,* pp. 102–103.

37. For Postmodernism, see Joe L. Kincheloe, *Toward a Critical Politics of Teacher Thinking: Mapping the Postmodern* (Westport, CT: Bergin and Garvey, 1993); William E. Doll, Jr., *A Post-Modern Perspective on Curriculum* (New York: Teachers College Press, 1993); Stanley Aronowitz and Henry Giroux, *Postmodern Education: Politics, Culture, and Social Criticism* (Minneapolis: University of Minnesota Press, 1991).

Index